EVERYDAY INDIAN AESTHETIC

sayali goyal

Lustre Press
Roli Books

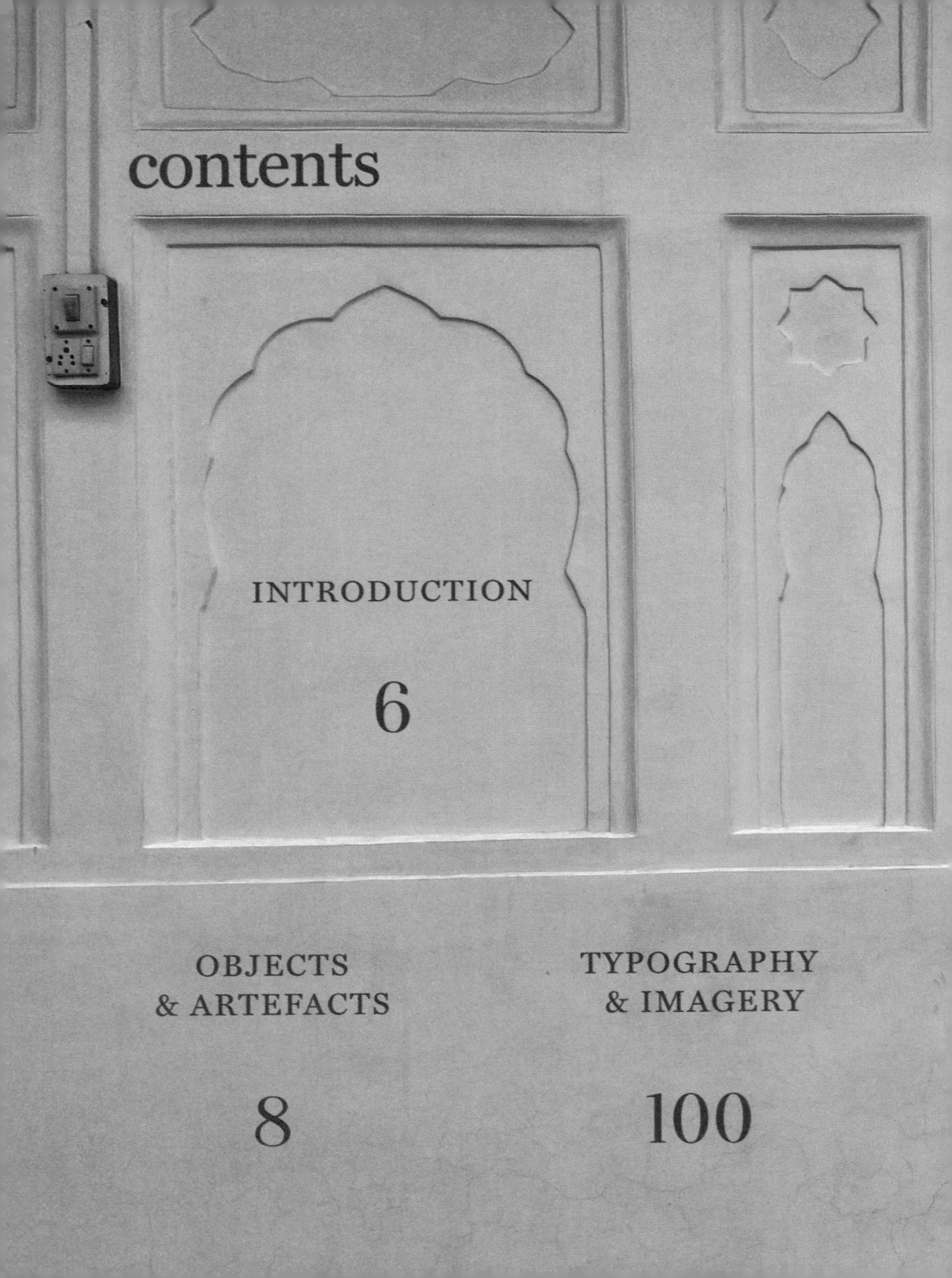

contents

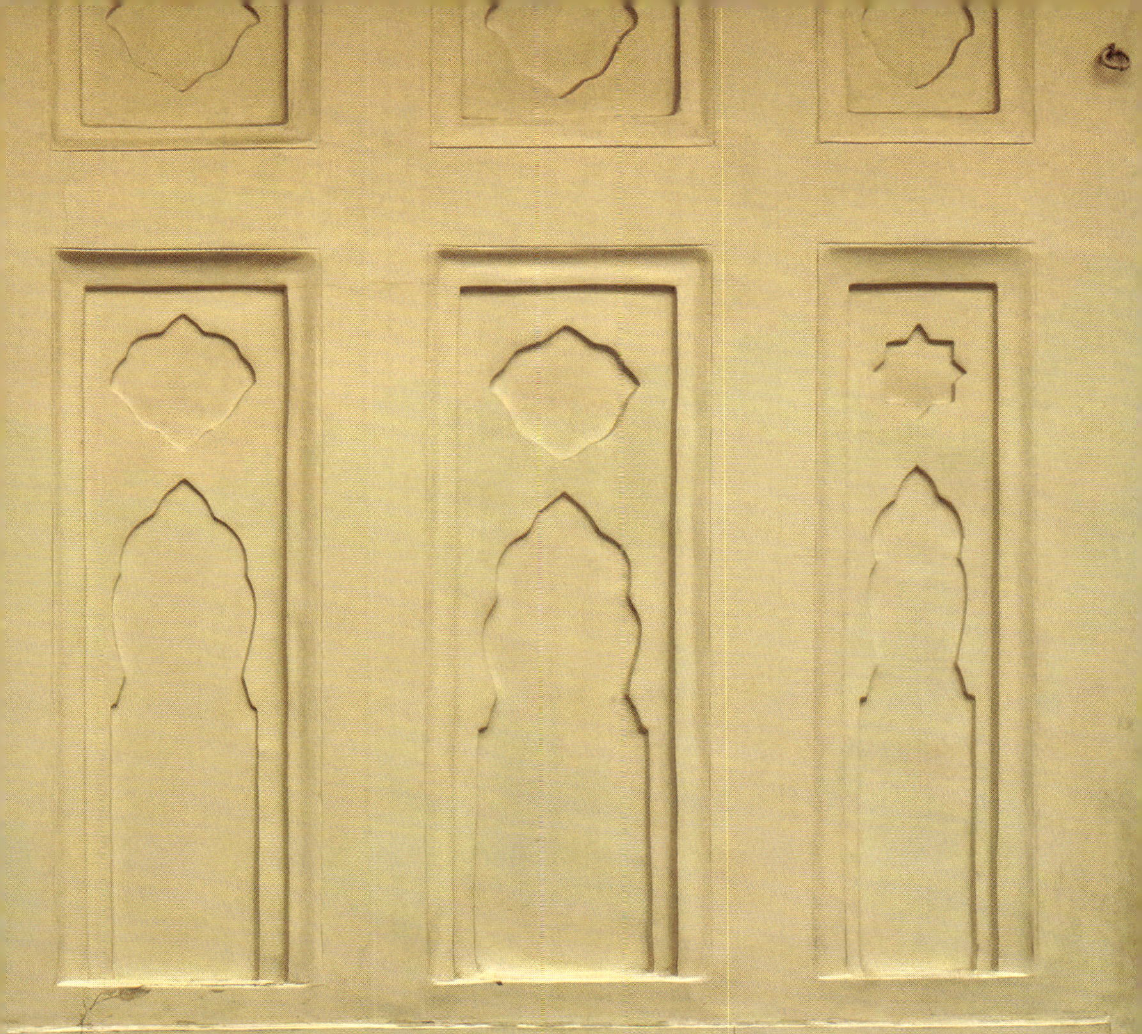

introduction

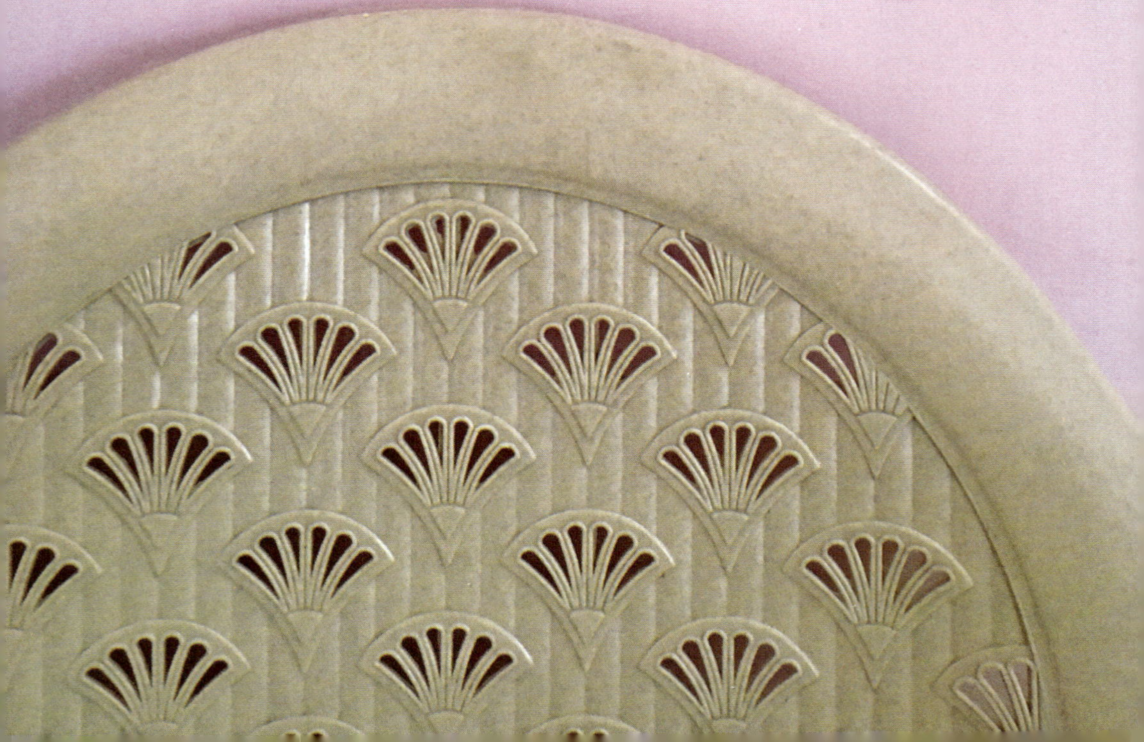

Everyday Indian Aesthetic is a collection of photographs taken during my travels across India in the last seven years, starting 2016. It is a compilation of visuals shot spontaneously in the course of my many travels. The photos have been put together under themes in retrospect, as themes emerge and patterns appear common across India's geography. This book is a peek into rural and small-town India, and the lifestyles of common people, through everyday design and architecture, adornments, colours, textures, patterns, and typography. My encounters with such details were instinctive and accidental, evident through the composition of the images. There is no staging of the objects that appear in the photographs, nor are we prepared to see something based on preconceived stereotypes. What greets us at the end of the photo book is an anthropological capture of India's lived realities and a visual aesthetic that is able to present people and places as they are.

In this project, I see everyday objects, practices and materiality of India with curiosity and admiration. It is a look at her design culture rooted in functionality and daily needs of the people. What becomes apparent through the myriad colours, shapes, forms, and textures is the sheer diversity of this mainland. Is design universal? Is everyday design conceptualized, or do concepts emerge through the functions it serves? Do colours speak of community identities? *Everyday Indian Aesthetic* begins to take a look at these questions and many more.

The book aims to allow each individual to make it their own. I imagine each viewer to use it like a library, and pull out visual information that fascinates them. Hence, the omission of captions for the images is a conscious choice to invite interpretations unhindered by any descriptive texts, and let the visual communication be infinite. The book has many layers, many 'ways of seeing' open to varied meanings. It also documents the synthesis of Indian design over the last few decades (since the 1960s through 2000s) along with the cities that came into existence in 18th and 19th centuries, thus opening a dialogue to global gaze on what Indian design stands for. The book may create connections to other cultures too, and put light on how design has the capacity to document cultural exchange and hold the past in the present.

So what is everyday Indian aesthetics? It's the systematic display at many retailers in a bazaar, it's the minimalistic borders and terrazzo flooring in a haveli combined with the floral decorative ones, it's the in between shades of eclectic and pastel colours, it's the European-influenced Art Deco details along with retro grill designs, it's the loud temple aesthetics, makeshift purposeful design, old handmade objects with new industrial objects, merging formal settings with informal, residential with commercial, it's in use of natural materials, it's in the traditions borrowed over generations, it's in the many drapes, the multilingual typography styles, geometric symbols and motifs, and everything in between.

Sayali Goyal

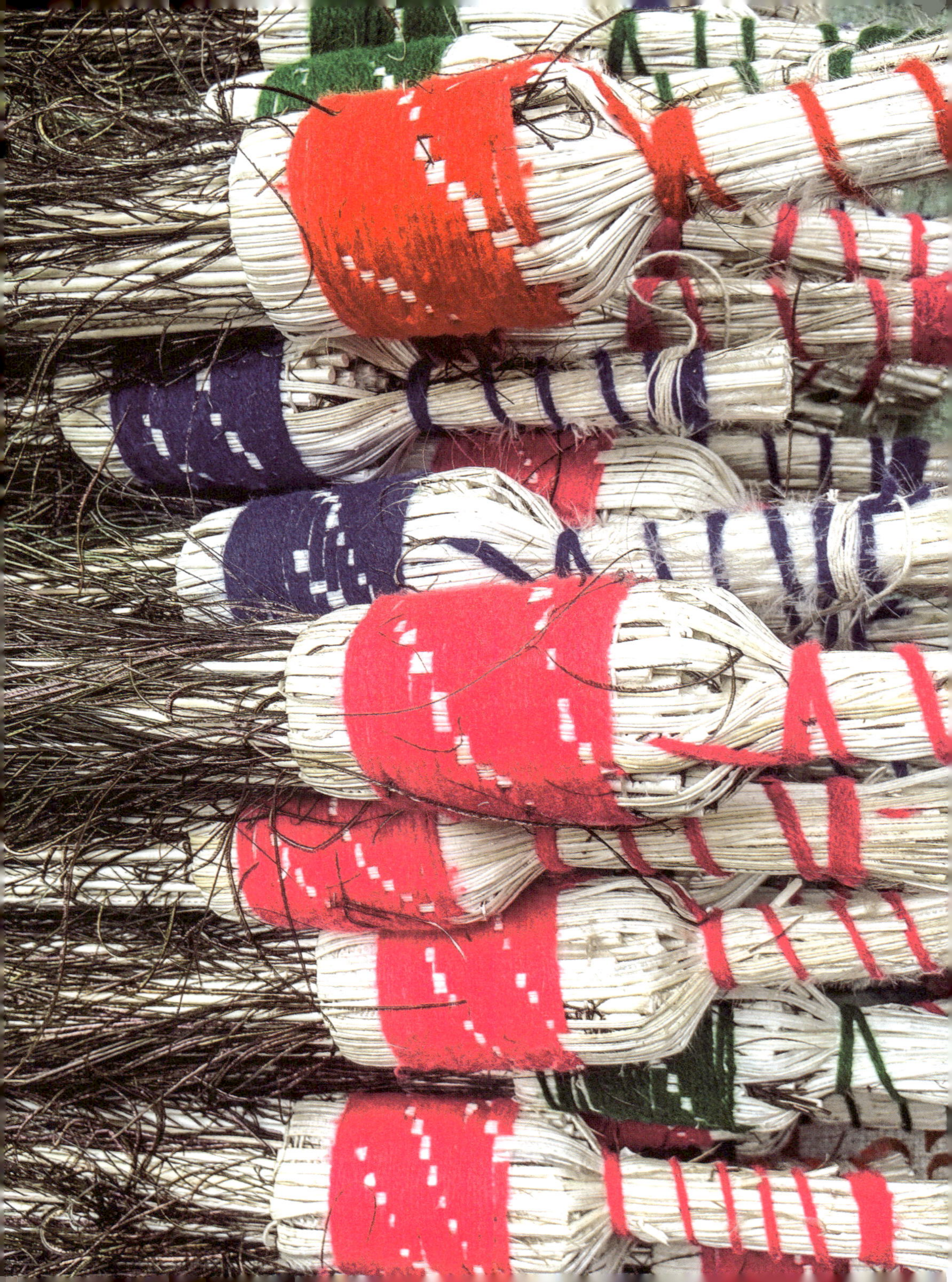

objects & artefacts

Colours and sculptures, textures and totems, materials and motifs – streets, markets and homes in India are filled with a multitude of objects that defy any definitive style or easy categorization. They hold the material memory of a place, while the place influences the making of every creation.

A cornucopia of shapes and sizes emerges in this collection of photographs from travels around the country. Shapes of all kinds; lines, both straight and angular; carvings and painted iconography mounted on walls; a range of kitchen utensils customized for local cuisine – in the curves of the lota, the ubiquity of the plastic armchairs, and the utility of the suitcase – lies the wonders of India.

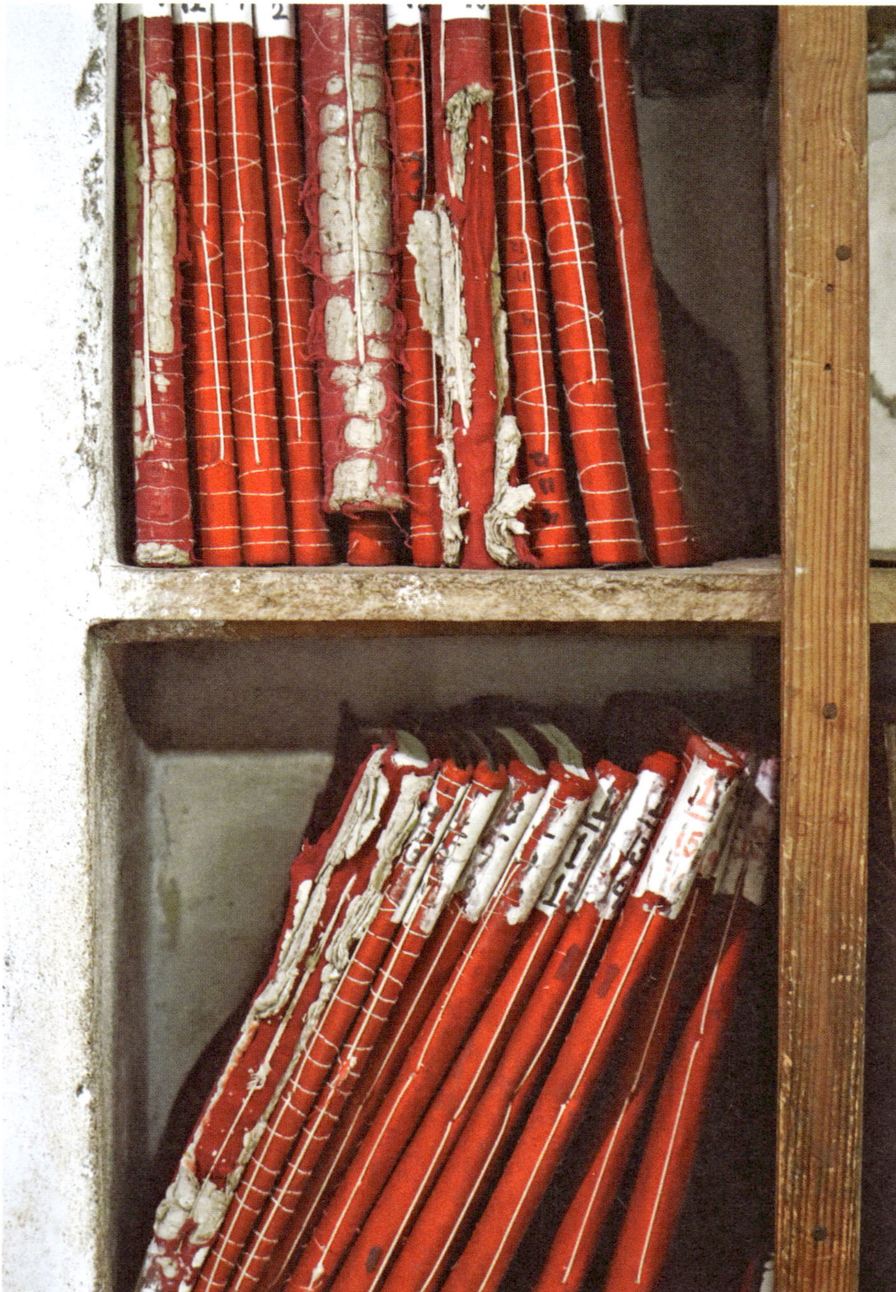

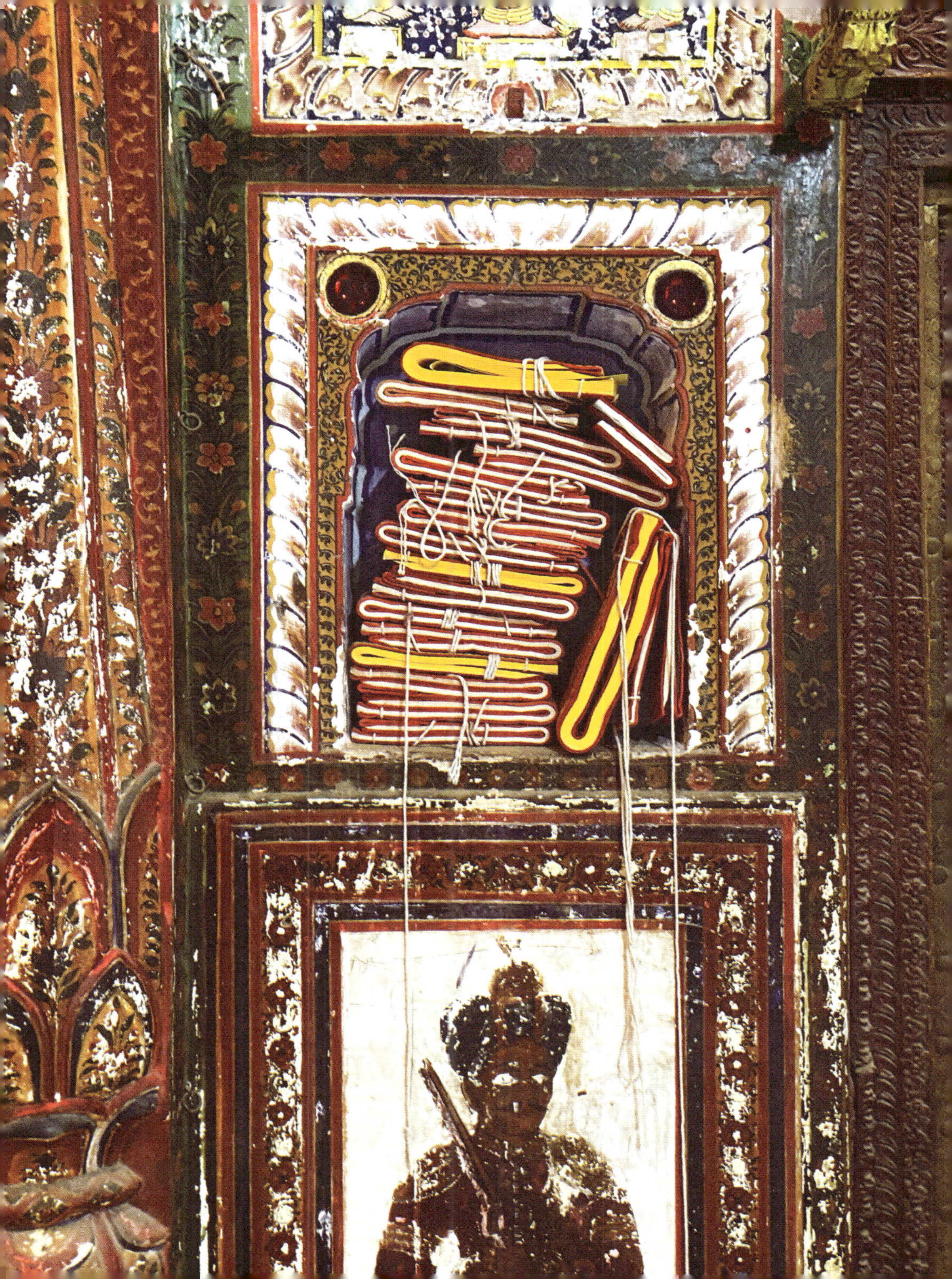

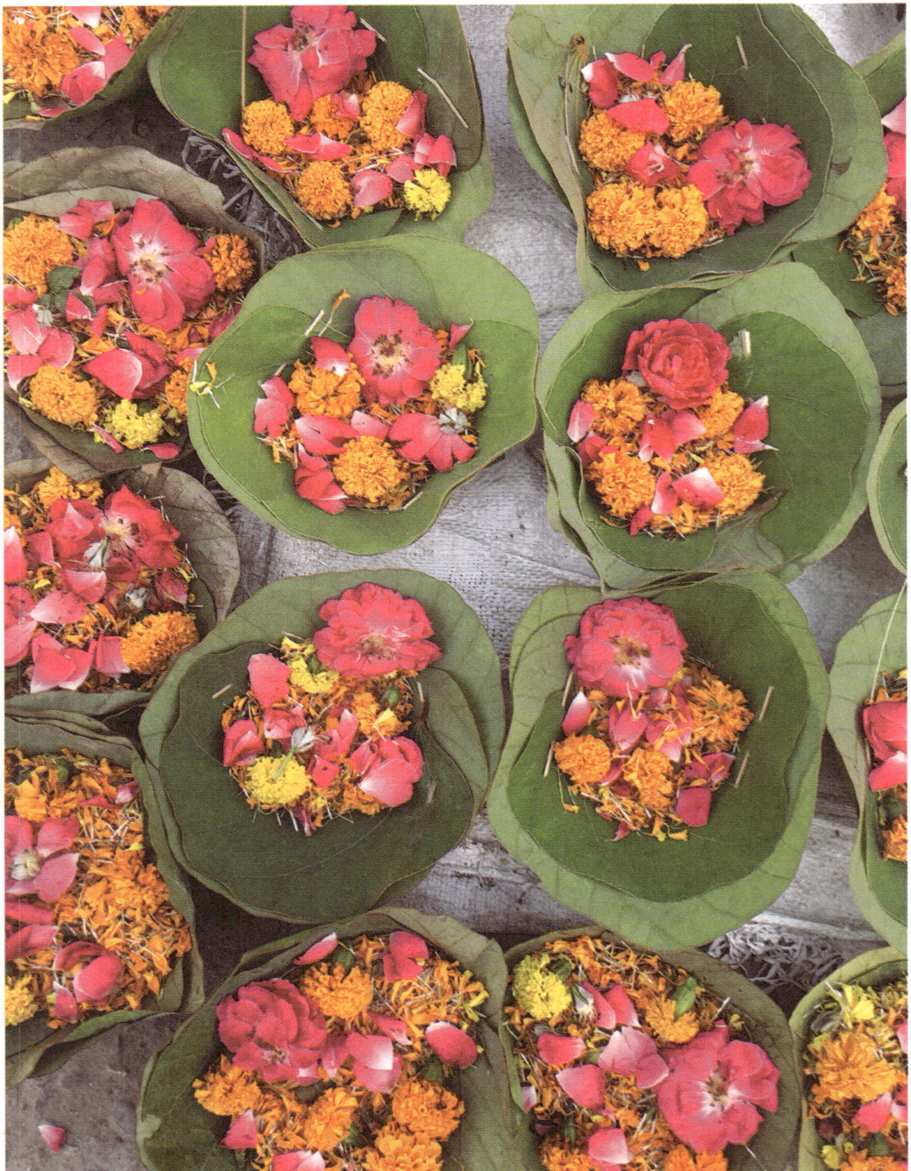

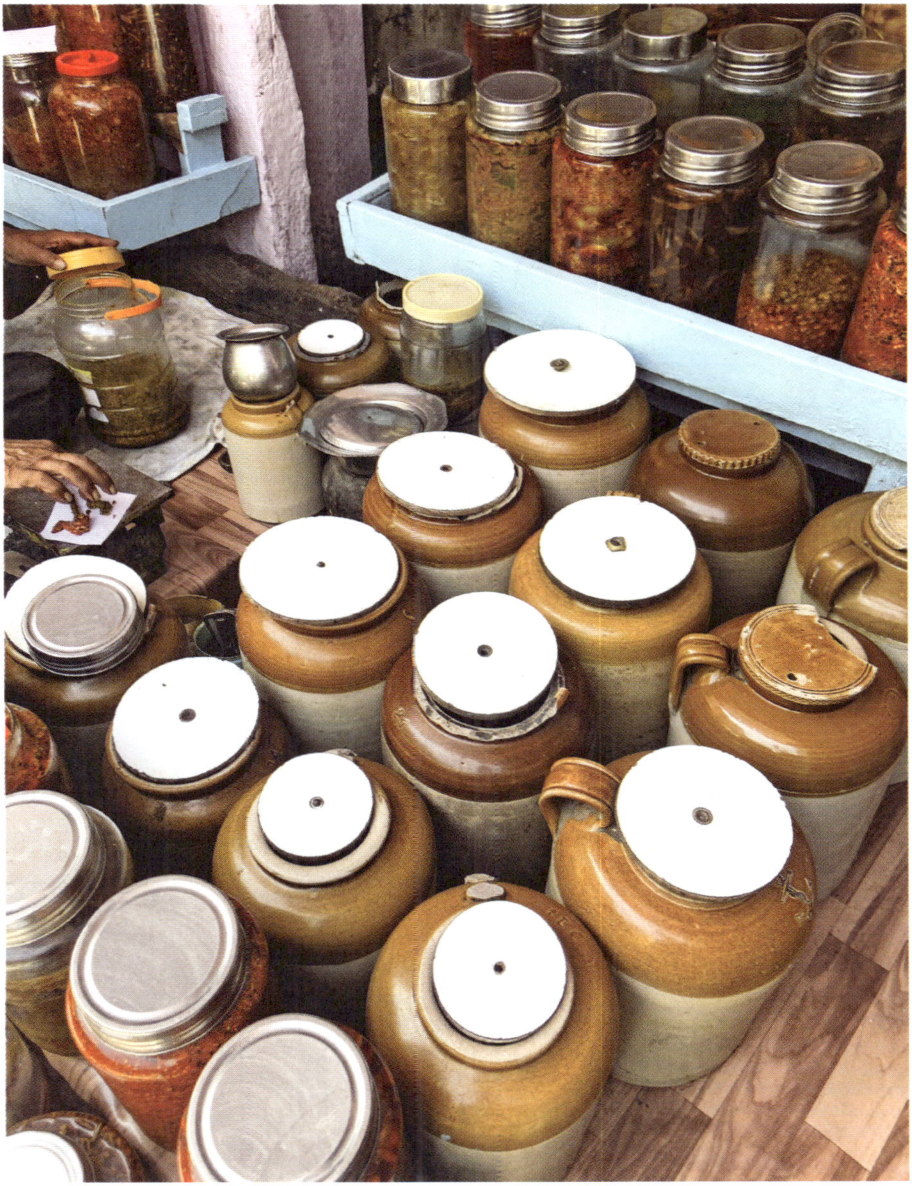

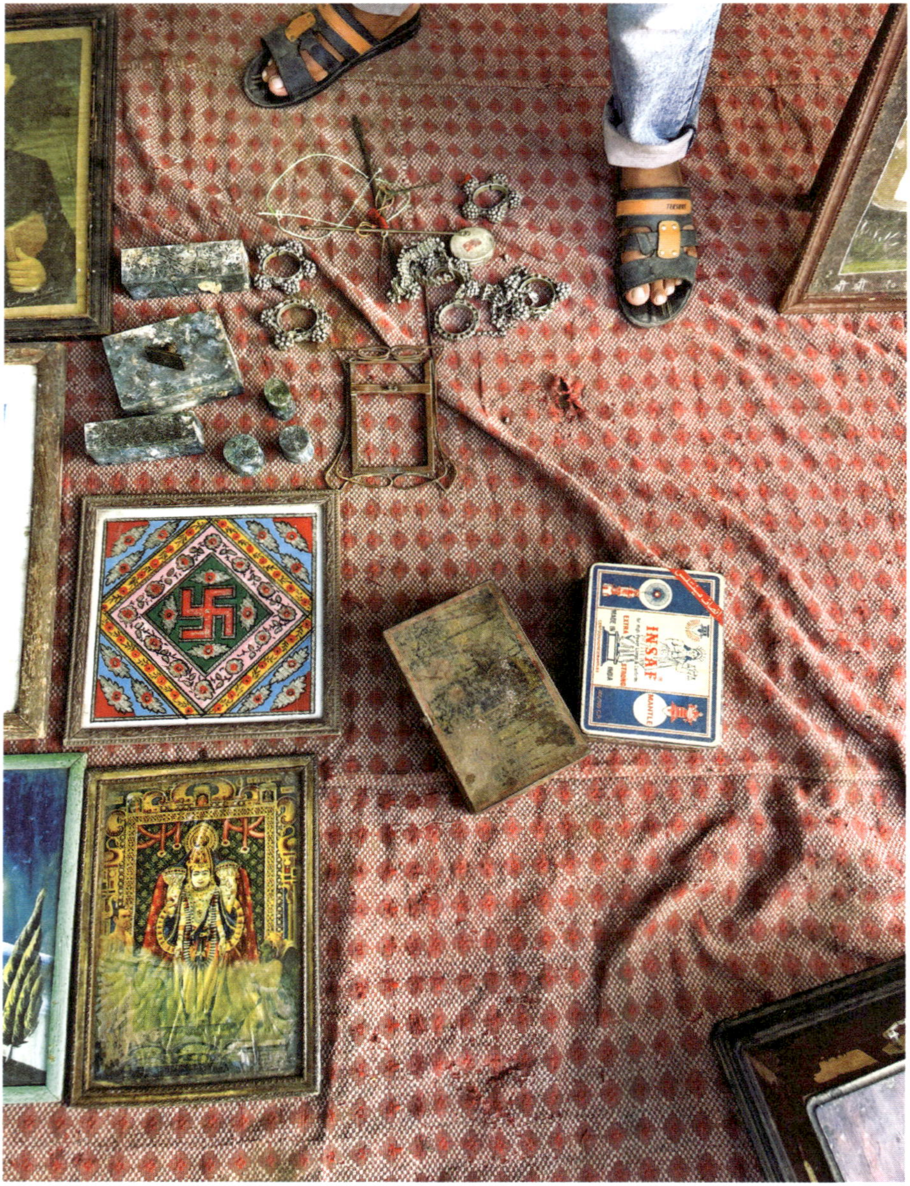
INSAF

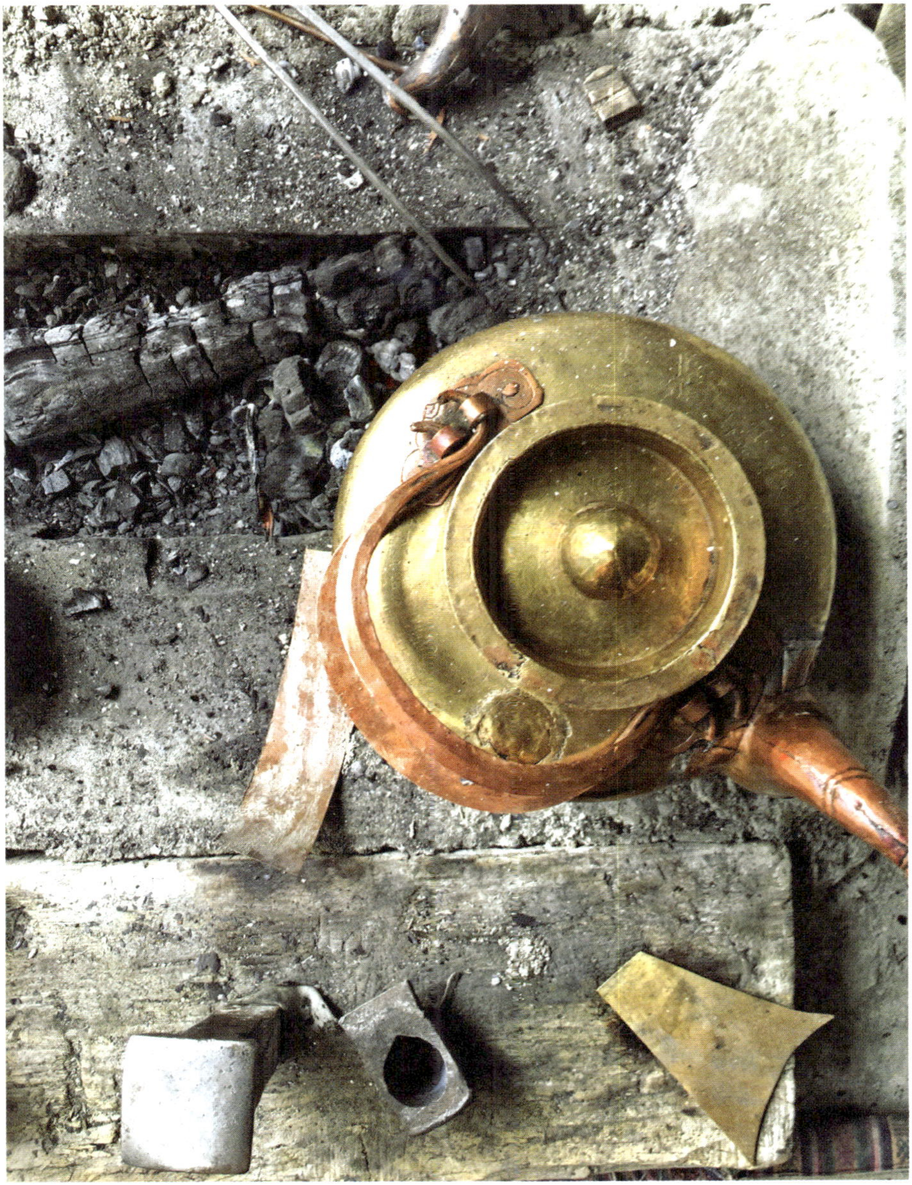

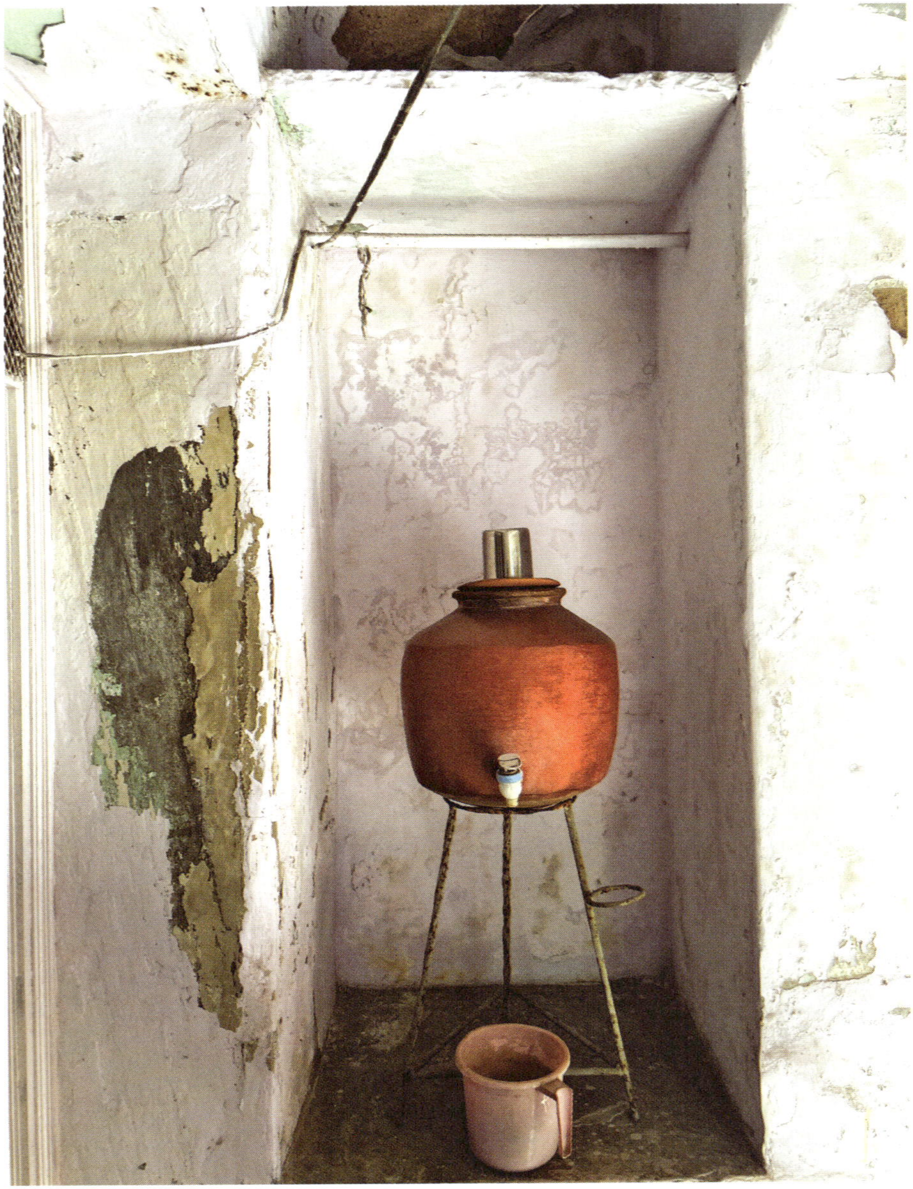

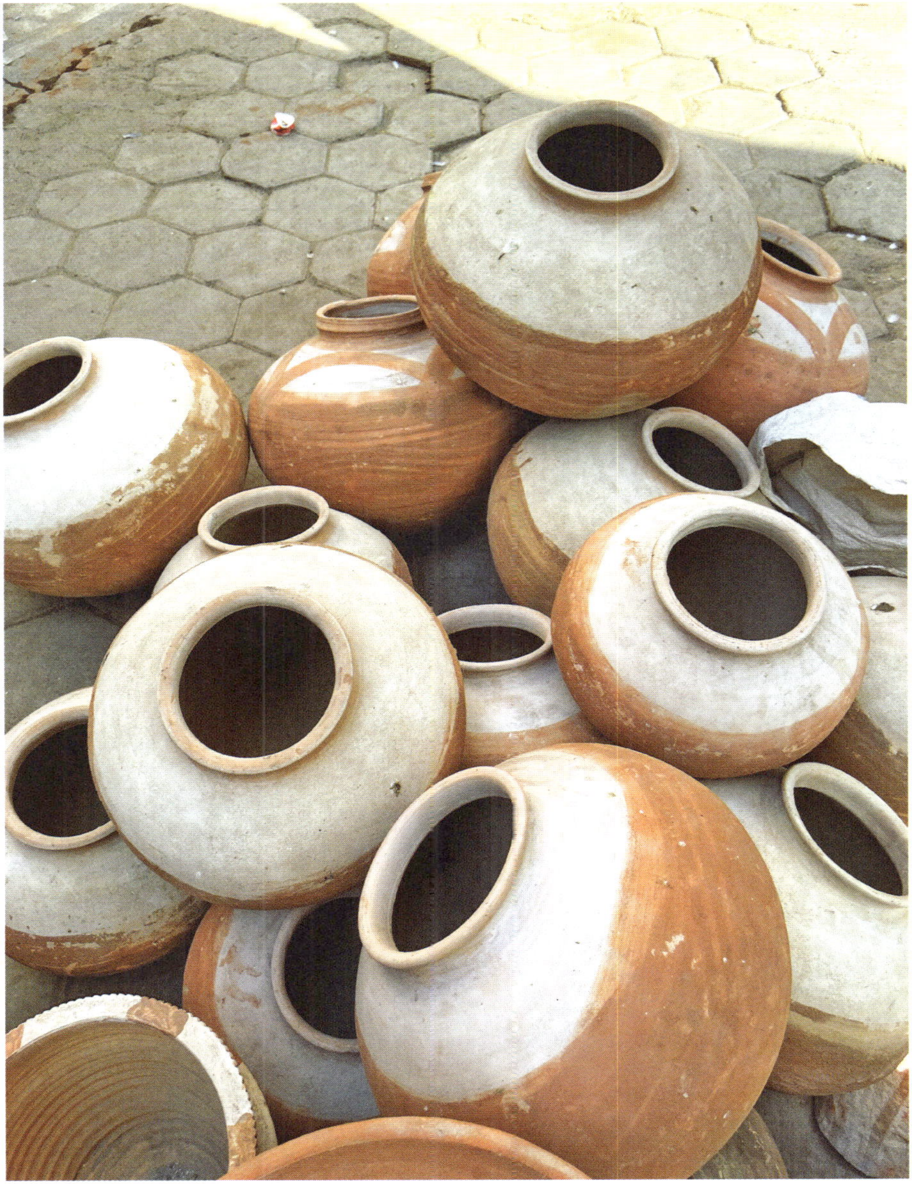

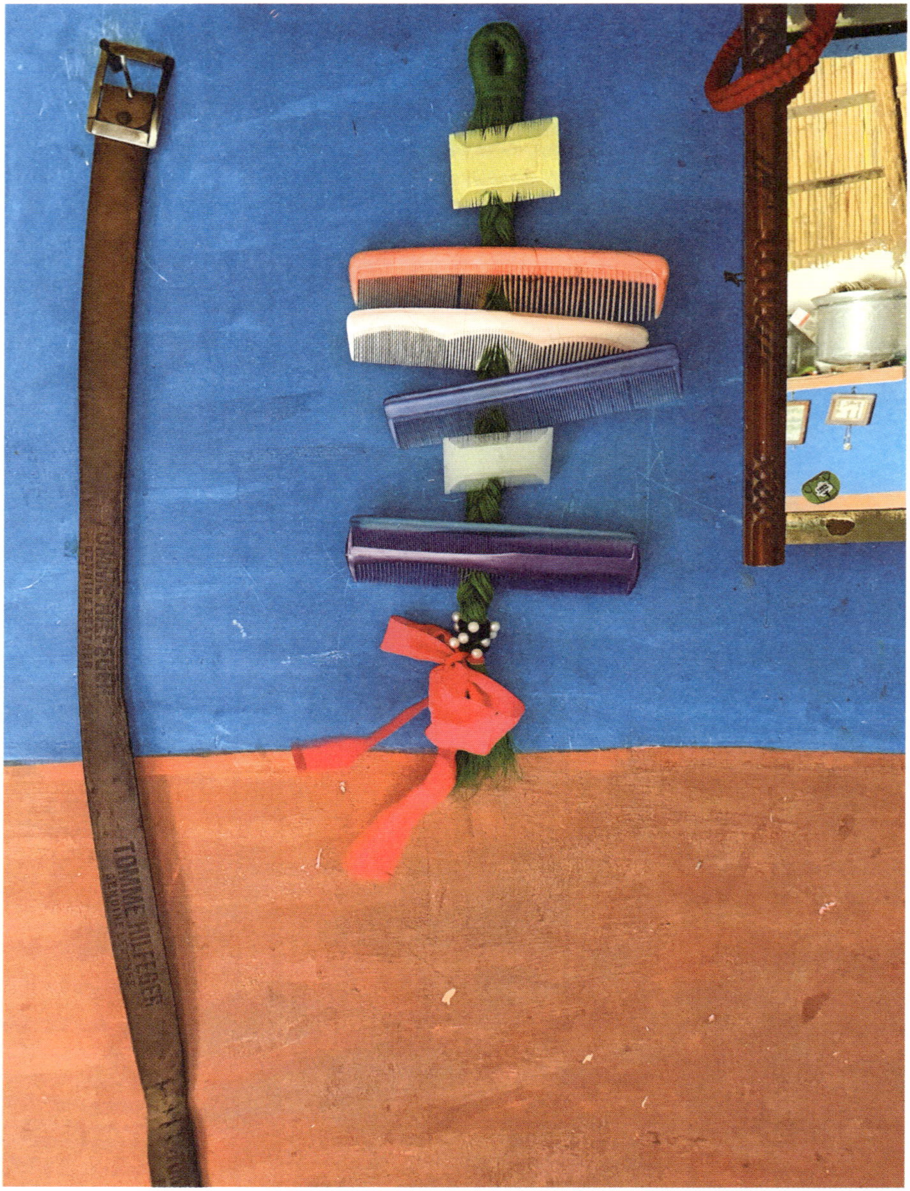

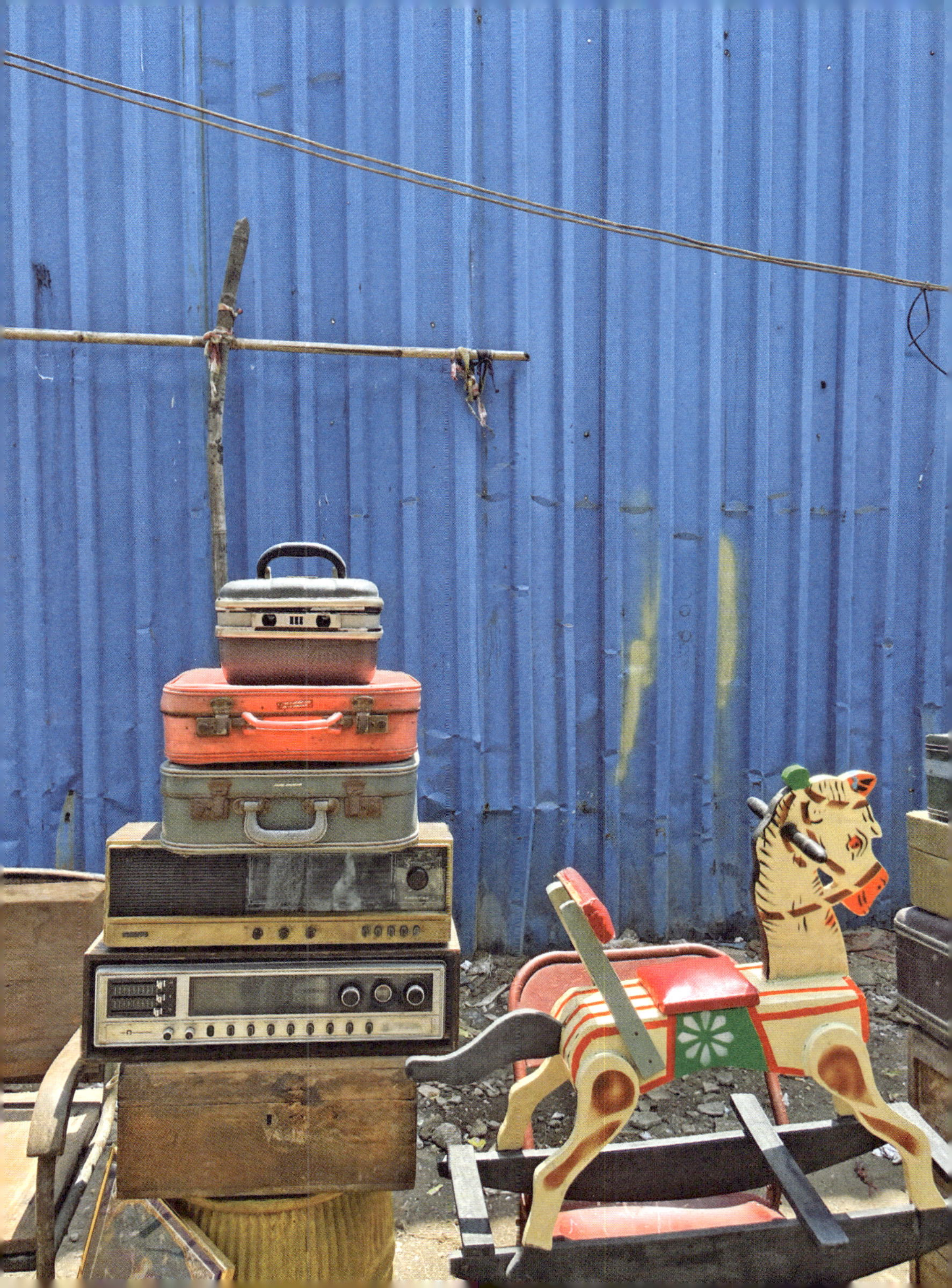

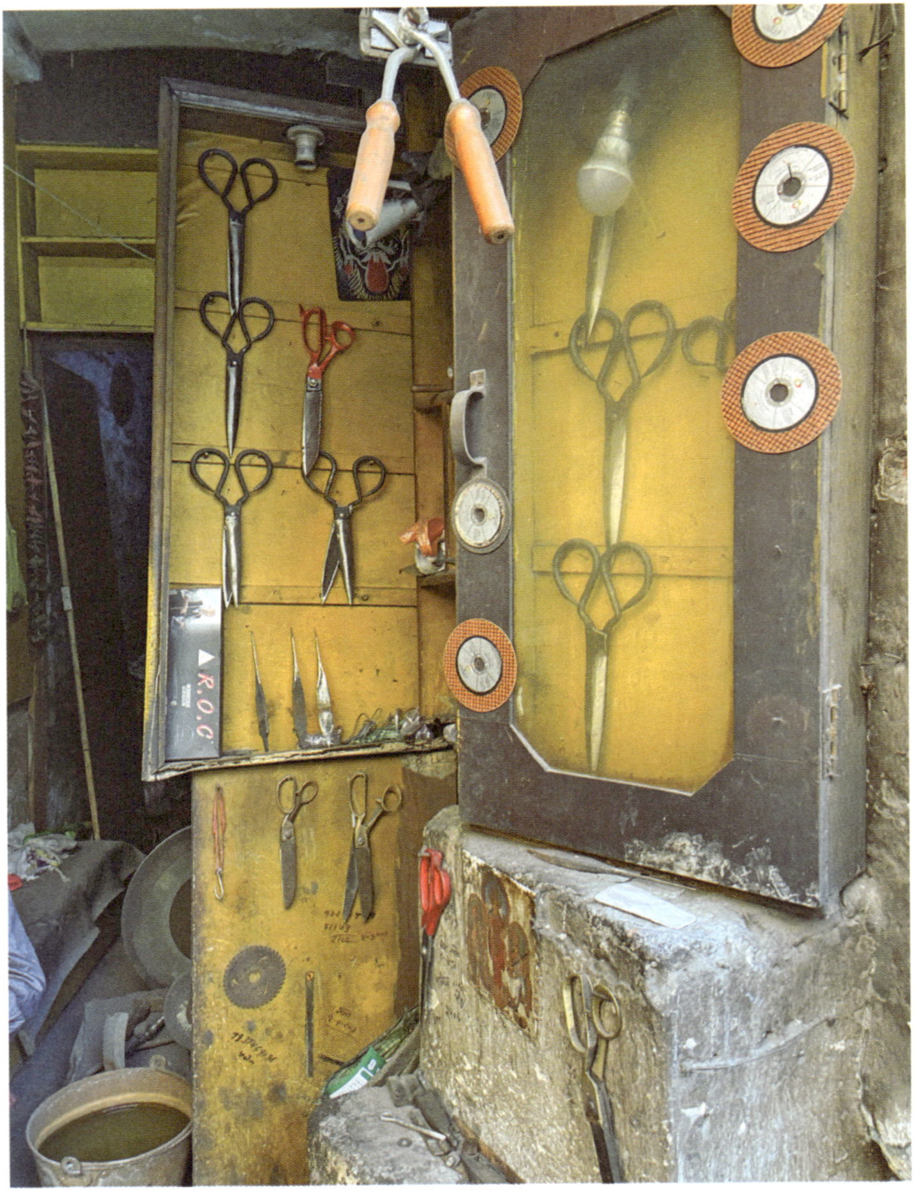
R.O.C

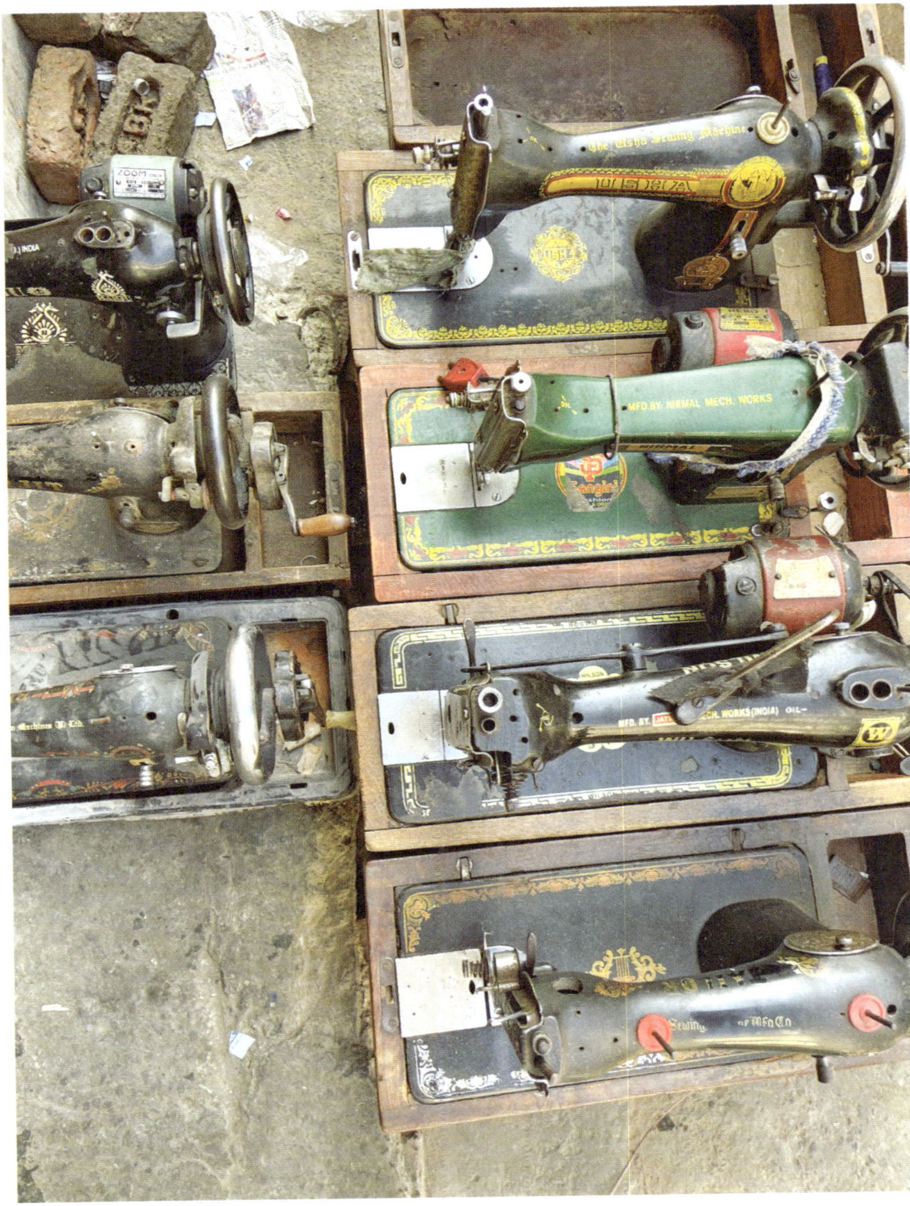
ZOOM
The Usha Sewing Machine
USHA
MFD.BY. NIRMAL MECH. WORKS

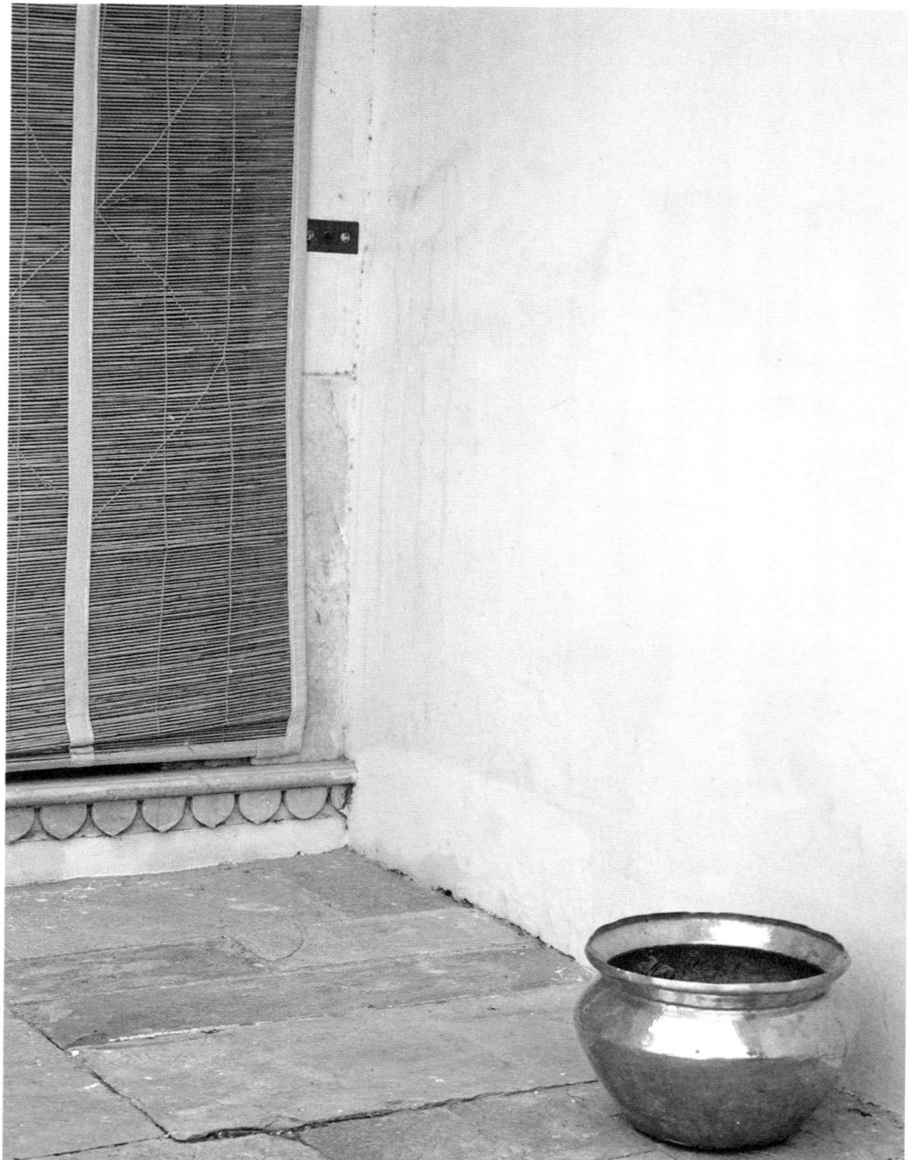

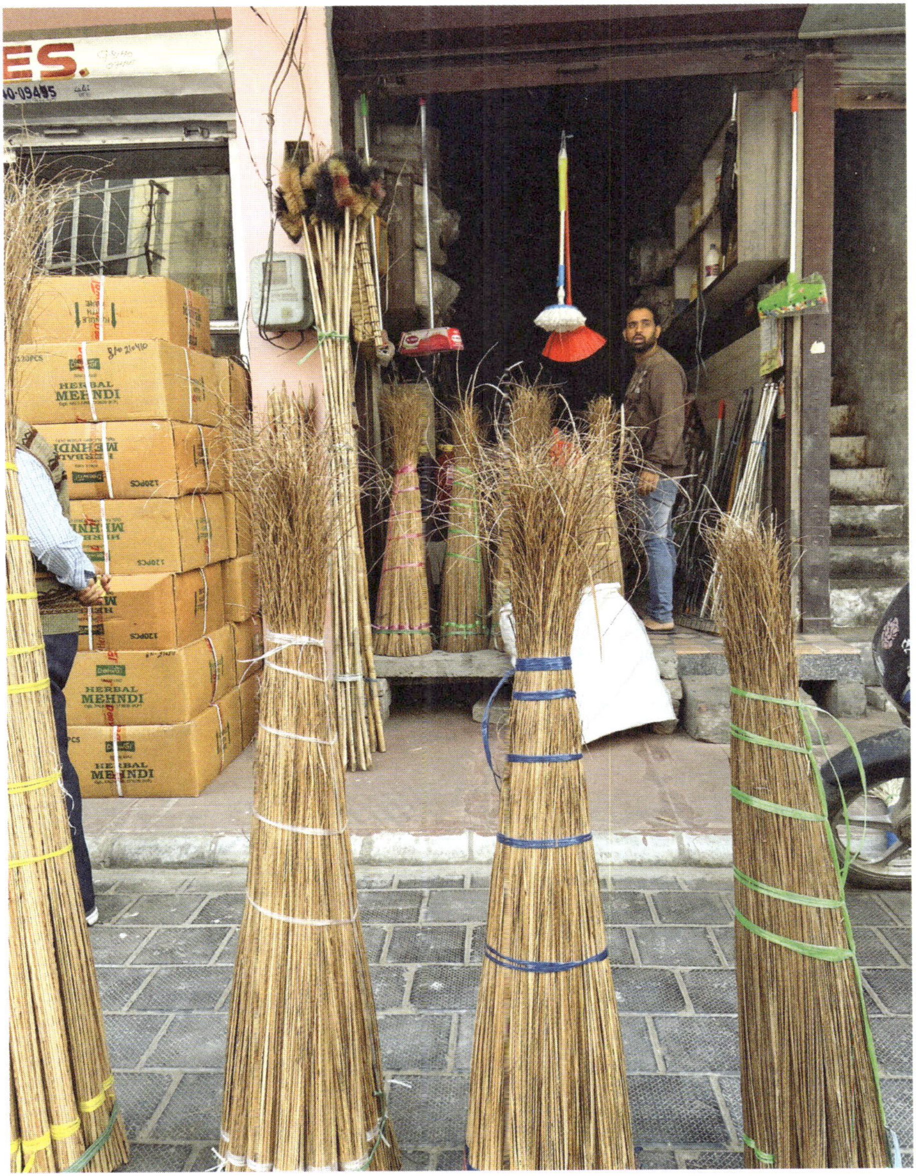
ES.
HERBAL MEHNDI
HERBAL MEHNDI
HERBAL MEHNDI

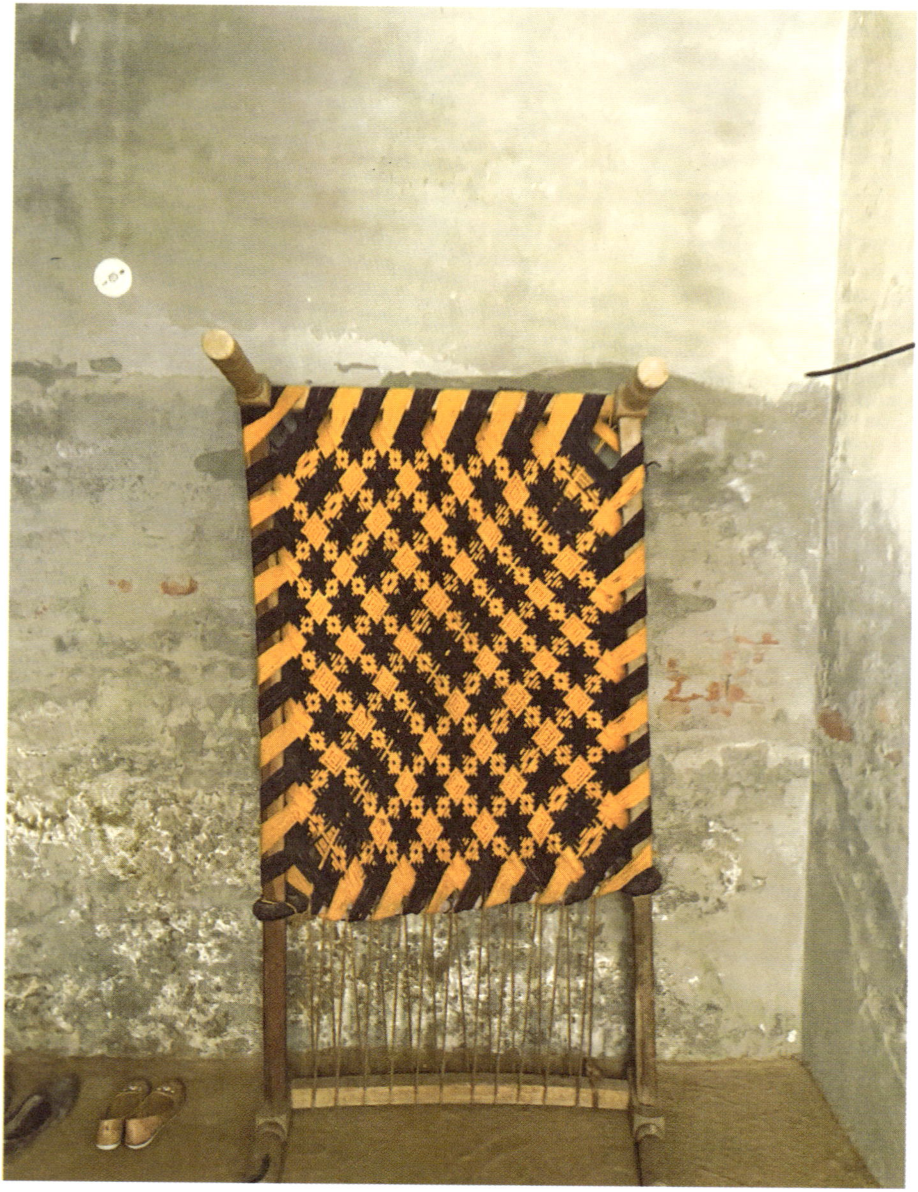

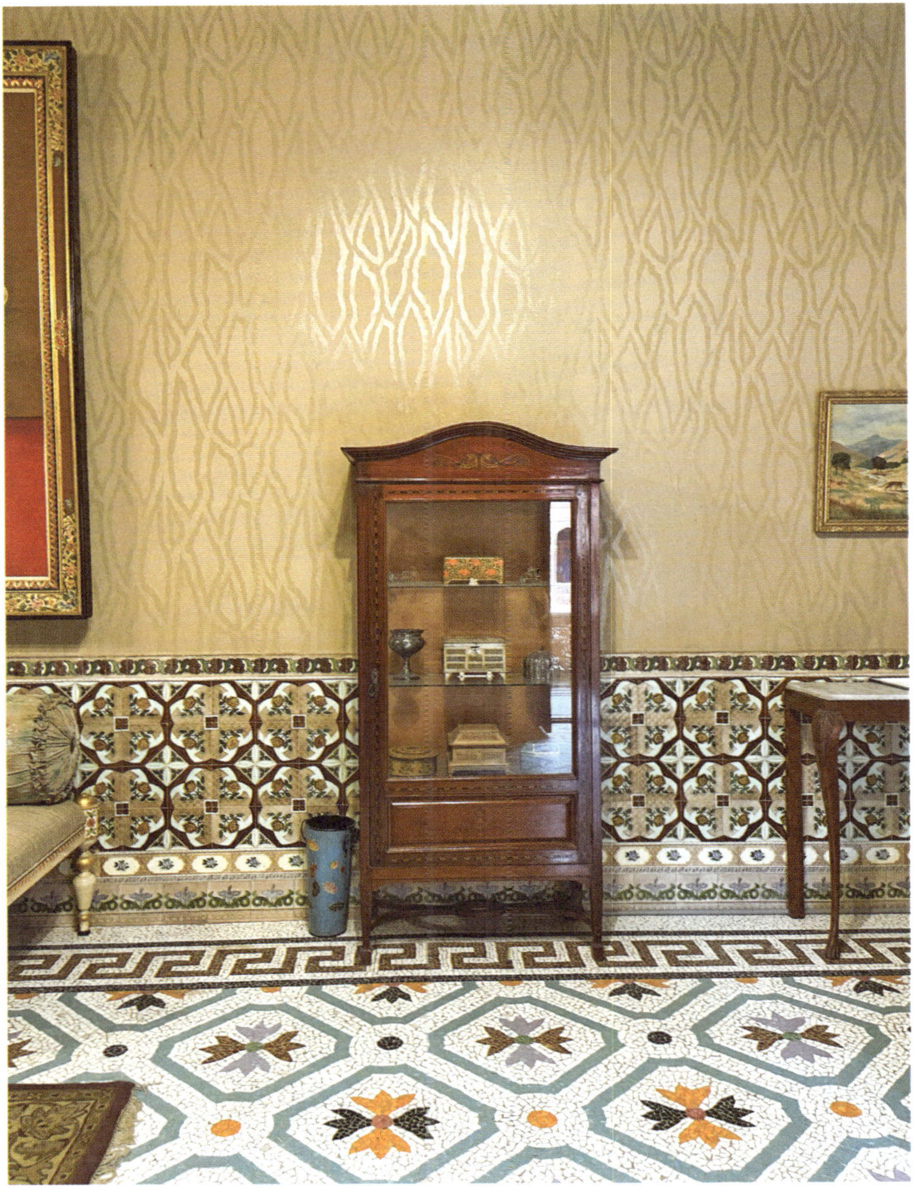

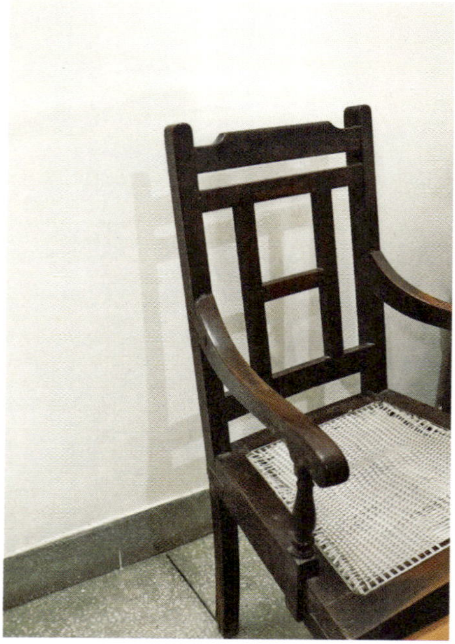
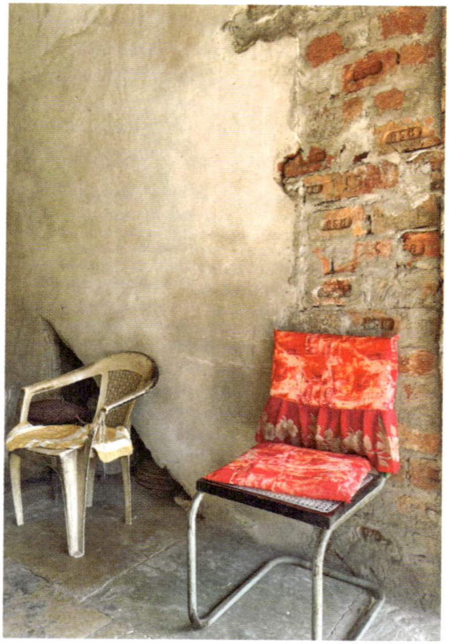
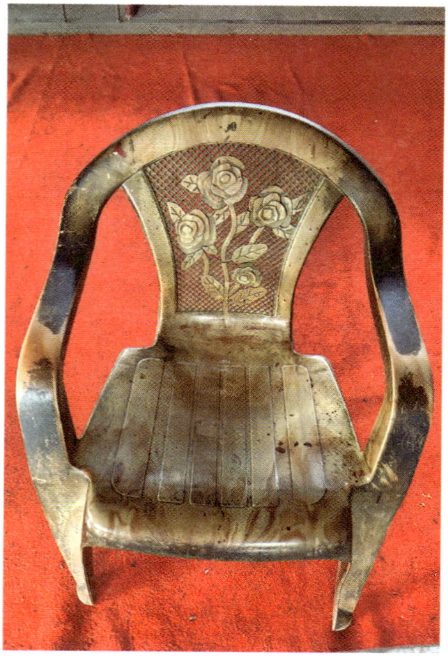
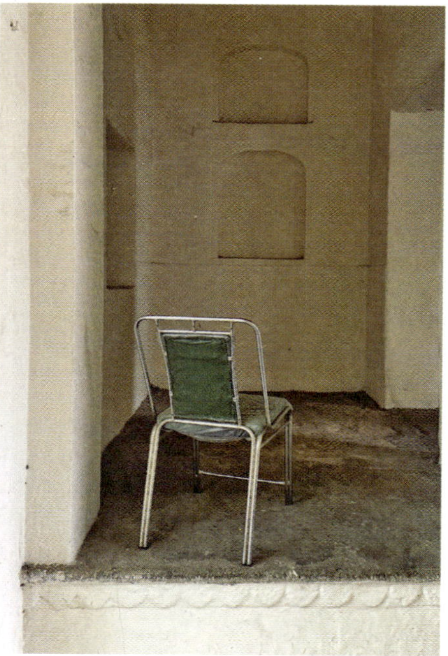

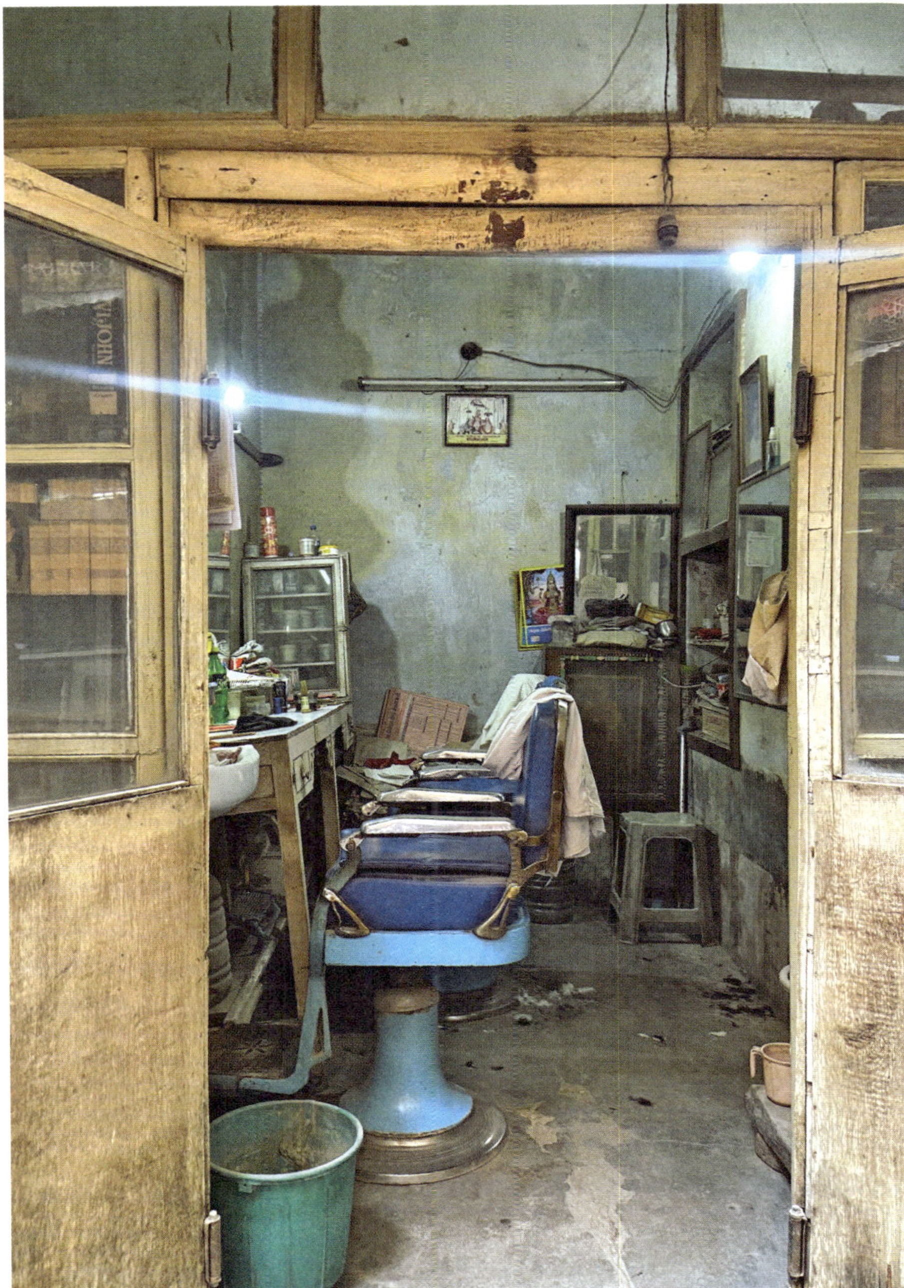

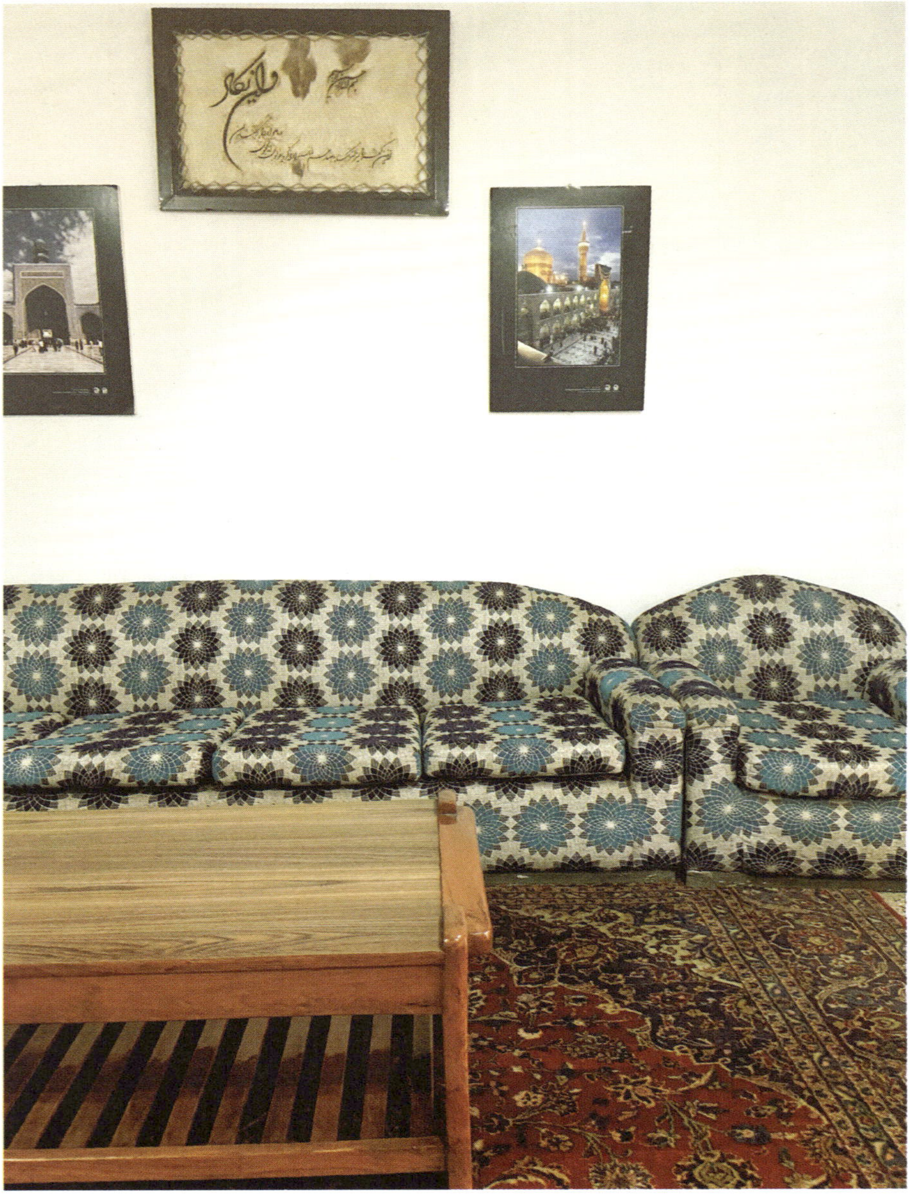

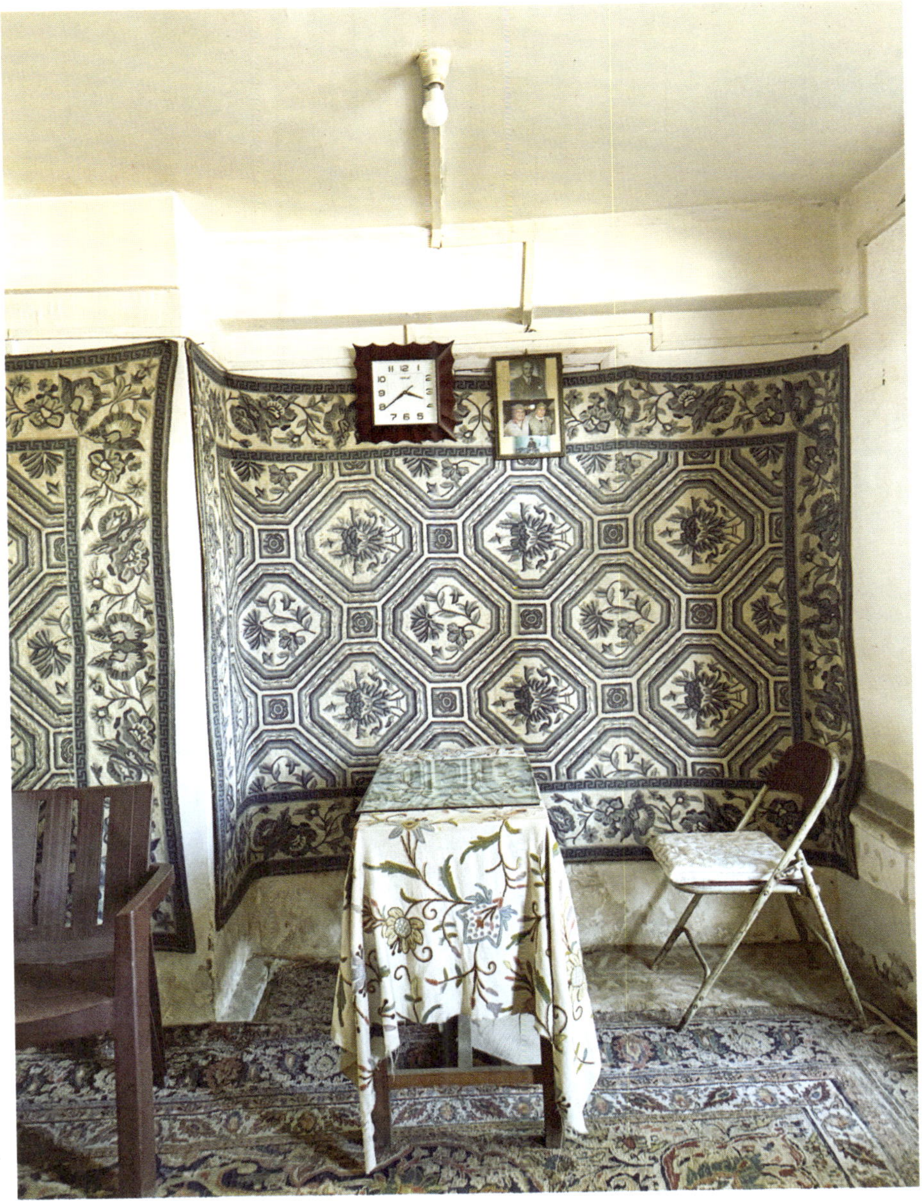

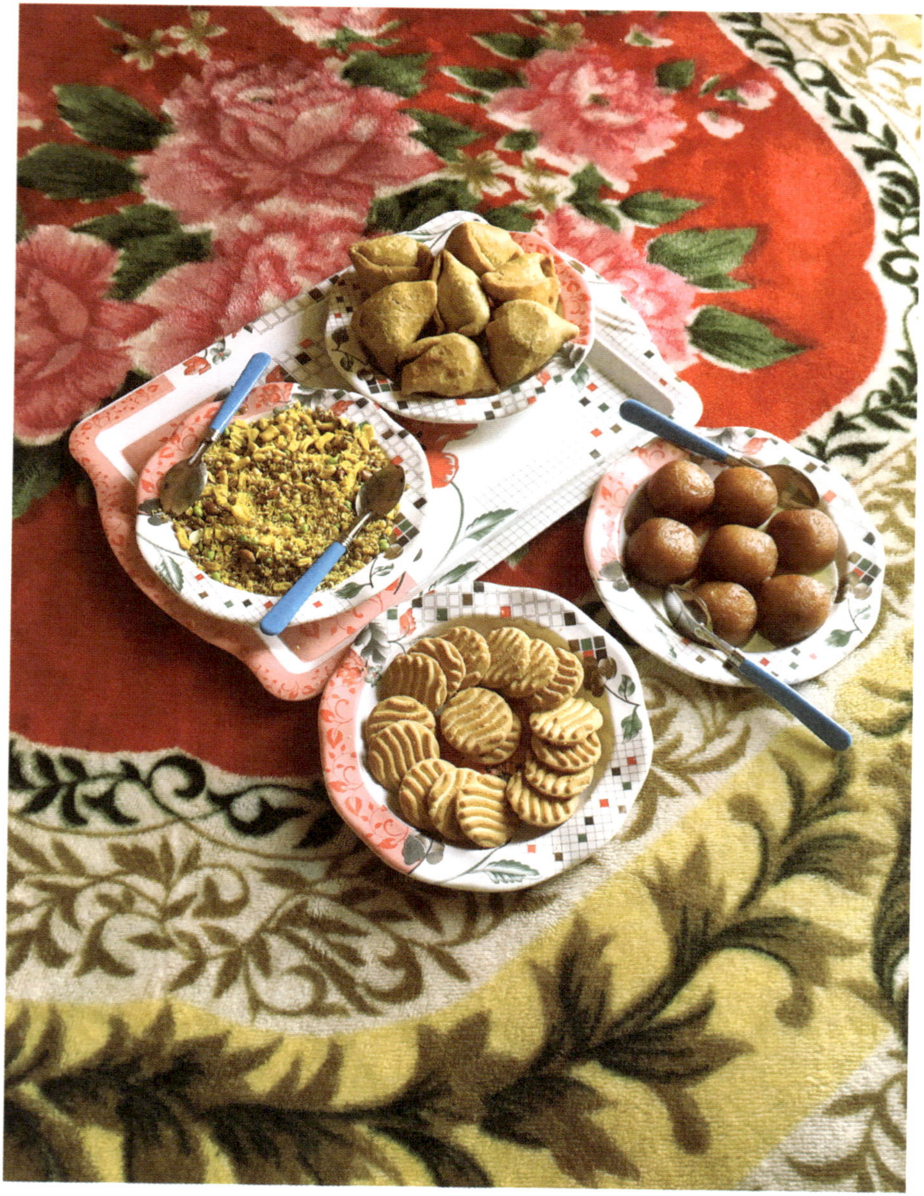

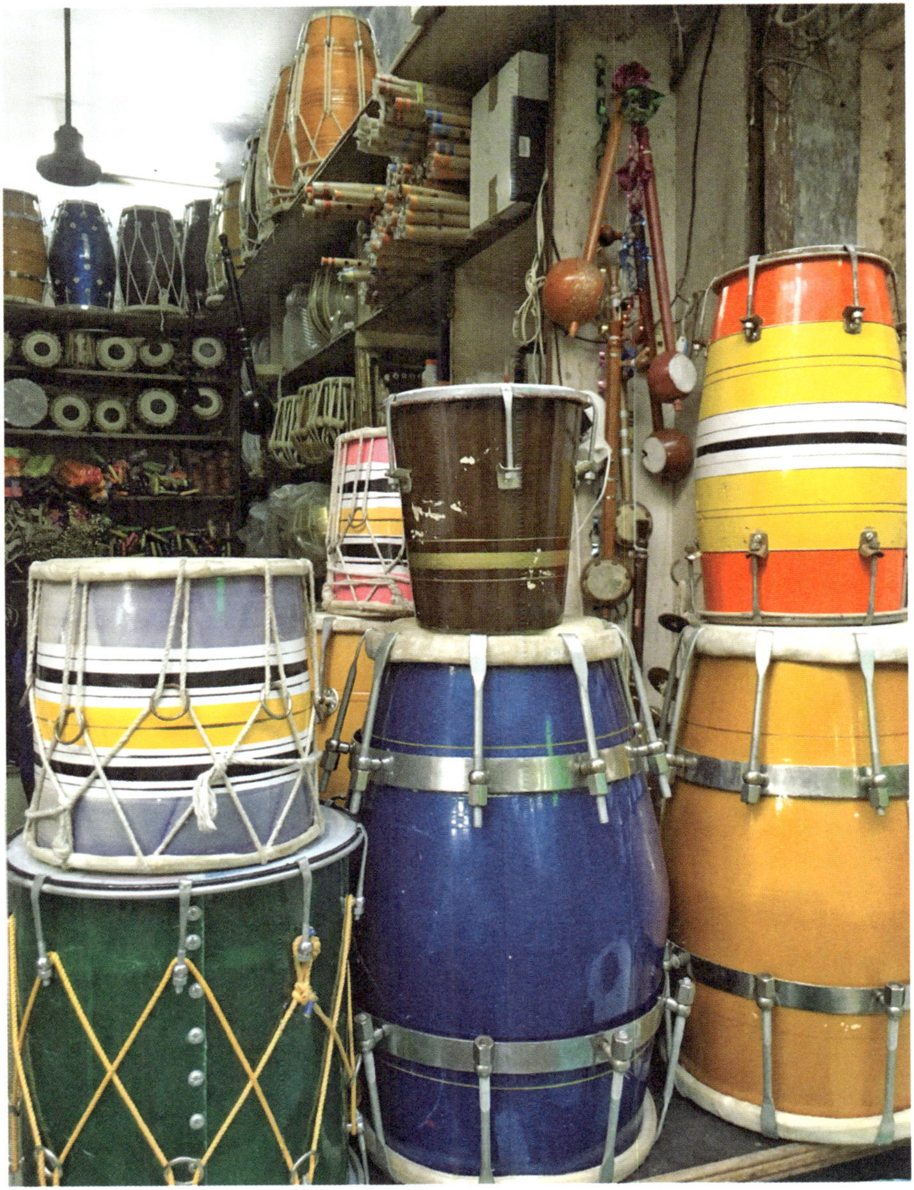

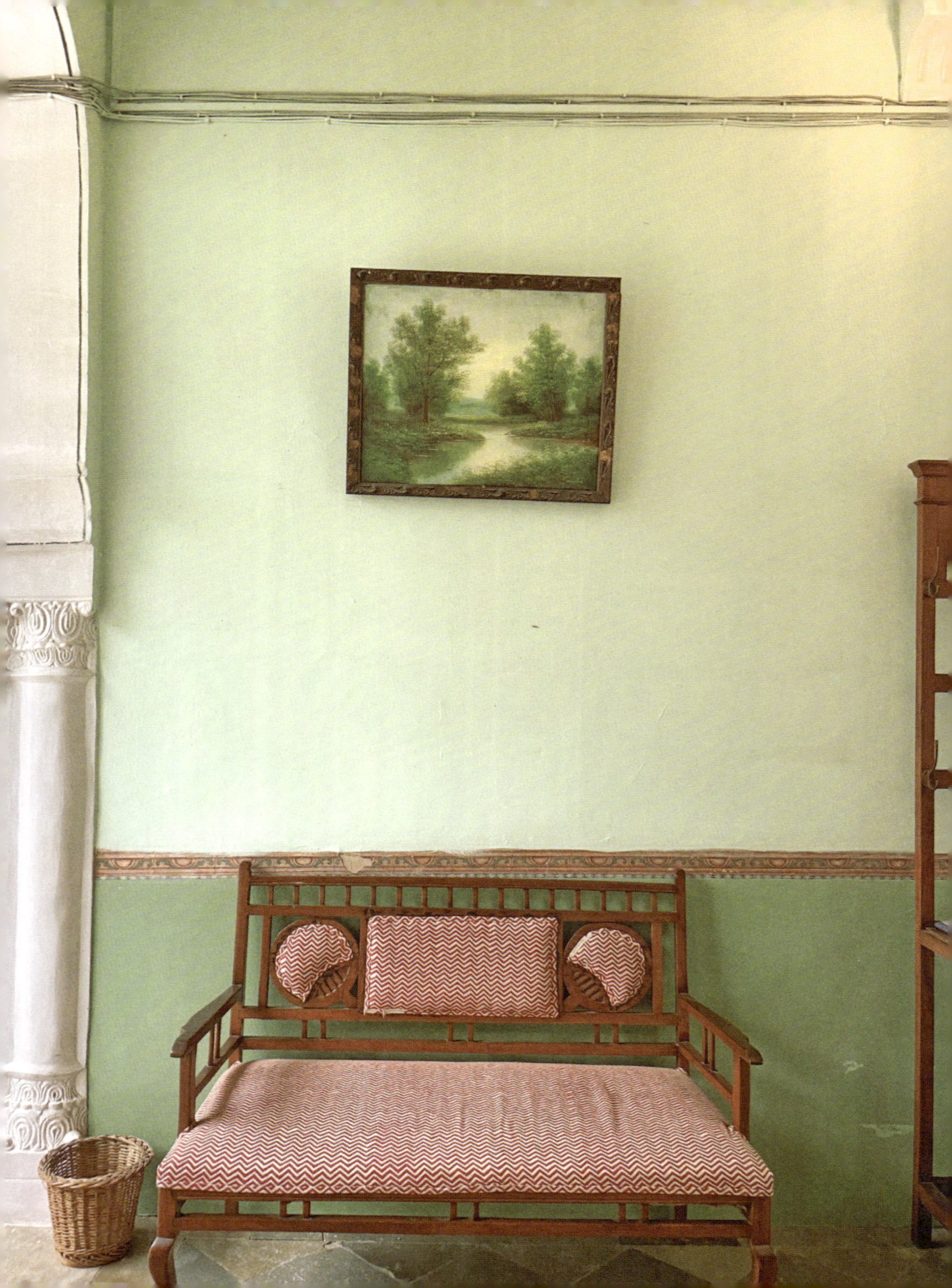

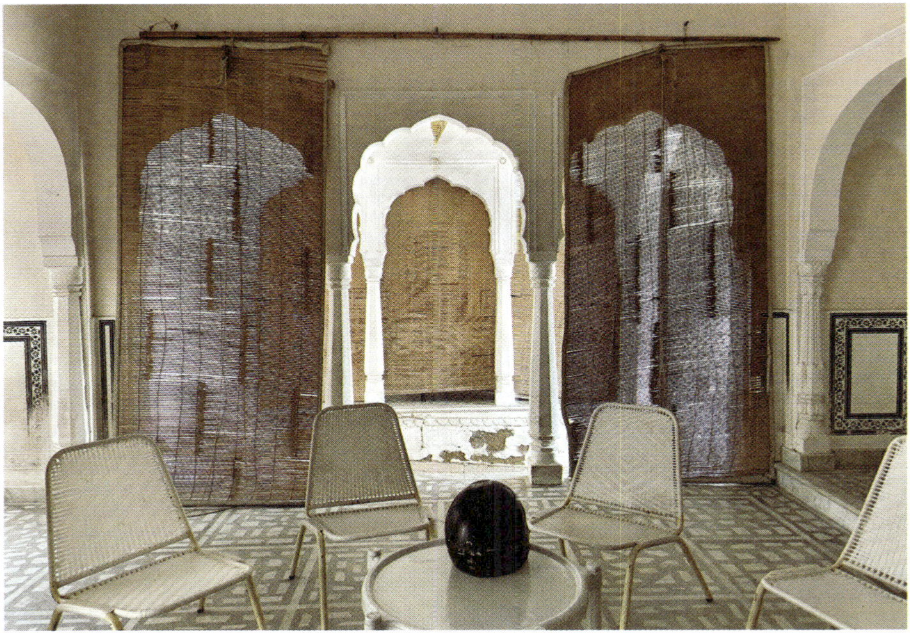

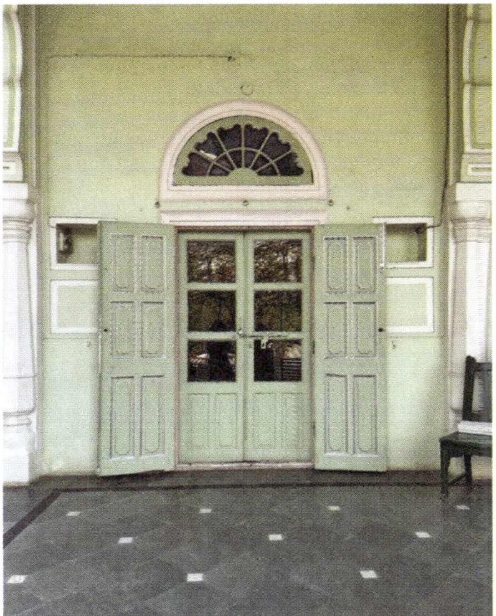

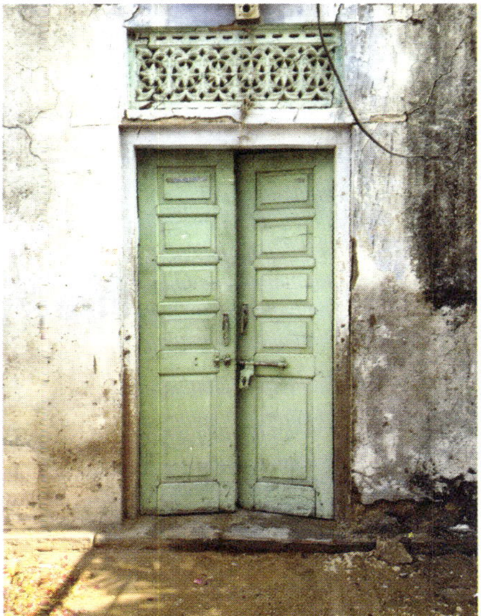

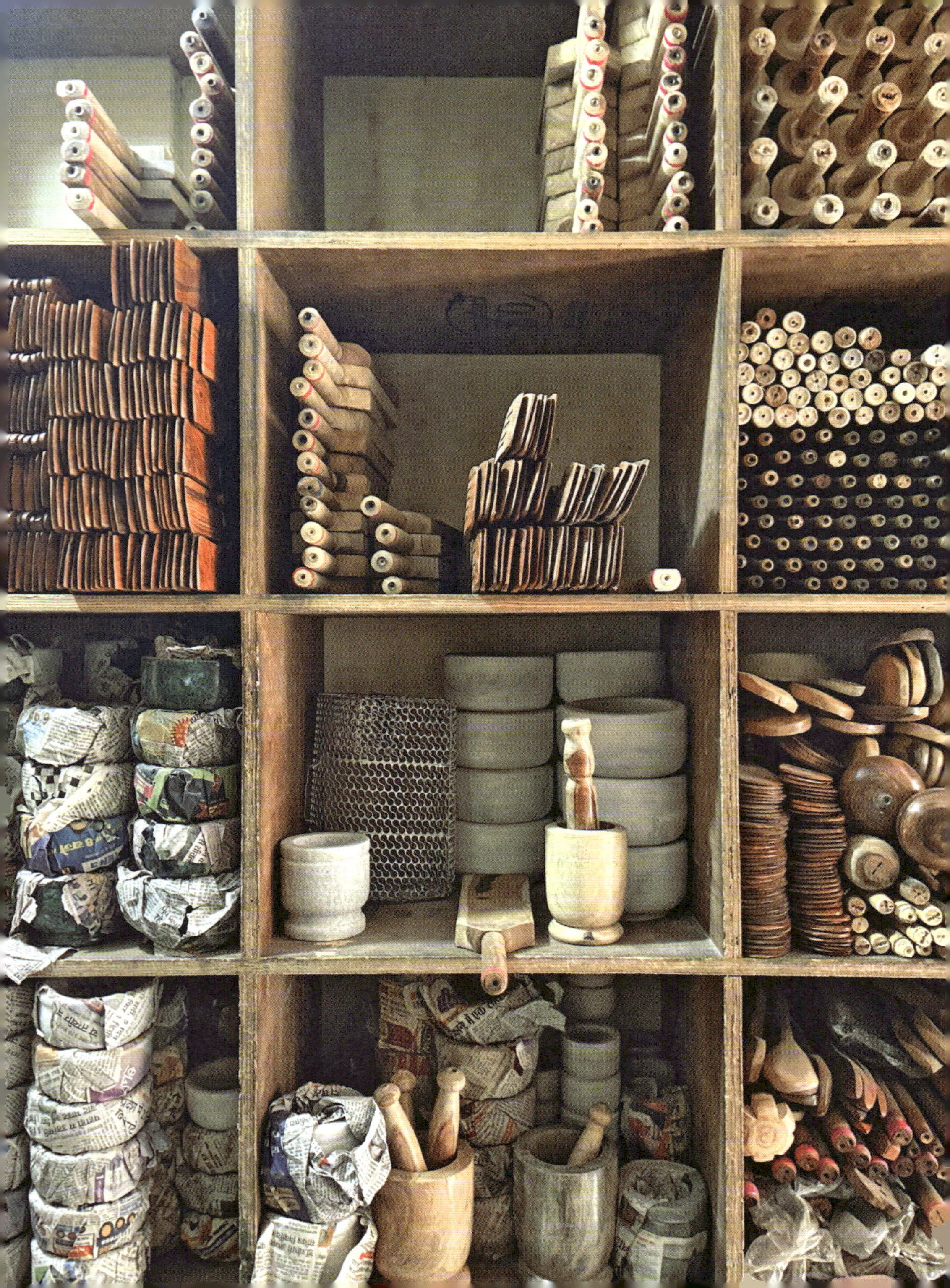

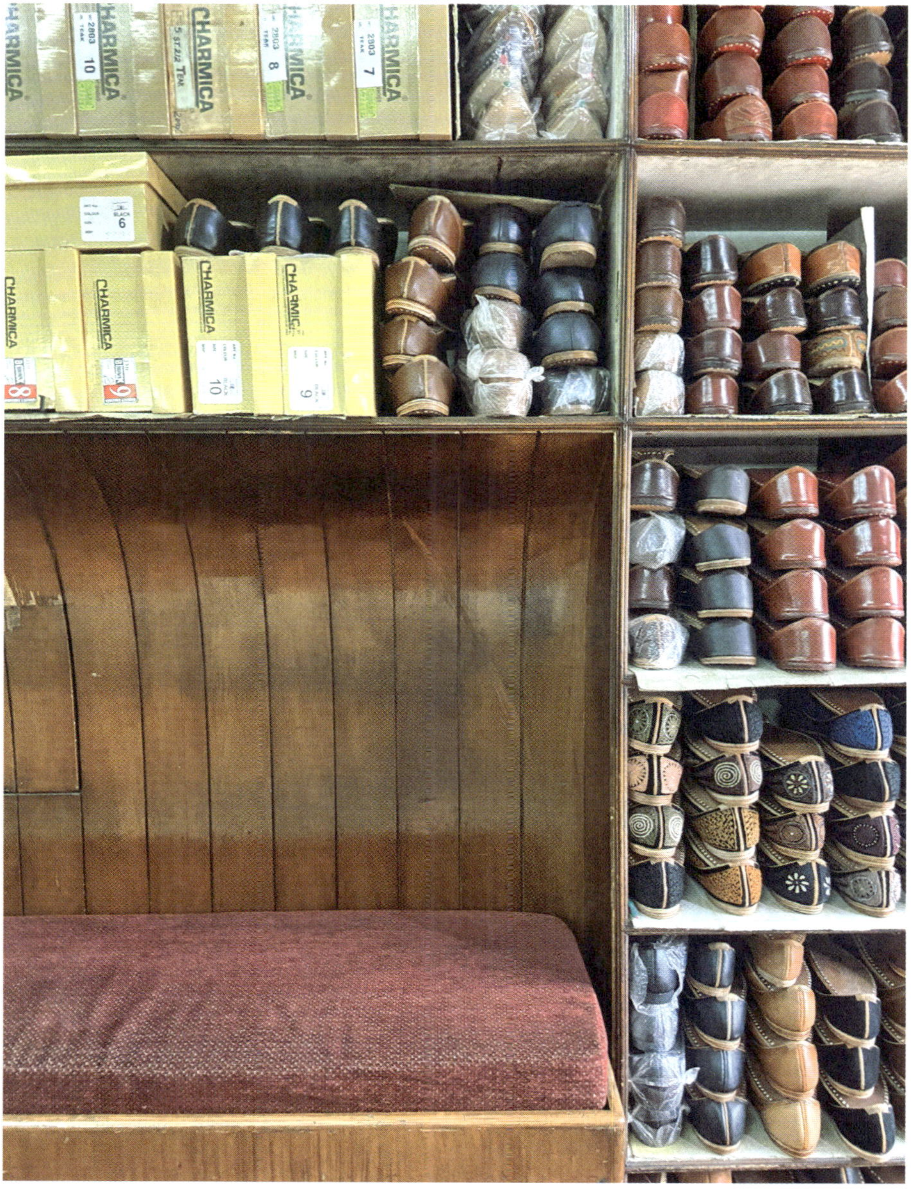
CHARMICA
CHARMICA
CHARMICA
CHARMICA

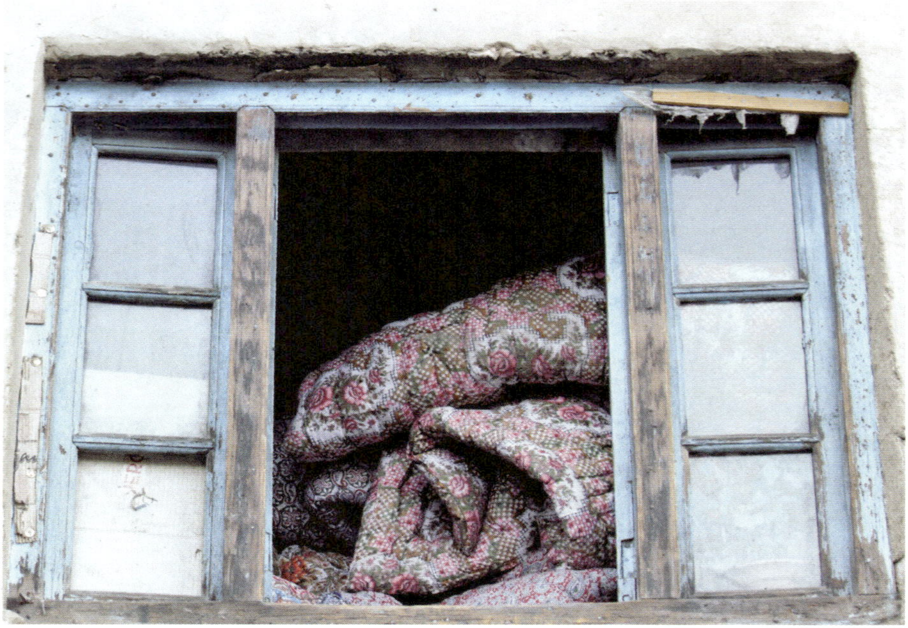

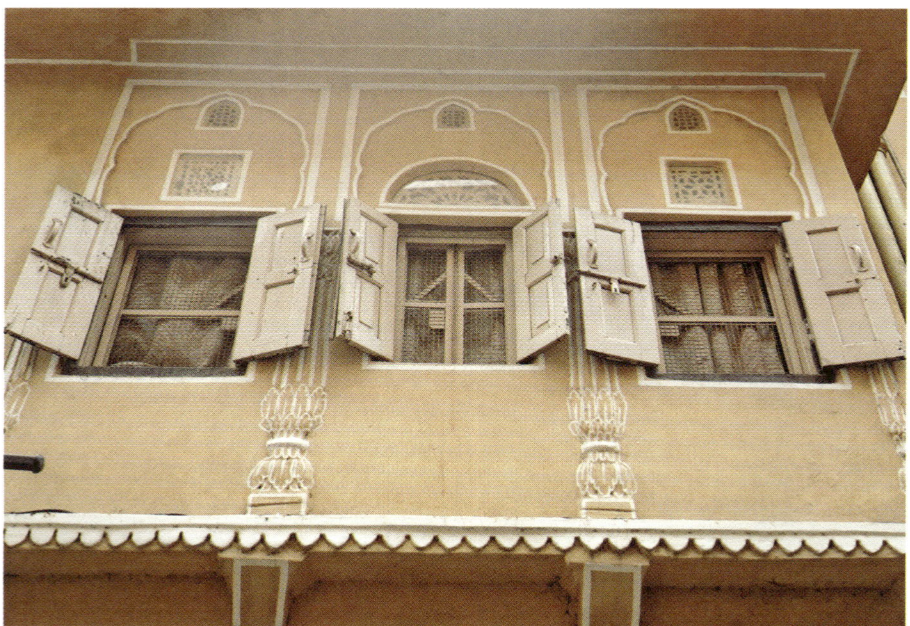

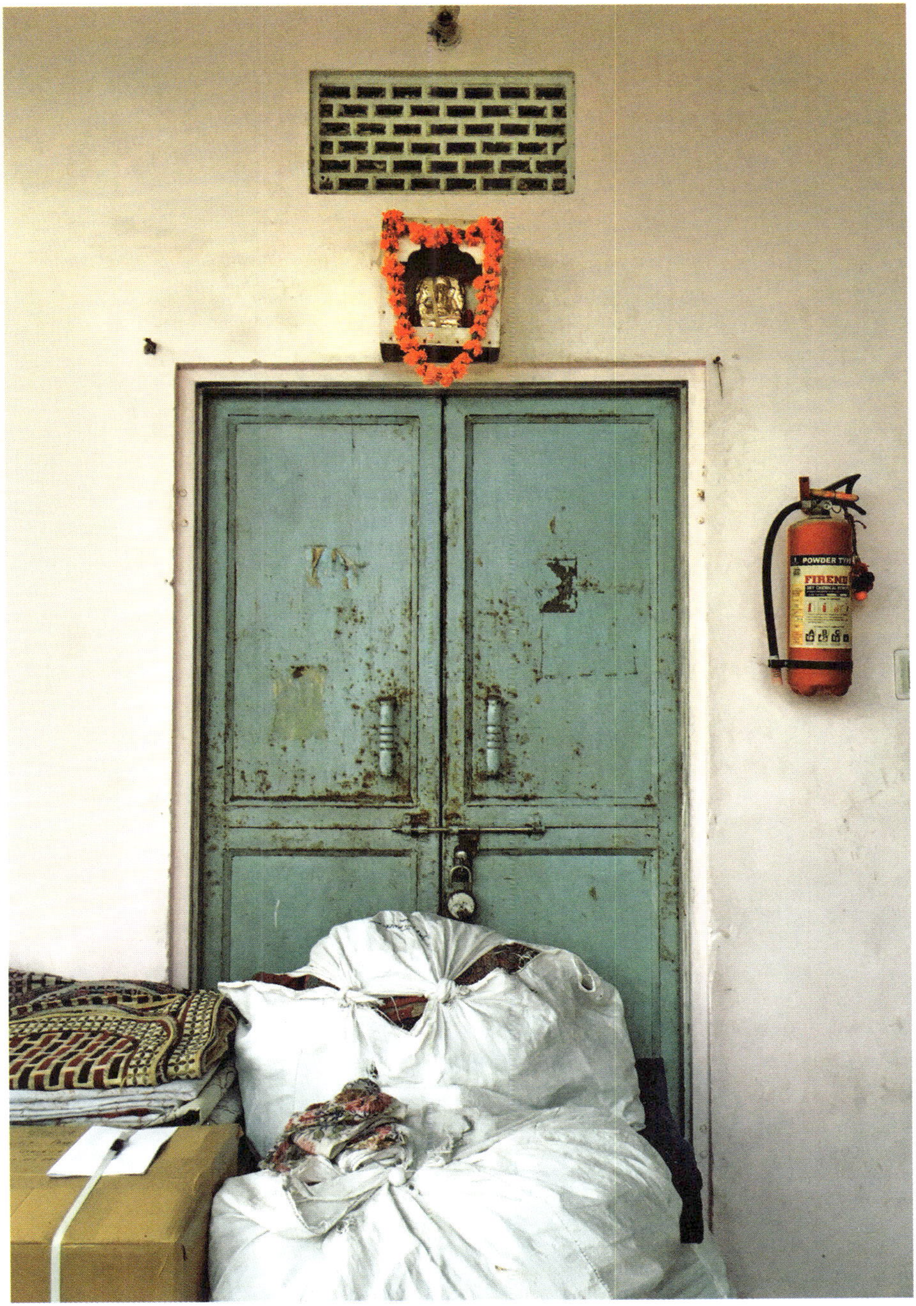

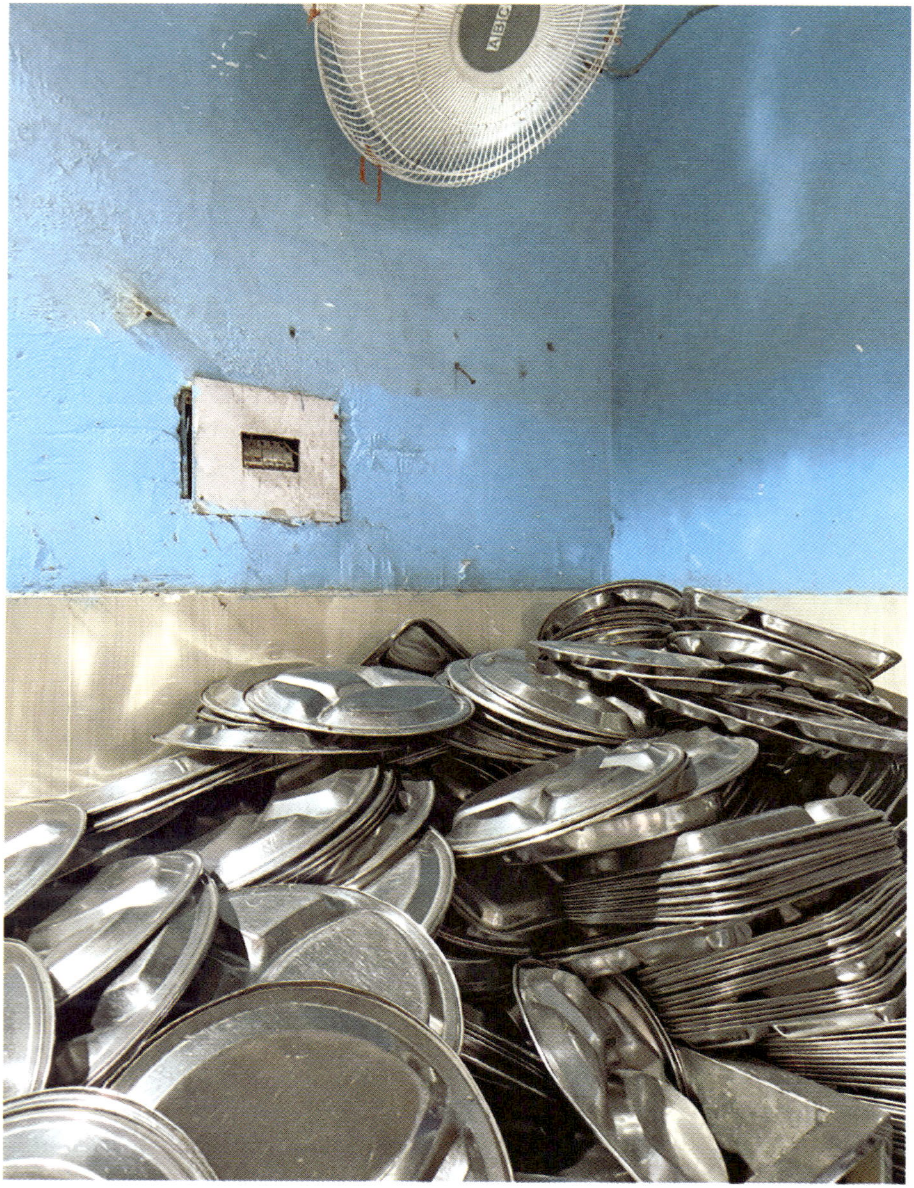
ABC

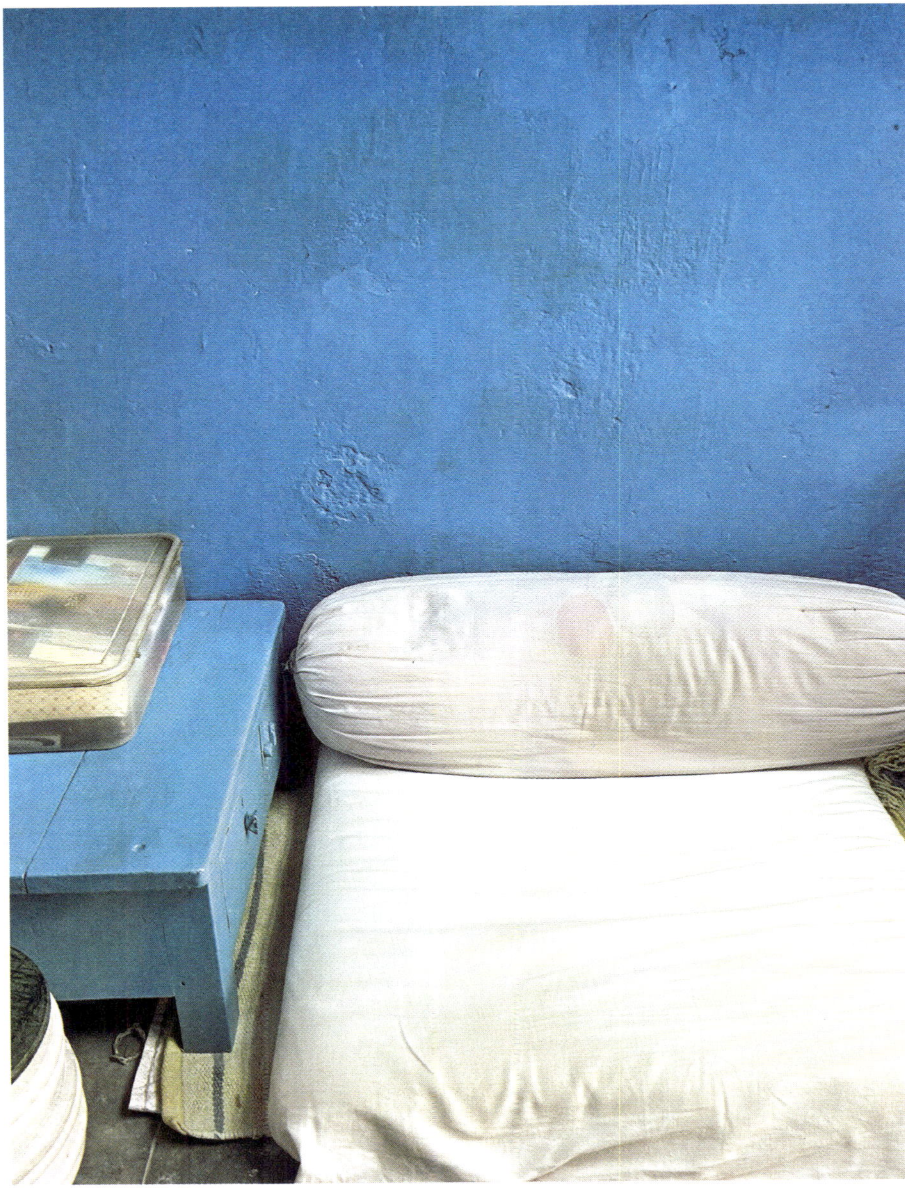

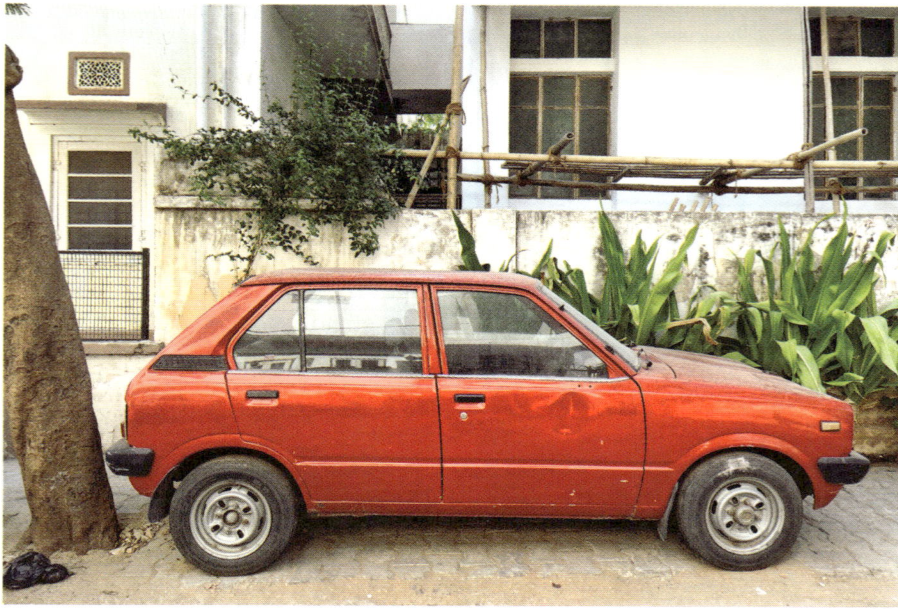

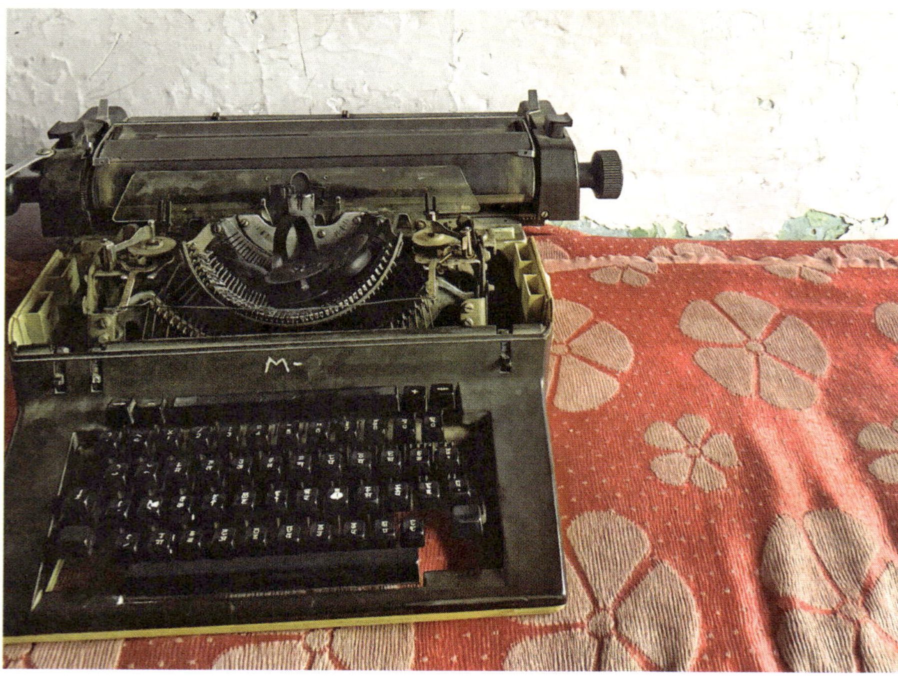
M-

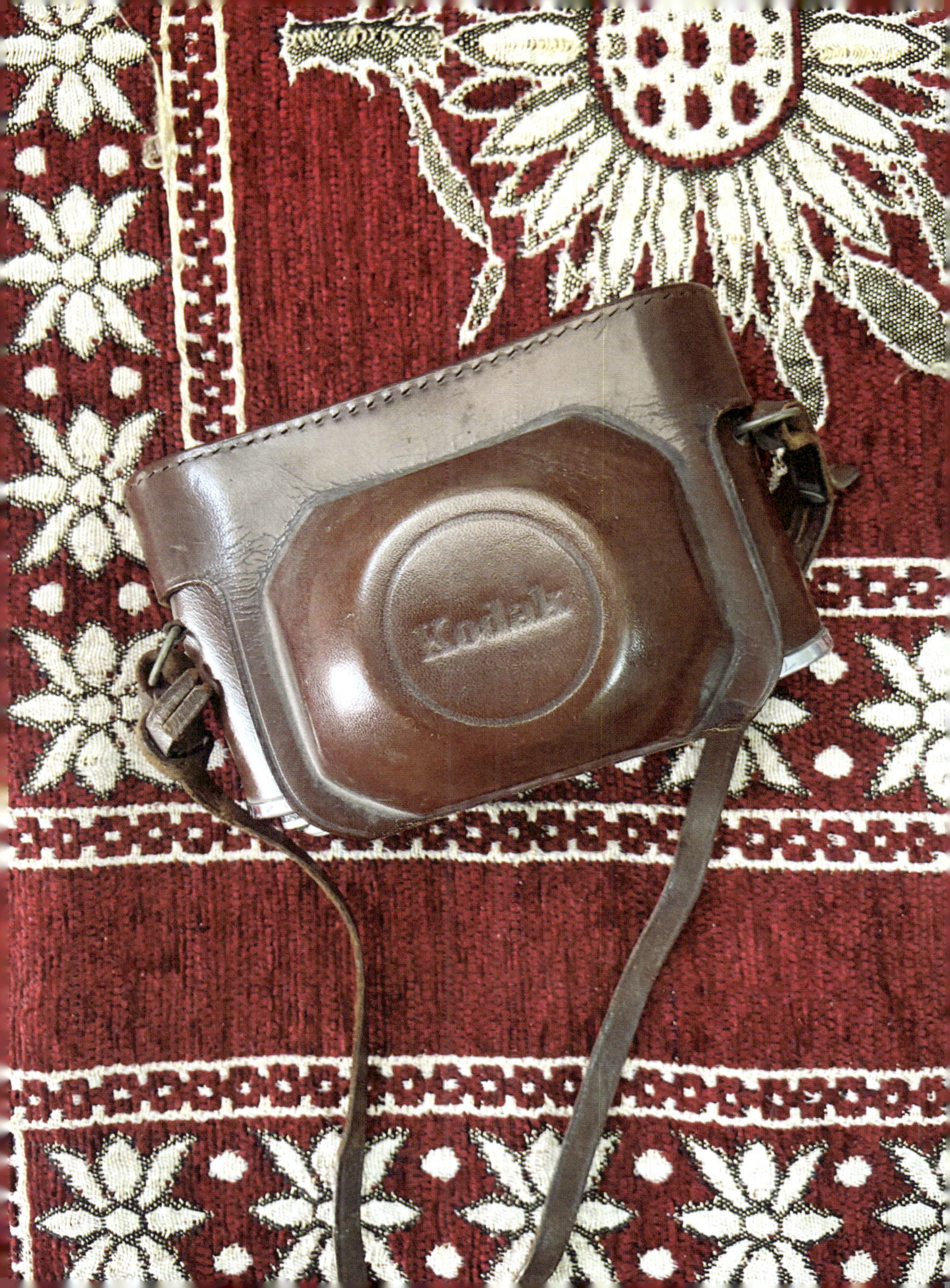
Kodak

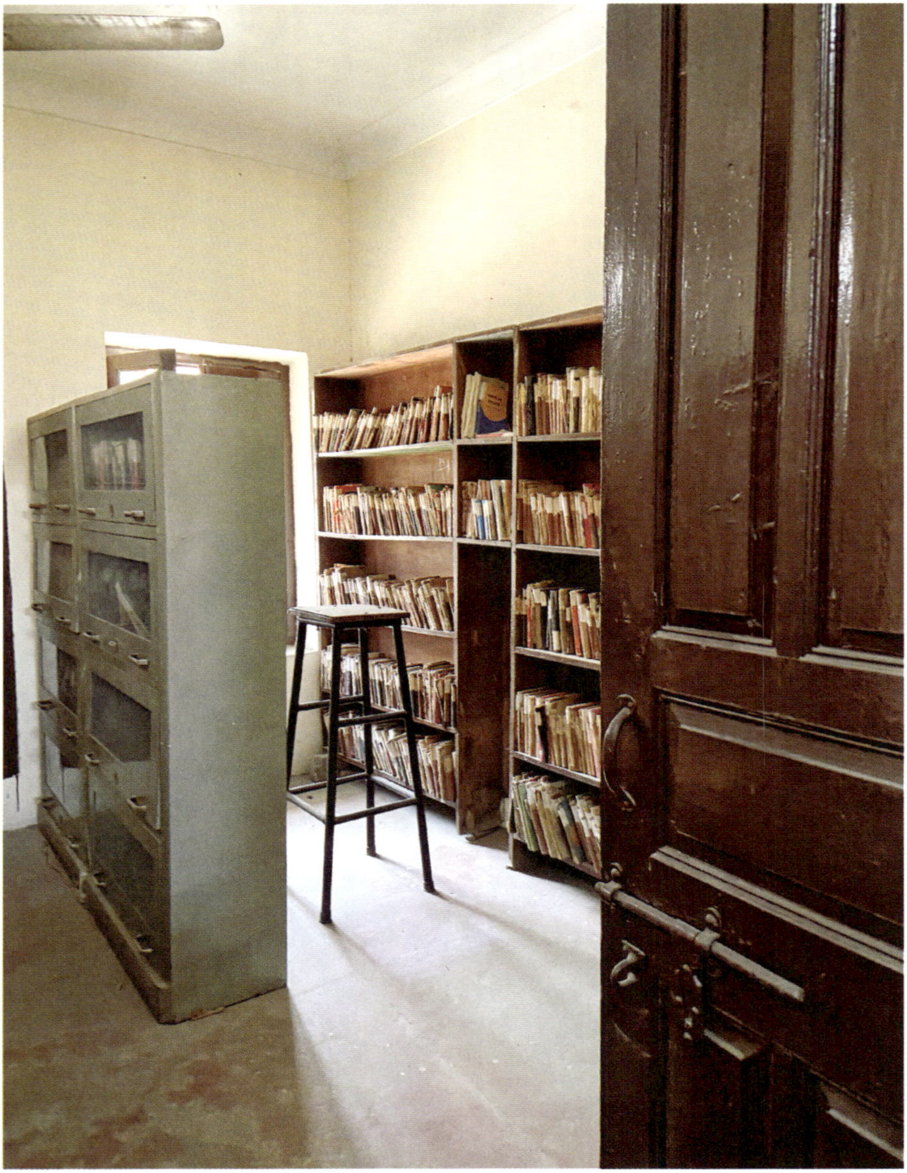

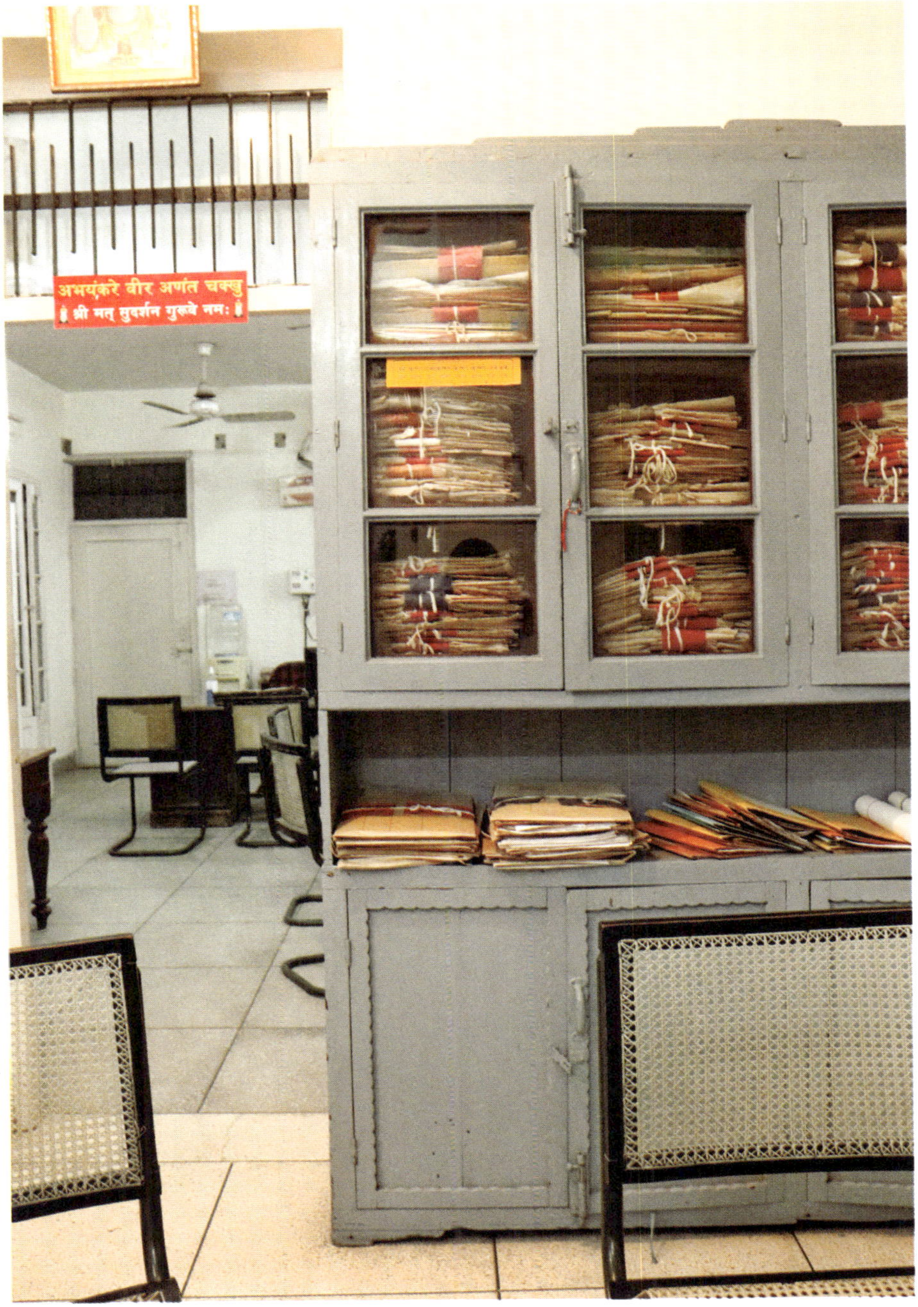
अभयंकरे वीर अणंत चक्खु
श्री मत् सुदर्शन गुरुवे नमः

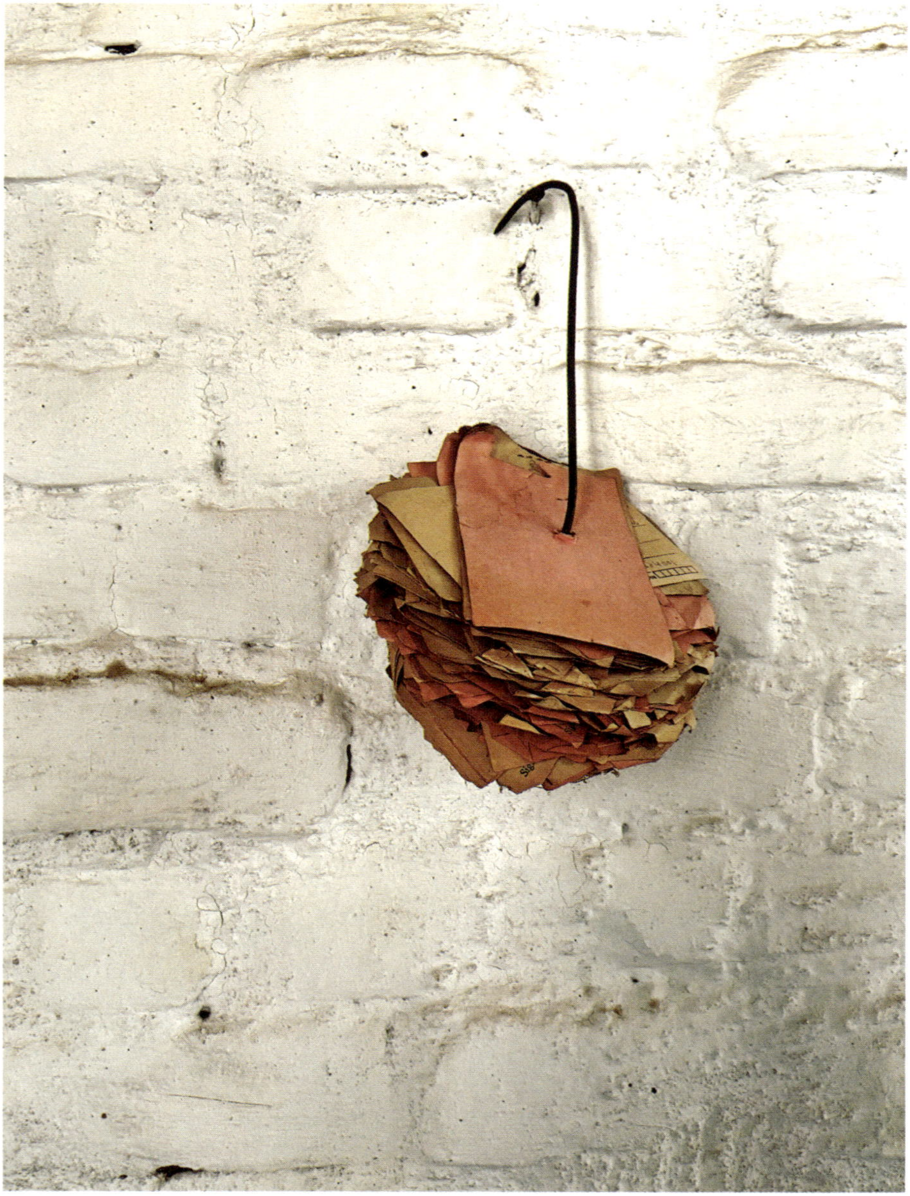

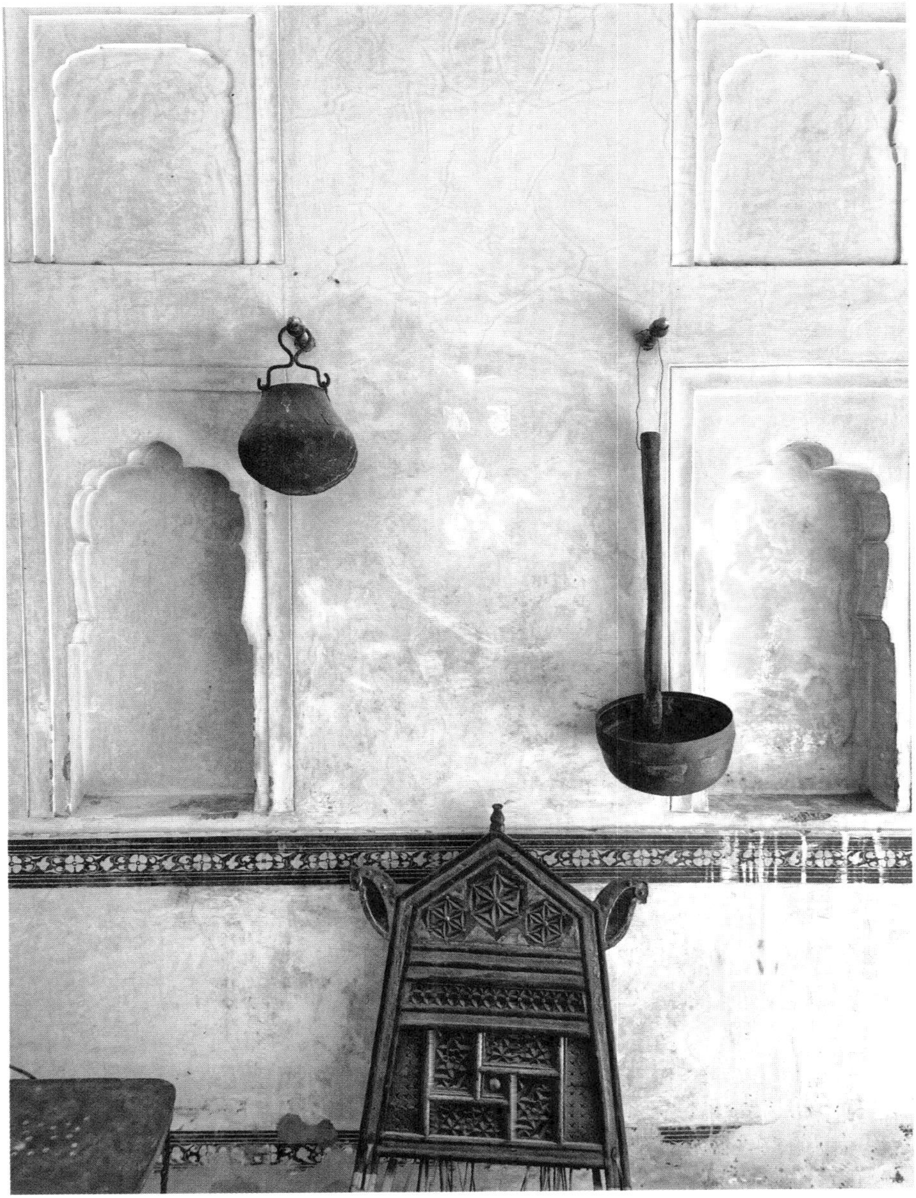

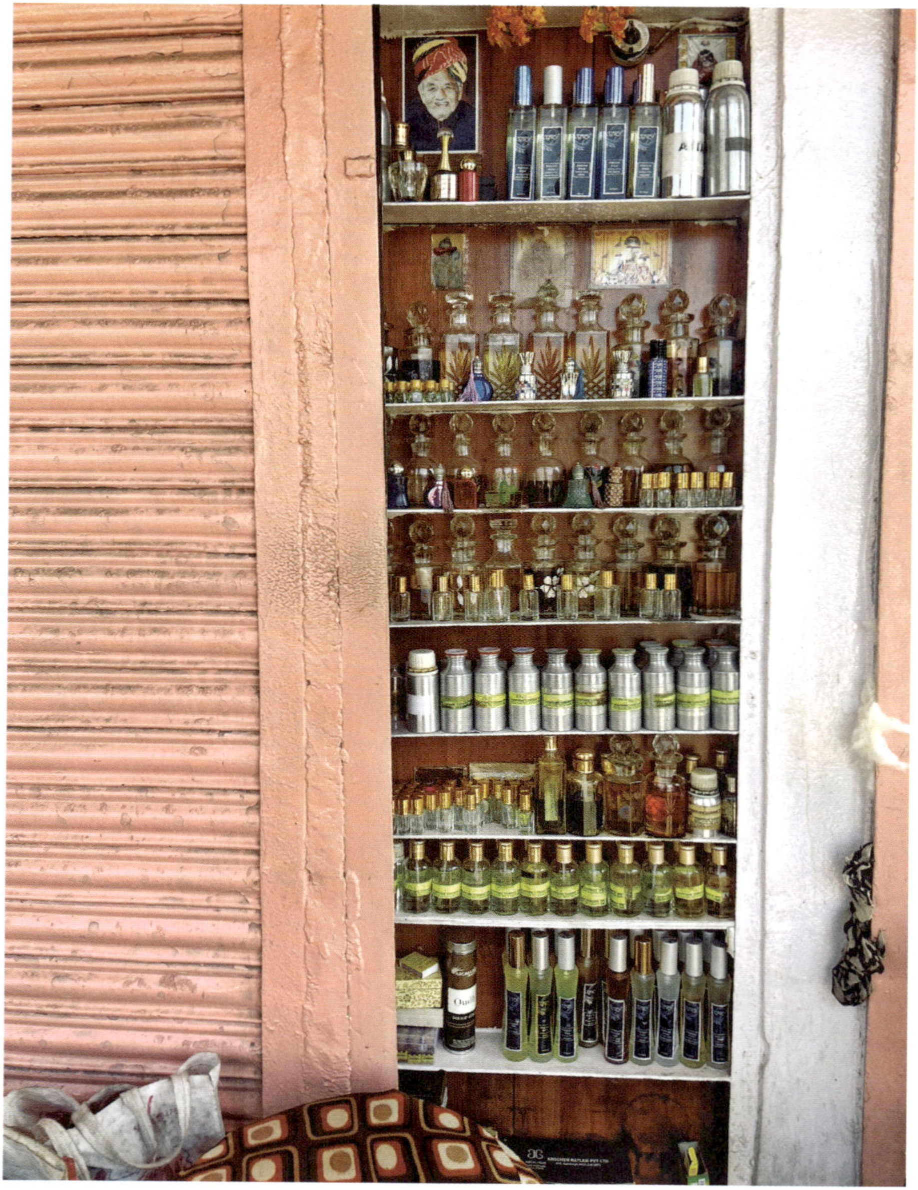

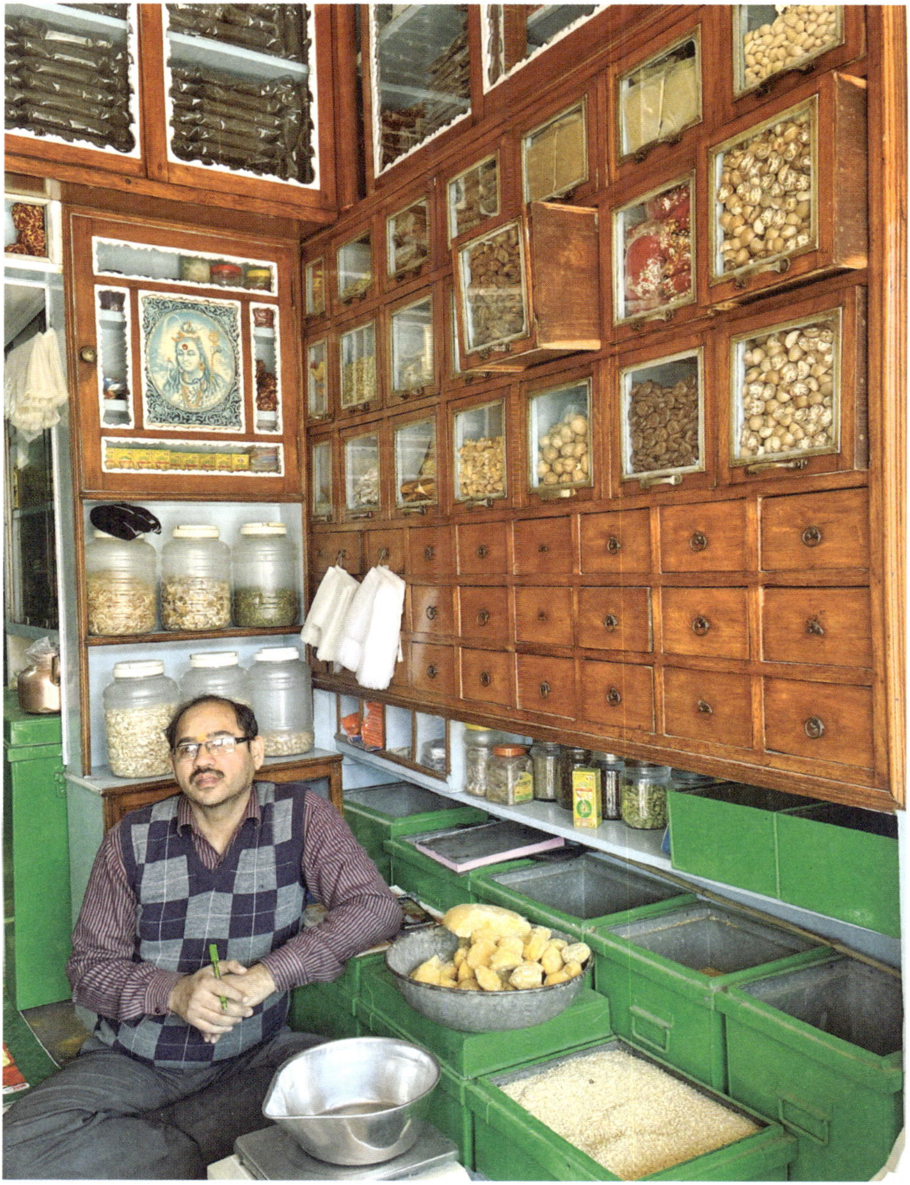

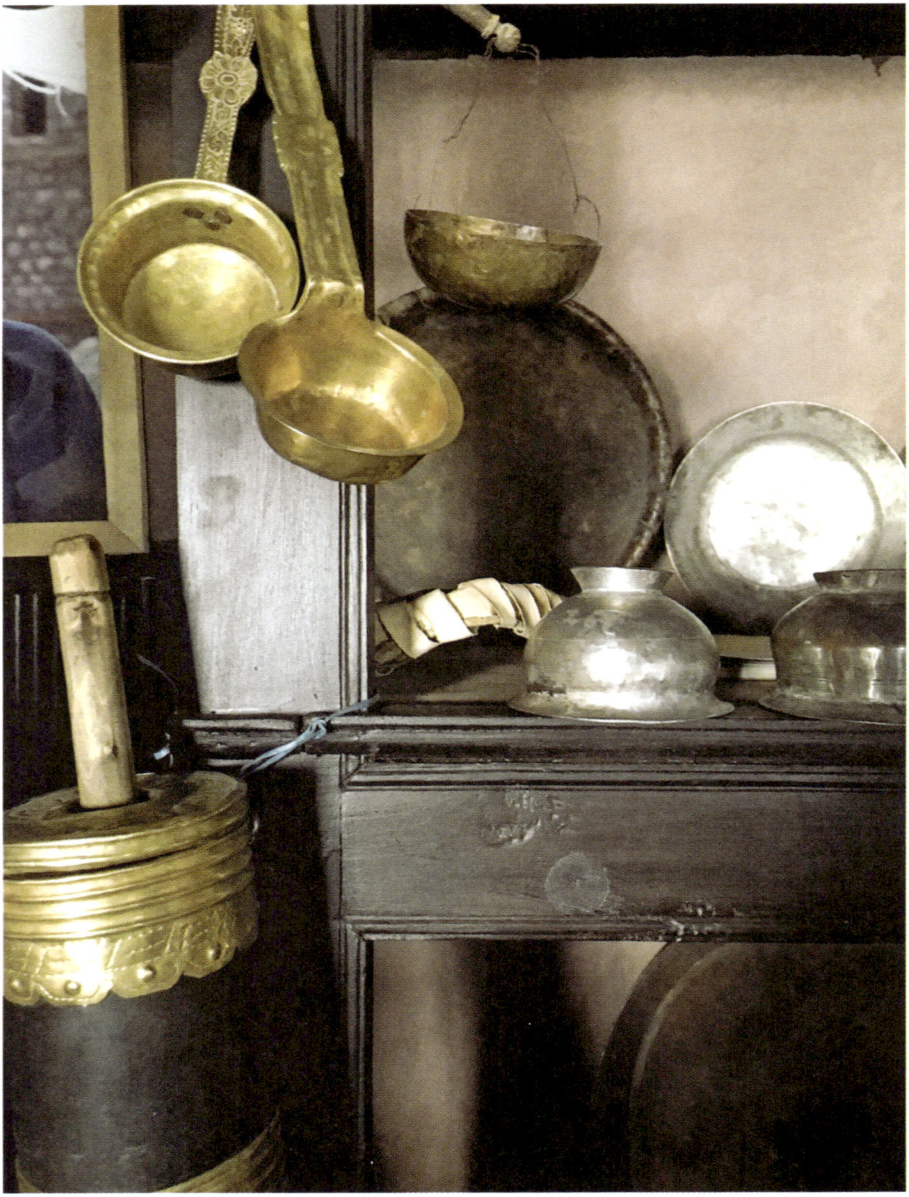

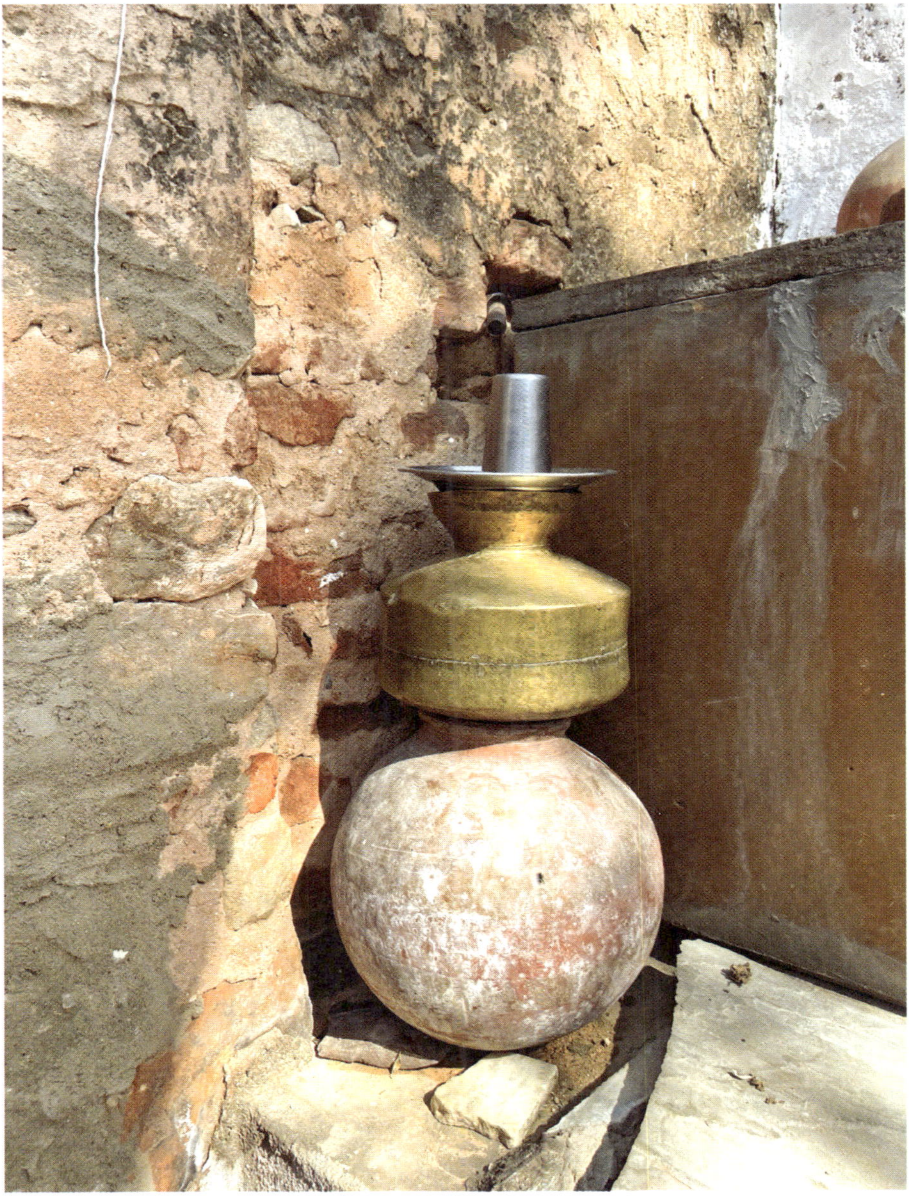

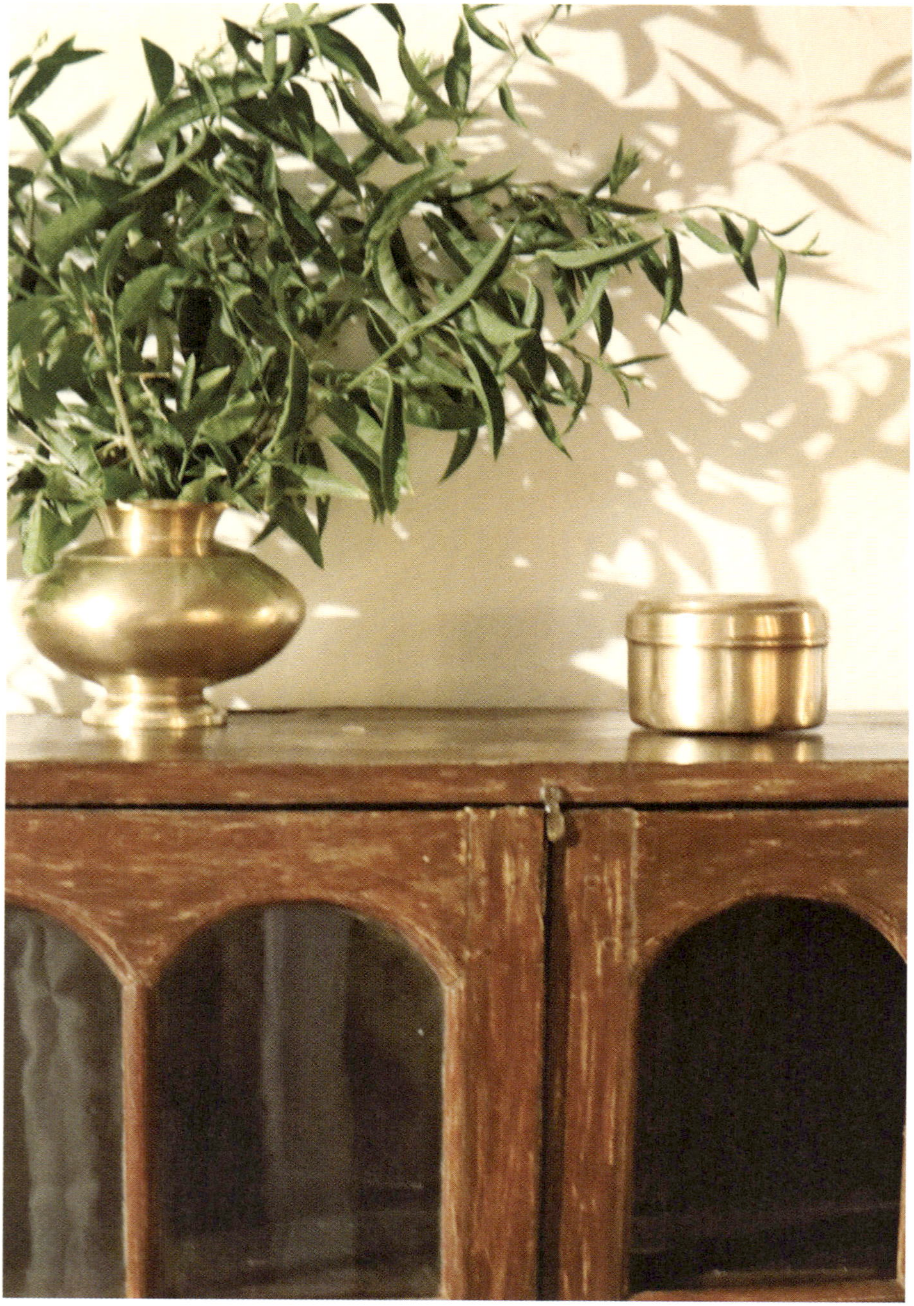

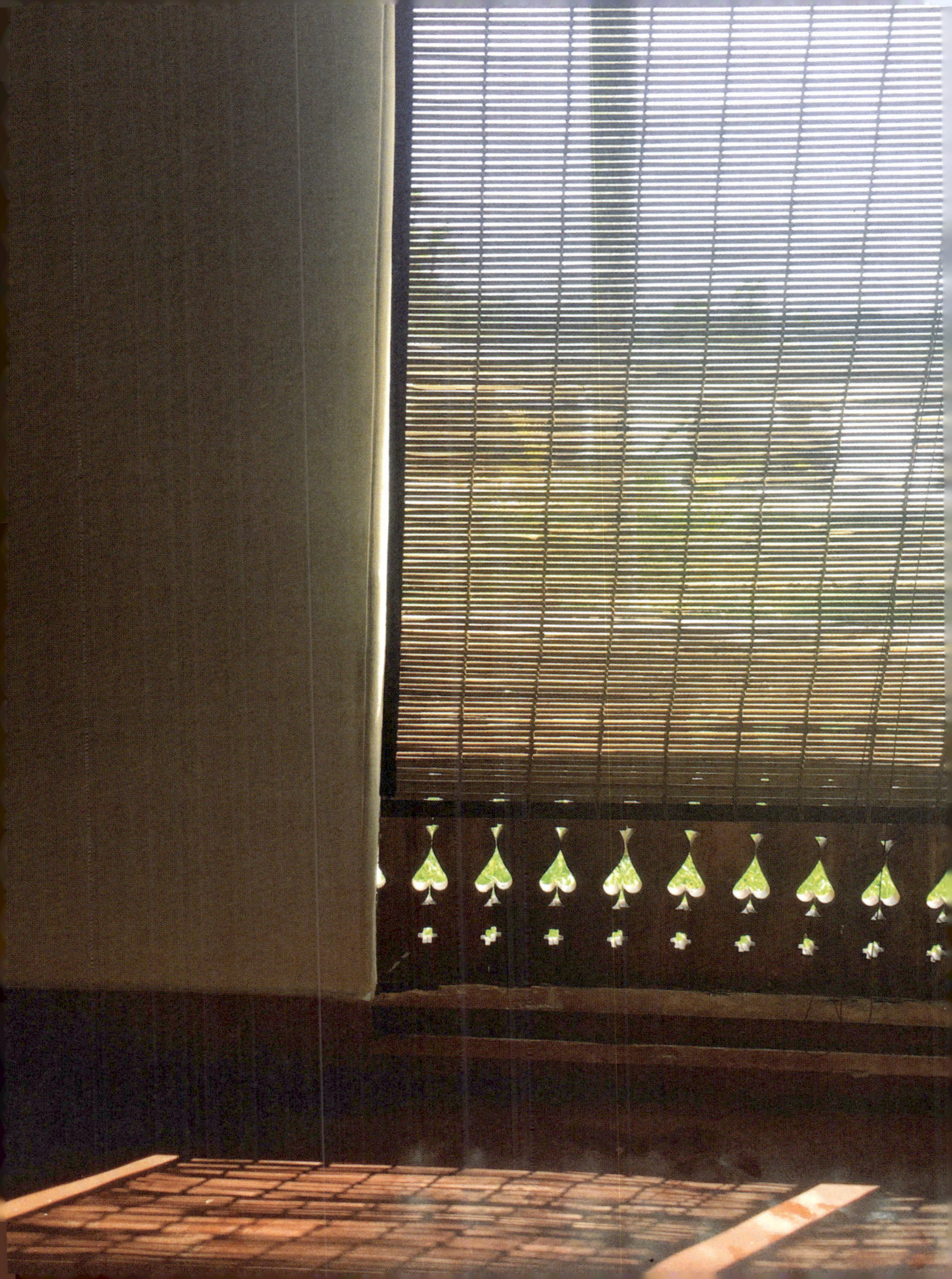

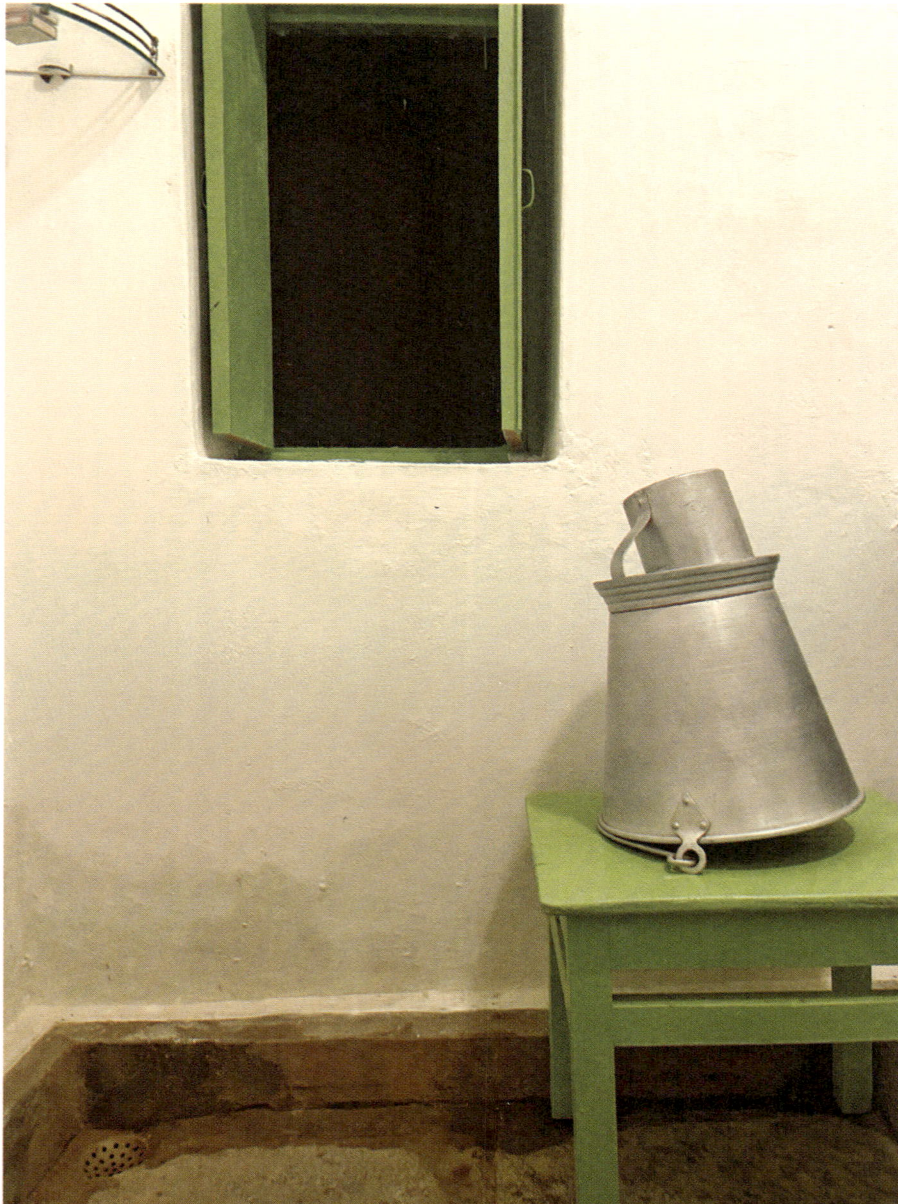

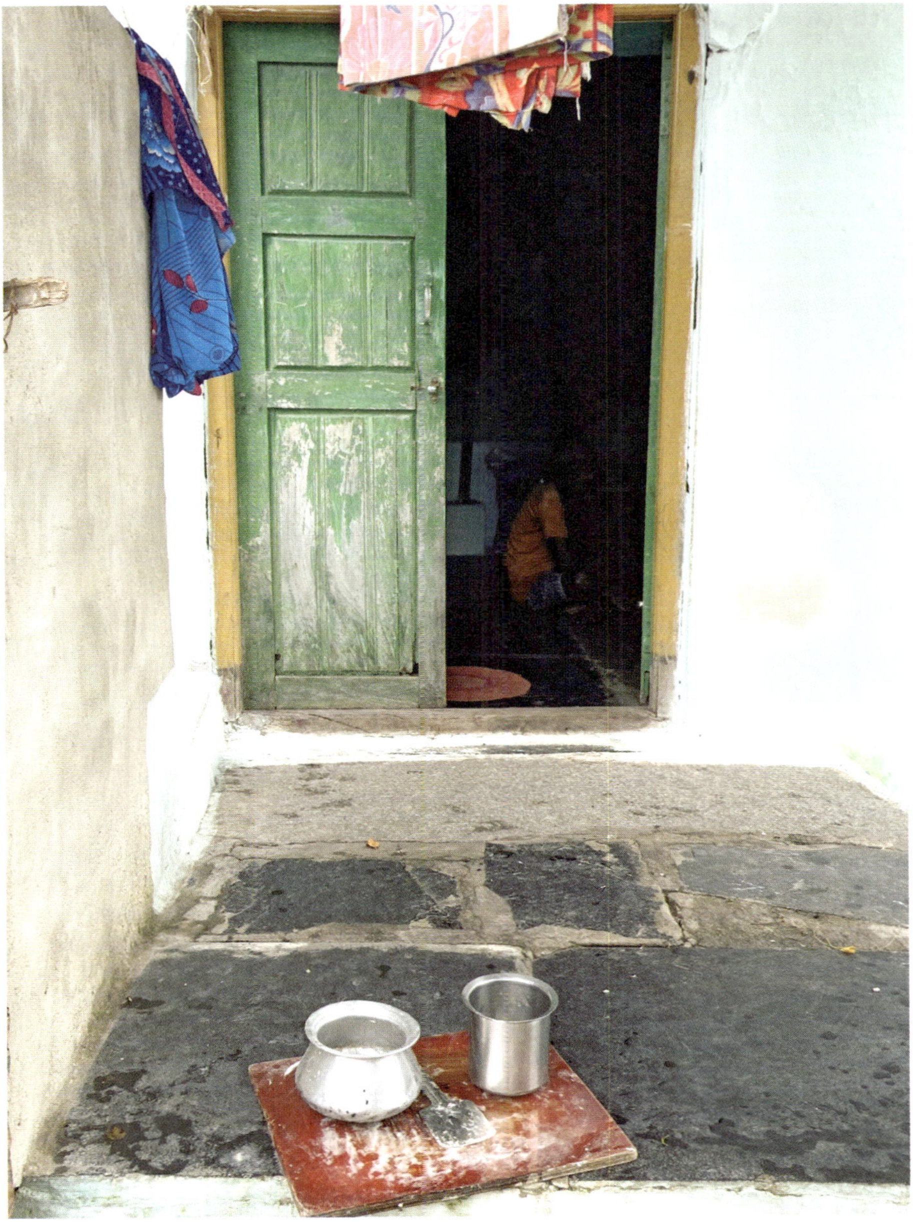

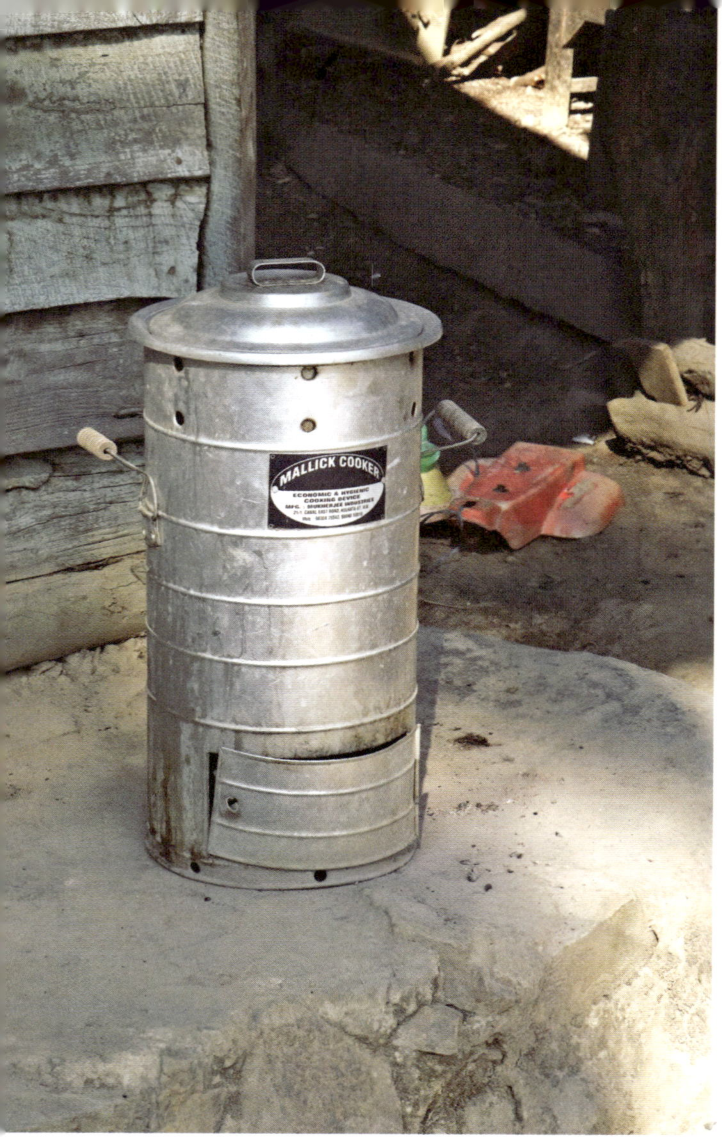
MALLICK COOKER
ECONOMIC & HYGIENIC
COOKING DEVICE
MFG. : MUKHERJEE INDUSTRIES

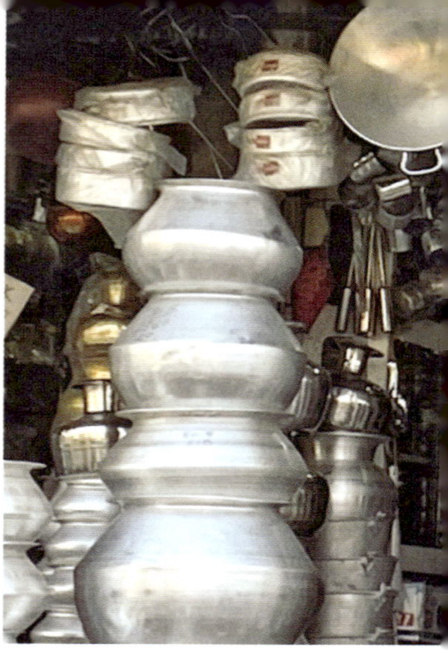

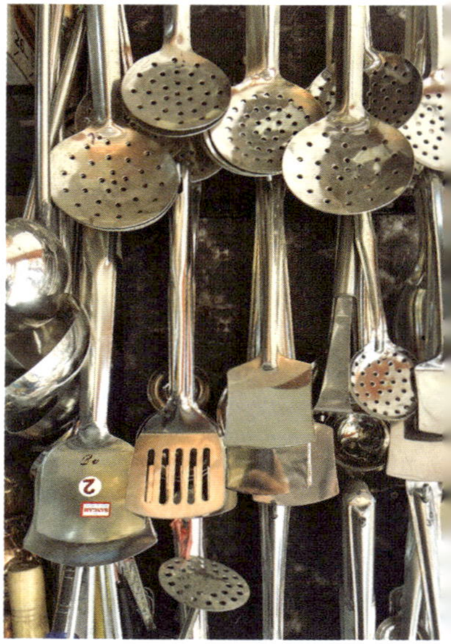

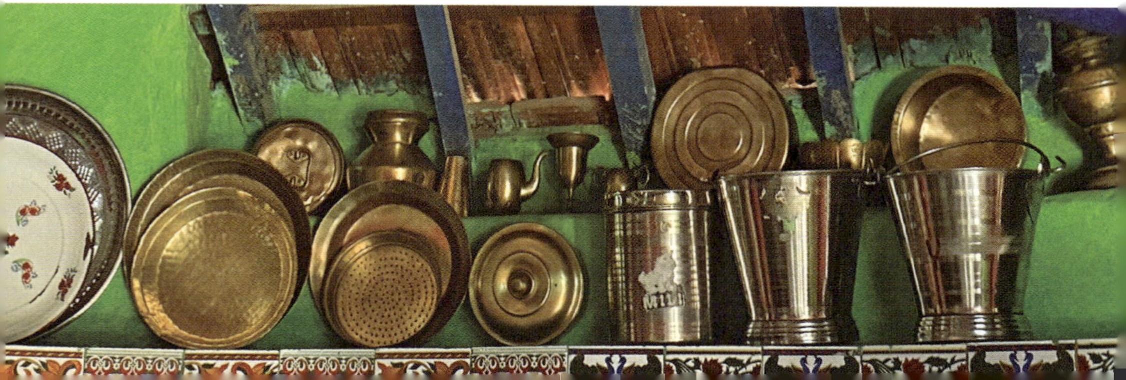

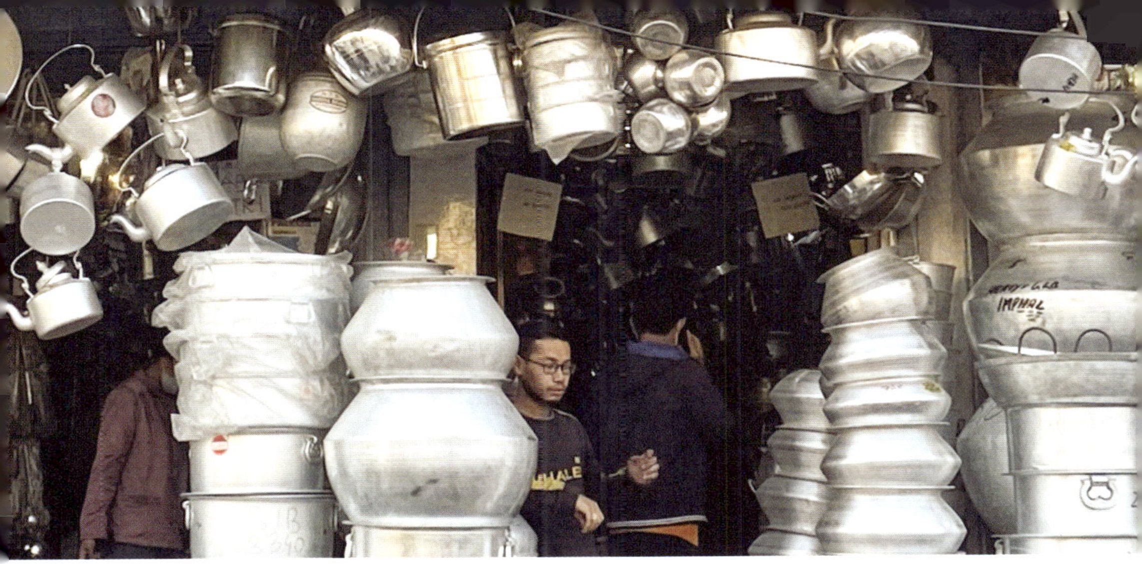
IMPHAL
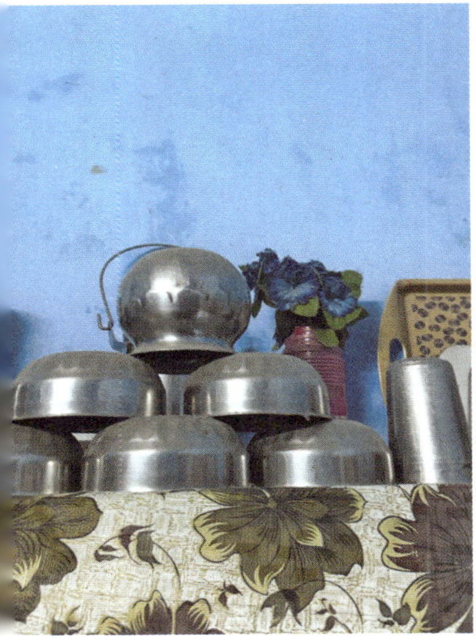
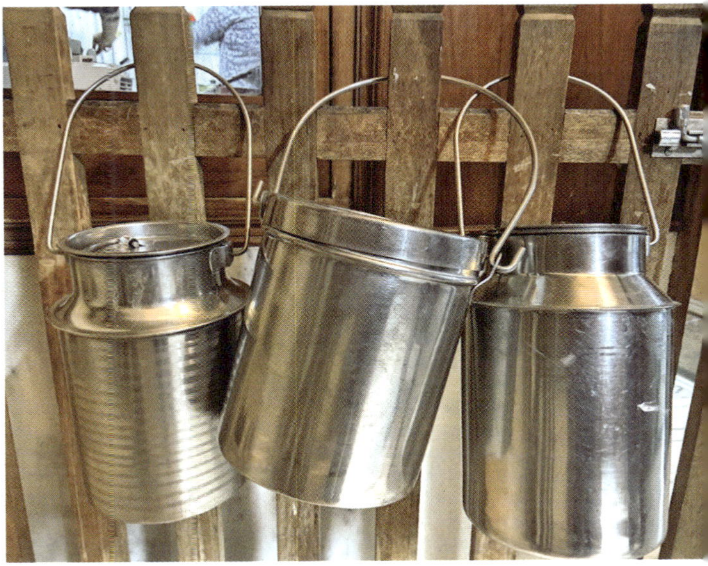
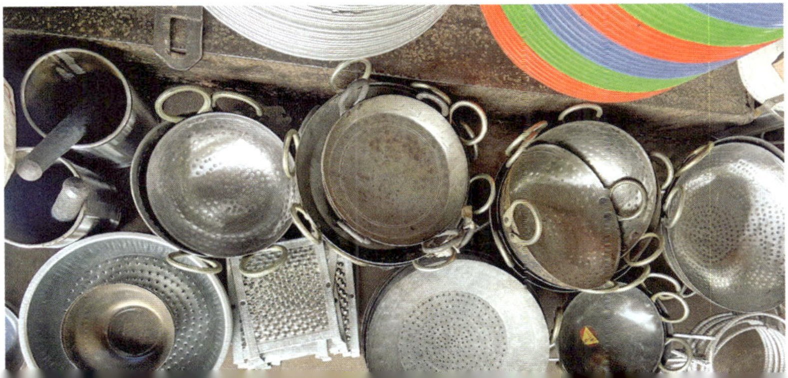
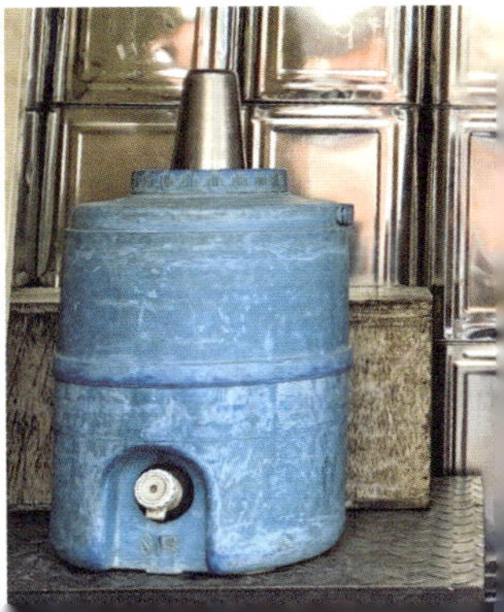

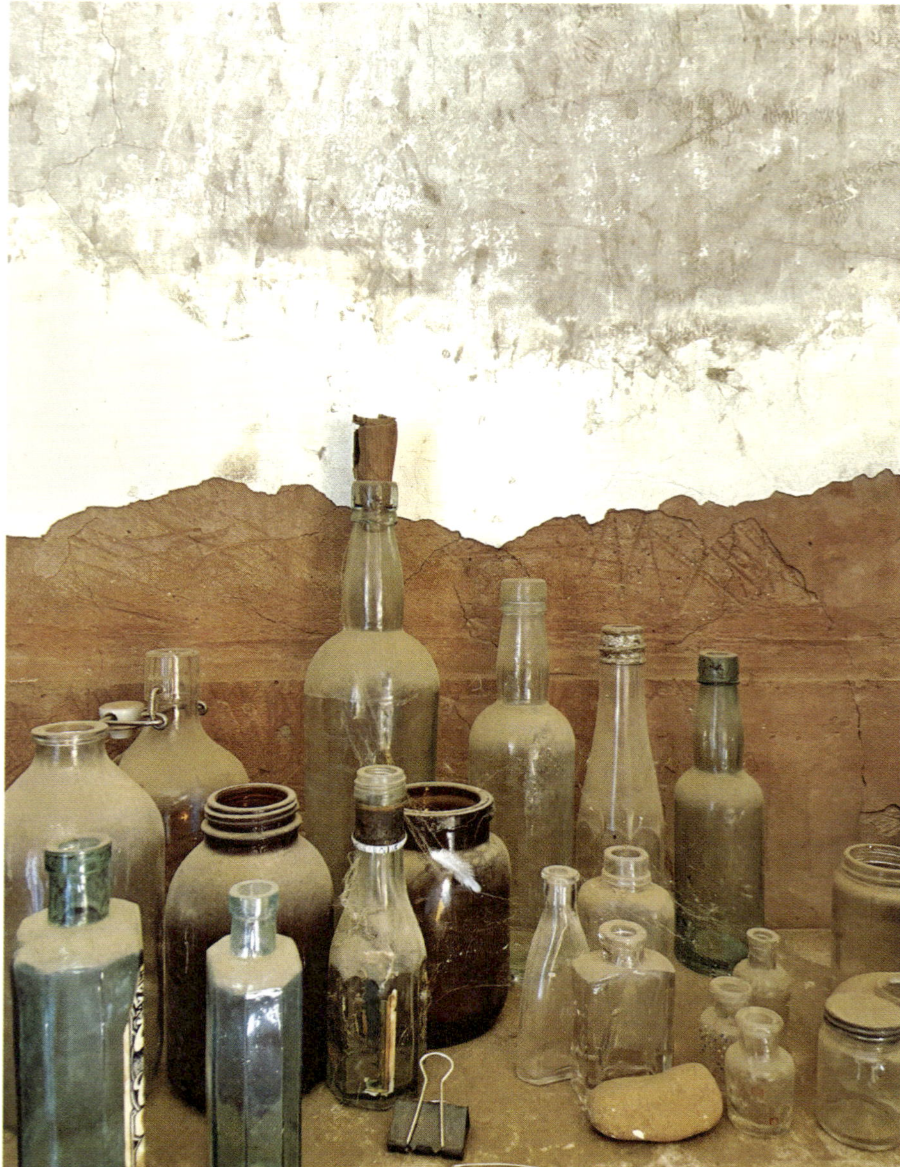

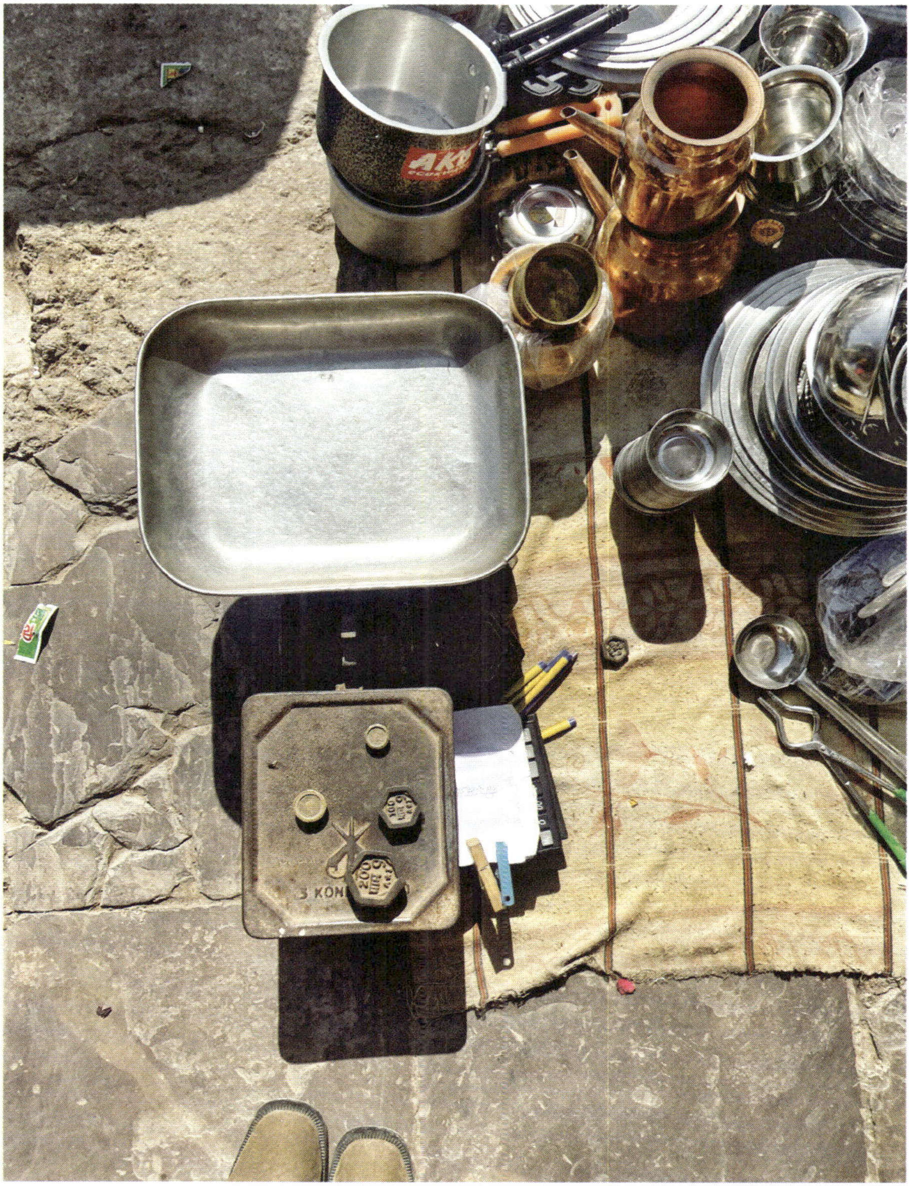

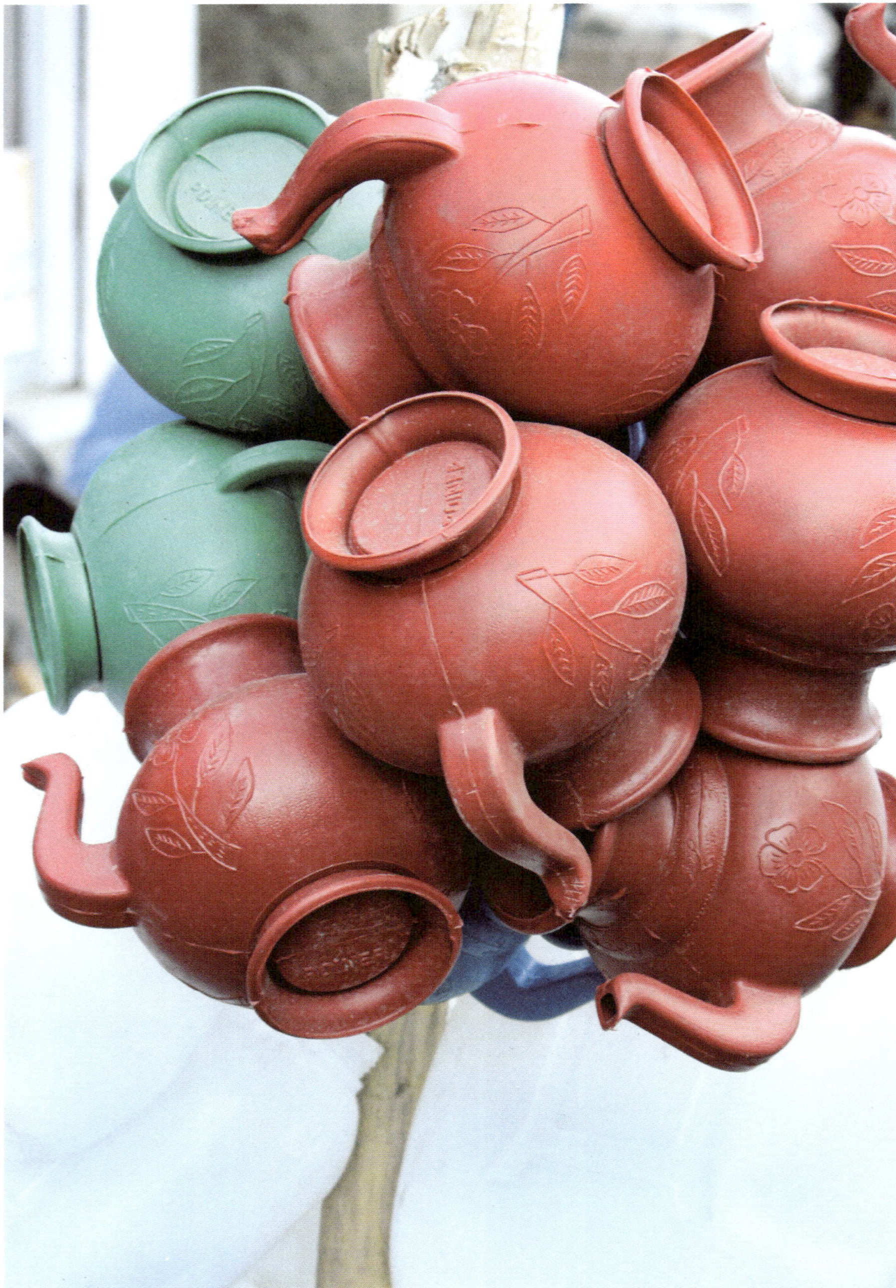

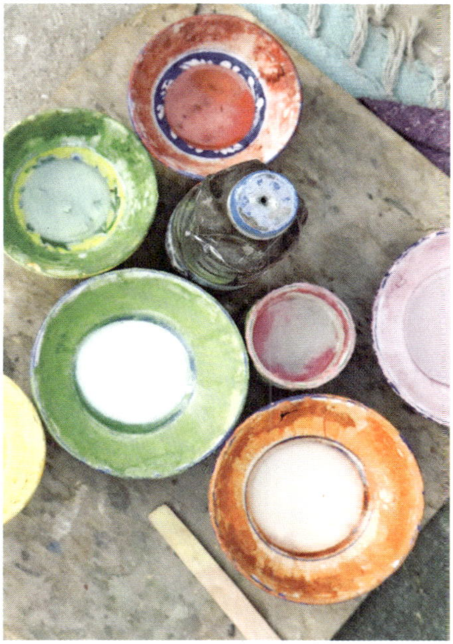

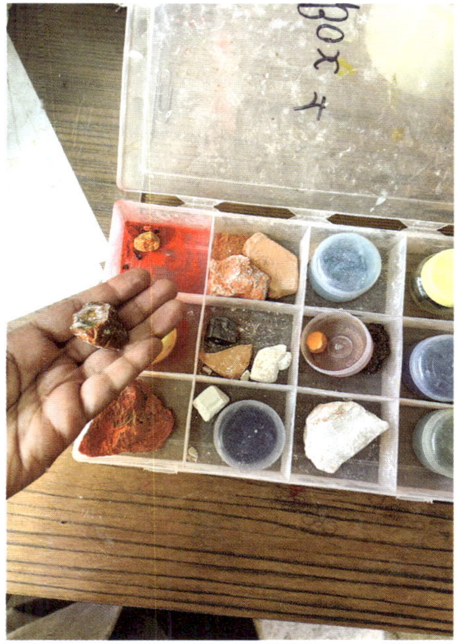
Box 4

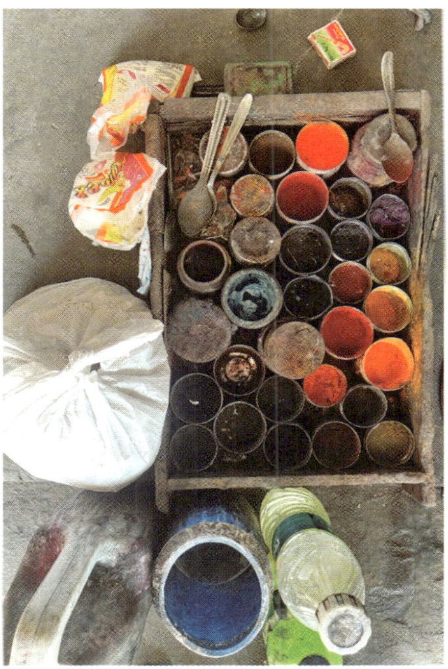

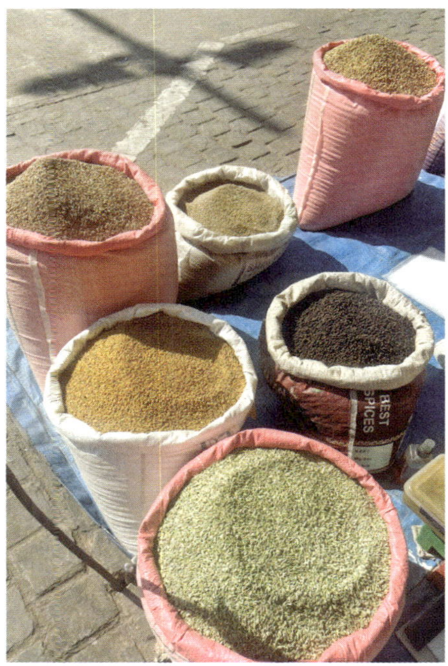
BEST

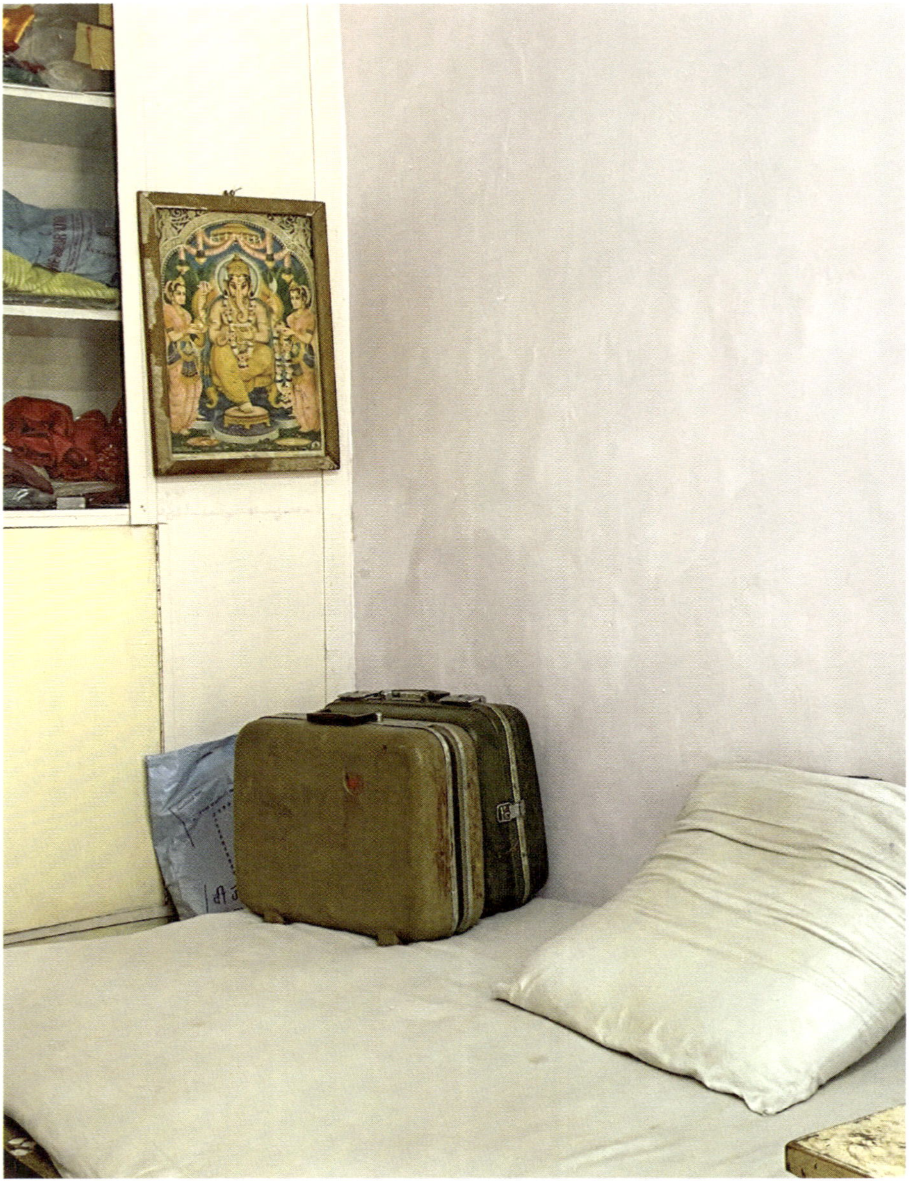

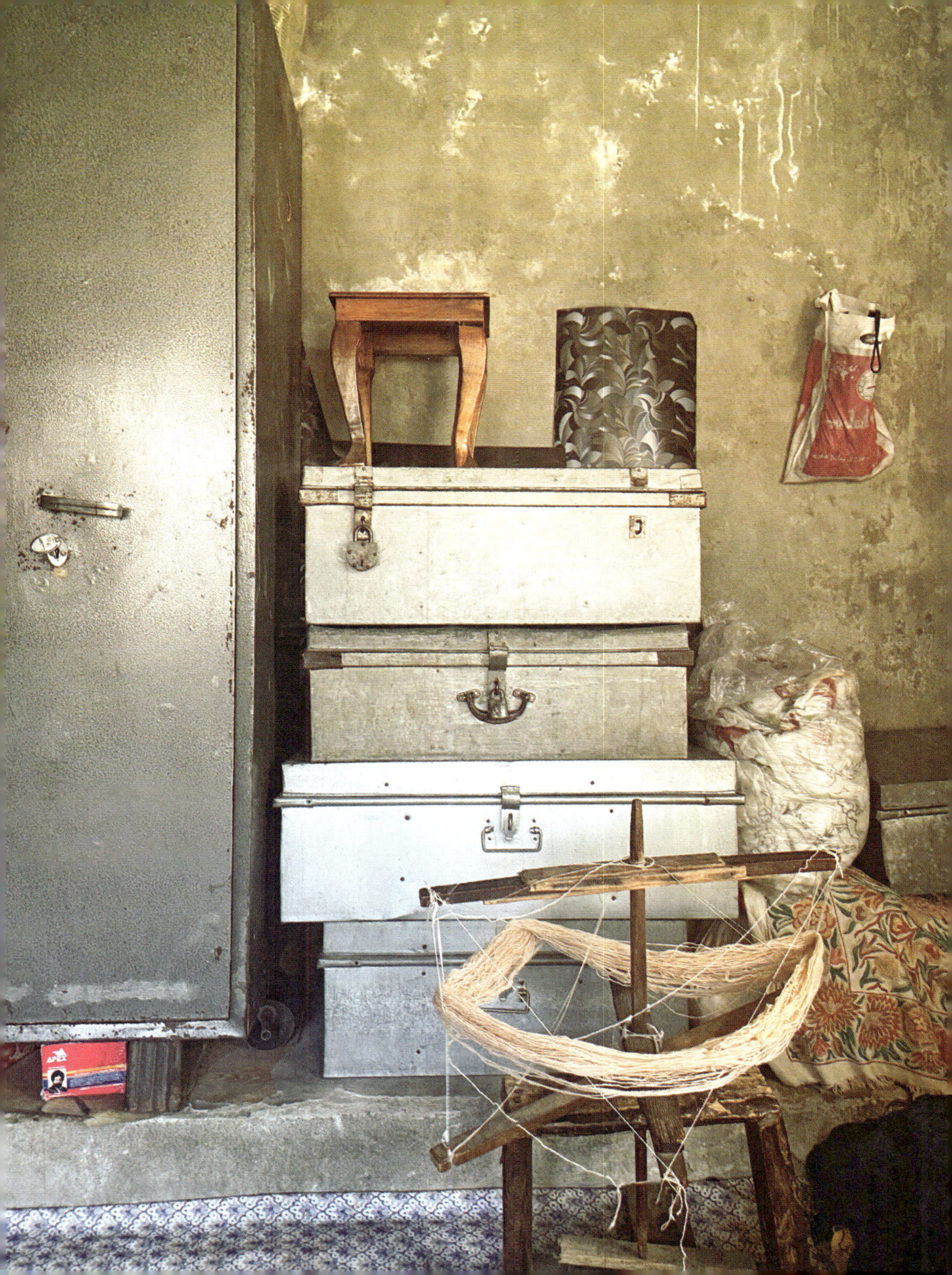

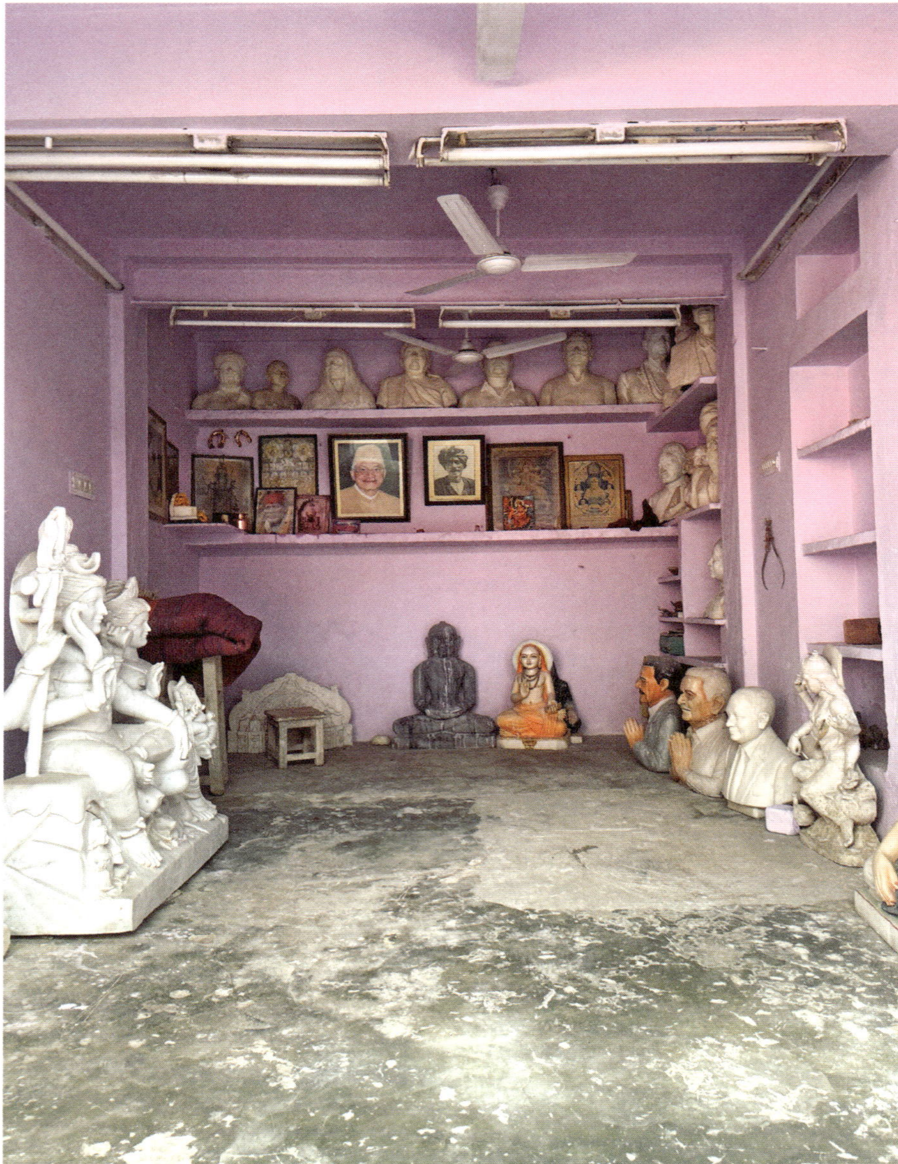

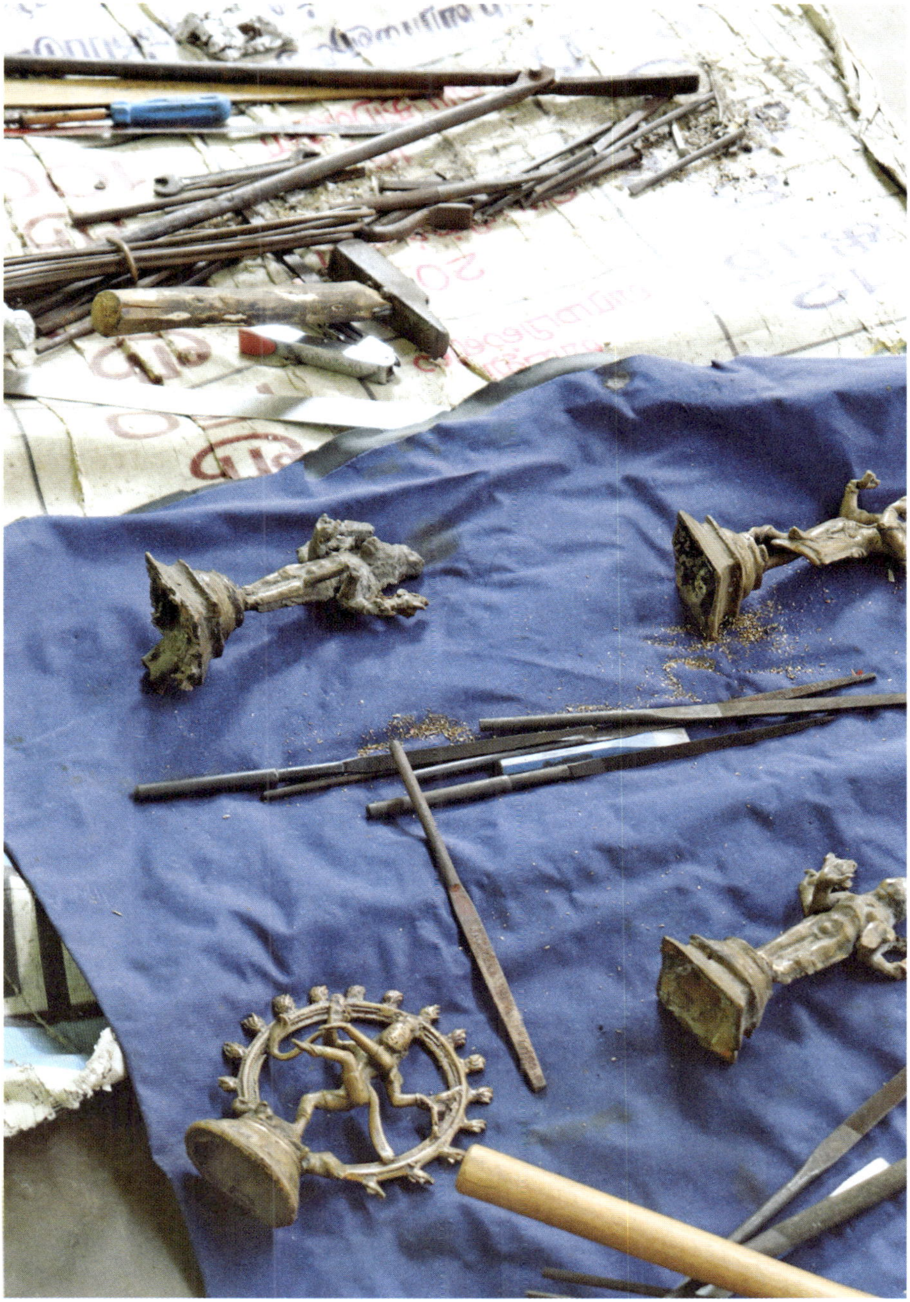

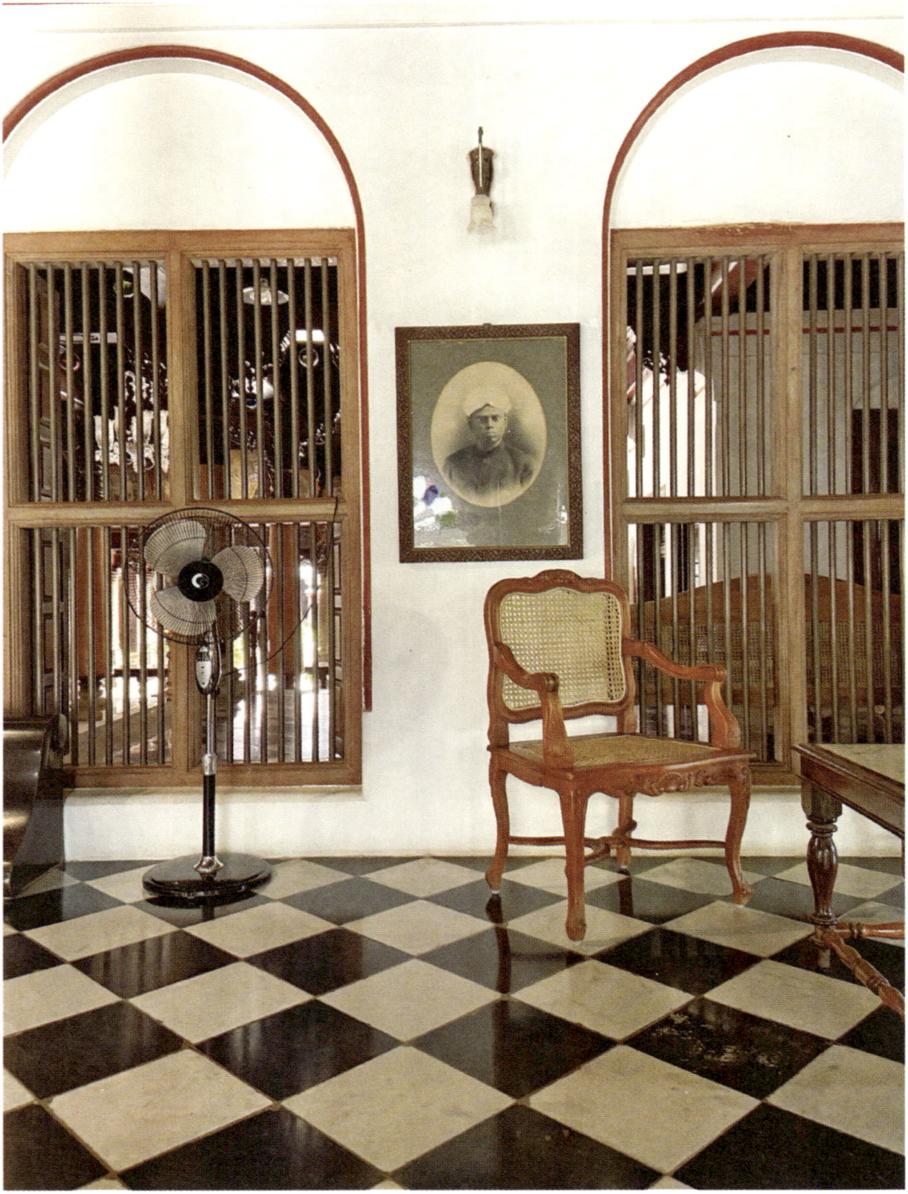

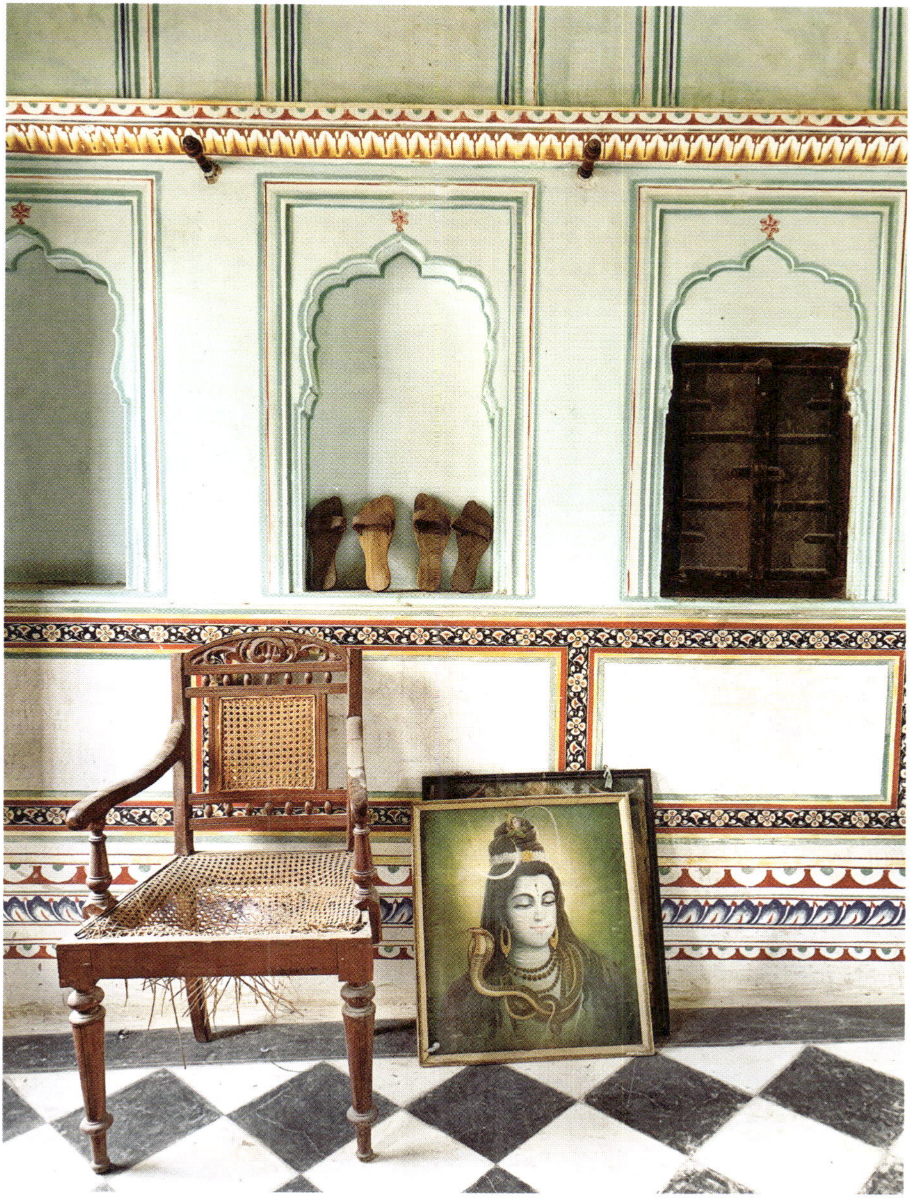

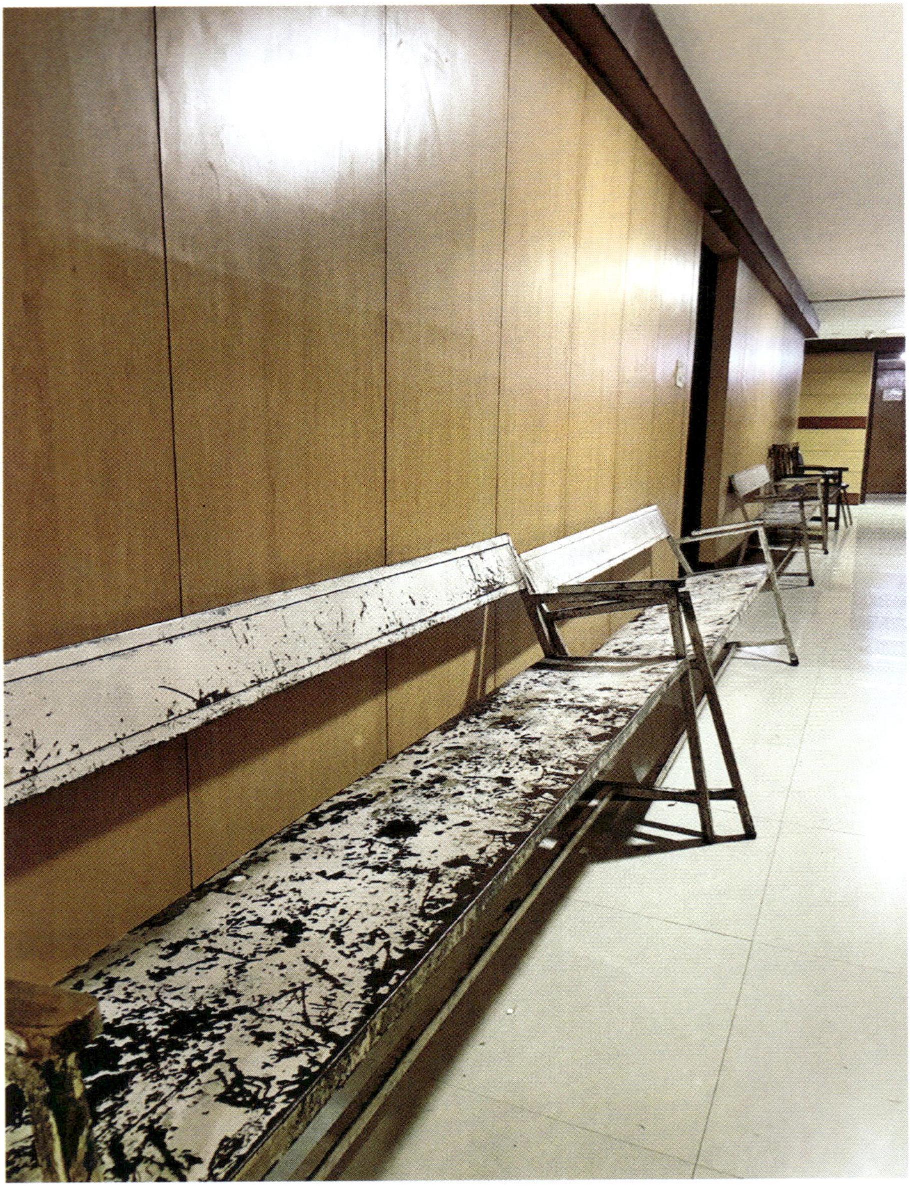

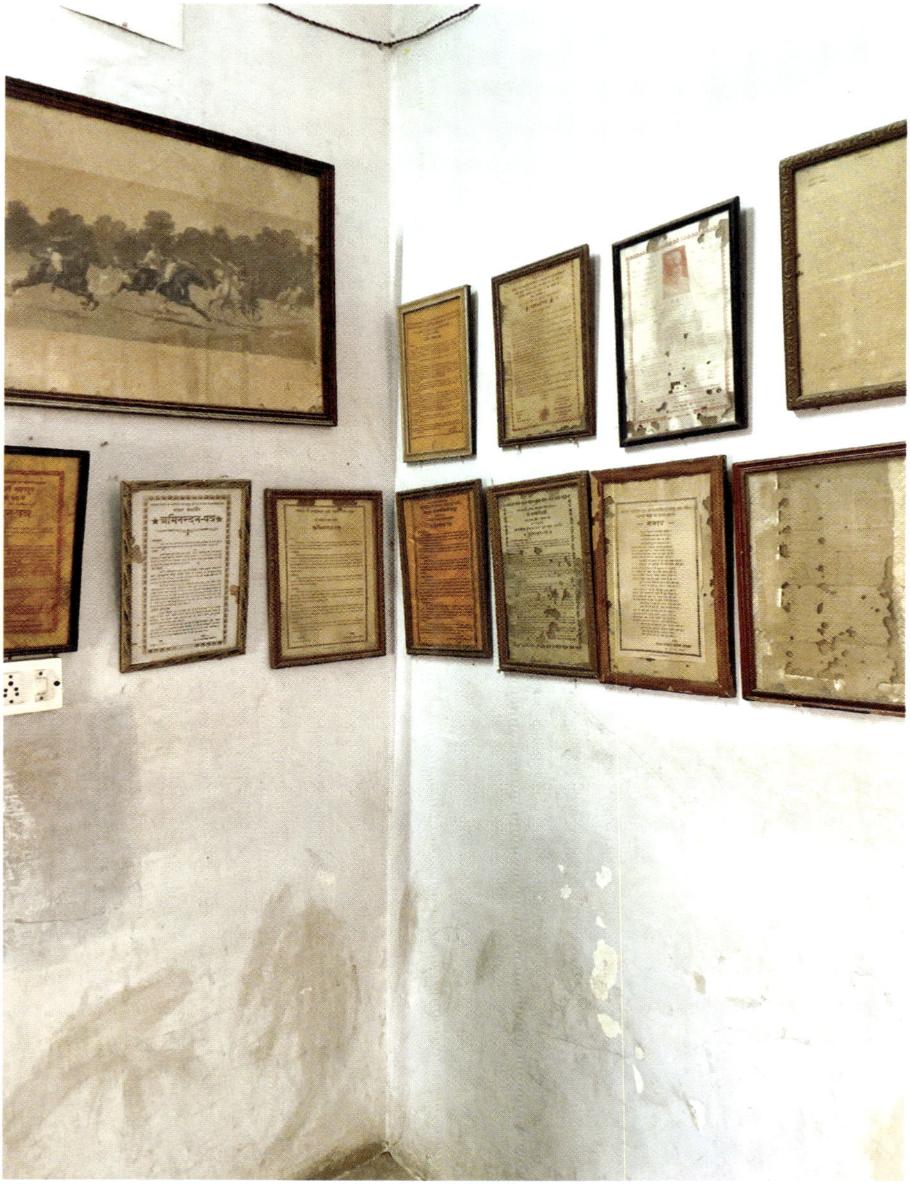
अभिनन्दन-पत्र

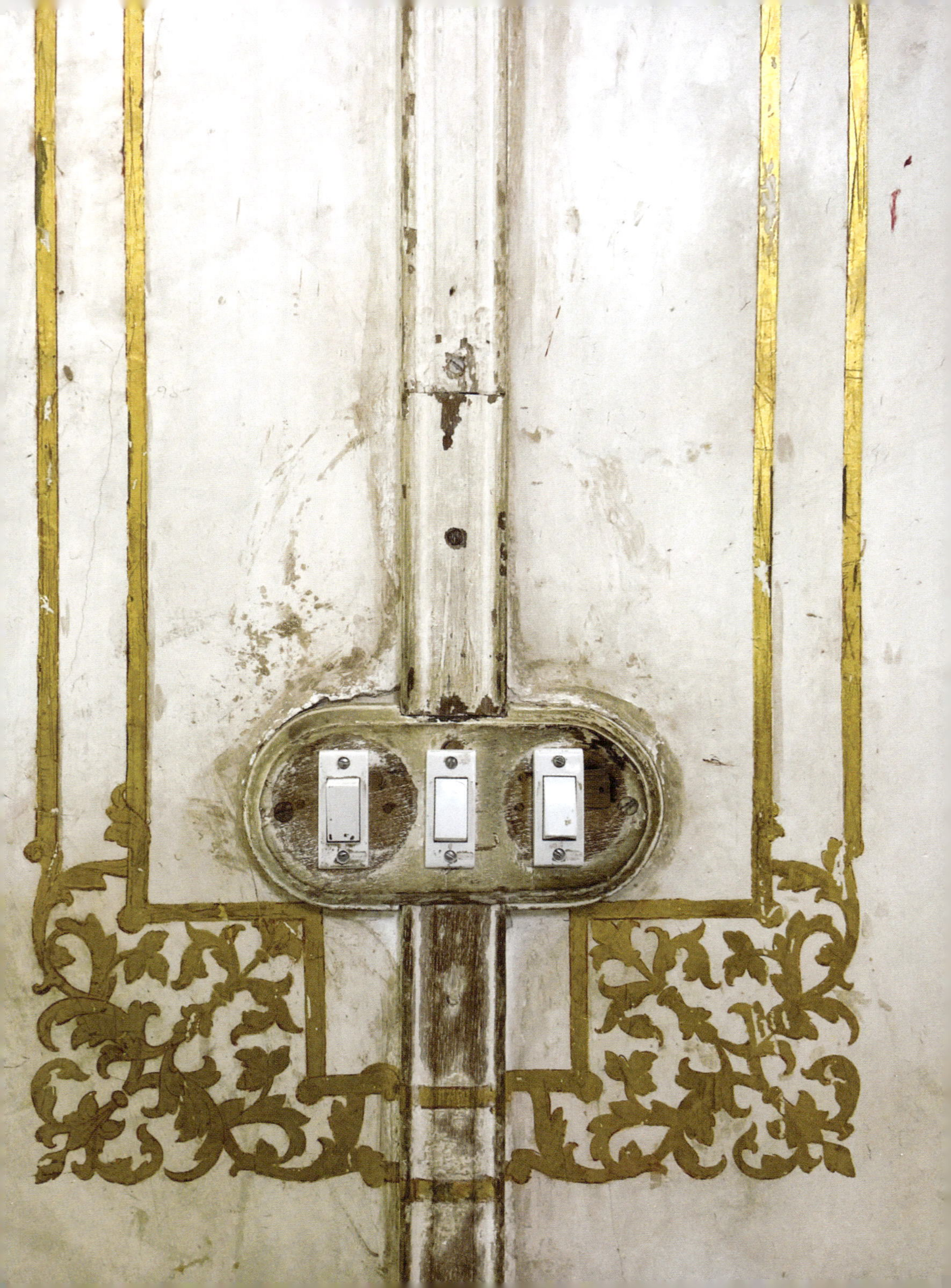

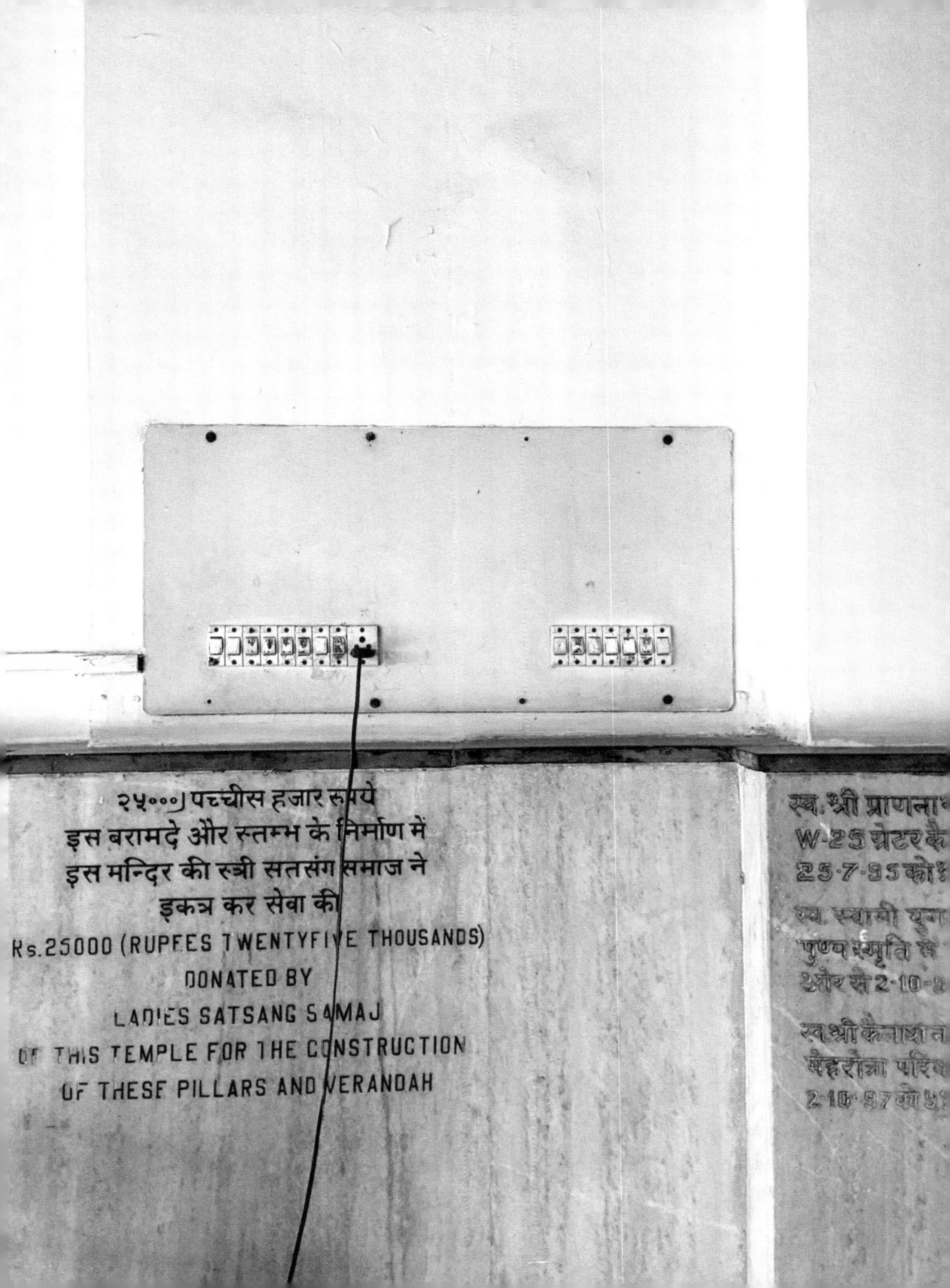
२५०००) पच्चीस हजार रुपये
इस बरामदे और स्तम्भ के निर्माण में
इस मन्दिर की स्त्री सतसंग समाज ने
इकत्र कर सेवा की
Rs.25000 (RUPEES TWENTYFIVE THOUSANDS)
DONATED BY
LADIES SATSANG SAMAJ
OF THIS TEMPLE FOR THE CONSTRUCTION
OF THESE PILLARS AND VERANDAH

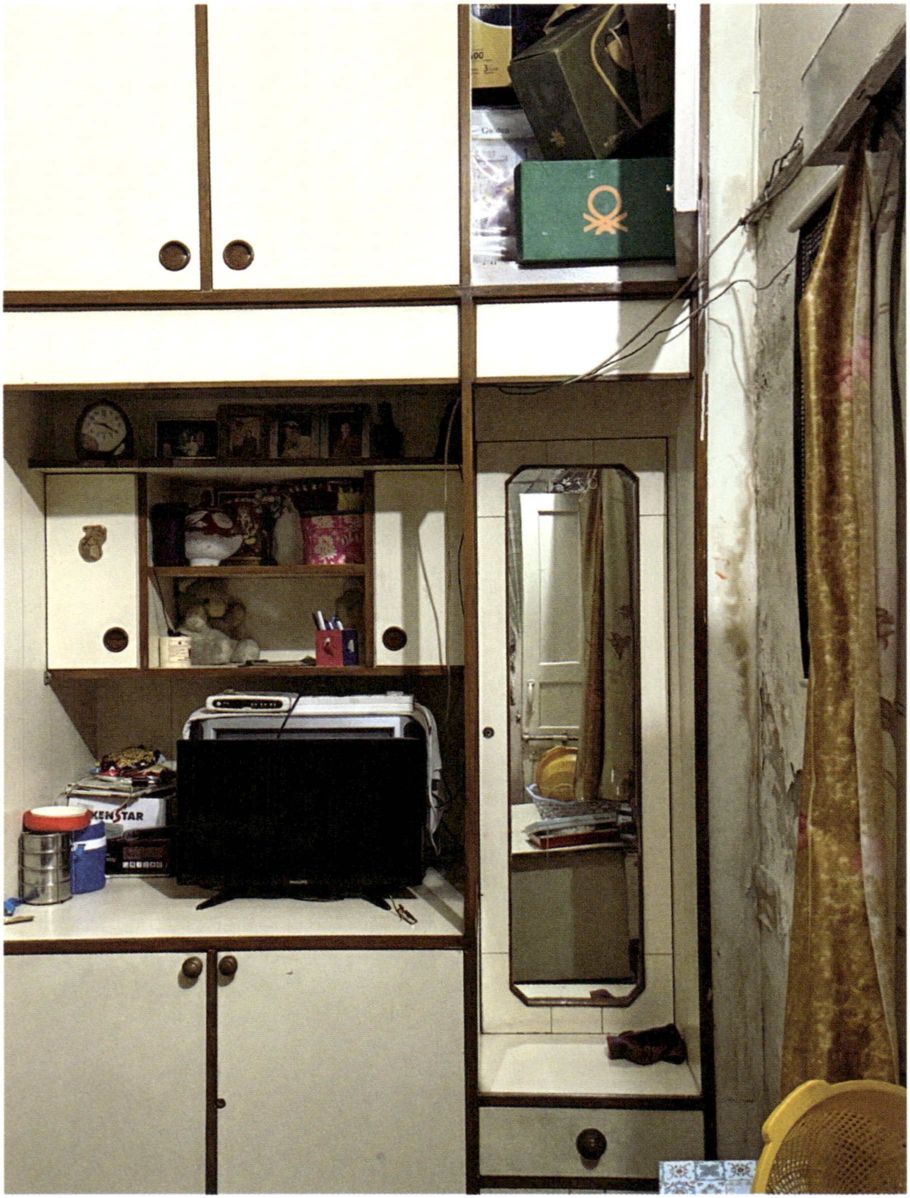
KENSTAR

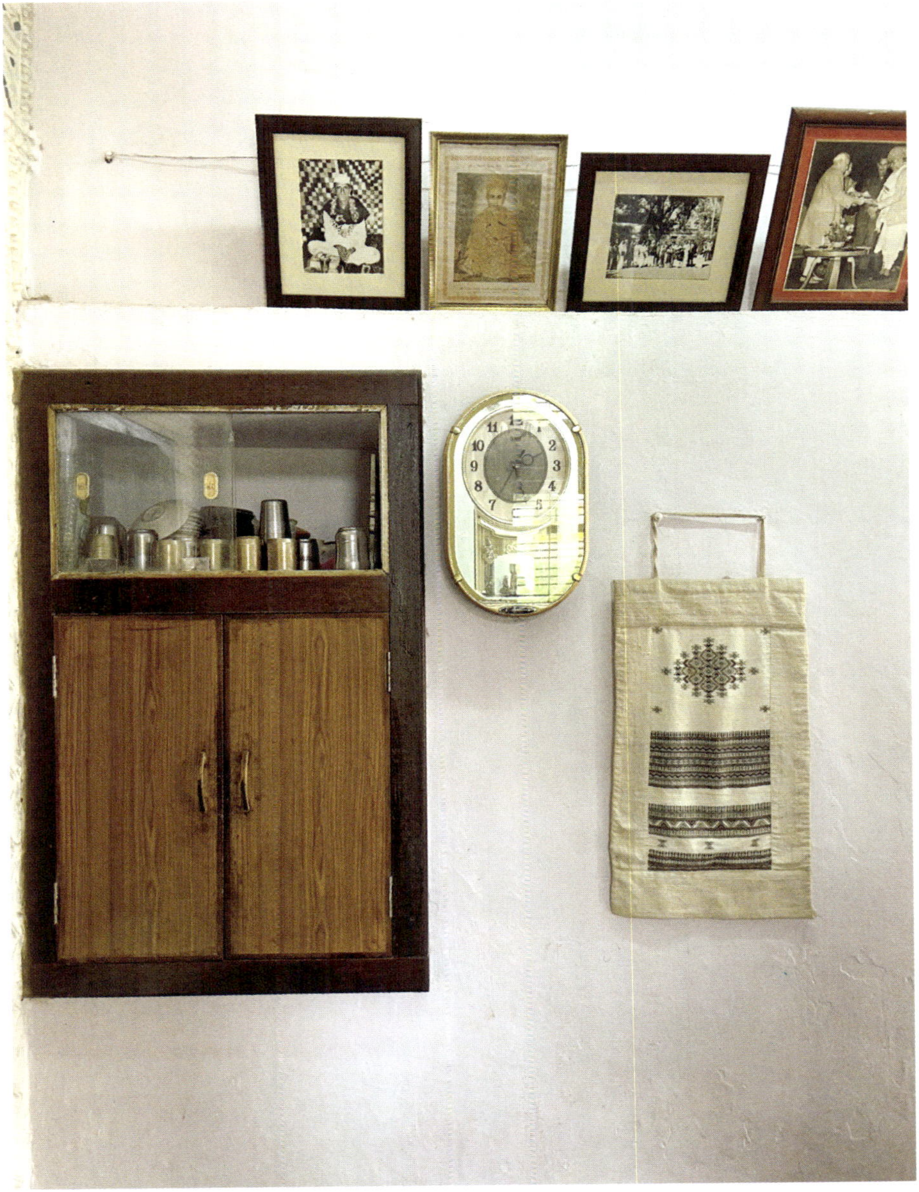

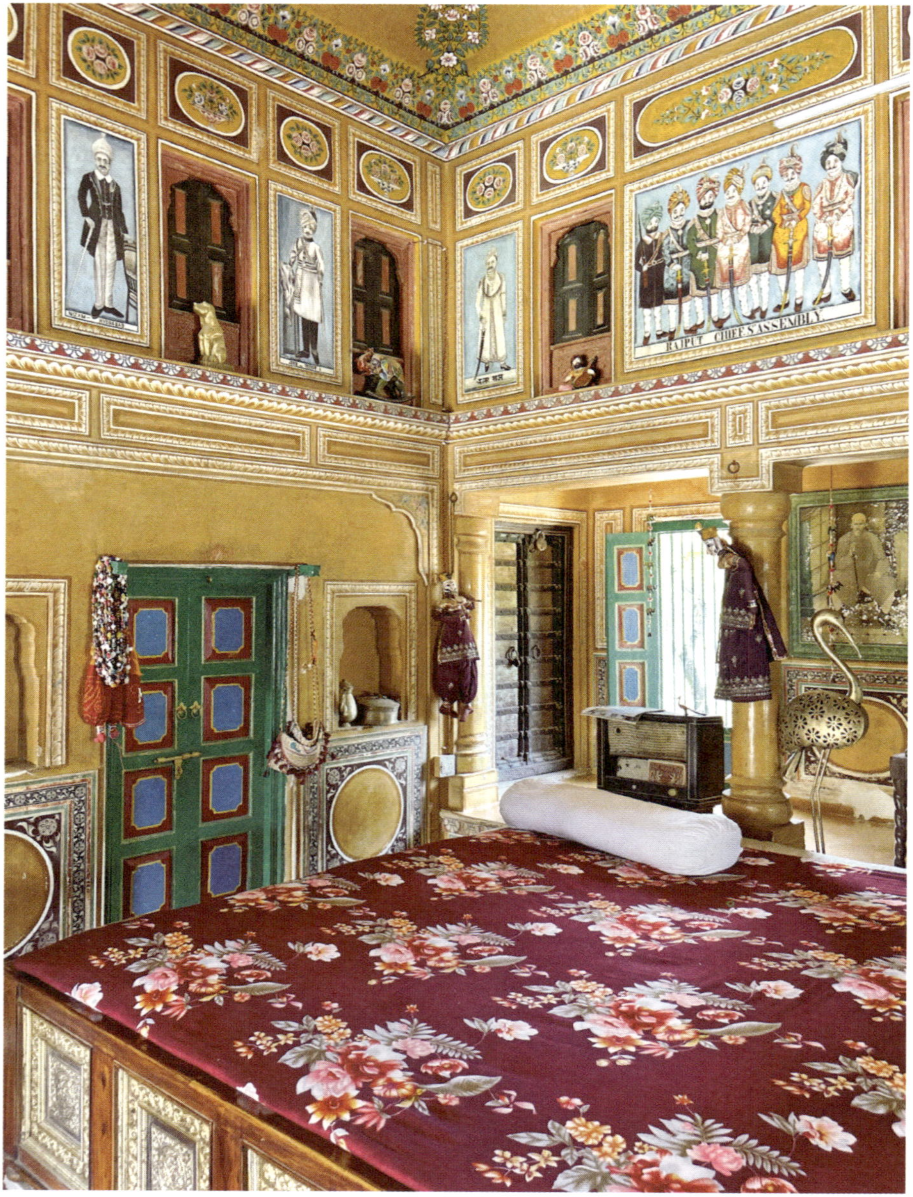
RAJPUT CHIEF'S ASSEMBLY

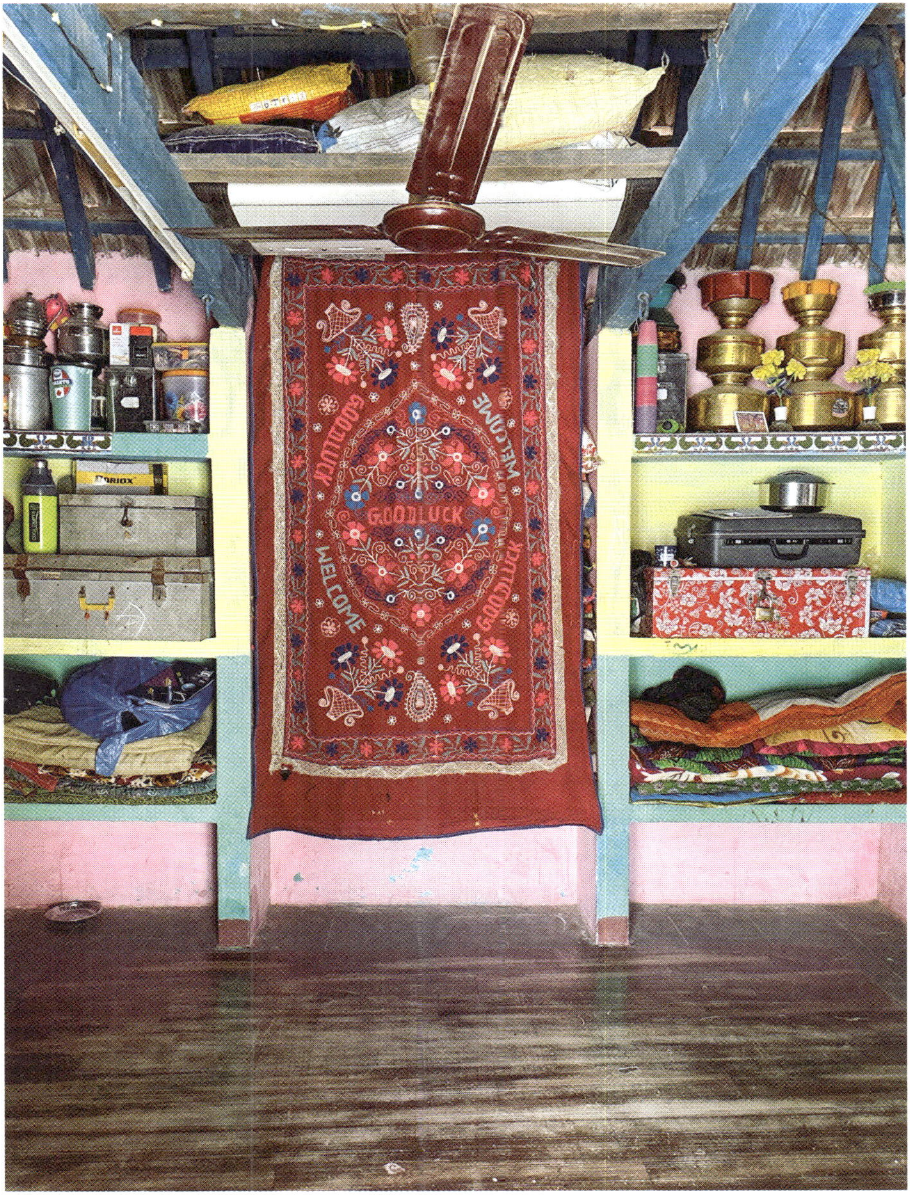
GOODLUCK
WELCOME
GOODLUCK
WELCOME
GOODLUCK

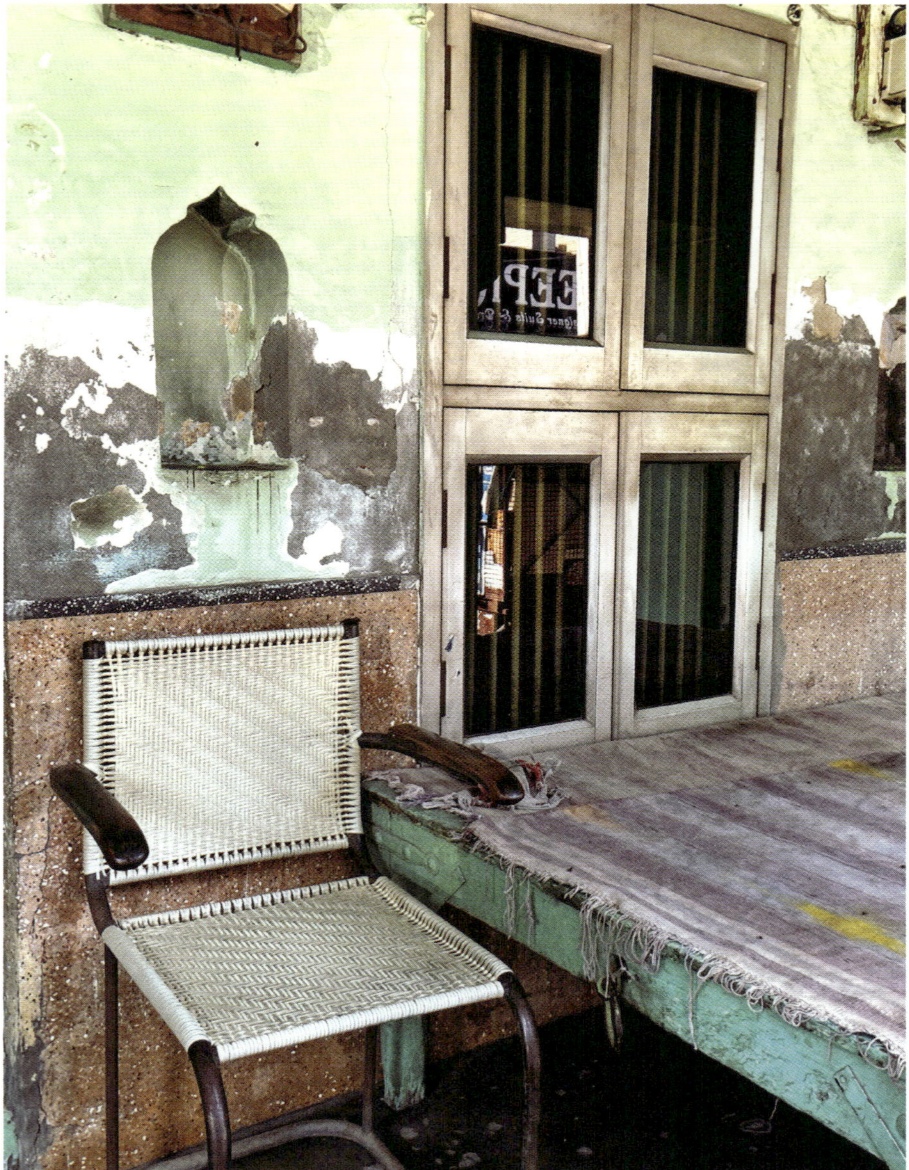

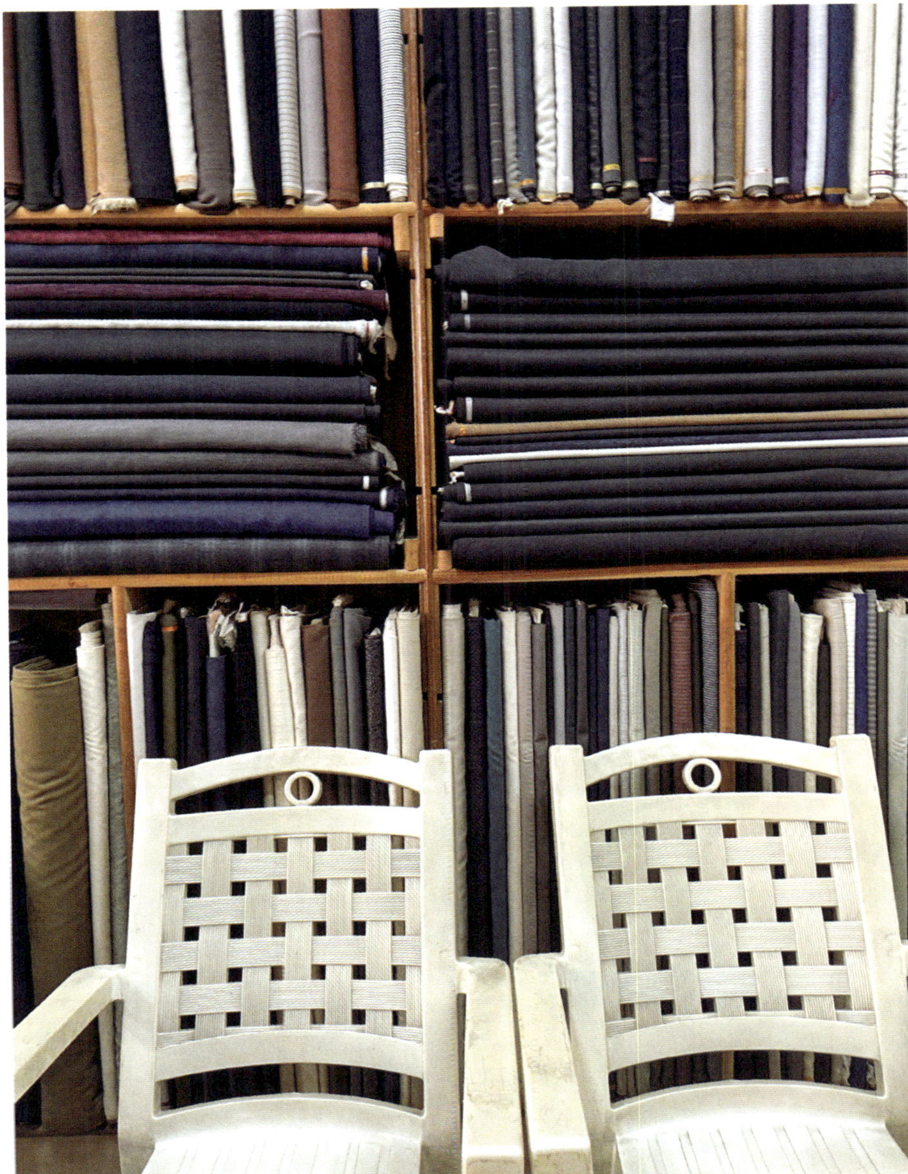

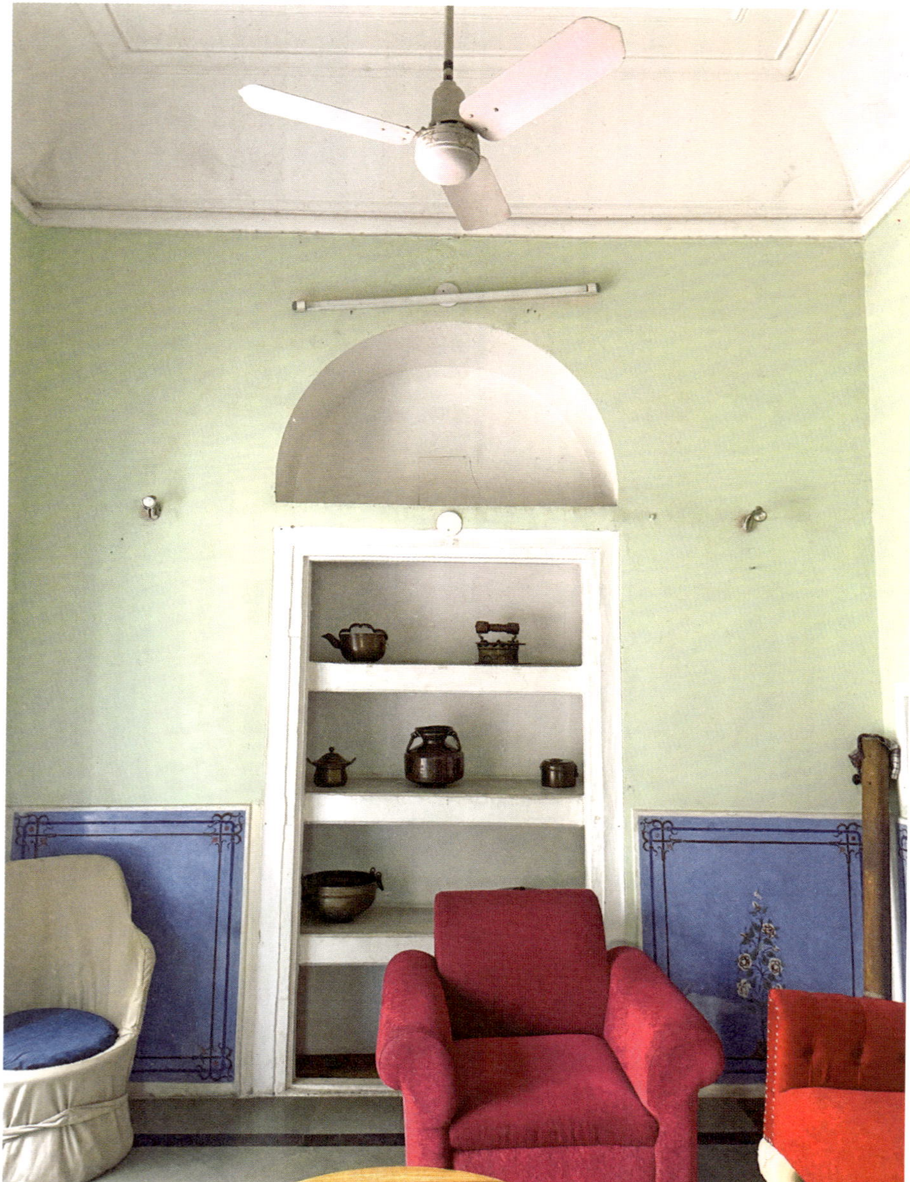

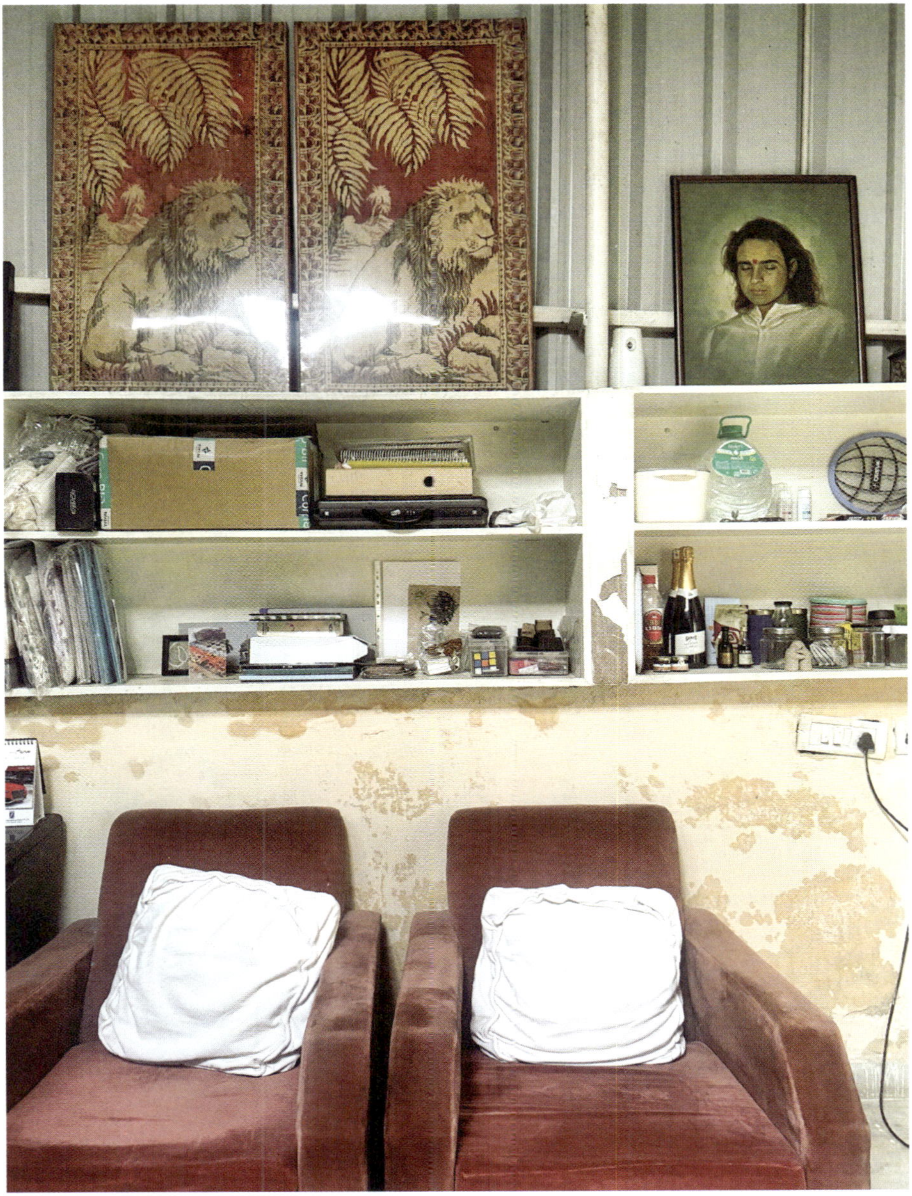

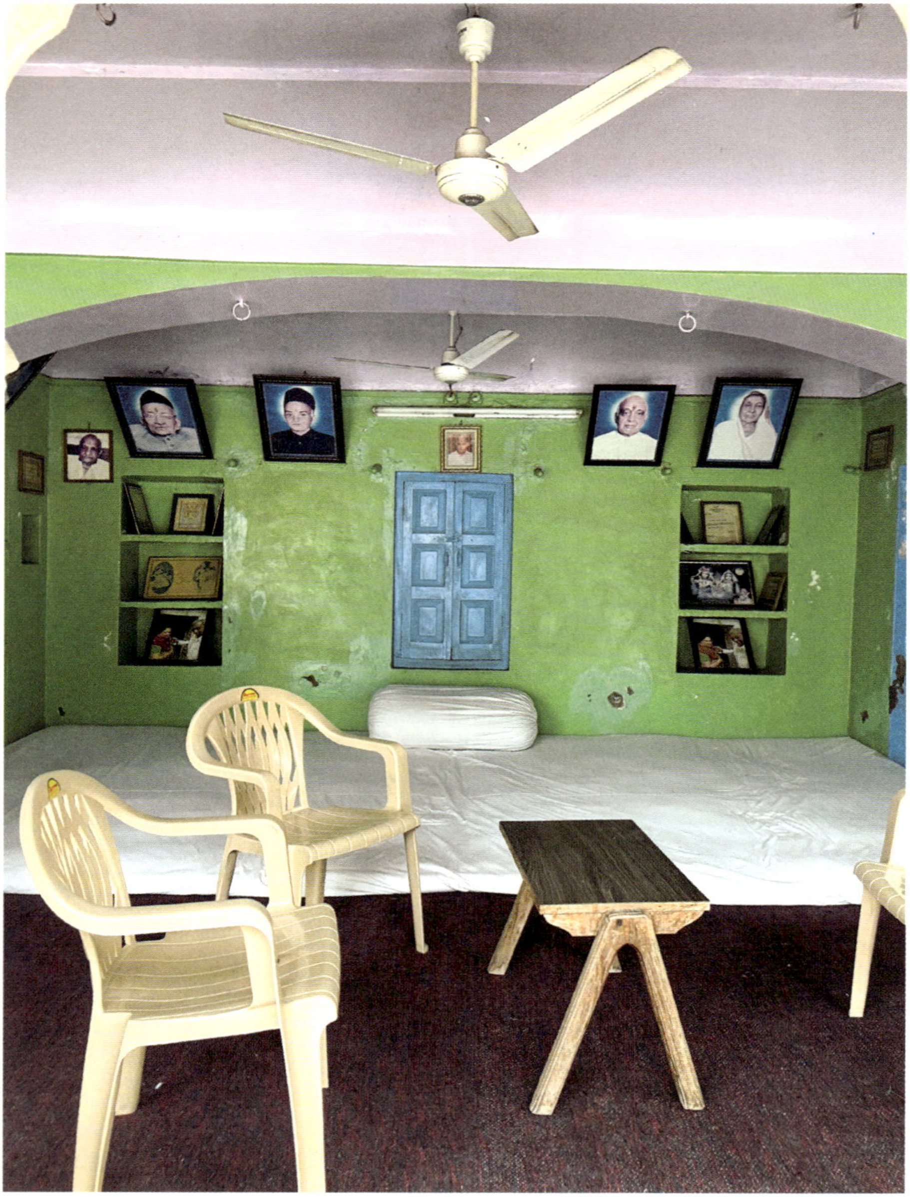

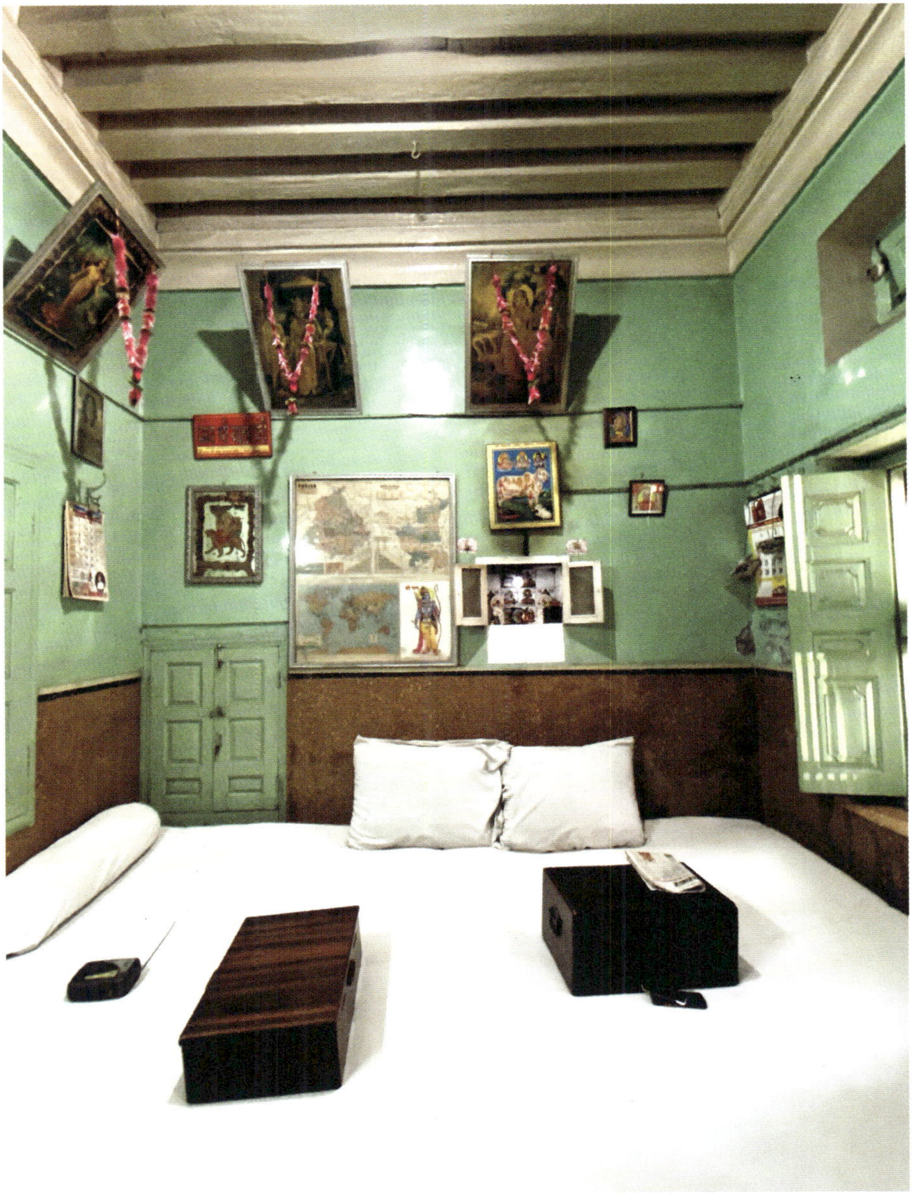

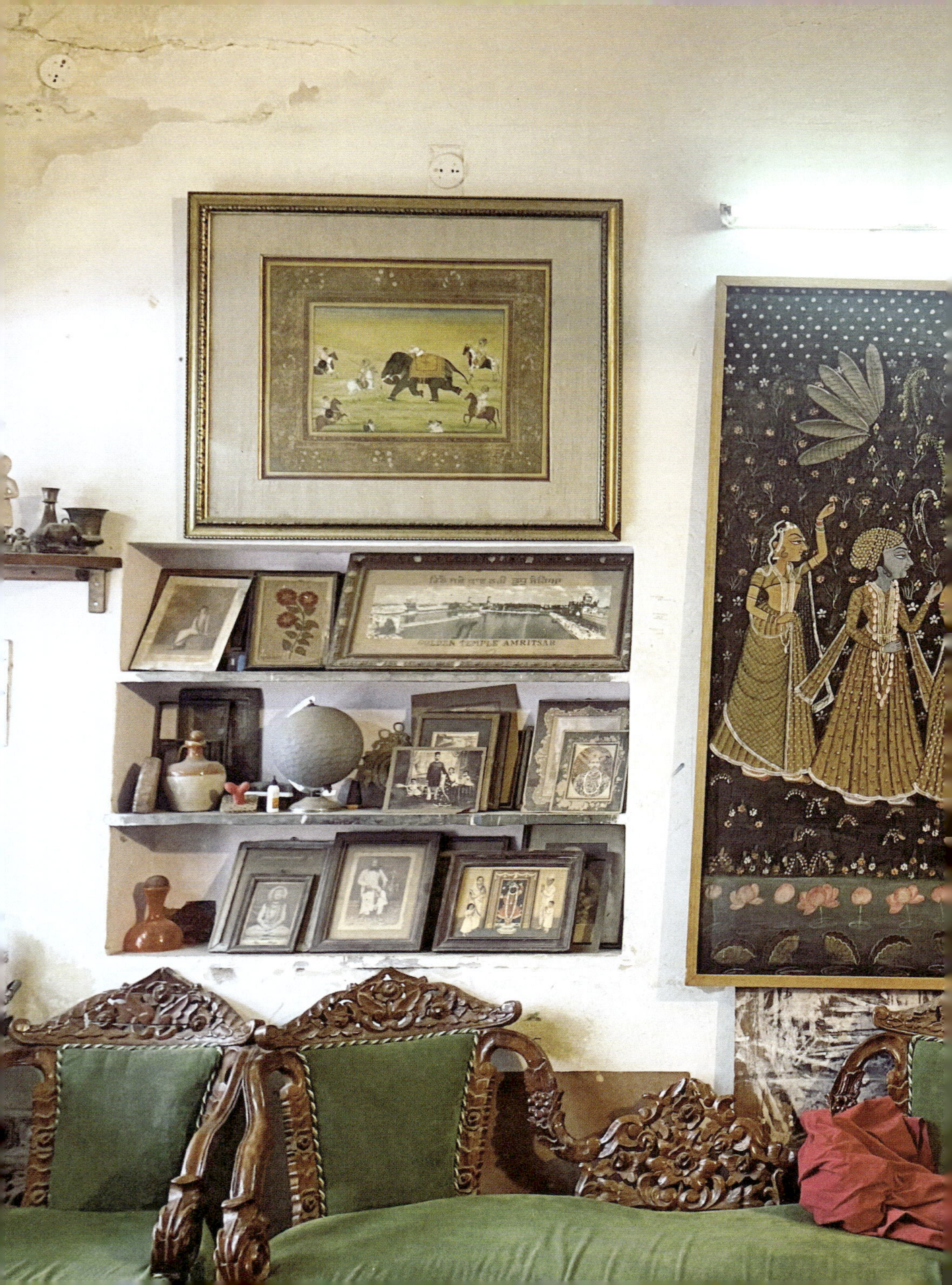
GOLDEN TEMPLE AMRITSAR

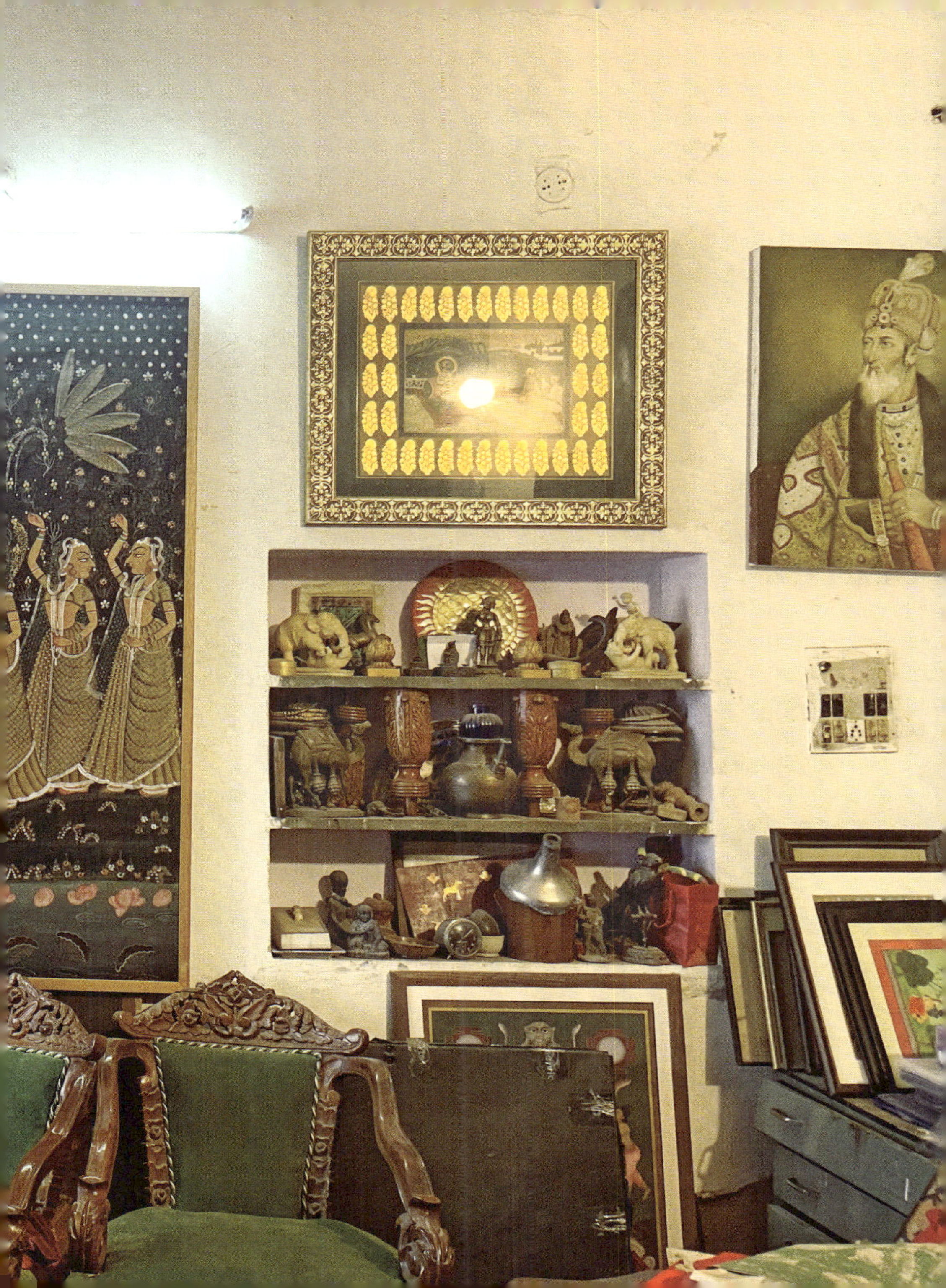

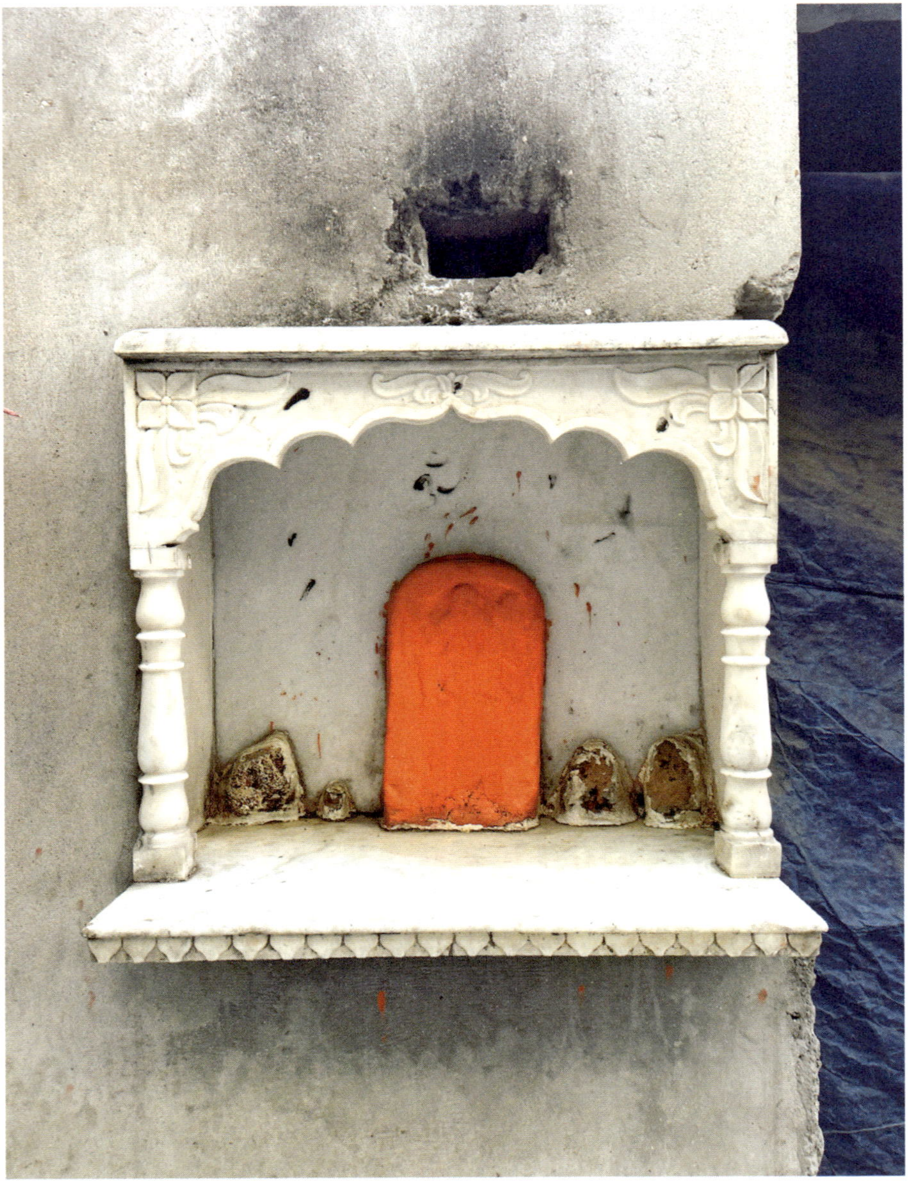

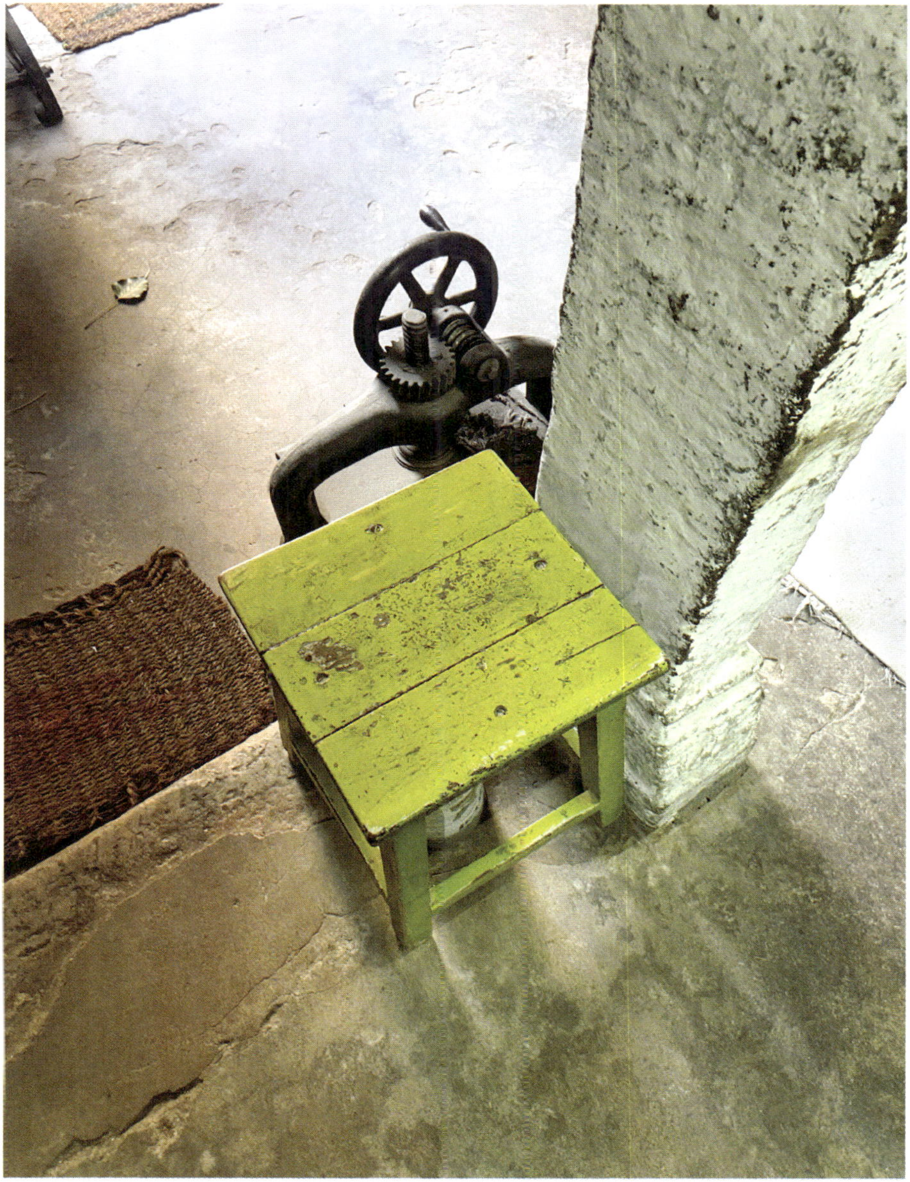

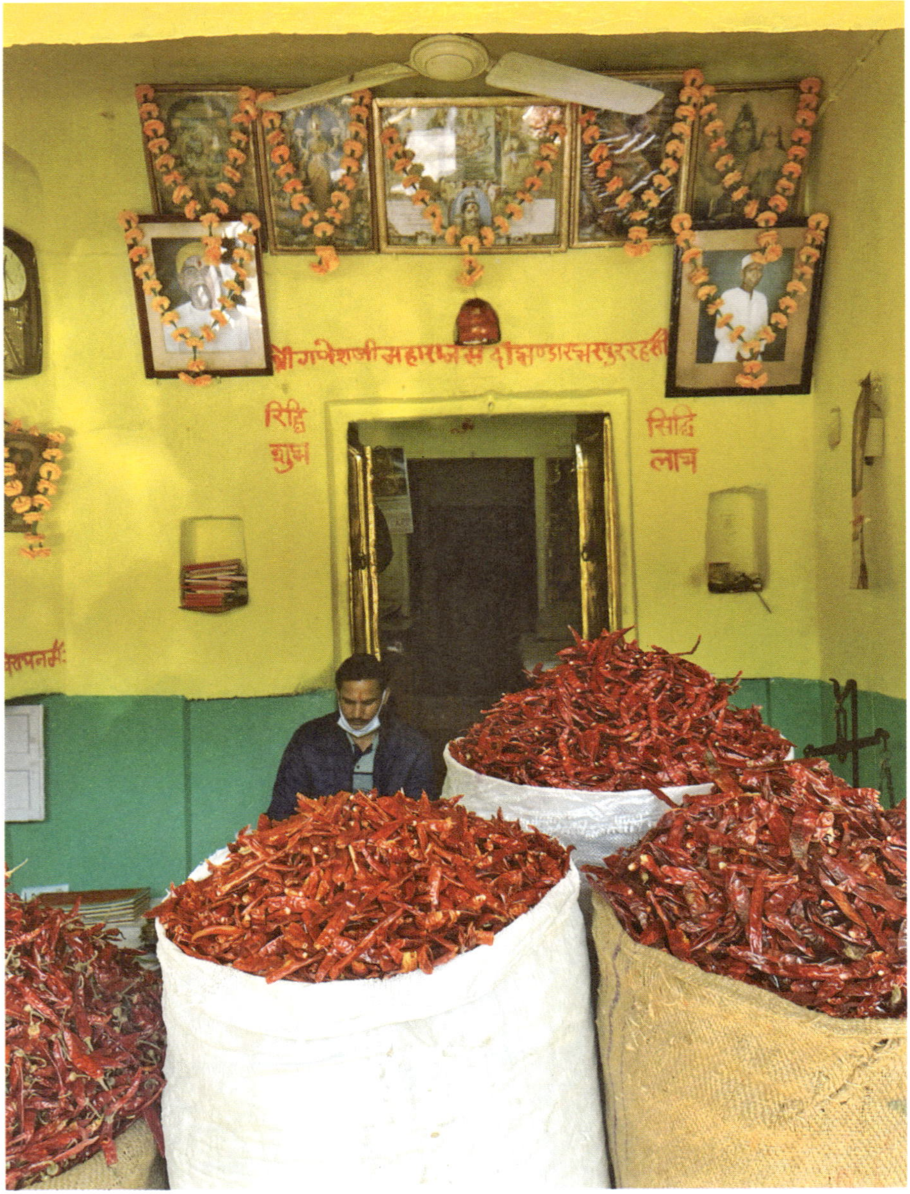
रिद्धि
शुभ
सिद्धि
लाभ

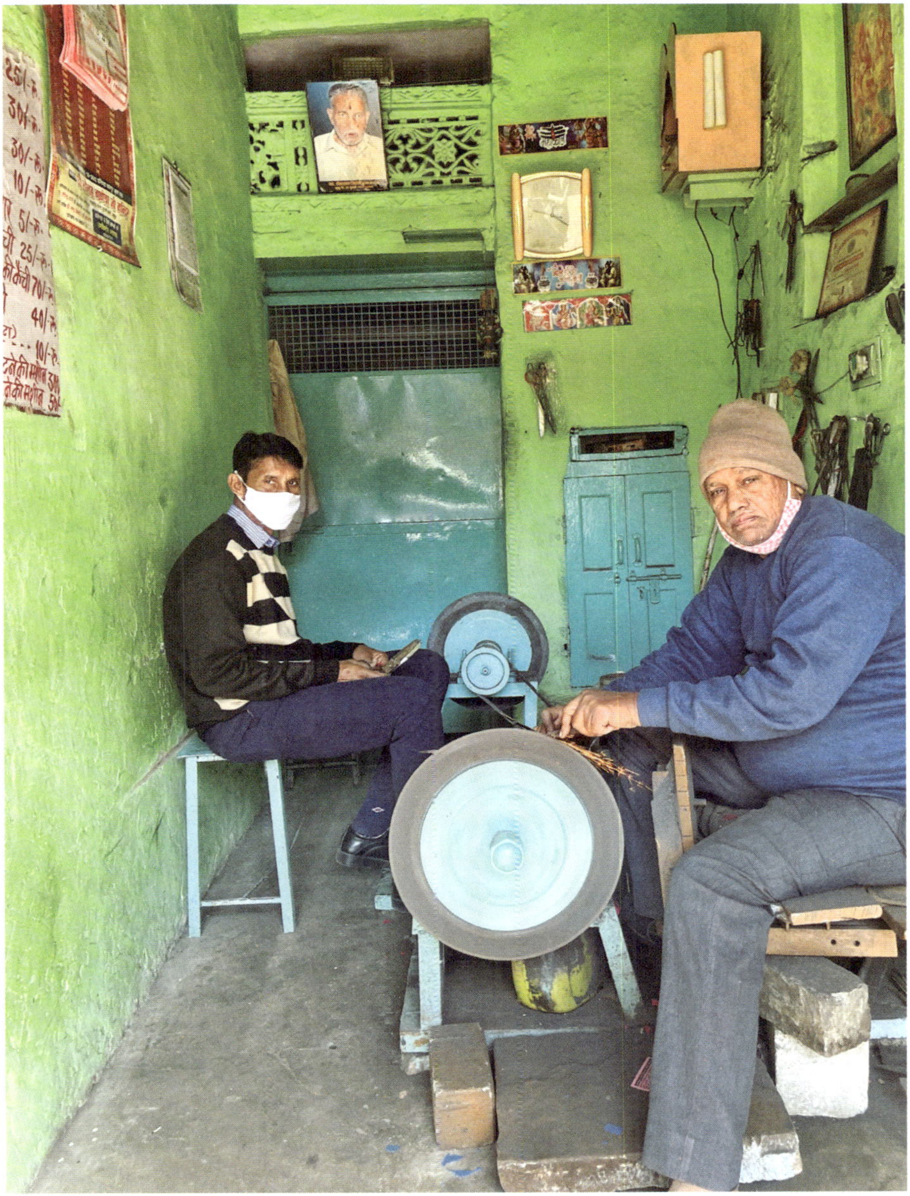

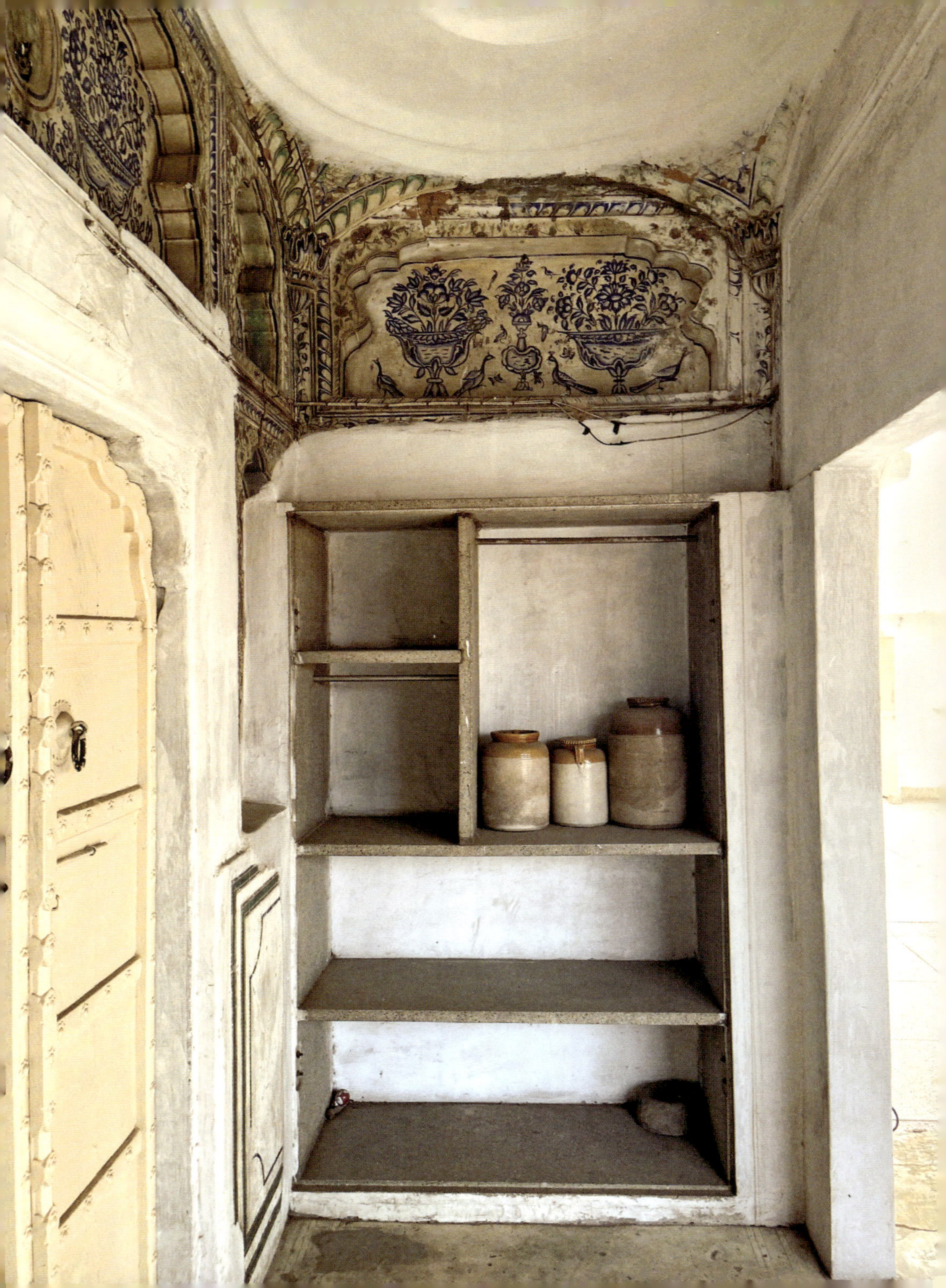

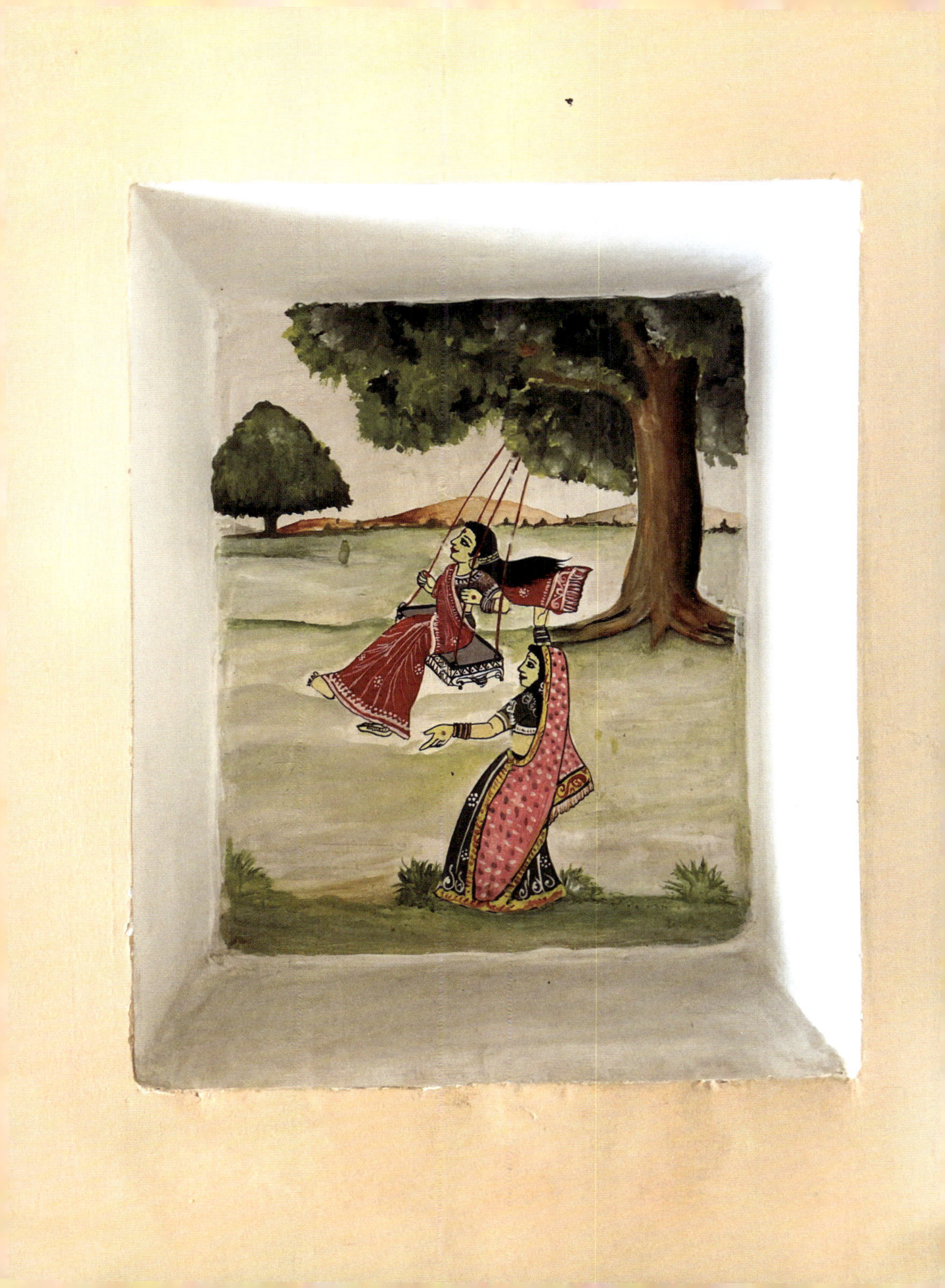

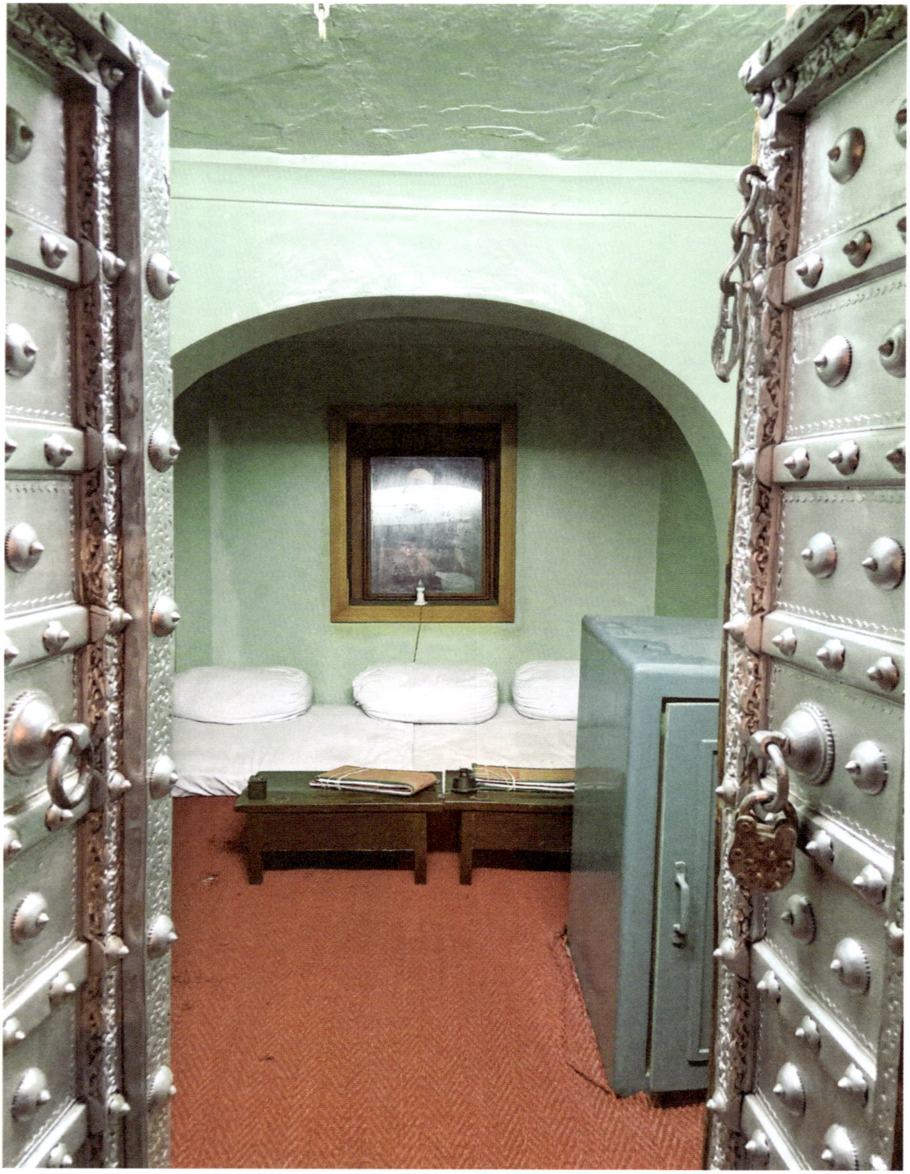

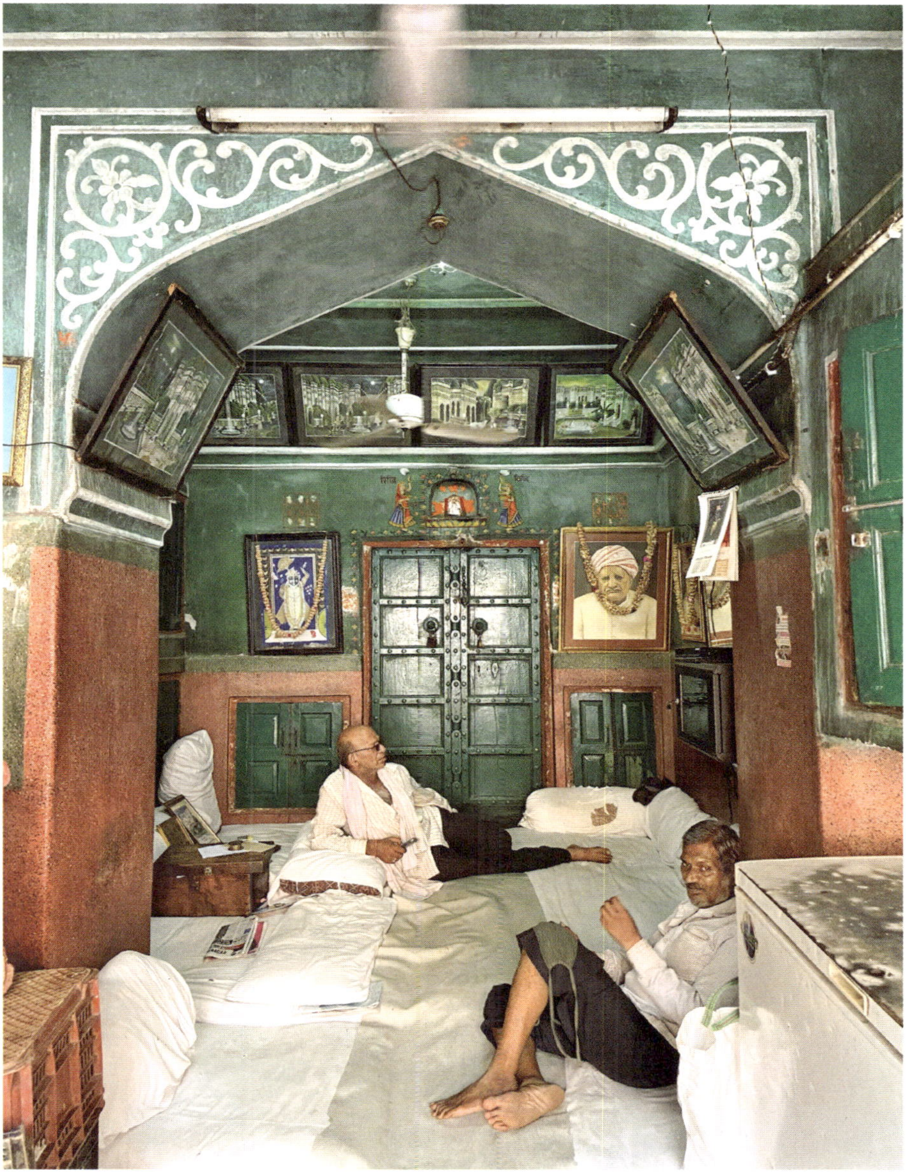

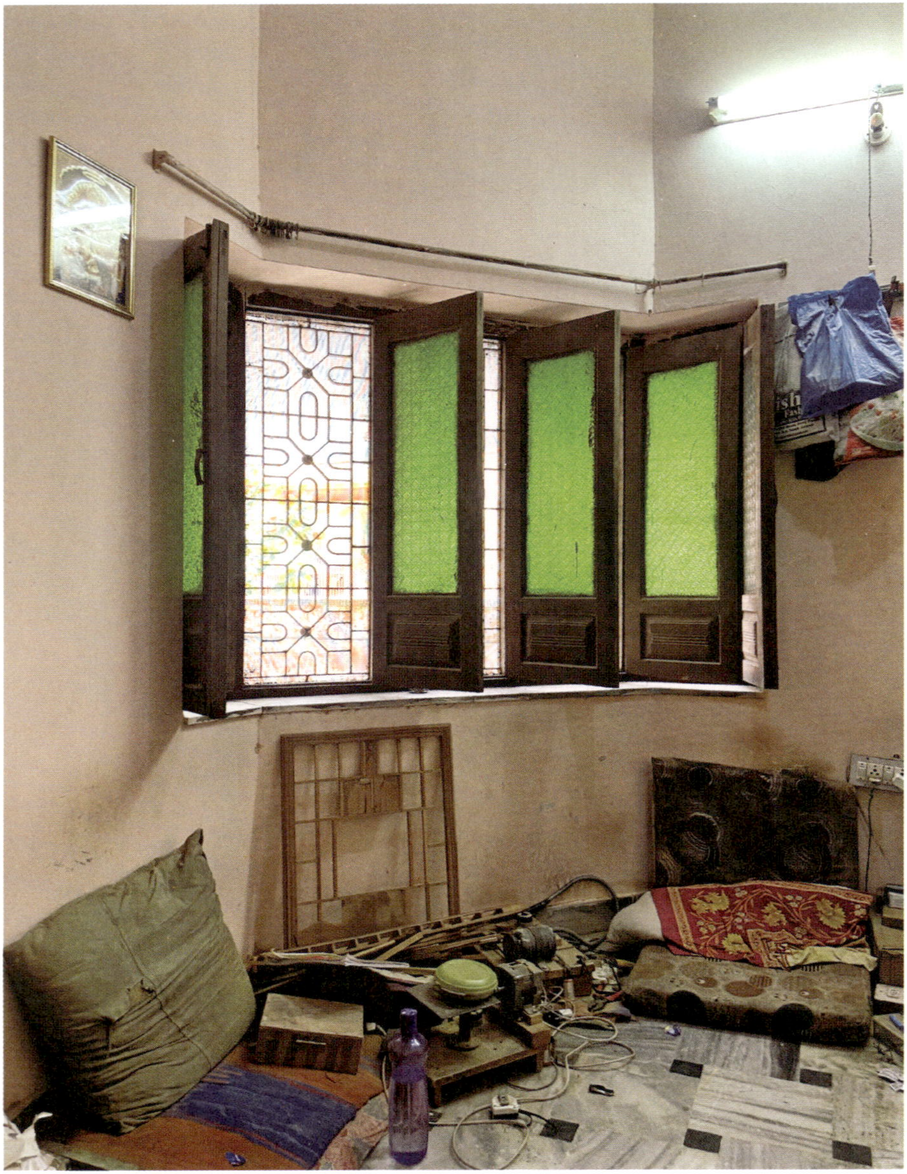

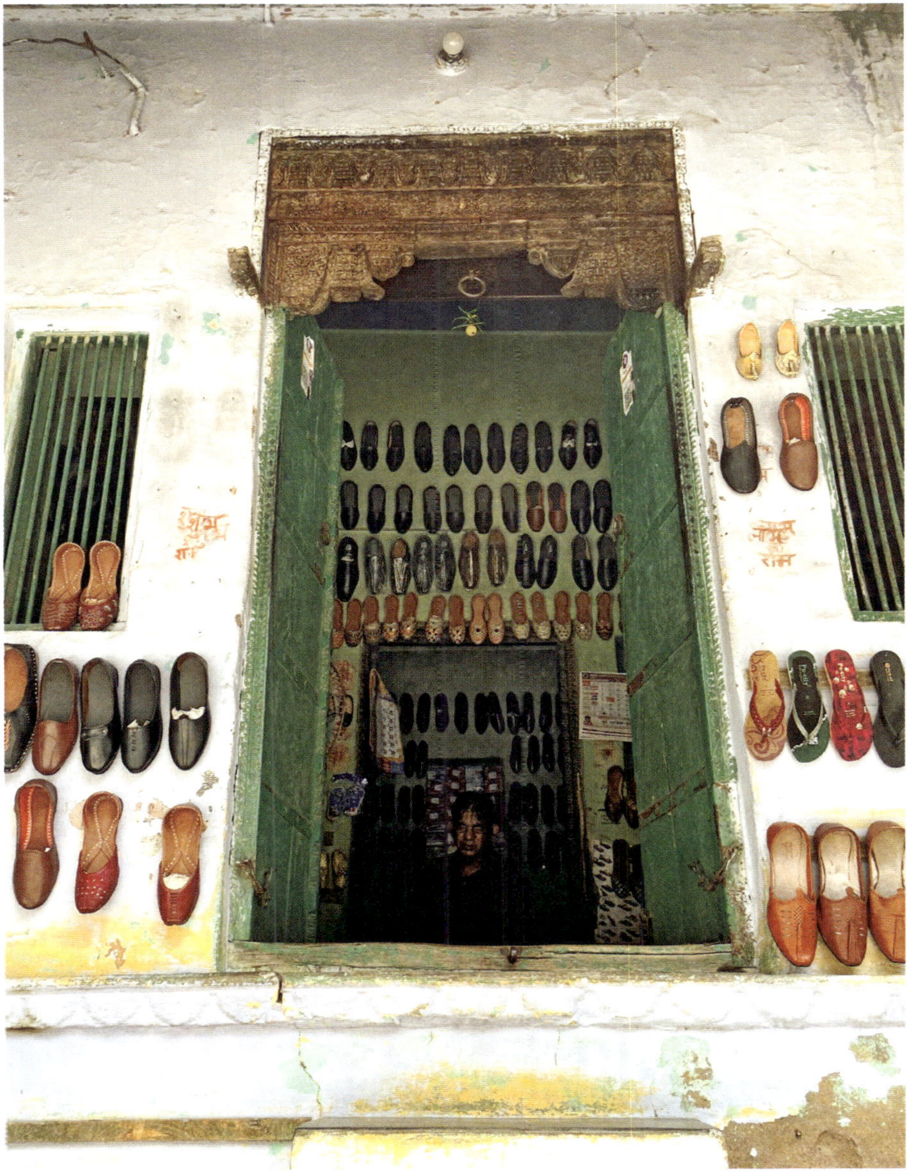

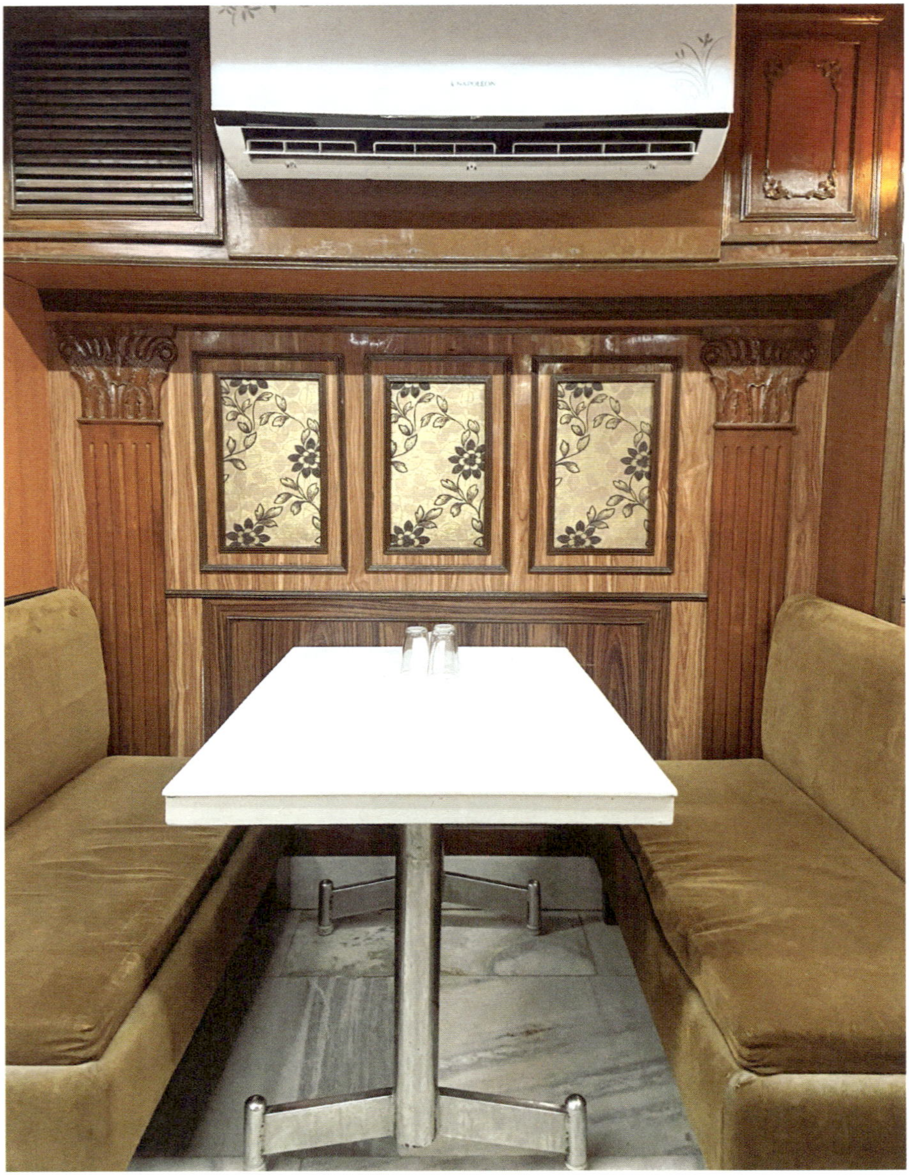

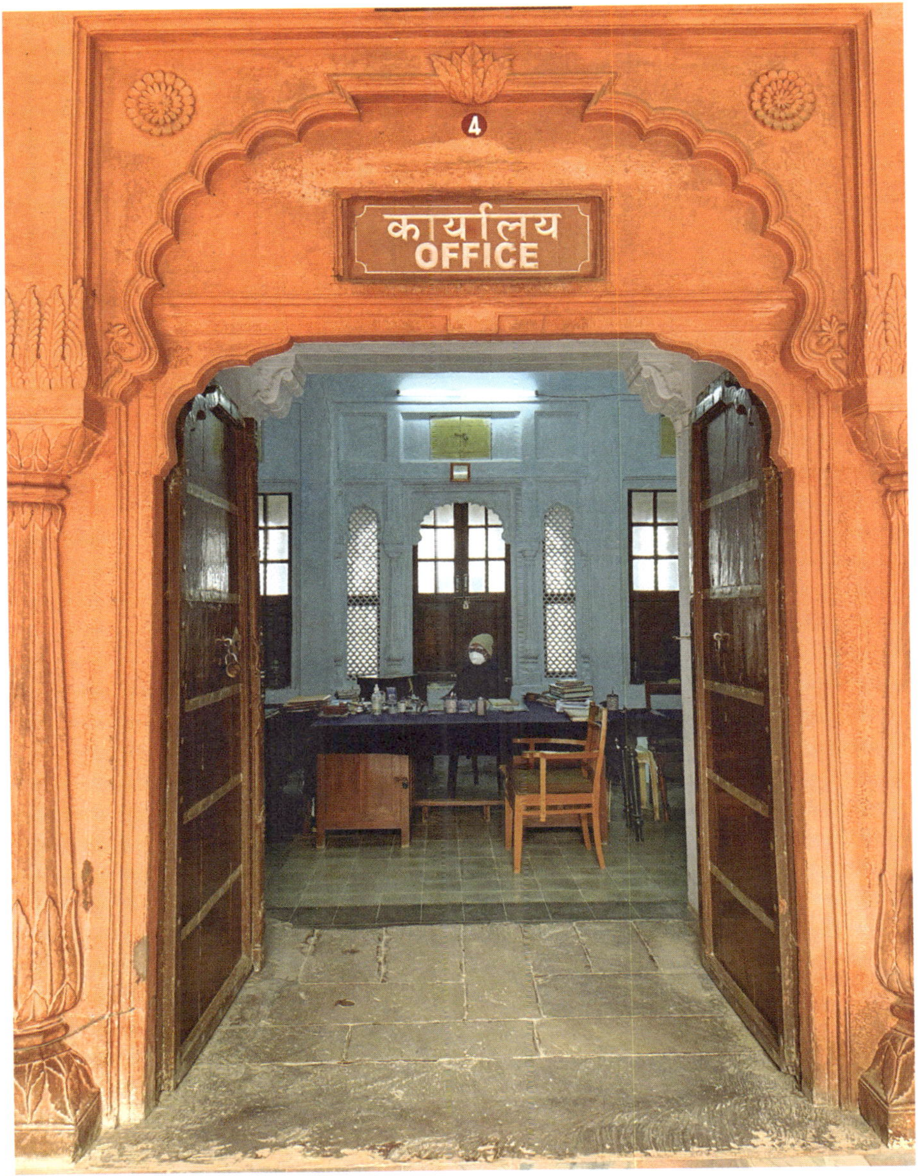
4
कार्यालय
OFFICE

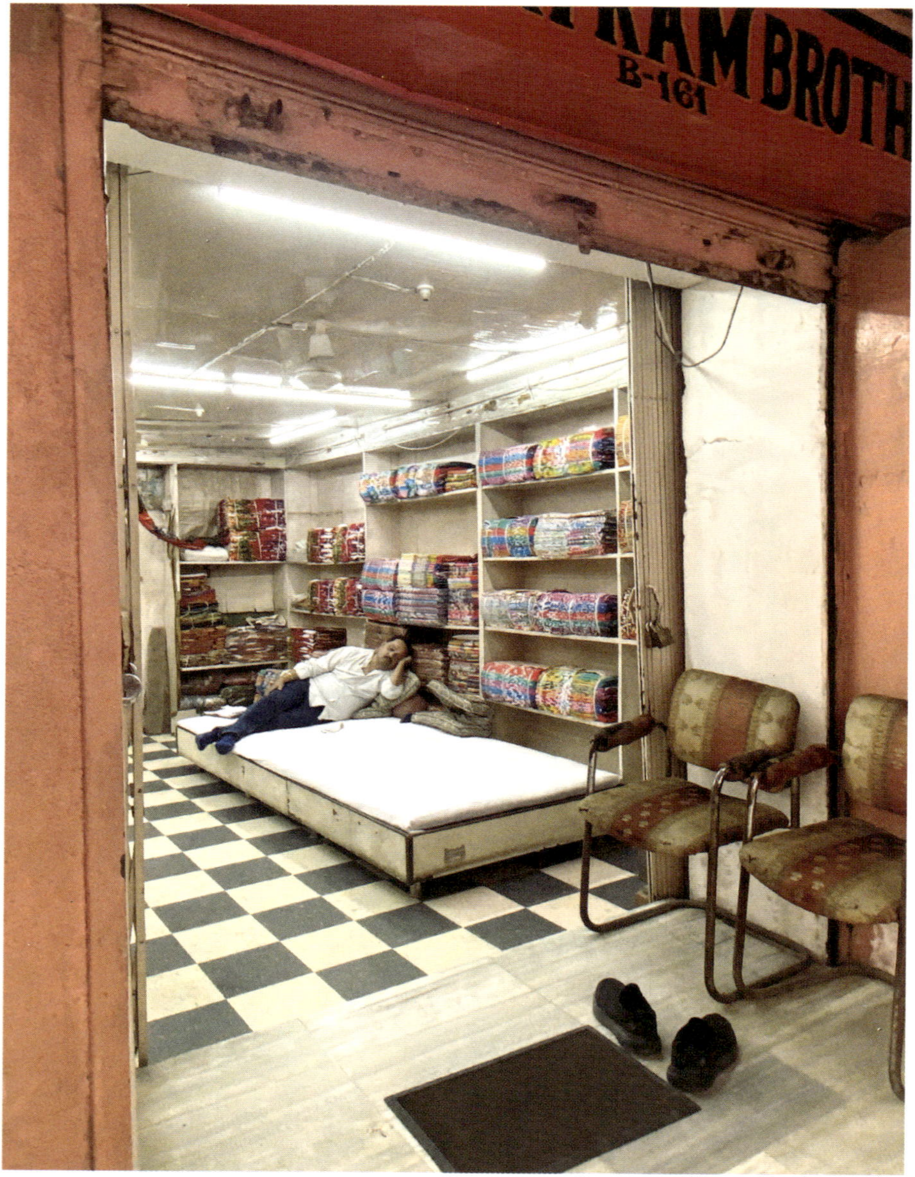
RAM BROTH
B-161

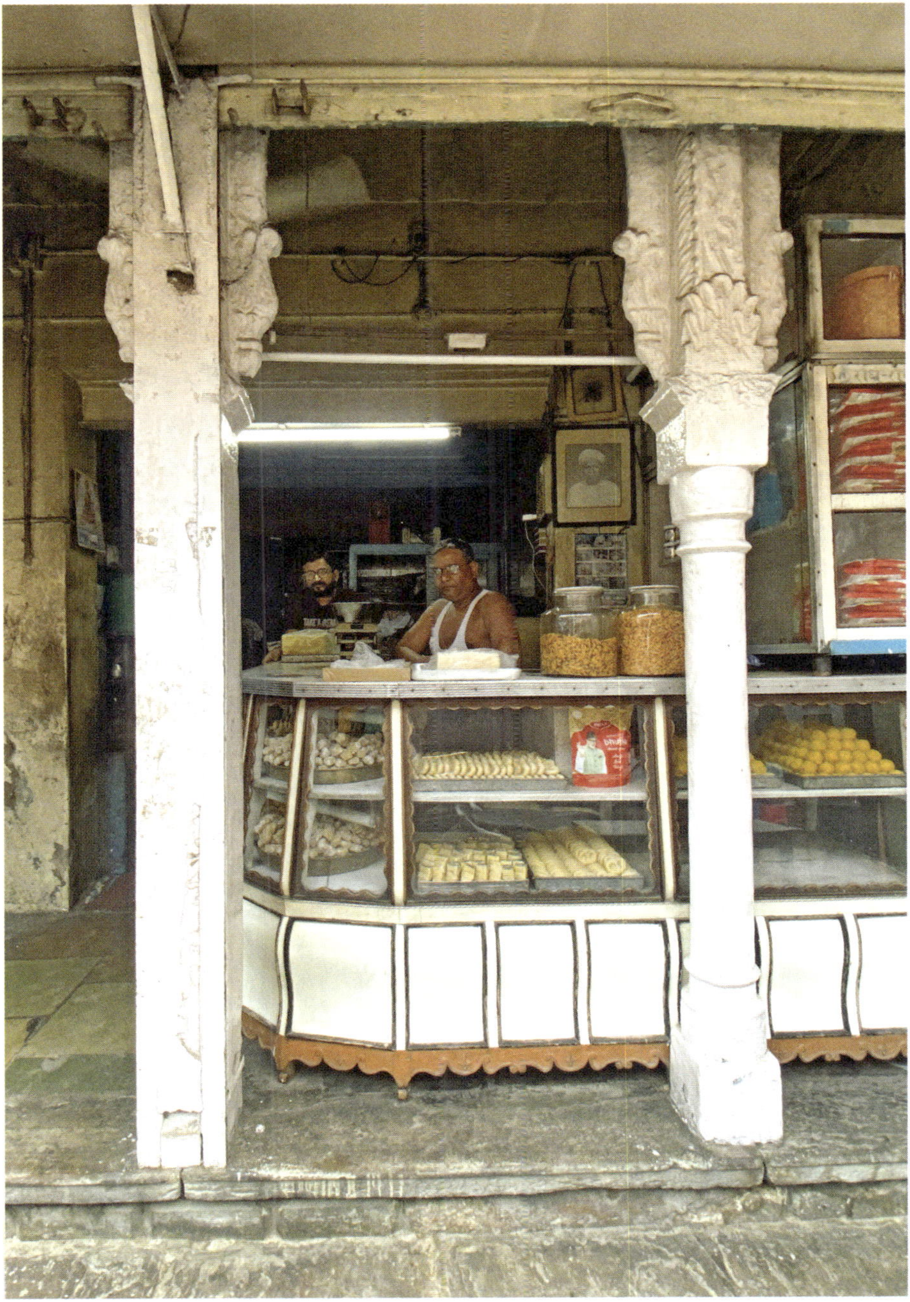

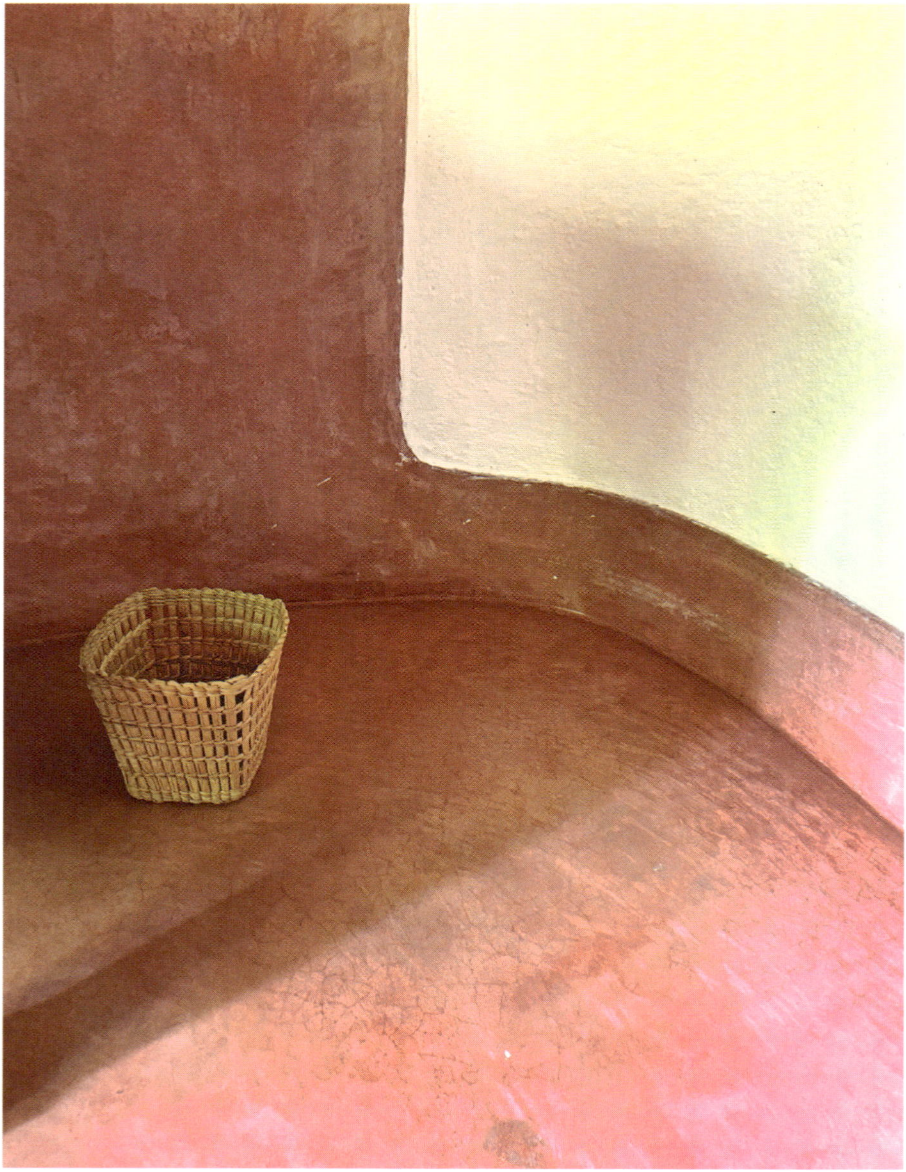

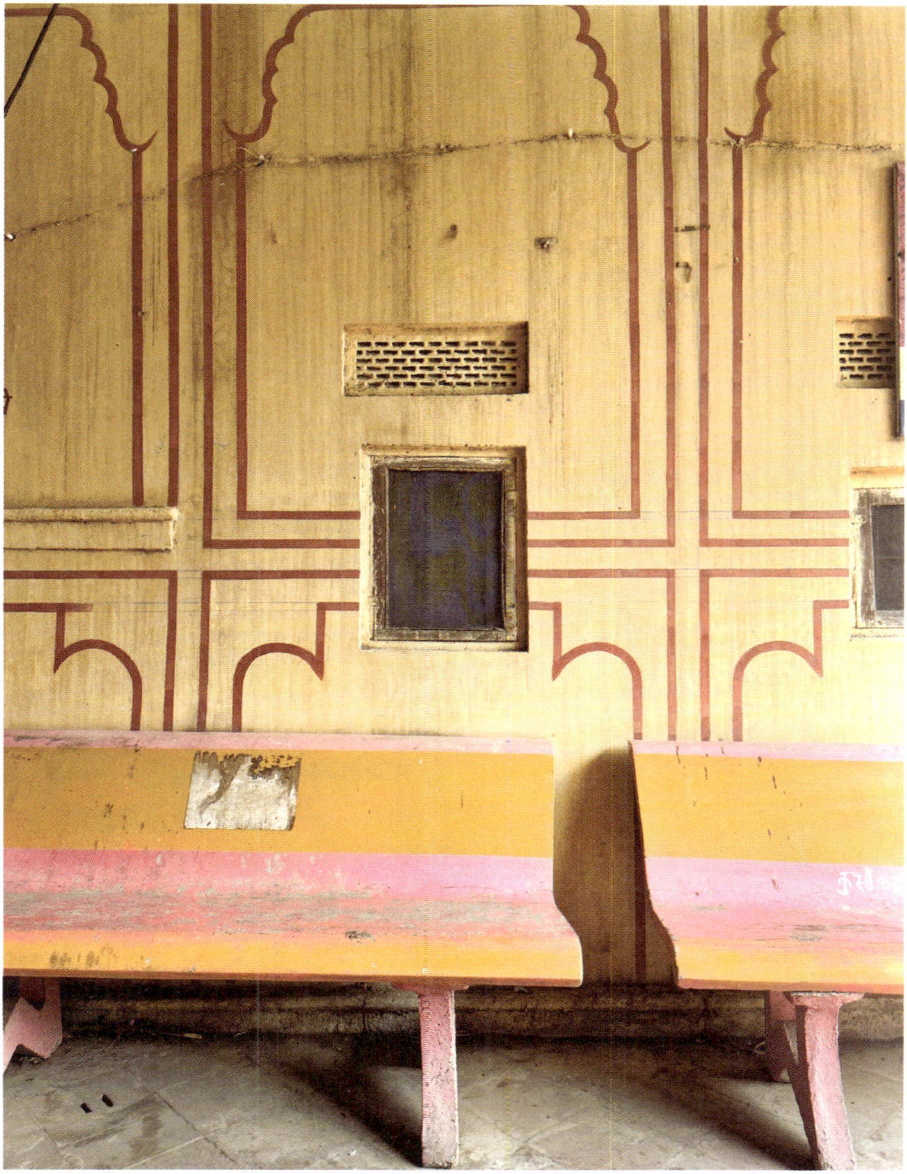

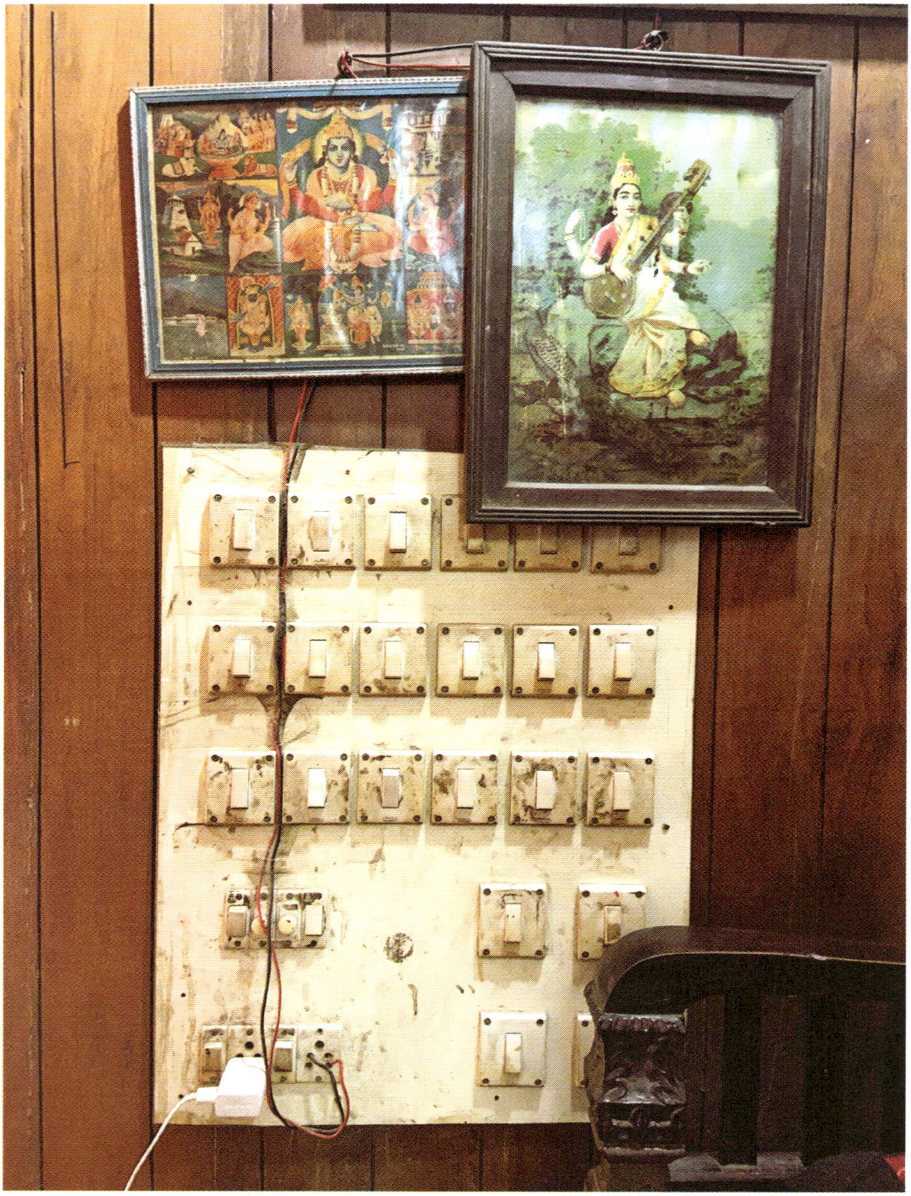

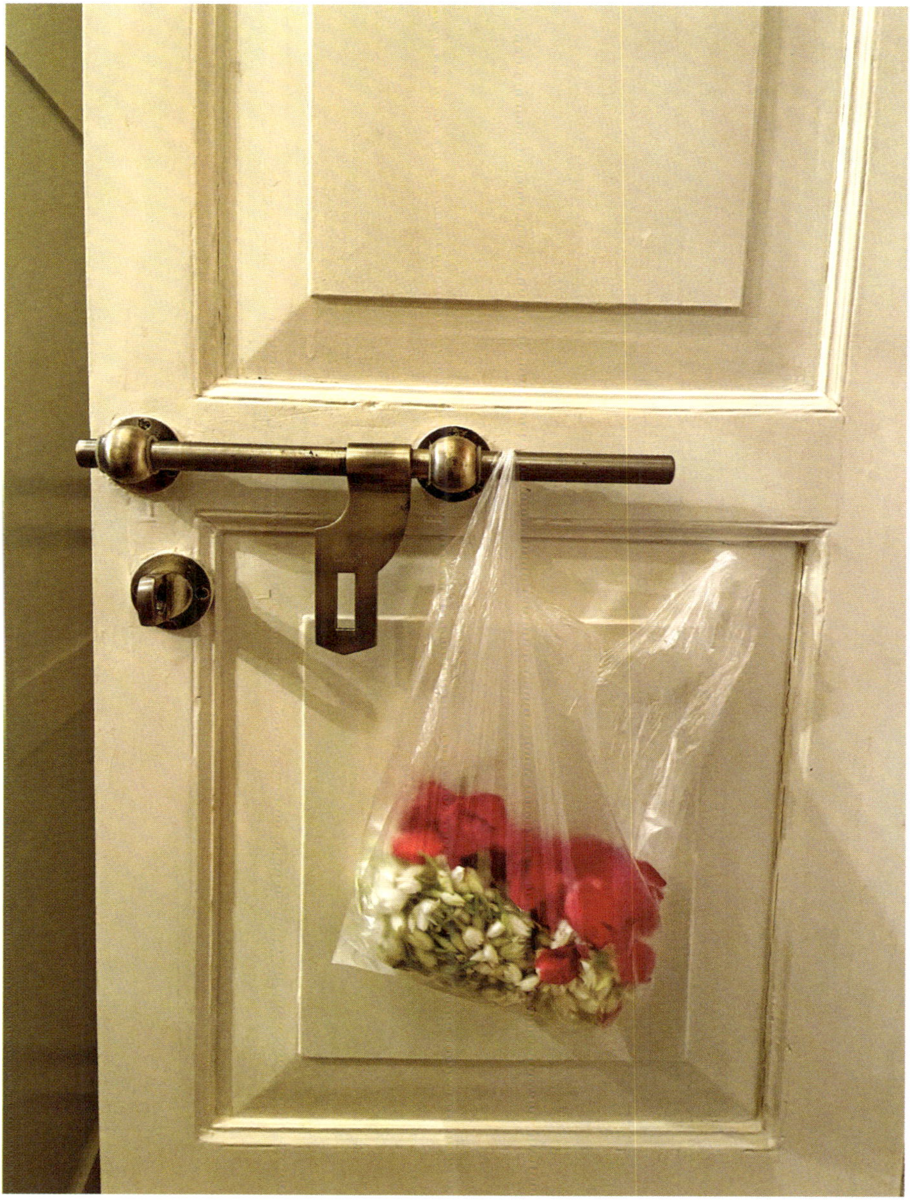

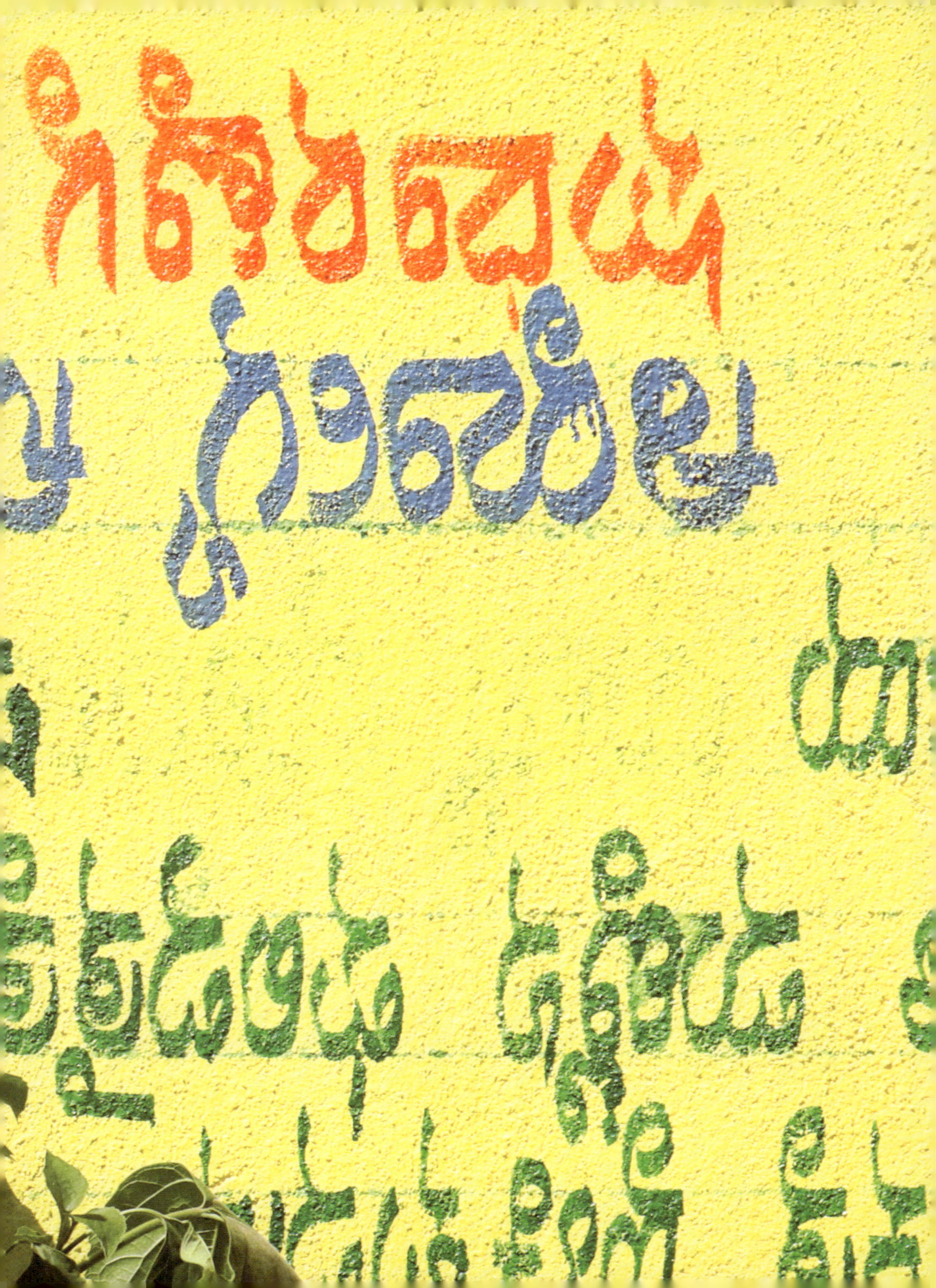

typography & imagery

Spiritual mantra and vastu yantra, hand-painted menus and directional signposts – everywhere one looks, from the living rooms to the shop fronts – a plethora of creative inspiration awaits the attention of onlookers.

Type fonts and calligraphy, signage and listicles, engravings and notice boards, banners and bills, posters and pamphlets – these photographs aim to capture a semblance of the Indian graphic traditions through ordinary vignettes. Whether it's the men's saloons or the roadside dhabas, the written word and the drawn designs have no standardized technique, yet within the stylistic dissonance emerges a visual unity. India's linguistic diversity is reflected through the striking bright and bold coloured letters that catch the eyes of every passer-by.

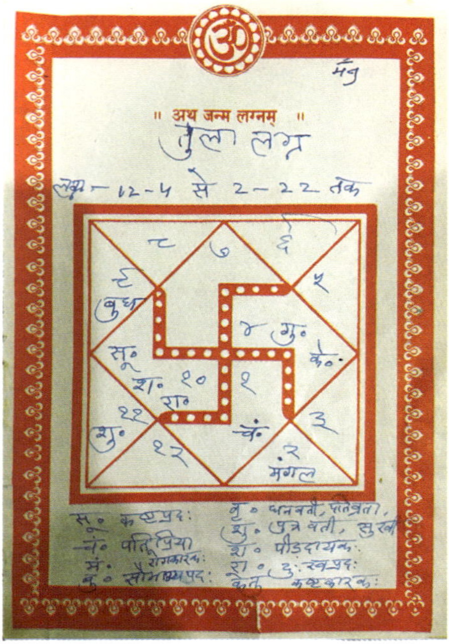
॥ अथ जन्म लग्नम् ॥
तुला लग्न
मंगल

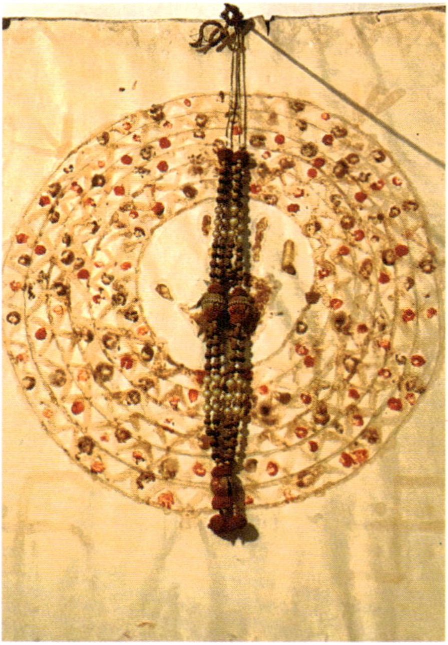

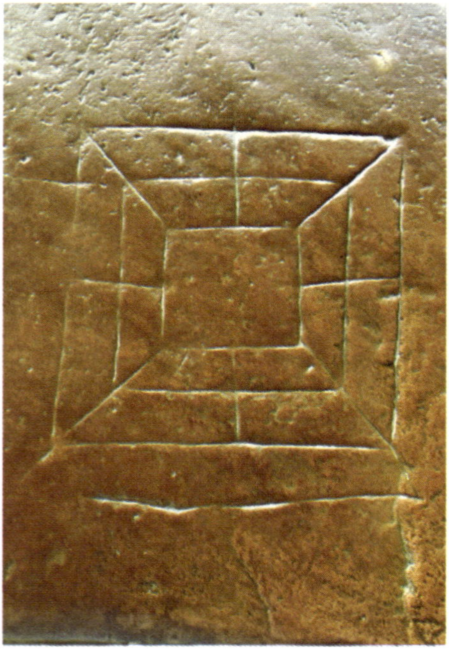

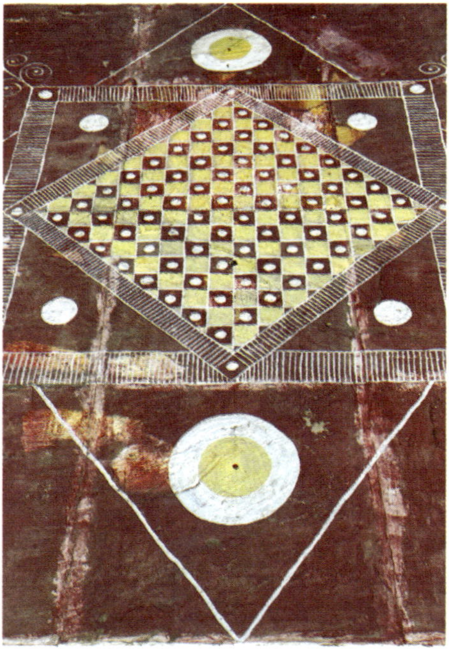

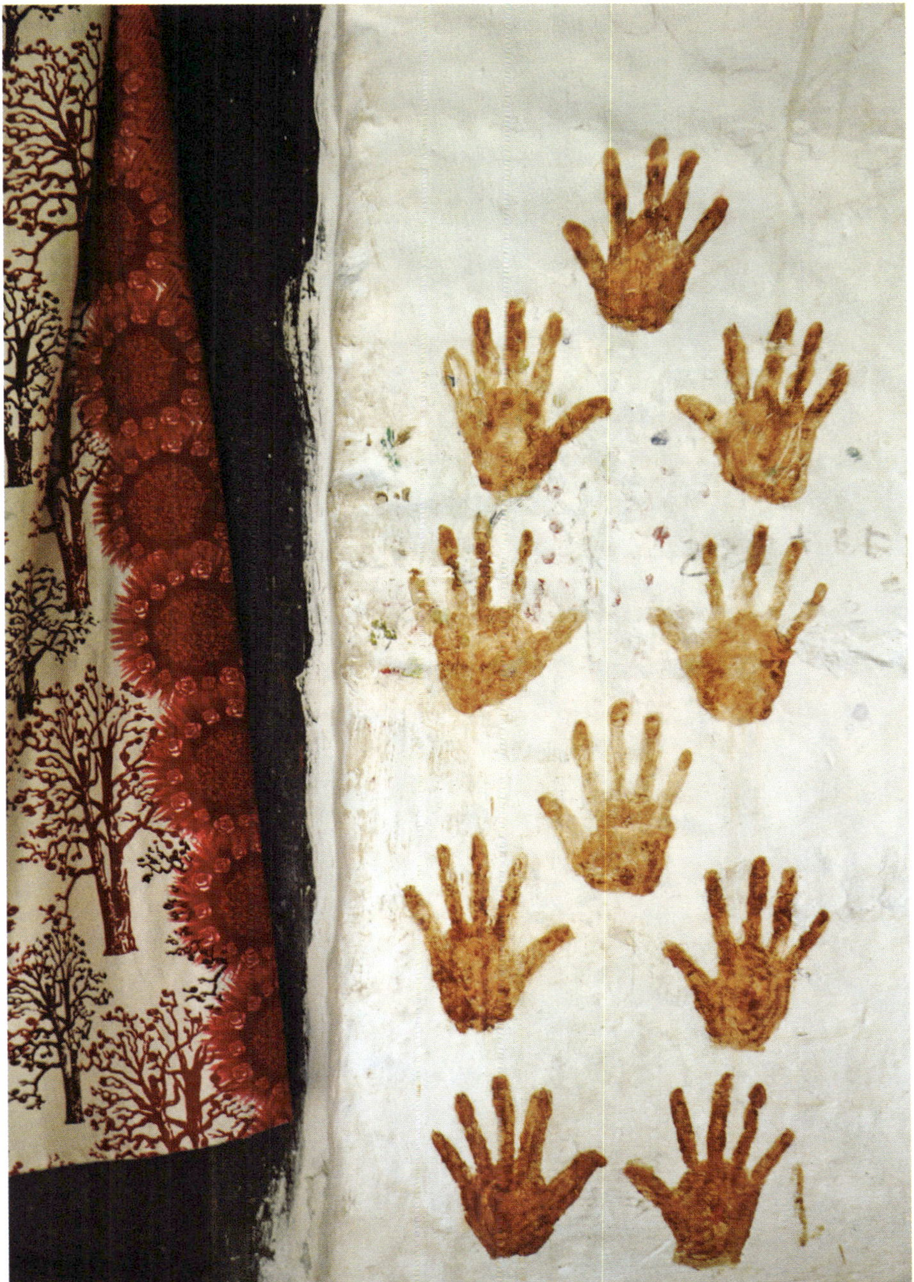

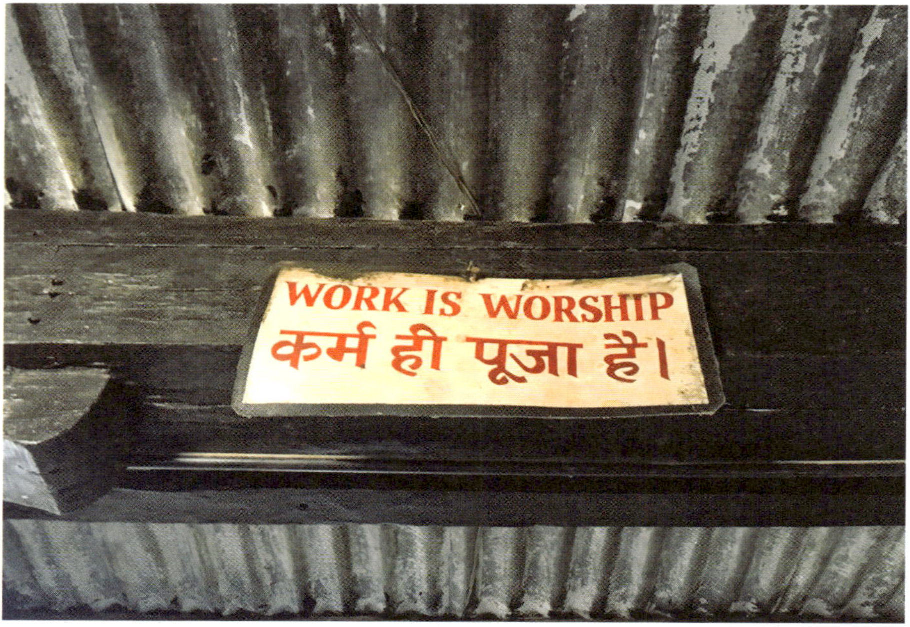
WORK IS WORSHIP
कर्म ही पूजा है।

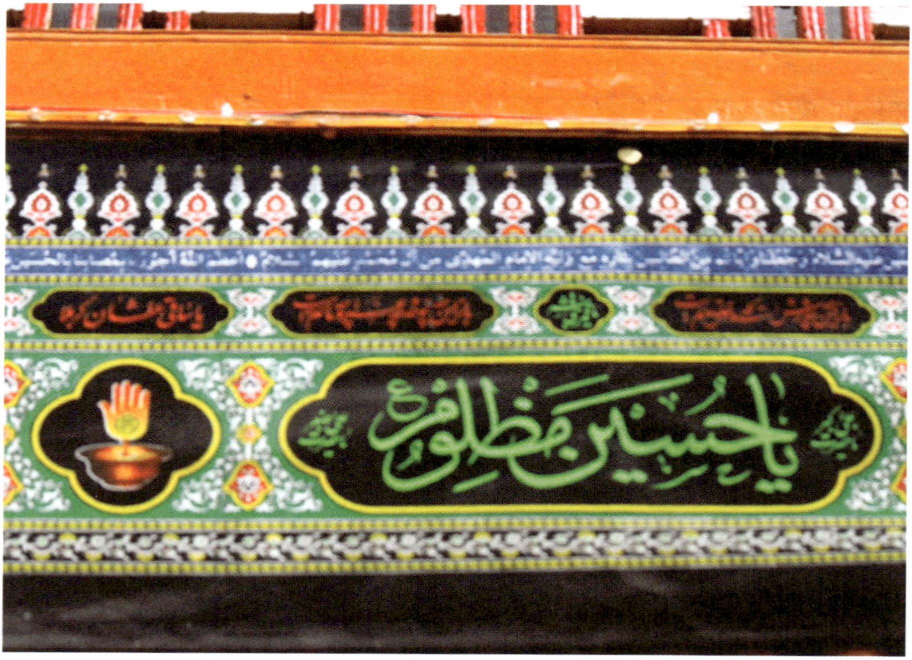
يا حسين مظلوم

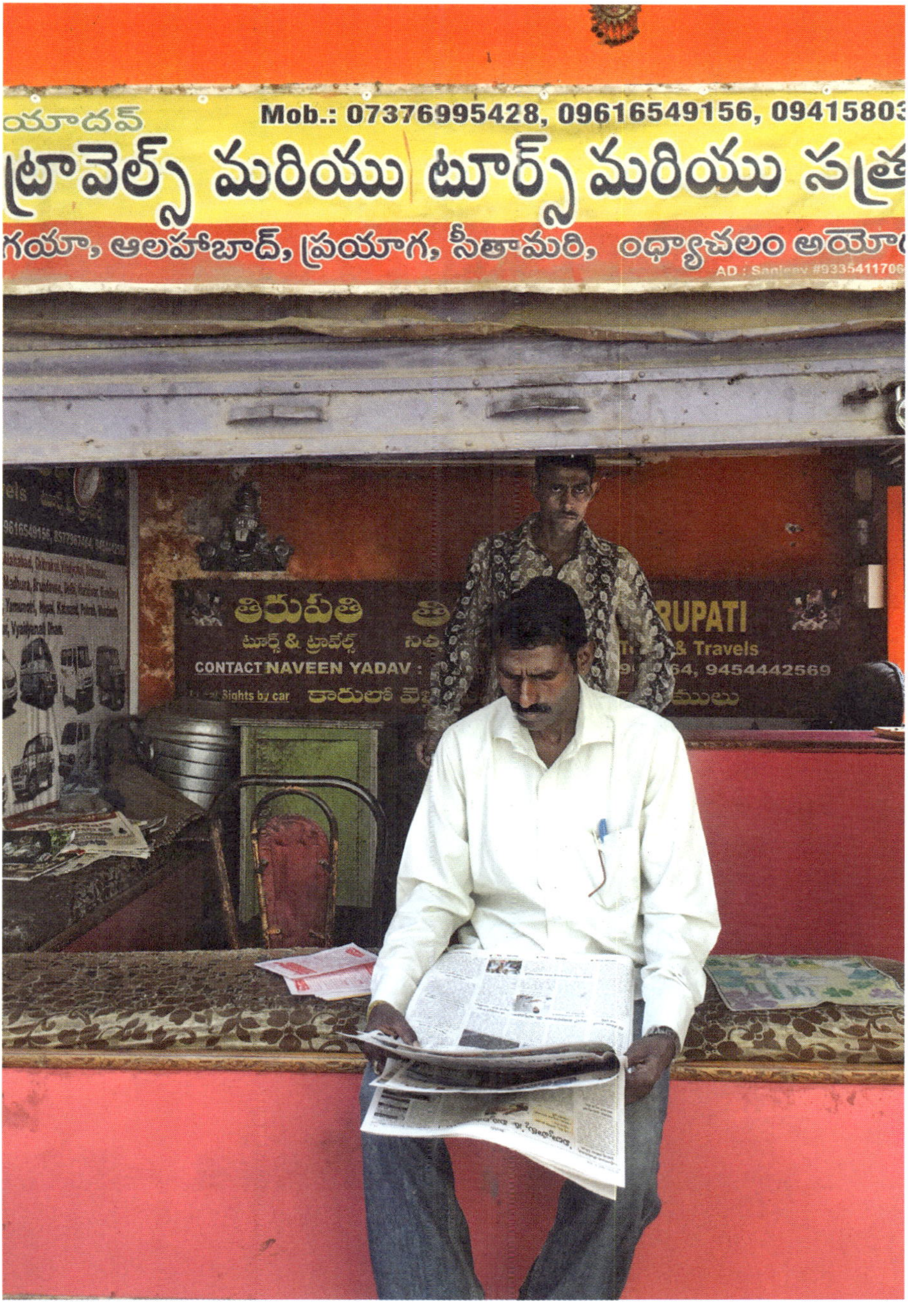
Mob.: 07376995428, 09616549156, 0941580
ట్రావెల్స్ మరియు టూర్స్ మరియు
గయా, అలహాబాద్, ప్రయాగ, సీతామరి,
తిరుపతి
టూర్స్ & ట్రావెల్స్
RUPATI
& Travels
CONTACT NAVEEN YADAV :
9454442569
Sights by car

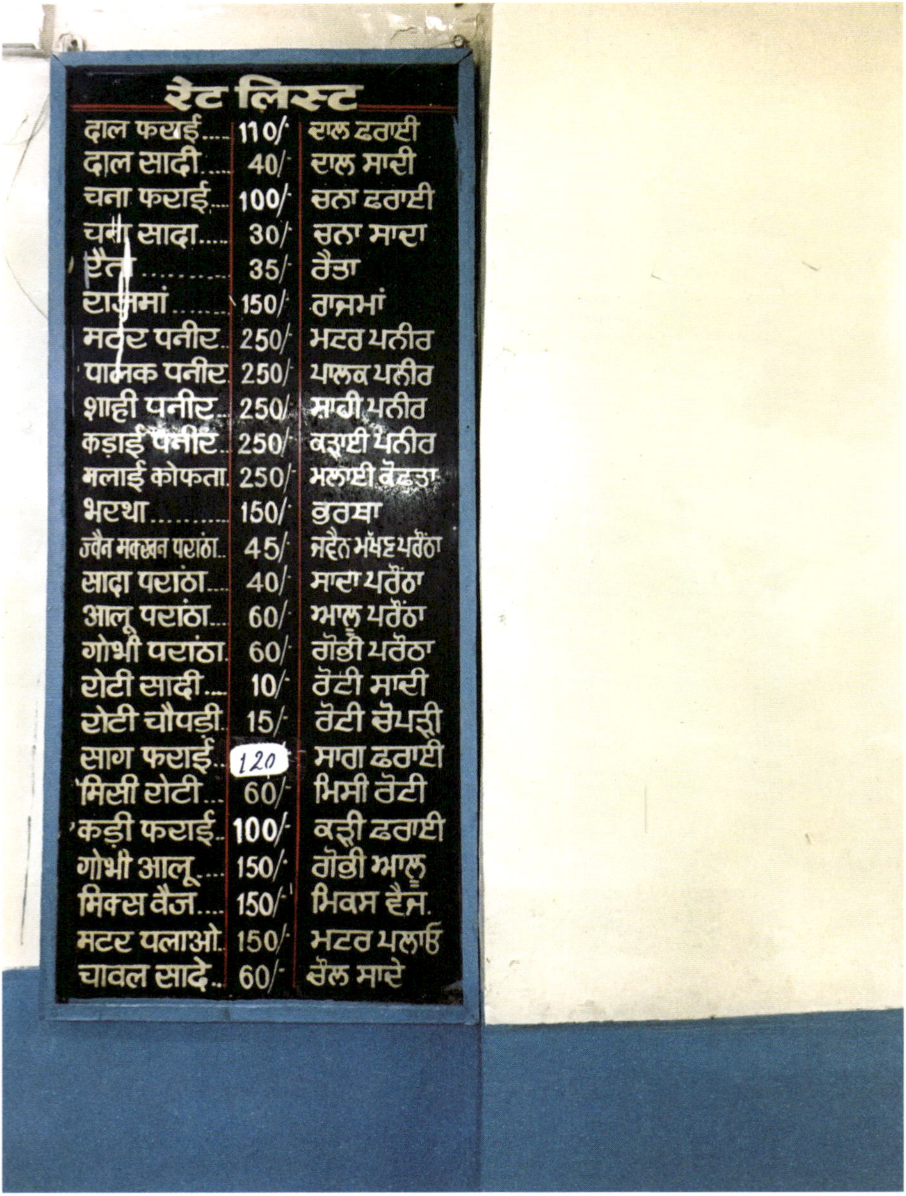
ਰੇਟ ਲਿਸਟ
दाल फराई 110/- ਦਾਲ ਫਰਾਈ
दाल सादी 40/- ਦਾਲ ਸਾਦੀ
चना फराई 100/- ਚਨਾ ਫਰਾਈ
चना सादा 30/- ਚਨਾ ਸਾਦਾ
रैता 35/- ਰੈਤਾ
राजमां 150/- ਰਾਜਮਾਂ
मटर पनीर 250/- ਮਟਰ ਪਨੀਰ
पालक पनीर 250/- ਪਾਲਕ ਪਨੀਰ
शाही पनीर 250/- ਸਾਹੀ ਪਨੀਰ
कड़ाई पनीर 250/- ਕੜਾਈ ਪਨੀਰ
मलाई कोफता 250/- ਮਲਾਈ ਕੋਫਤਾ
भरथा 150/- ਭਰਥਾ
ज्वैन मक्खन परांठा 45/- ਜਵੈਨ ਮੱਖਣ ਪਰੌਂਠਾ
सादा परांठा 40/- ਸਾਦਾ ਪਰੌਂਠਾ
आलू परांठा 60/- ਆਲੂ ਪਰੌਂਠਾ
गोभी परांठा 60/- ਗੋਭੀ ਪਰੌਂਠਾ
रोटी सादी 10/- ਰੋਟੀ ਸਾਦੀ
रोटी चौपड़ी 15/- ਰੋਟੀ ਚੋਪੜੀ
साग फराई 120 ਸਾਗ ਫਰਾਈ
मिसी रोटी 60/- ਮਿਸੀ ਰੋਟੀ
कड़ी फराई 100/- ਕੜੀ ਫਰਾਈ
गोभी आलू 150/- ਗੋਭੀ ਆਲੂ
मिक्स वैज 150/- ਮਿਕਸ ਵੈਜ.
मटर पलाओ 150/- ਮਟਰ ਪਲਾਓ
चावल सादे 60/- ਚੌਲ ਸਾਦੇ

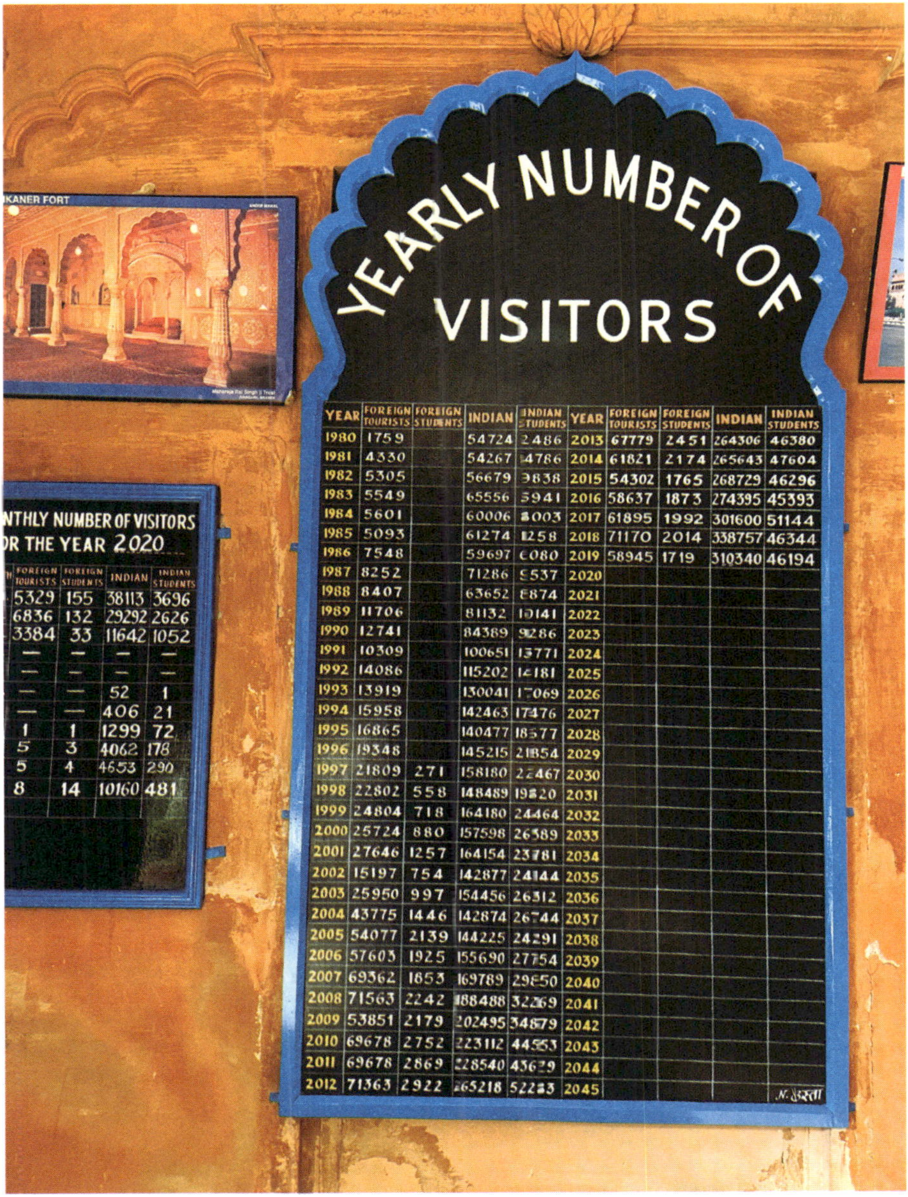
YEARLY NUMBER OF VISITORS
YEAR FOREIGN TOURISTS FOREIGN STUDENTS INDIAN INDIAN STUDENTS YEAR FOREIGN TOURISTS FOREIGN STUDENTS INDIAN INDIAN STUDENTS
1980 1759 54724 2486 2013 67779 2451 264306 46380
1981 4330 54267 4786 2014 61821 2174 265643 47604
1982 5305 56679 9838 2015 54302 1765 268729 46296
1983 5549 65556 5941 2016 58637 1873 274395 45393
1984 5601 60006 8003 2017 61895 1992 301600 51144
1985 5093 61274 1258 2018 71170 2014 338757 46344
1986 7548 59697 6080 2019 58945 1719 310340 46194
1987 8252 71286 5537 2020
1988 8407 63652 8874 2021
1989 11706 81132 10141 2022
1990 12741 84389 9286 2023
1991 10309 100651 13771 2024
1992 14086 115202 14181 2025
1993 13919 130041 17069 2026
1994 15958 142463 17476 2027
1995 16865 140477 18577 2028
1996 19348 145215 21854 2029
1997 21809 271 158180 22467 2030
1998 22802 558 148489 19820 2031
1999 24804 718 164180 24464 2032
2000 25724 880 157598 26589 2033
2001 27646 1257 164154 23781 2034
2002 15197 754 142877 24144 2035
2003 25950 997 154456 26312 2036
2004 43775 1446 142874 26744 2037
2005 54077 2139 144225 24291 2038
2006 57603 1925 155690 27754 2039
2007 69362 1853 169789 29850 2040
2008 71563 2242 188488 32269 2041
2009 53851 2179 202495 34879 2042
2010 69678 2752 223112 44553 2043
2011 69678 2869 228540 43629 2044
2012 71363 2922 265218 52283 2045

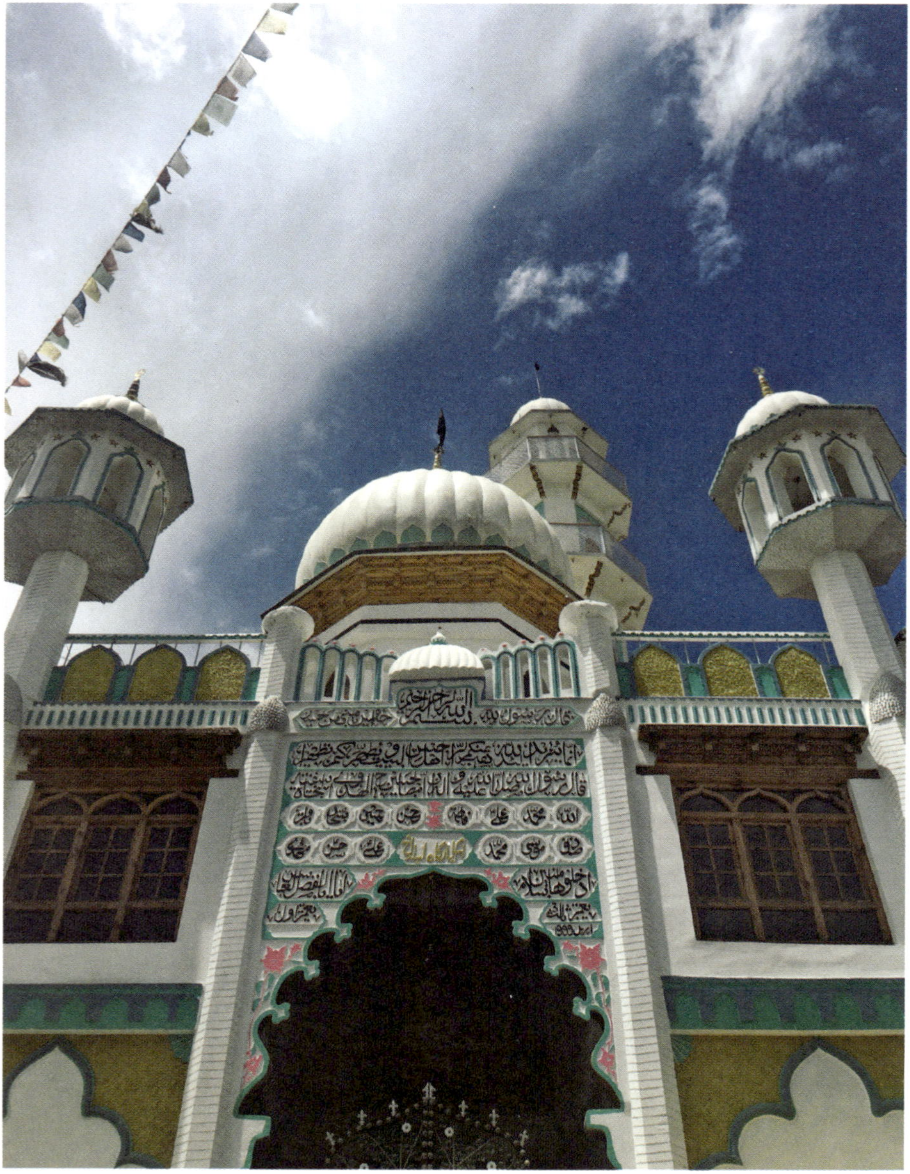

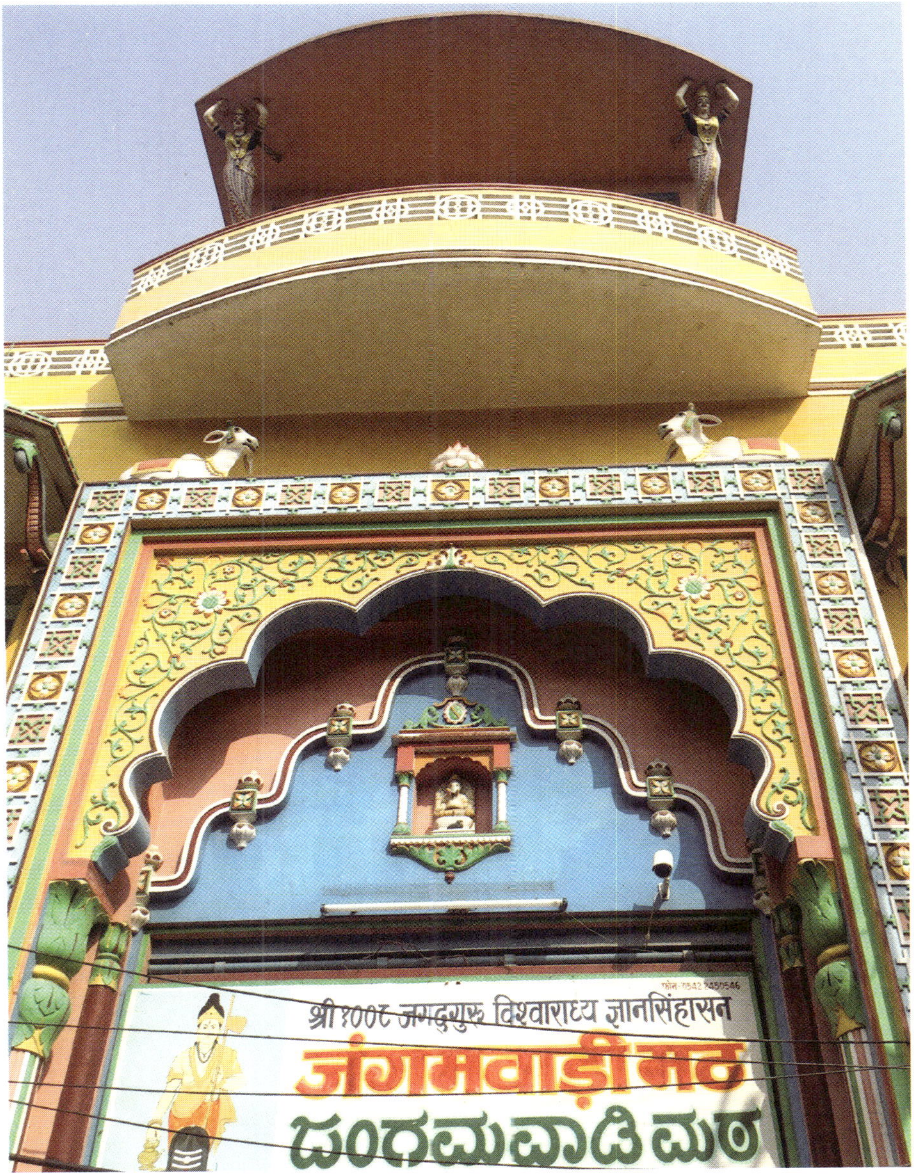
फोन-0542 2450546
श्री १००८ जगद्गुरु विश्वाराध्य ज्ञानसिंहासन
जंगमवाड़ी मठ
ಜಂಗಮವಾಡಿ ಮಠ

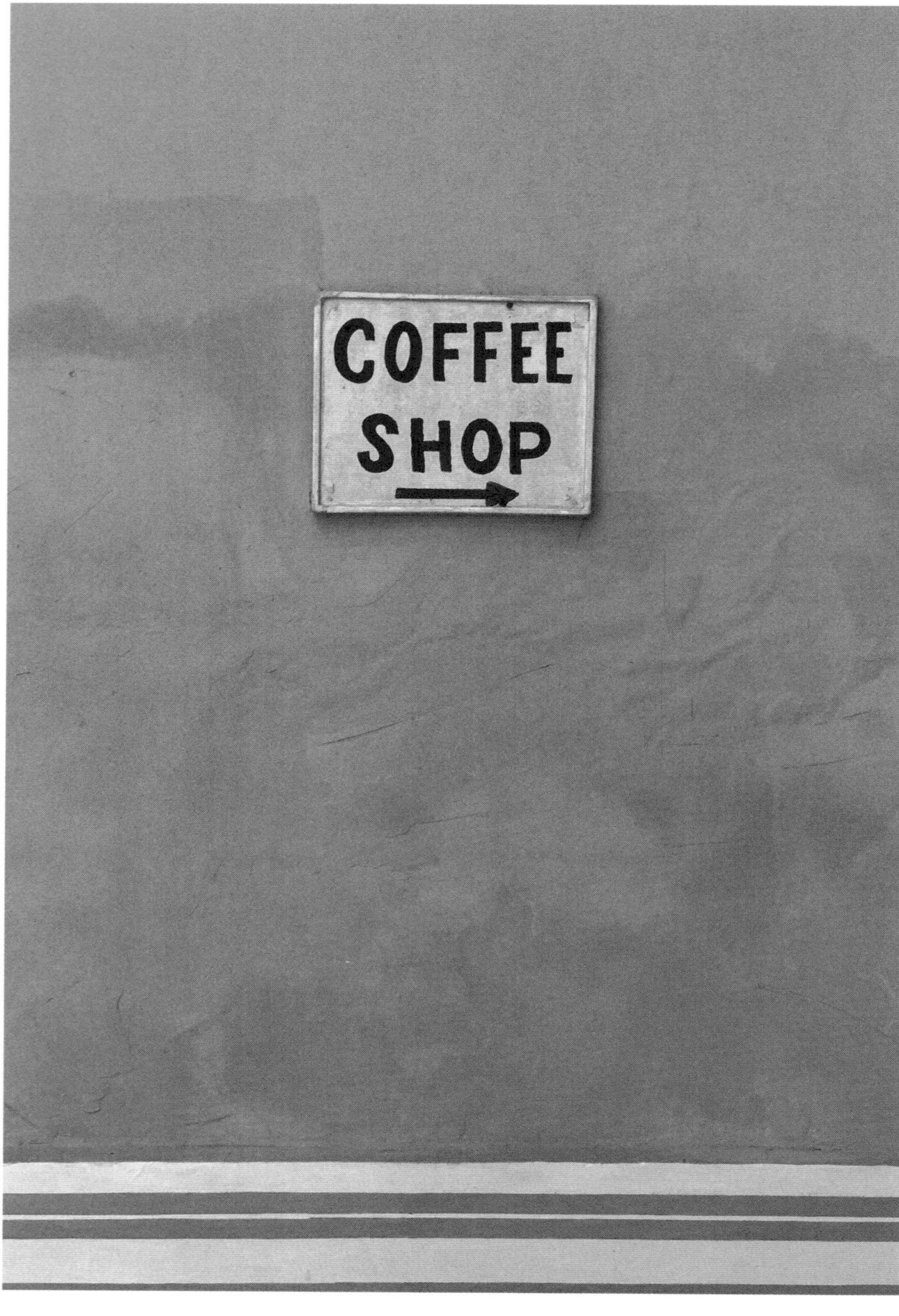
COFFEE
SHOP

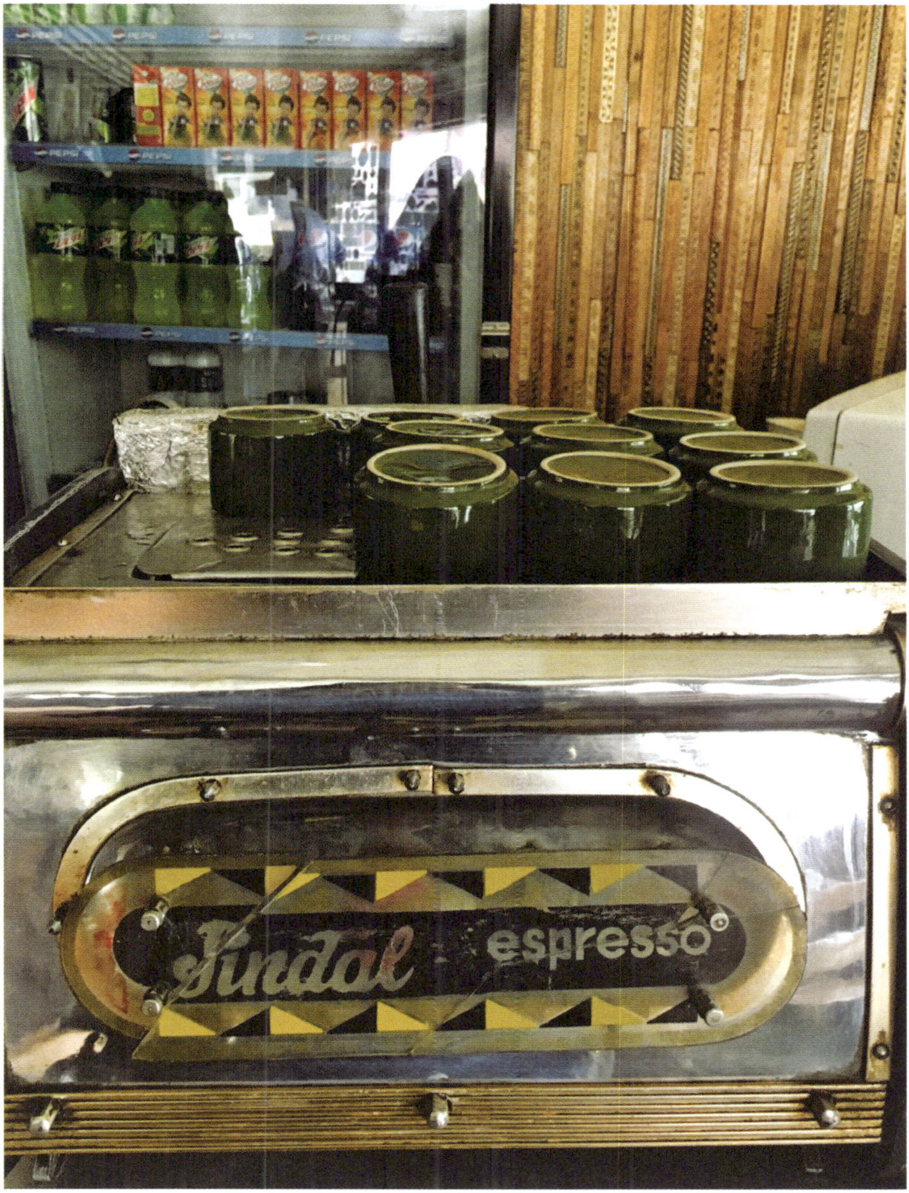
Jindal espresso

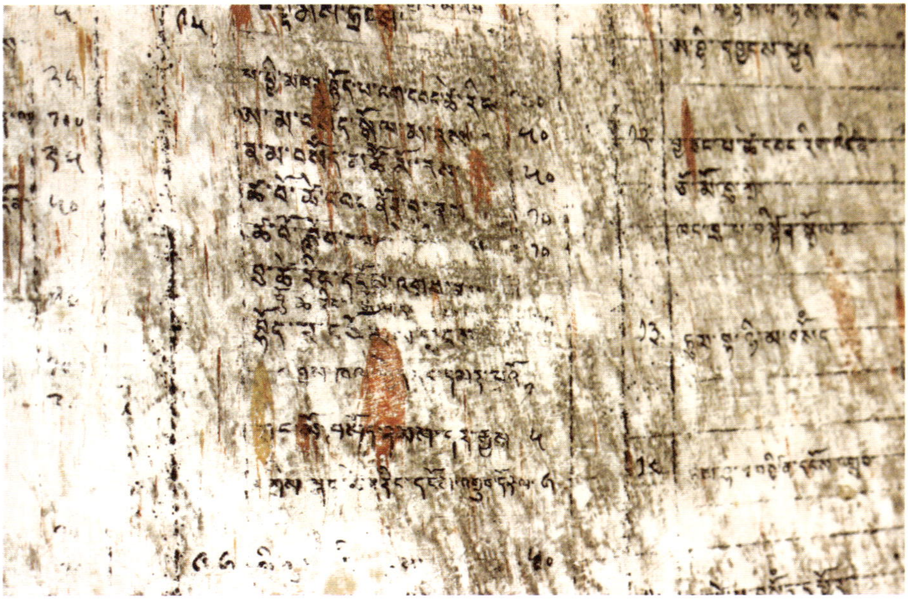

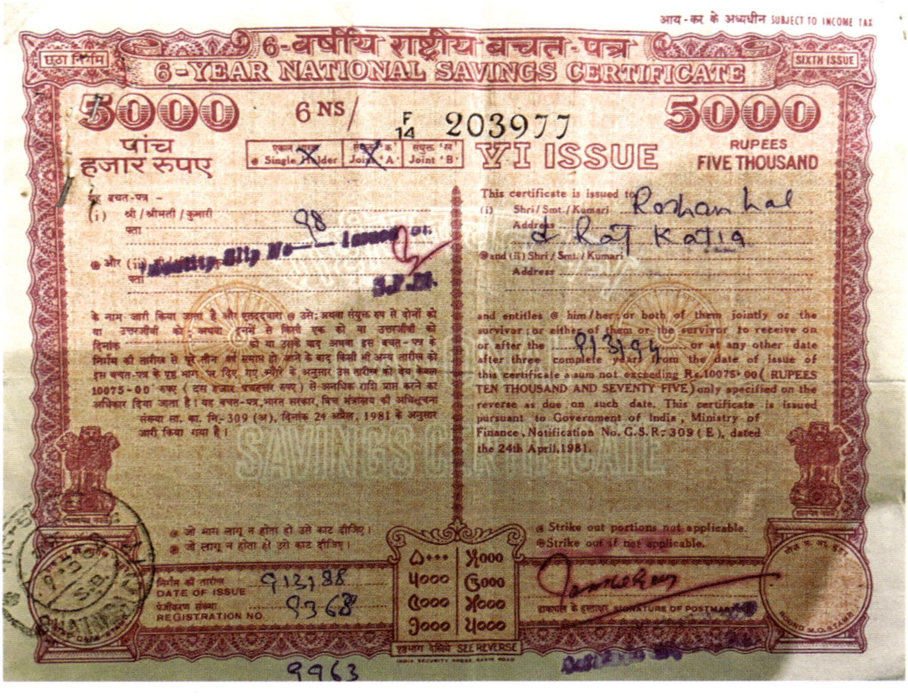

आय-कर के अध्यधीन SUBJECT TO INCOME TAX

छठा निर्गम — 6-वर्षीय राष्ट्रीय बचत-पत्र — SIXTH ISSUE

6-YEAR NATIONAL SAVINGS CERTIFICATE

5000 6 NS/ F 14 203977 5000

पांच हजार रुपए — VI ISSUE — RUPEES FIVE THOUSAND

@ Single Holder / Joint 'A' / Joint 'B'

यह बचत-पत्र -
(i) श्री / श्रीमती / कुमारी
पता
@ और (ii) श्री / श्रीमती / कुमारी
पता

के नाम जारी किया जाता है और इनको @ उसे; अथवा संयुक्त रूप से दोनों को या उत्तरजीवी को; अथवा इनमें से किसी एक को या उत्तरजीवी को दिनांक .... को या उसके बाद अथवा इस बचत-पत्र के निर्गम की तारीख से पूरे तीन वर्ष समाप्त हो जाने के बाद किसी भी अन्य तारीख को इस बचत-पत्र के पृष्ठ भाग पर दिए गए ब्यौरे के अनुसार उस तारीख को देय केवल 10075-00 रुपए (दस हजार पचहत्तर रुपए) से अनधिक राशि प्राप्त करने का अधिकार दिया जाता है। यह बचत-पत्र, भारत सरकार, वित्त मंत्रालय की अधिसूचना संख्या सा. का. नि.-309 (अ), दिनांक 24 अप्रैल, 1981 के अनुसार जारी किया गया है।

This certificate is issued to
(i) Shri / Smt. / Kumari Roshan Lal
Address ....
@ and (ii) Shri / Smt. / Kumari
Address

and entitles @ him / her; or both of them jointly or the survivor; or either of them or the survivor to receive on or after the 9.13.94 or at any other date after three complete years from the date of issue of this certificate a sum not exceeding Rs. 10075-00 (RUPEES TEN THOUSAND AND SEVENTY FIVE) only specified on the reverse as due on such date. This certificate is issued pursuant to Government of India, Ministry of Finance, Notification No. G.S.R. 309 (E), dated the 24th April, 1981.

@ जो भाग लागू न होता हो उसे काट दीजिए।
@ Strike out portions not applicable.

निर्गम की तारीख DATE OF ISSUE 9.13.88
पंजीकरण संख्या REGISTRATION NO. 9368

डाकपाल के हस्ताक्षर SIGNATURE OF POSTMASTER

पृष्ठभाग देखिए SEE REVERSE

INDIA SECURITY PRESS NASIK ROAD

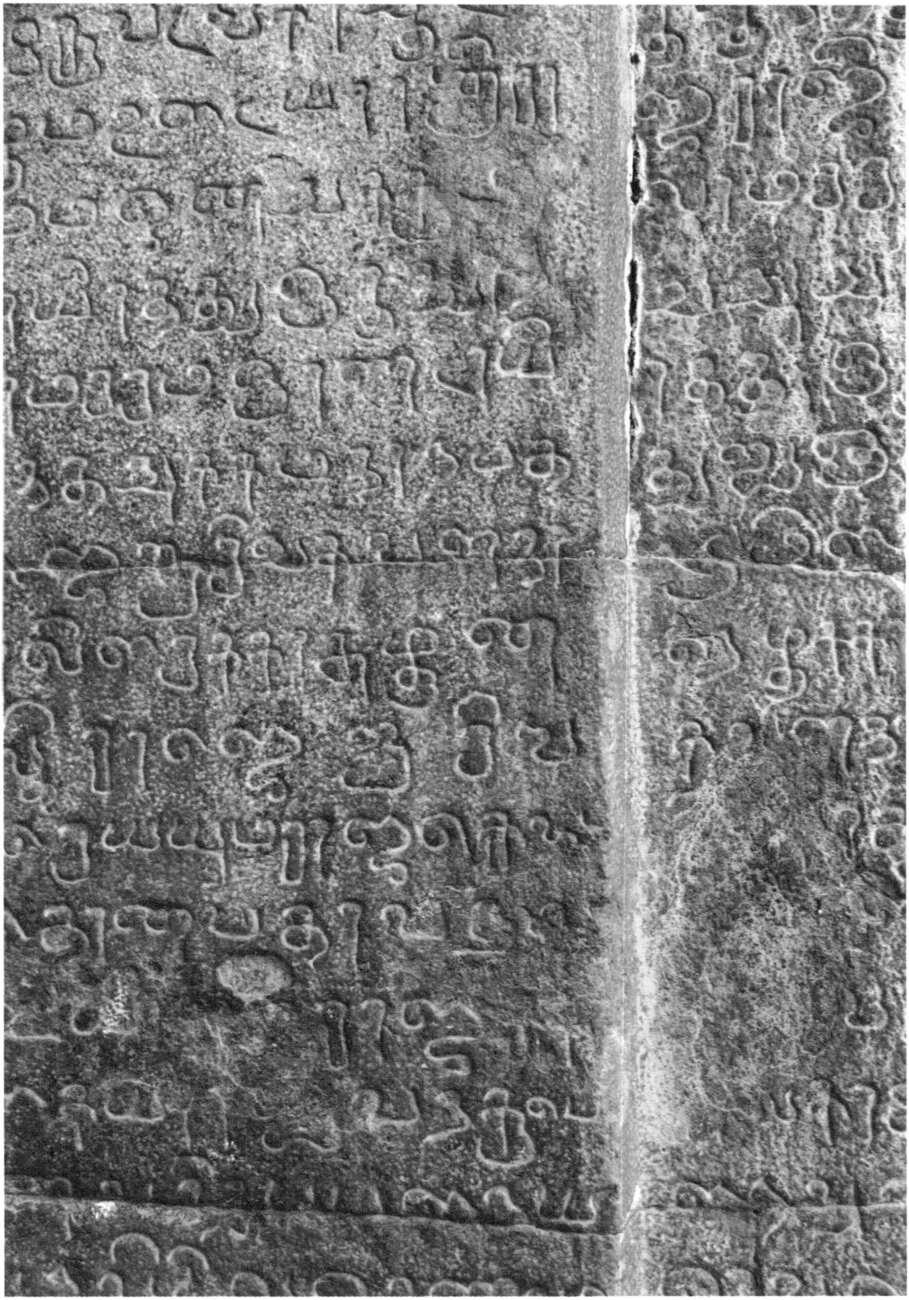

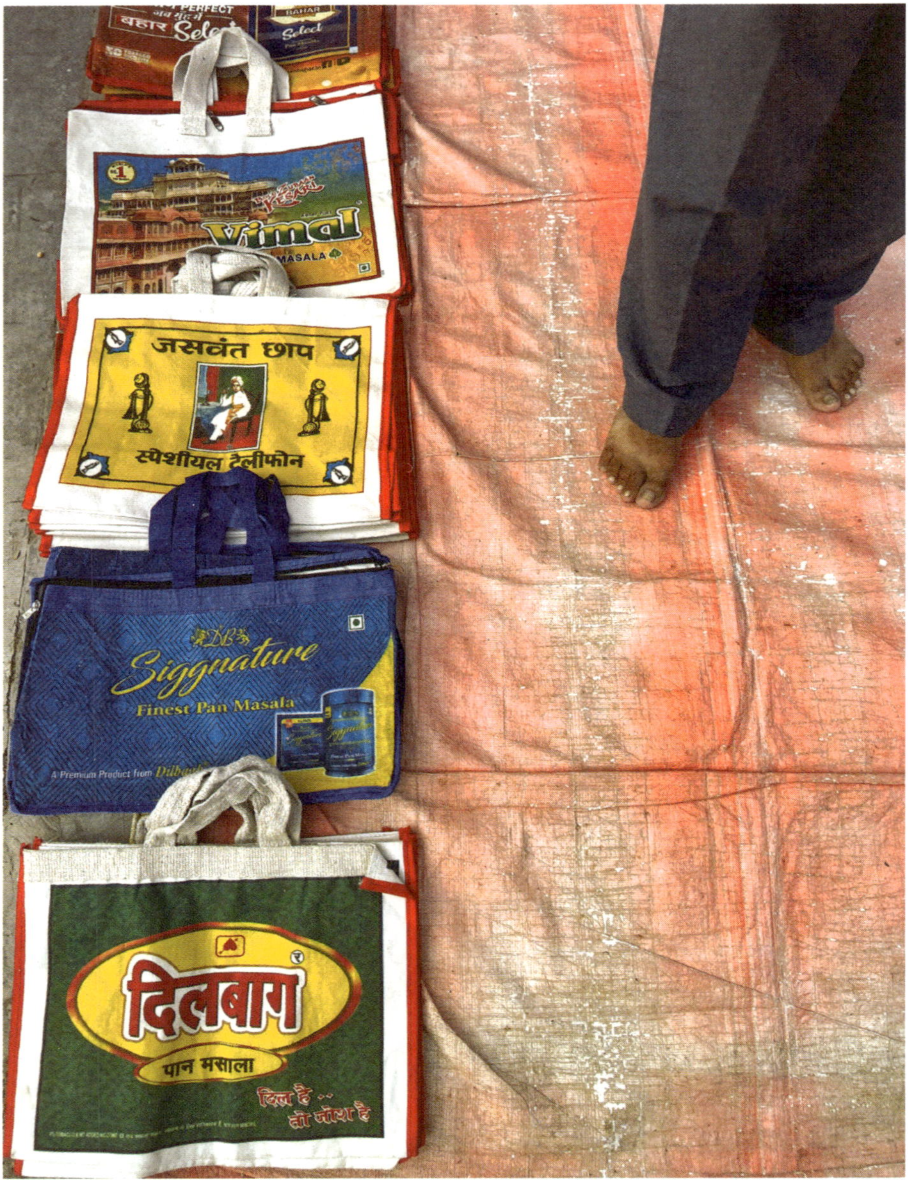
Vimal
MASALA
जसवंत छाप
स्पेशीयल टेलीफोन
Siggnature
Finest Pan Masala
A Premium Product from
दिलबाग
पान मसाला
दिल है ..
तो जोश है

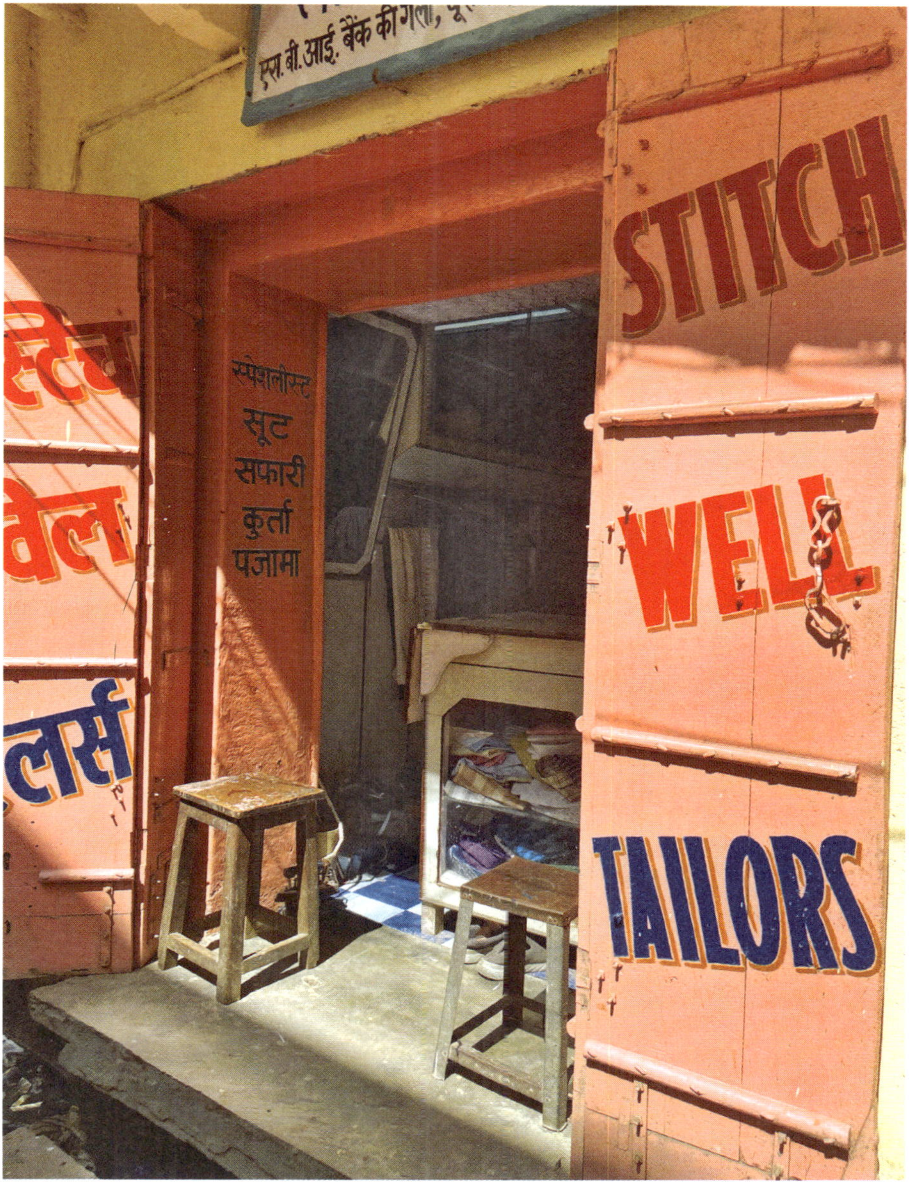
एस.बी.आई. बैंक की गली,
स्पेशलीस्ट
सूट
सफारी
कुर्ता
पजामा
STITCH
WELL
TAILORS

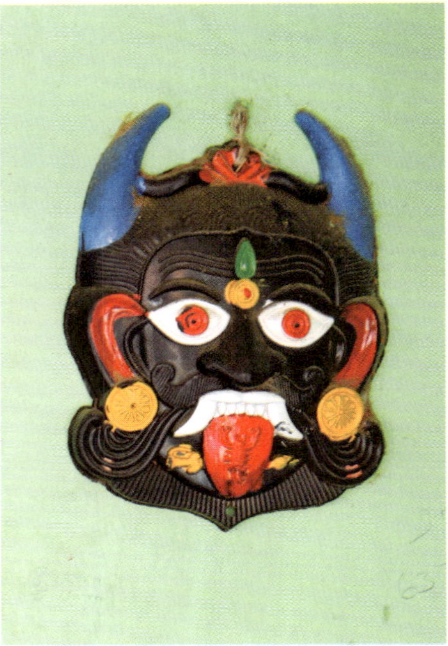

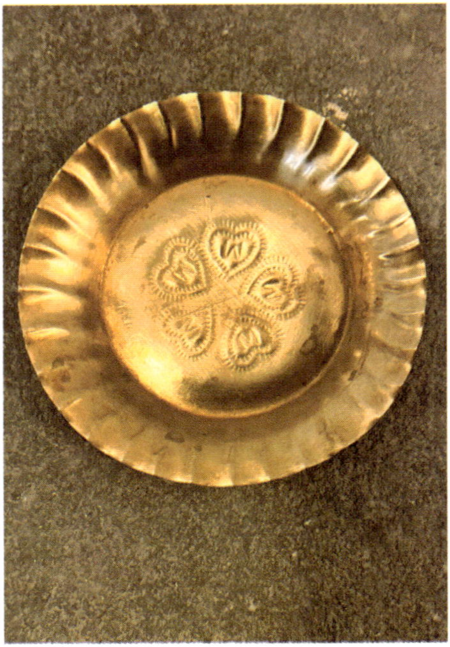

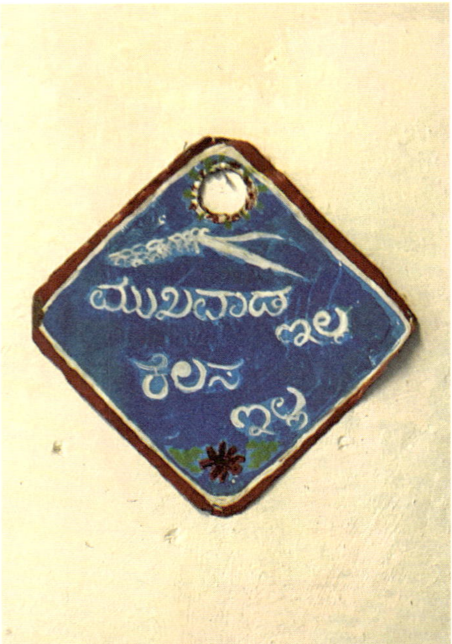
ಮುಖವಾಡ ಇಲ್ಲ
ಕೆಲಸ
ಇಲ್ಲ

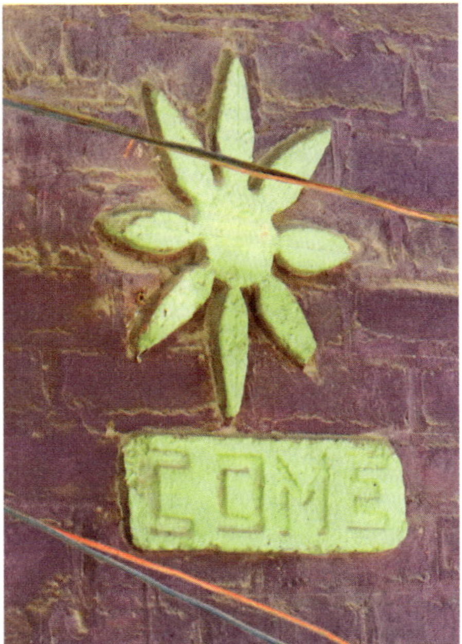
COME

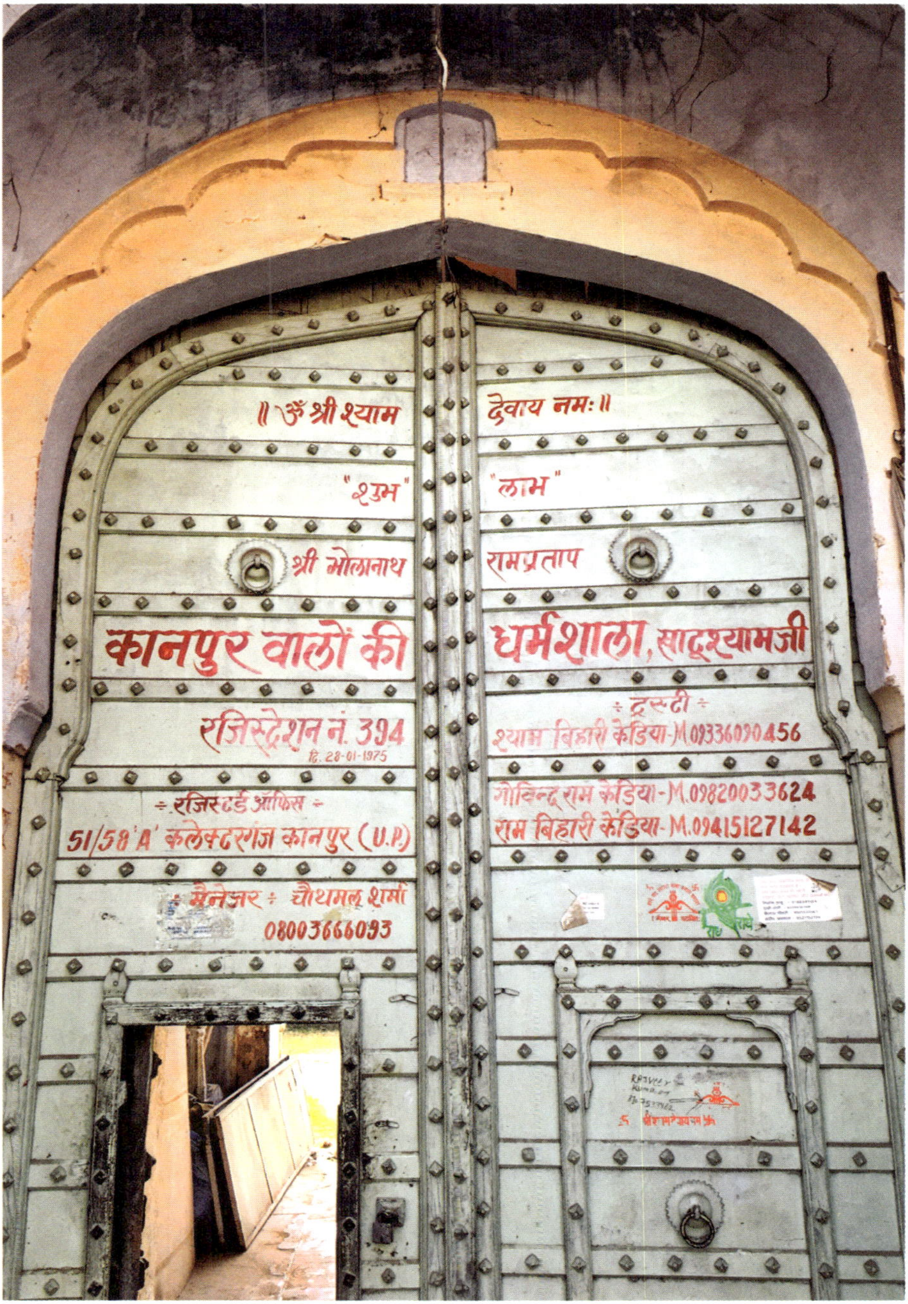
॥ ॐ श्री श्याम देवाय नमः ॥
"शुभ" "लाभ"
श्री भोलानाथ रामप्रताप
कानपुर वालों की धर्मशाला, सादूश्यामजी
रजिस्ट्रेशन नं. 394
दि. 28-01-1975
÷ रजिस्टर्ड ऑफिस ÷
51/58 'A' कलेक्टरगंज कानपुर (U.P.)
÷ मैनेजर ÷ चौथमल शर्मा
08003666093
÷ ट्रस्टी ÷
श्याम बिहारी केडिया-M.09336090456
गोविन्द राम केडिया-M.09820033624
राम बिहारी केडिया-M.09415127142

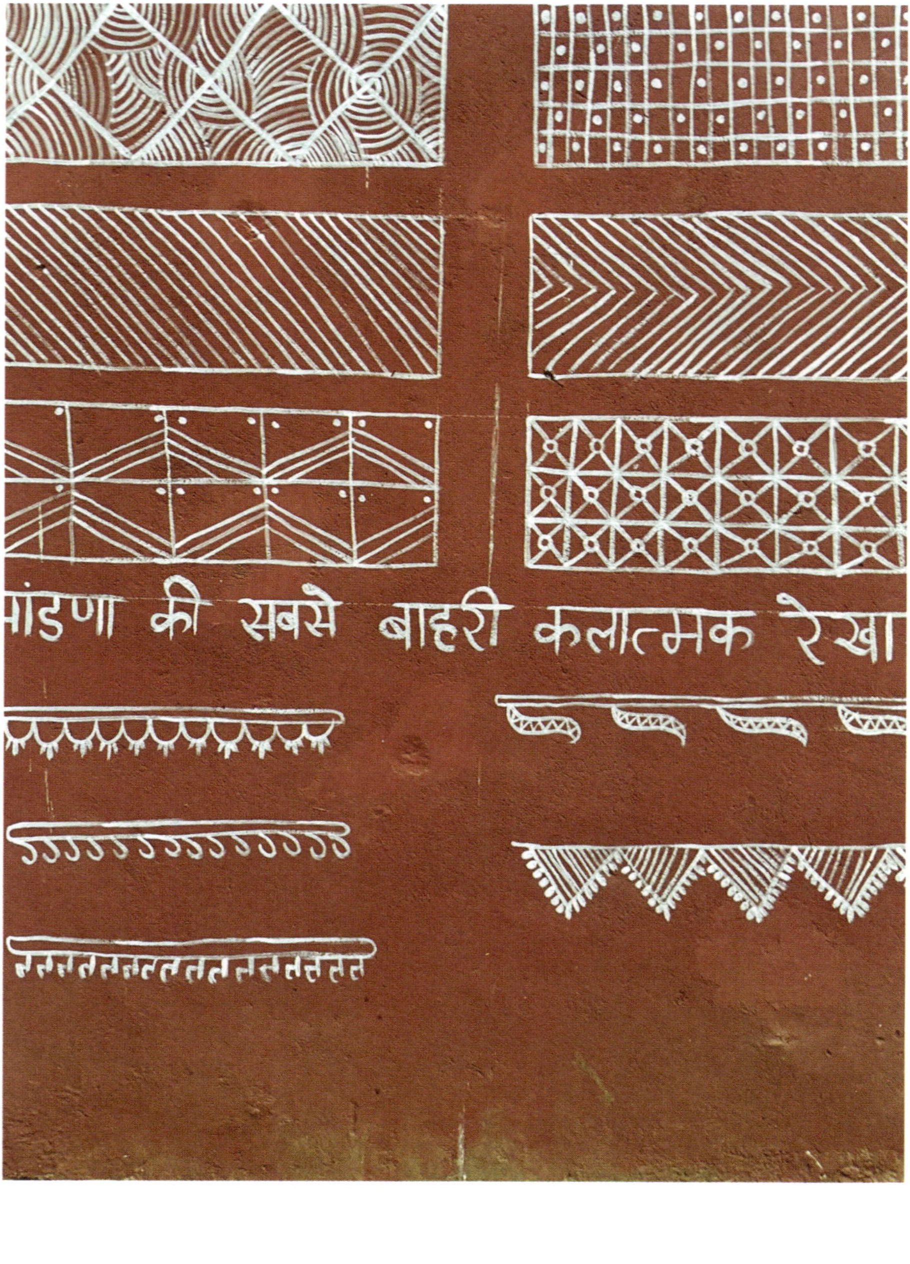
ांडणा की सबसे बाहरी कलात्मक रेखा

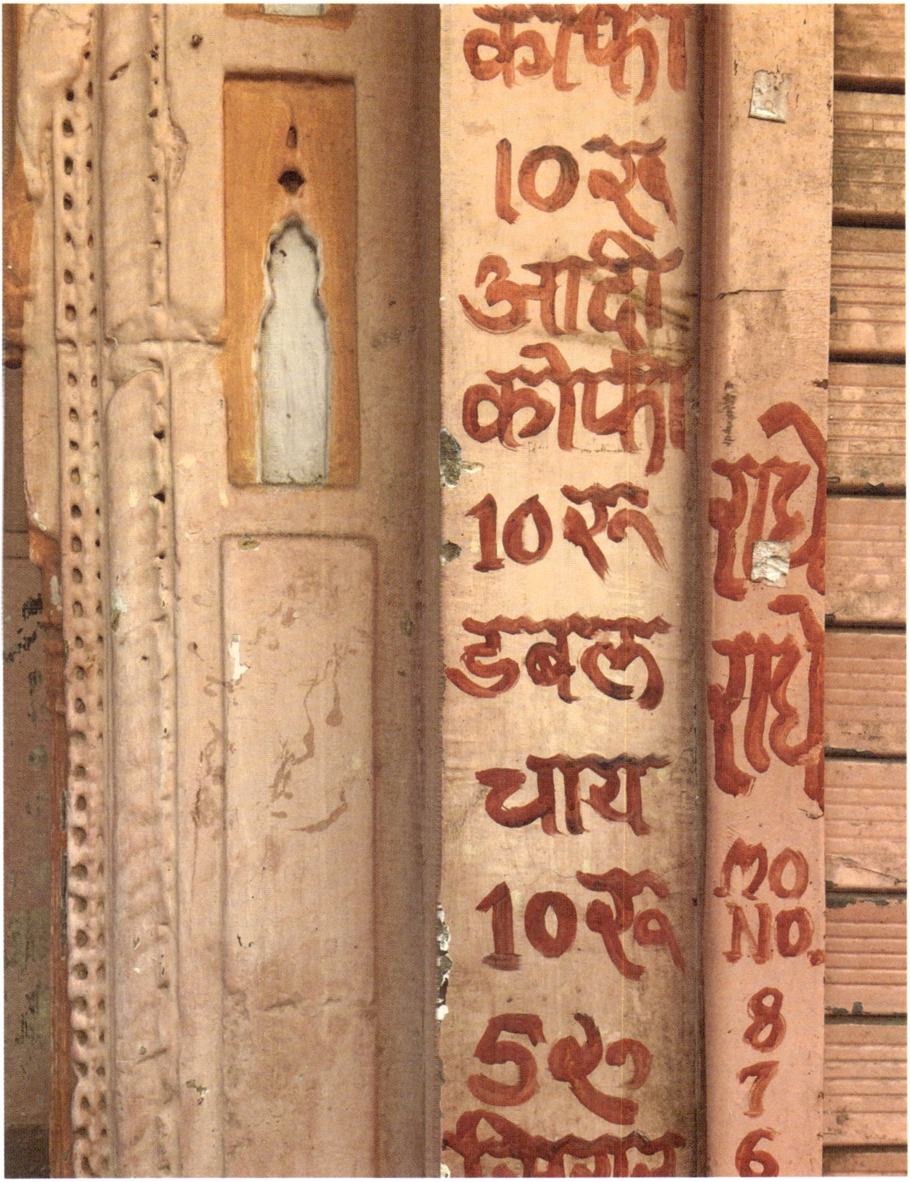
10 रु
आधी
कॉफी
10 रु
डबल
चाय
10 रु
5 रु
राधे
राधे
No.
8
7
6

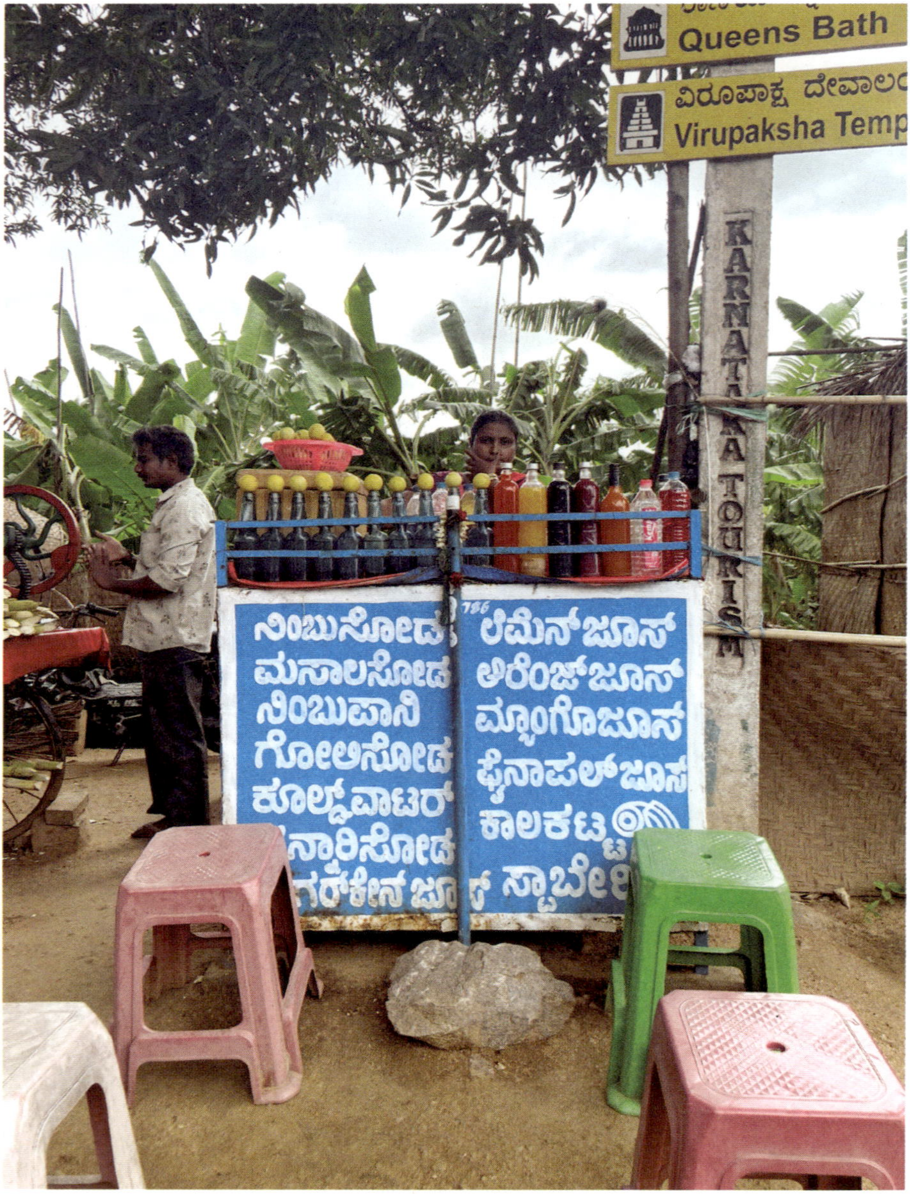
Queens Bath
ವಿರೂಪಾಕ್ಷ ದೇವಾಲ
Virupaksha Temp
KARNATAKA TOURISM
ನಿಂಬುಸೋಡ
ಲೆಮೆನ್ ಜ್ಯೂಸ್
ಮಸಾಲಸೋಡ
ಆರೆಂಜ್ ಜ್ಯೂಸ್
ನಿಂಬುಪಾನಿ
ಮ್ಯಾಂಗೋಜ್ಯೂಸ
ಗೋಲಿಸೋಡ
ಕೂಲ್ಡ್ ವಾಟರ್

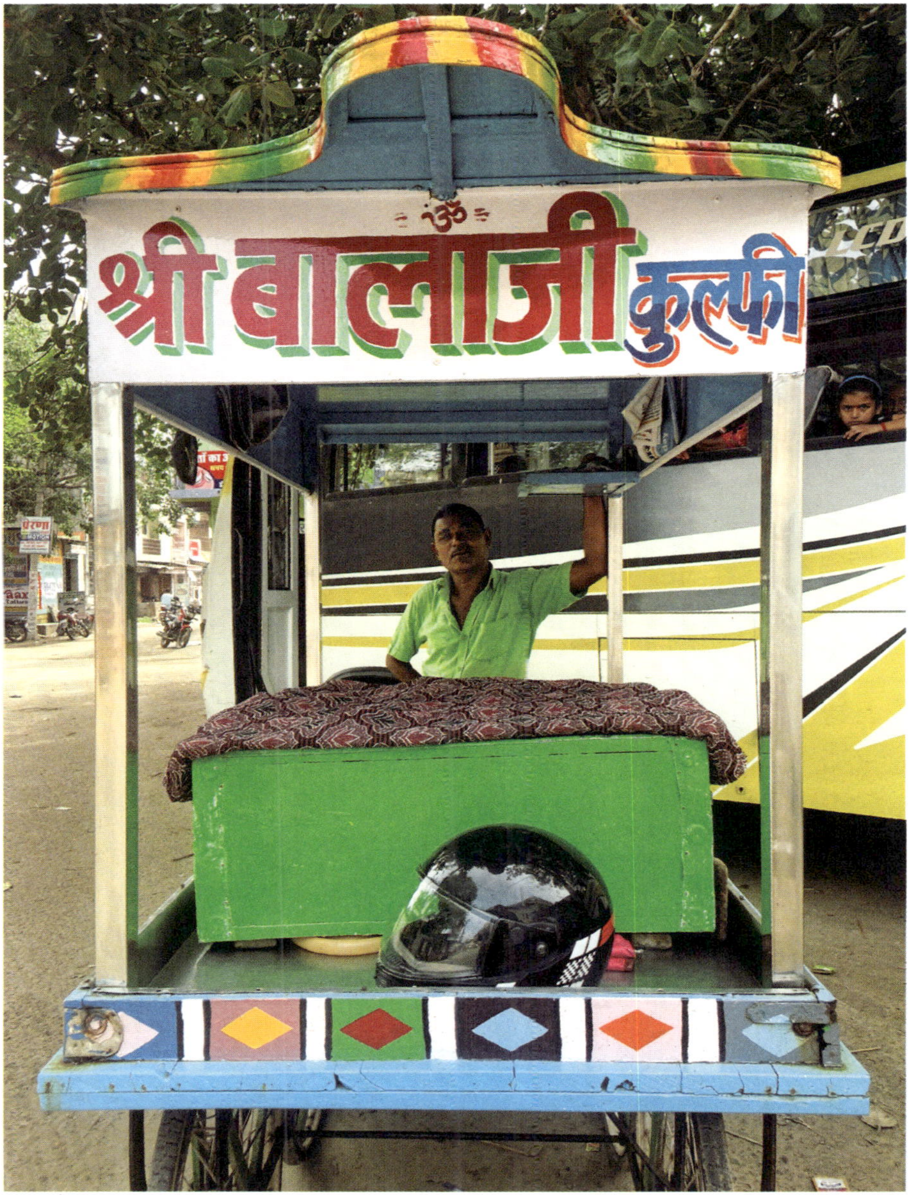
ॐ
श्री बालाजी कुल्फी

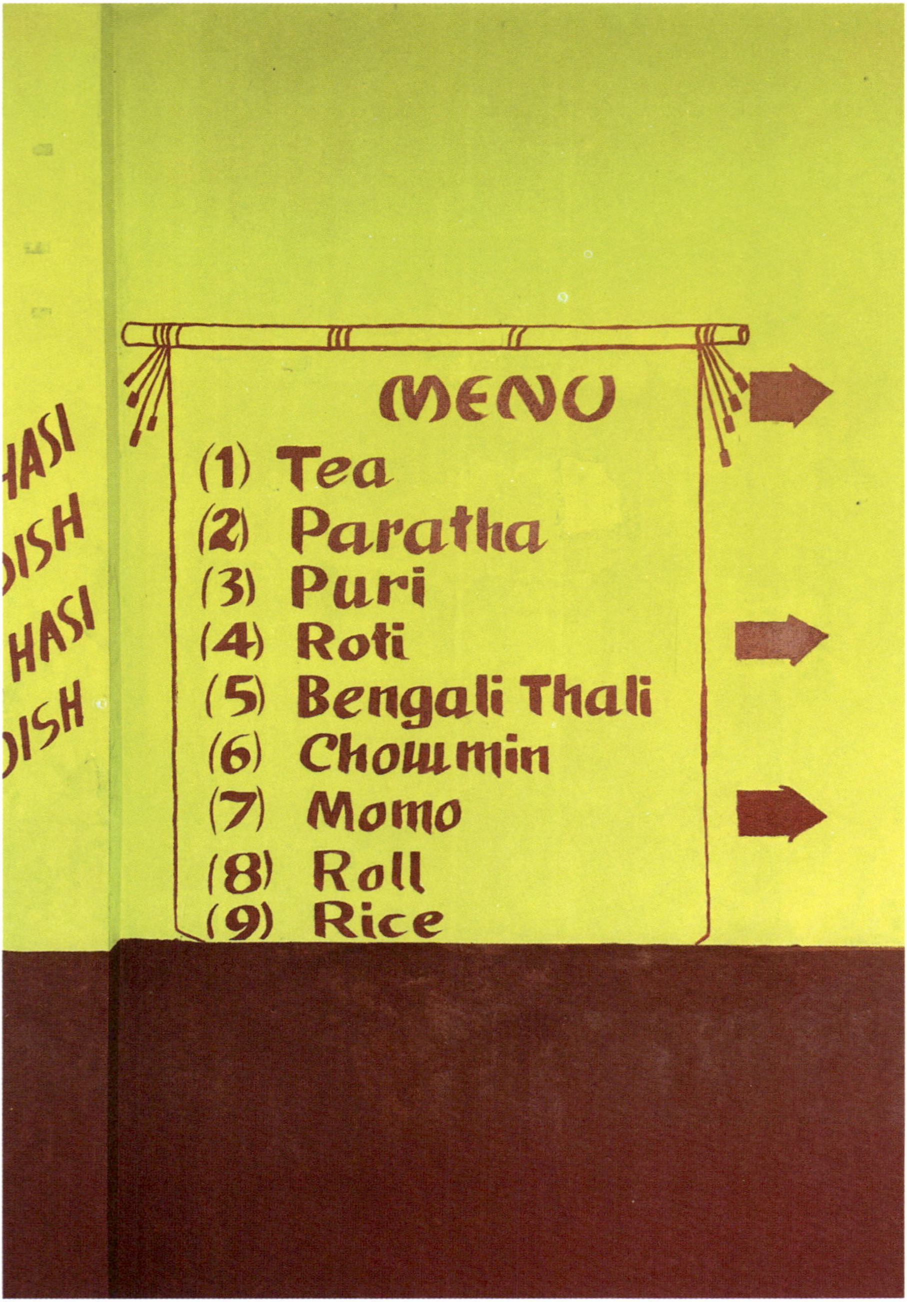
MENU
(1) Tea
(2) Paratha
(3) Puri
(4) Roti
(5) Bengali Thali
(6) Chowmin
(7) Momo
(8) Roll
(9) Rice
HASI
DISH
HASI
DISH

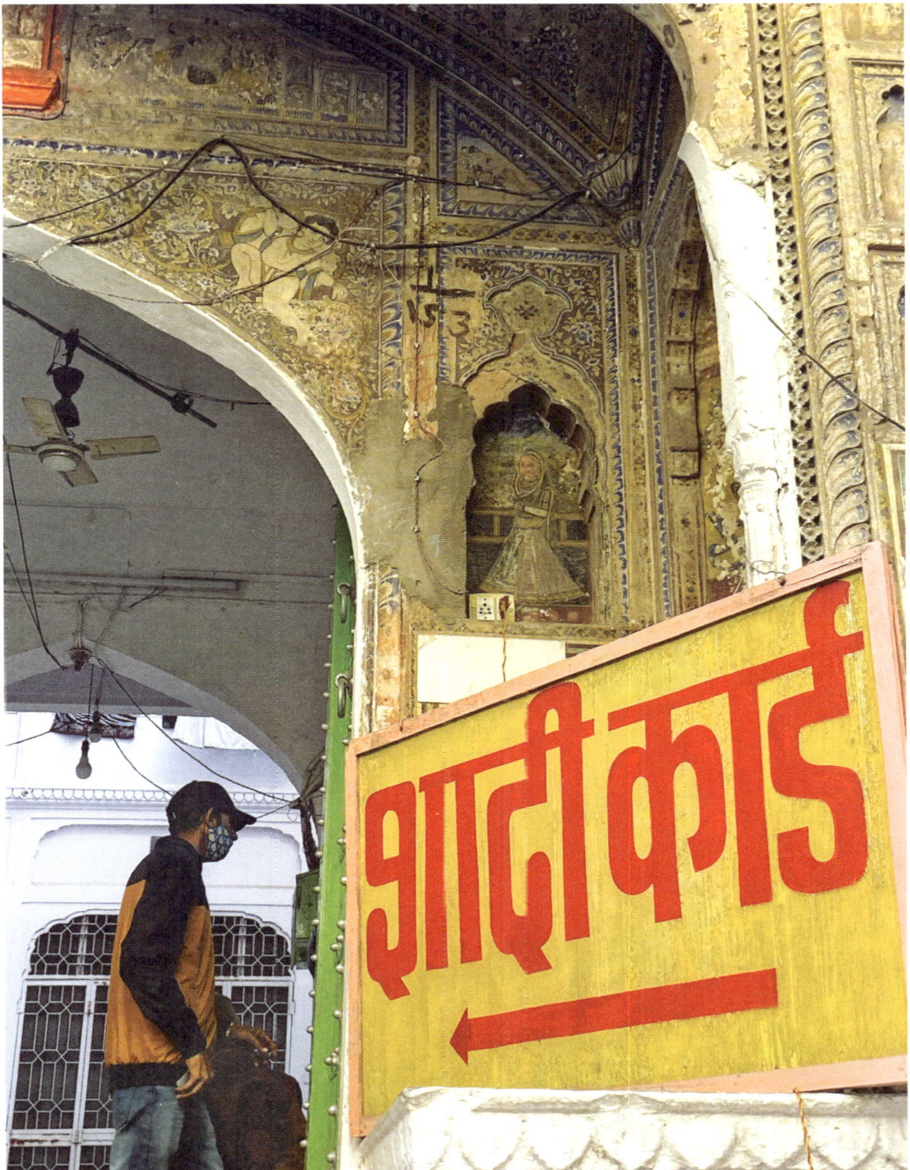
शादी कार्ड

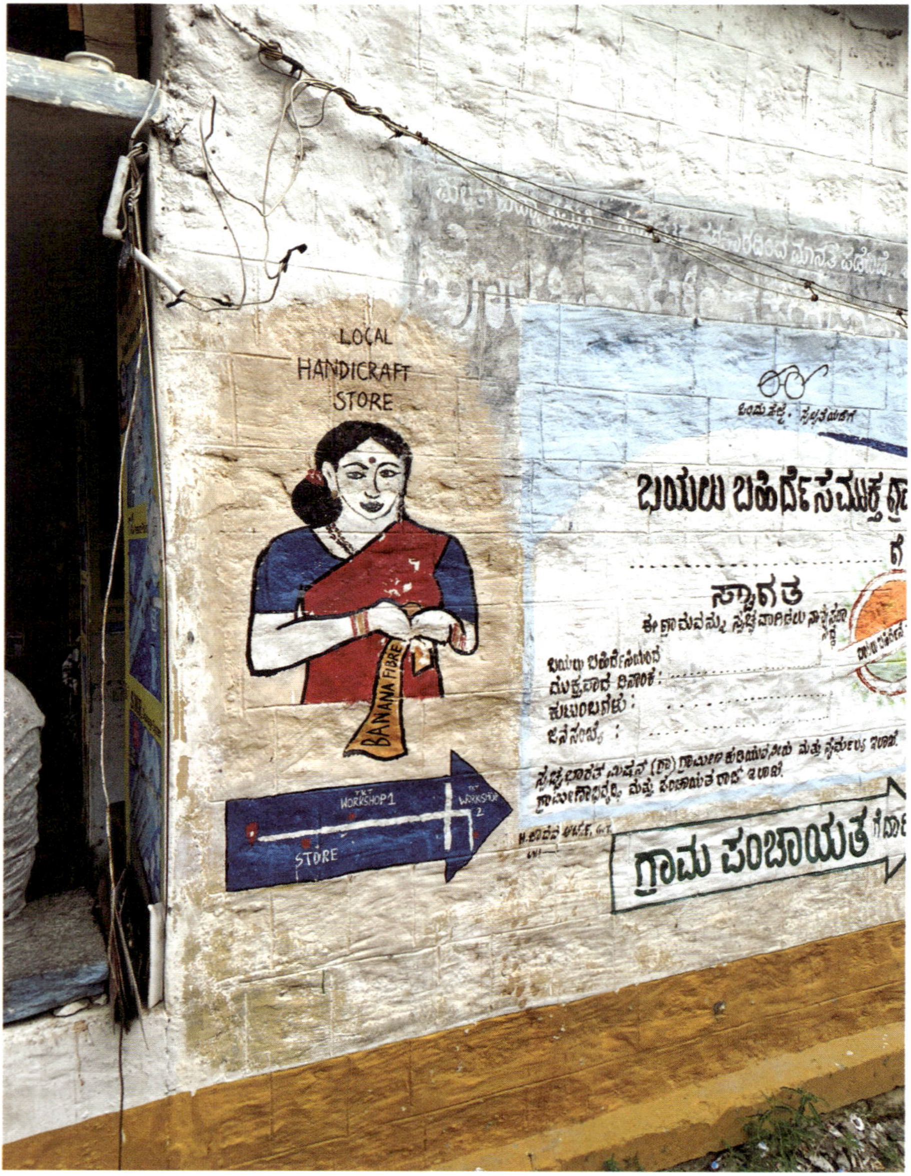
LOCAL
HANDICRAFT
STORE
BANANA FIBRE
WORKSHOP1
WORKSHOP 2
STORE
ಸ್ವಾಗತ
ಗ್ರಾಮ ಪಂಚಾಯತ

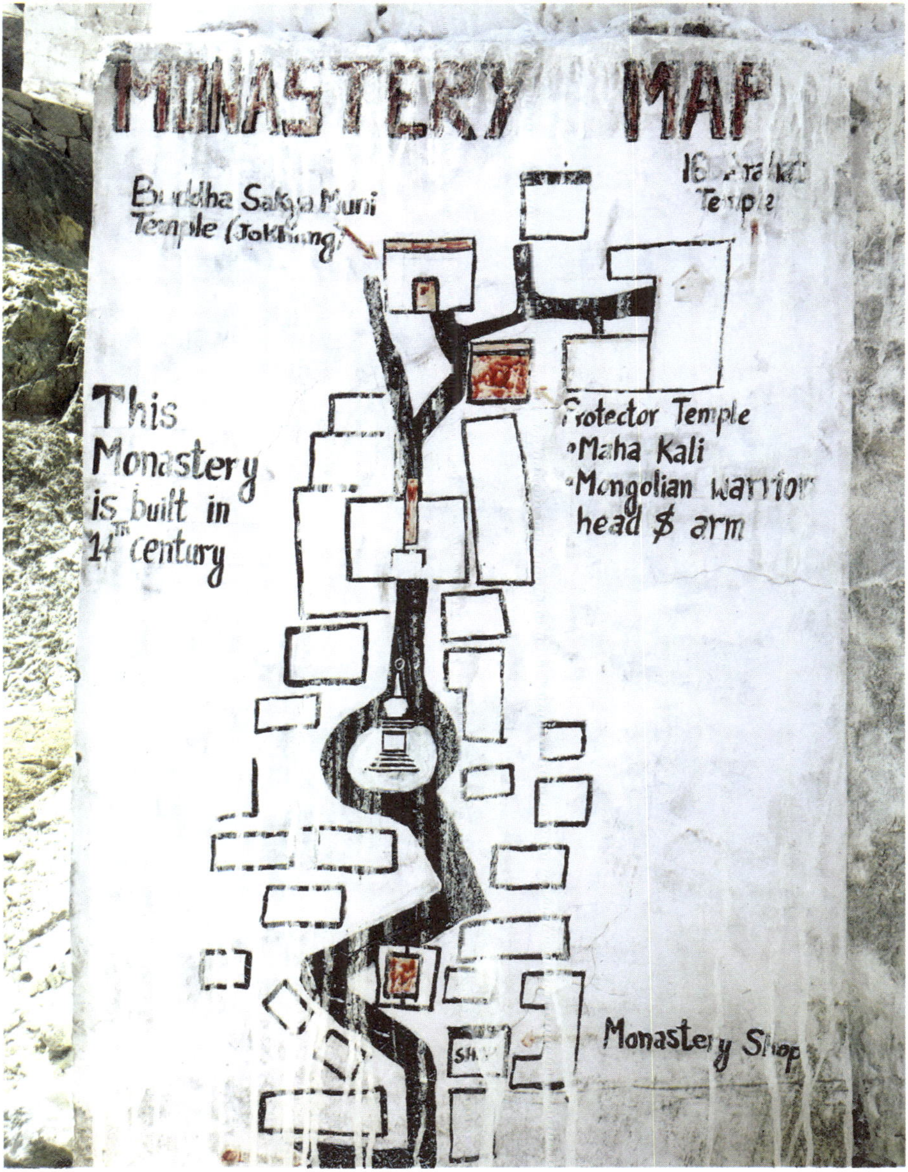
MONASTERY MAP
Buddha Sakya Muni Temple (JoKhang)
Temple
This Monastery is built in 14TH century
Protector Temple
•Maha Kali
•Mongolian warrior head $ arm
Monastery Shop

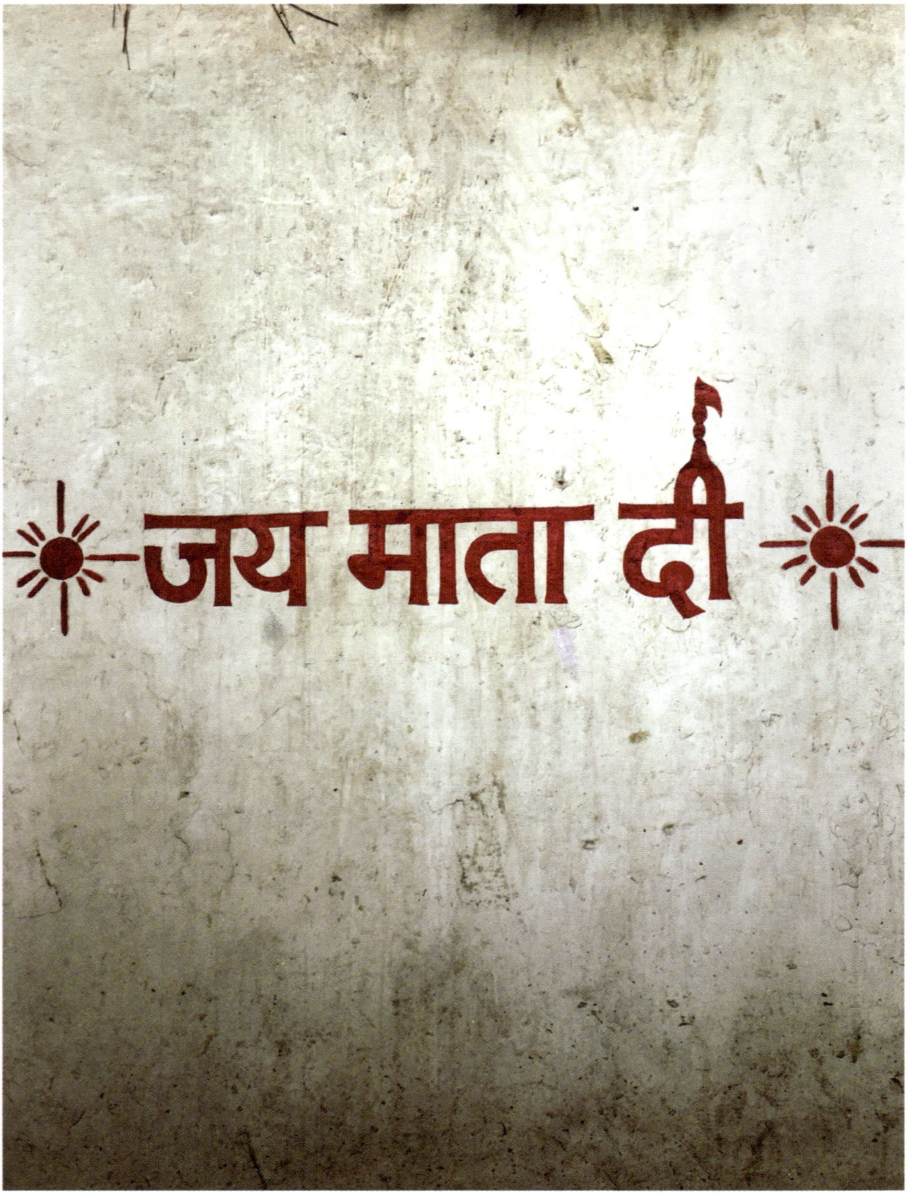
जय माता दी

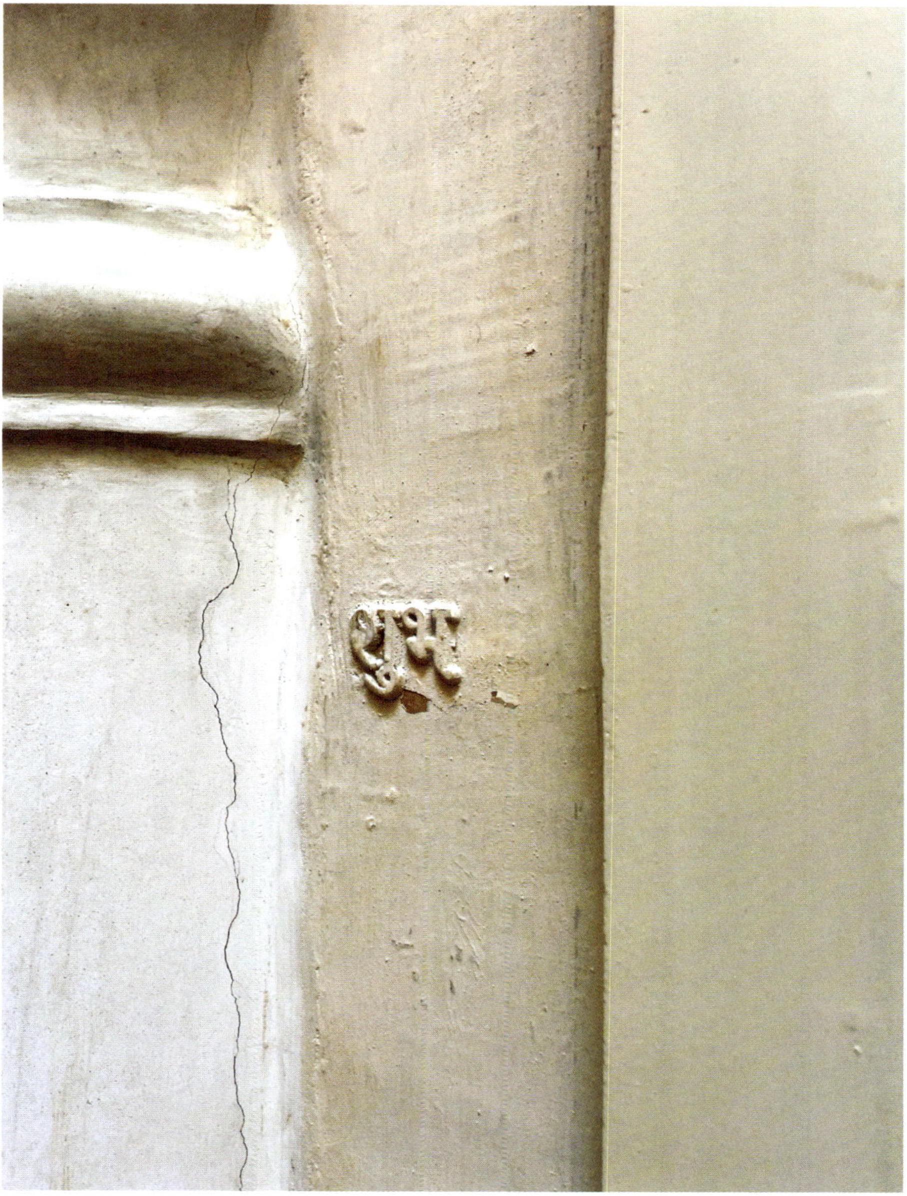
शुभ

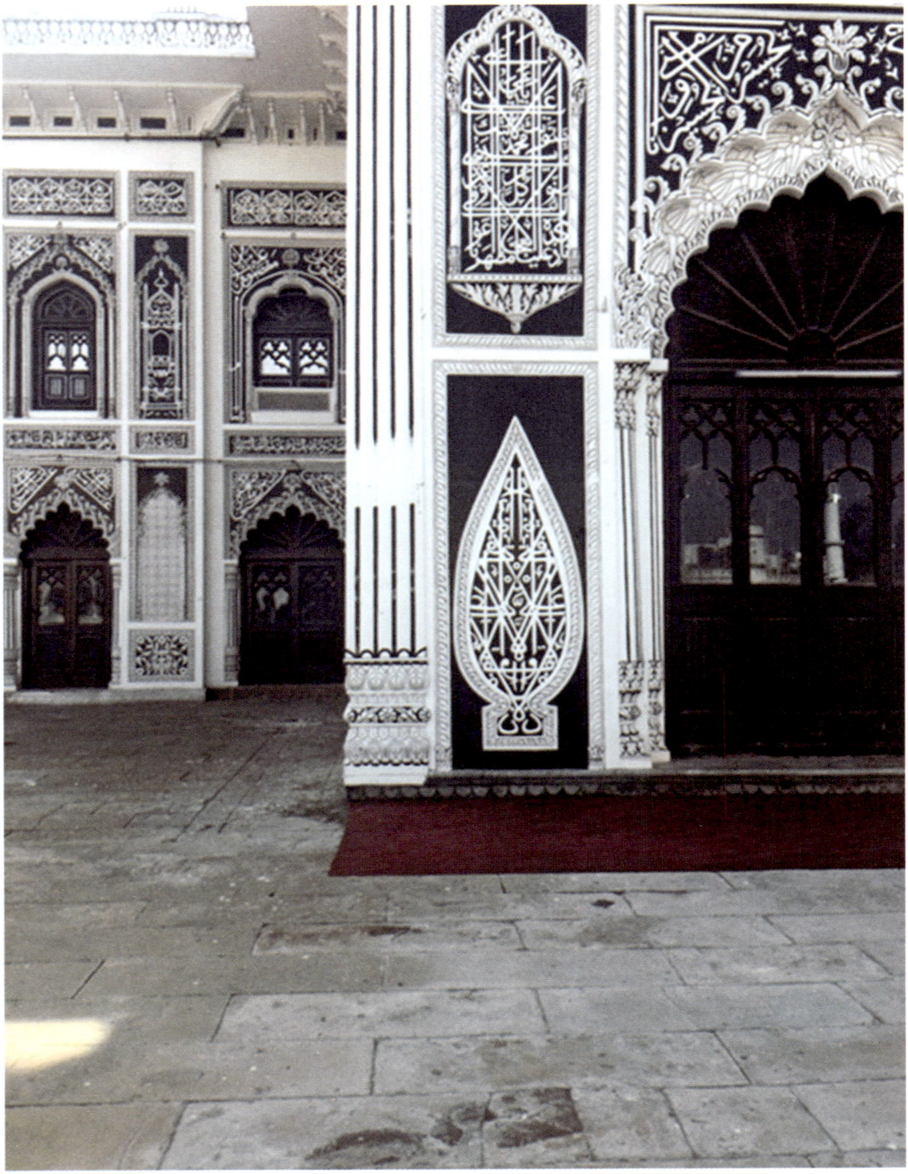

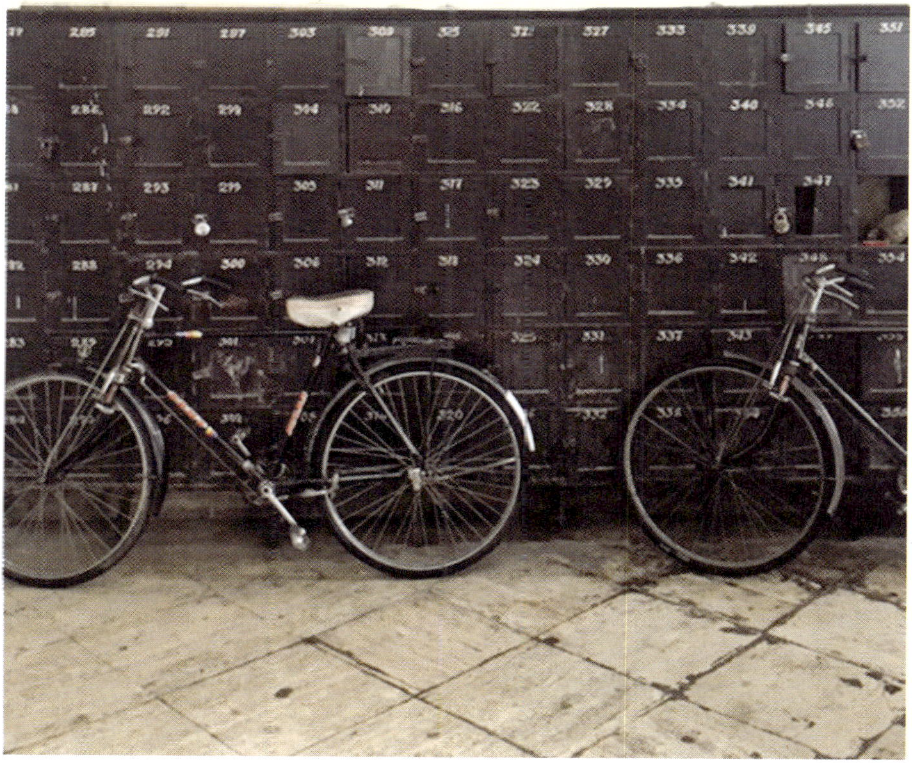

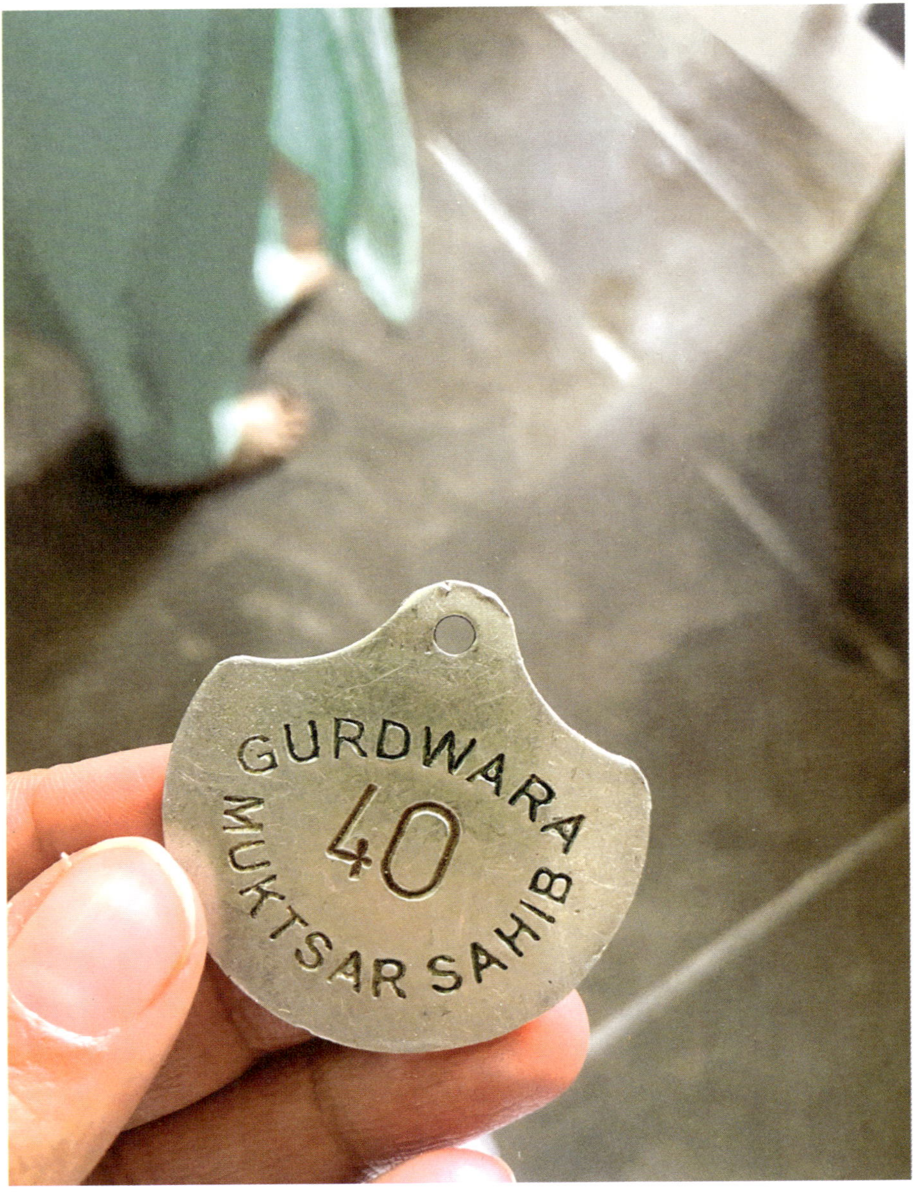
GURDWARA
40
MUKTSAR SAHIB

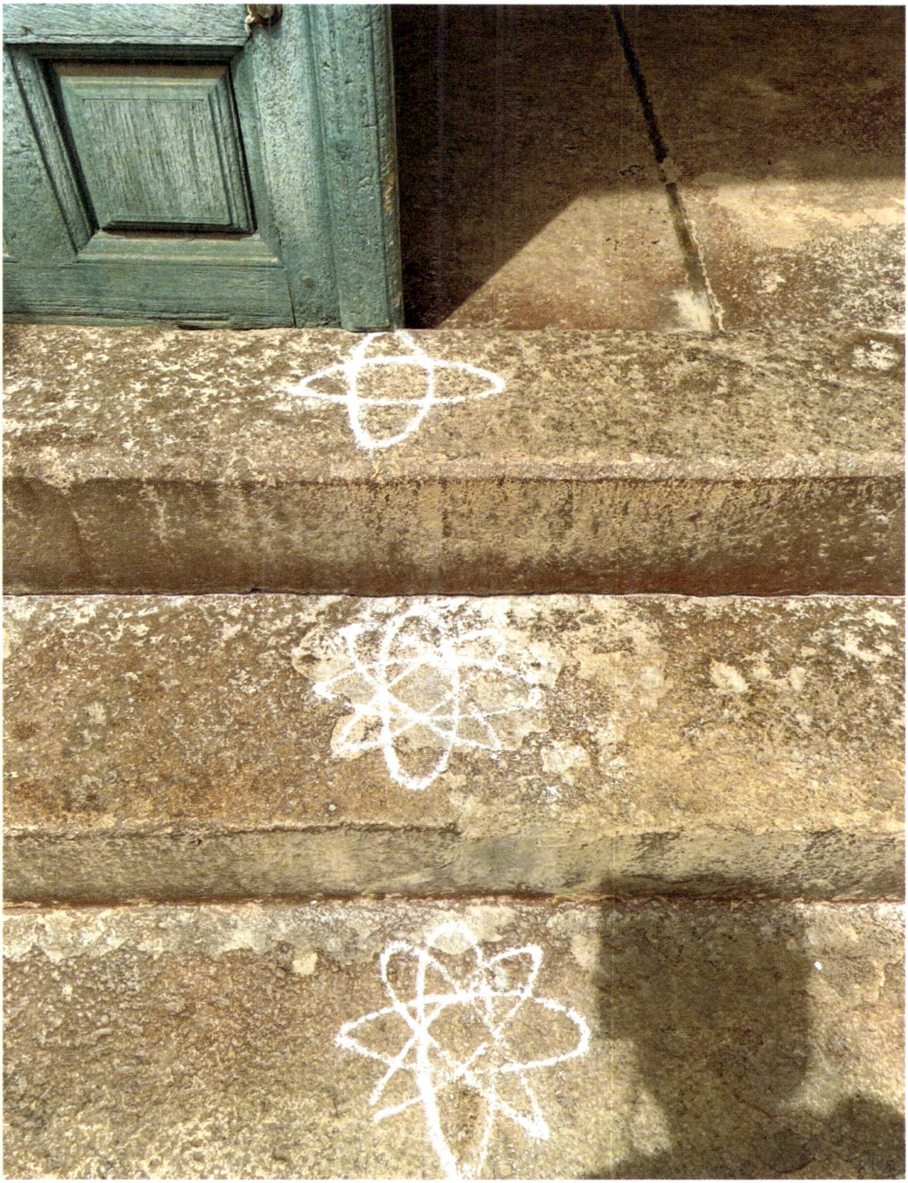

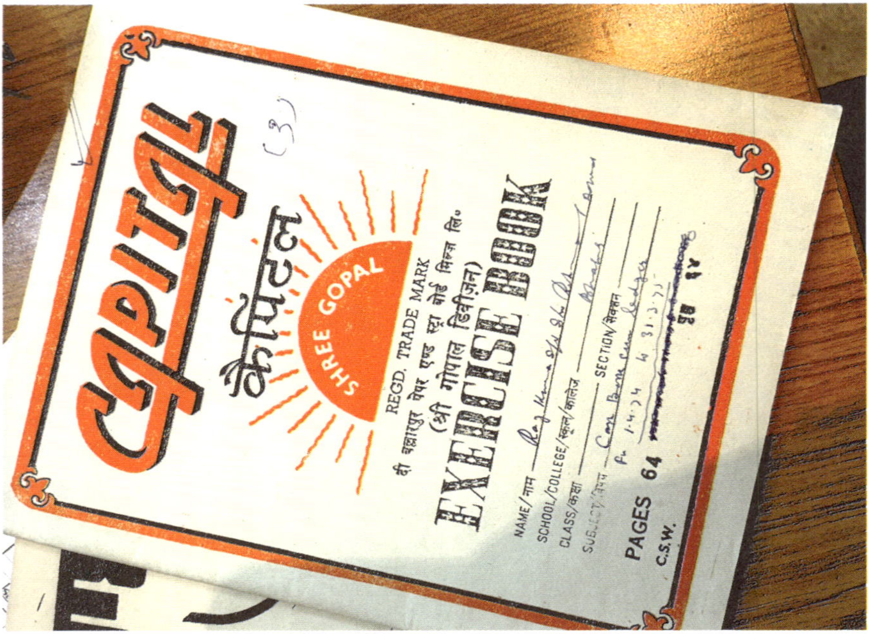
Capital
कैपिटल
SHREE GOPAL
REGD. TRADE MARK
दी बल्लारपुर पेपर एण्ड स्ट्रा बोर्ड मिल्स लि०
(श्री गोपाल डिवीज़न)
EXERCISE BOOK
NAME/नाम
SCHOOL/COLLEGE/स्कूल/कालेज
CLASS/कक्षा
SECTION/सेक्शन
PAGES 64
C.S.W.

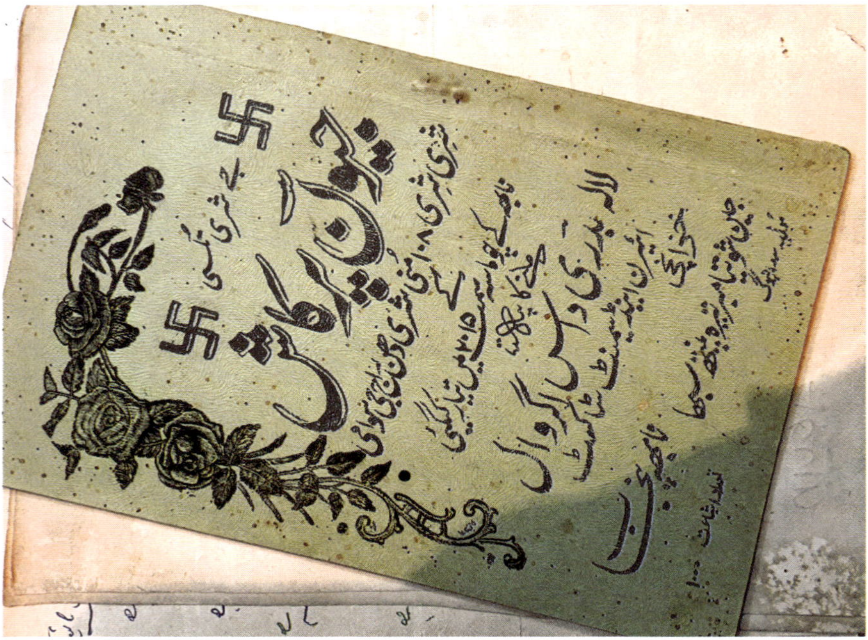

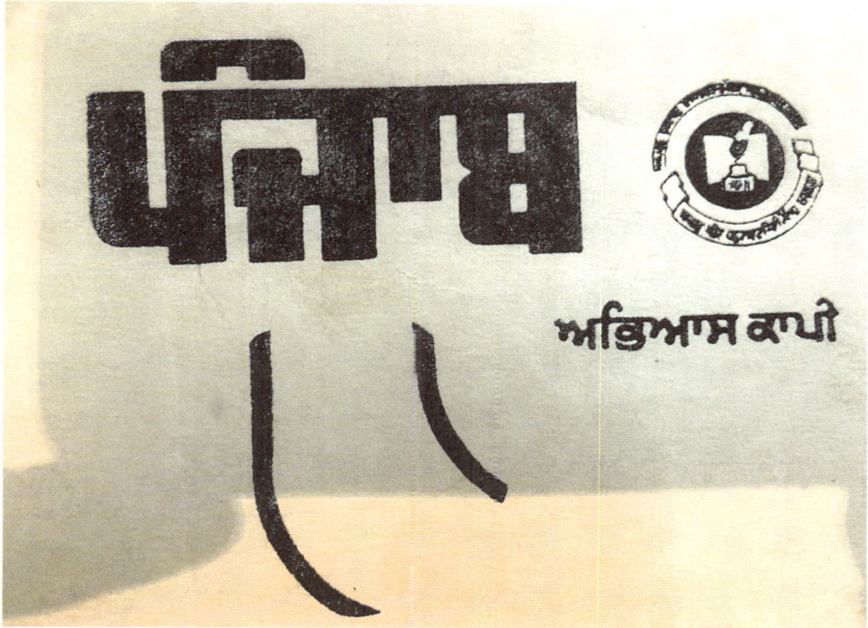
ਪੰਜਾਬ
ਅਭਿਆਸ ਕਾਪੀ

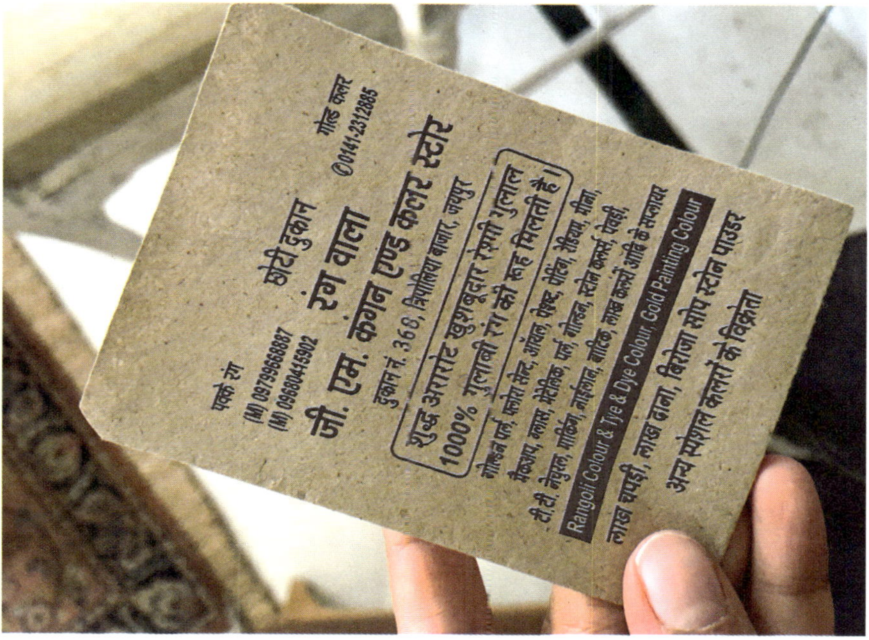
पक्के रंग
छोटी दुकान
गोल्ड कलर
(M) 09799668887
(M) 09680415902
जी. एम. कंगन एण्ड कलर स्टोर
रंग वाला
©0141-2312885
1000% गुलाली रंग की सह मिलती है।
Rangoli Colour & Tye & Dye Colour, Gold Painting Colour
अन्य स्पेशल कलरों के विक्रेता

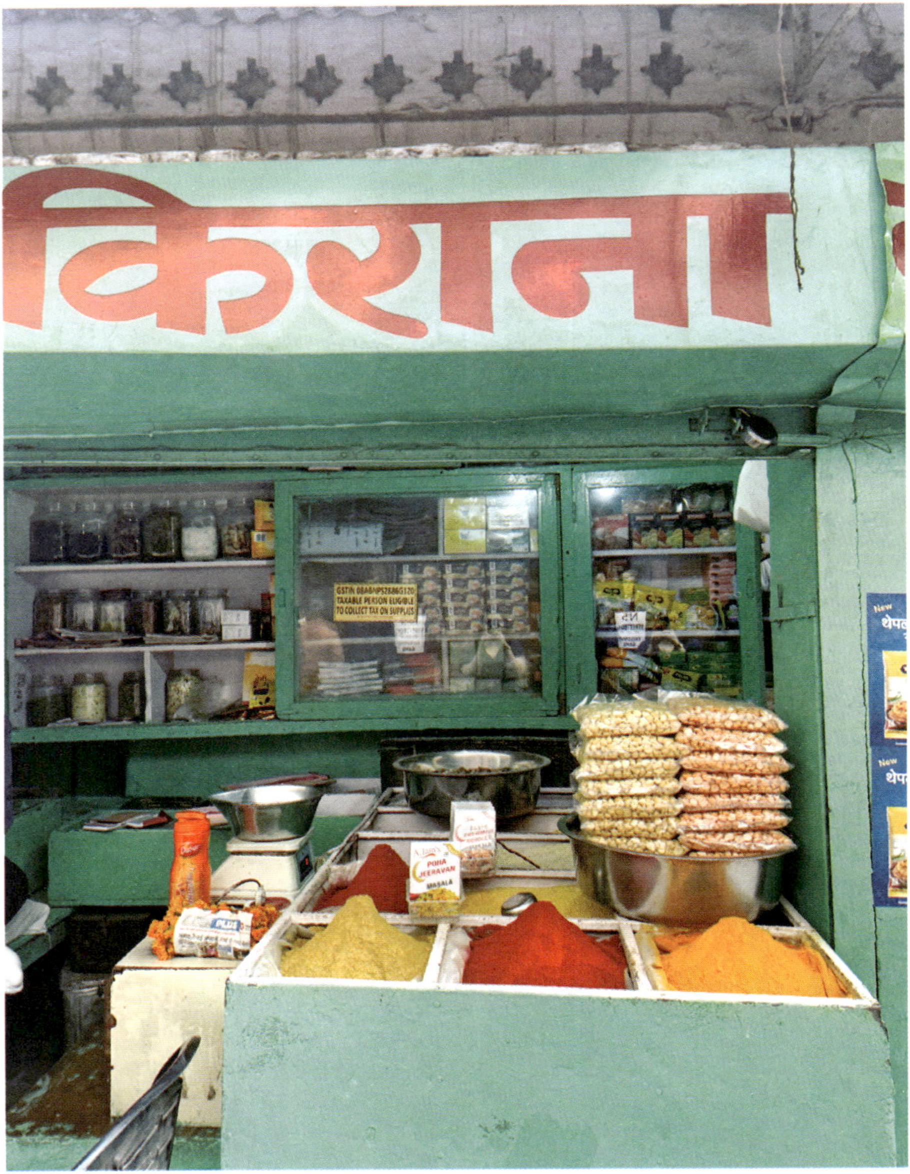
किराना
TAXABLE PERSON ELIGIBLE
TO COLLECT TAX ON SUPPLIES
POHA
JEERAVAN
MASALA

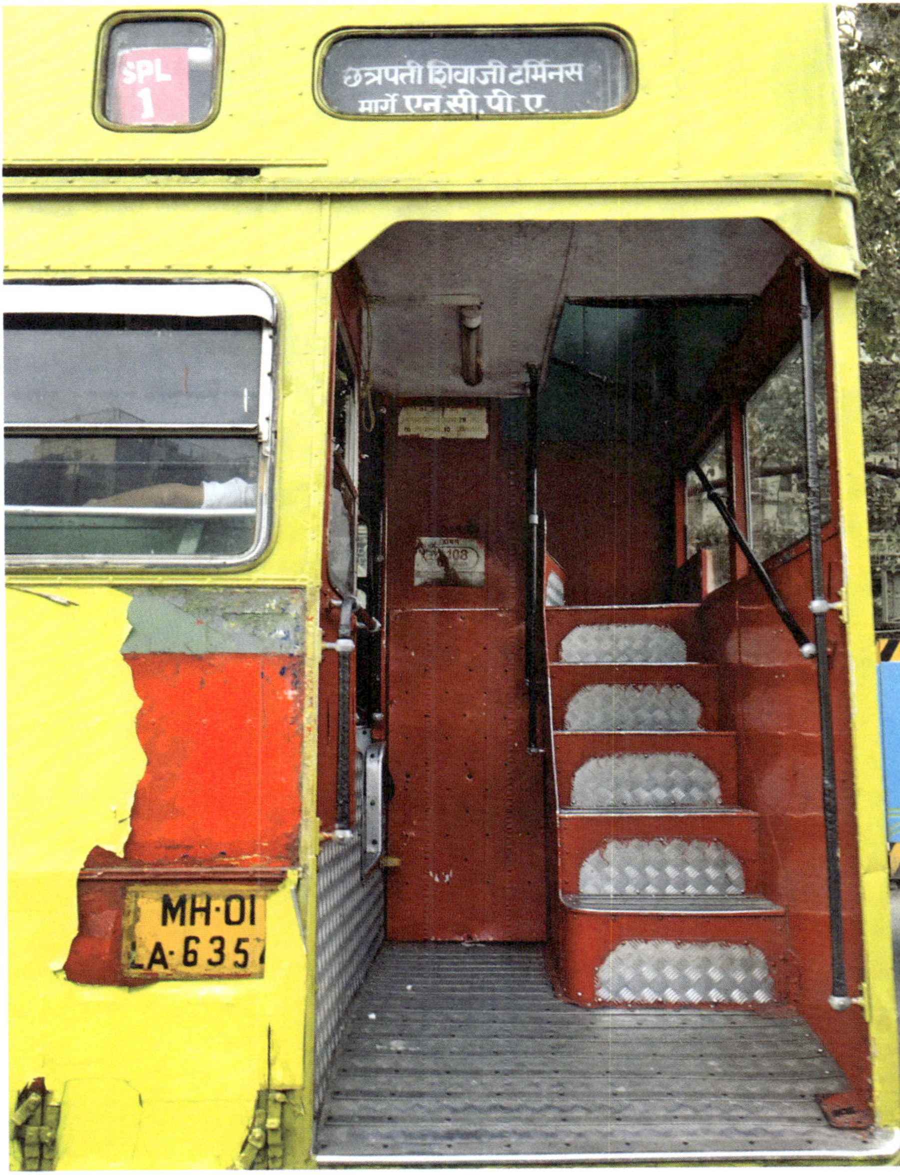
SPL
1
छत्रपती शिवाजी टर्मिनस
MH·01
LA·635

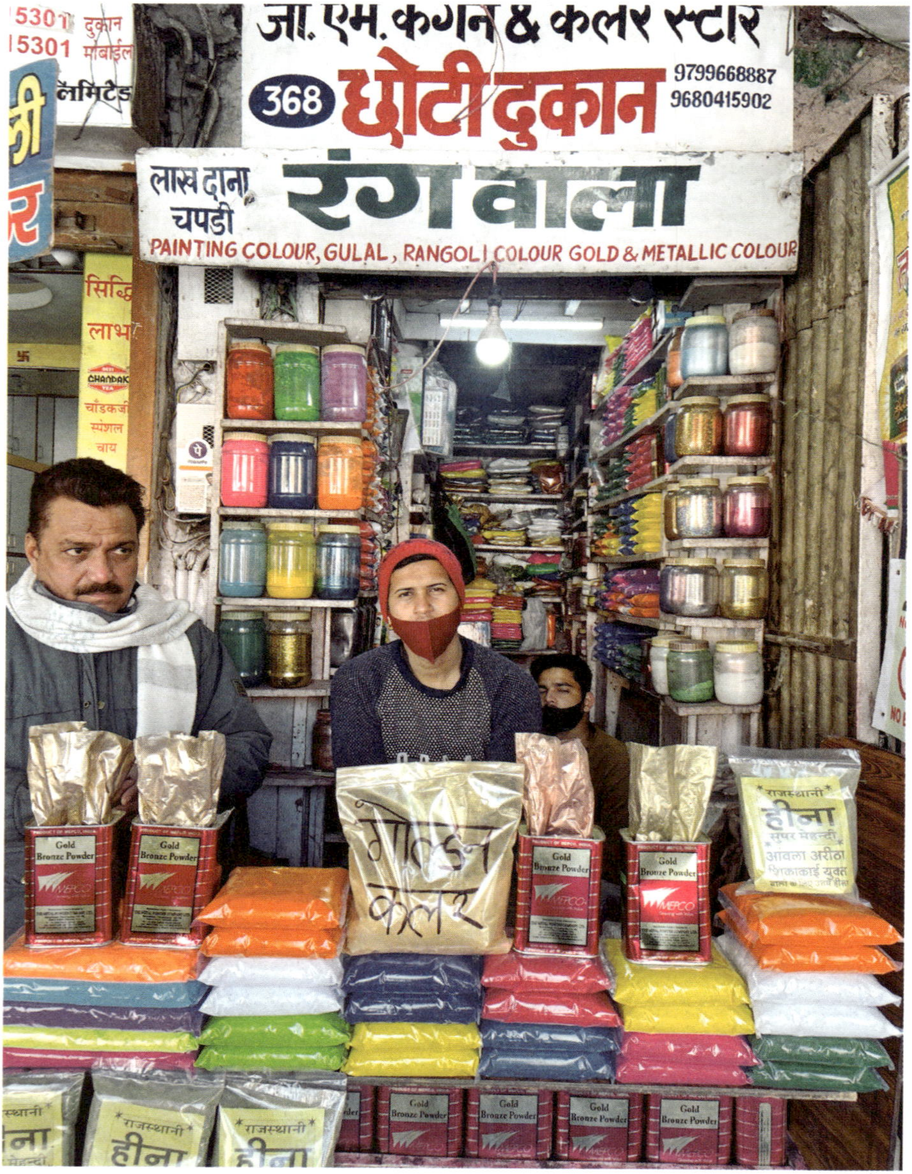
368 छोटी दुकान
9799668887
9680415902
लाख दाना
चपडी
रंग वाला
PAINTING COLOUR, GULAL, RANGOLI COLOUR GOLD & METALLIC COLOUR
Gold Bronze Powder
गोल्डन कलर
राजस्थानी
हीना

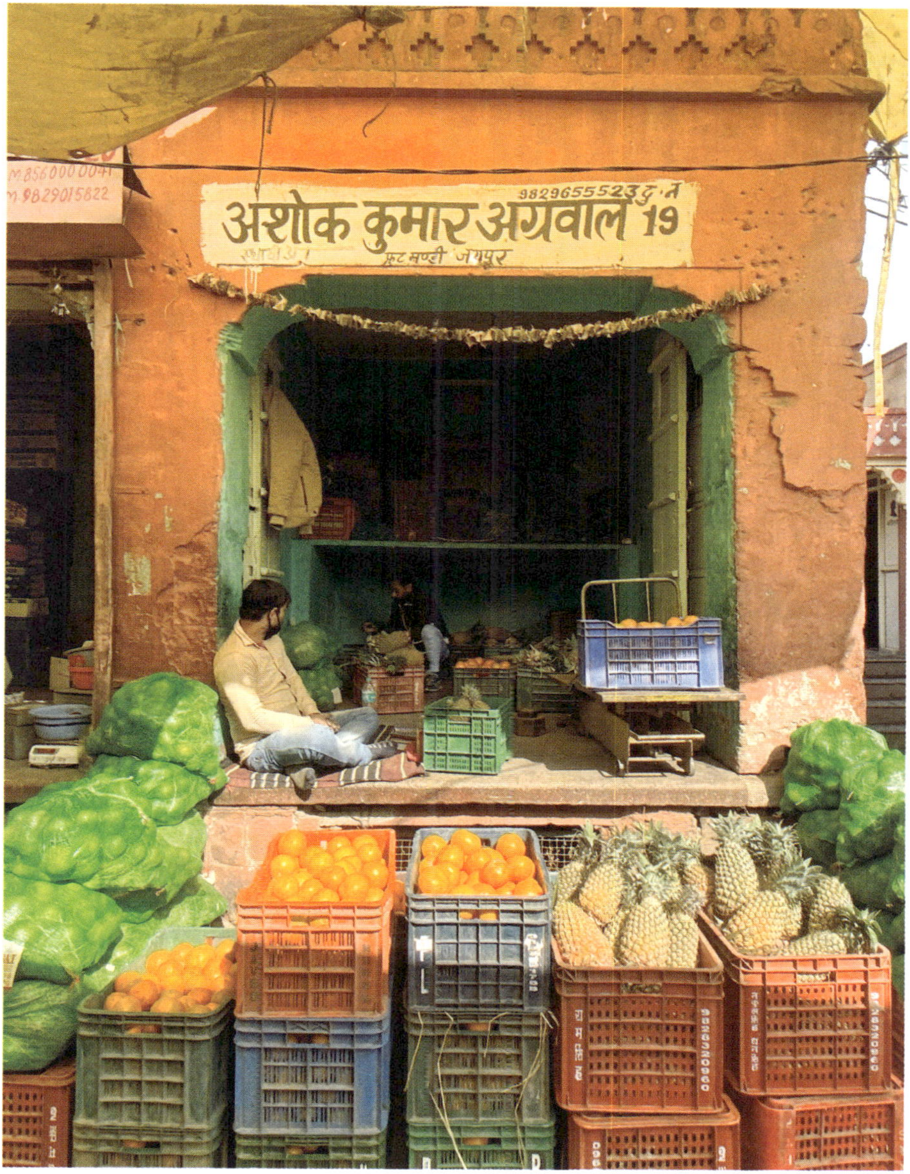
M.8560000041
M.9829015822
9829655523 दु.नं
अशोक कुमार अग्रवाल 19
फ्रूट मण्डी जयपुर

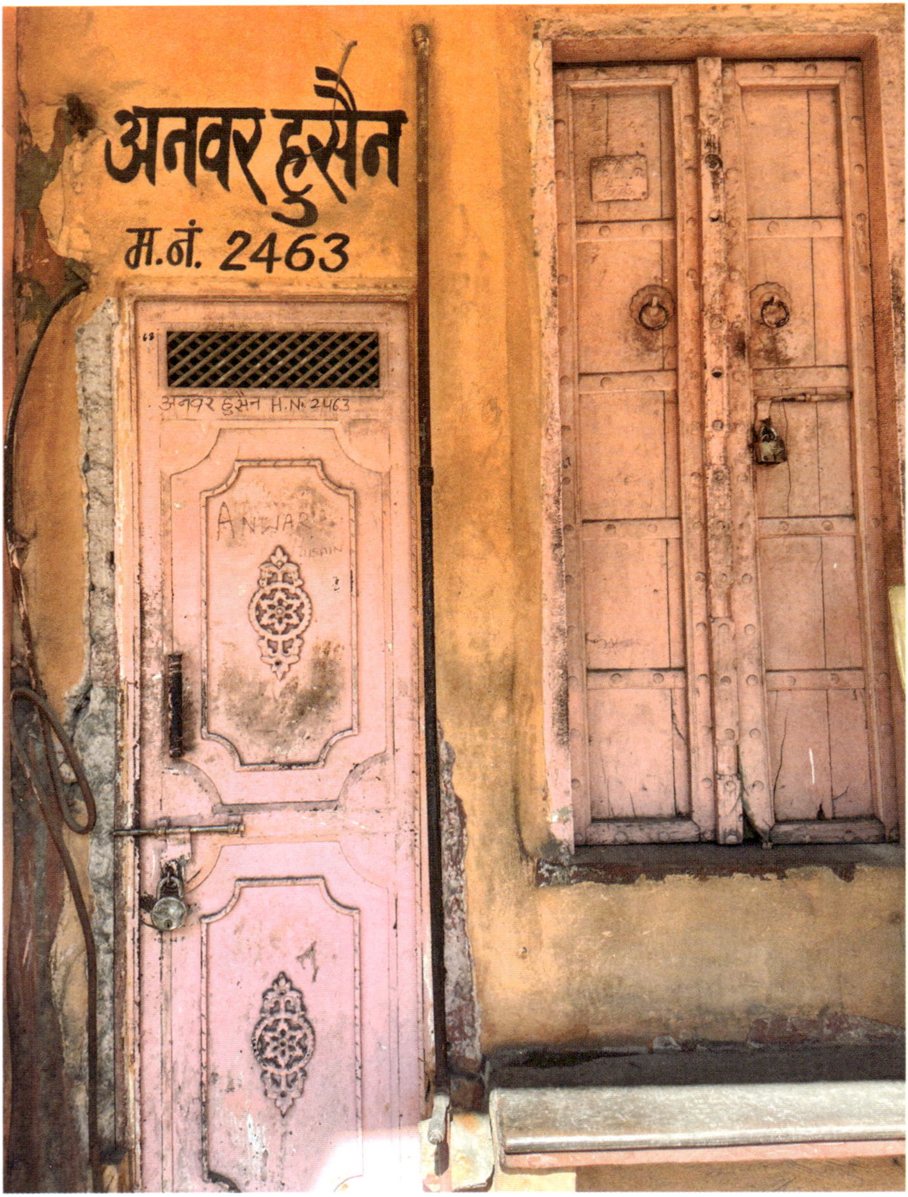
अनवर हुसैन
म.नं. 2463
अनवर हुसैन H.N. 2463
ANWAR

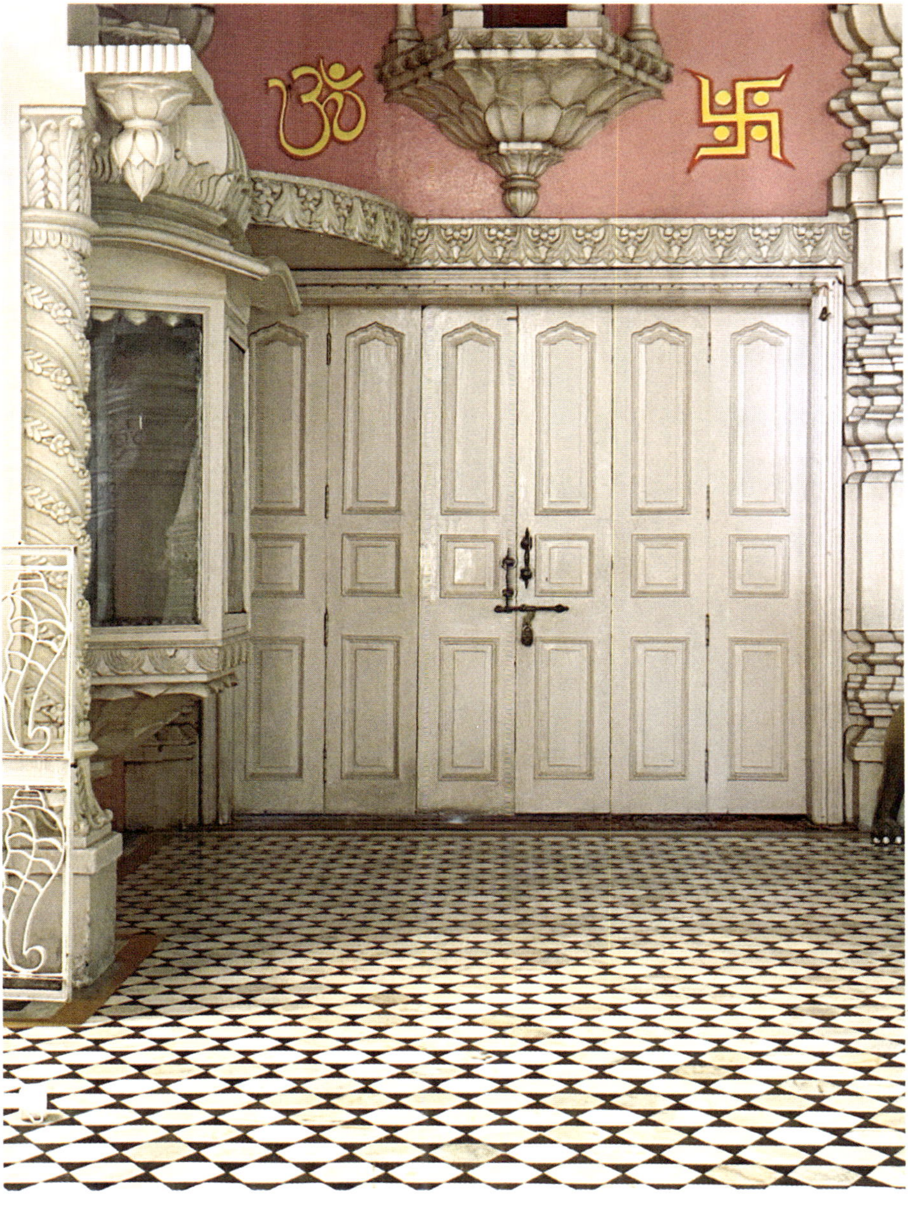

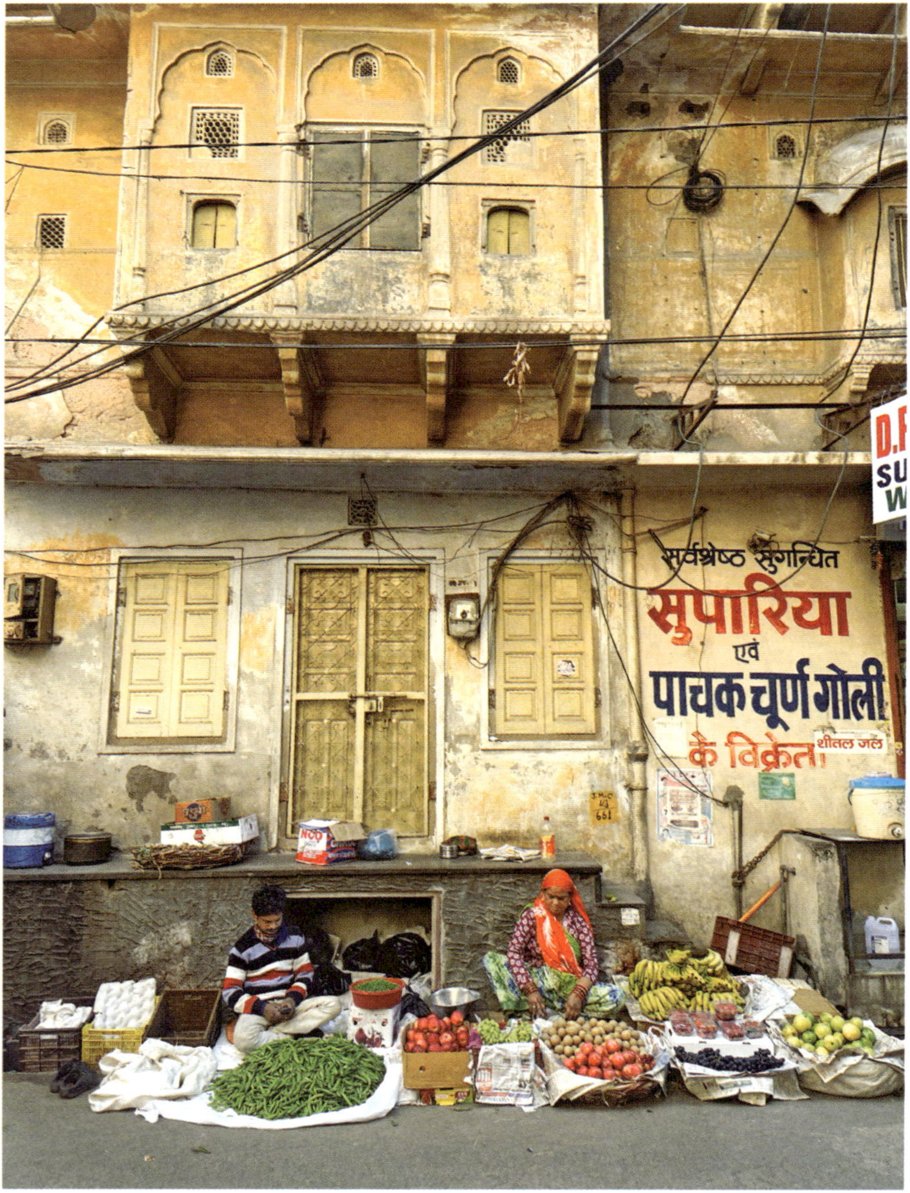
सर्वश्रेष्ठ सुगन्धित
सुपारिया
एवं
पाचक चूर्ण गोली
के विक्रेता
शीतल जल

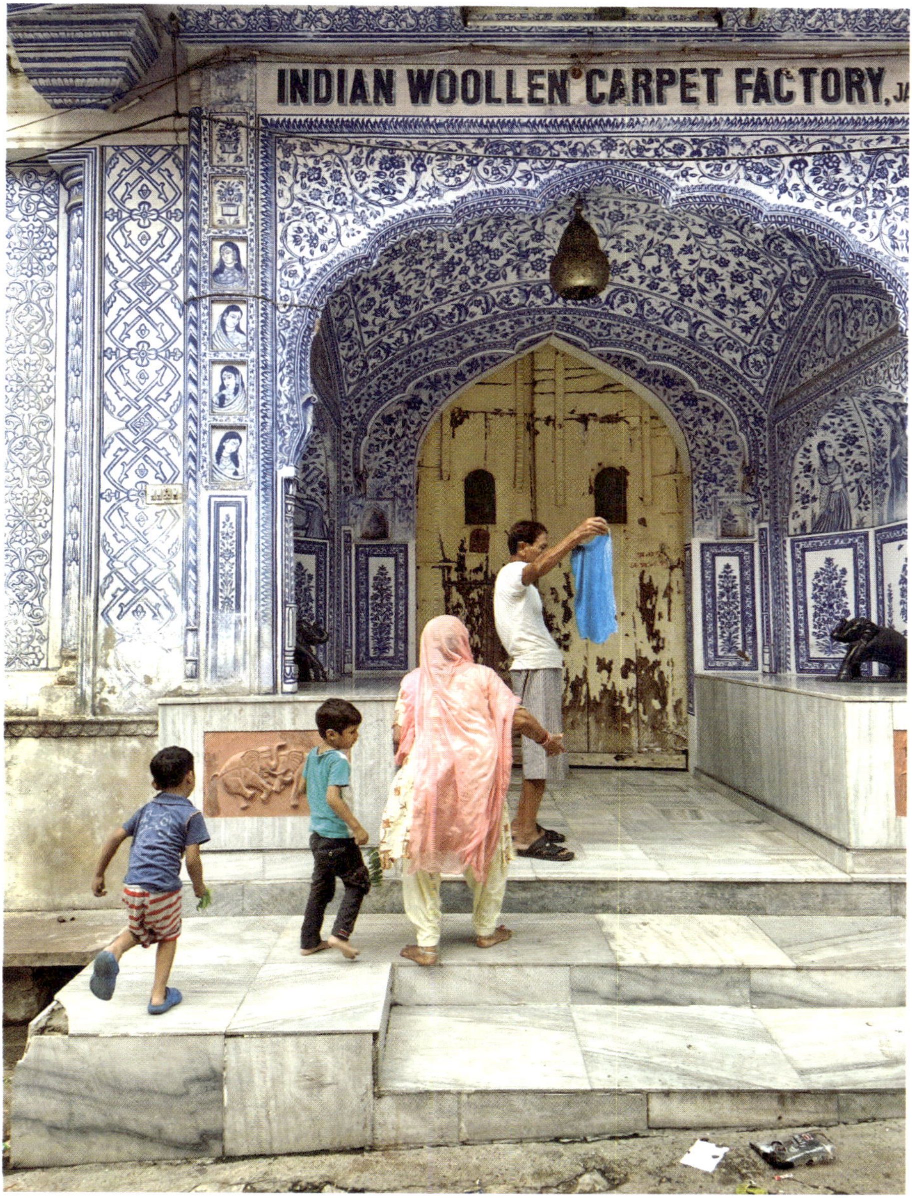
INDIAN WOOLLEN CARPET FACTORY, JA

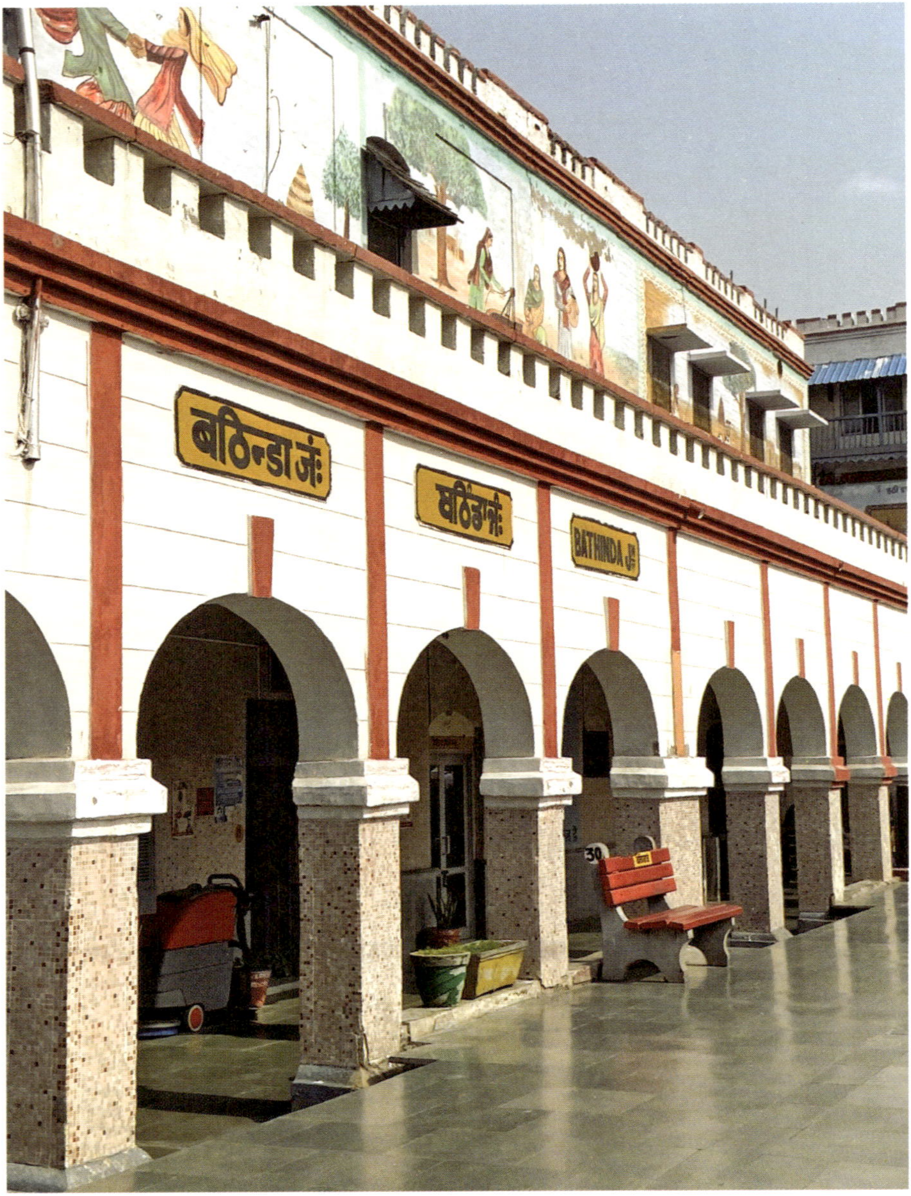
बठिण्डा जं:
BATHINDA

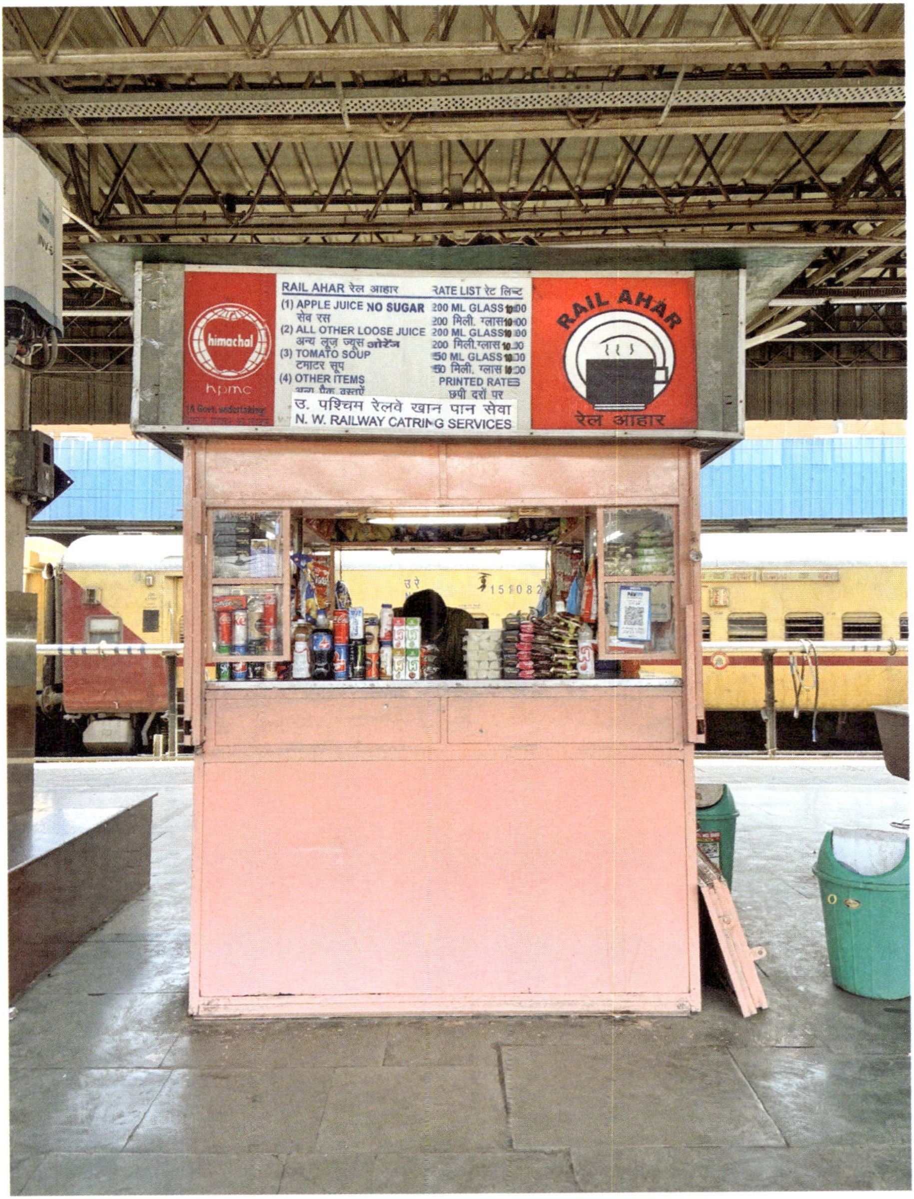

RAIL AHAR रेल आहार
RATE LIST रेट लिस्ट
(1) APPLE JUICE NO SUGAR
सेव रस
(2) ALL OTHER LOOSE JUICE
अन्य लूज़ ज्यूस ओरेंज
(3) TOMATO SOUP
टमाटर सूप
(4) OTHER ITEMS
200 ML GLASS
200 मिली. ग्लास
छपी दरों पर
उ. पश्चिम रेलवे खान पान सेवा
N. W. RAILWAY CATRING SERVICES
himachal
hpmc
RAIL AHAR
रेल आहार

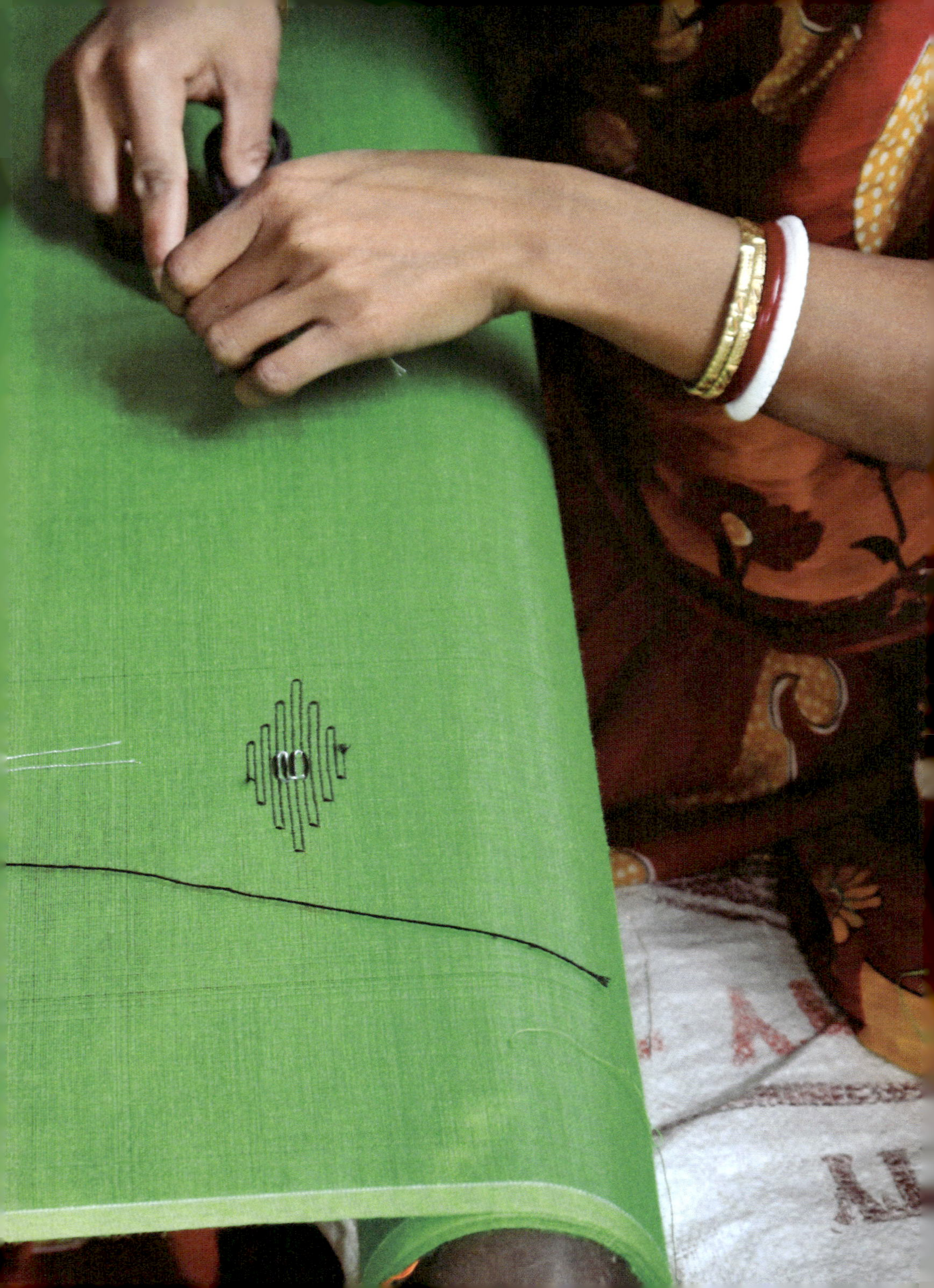

adornment & identity

The body becomes a canvas – accessories and sartorial choices are markers of the self and the community in India. A particular piece of jewellery can symbolize a woman's marital status while the drape, colours and cuts of draped cloth signify the wearer's religion and regional origins.

Everyday clothing captured in these images displays a variety of fabric and patterns – monochromatic and tessellating, checks and borders, shades of pastel or neon, embroidered and embellished – a concoction of customs and creativity. Unstitched textiles are common, with men draping turbans, lungees and dhotis, and women clothed in saris, hijabs, and *odhanis*. Anklets, *jutis,* and toe rings adorn the feet, ears stacked with hoops and danglers, wrists decked with bangles and necks carry beads, pendants, and chains.

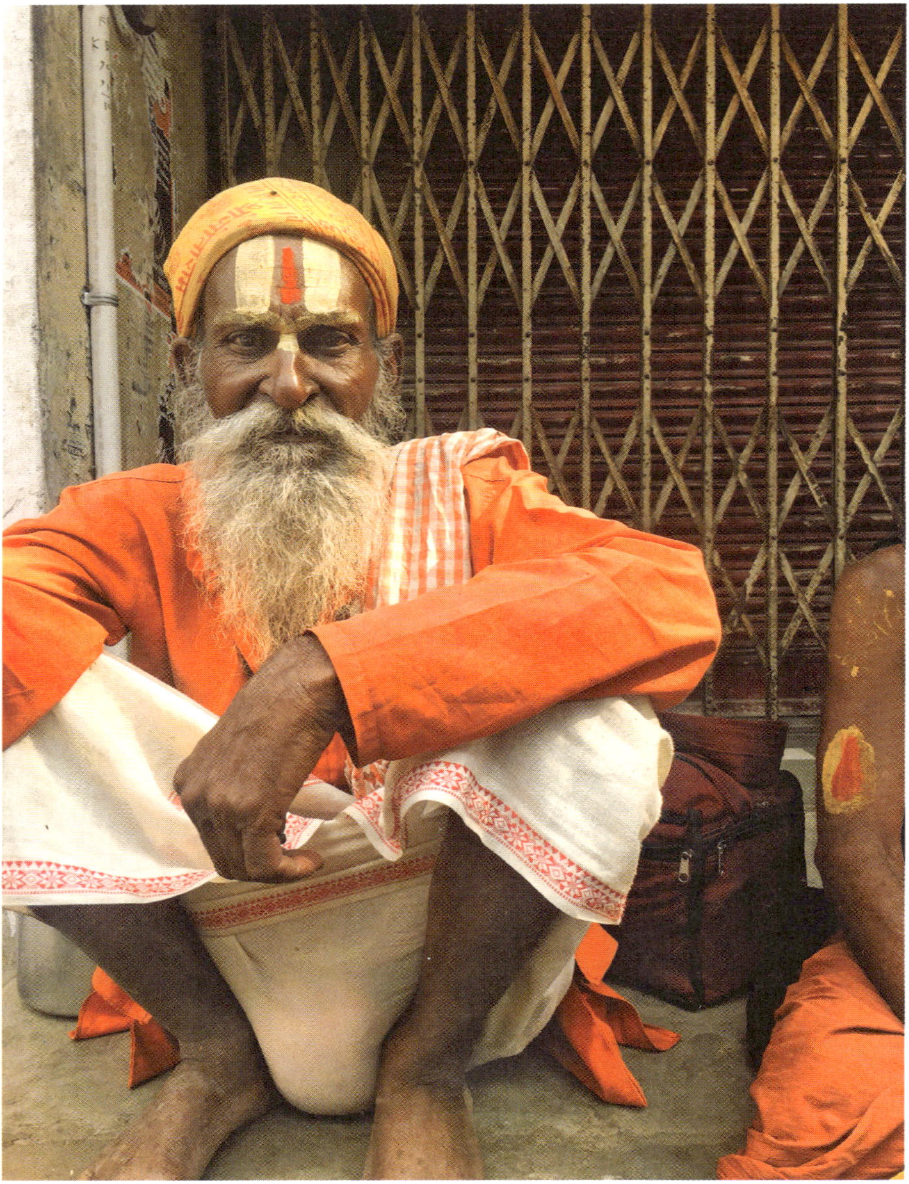

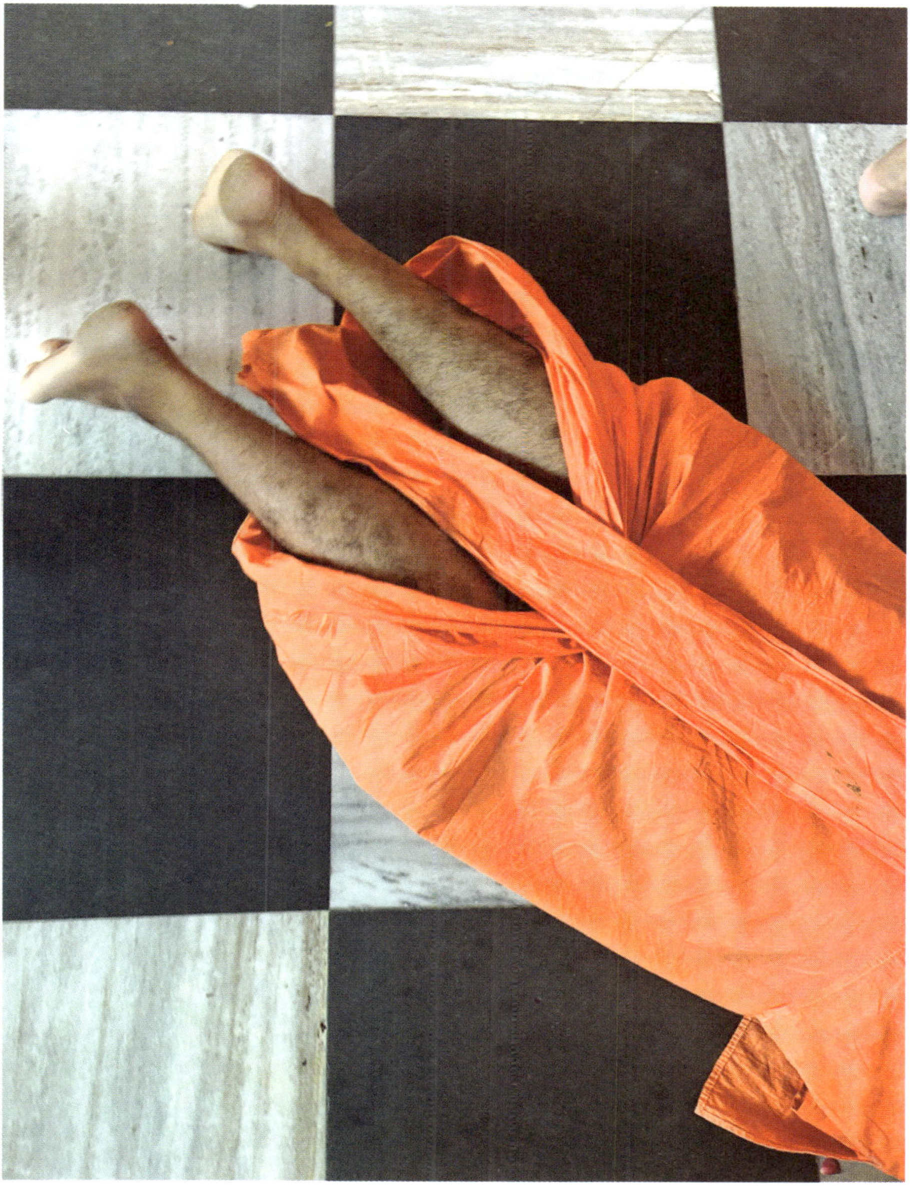

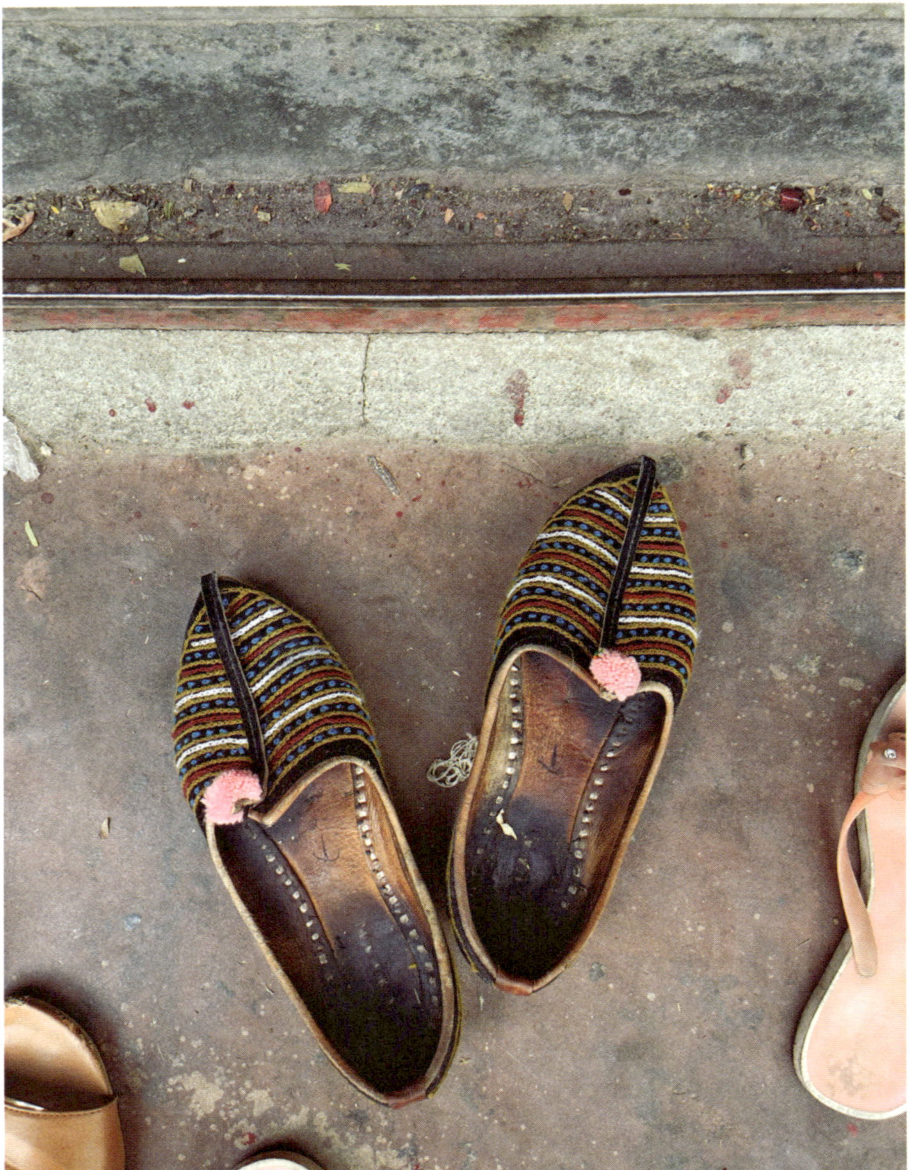

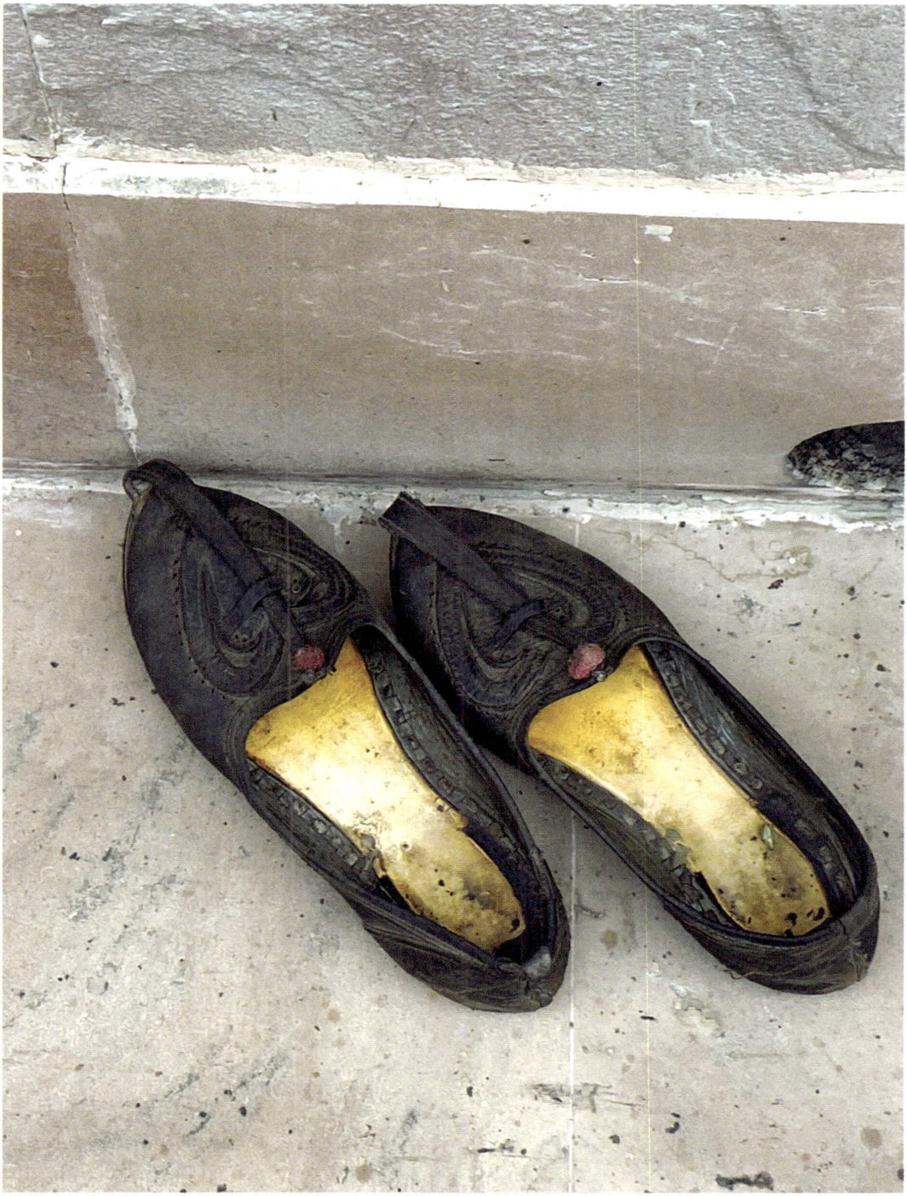

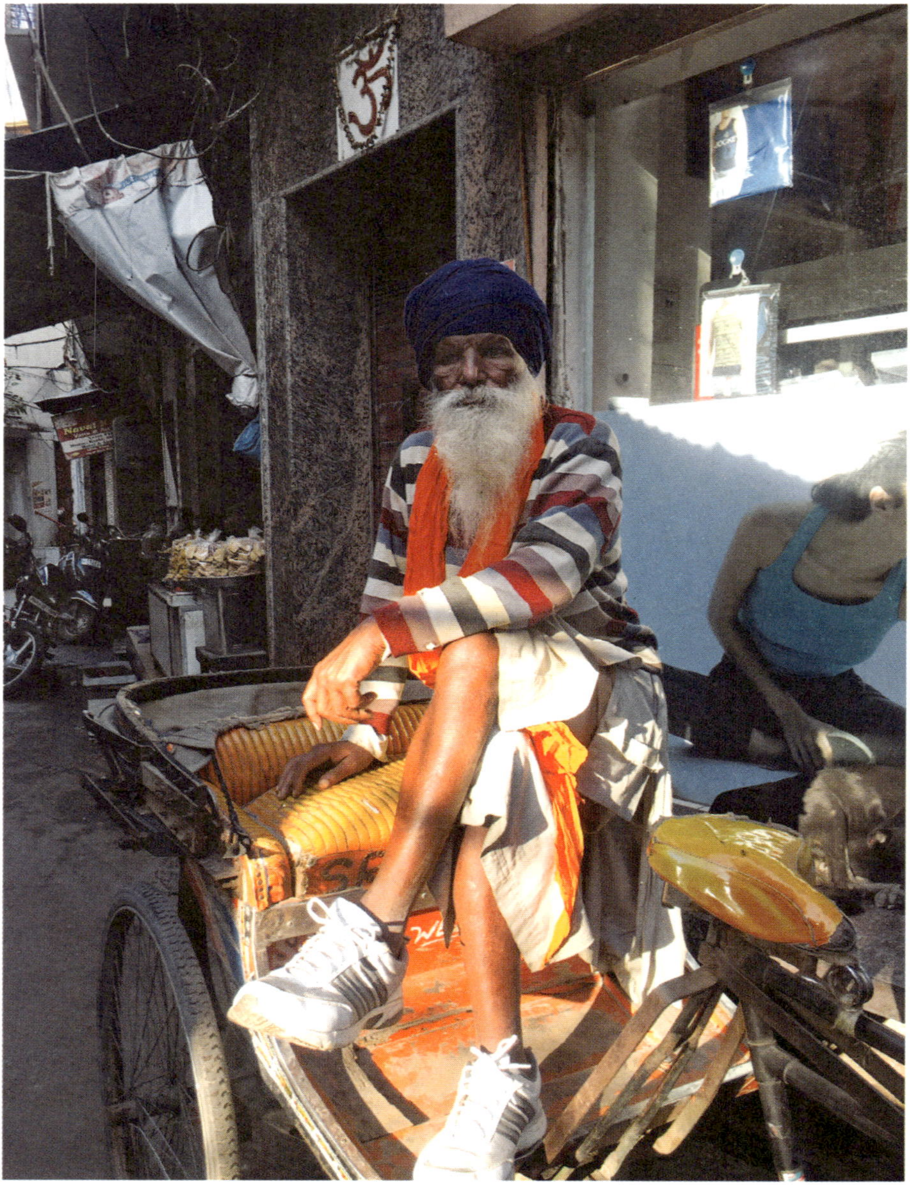

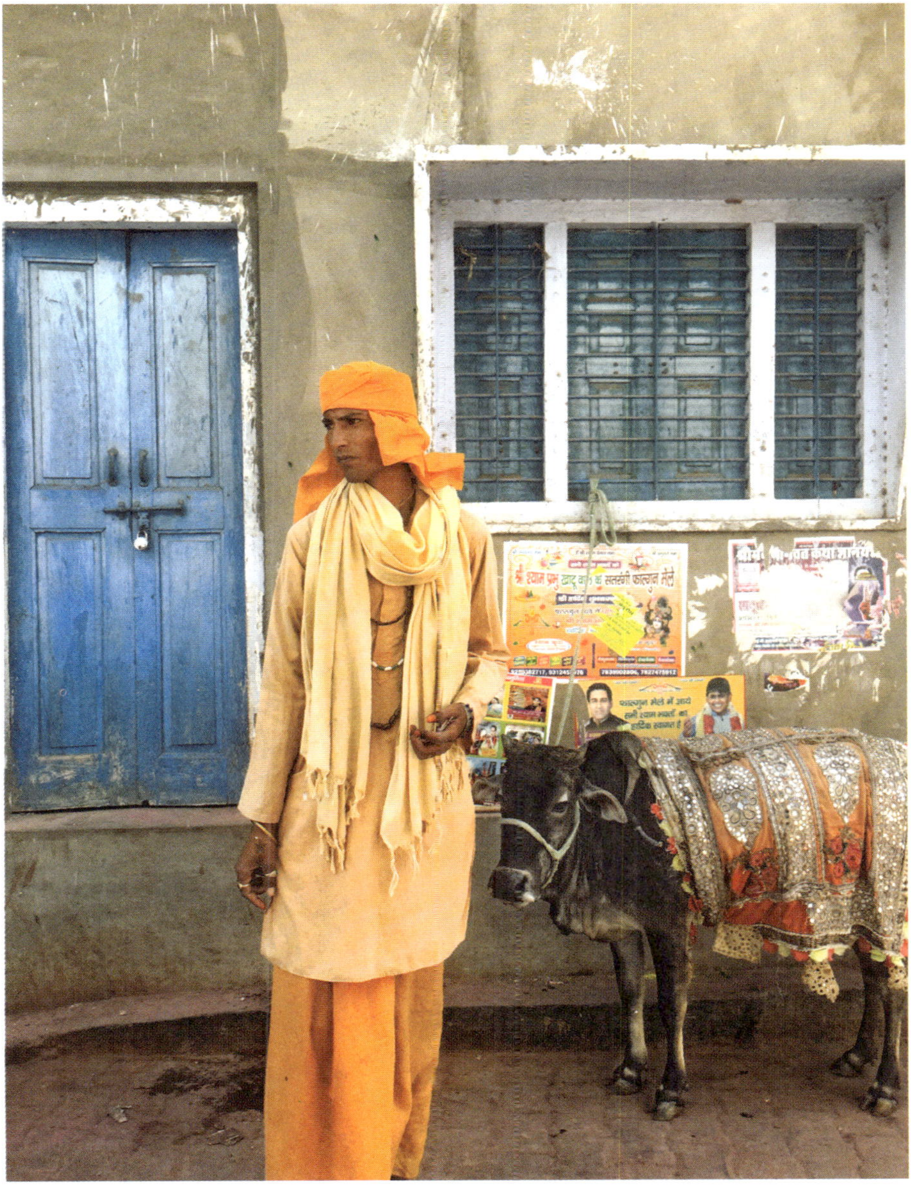
फाल्गुन मेले में आये
सभी श्याम भक्तों का
हार्दिक स्वागत है

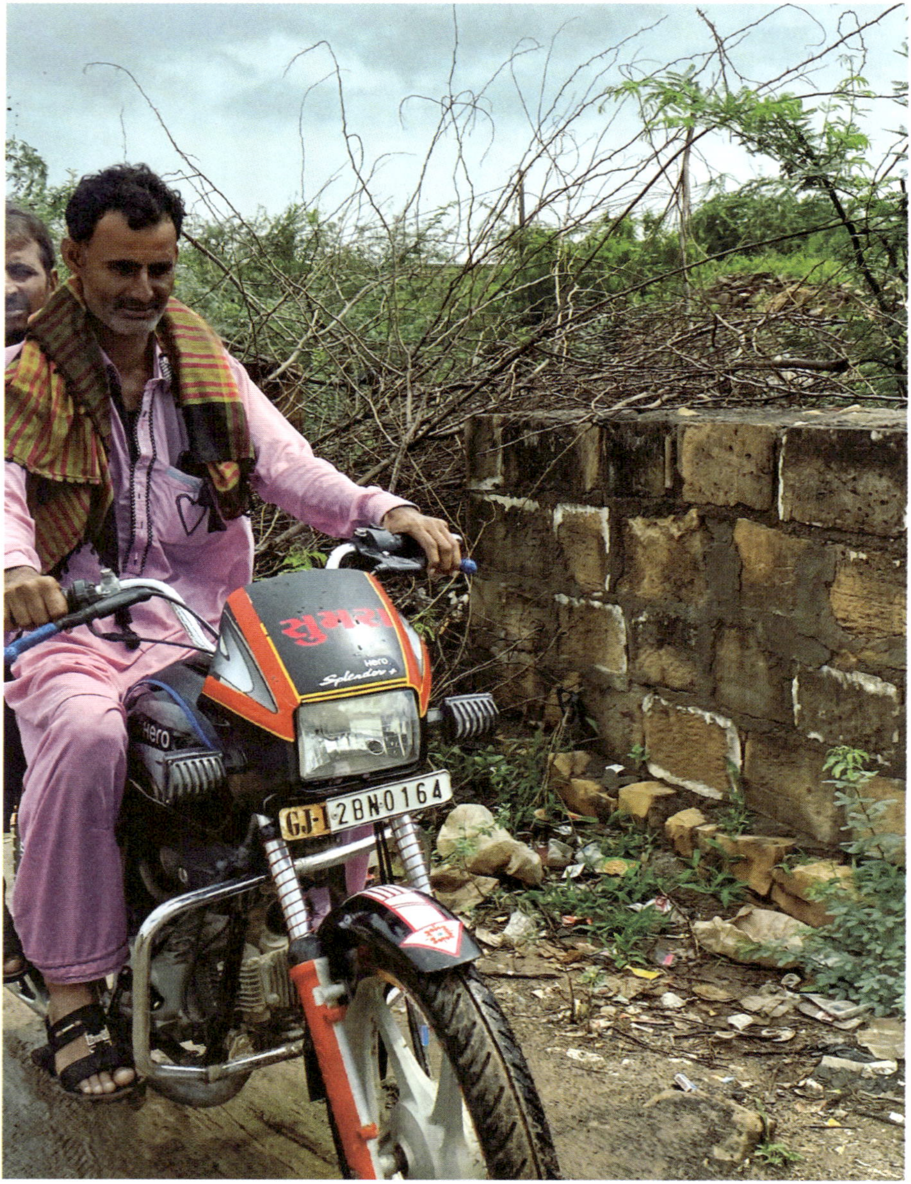
Hero
Splendor+
GJ-1 2BN0164

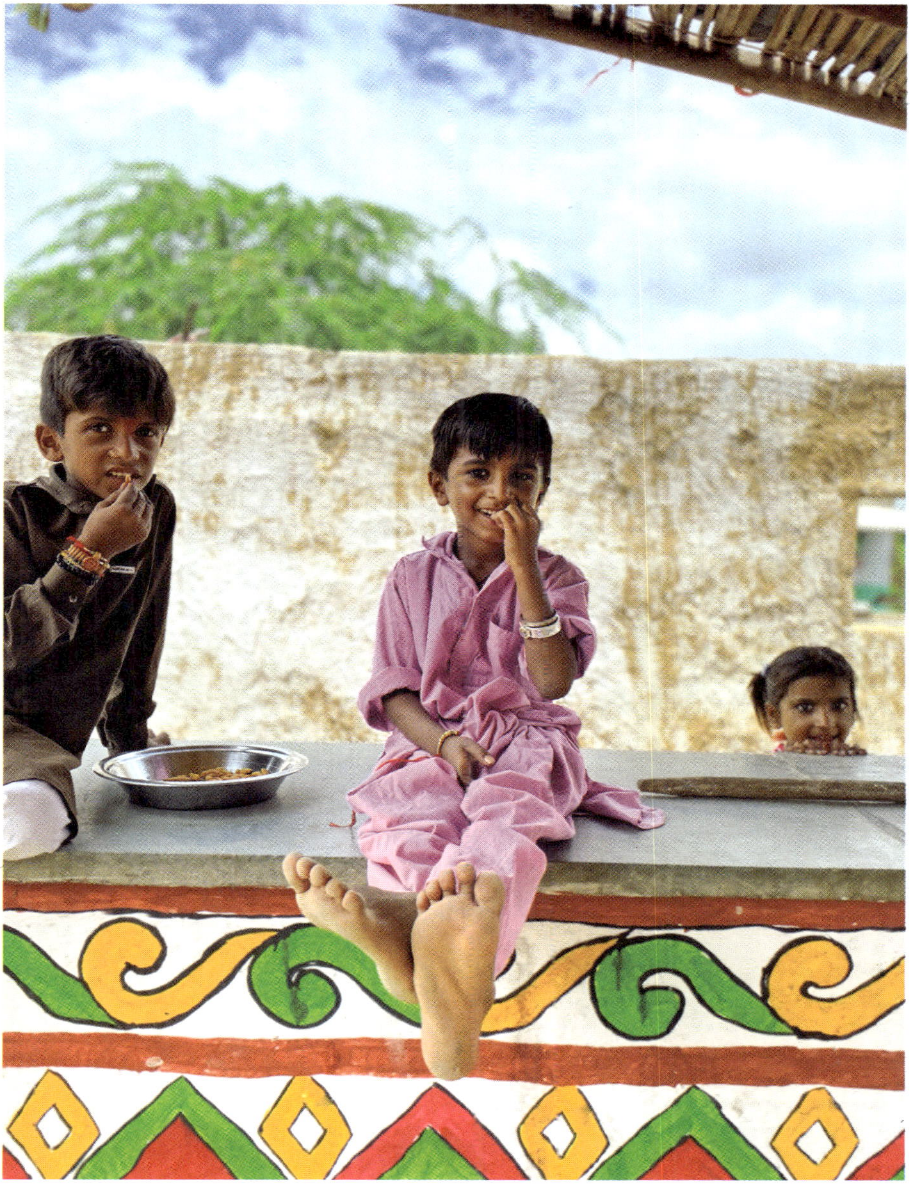

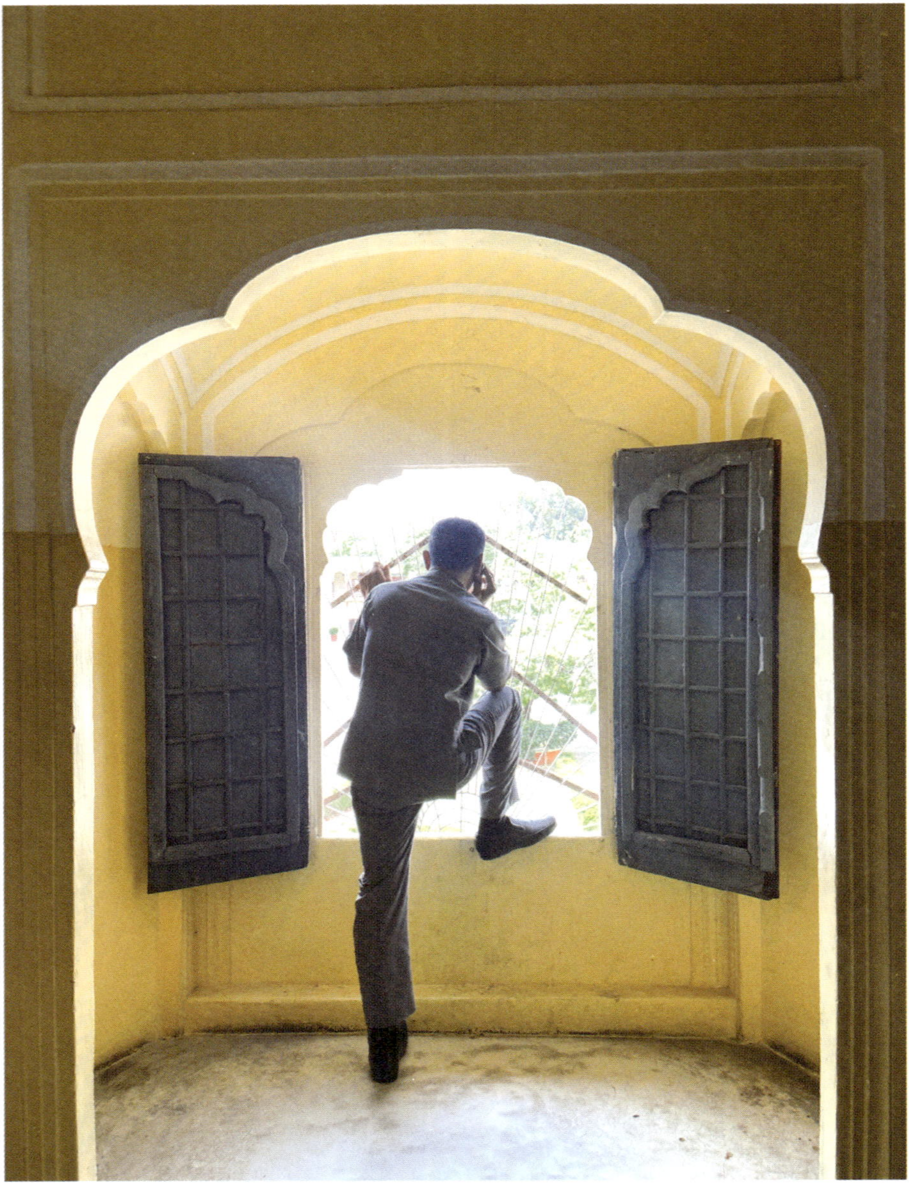

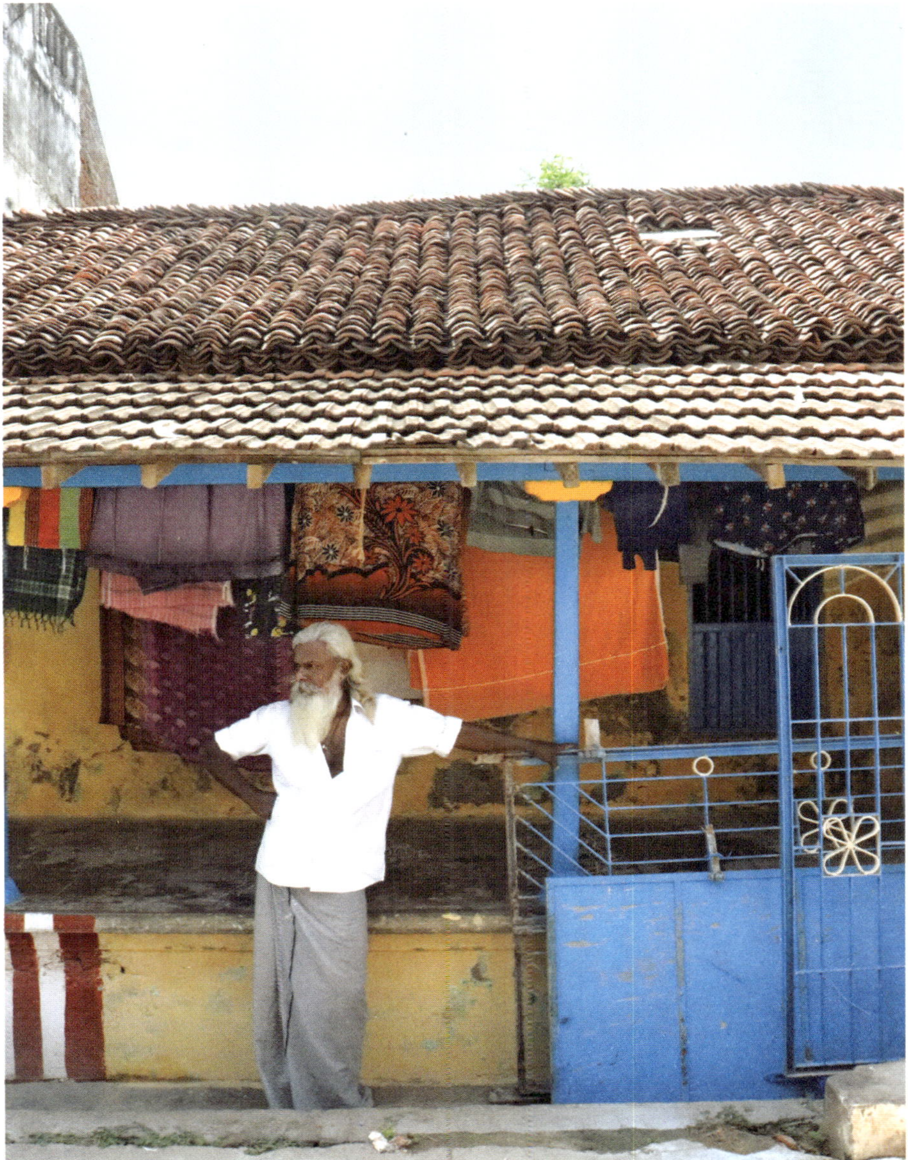

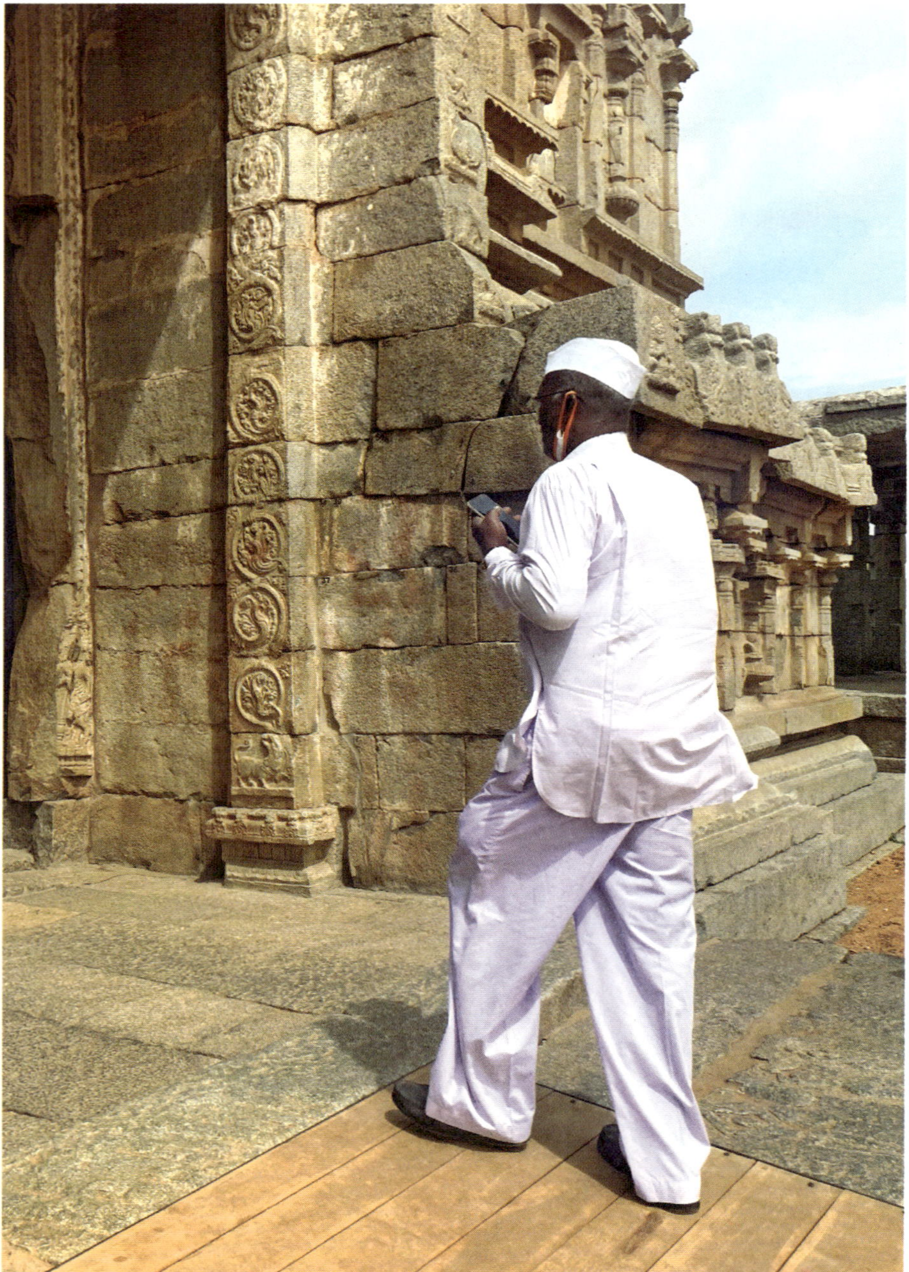

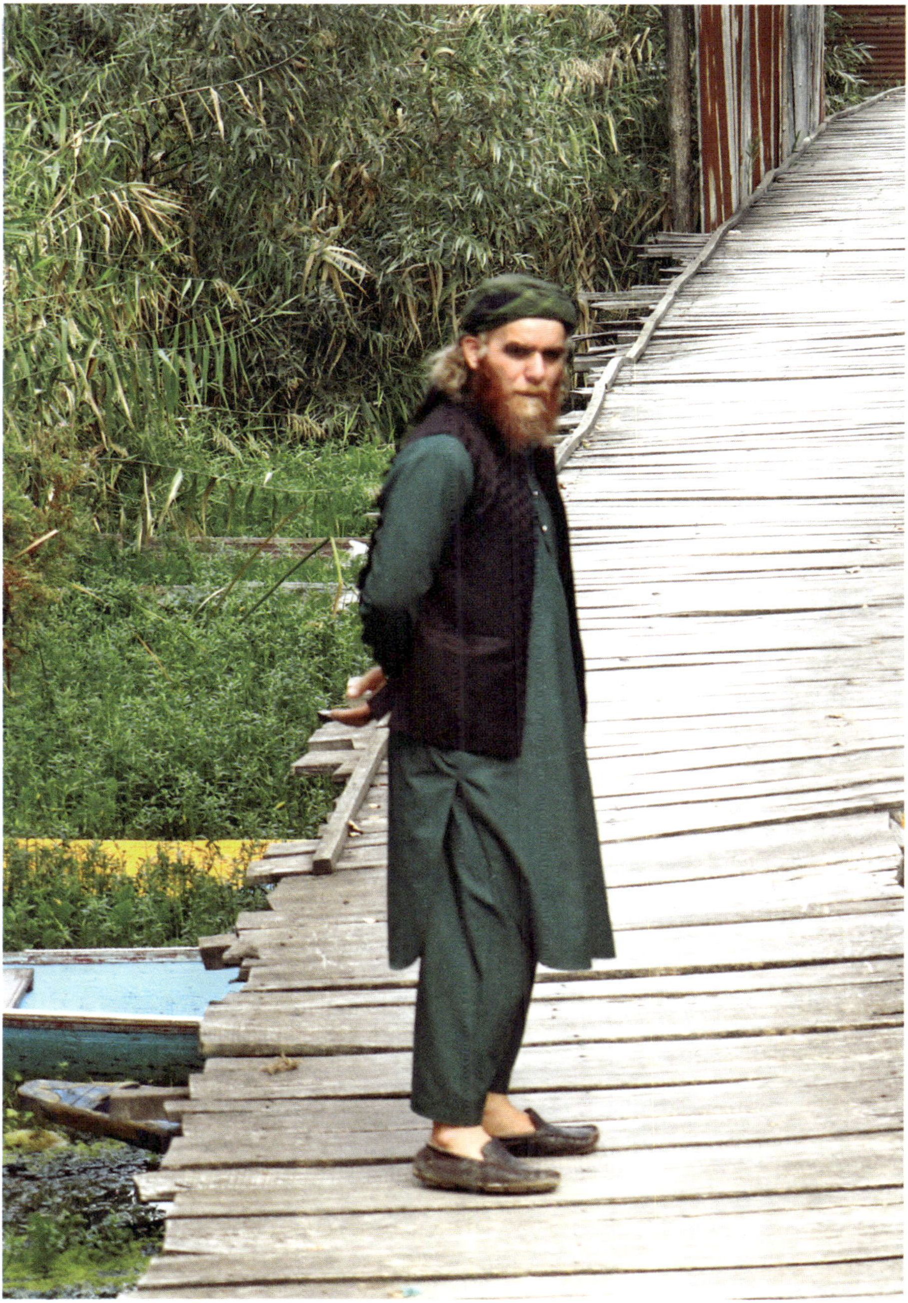

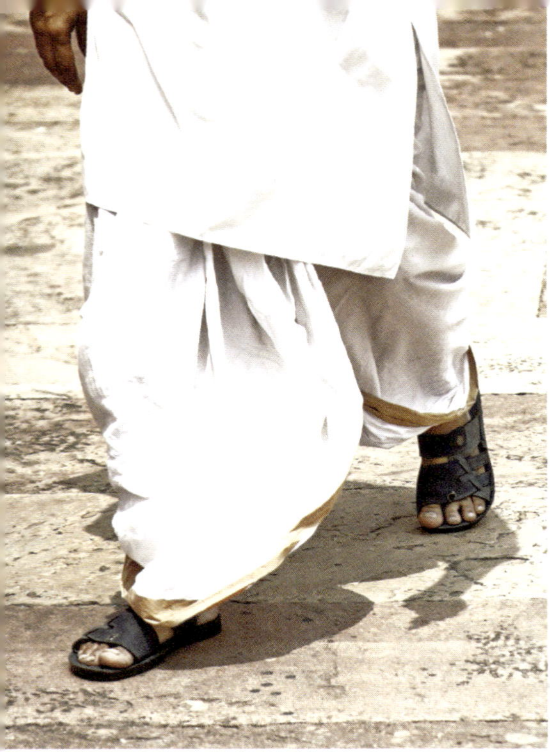

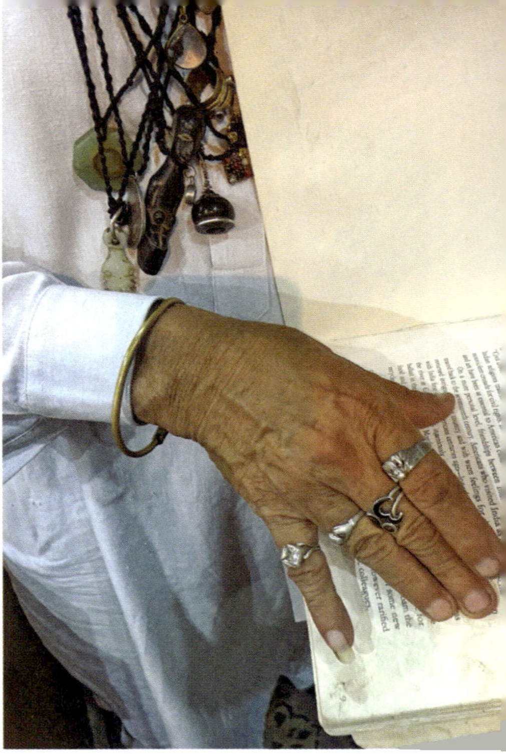

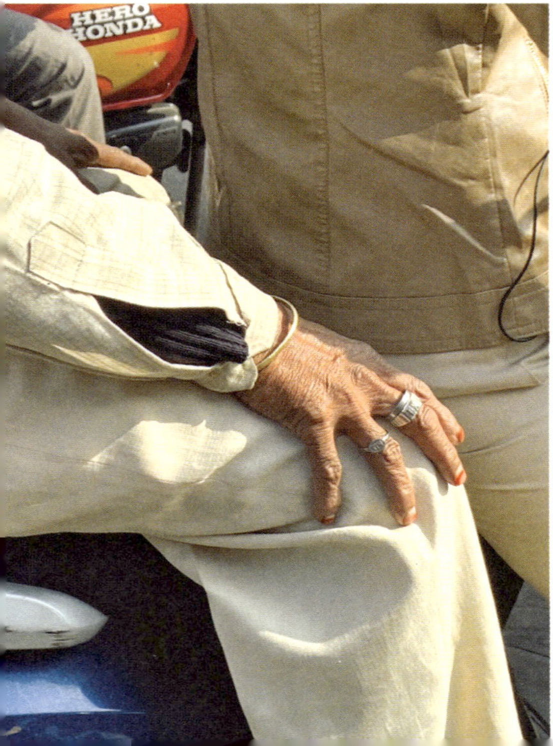
HERO
HONDA

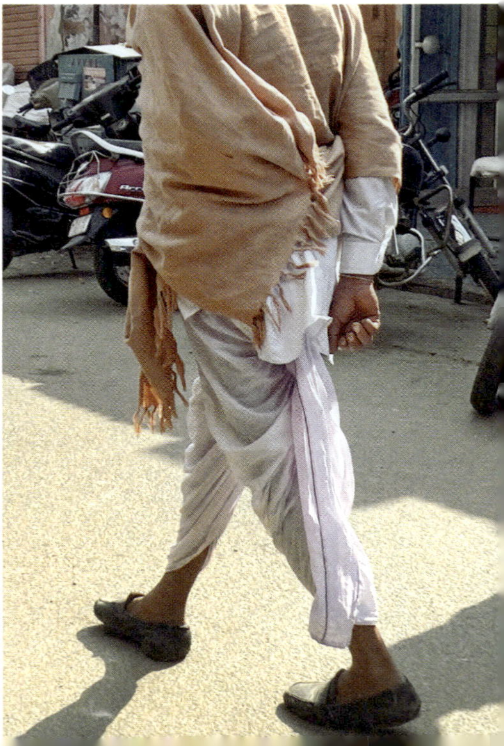

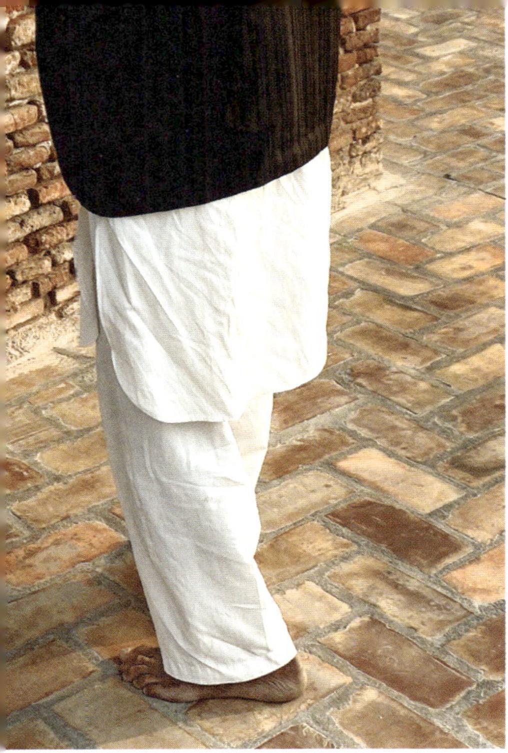
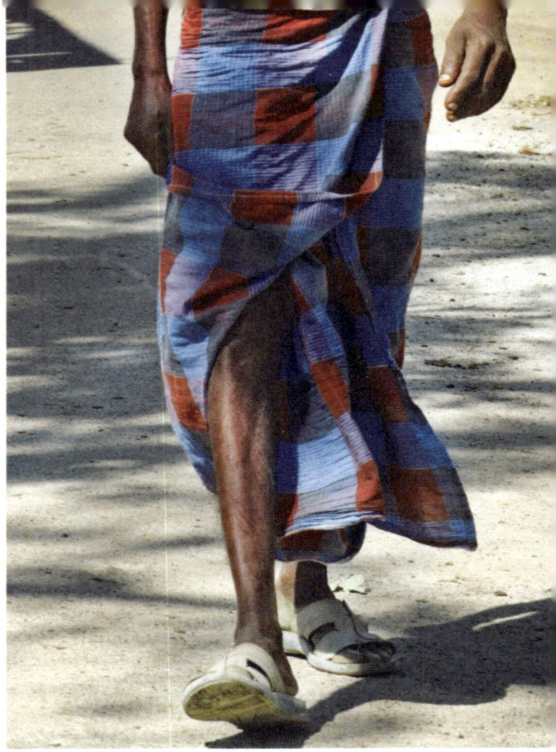
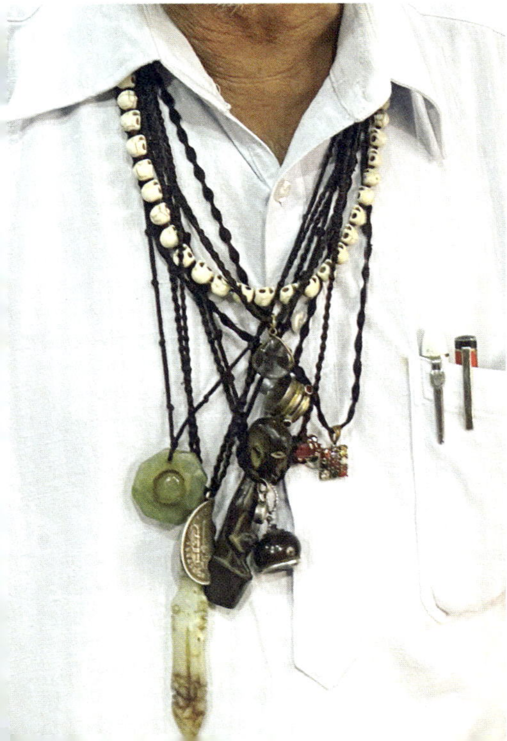
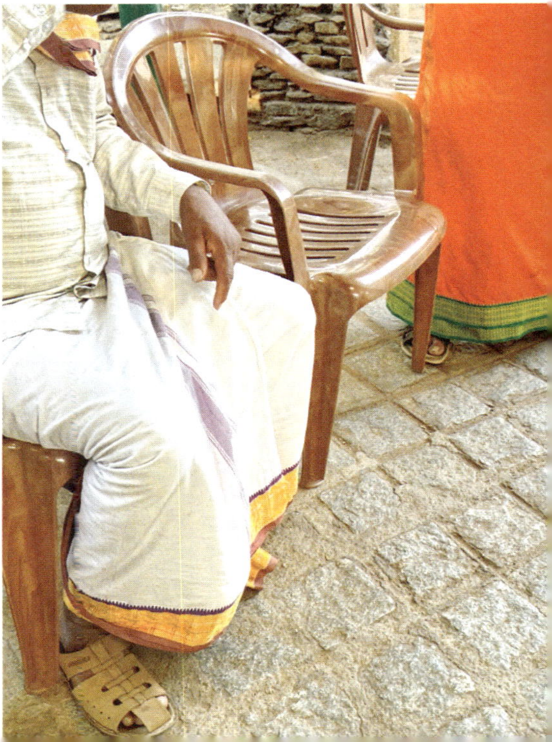

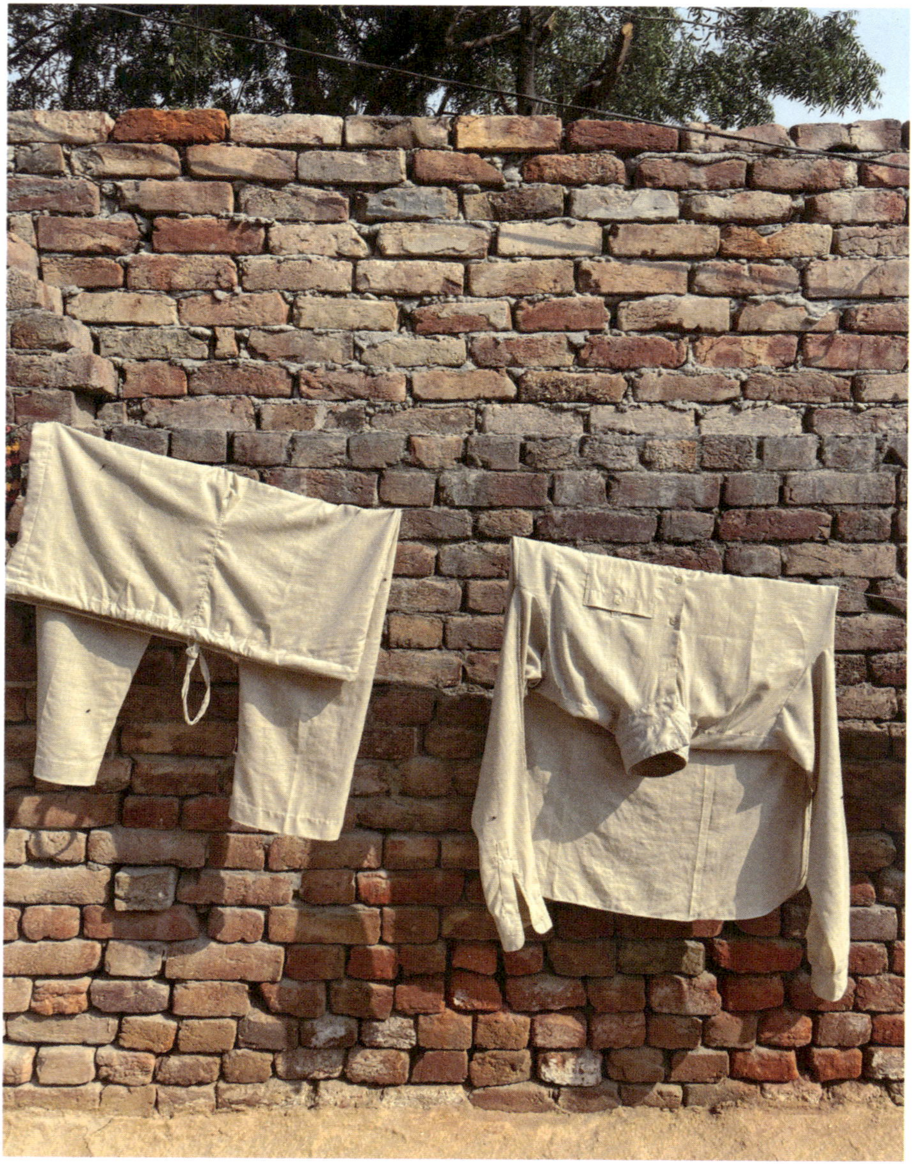

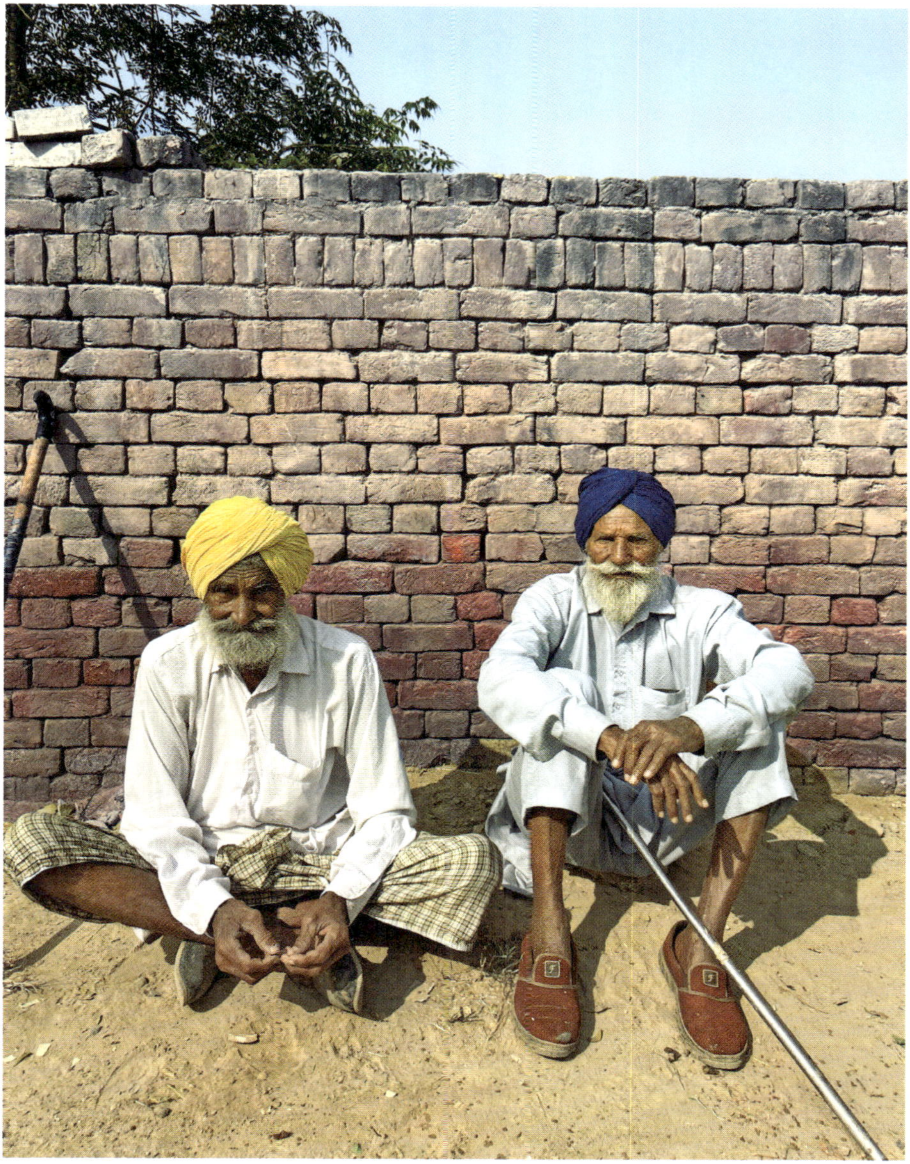

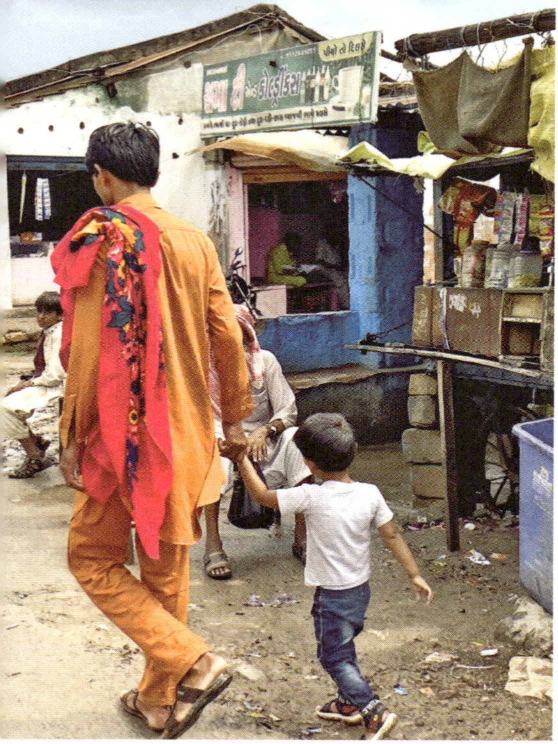

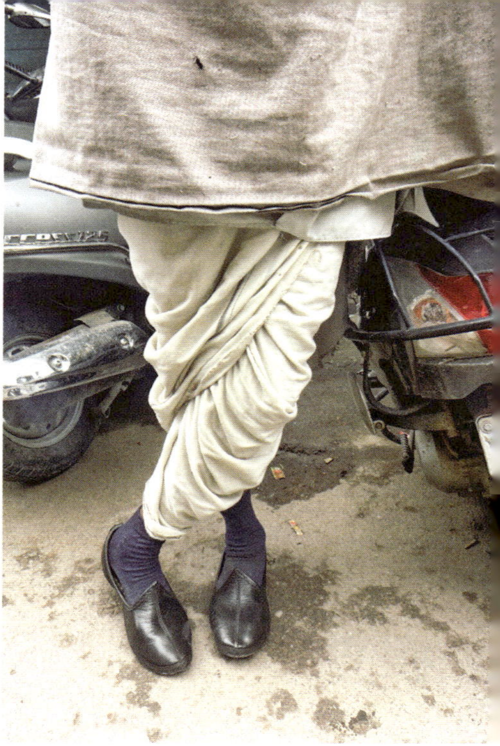

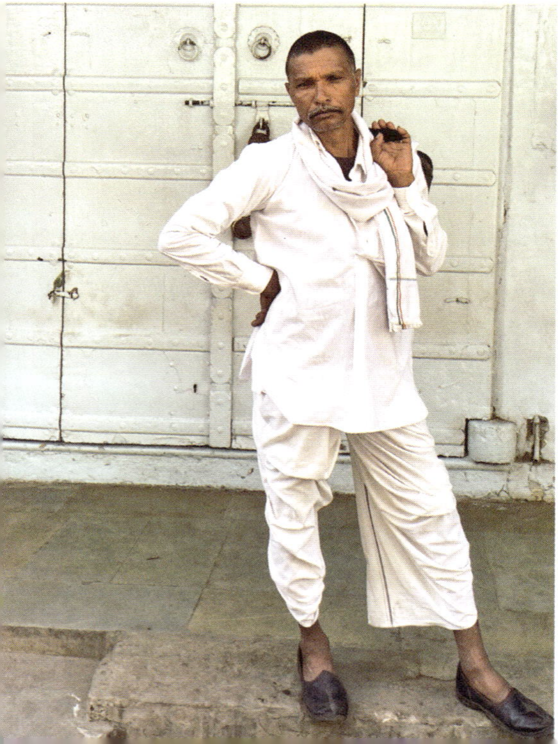

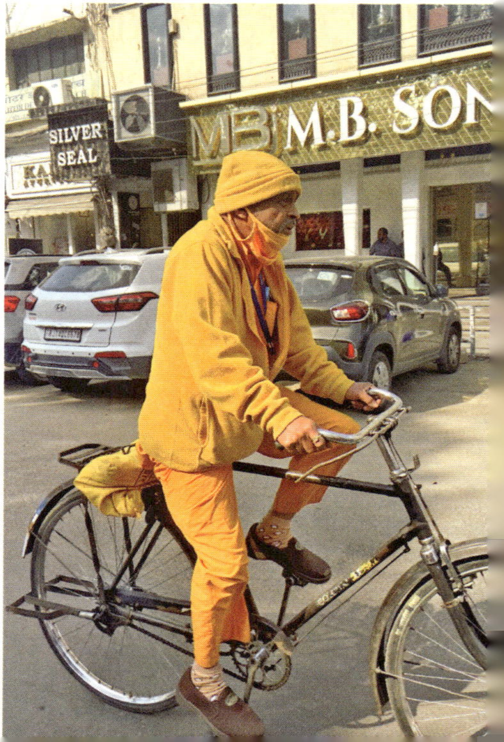

SILVER
SEAL
MB M.B. SON

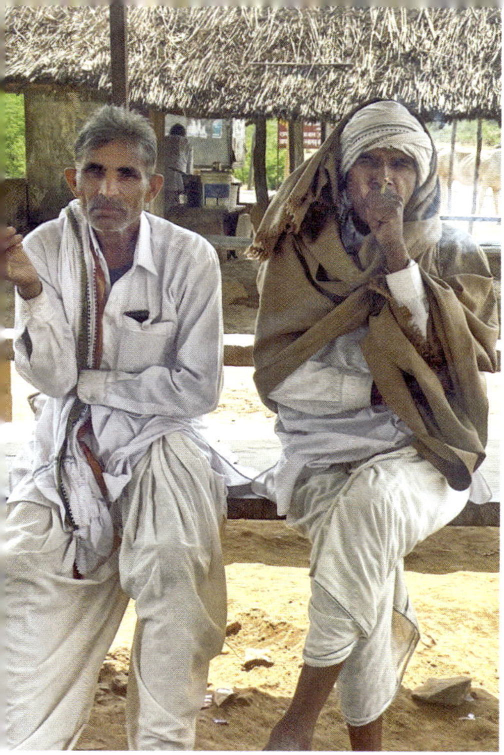
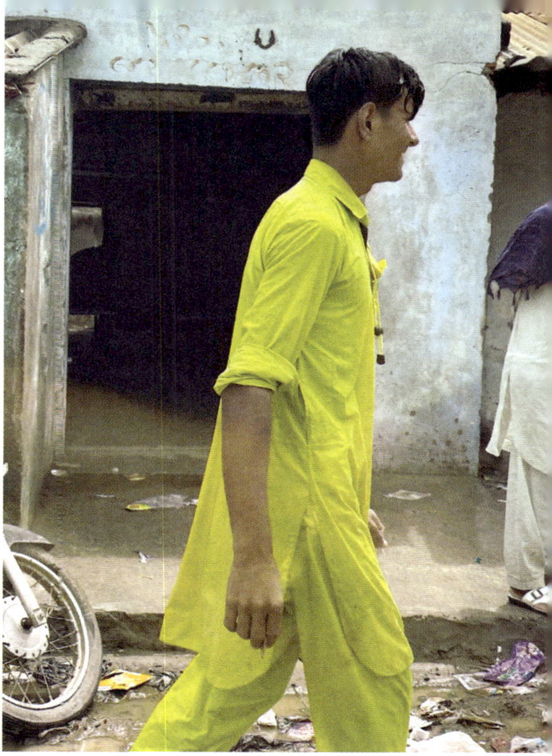
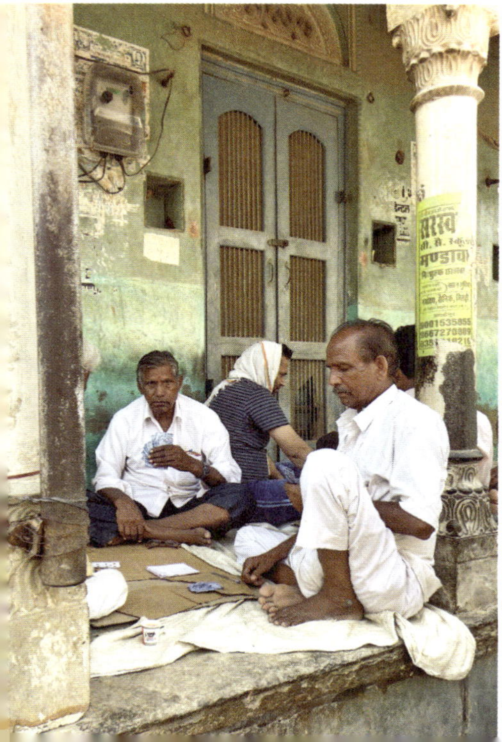
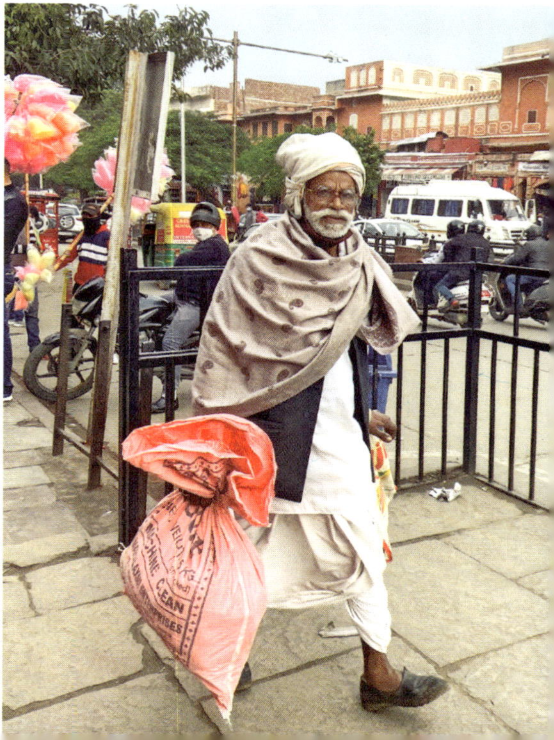

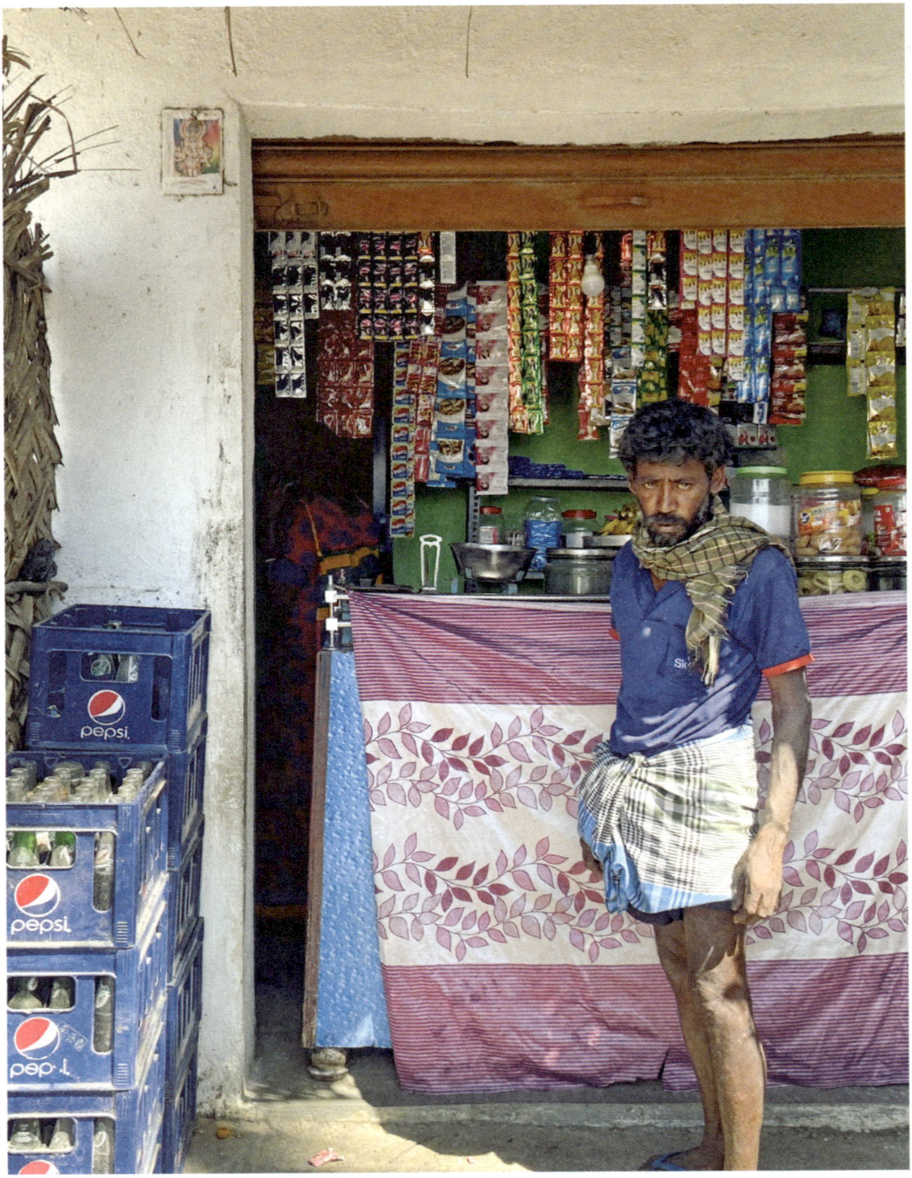
pepsi
pepsi

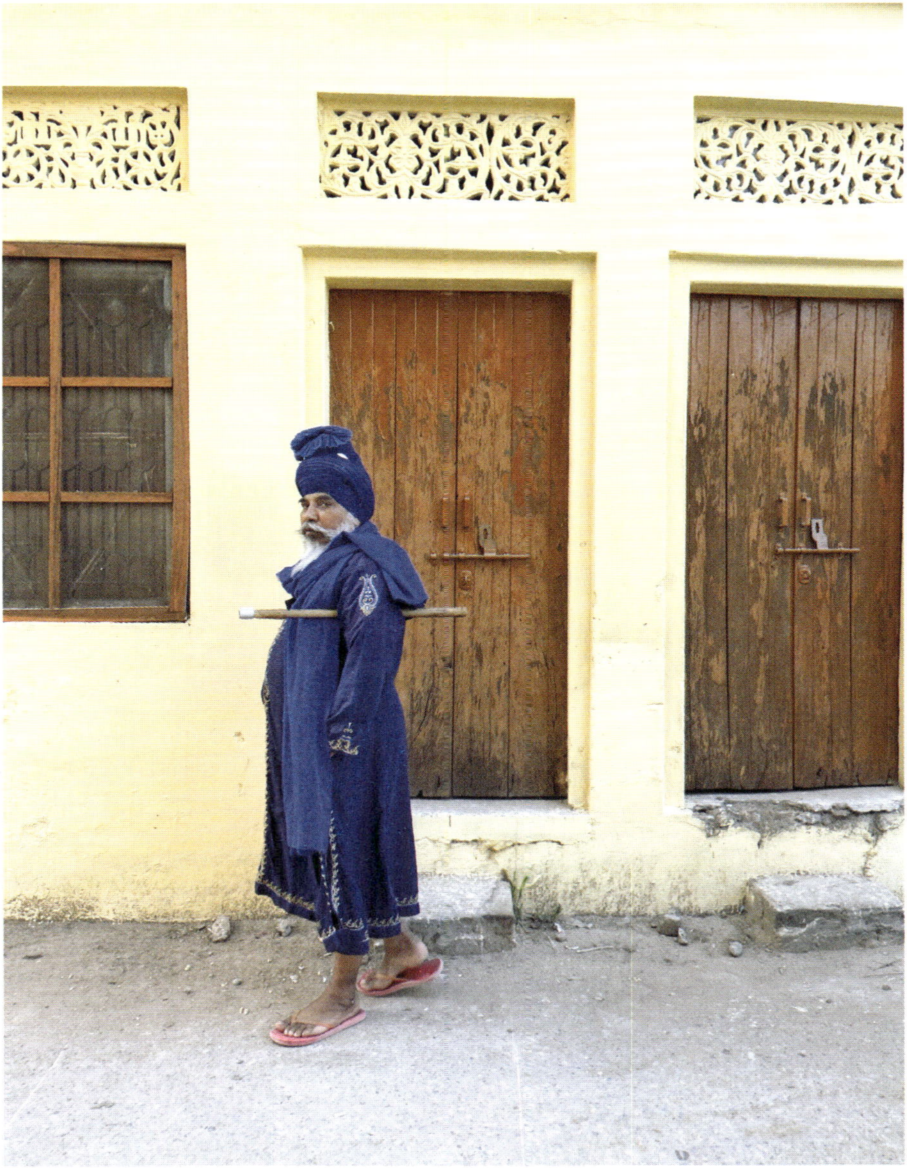

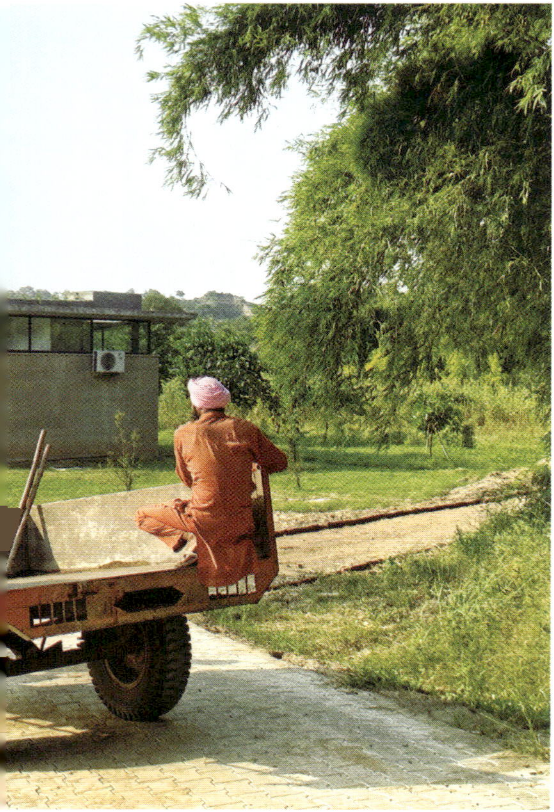

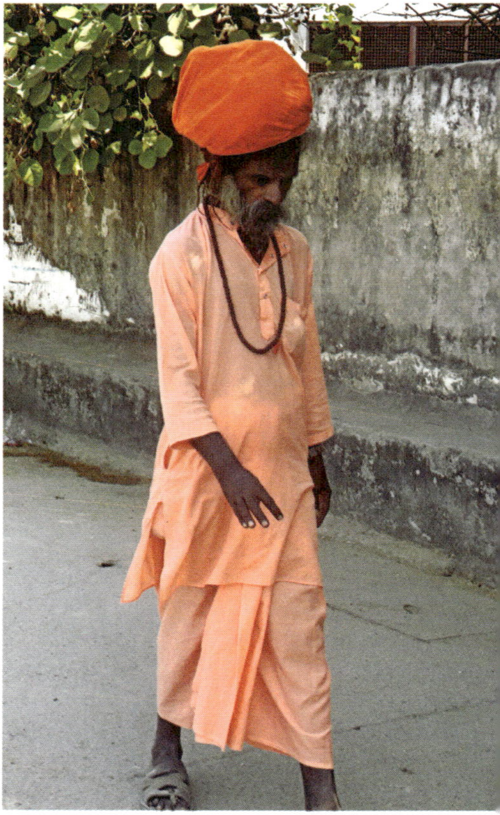

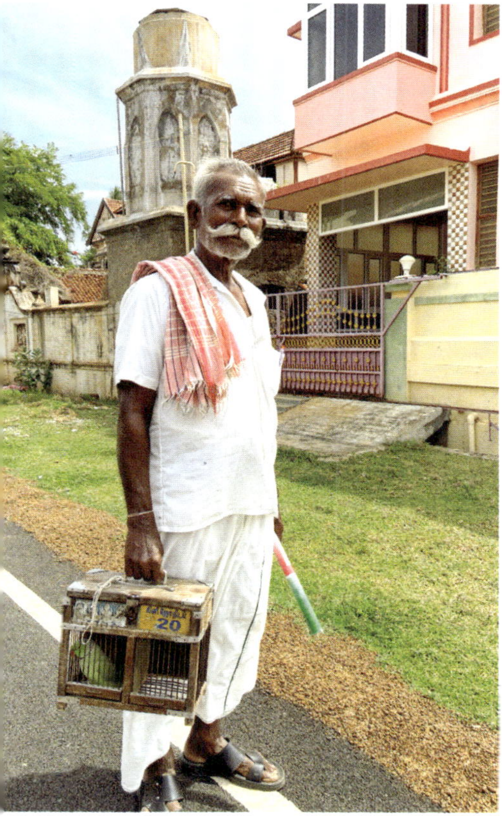
20

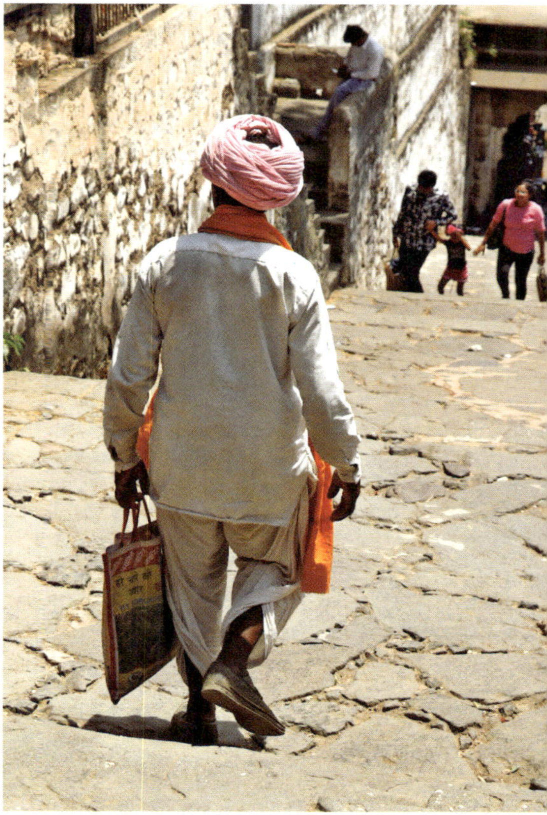

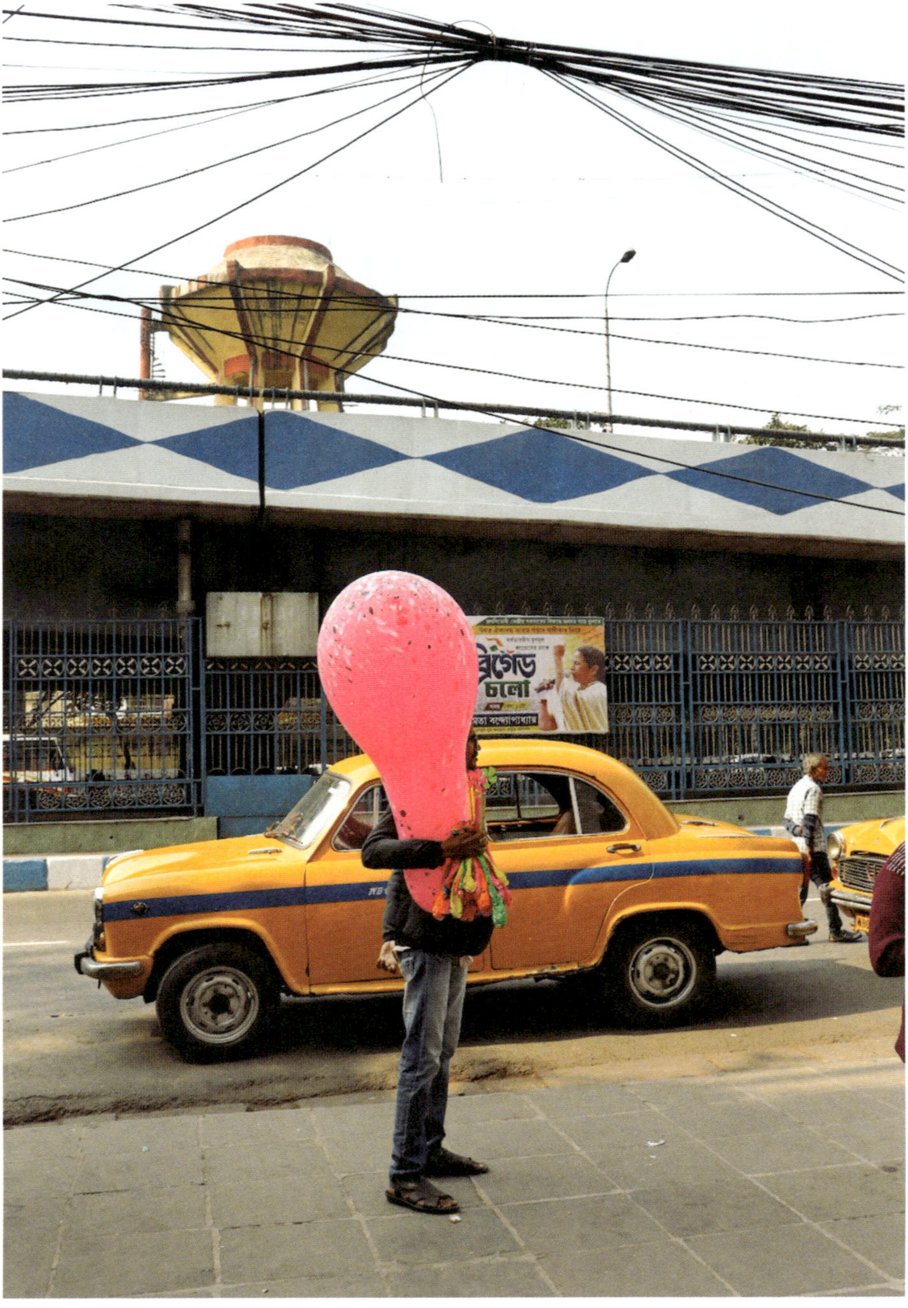
চলো

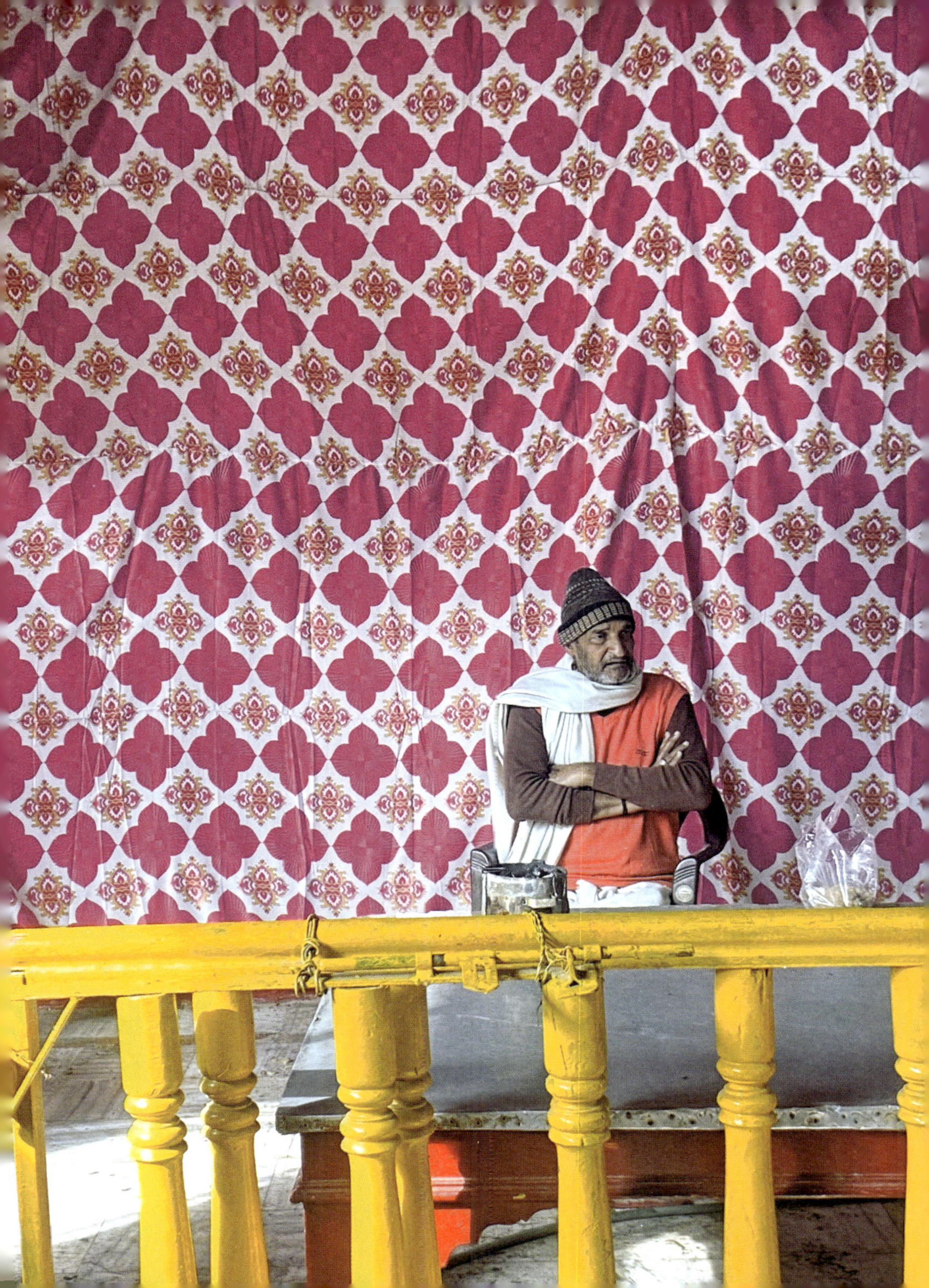

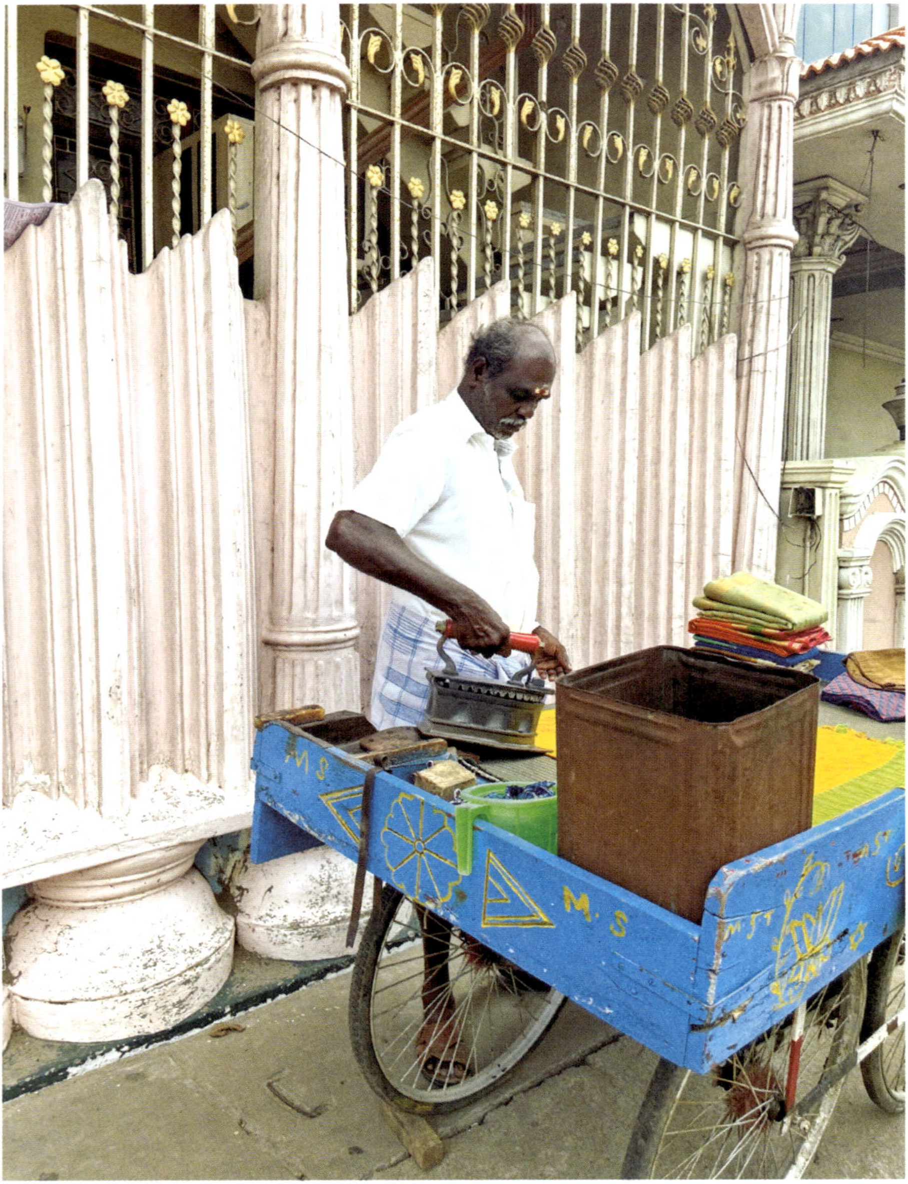
M S
M. S

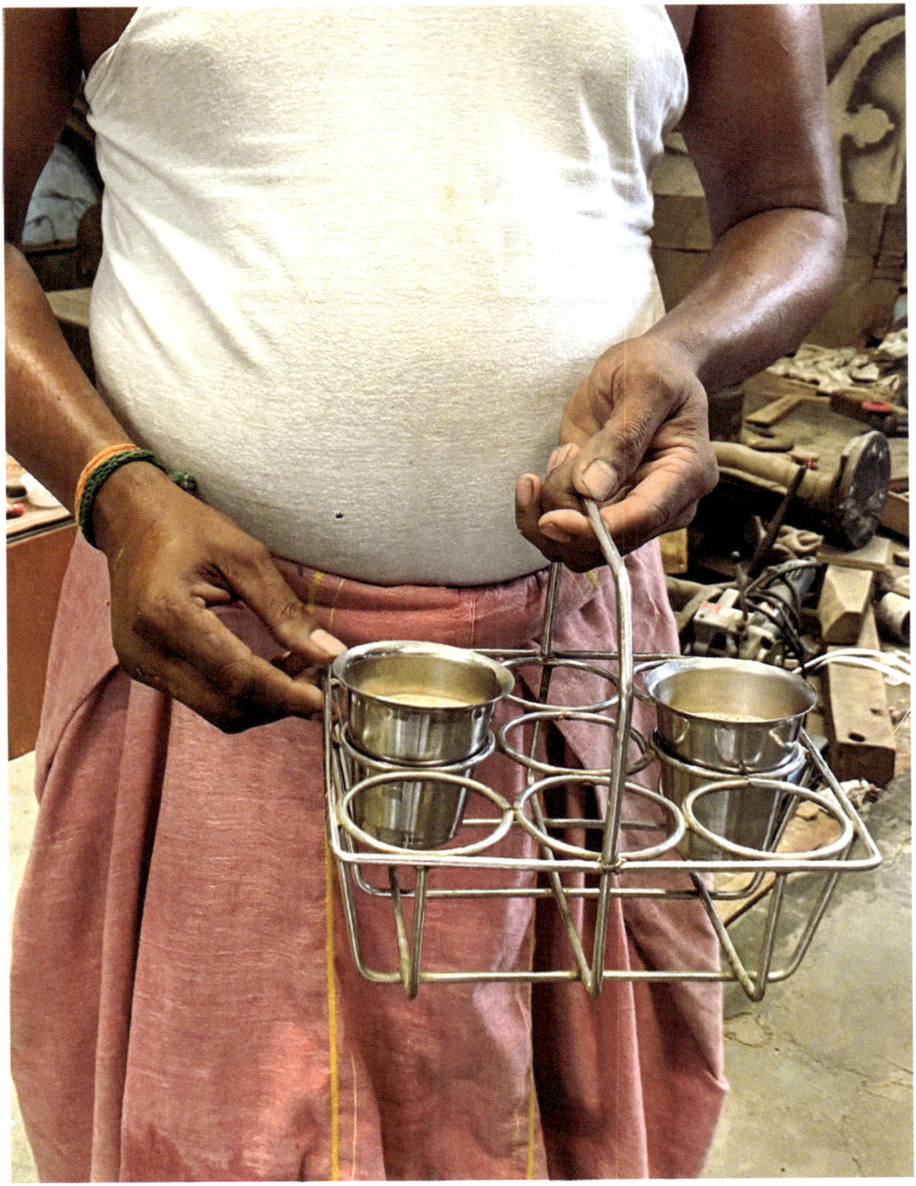

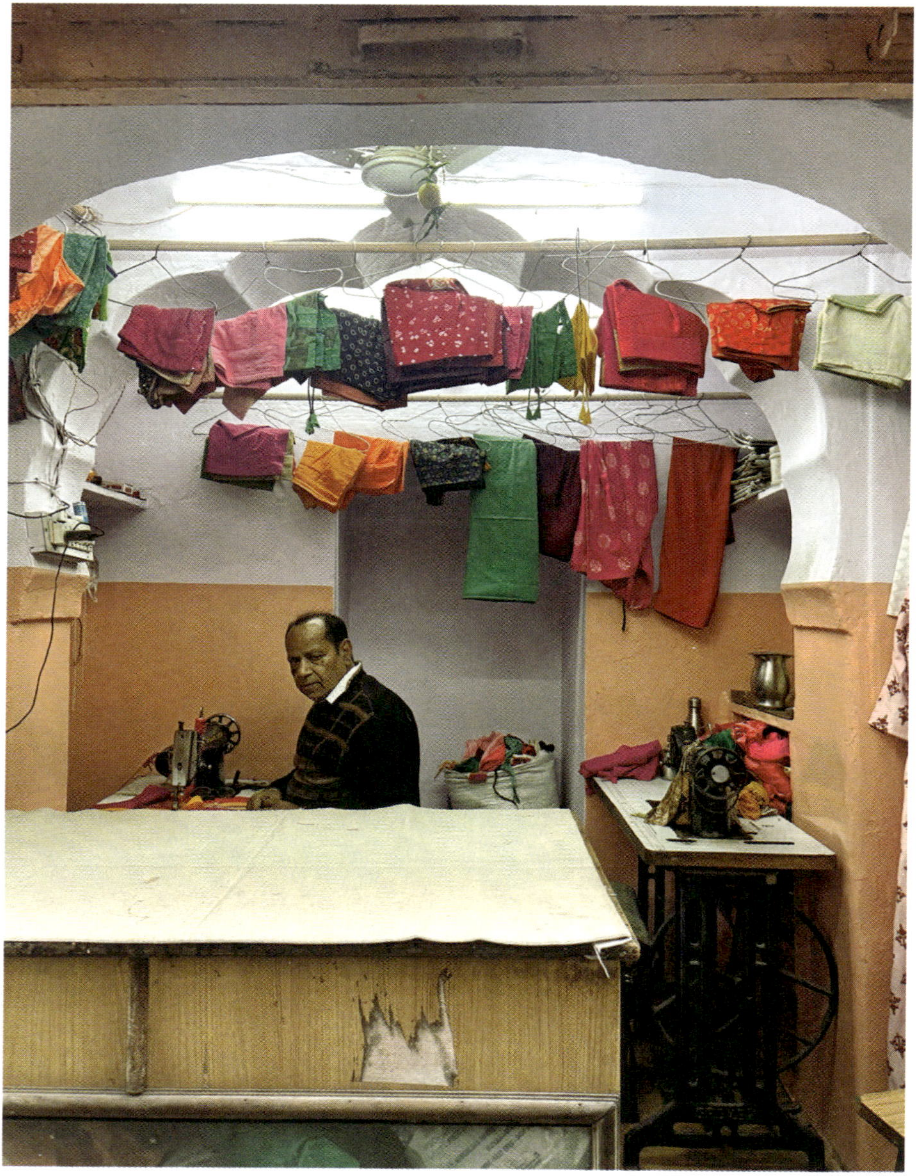

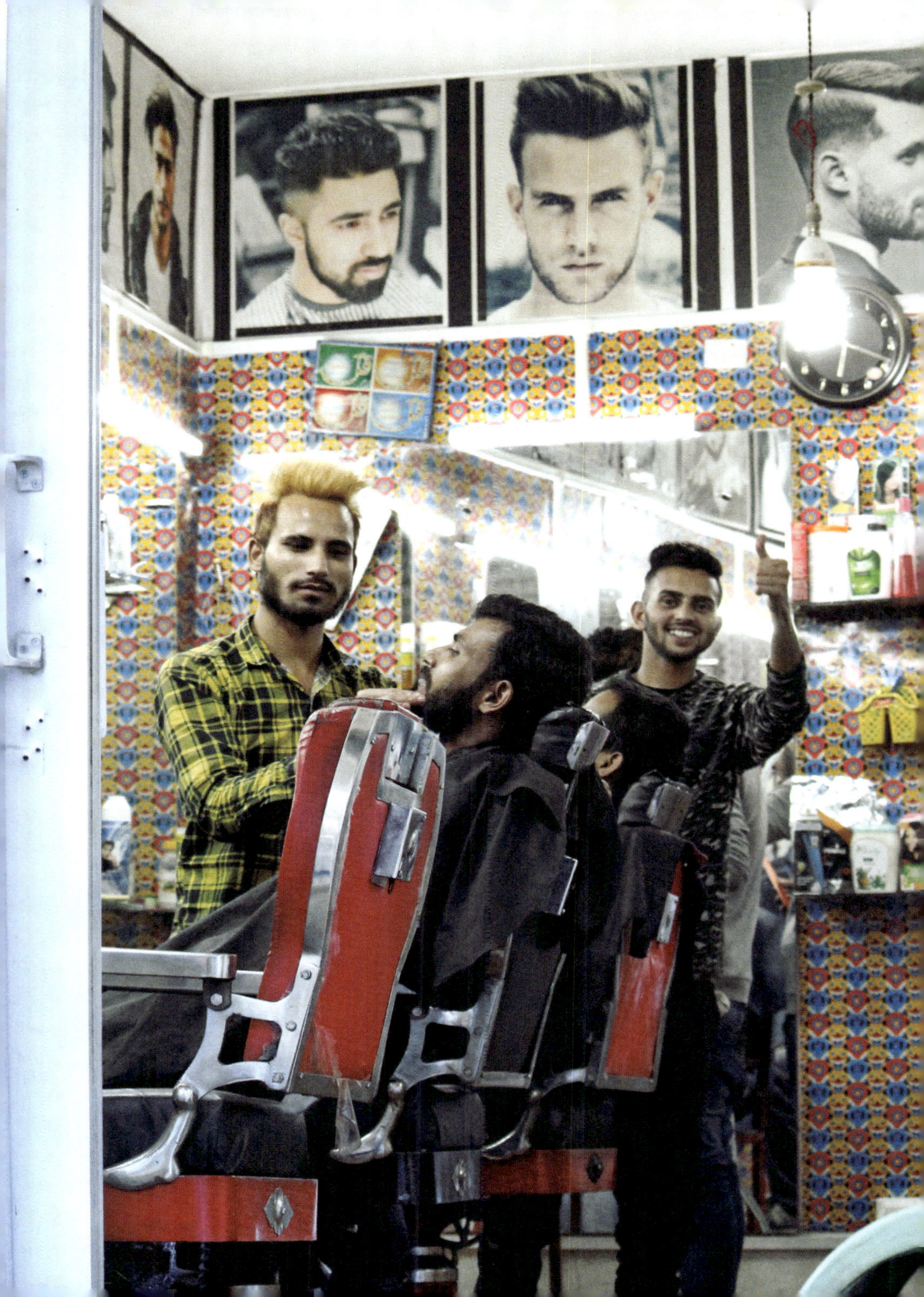

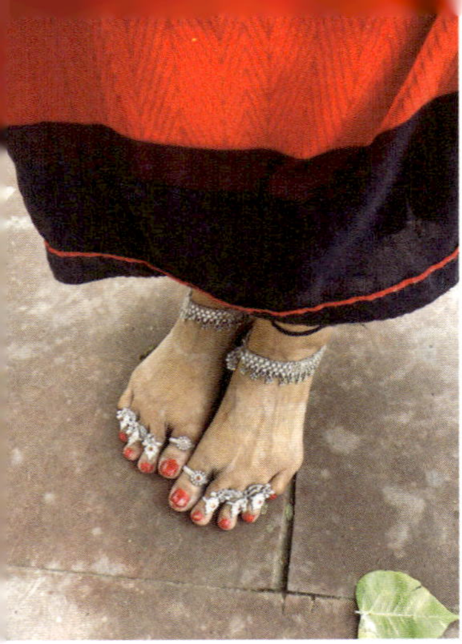
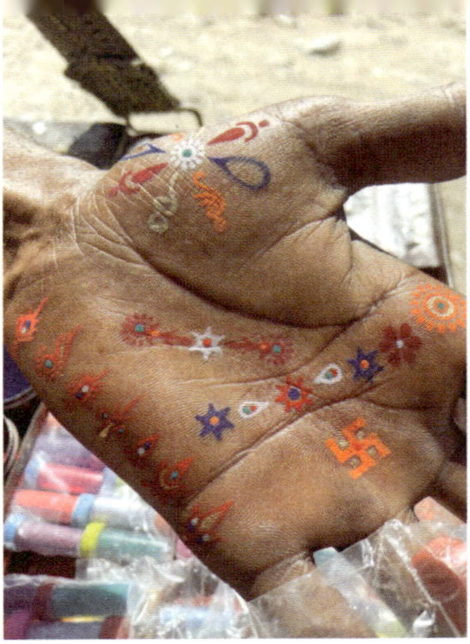
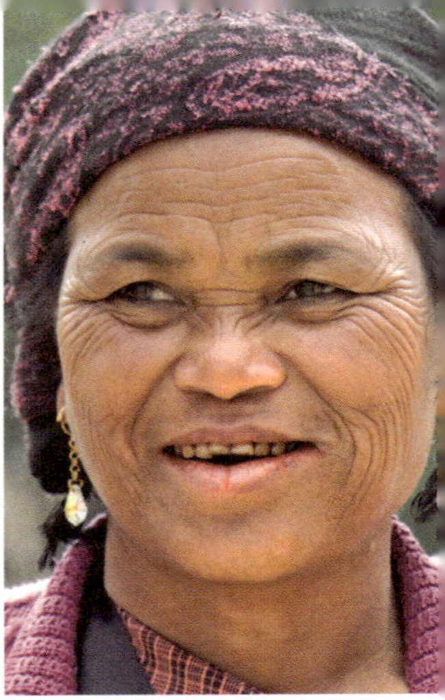
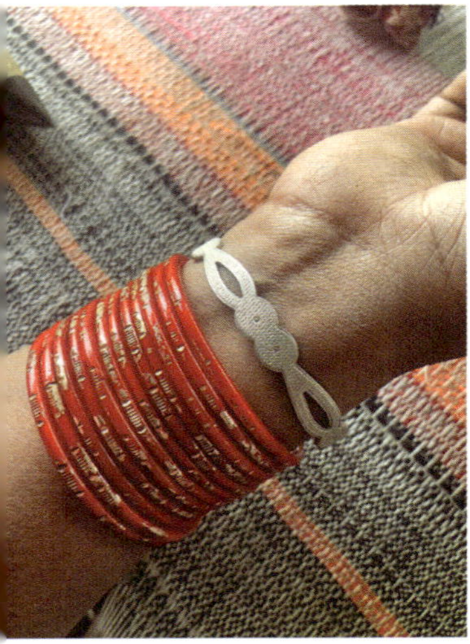
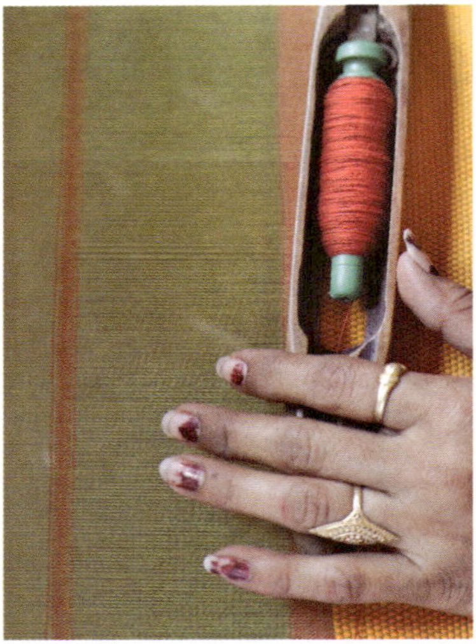
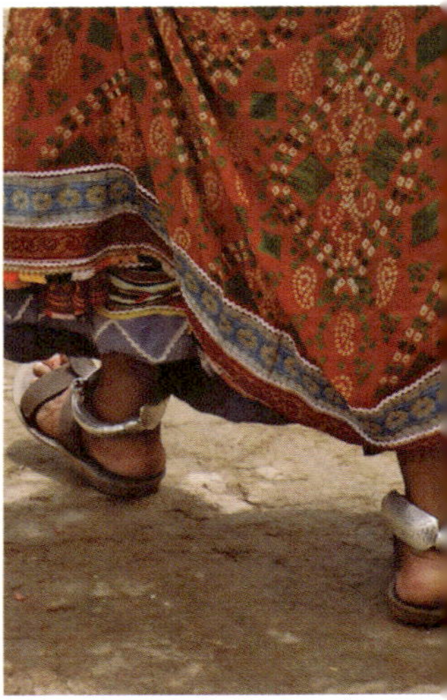
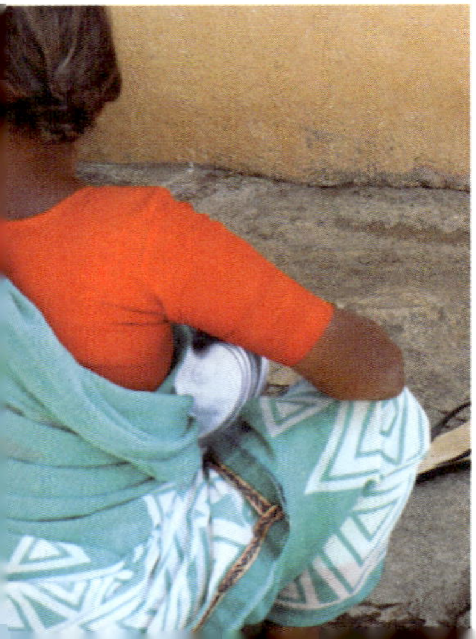
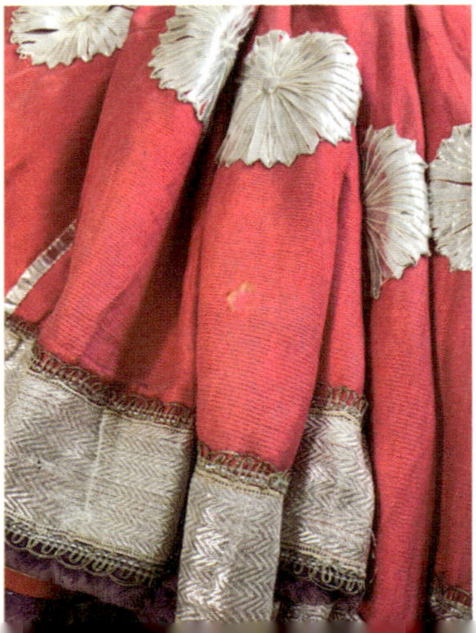
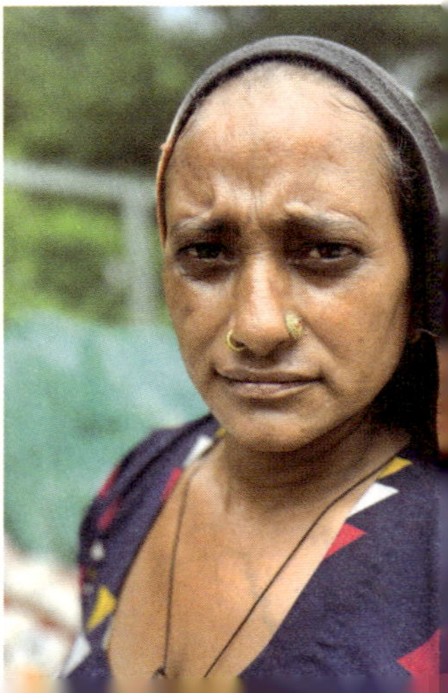

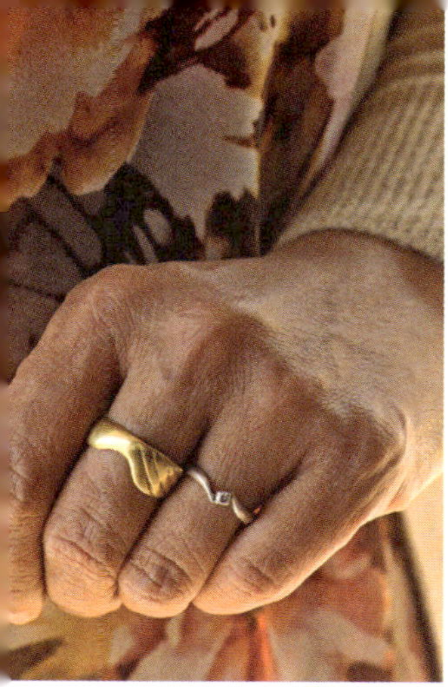
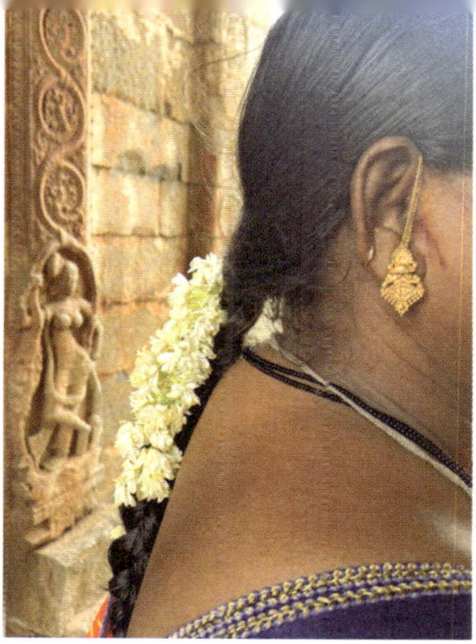
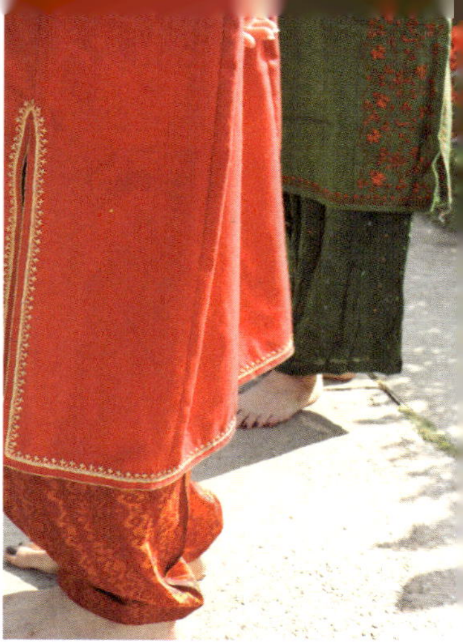
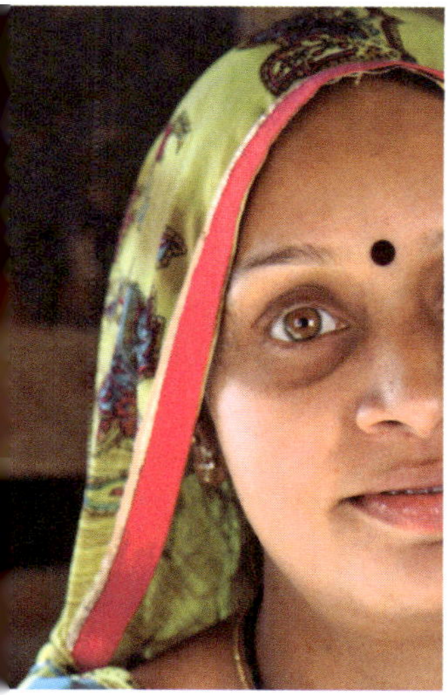
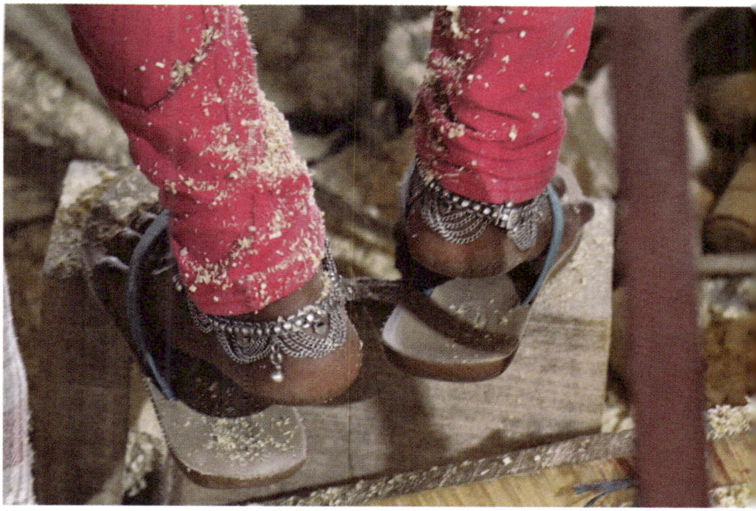
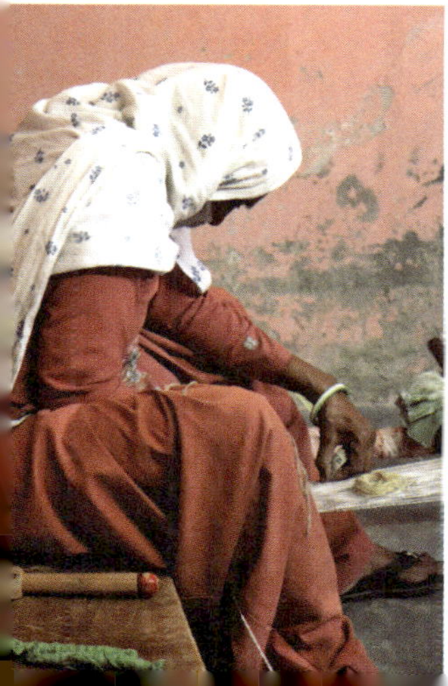
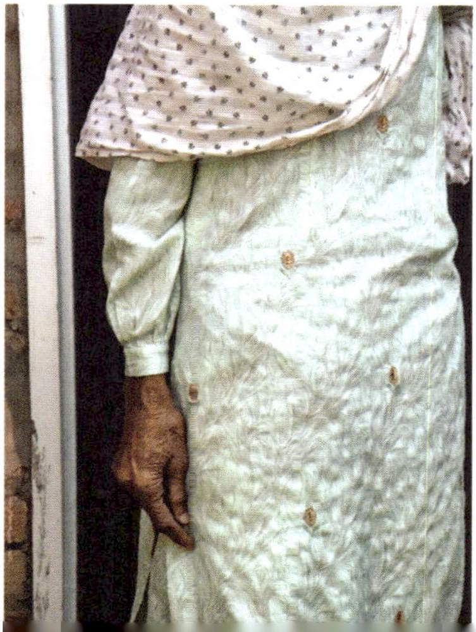
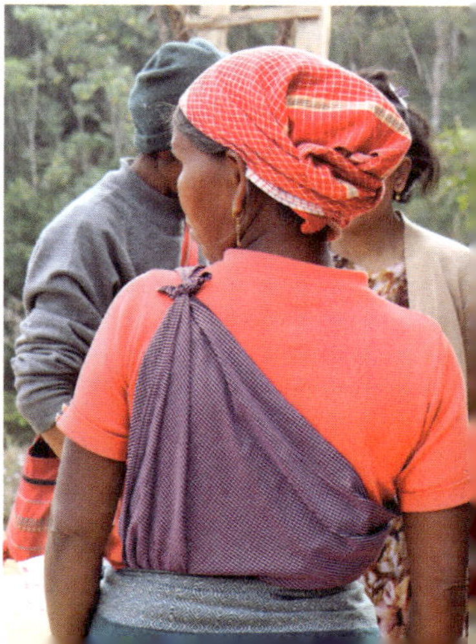

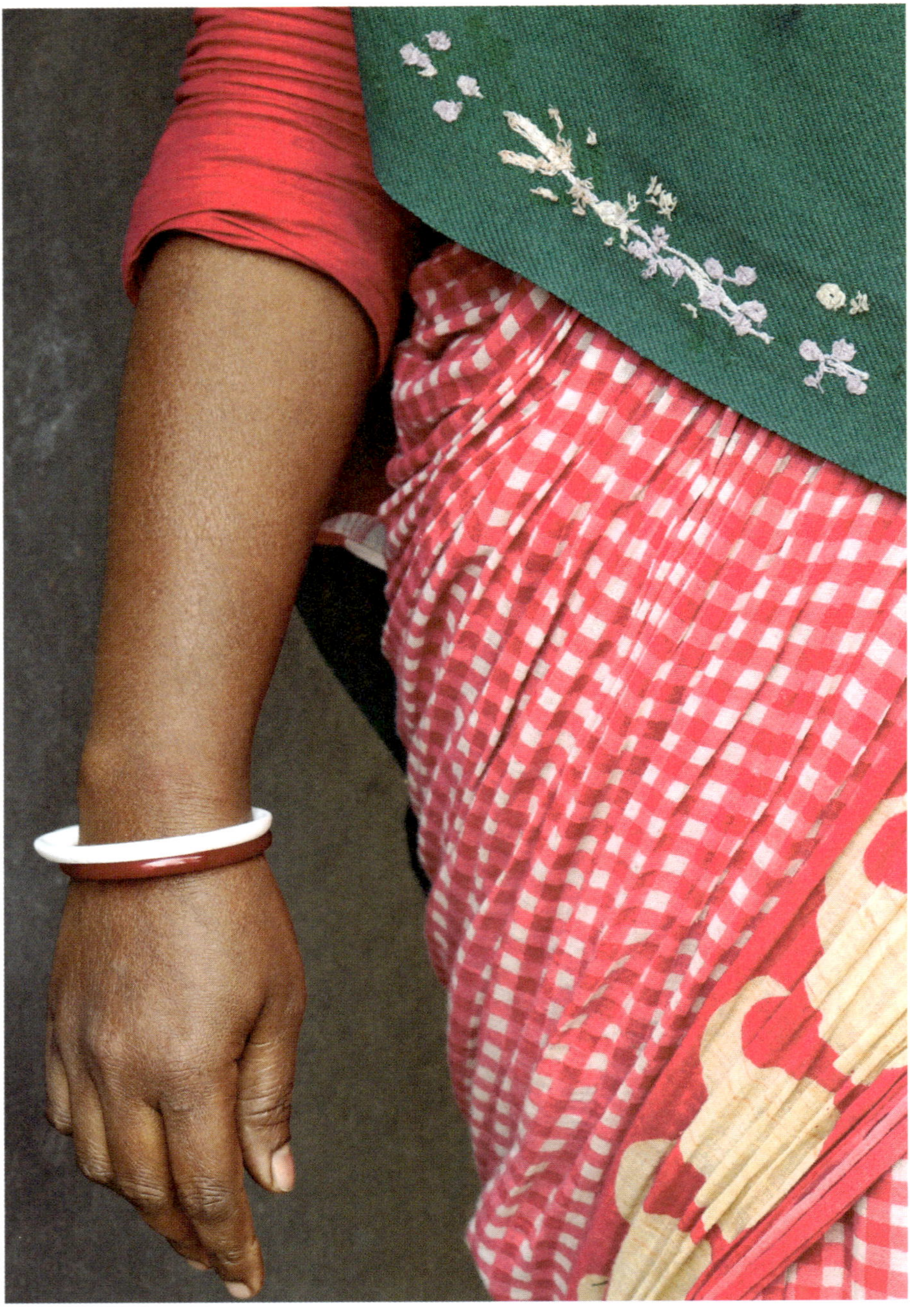

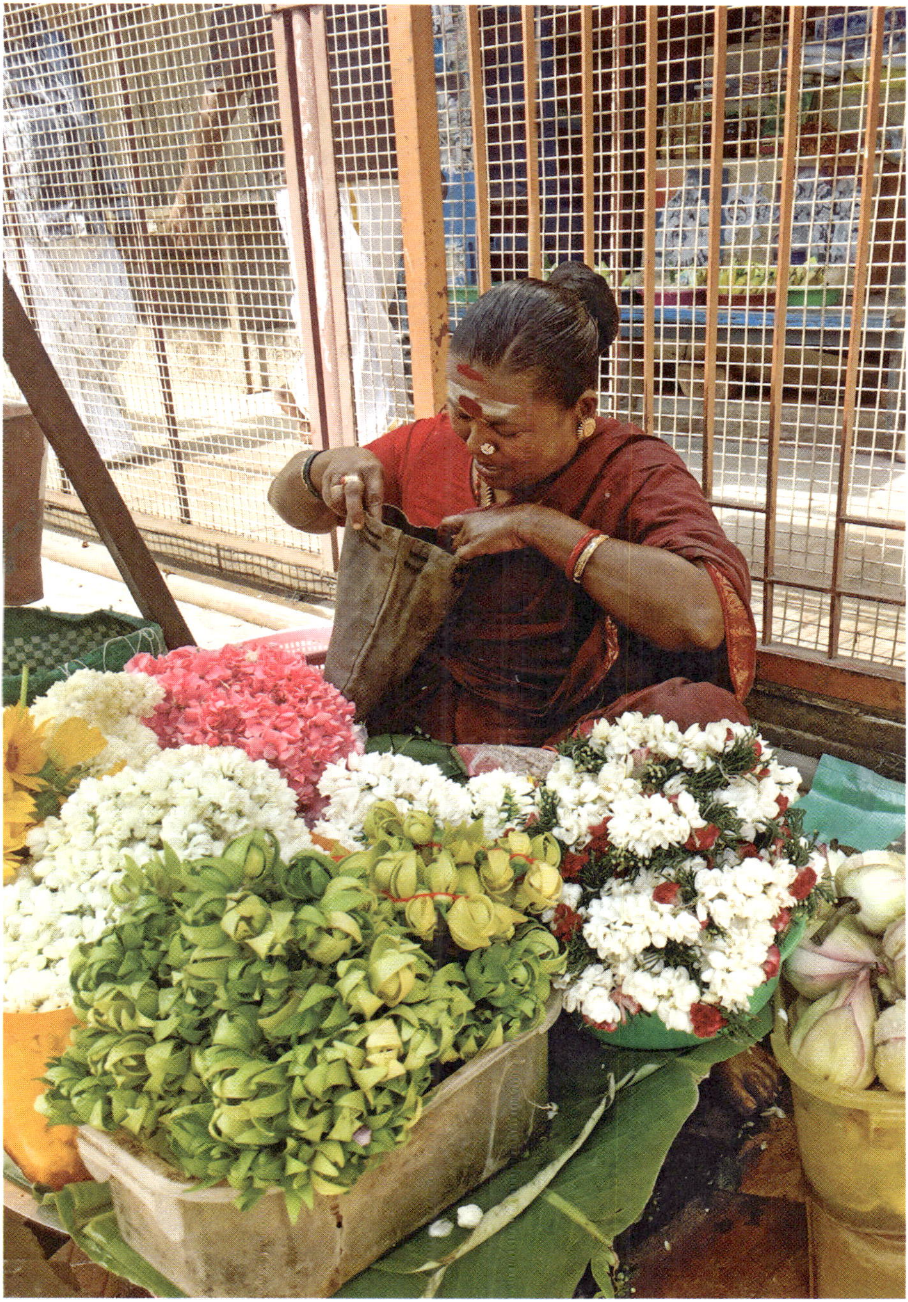

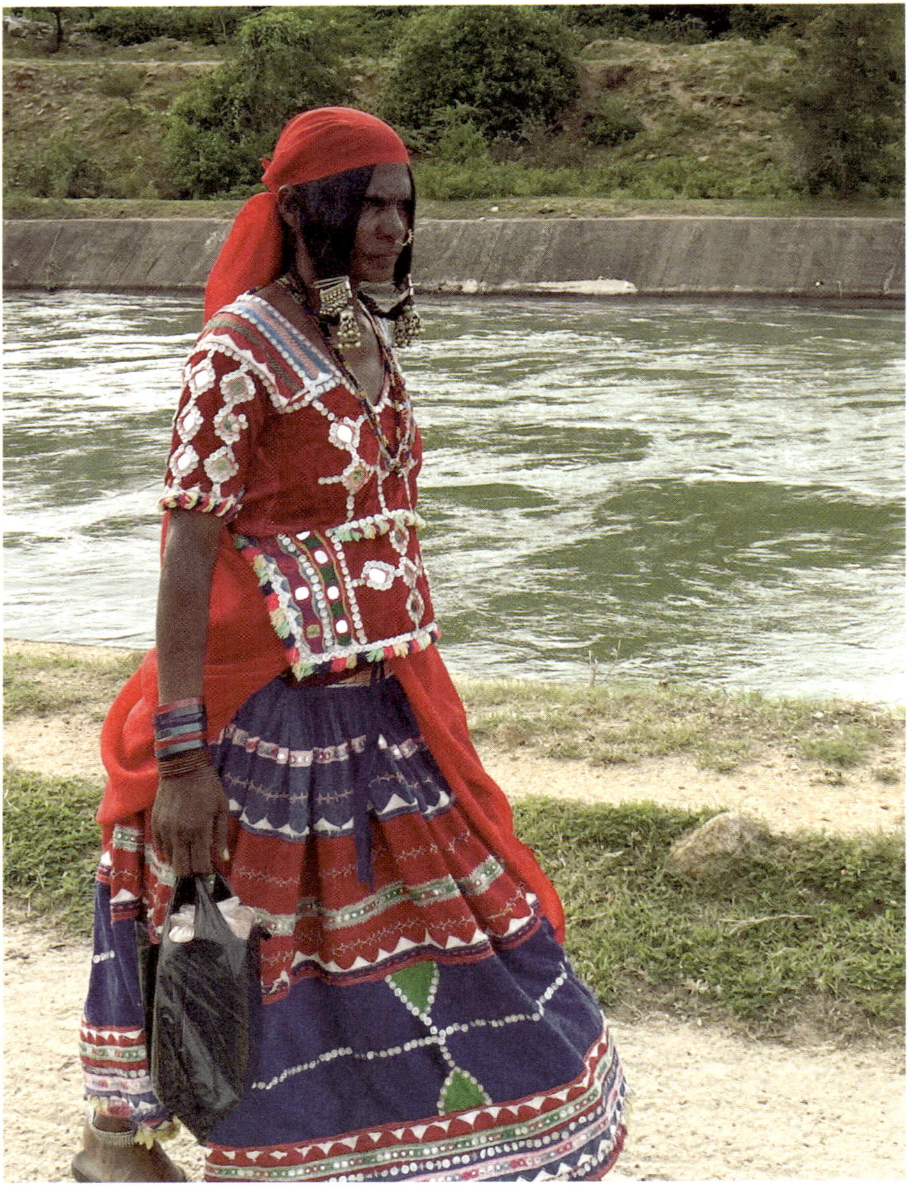

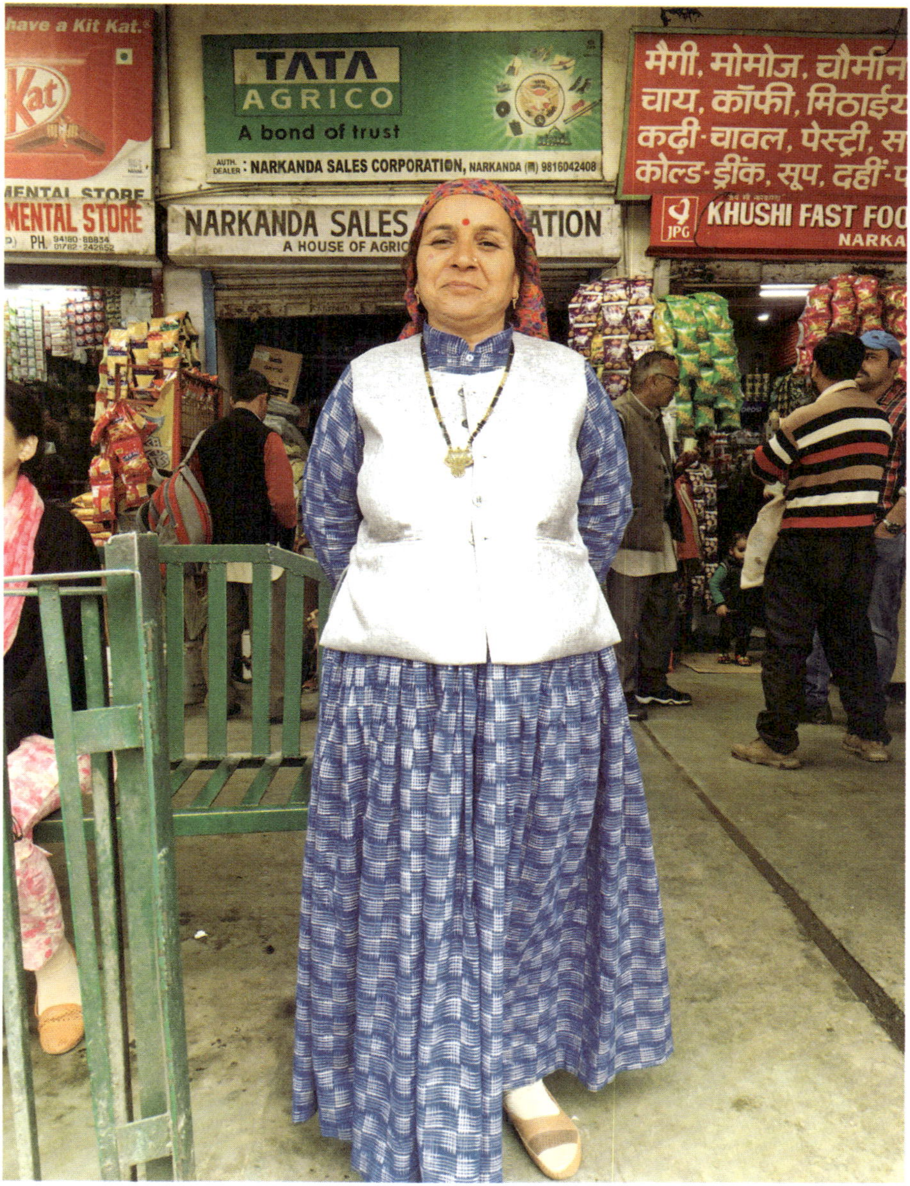
have a Kit Kat.
TATA
AGRICO
A bond of trust
AUTH. DEALER : NARKANDA SALES CORPORATION, NARKANDA 9816042408
NARKANDA SALES
A HOUSE OF AGRIC
मैगी, मोमोज, चौमीन
चाय, कॉफी, मिठाई
कढ़ी-चावल, पेस्ट्री,
कोल्ड-ड्रींक, सूप, दहीं
KHUSHI FAST FOO
MENTAL STORE

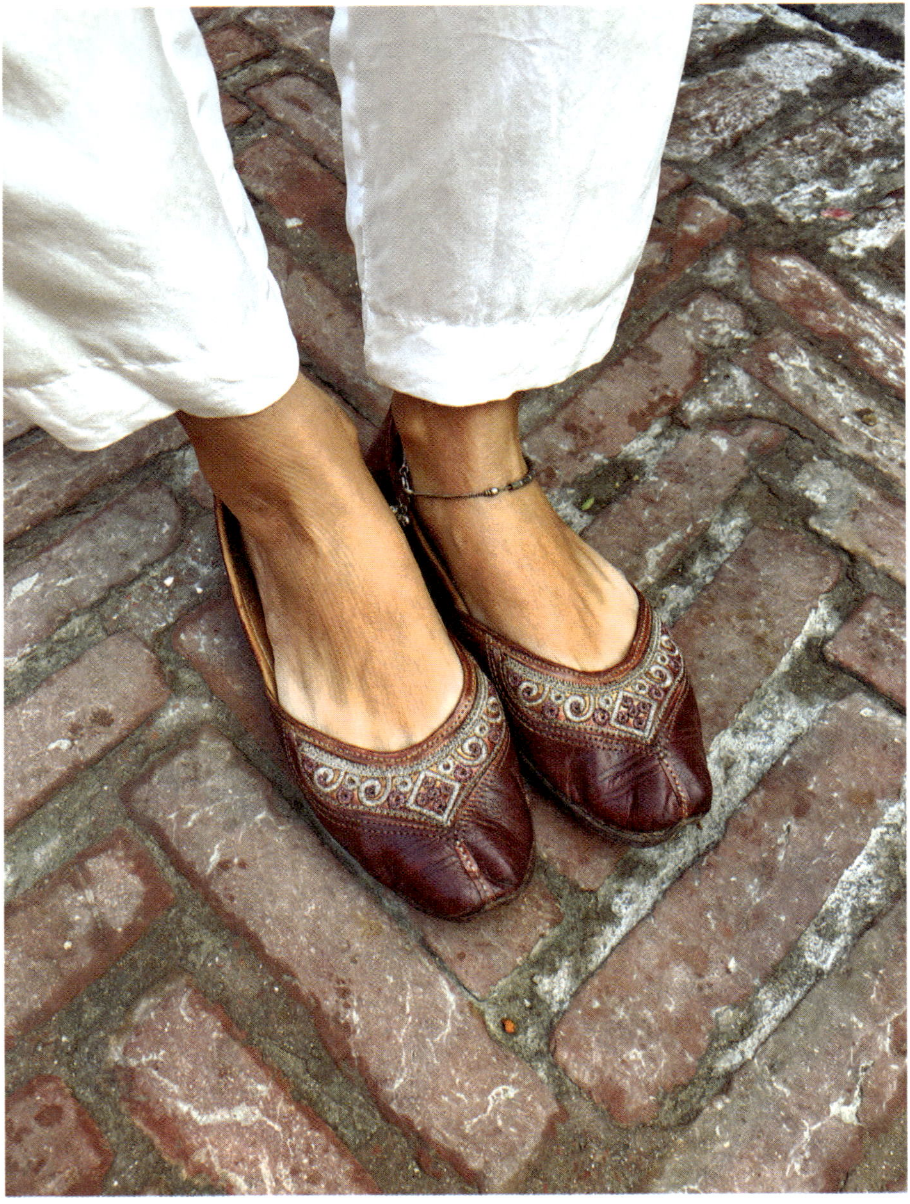

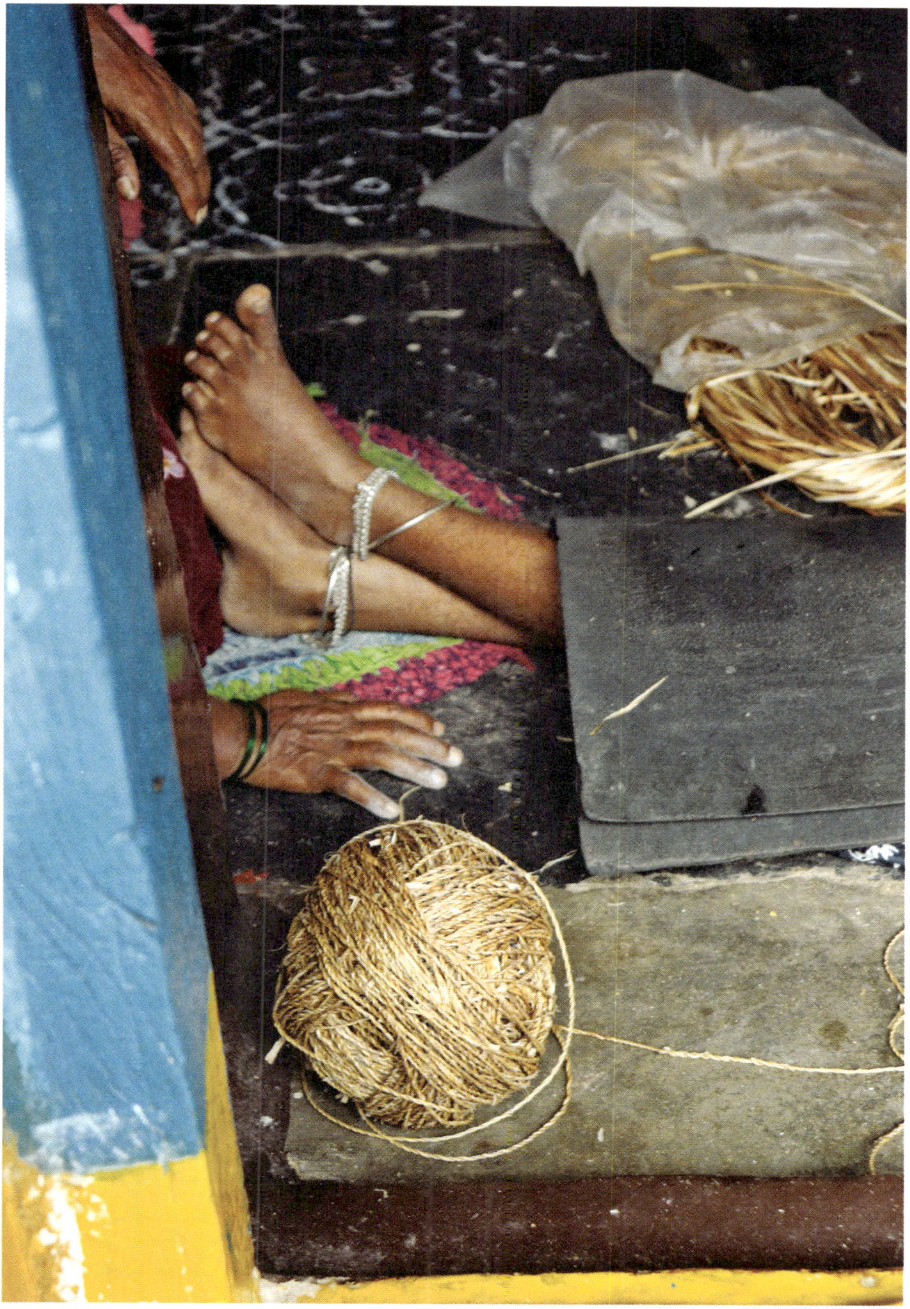

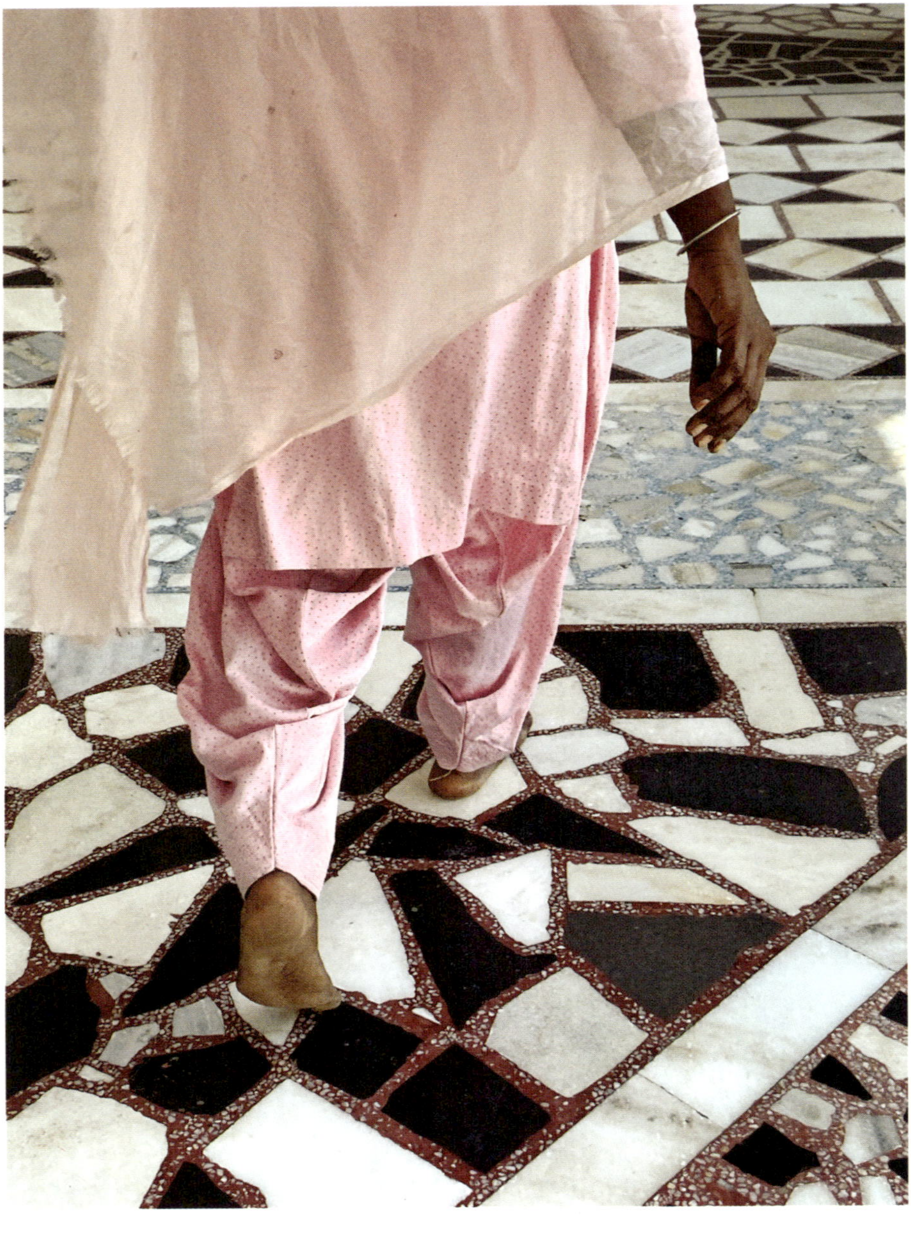

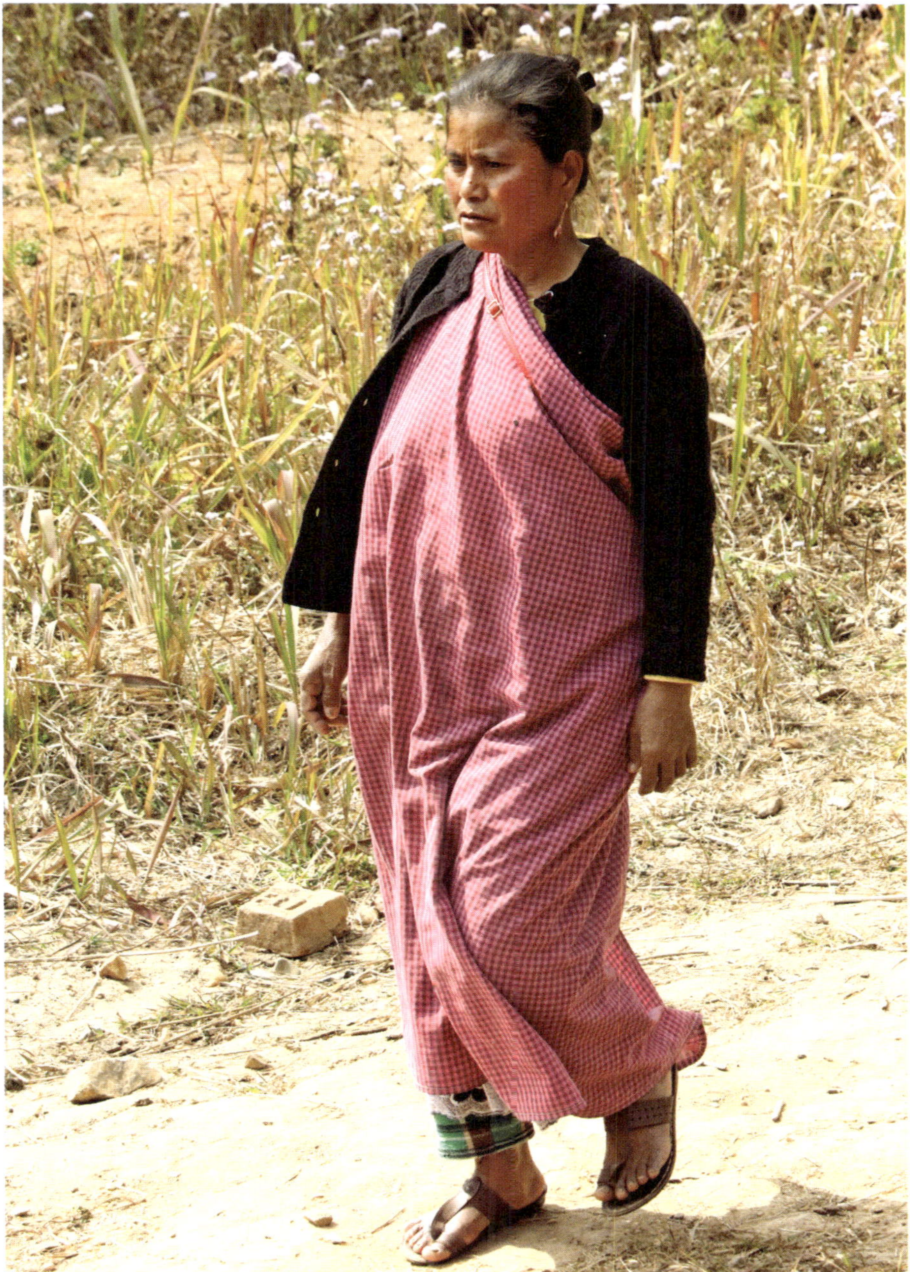

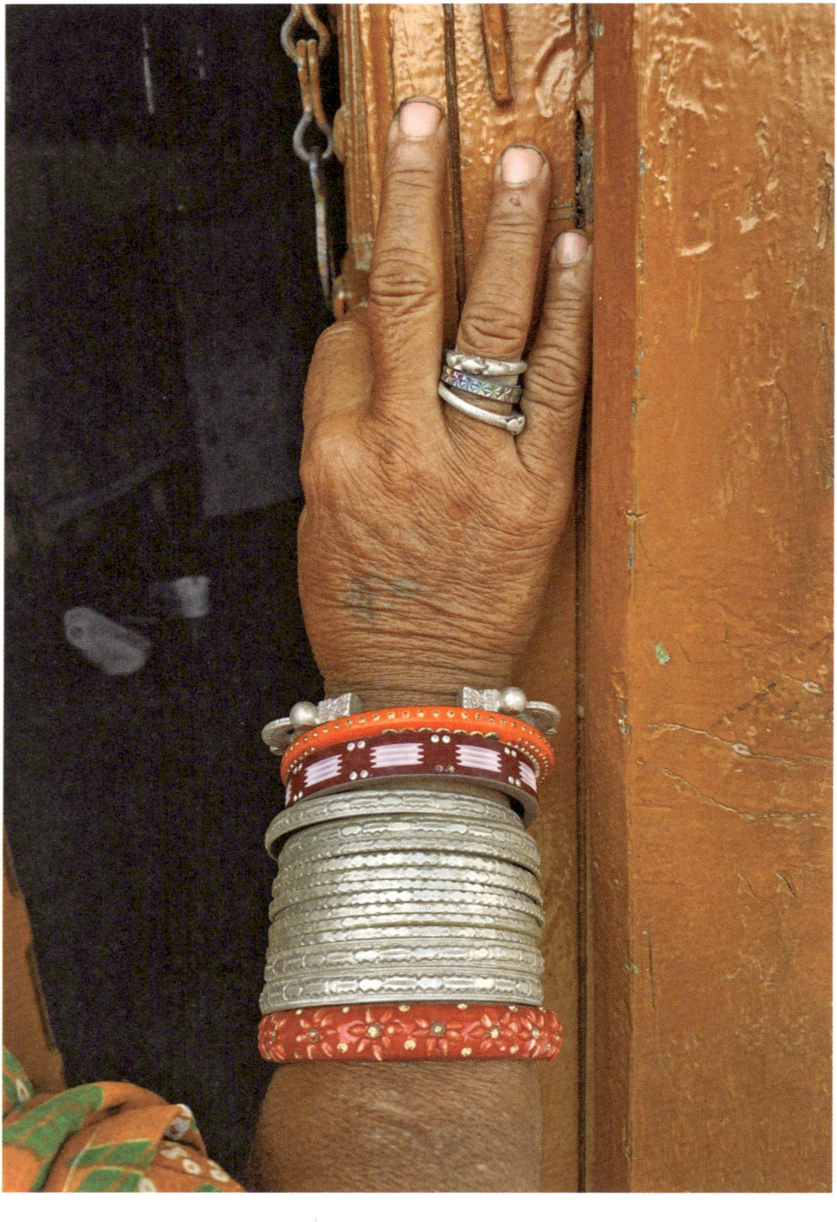

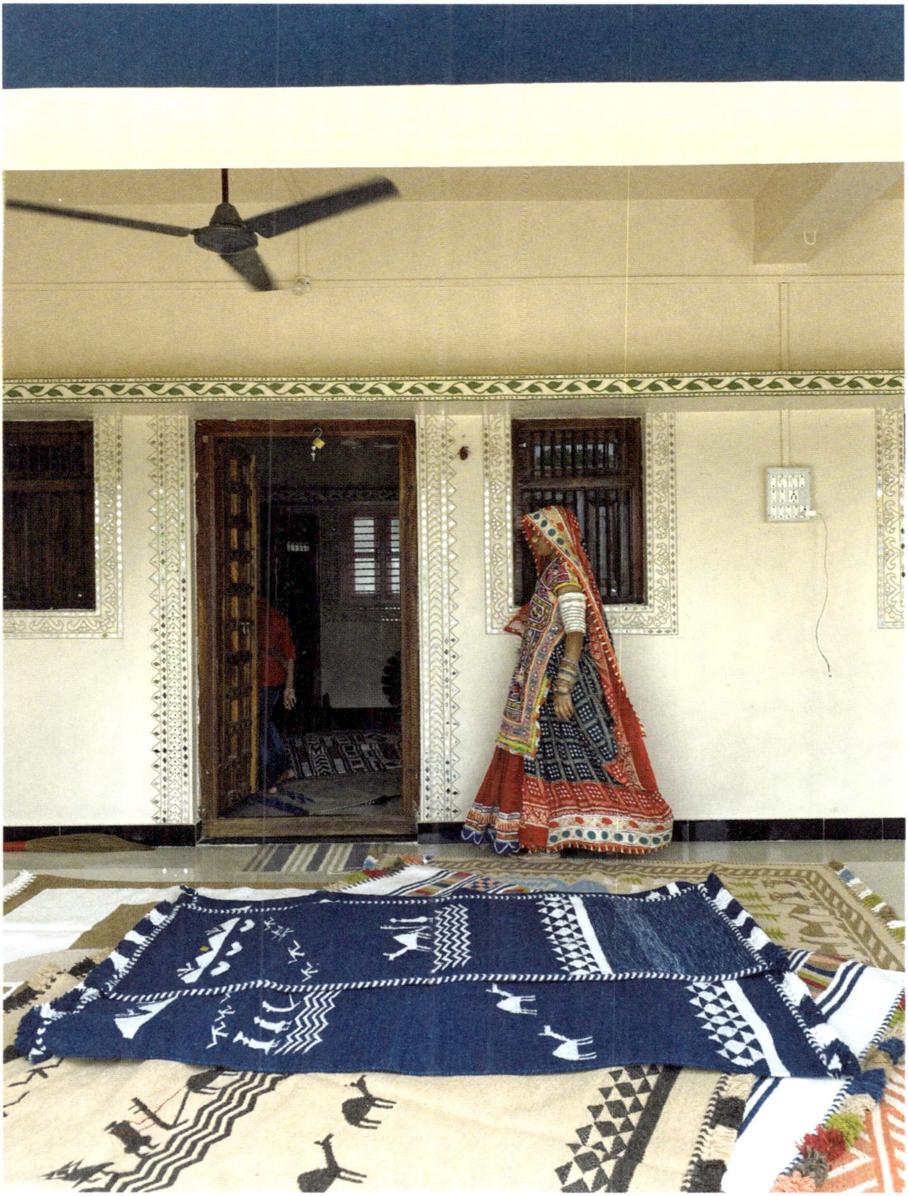

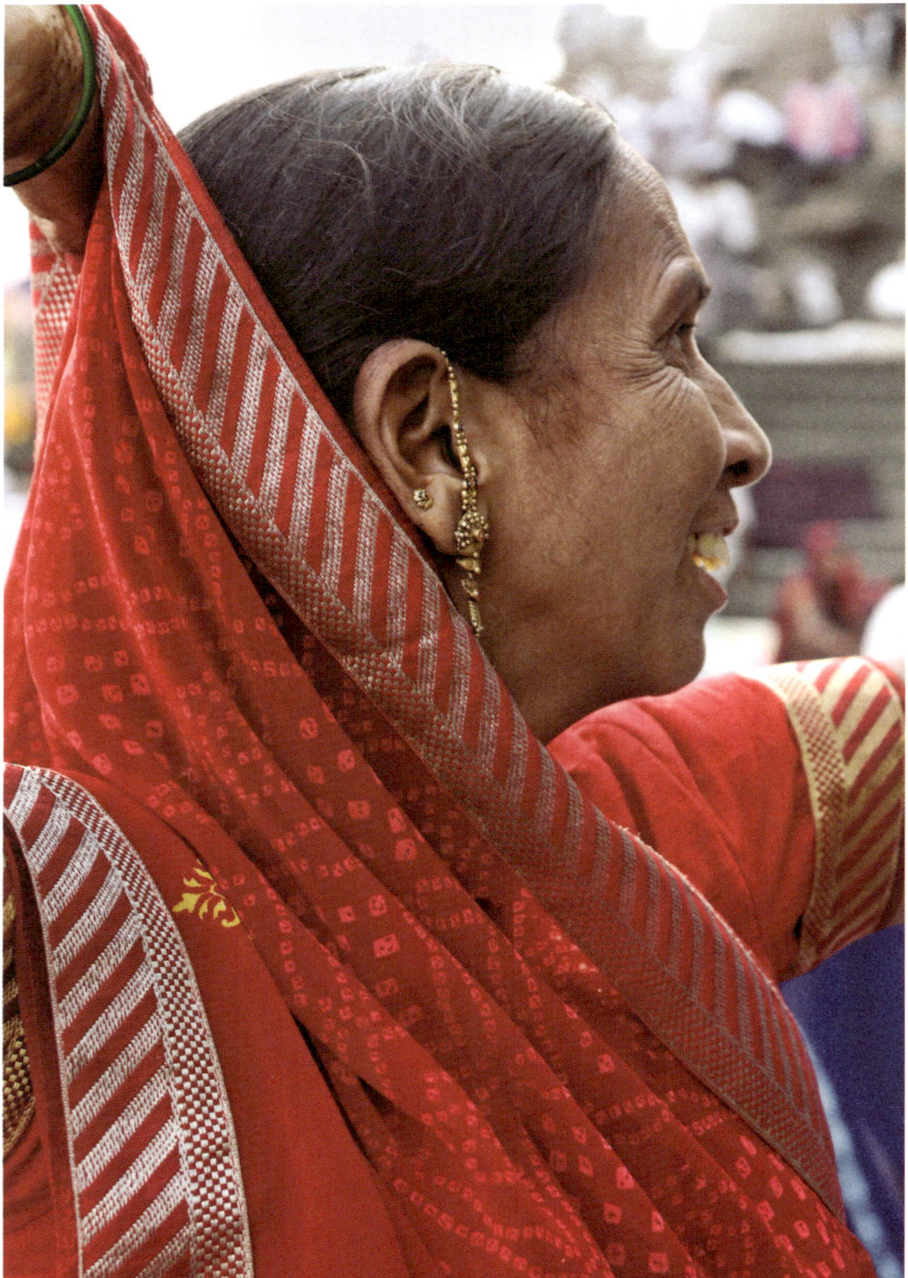

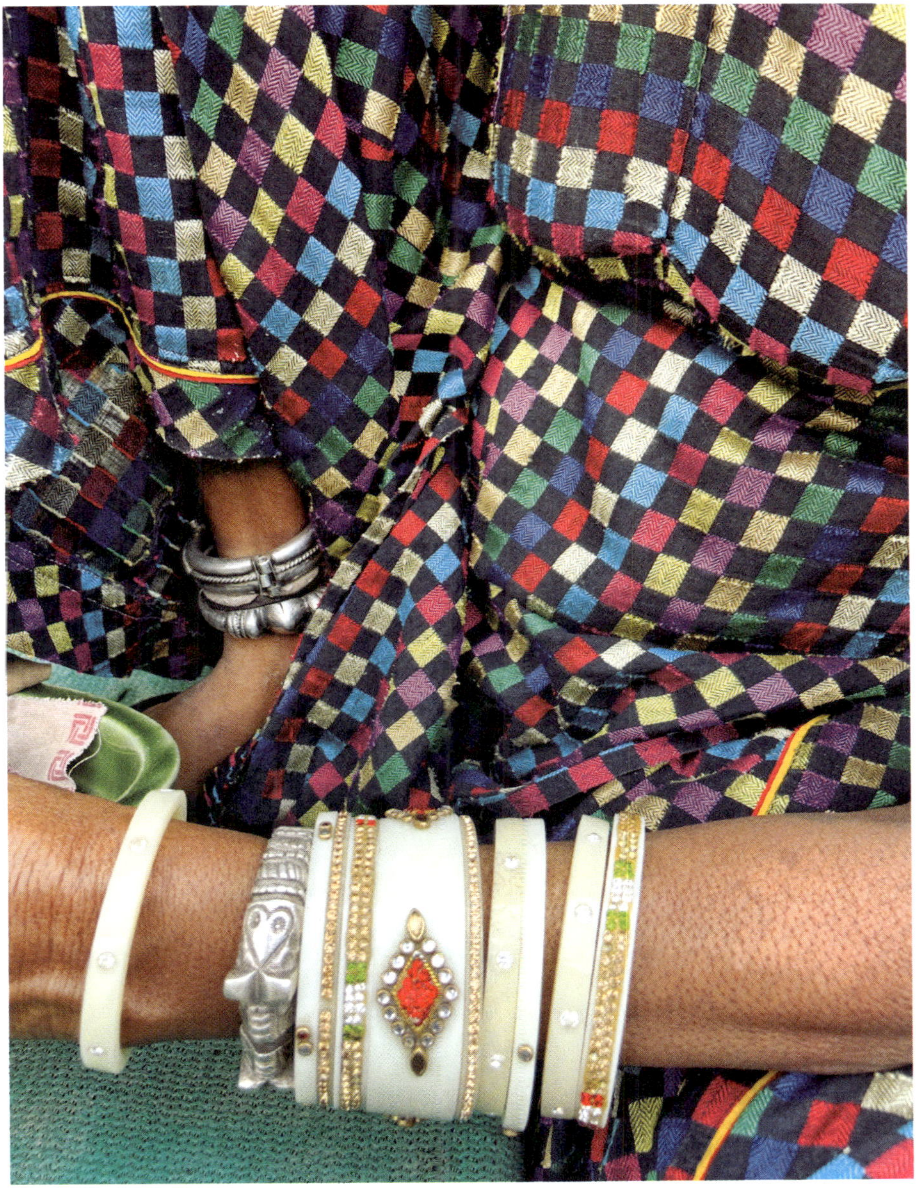

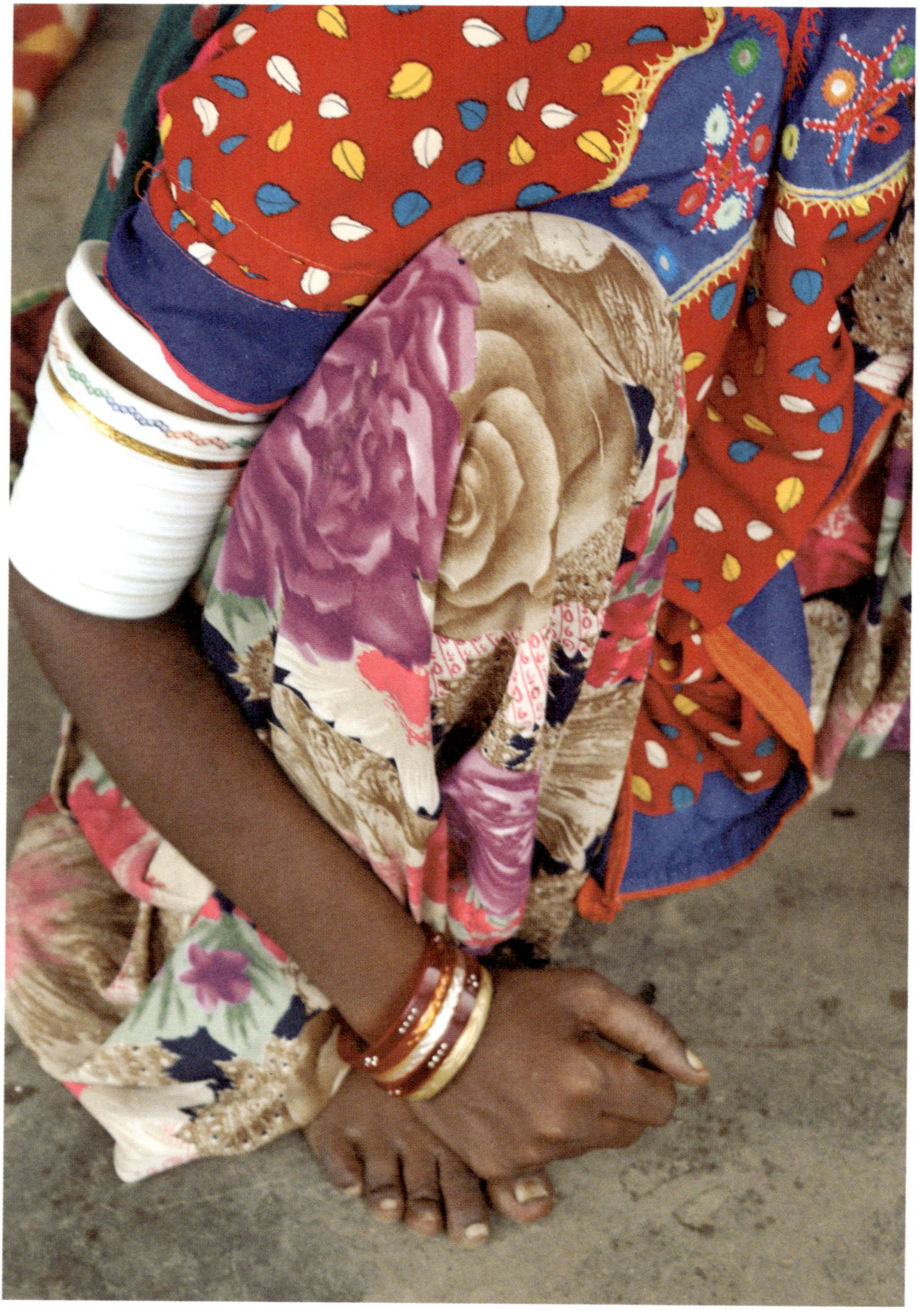

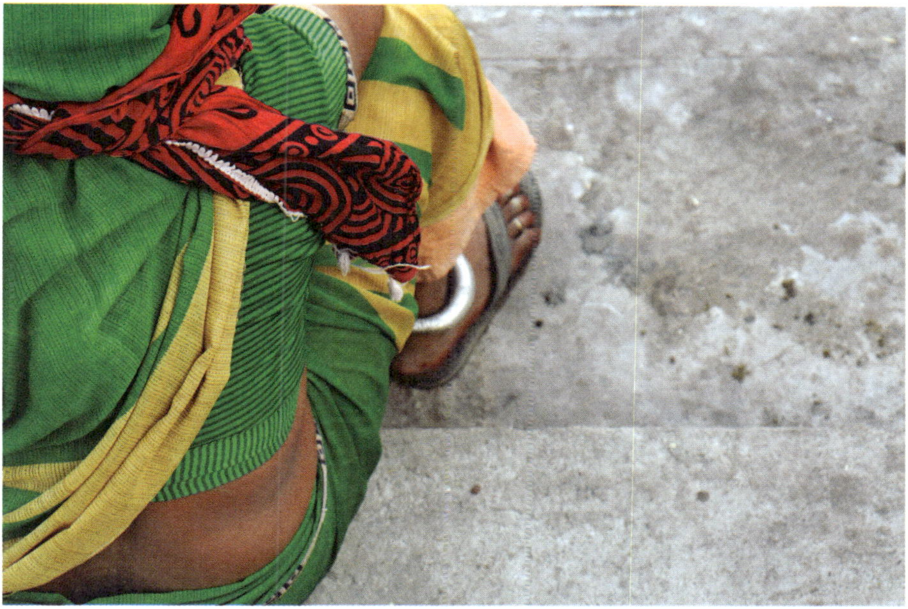

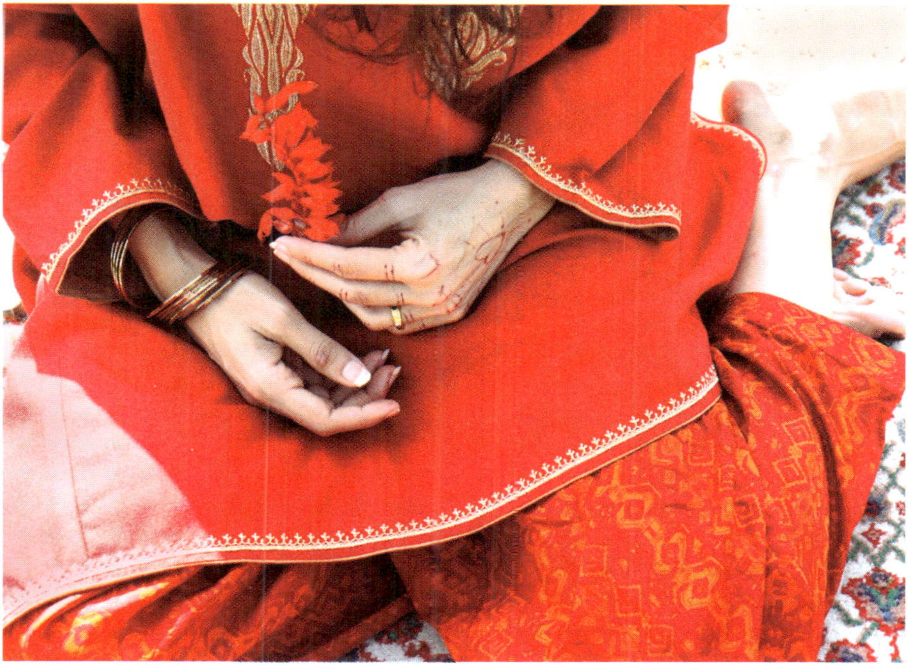

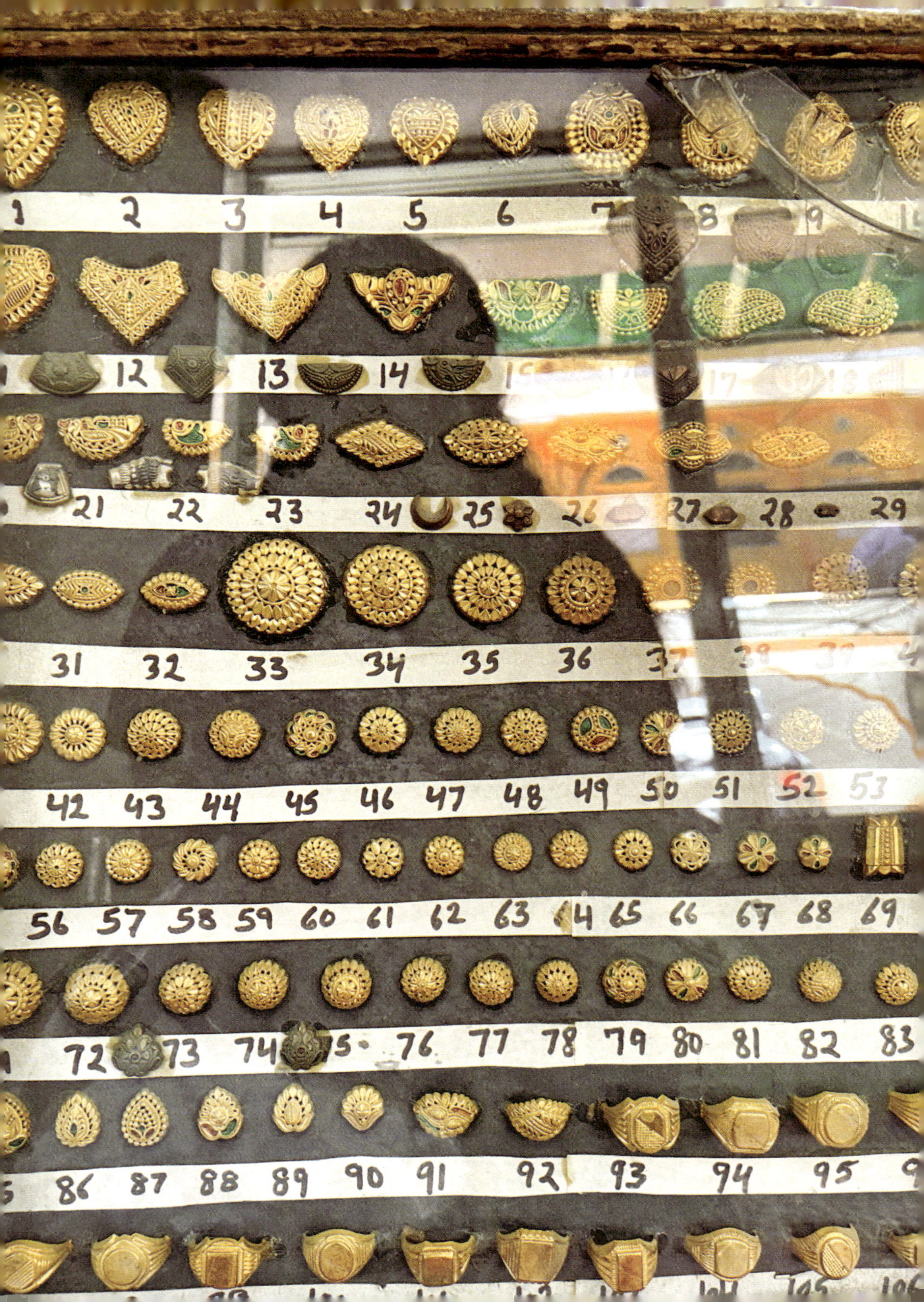
1 2 3 4 5 6 7 8 9
12 13 14
21 22 23 24 25 26 27 28 29
31 32 33 34 35 36
42 43 44 45 46 47 48 49 50 51 52 53
56 57 58 59 60 61 62 63 65 66 67 68 69
72 73 74 76 77 78 79 80 81 82 83
86 87 88 89 90 91 92 93 94 95

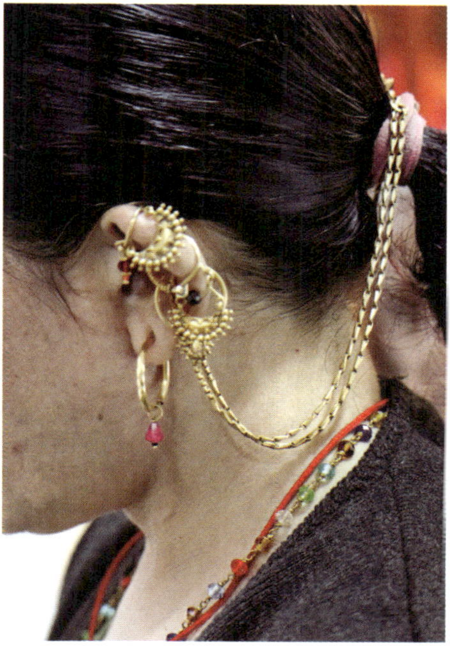

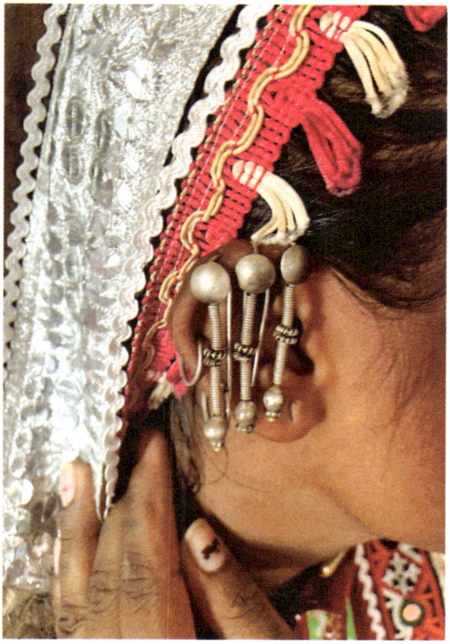

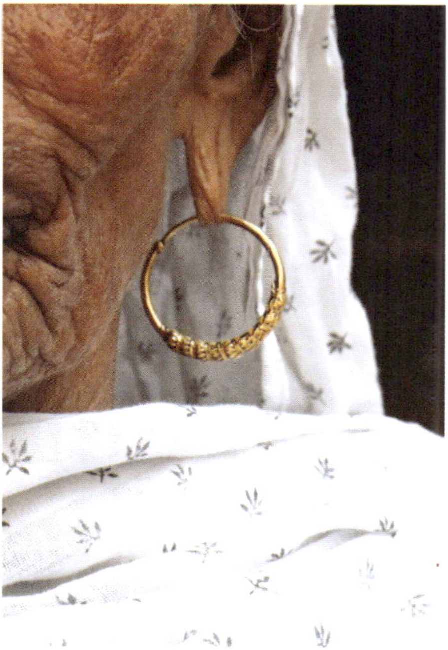

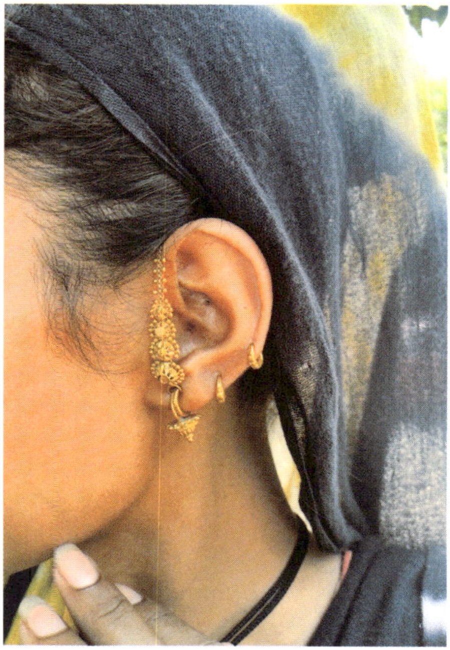

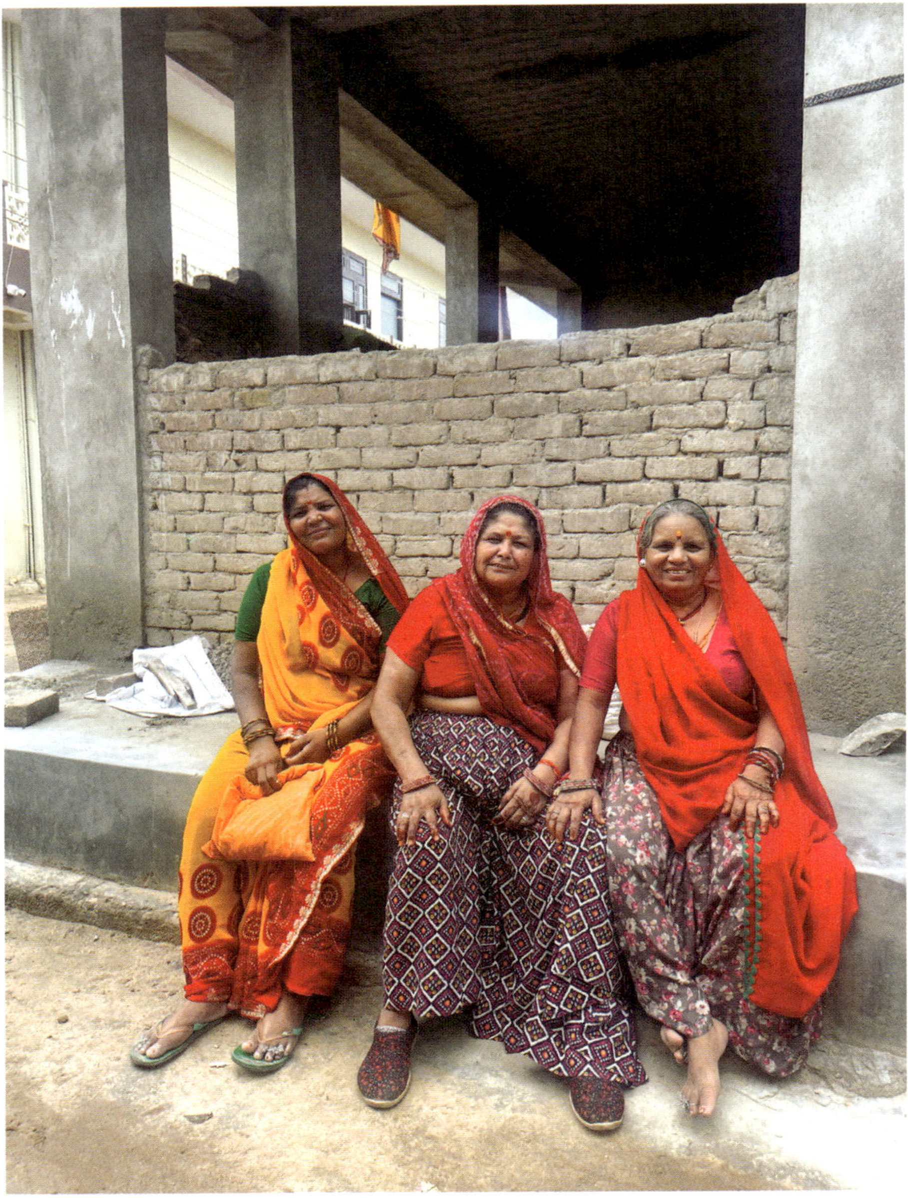

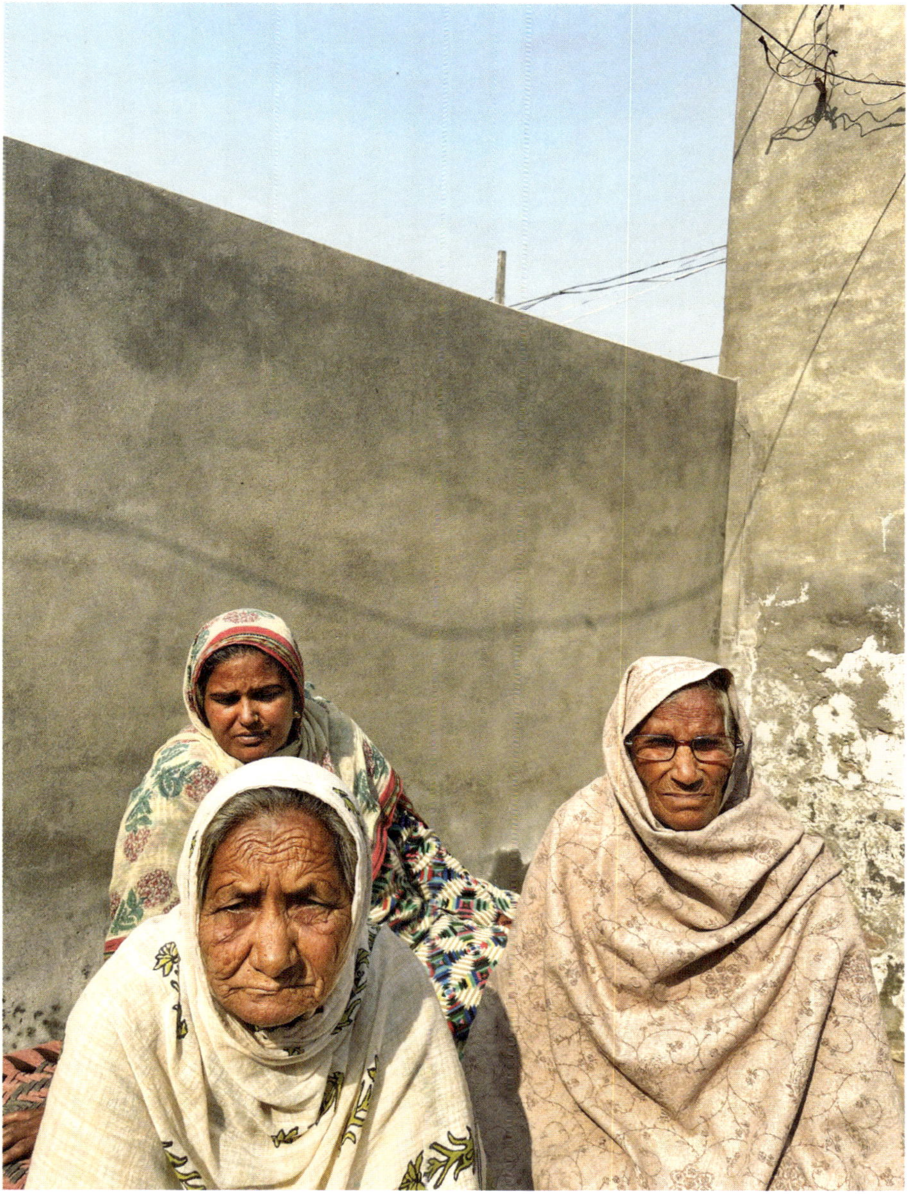

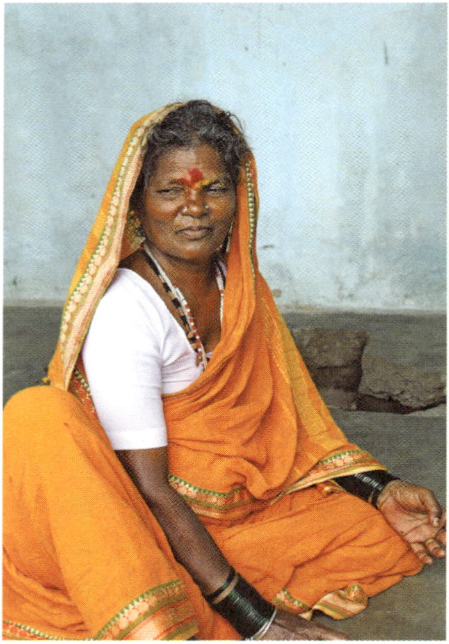
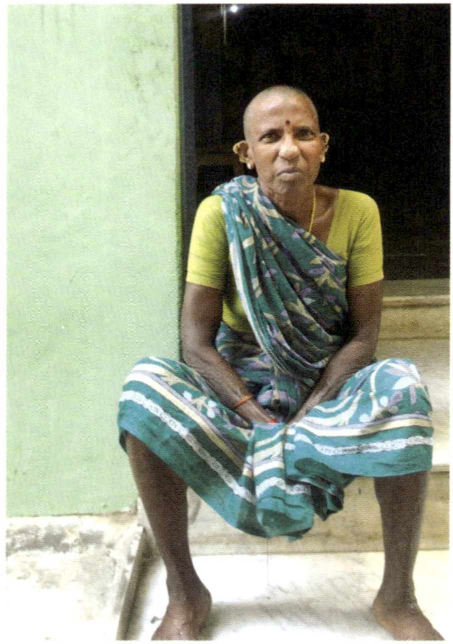
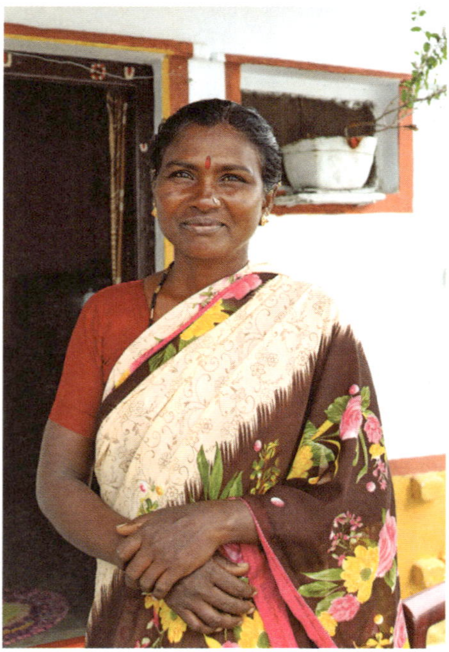
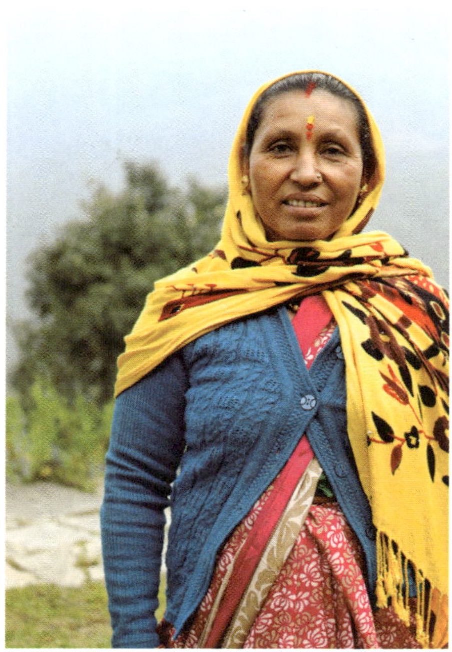

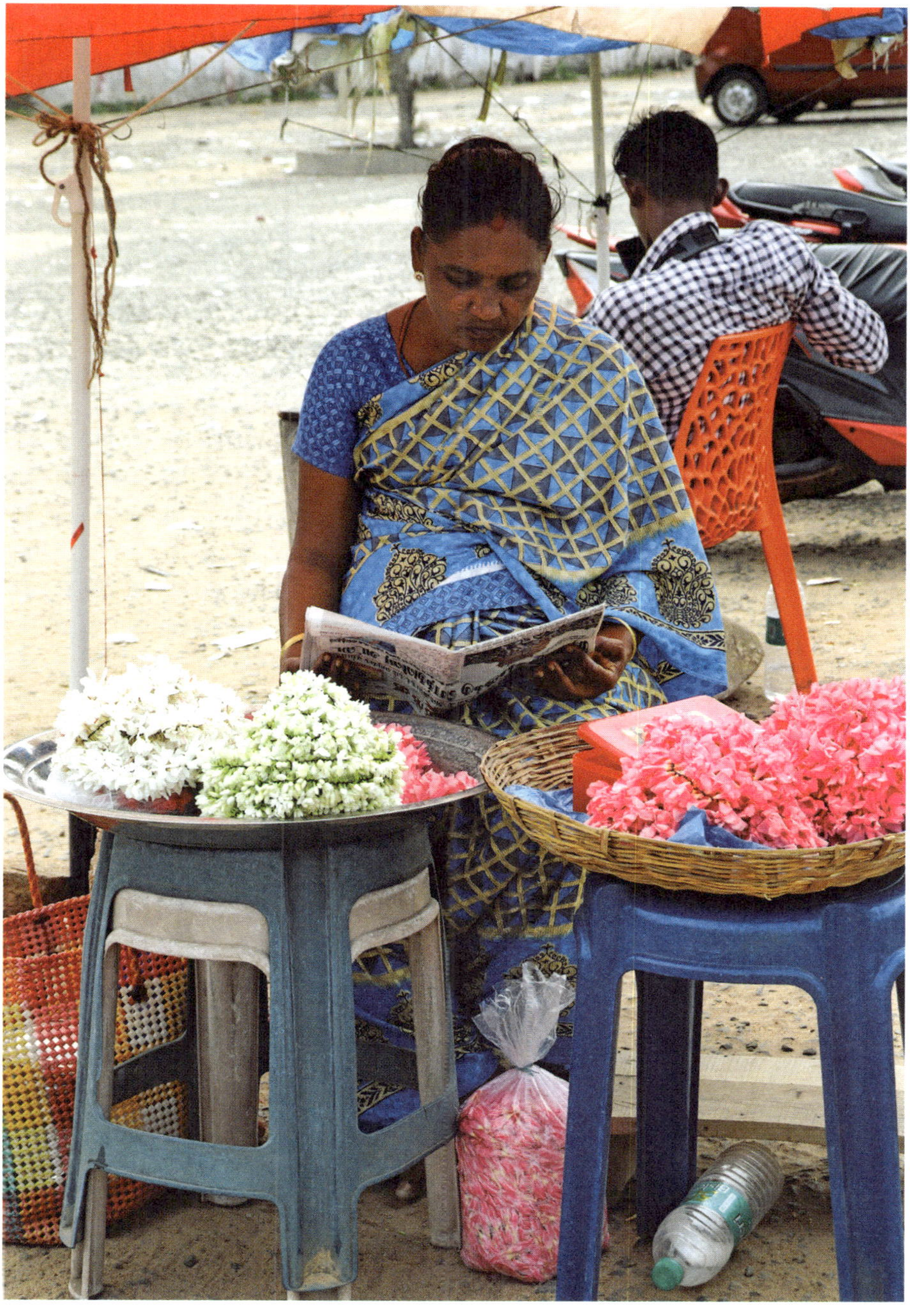

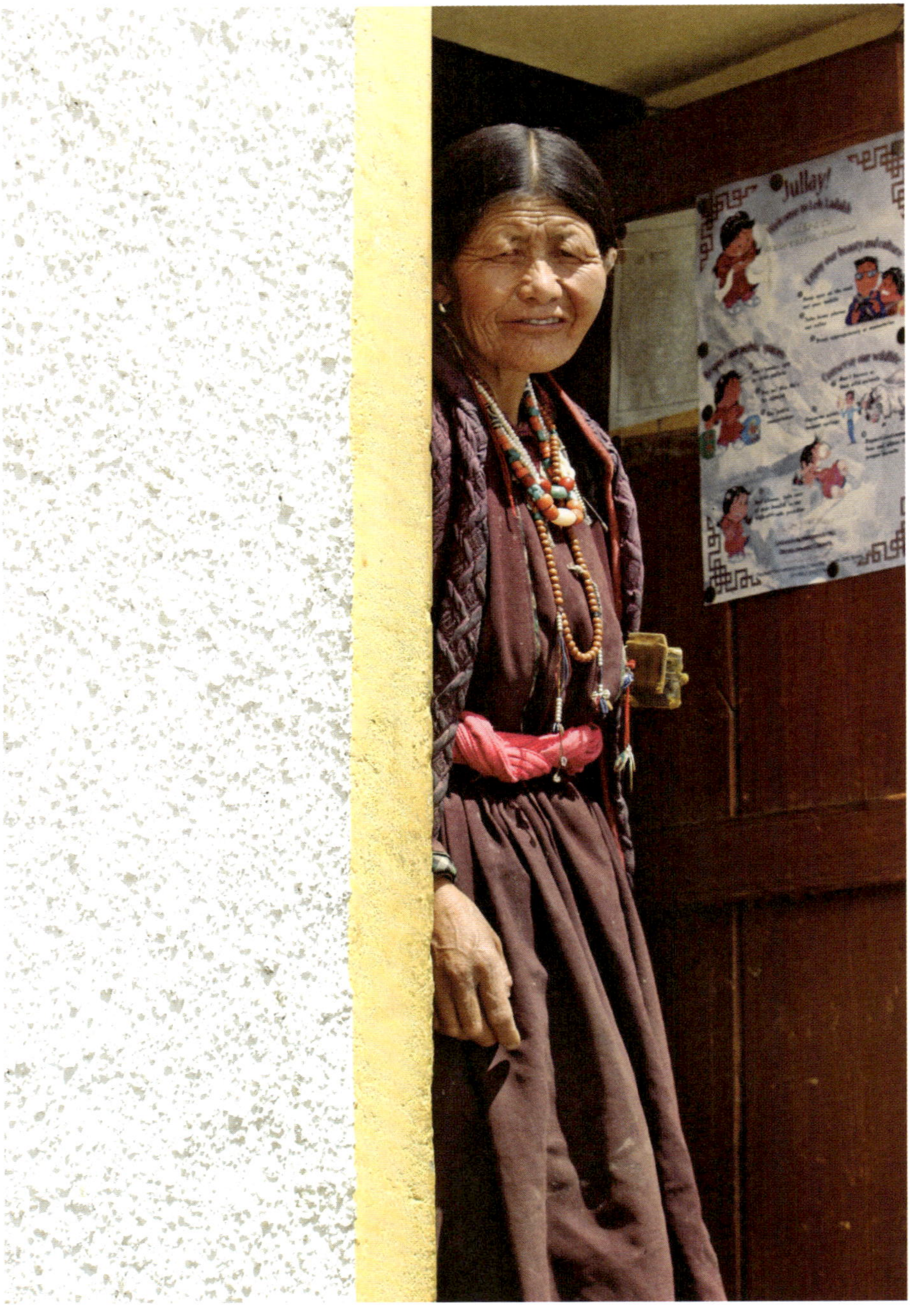
Jullay!

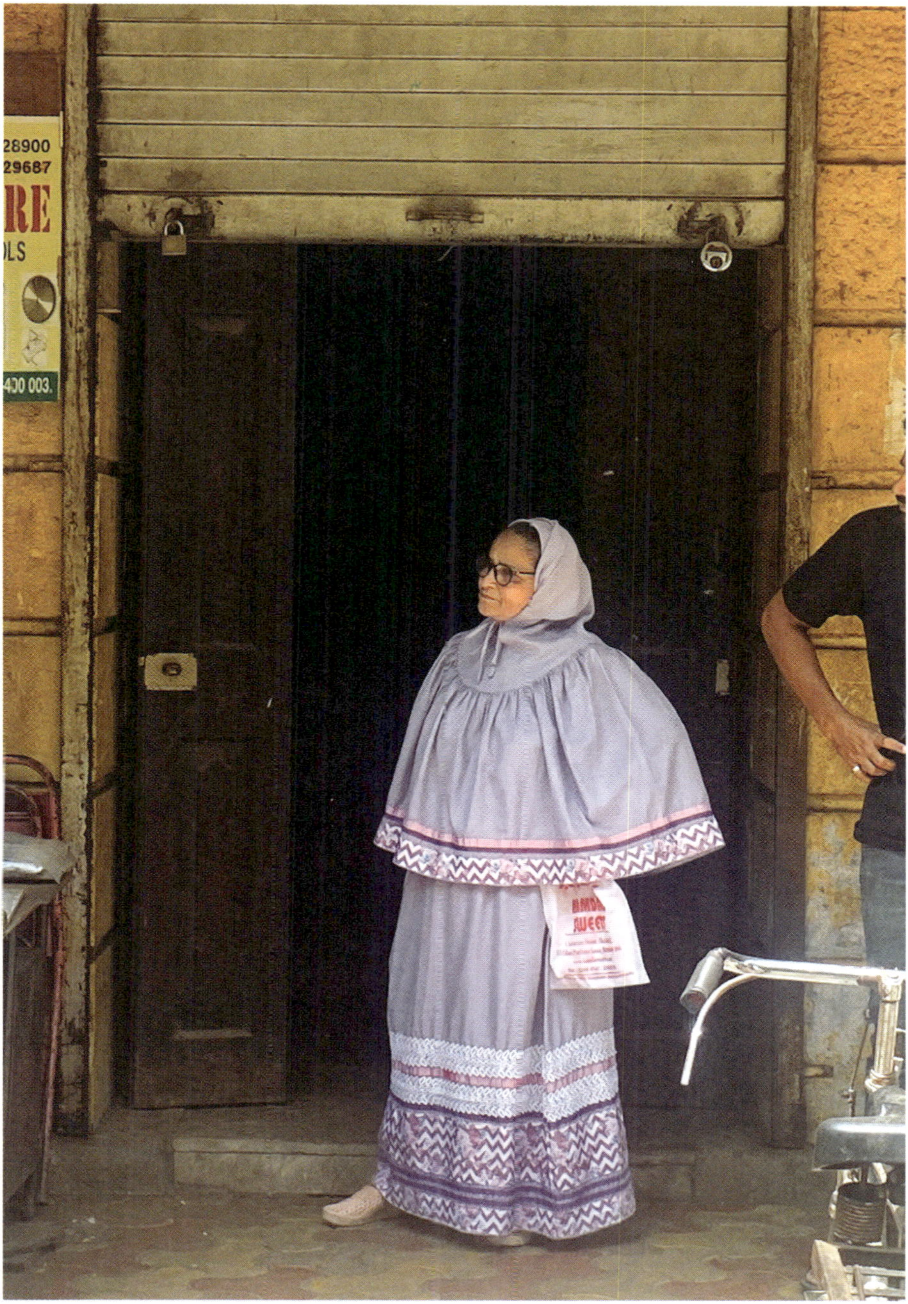
28900
29687
RE
OLS
400 003.

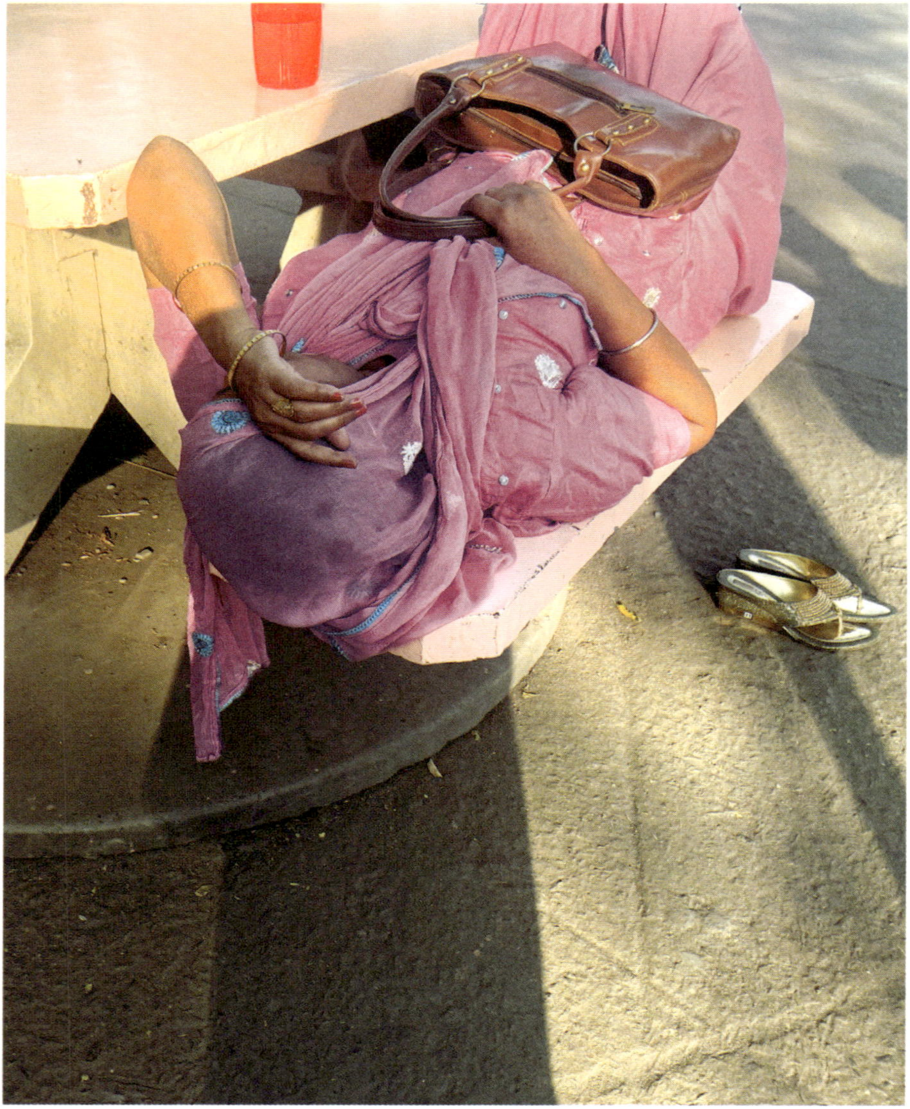

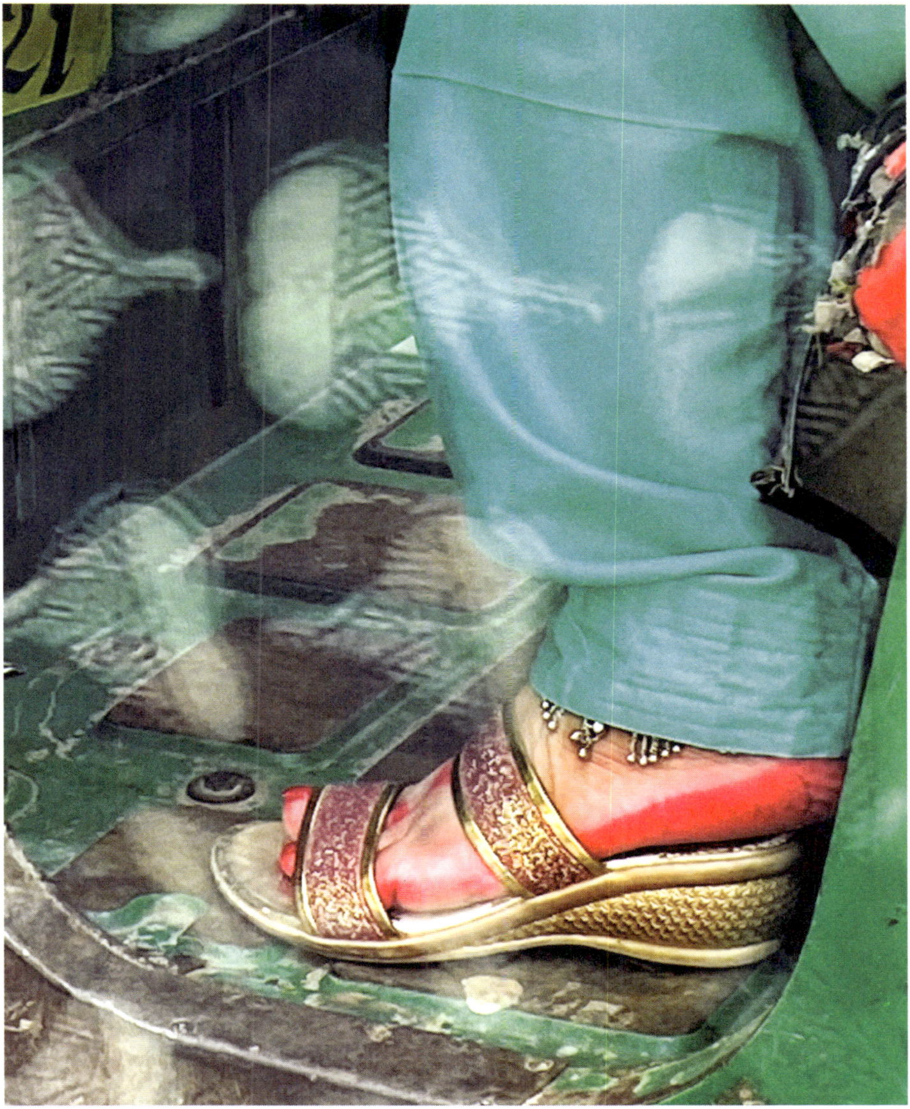

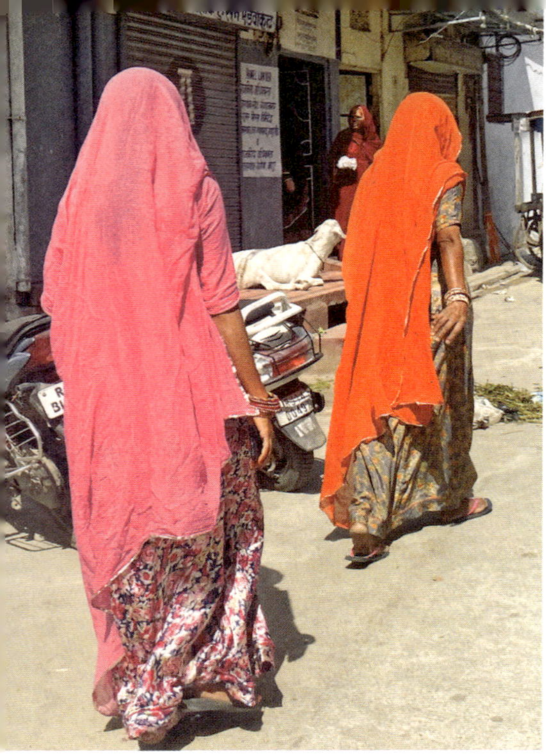

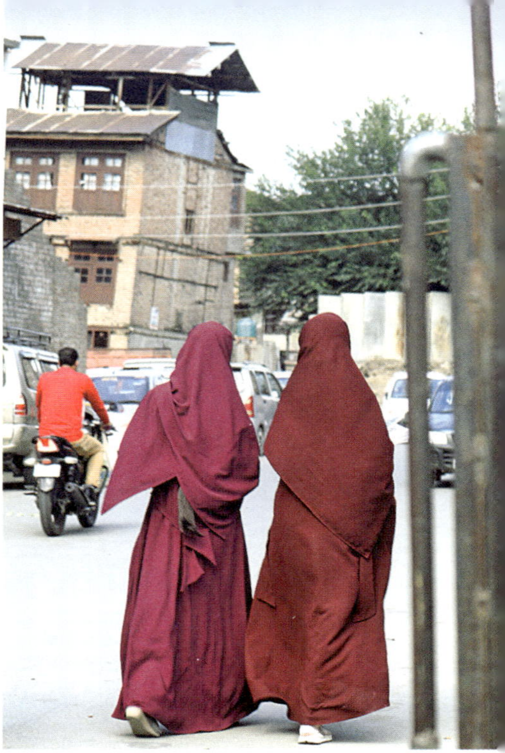

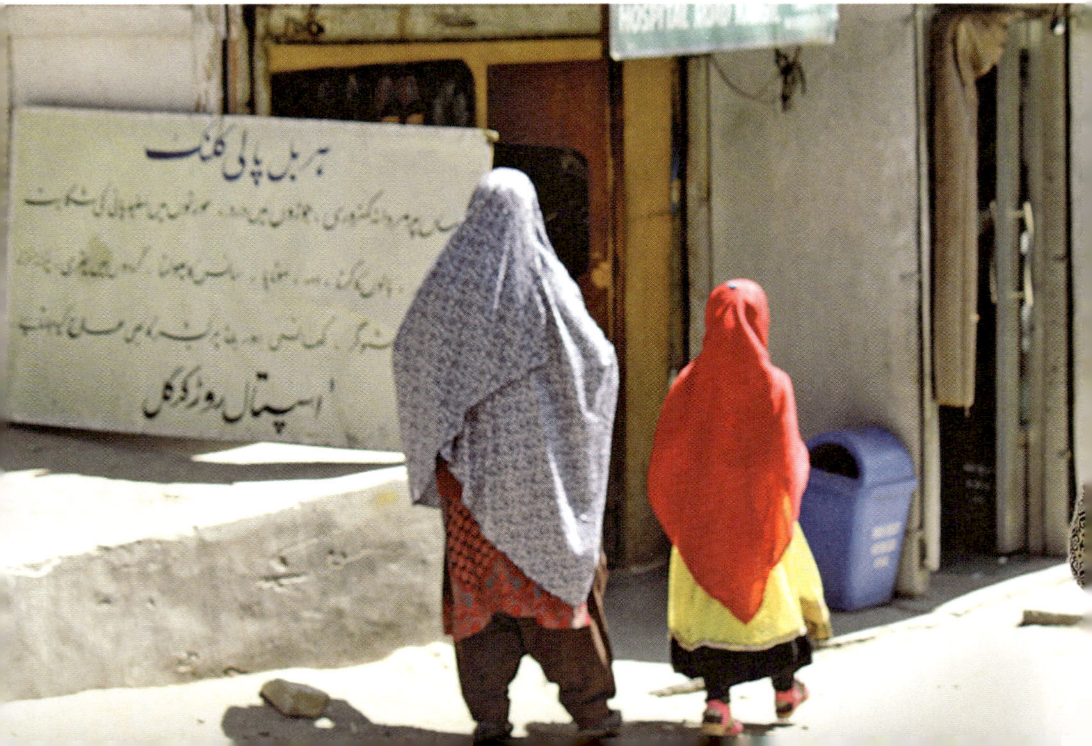
ہربل پالی کلنک
اسپتال روڈ کرگل

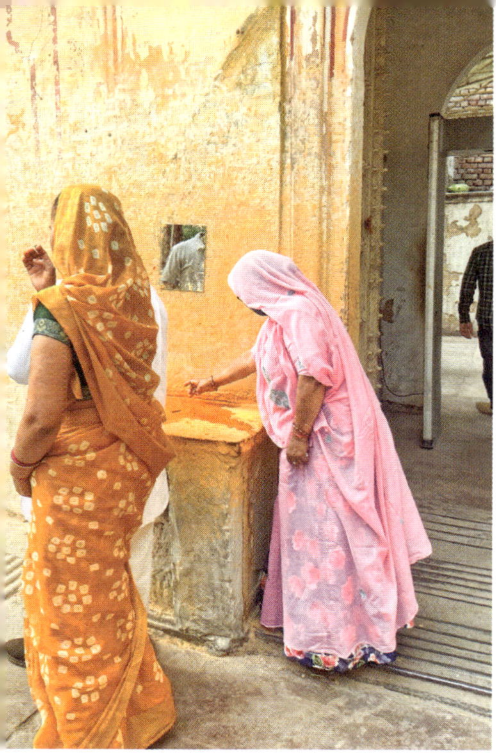

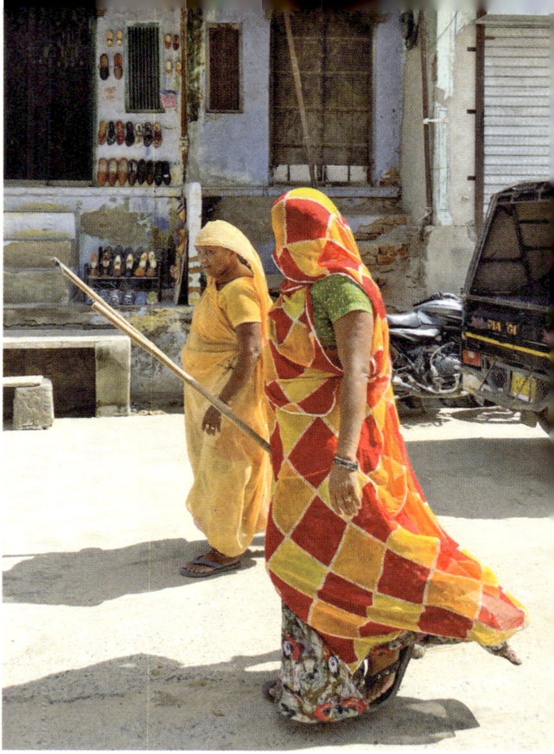

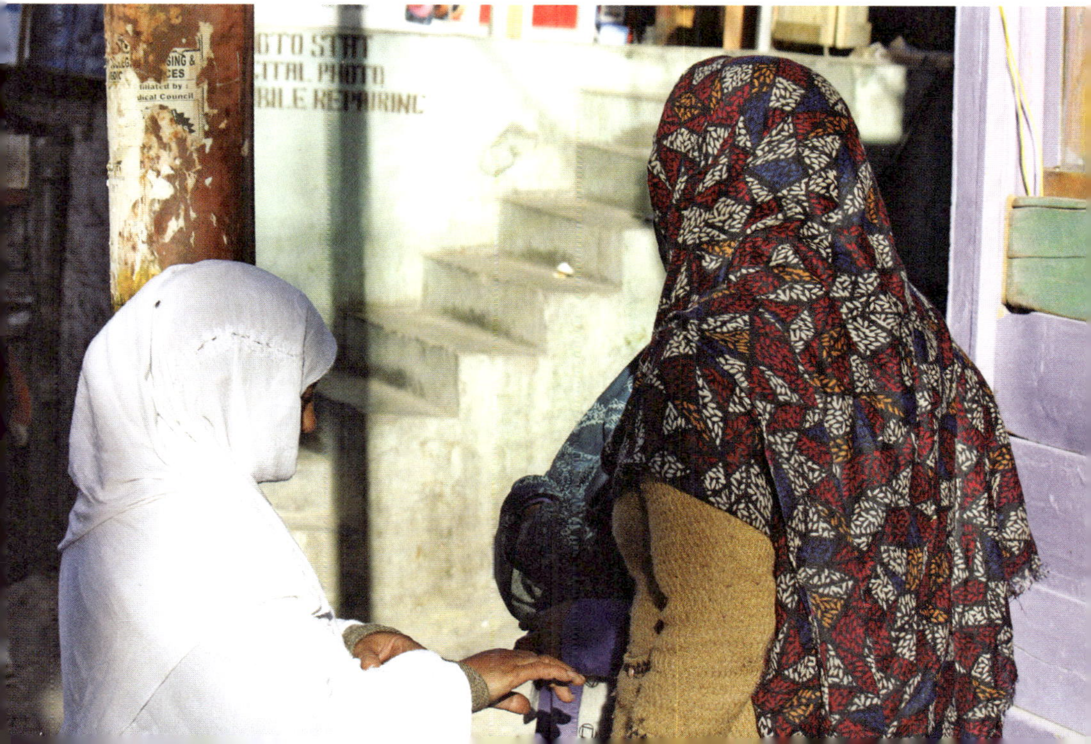
SING &
CES
filiated by :
dical Council

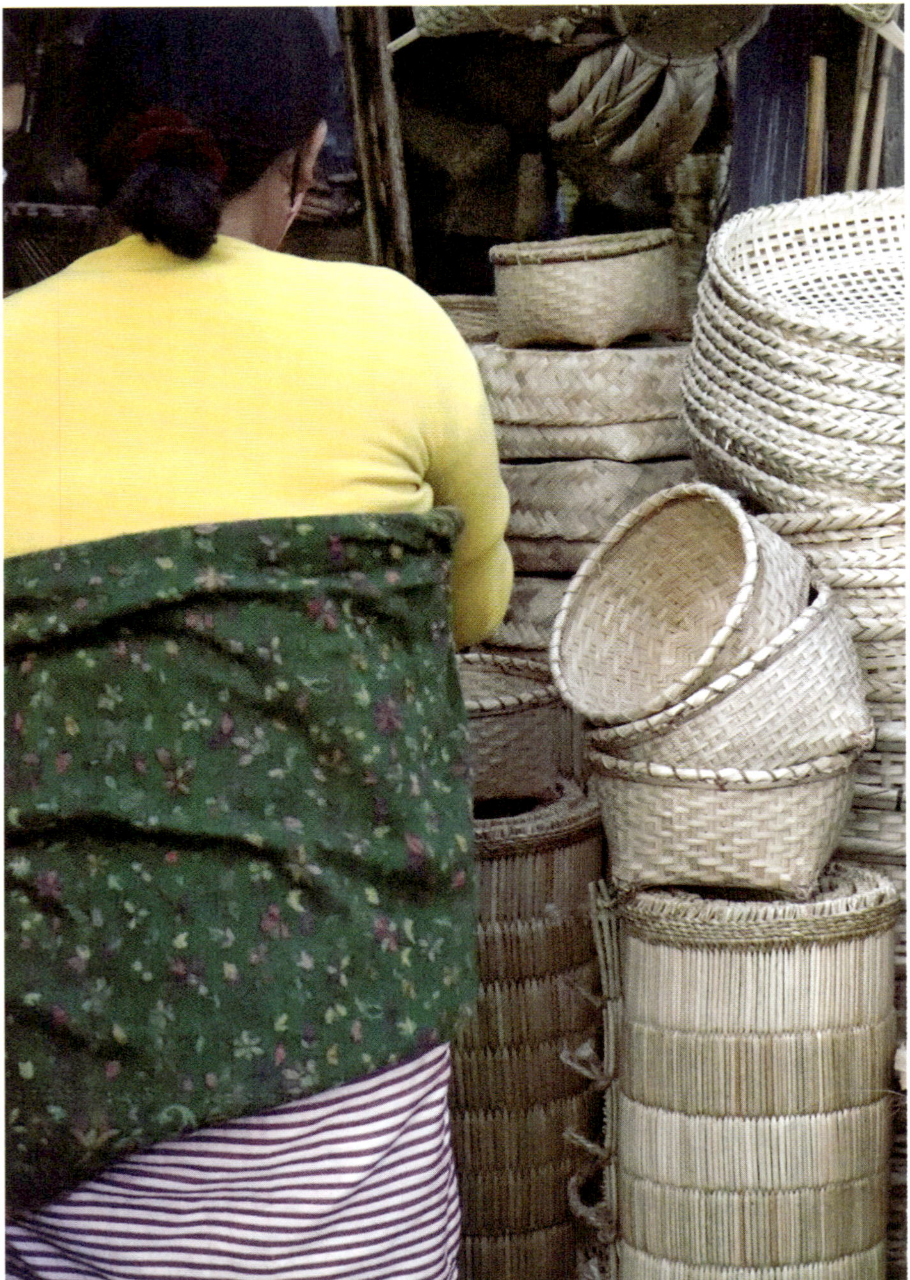

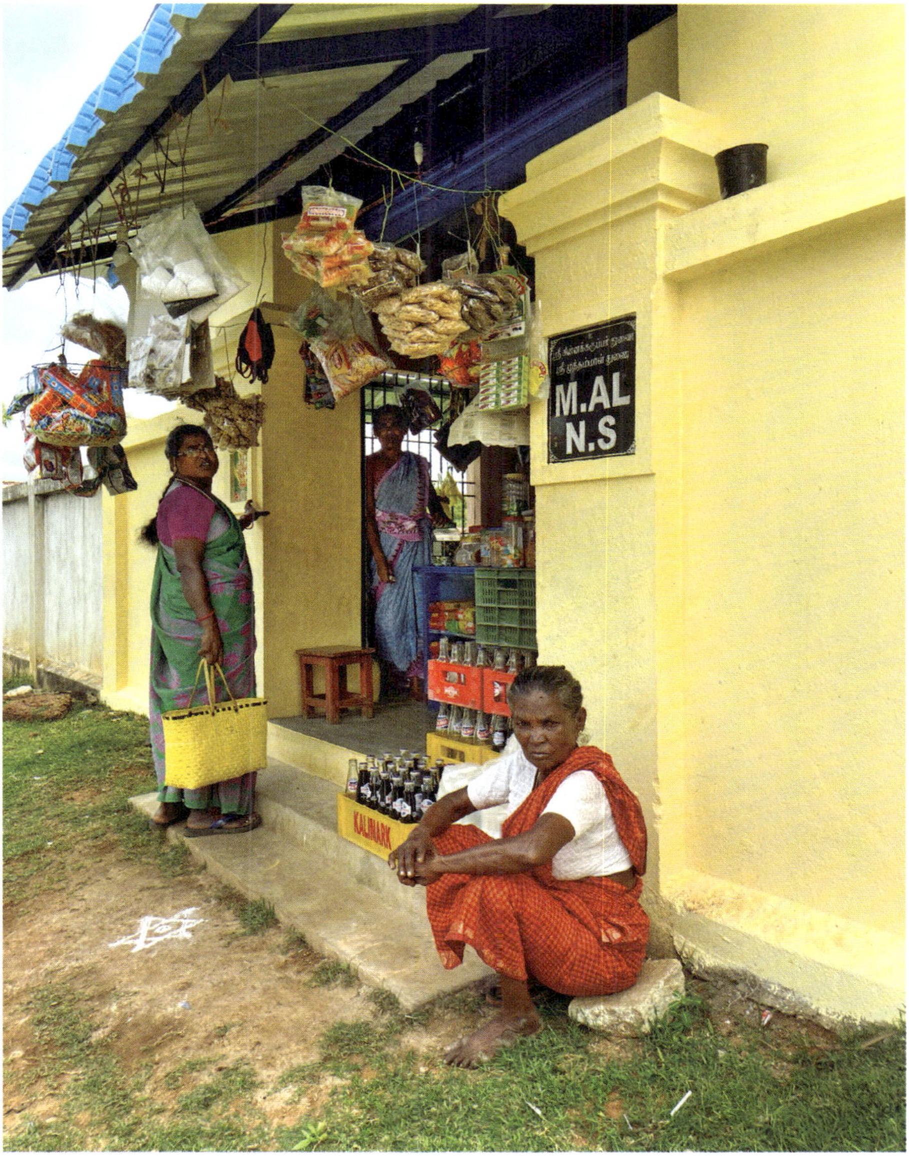
M.AL
N.S
KALIMARK

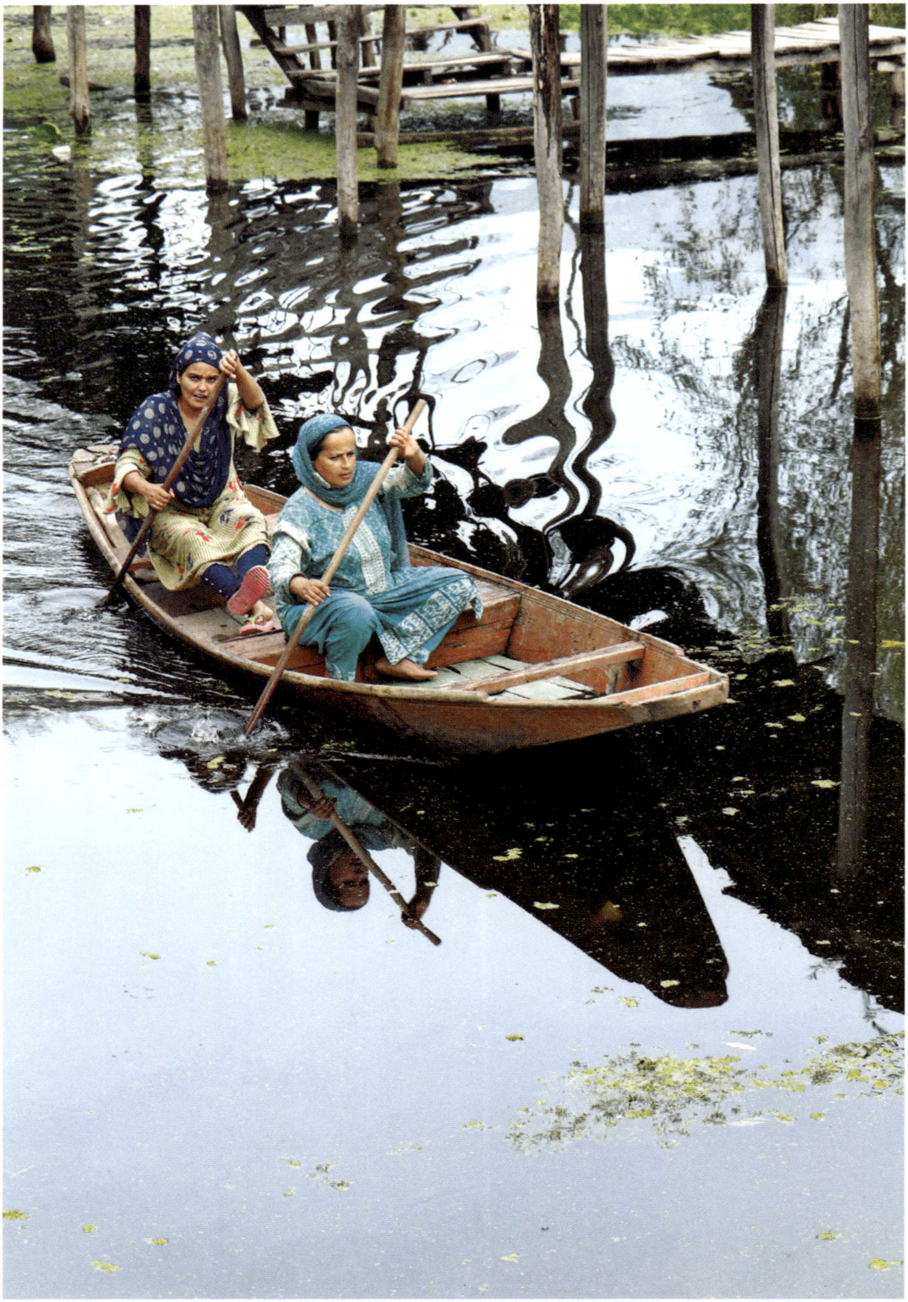

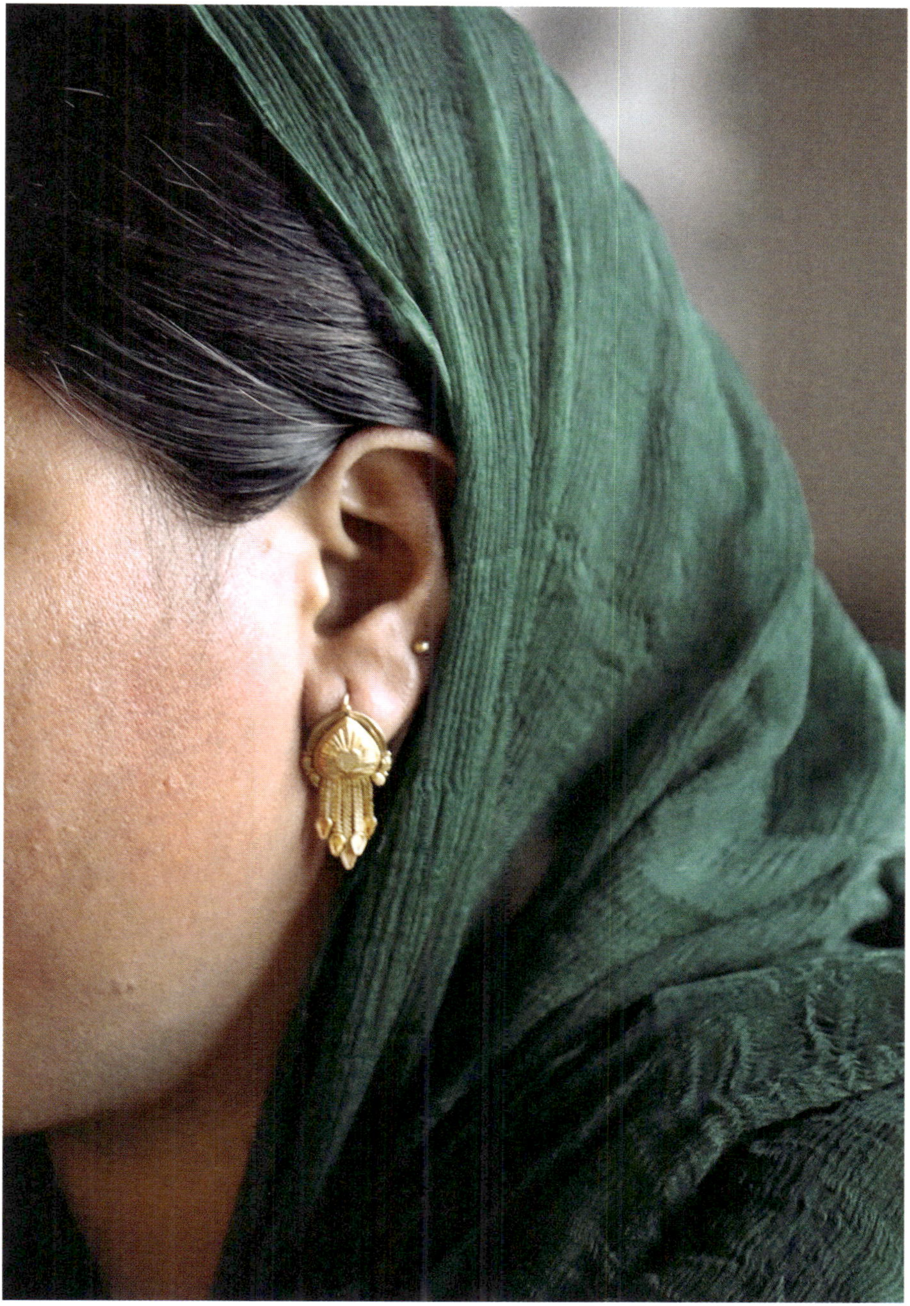

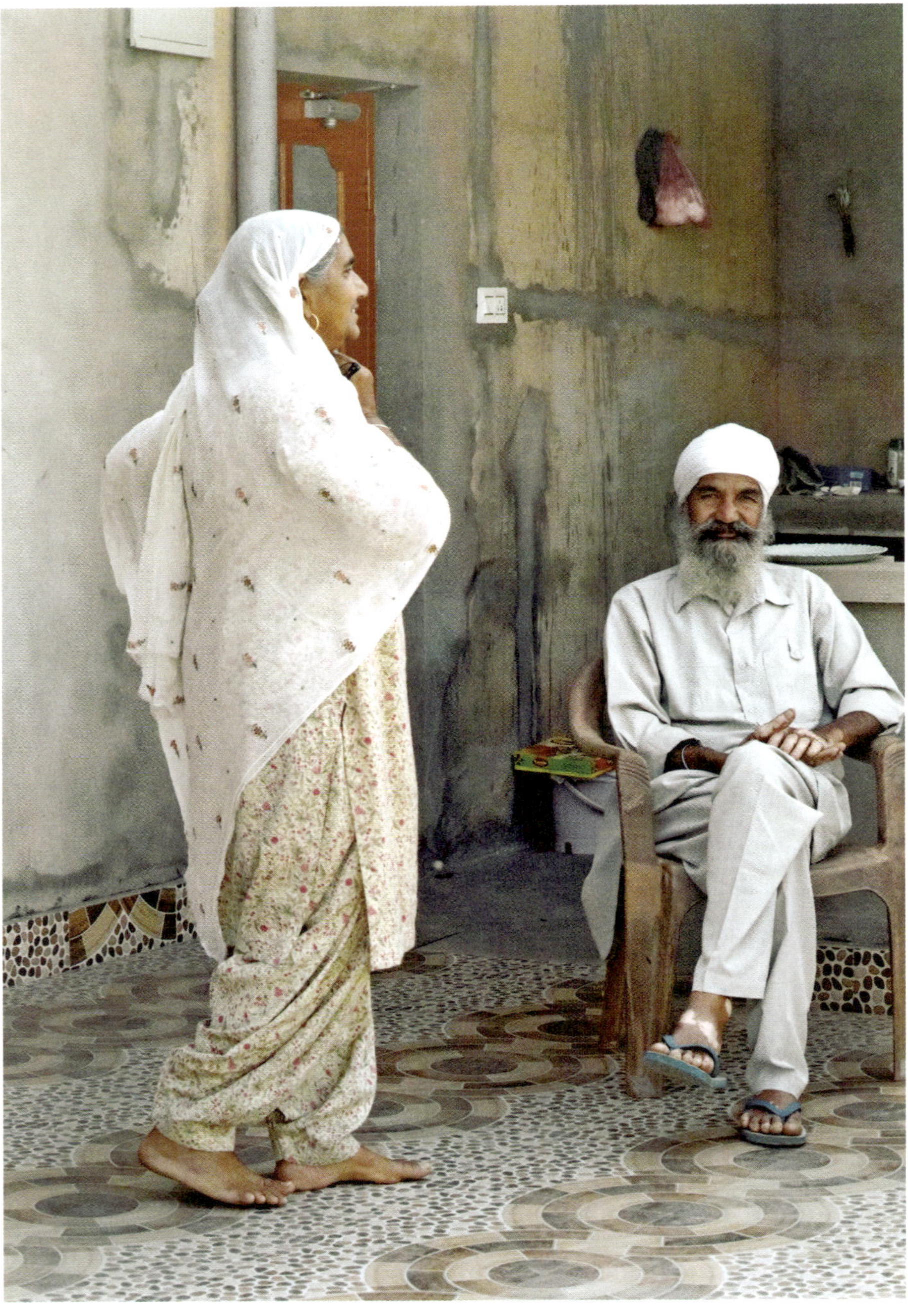

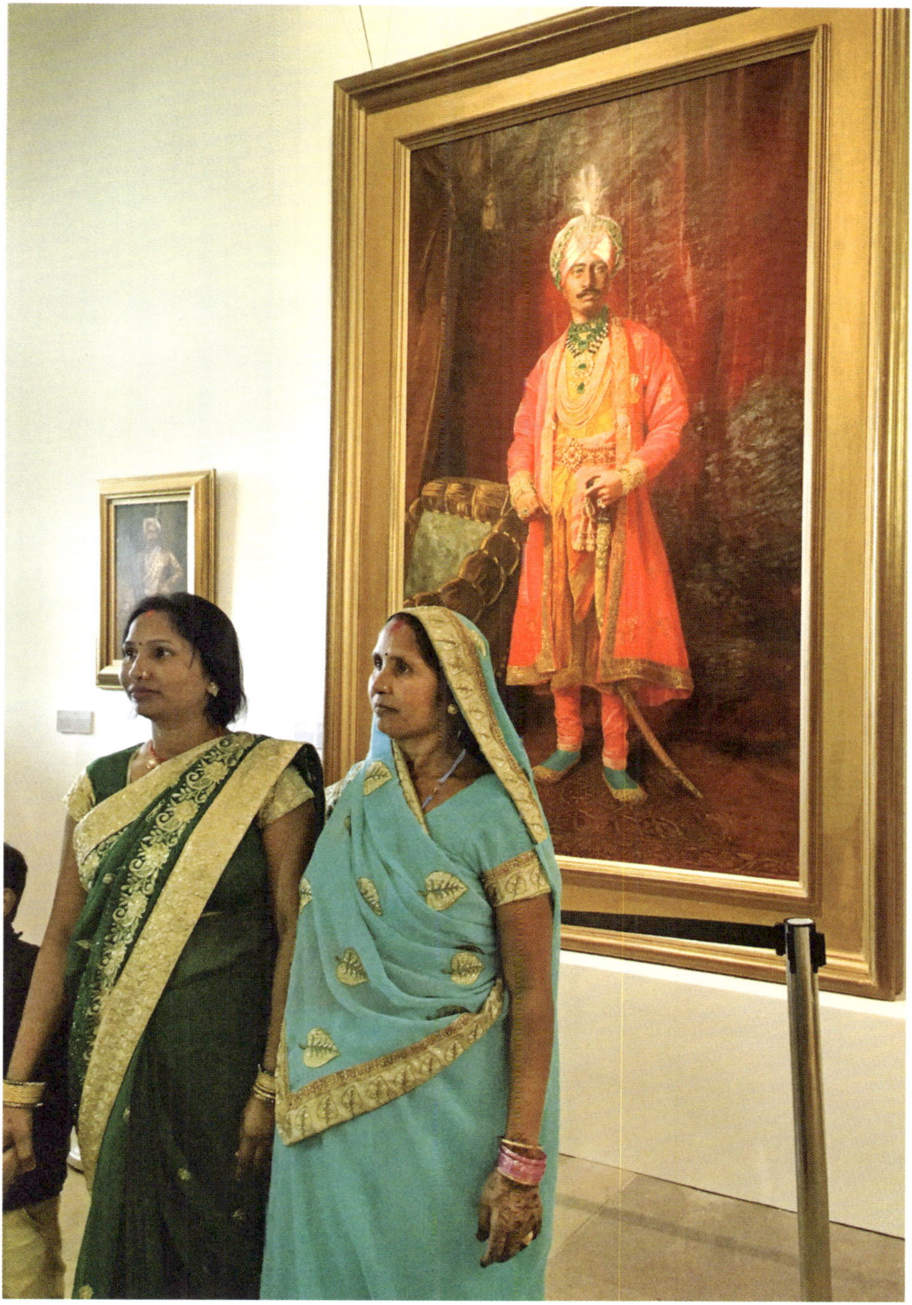

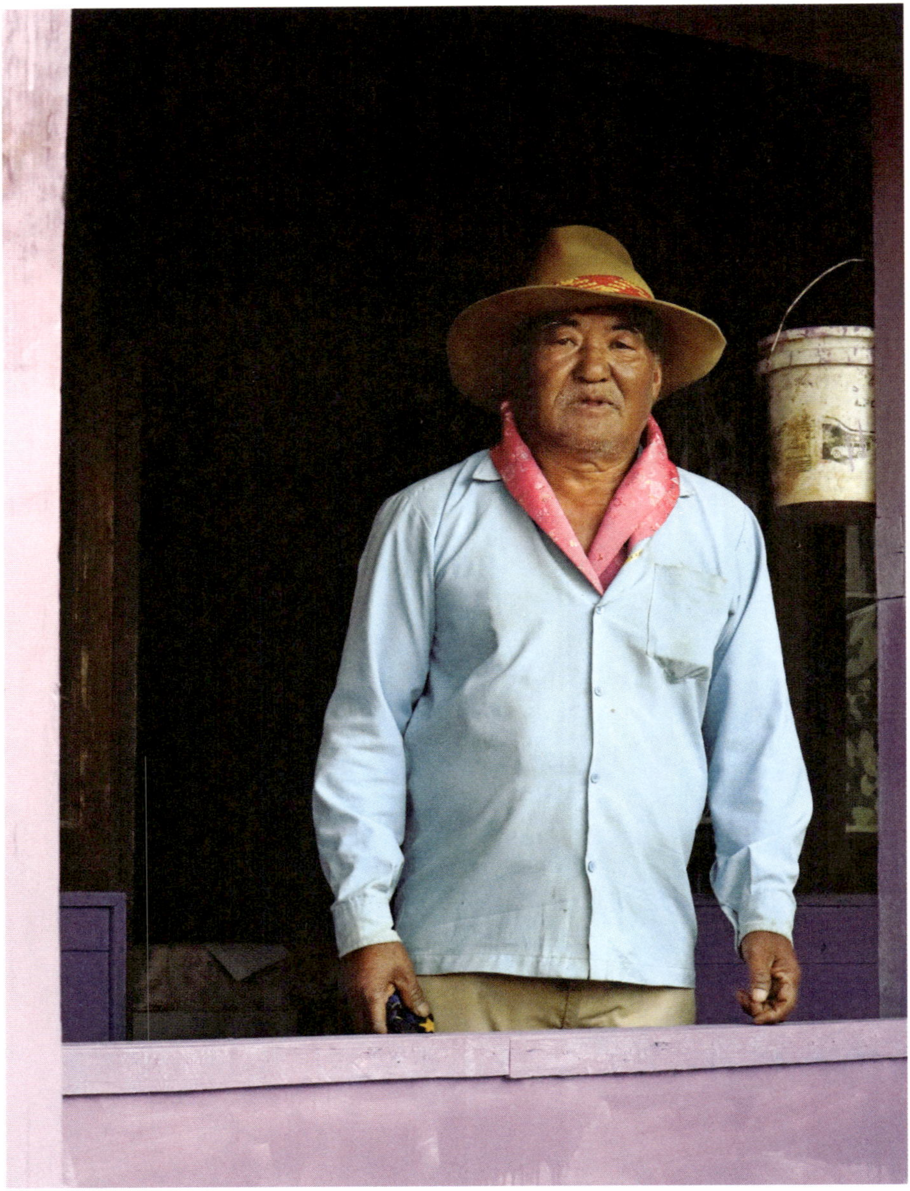

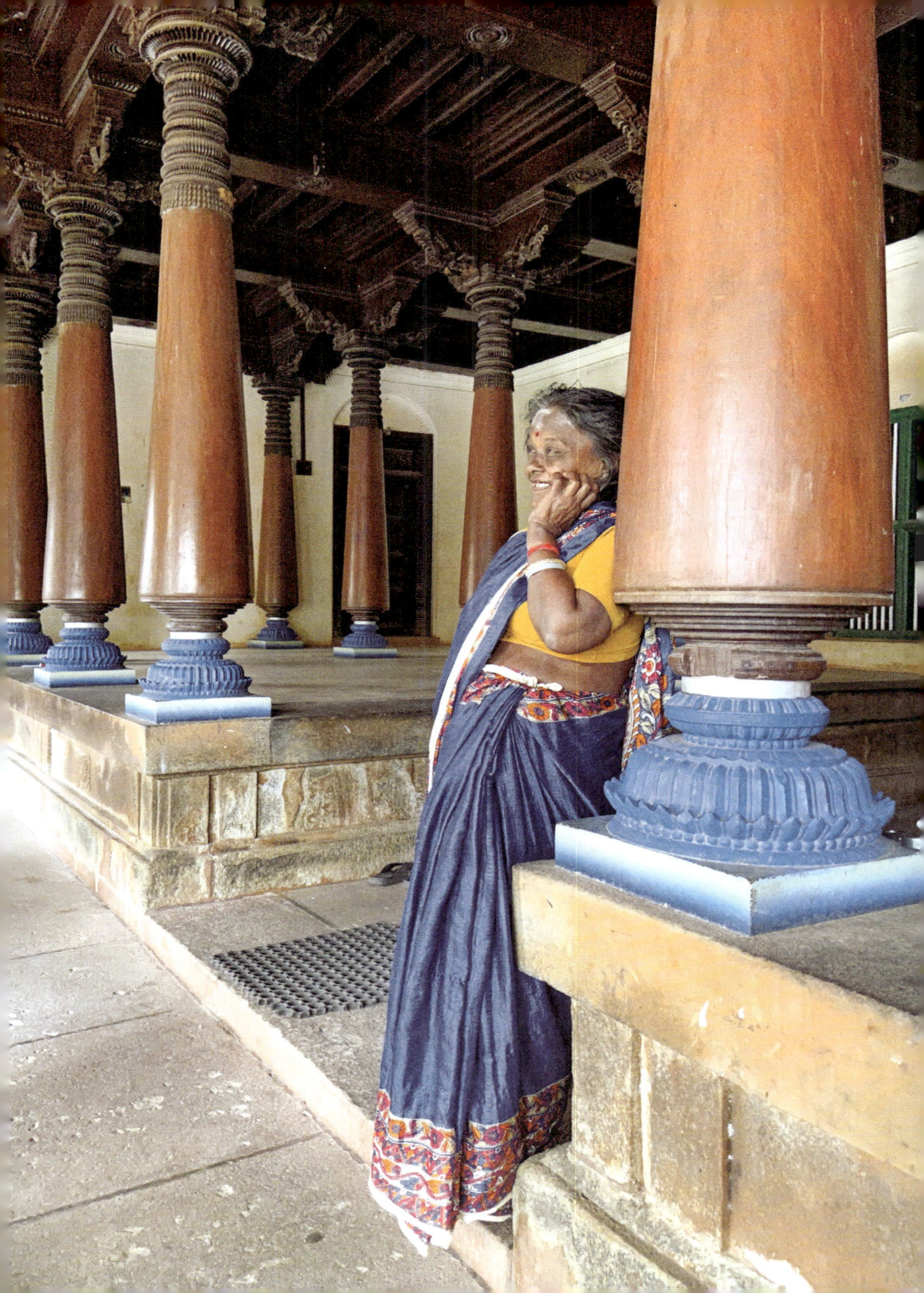

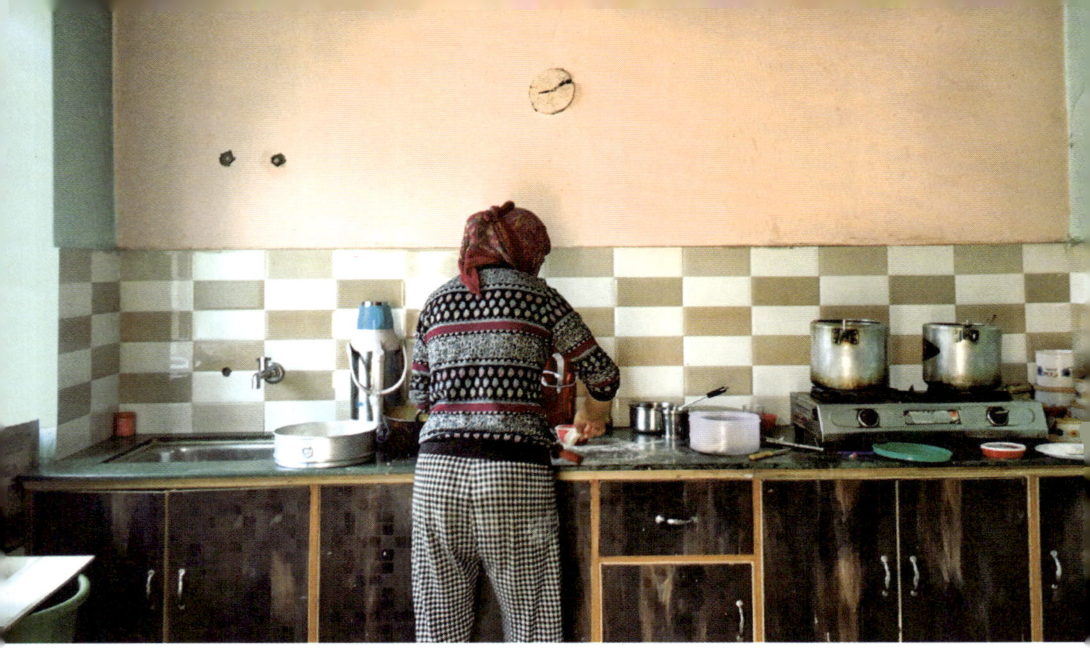

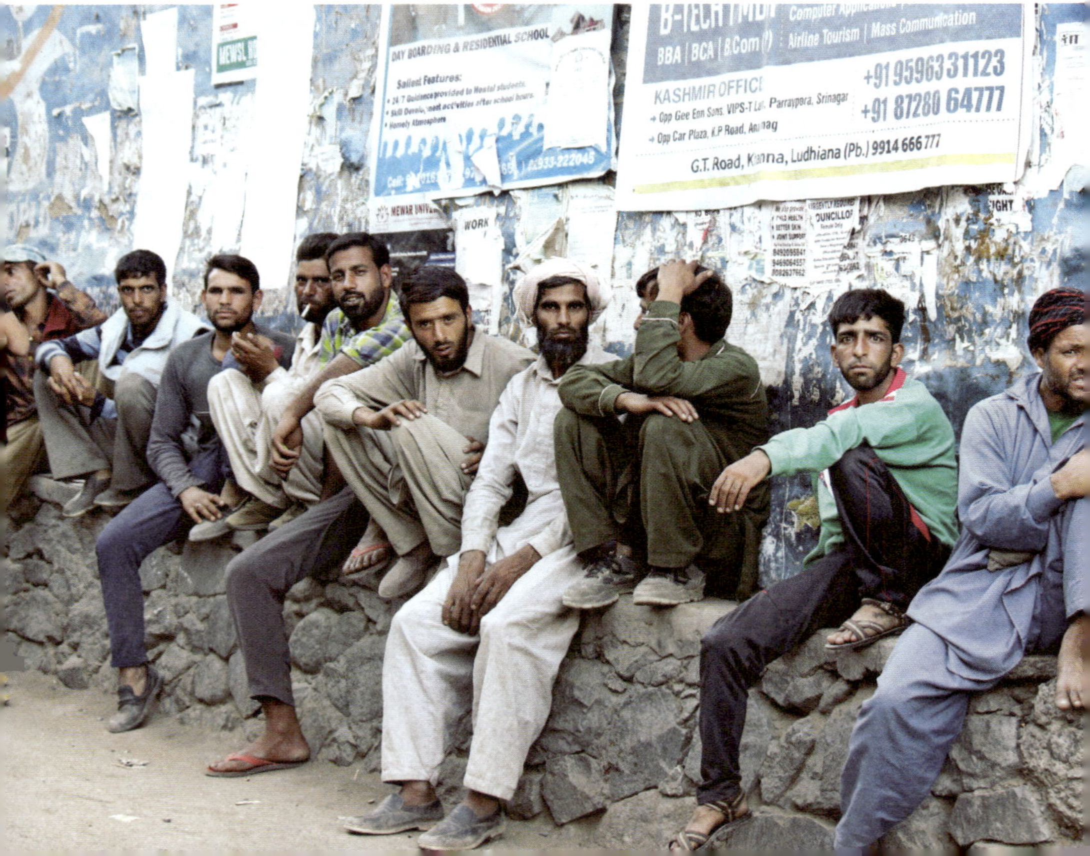

DAY BOARDING & RESIDENTIAL SCHOOL
Salient Features:
Homely Atmosphere
Computer Applications
BBA | BCA | B.Com
Airline Tourism | Mass Communication
+91 95963 31123
+91 87280 64777
G.T. Road
Ludhiana (Pb.) 9914 666 777
WORK

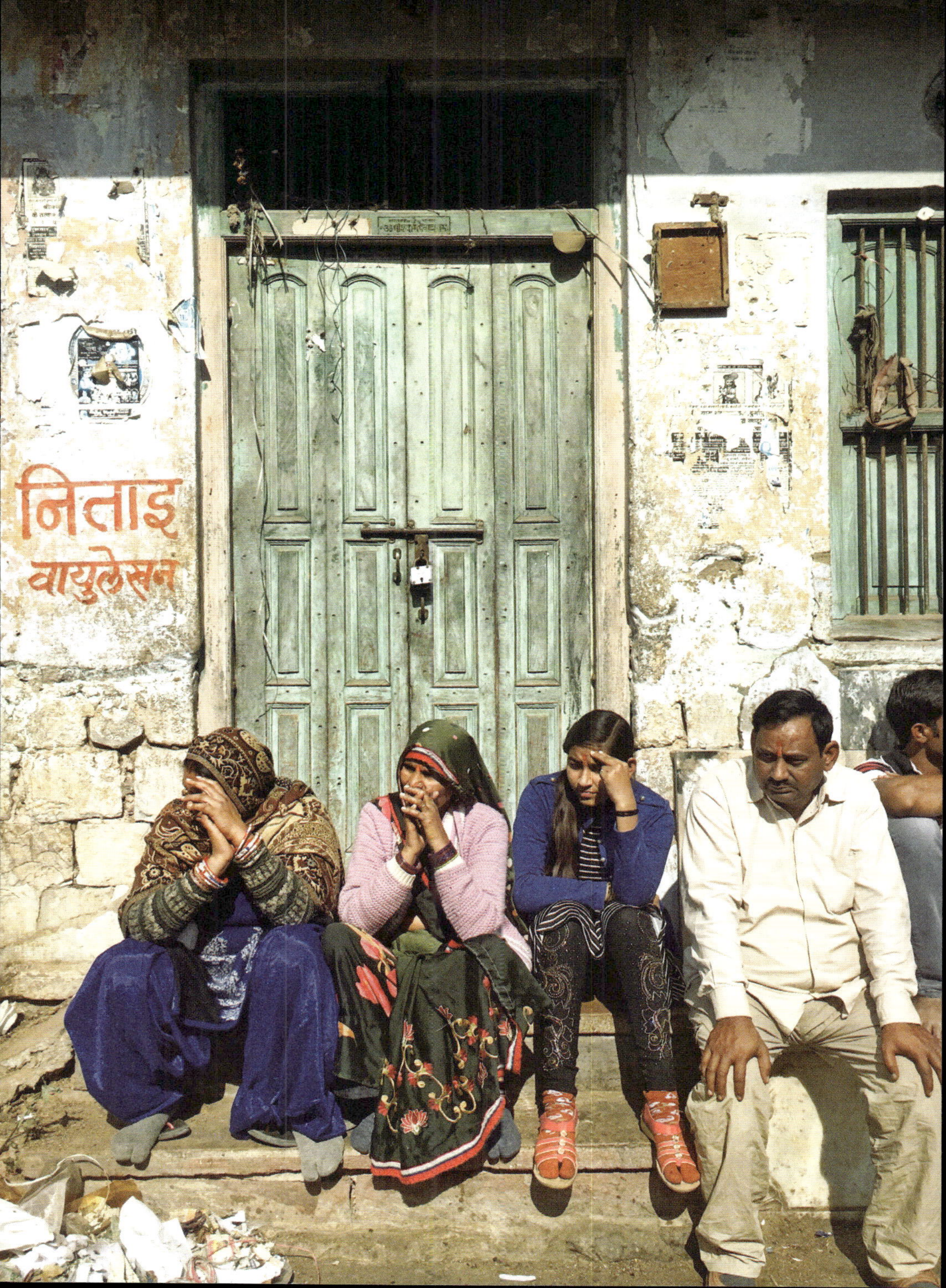
निताइ
वायुलेसन

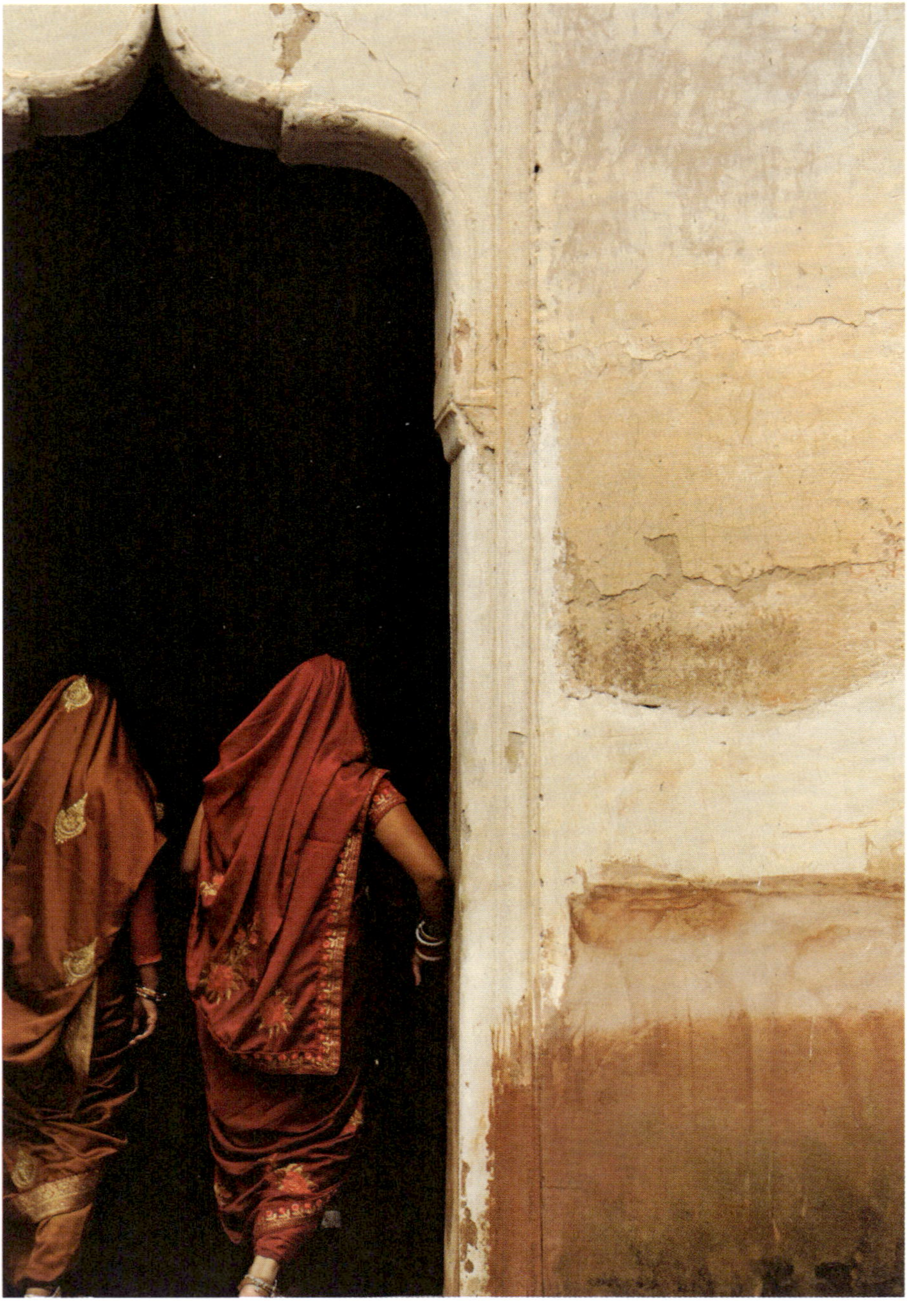

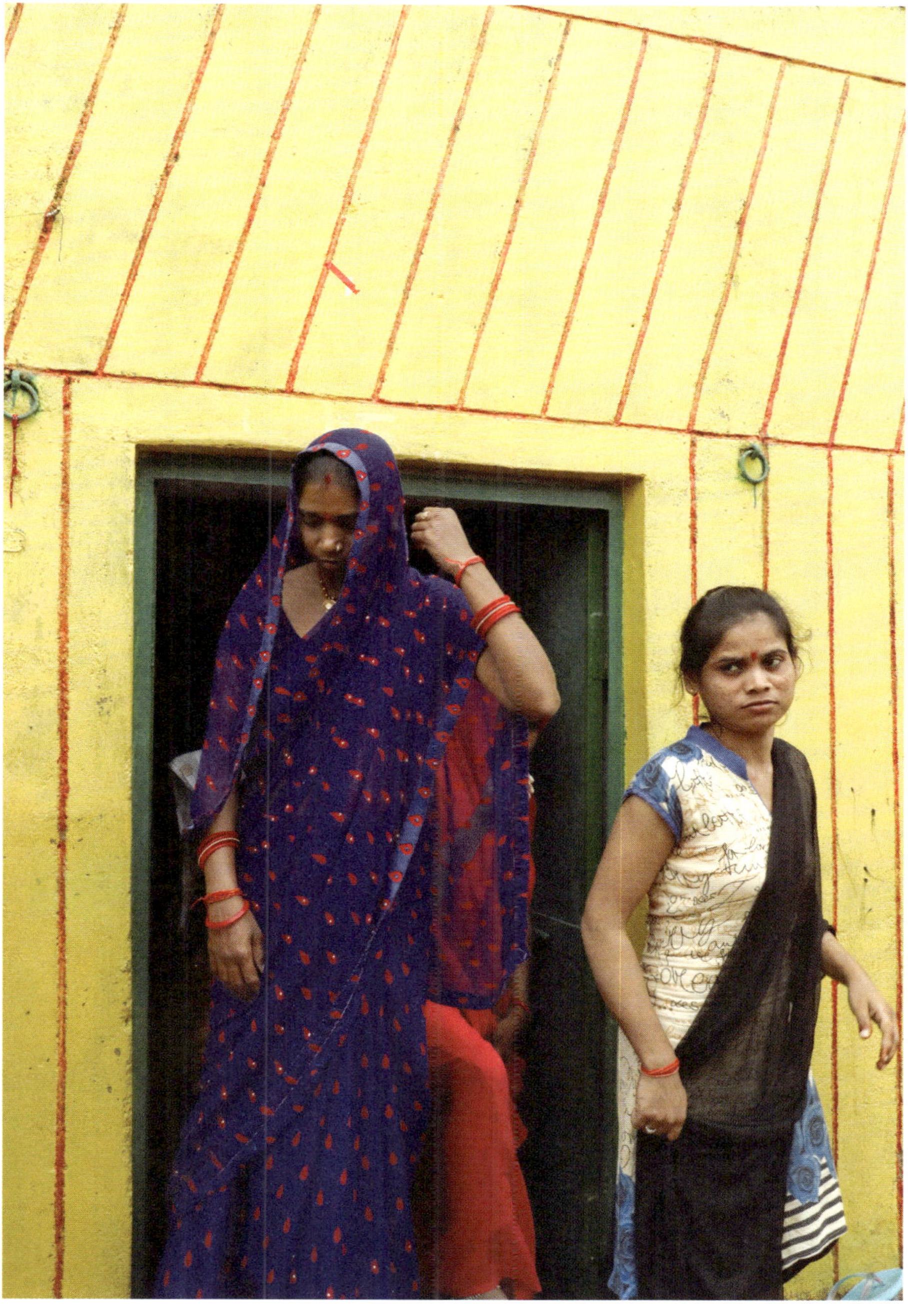

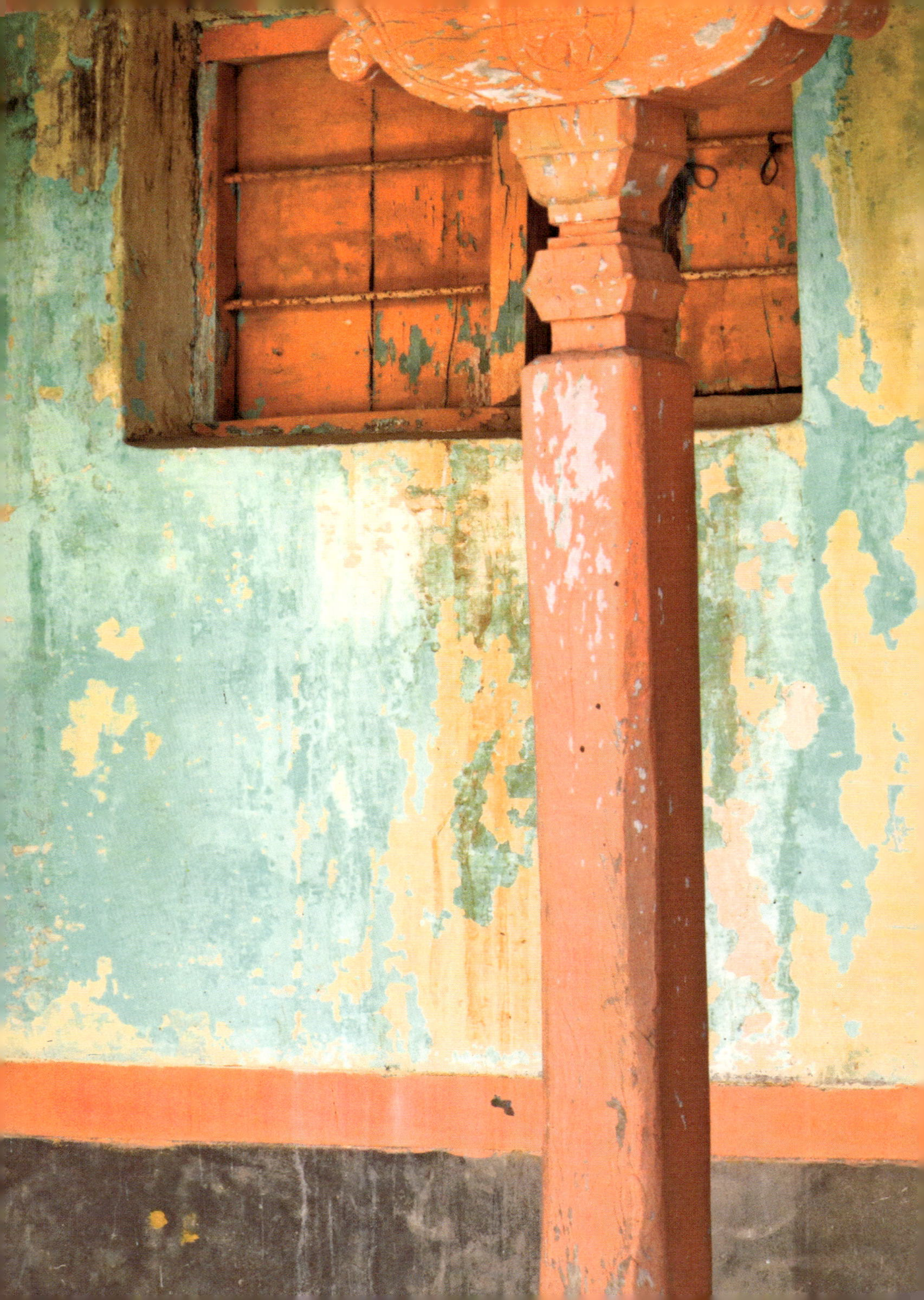

architecture & interiors

Space meets spirituality in the built world of India. Wrought-iron grills with geometric designs accompany windows and doors. Ornate doorframes with latch locks, knobs and knockers and floors with mosaic tiles of marble, stone, and quartz are a familiar sight. Window panes of stained glasses, balconies with arches and pillars, sculptures of domes and spires, walls with floral leitmotifs and painted borders, decorative cornices, sloping roofs of terracotta tiles, courtyards and columns, staircases and stuccos are found across the country. The interiors in rural dwellings have charpoys, while city homes' seating arrangements include upholstered sofa sets to welcome guests.

Whether it's Chandigarh or Chettinad – Indo-Islamic, Art Deco, Modernism or traditional vernacular architecture design – every structure tells a distinct story.

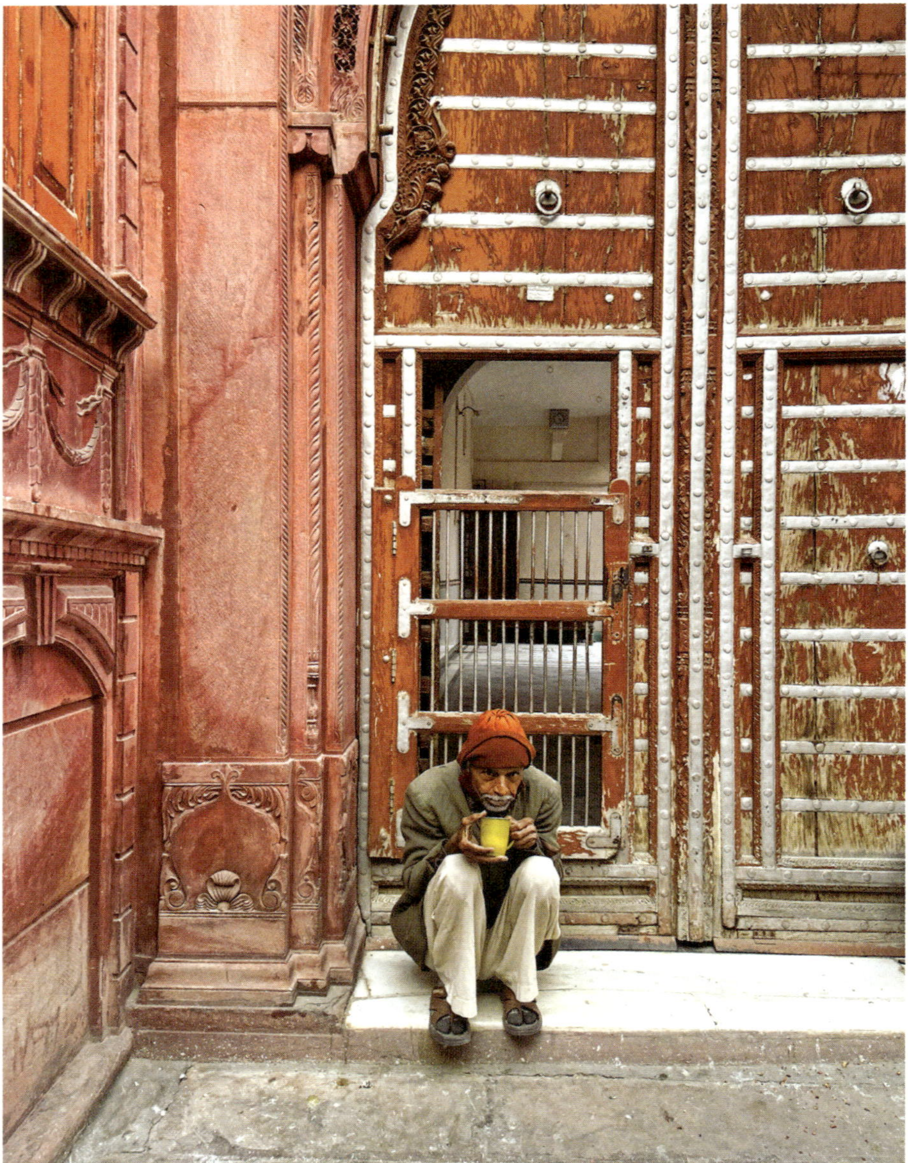

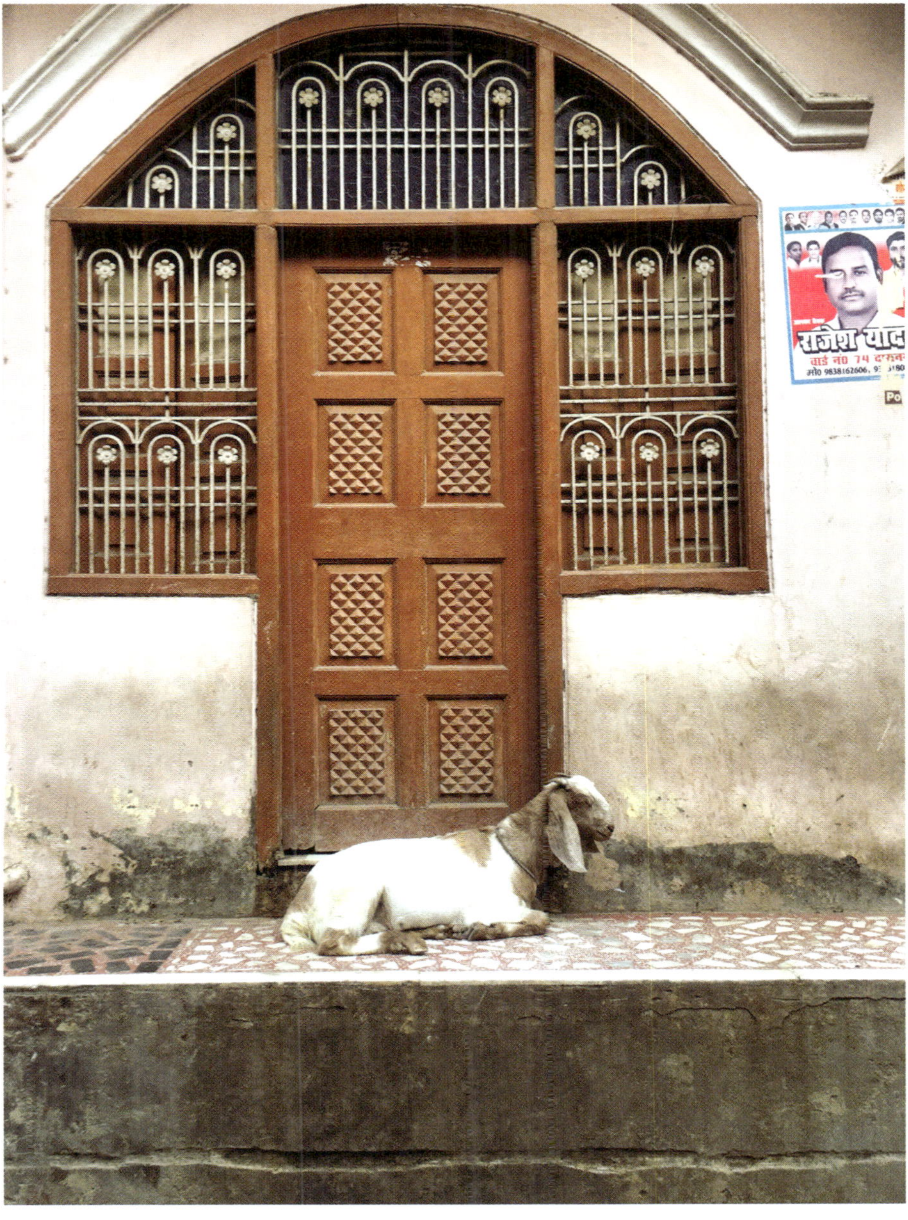
राजेश याद
मो0 9838162606

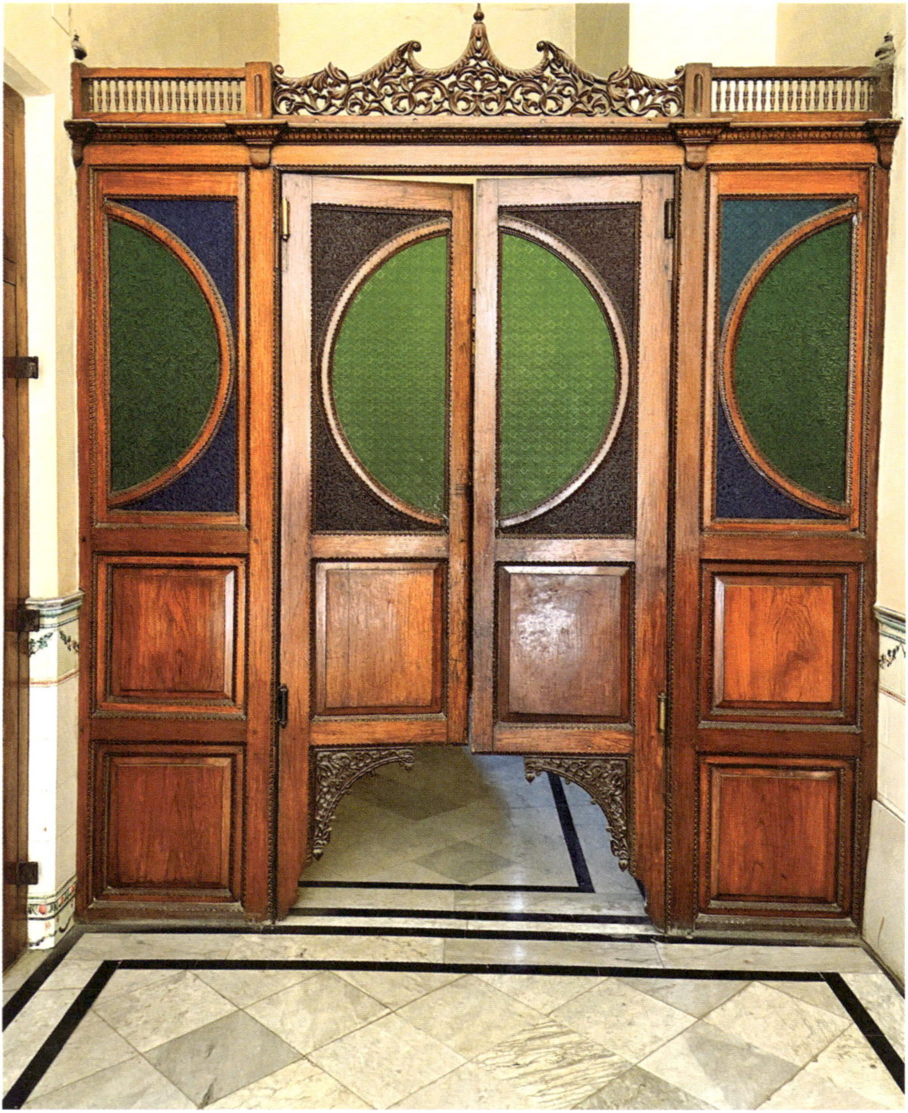

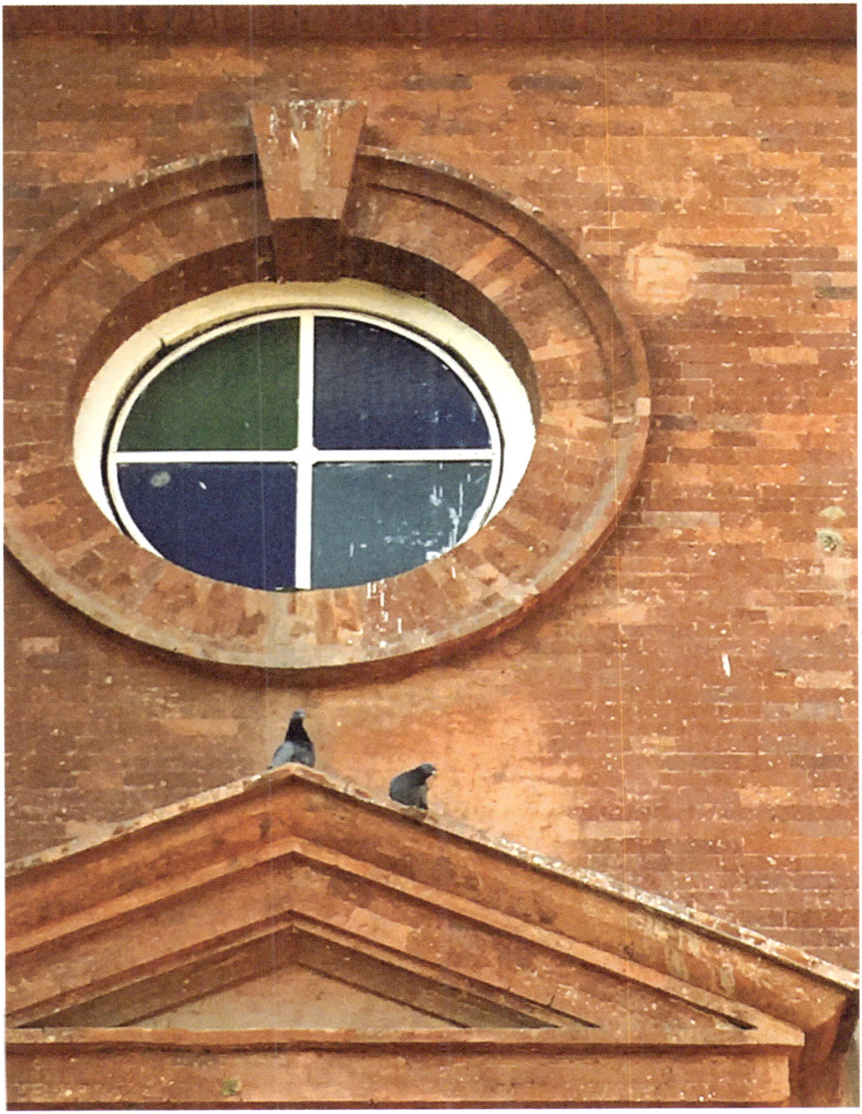

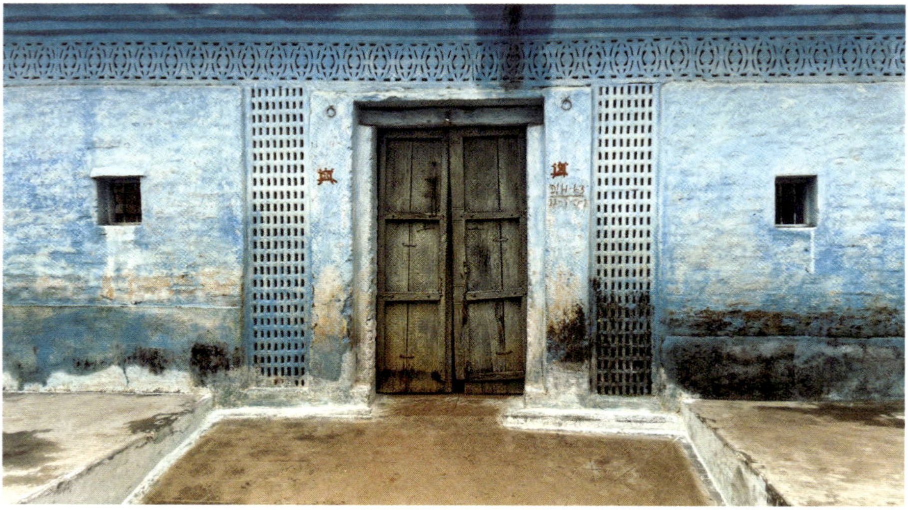

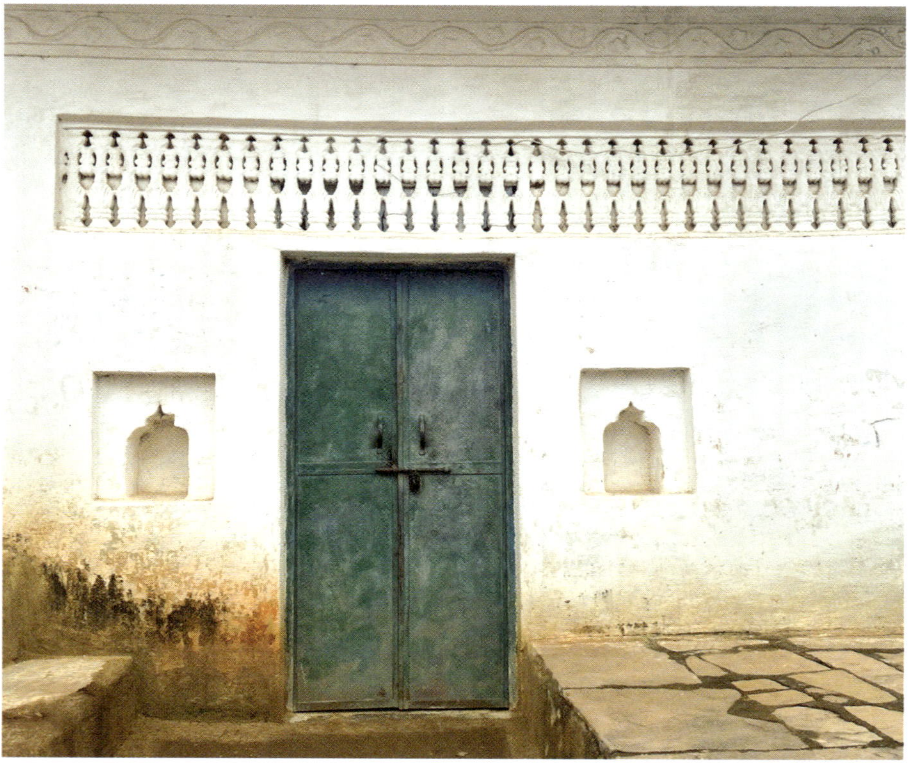

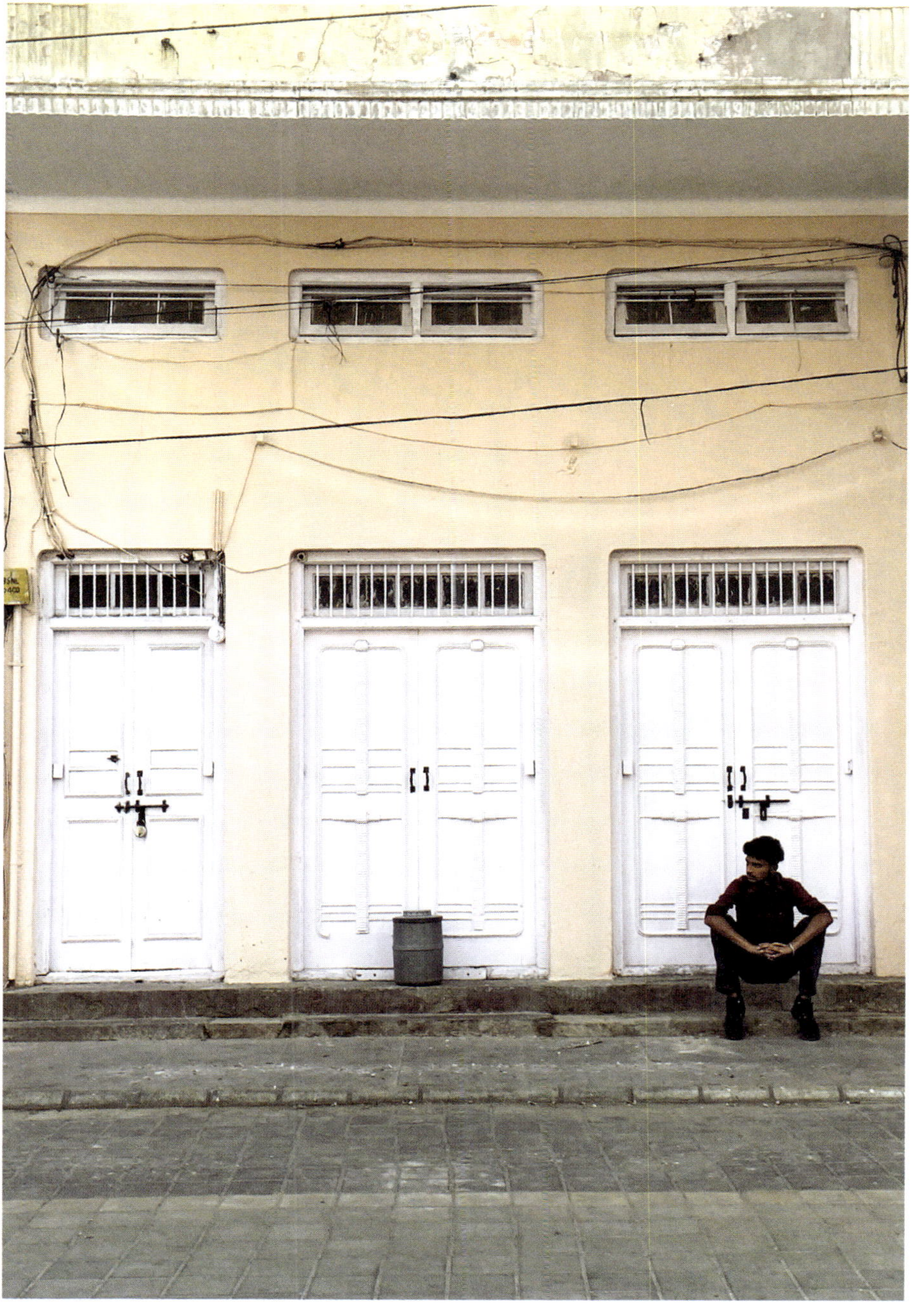

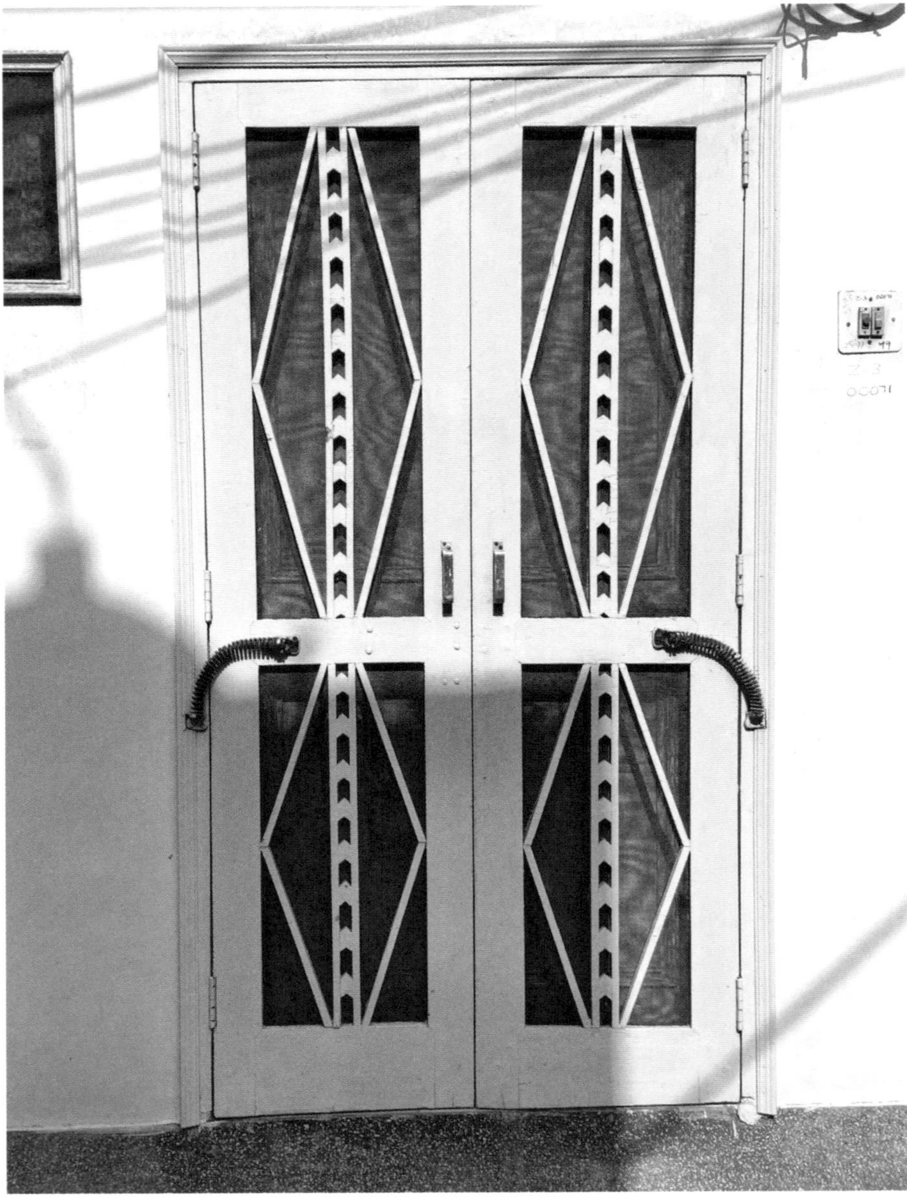

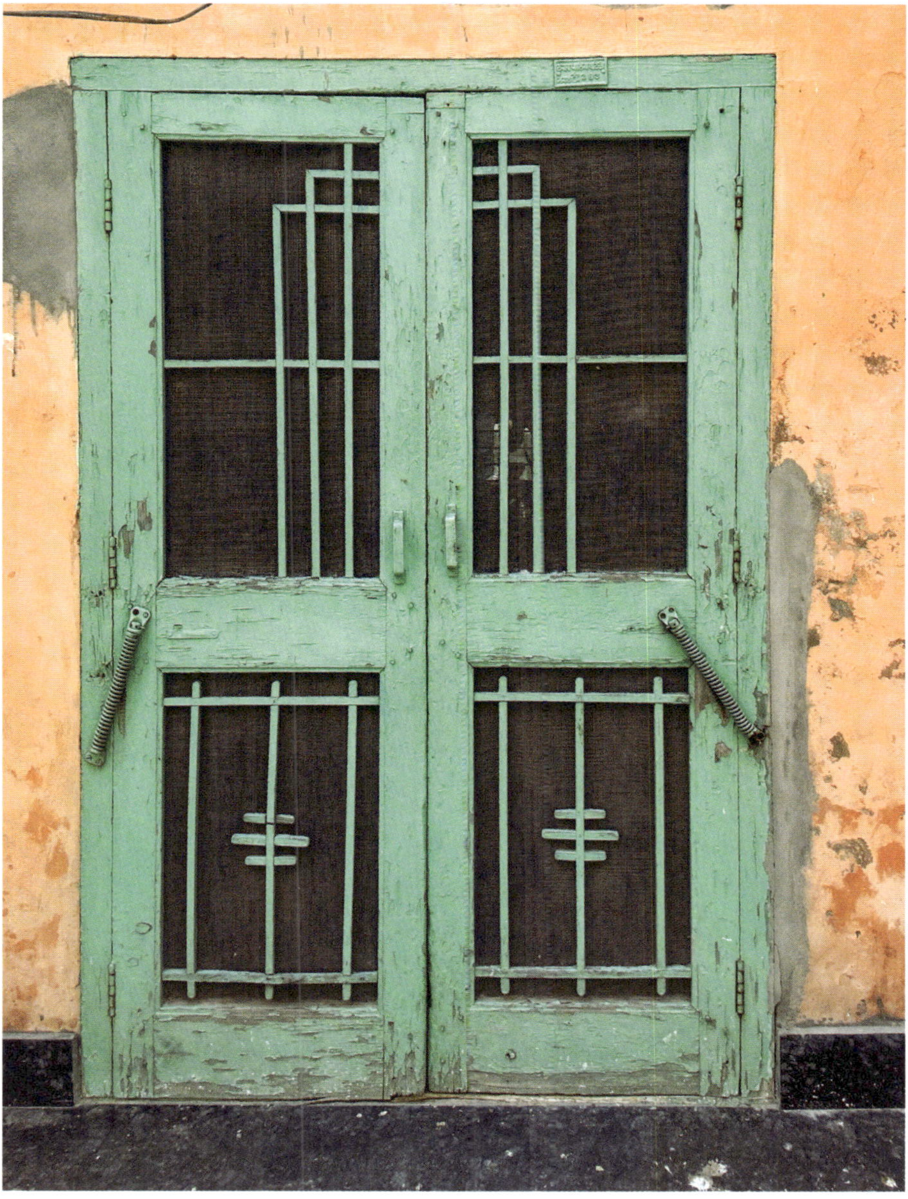

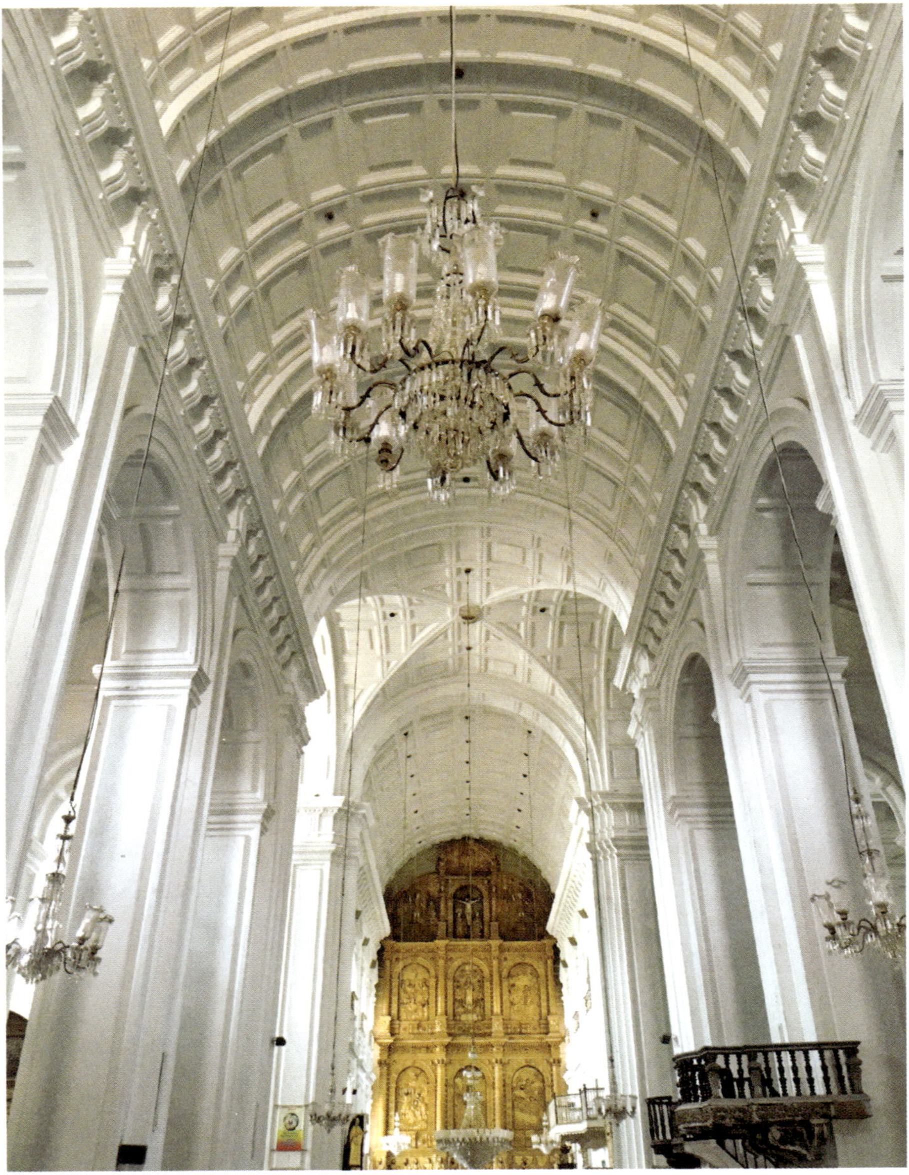

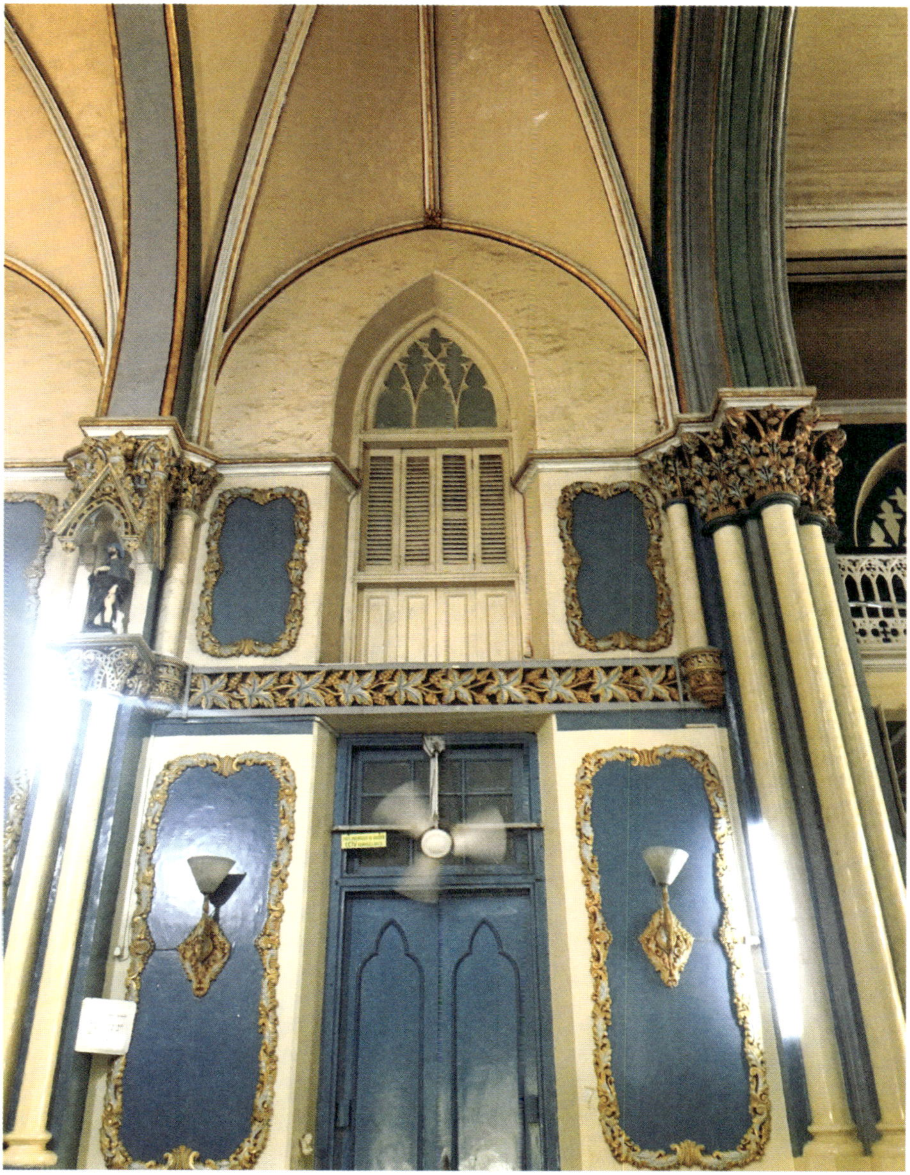

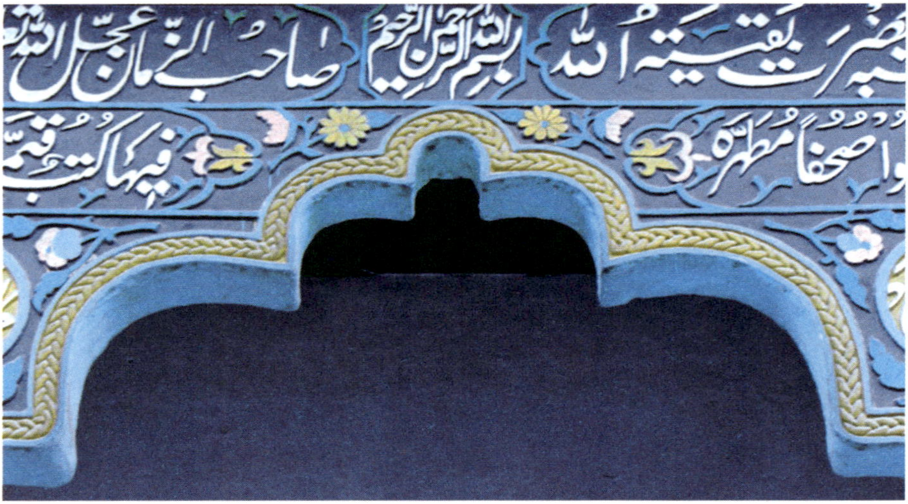
بسم الله الرحمن الرحيم

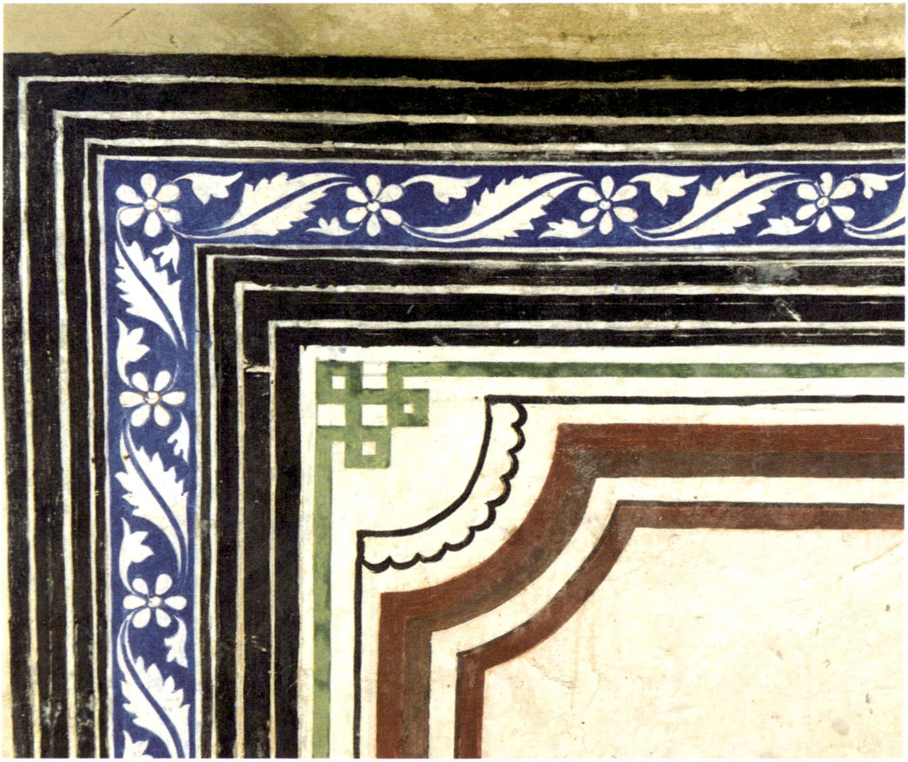

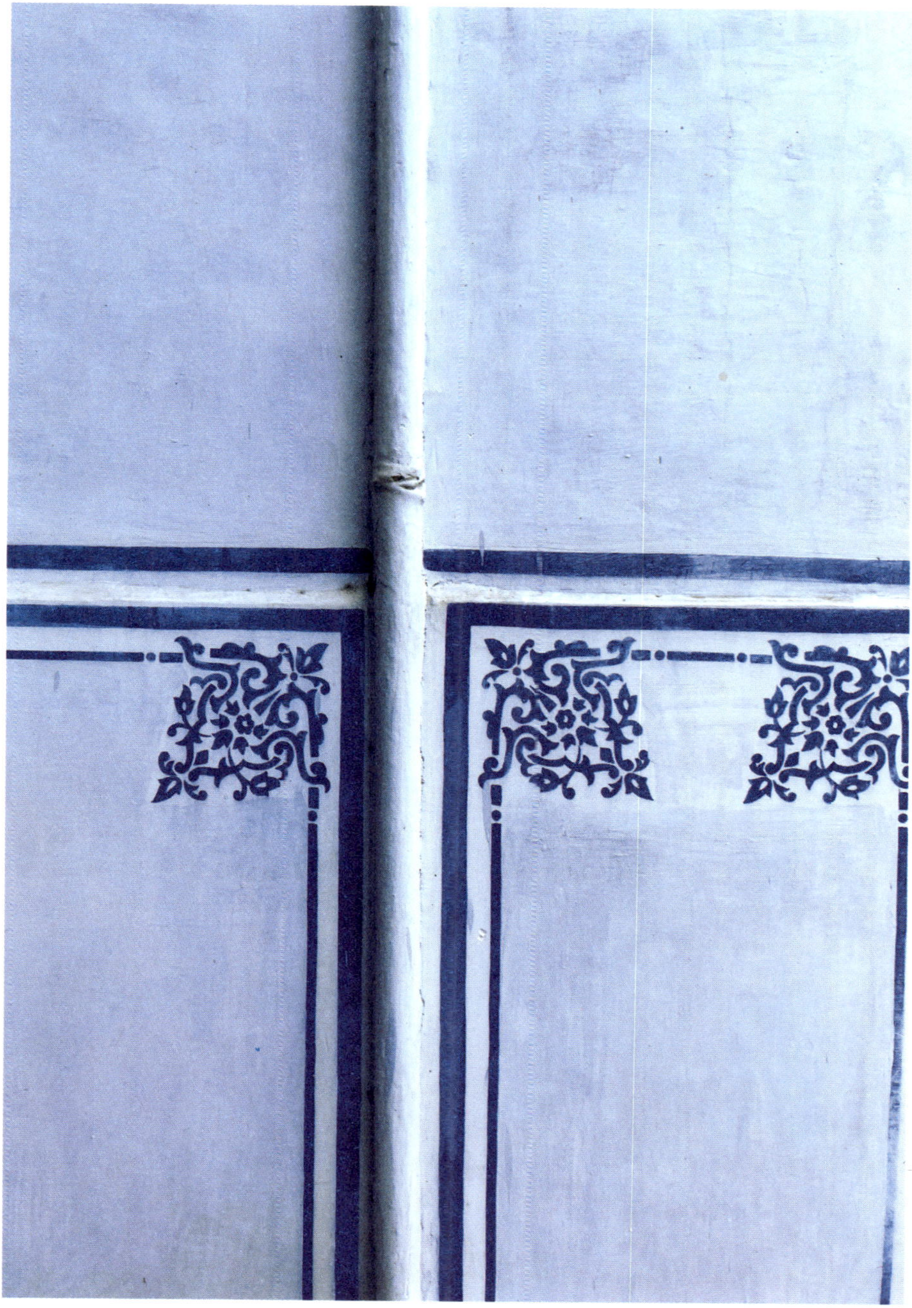

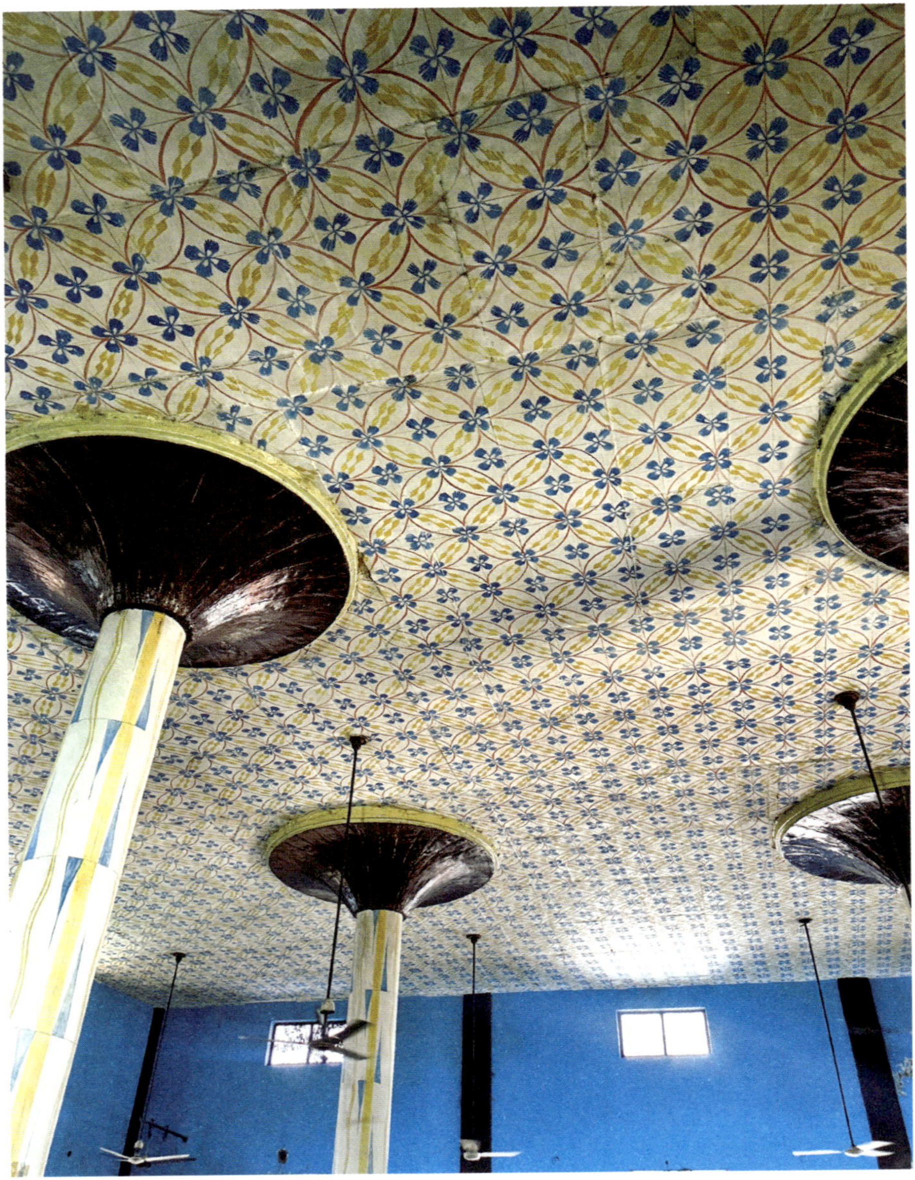

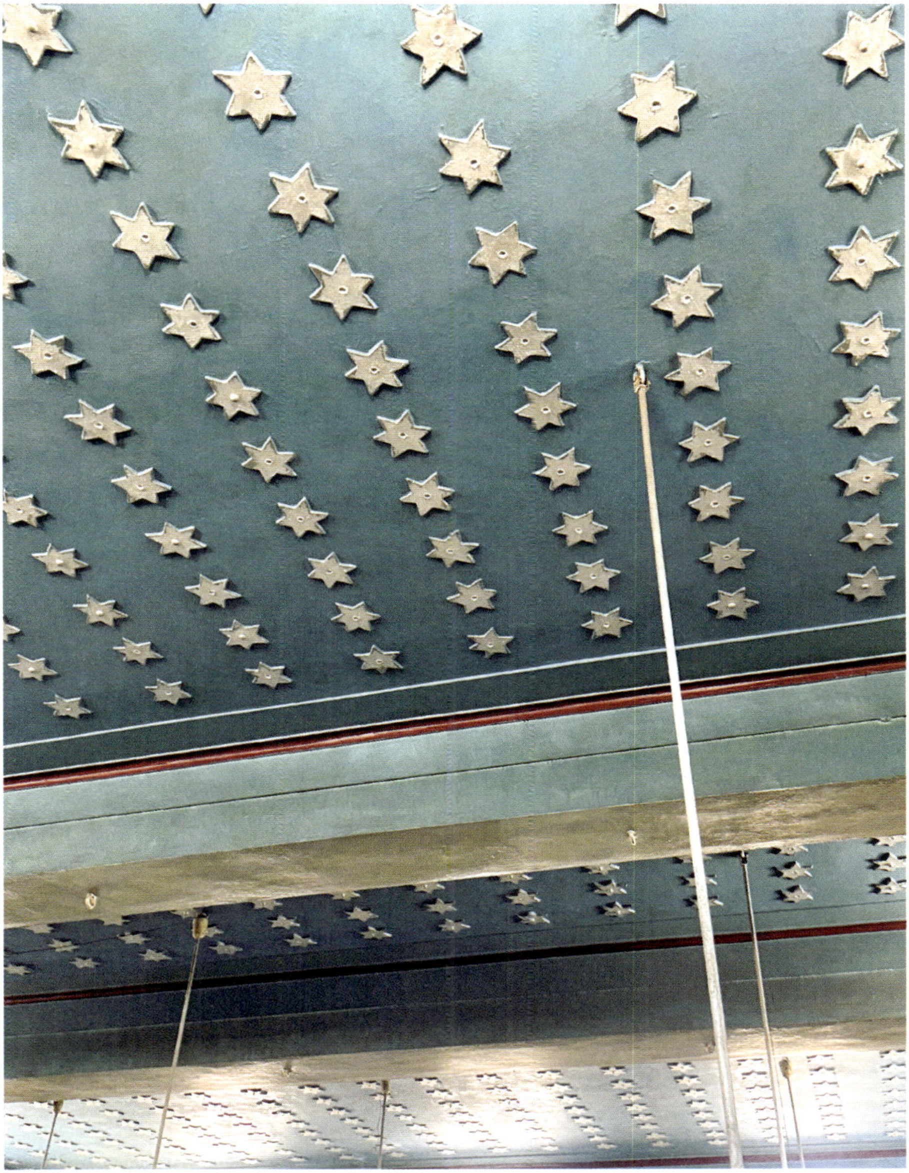

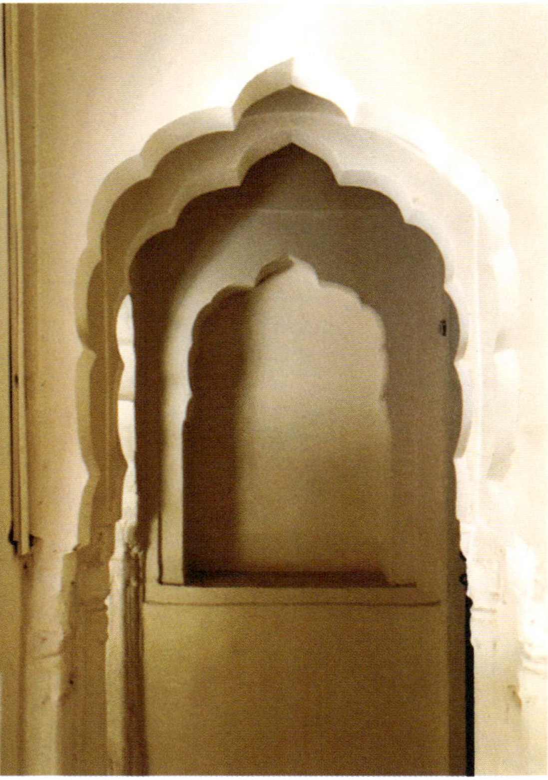

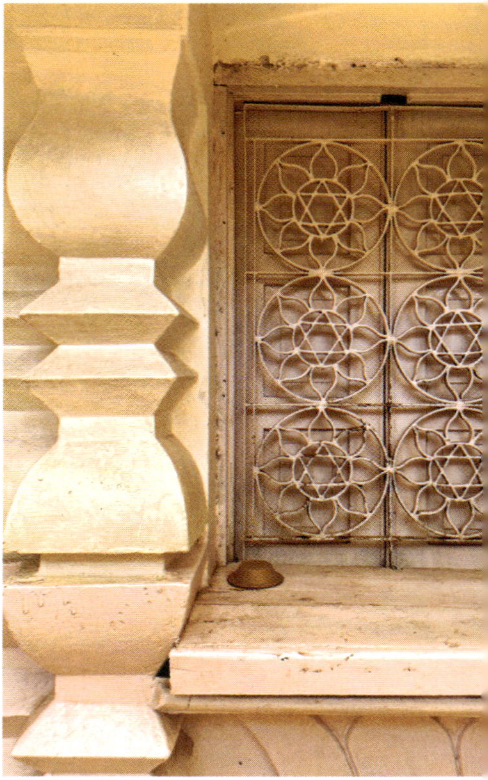

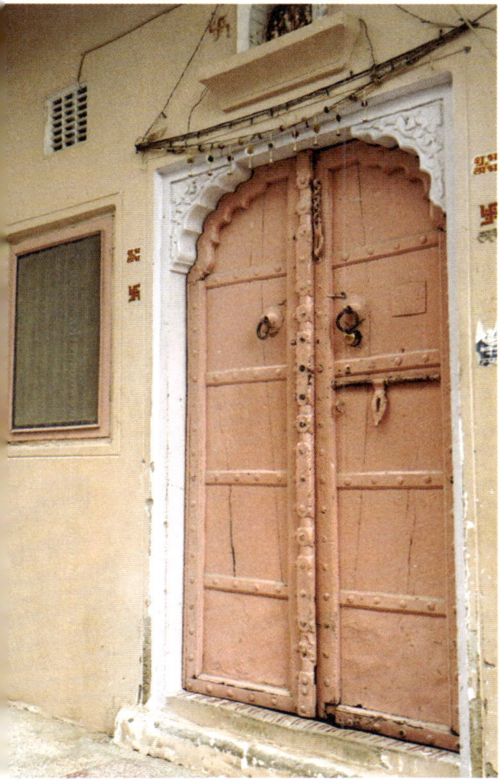

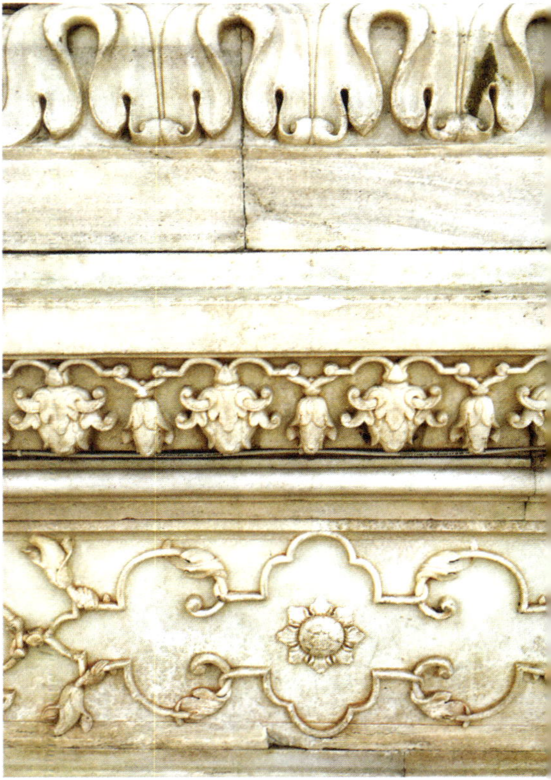

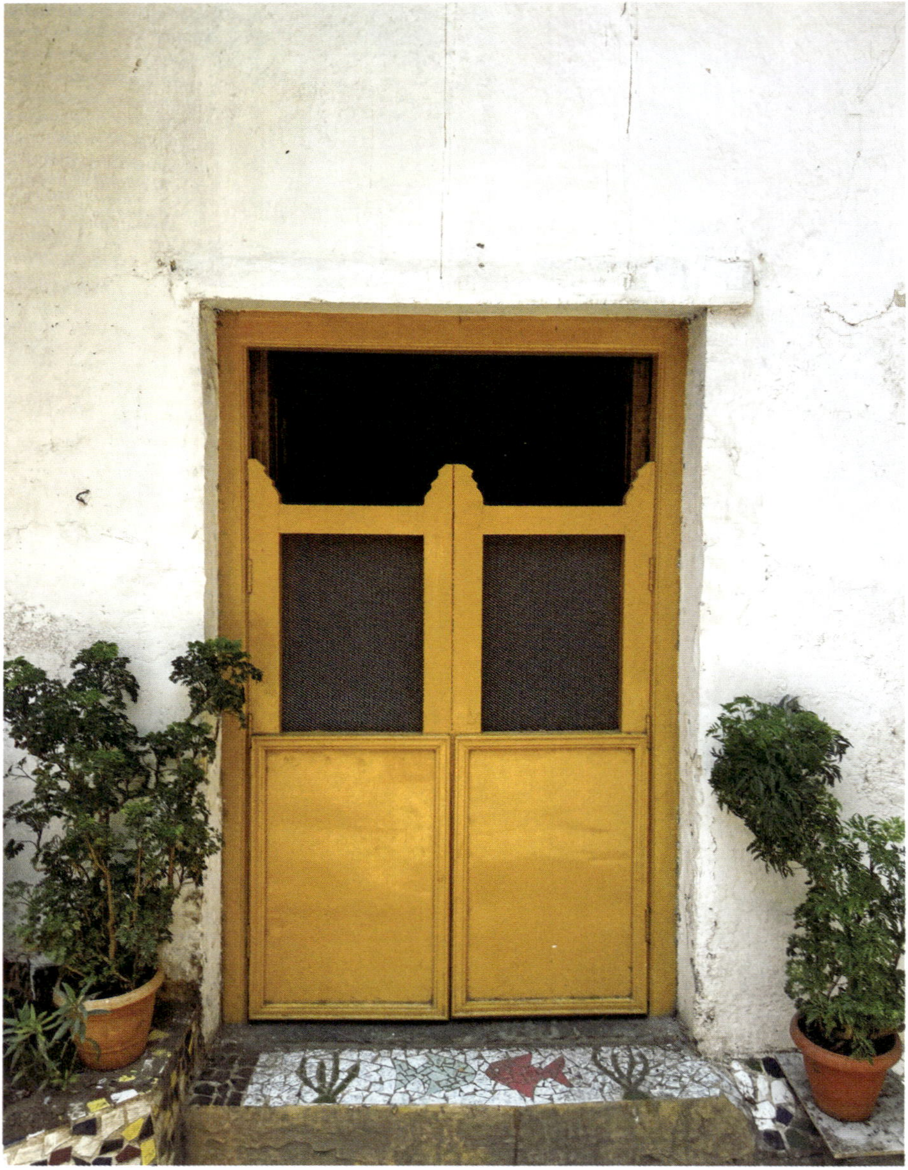

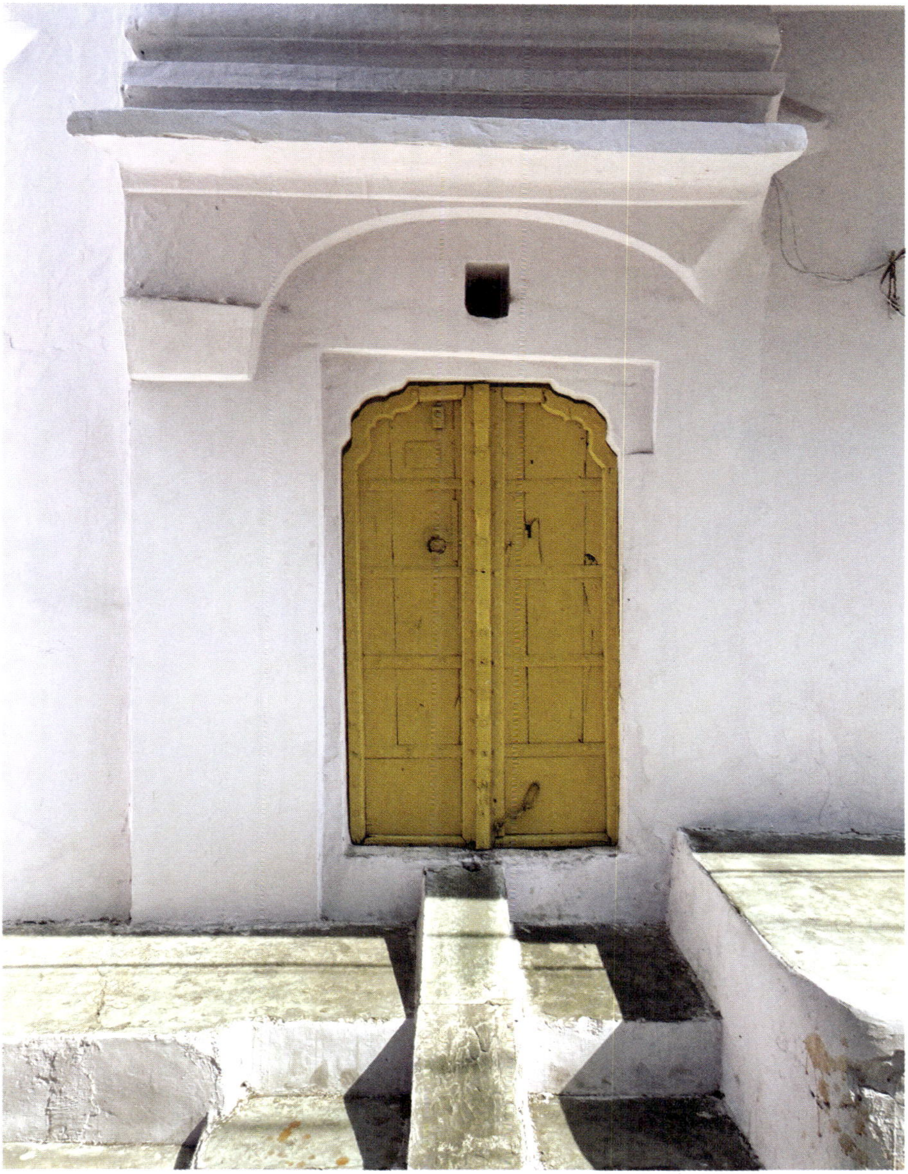

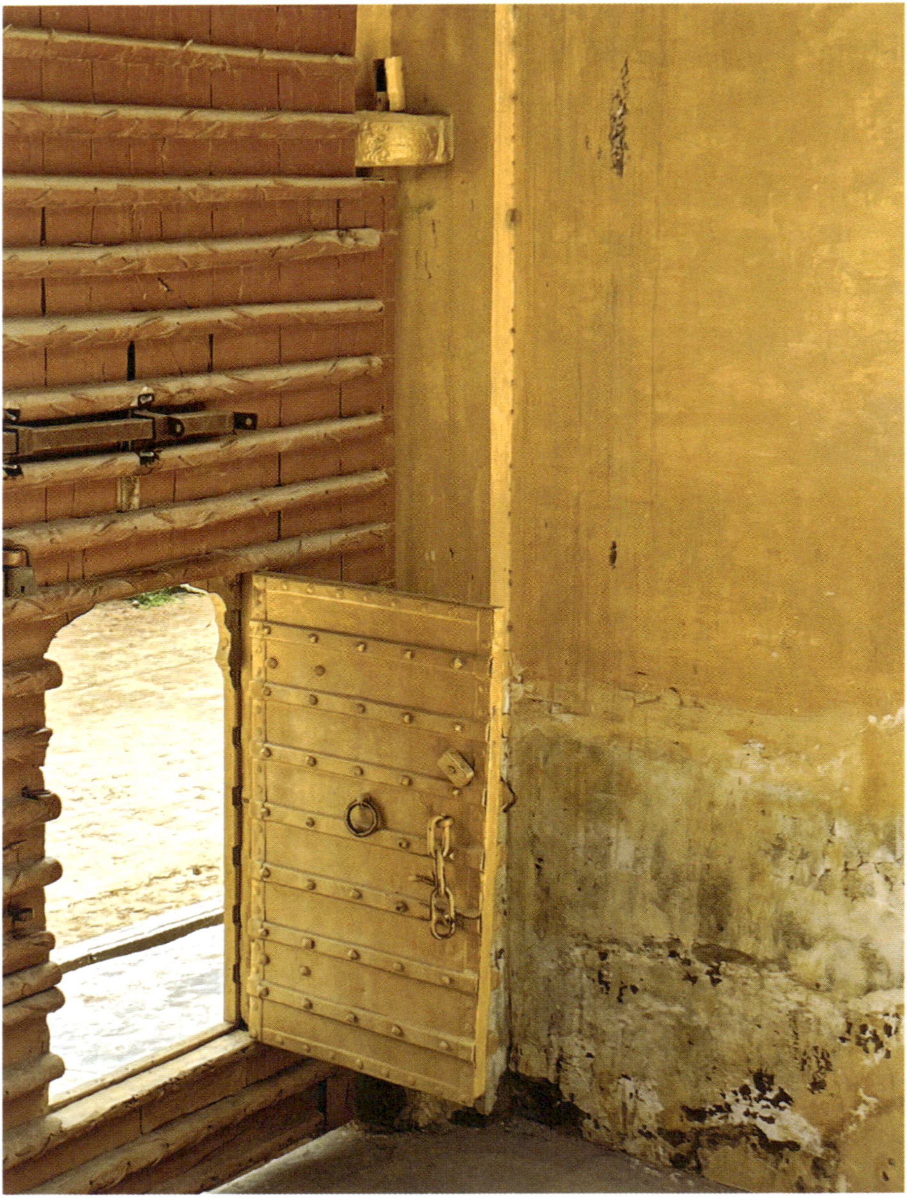

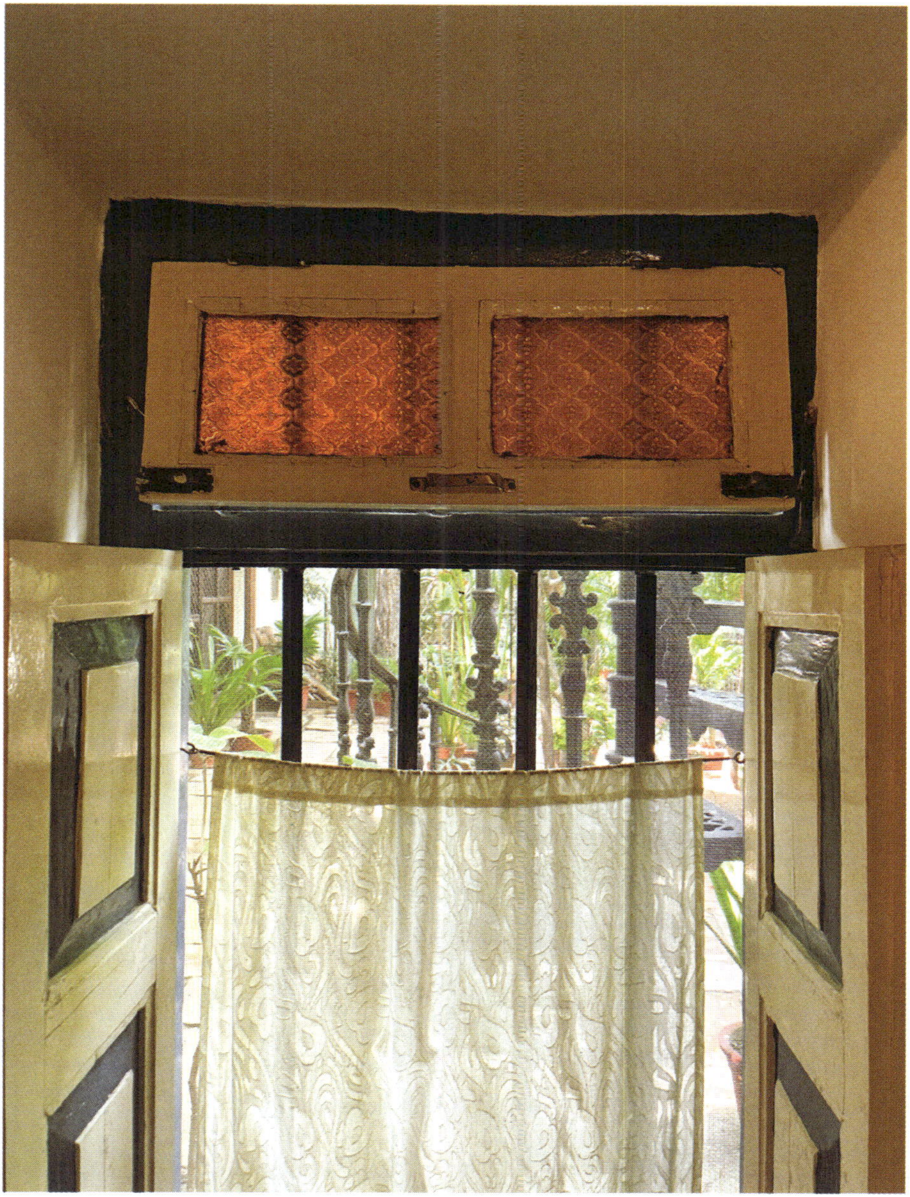

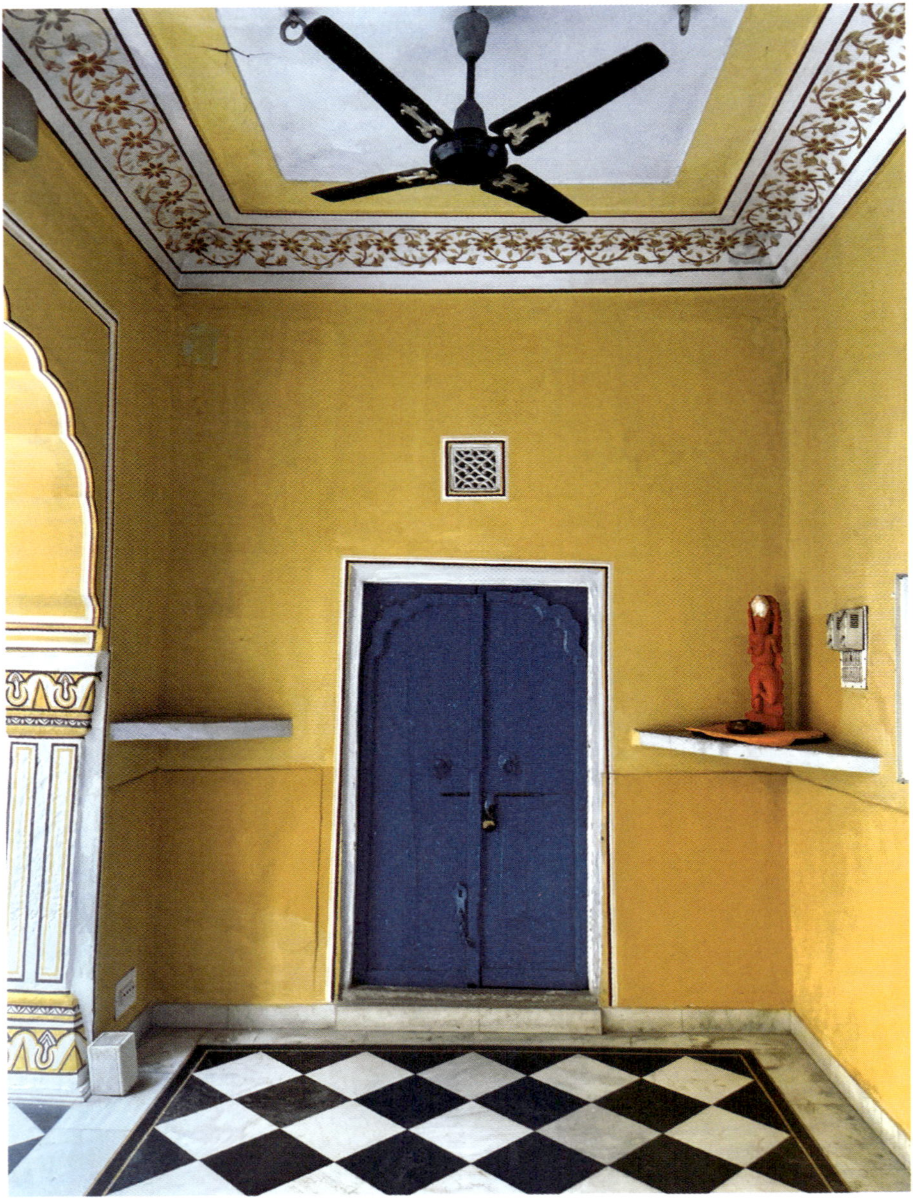

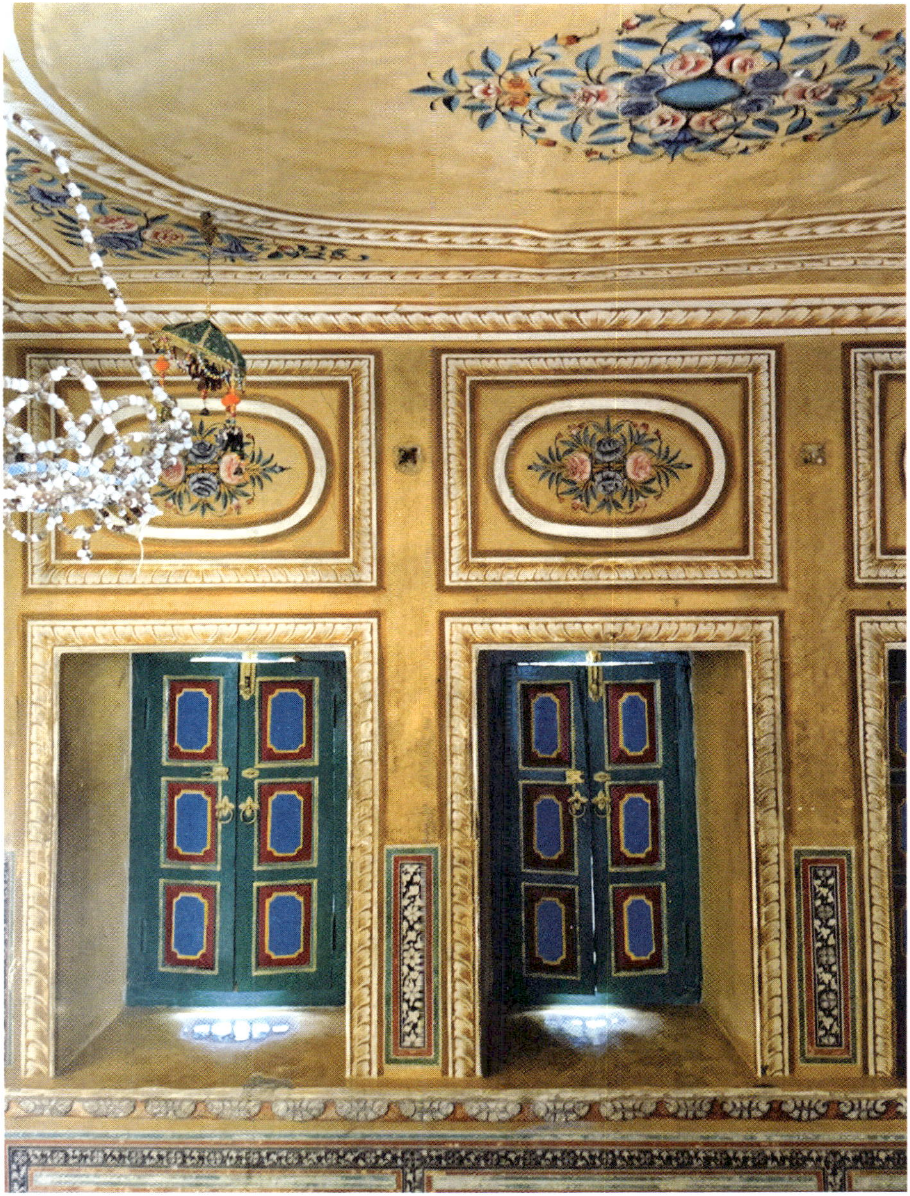

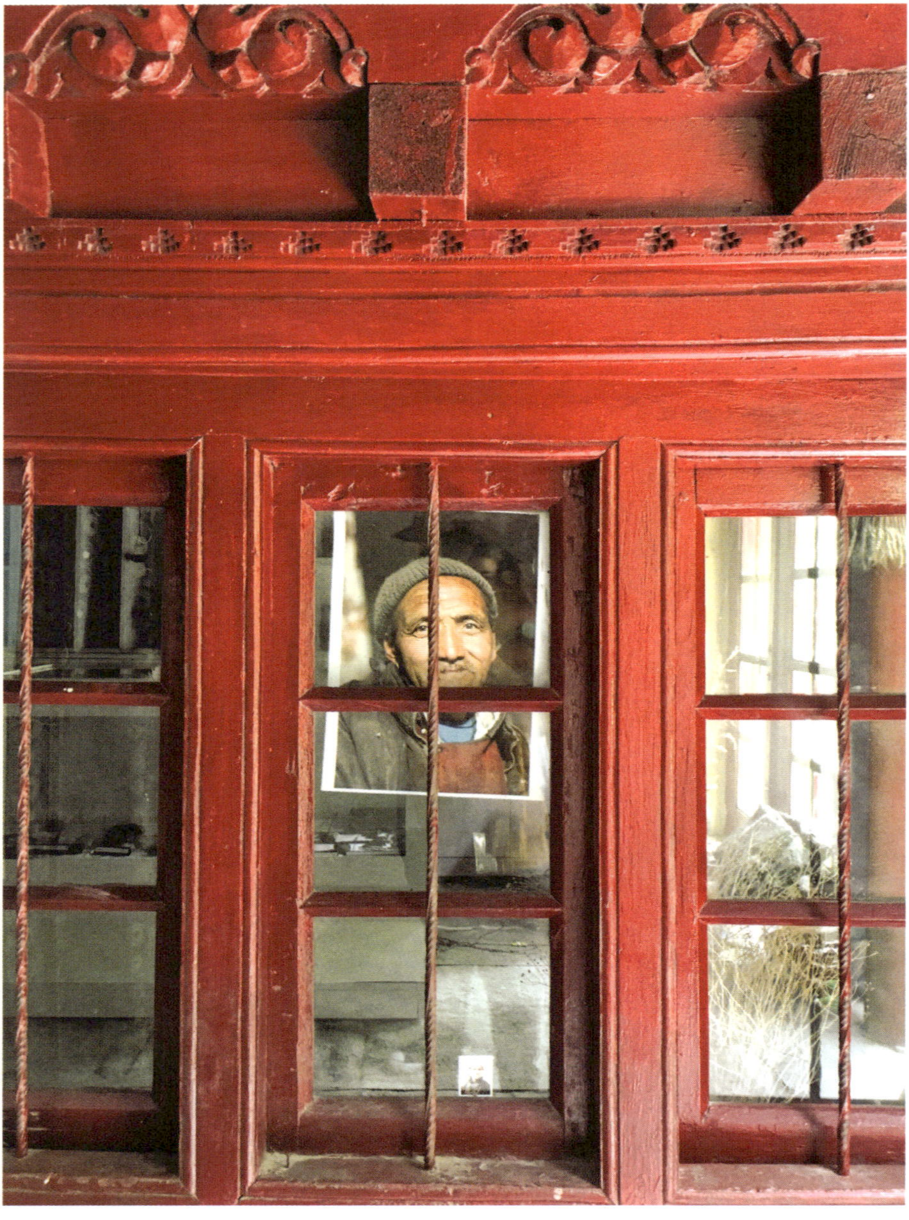

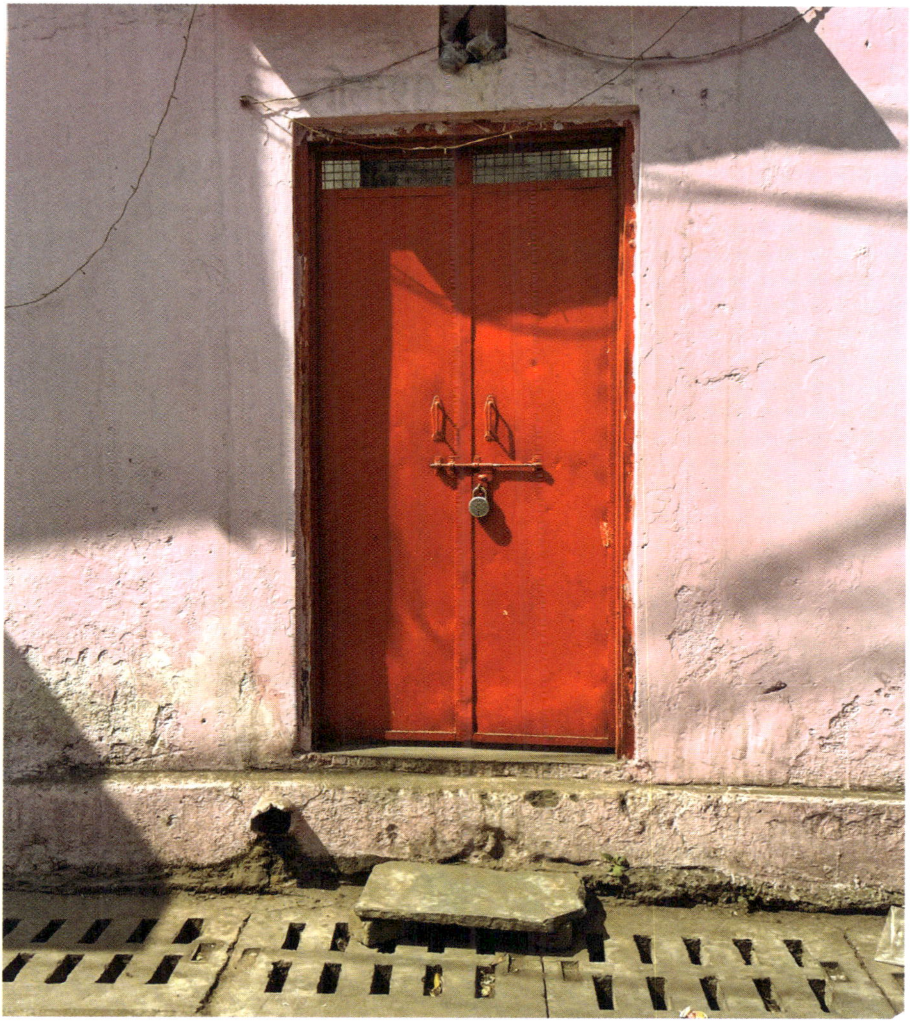

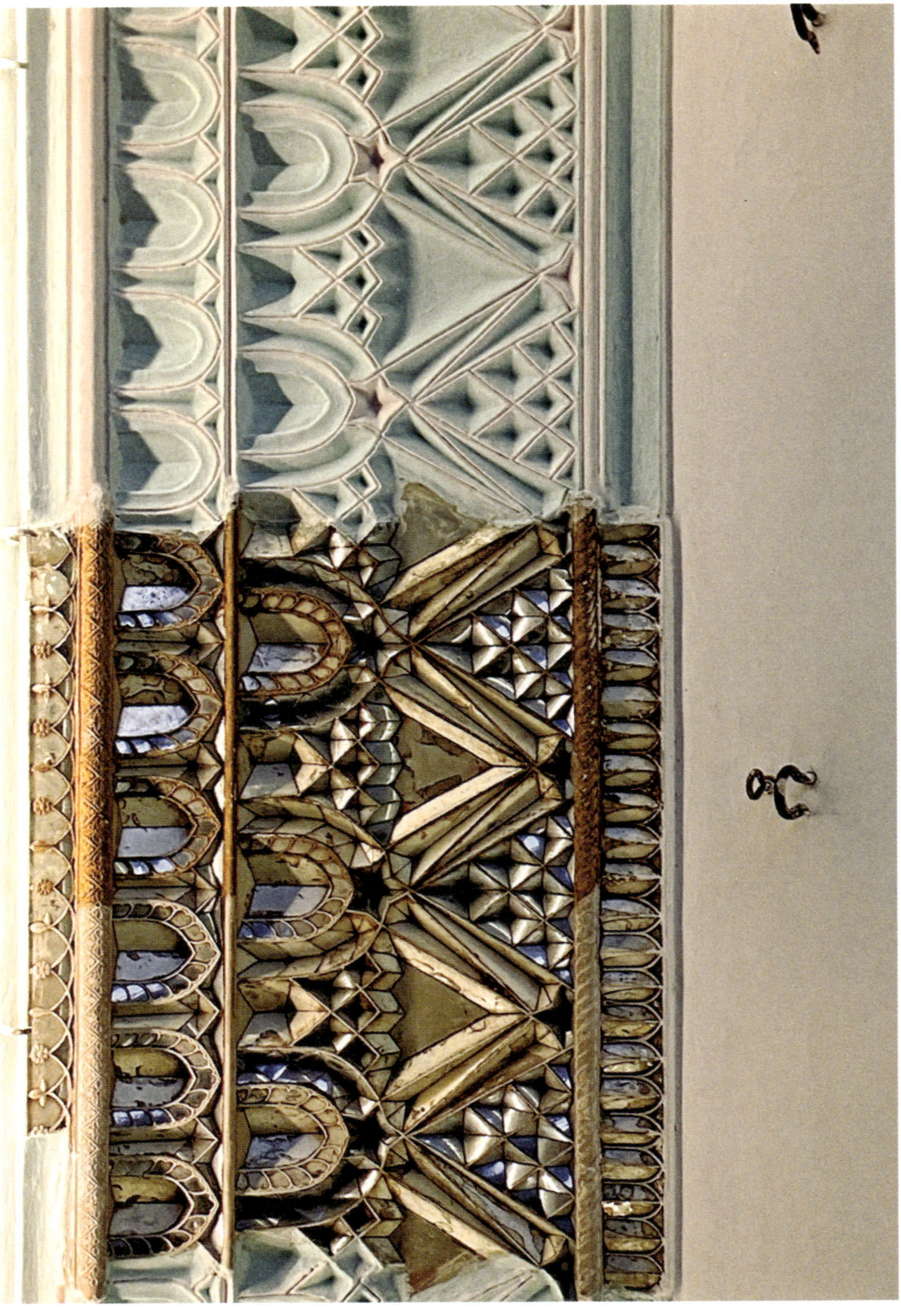

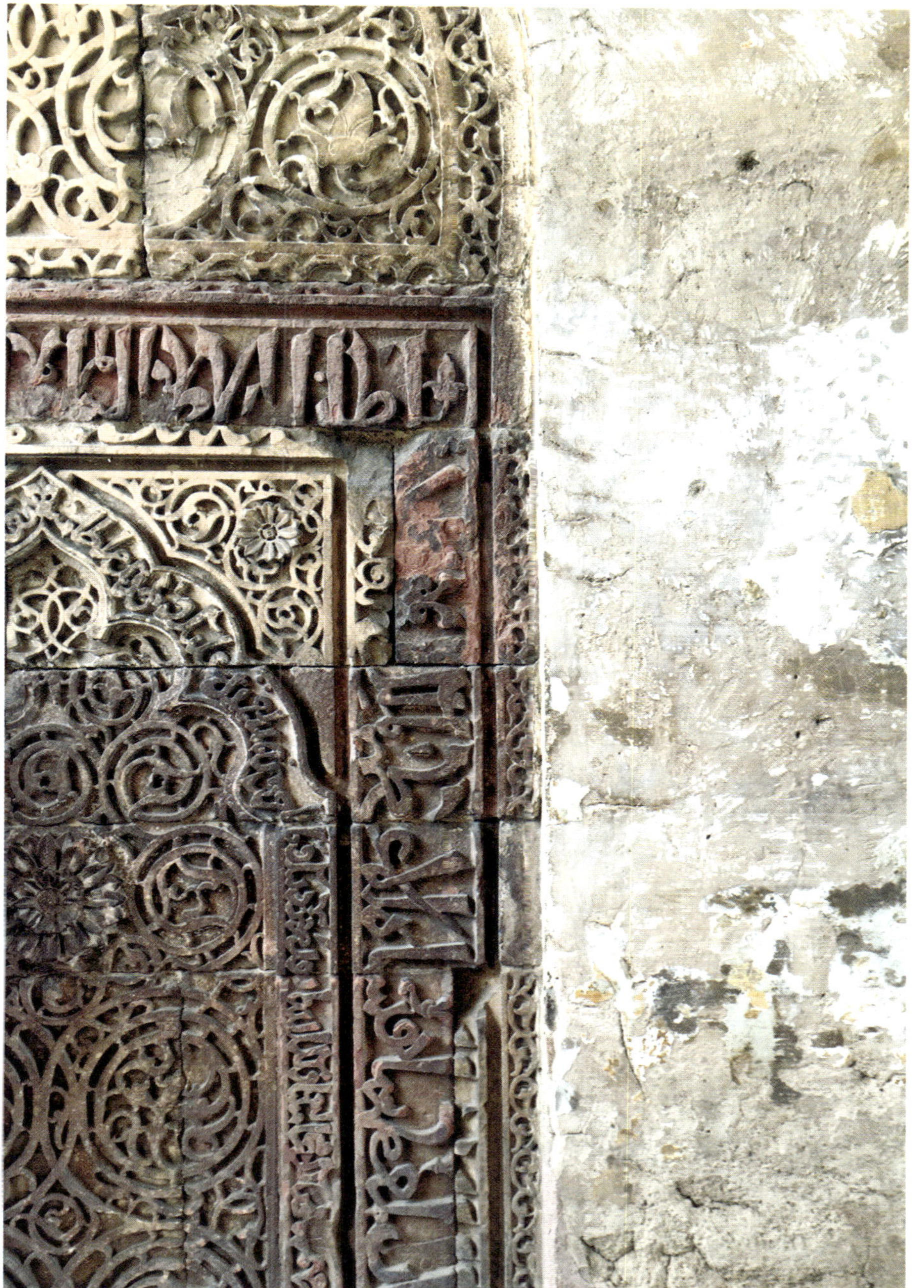

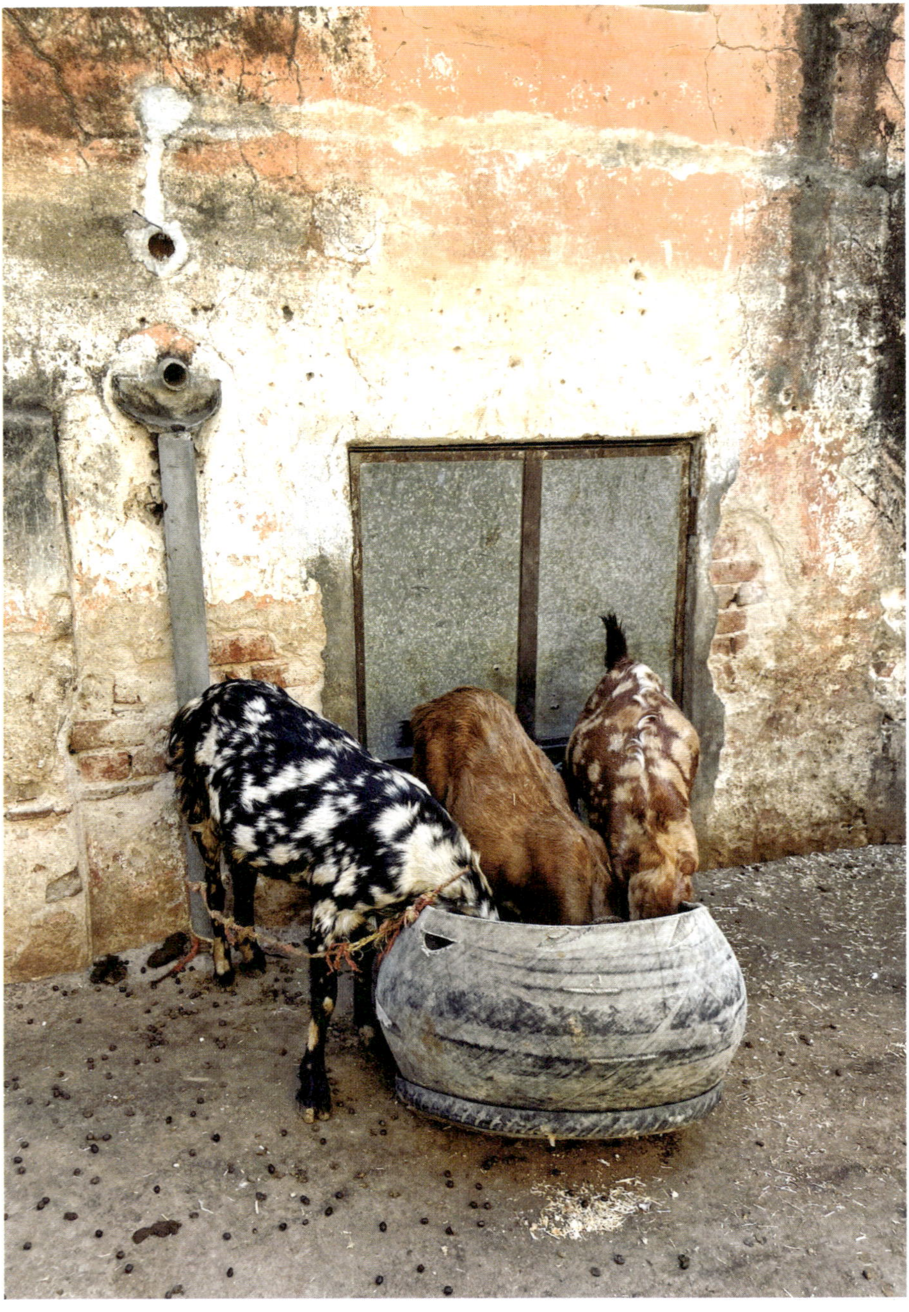

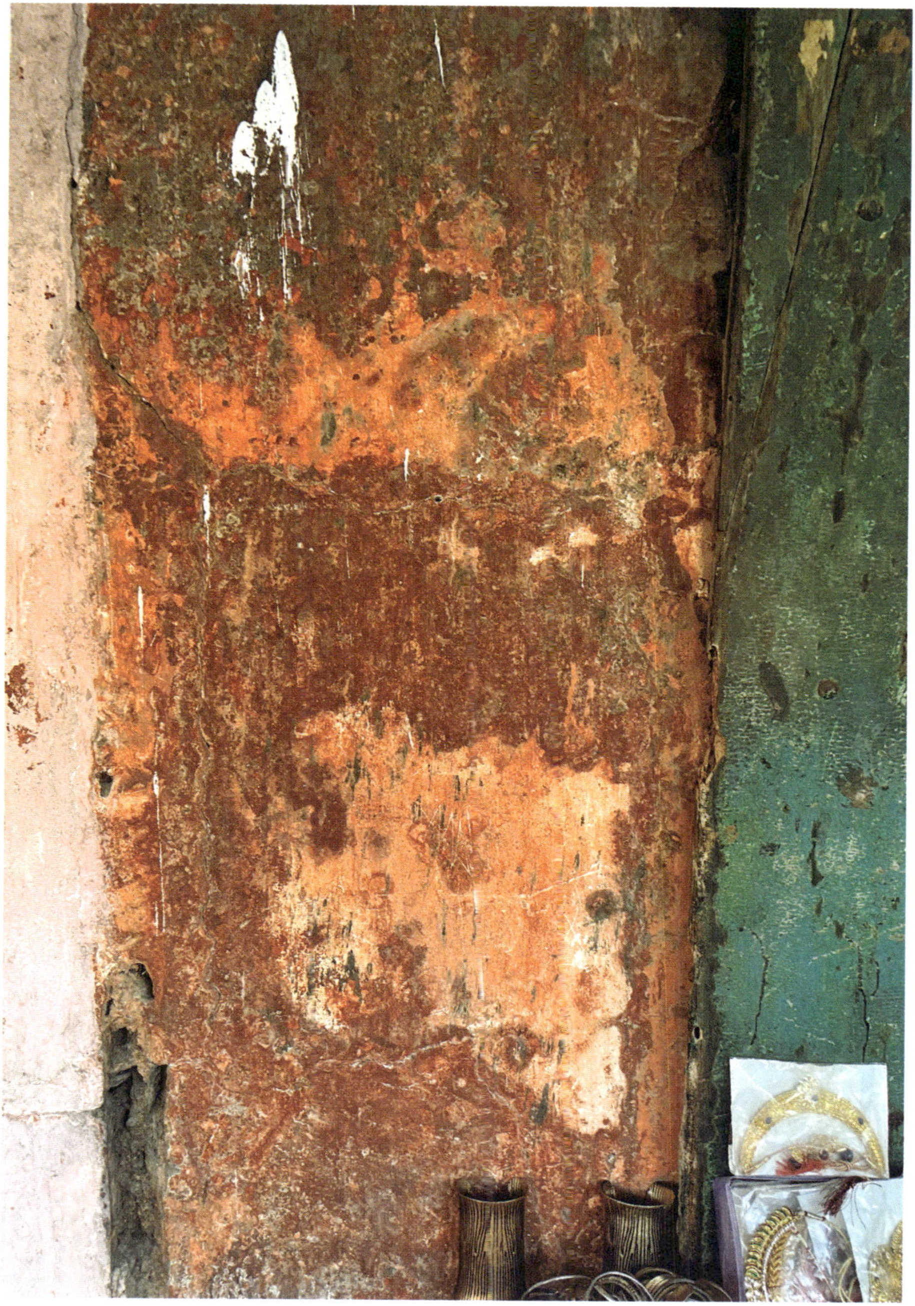

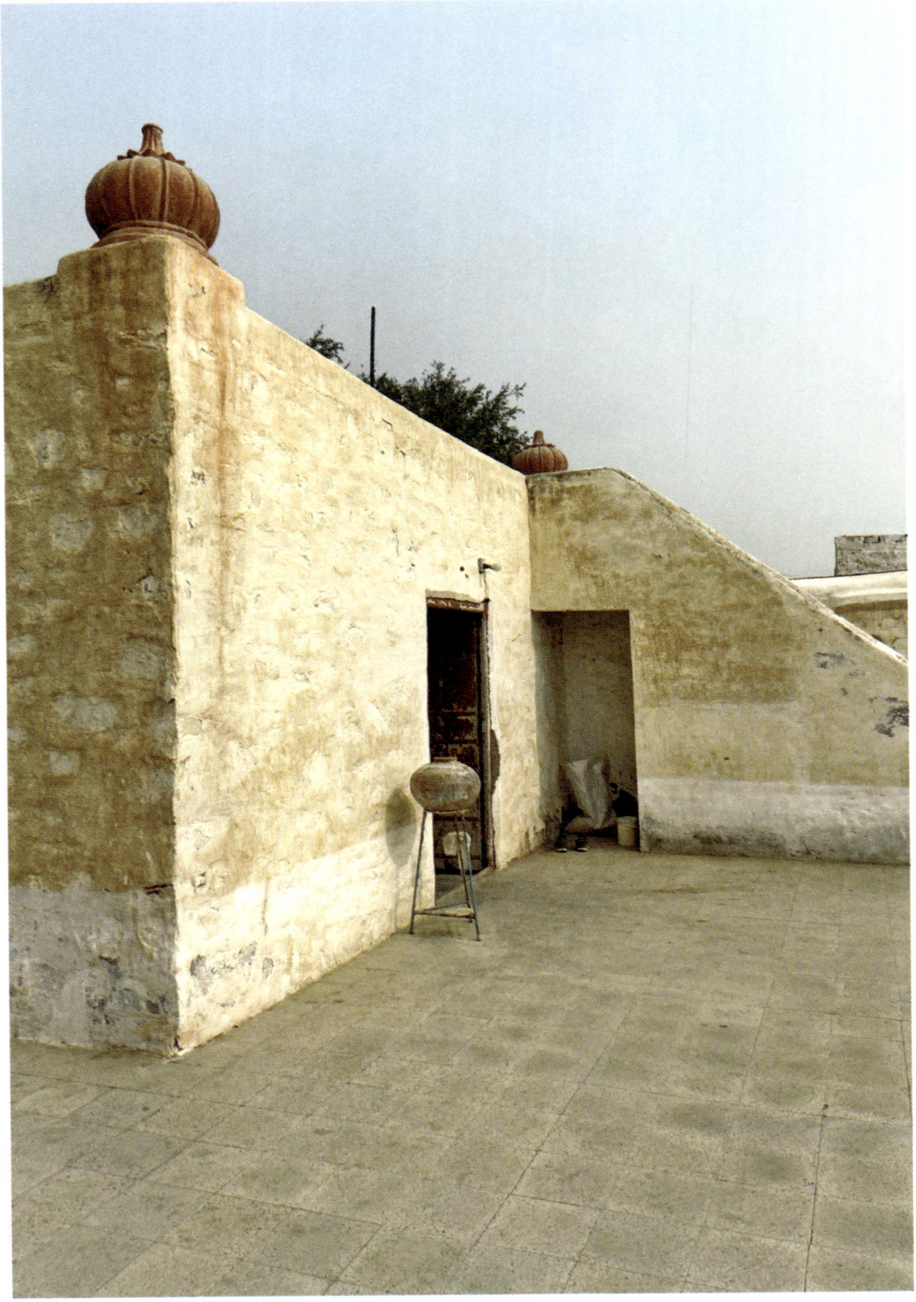

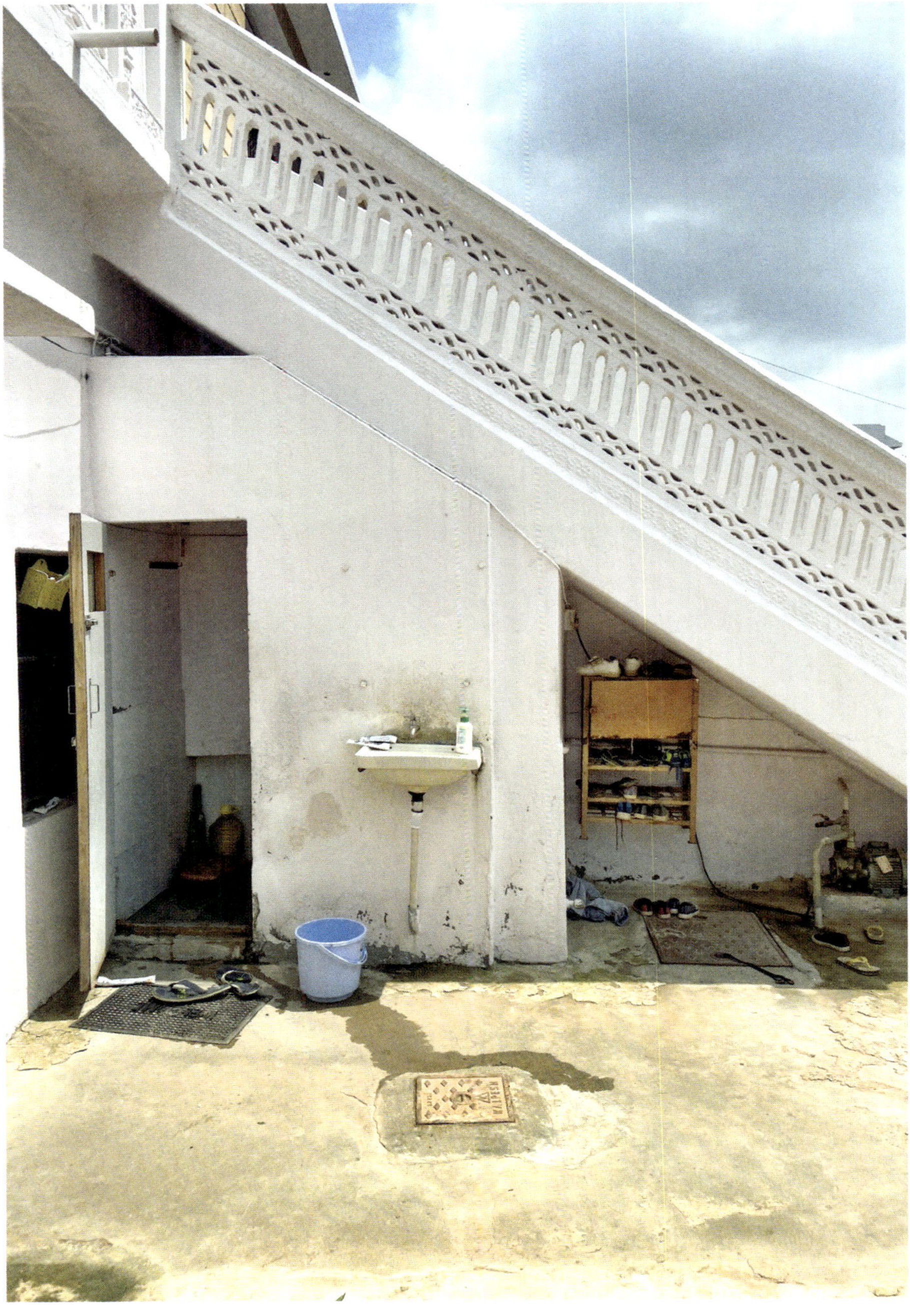

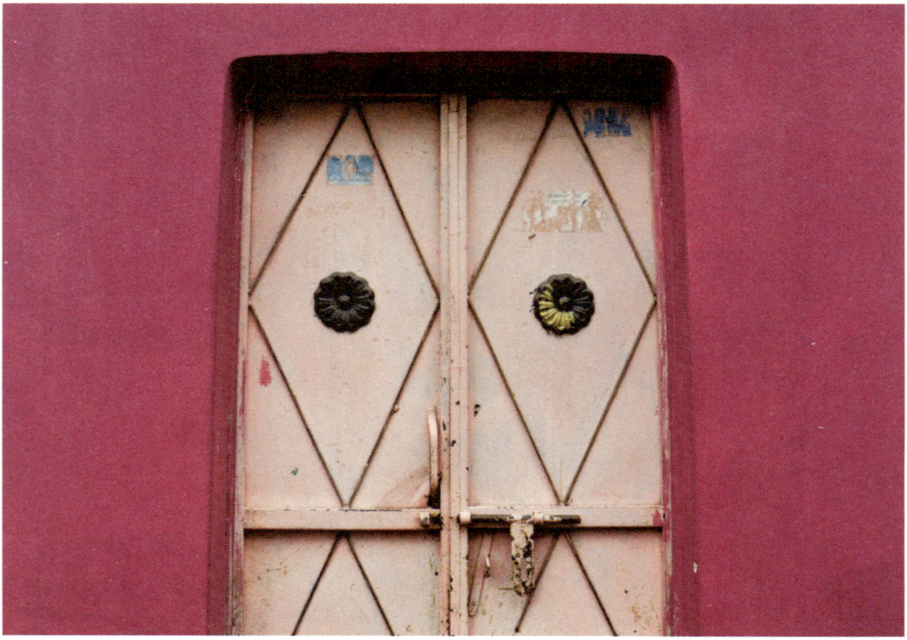

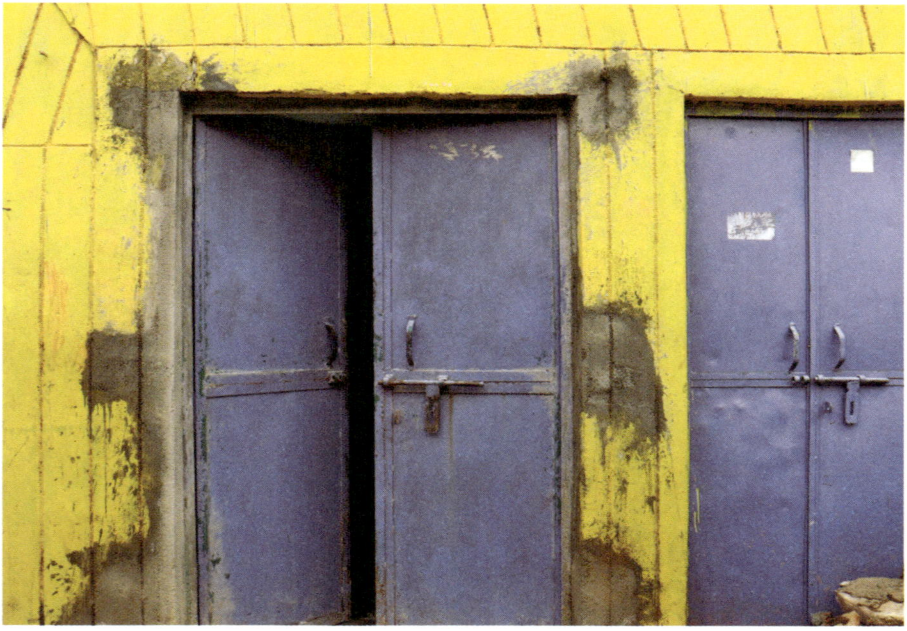

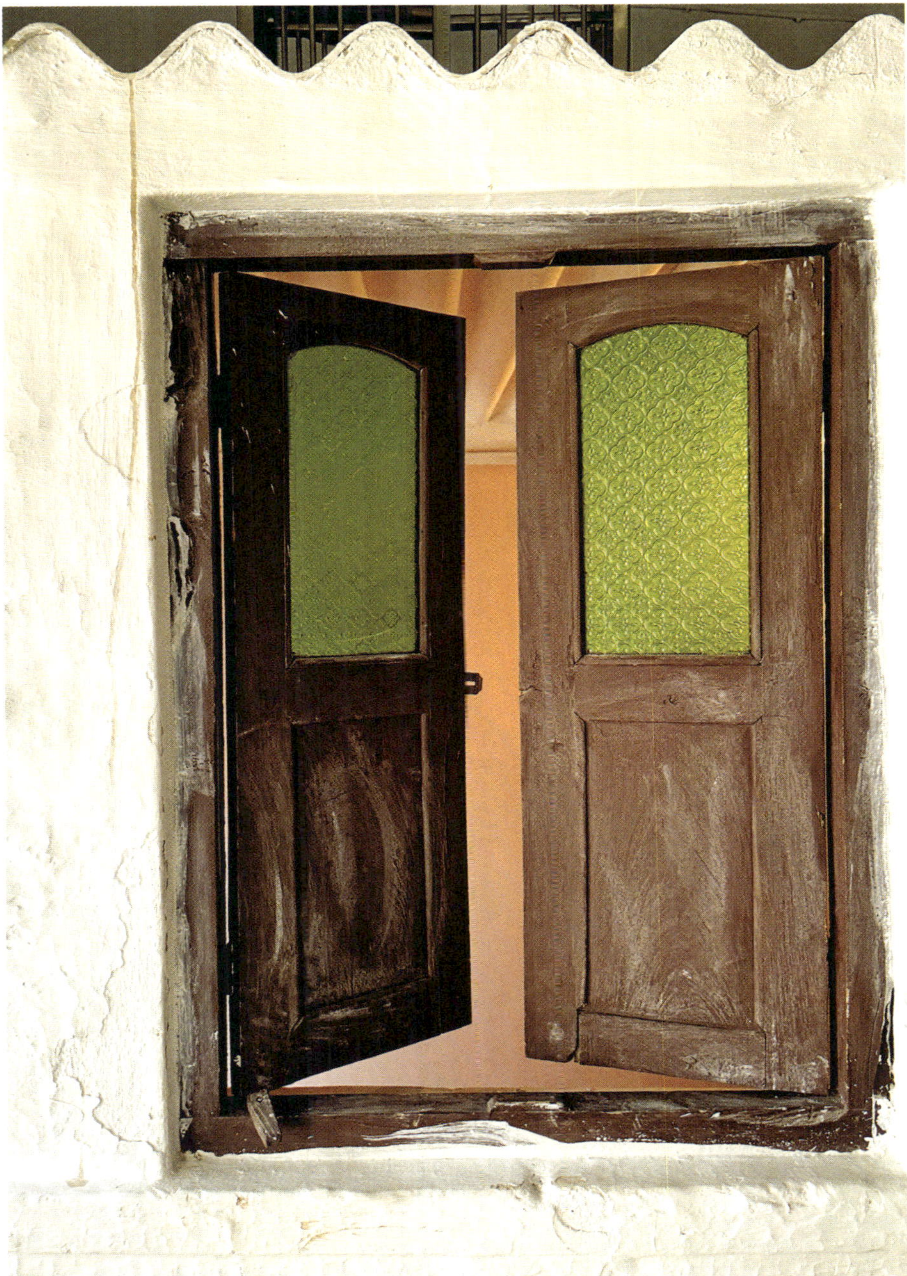

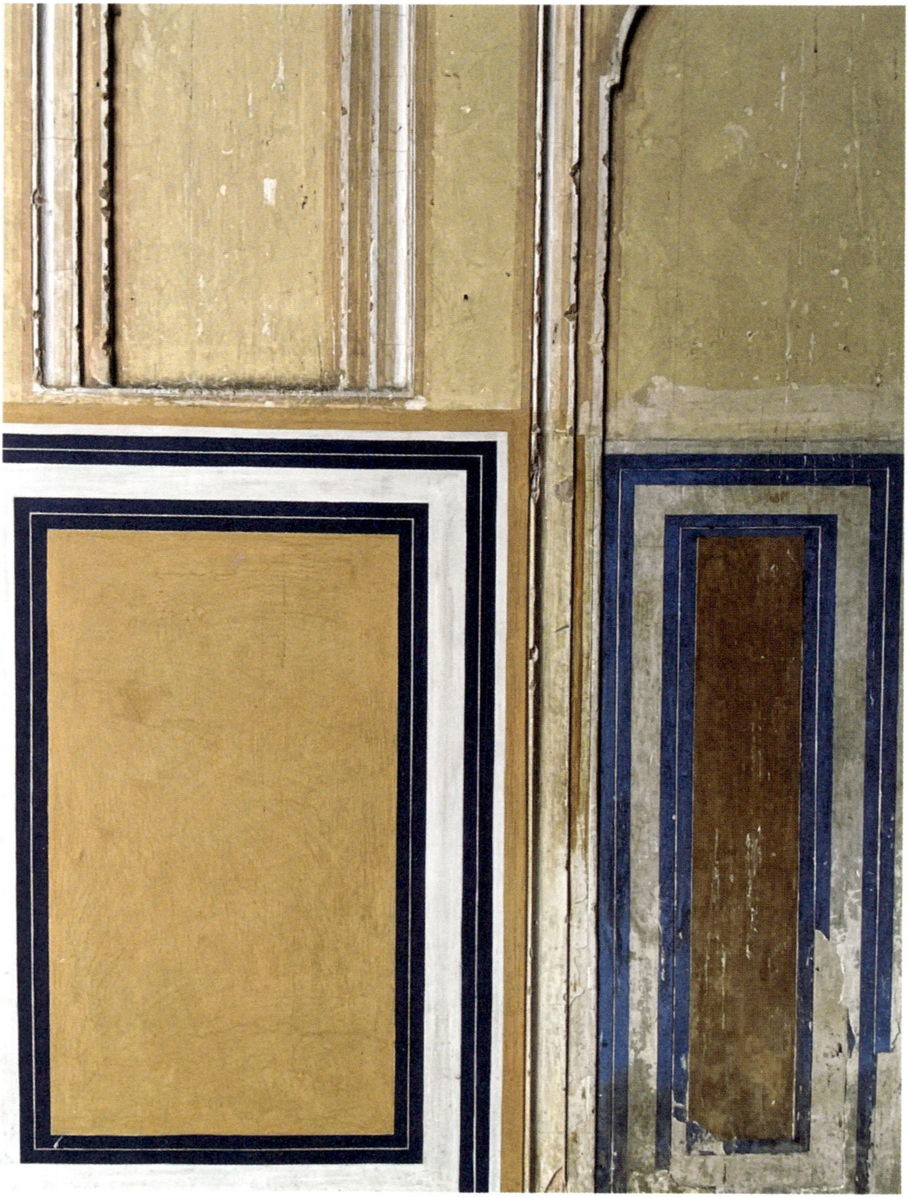

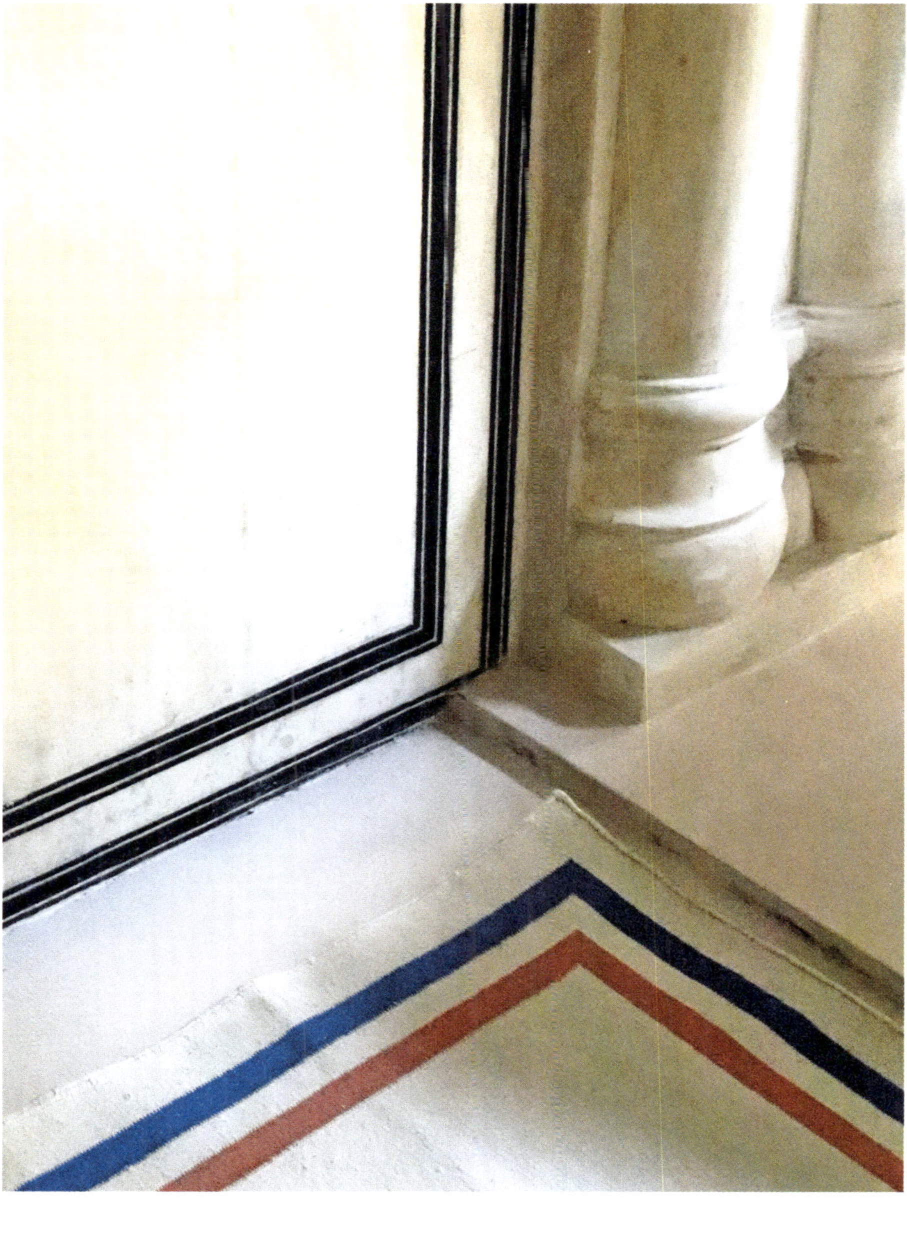

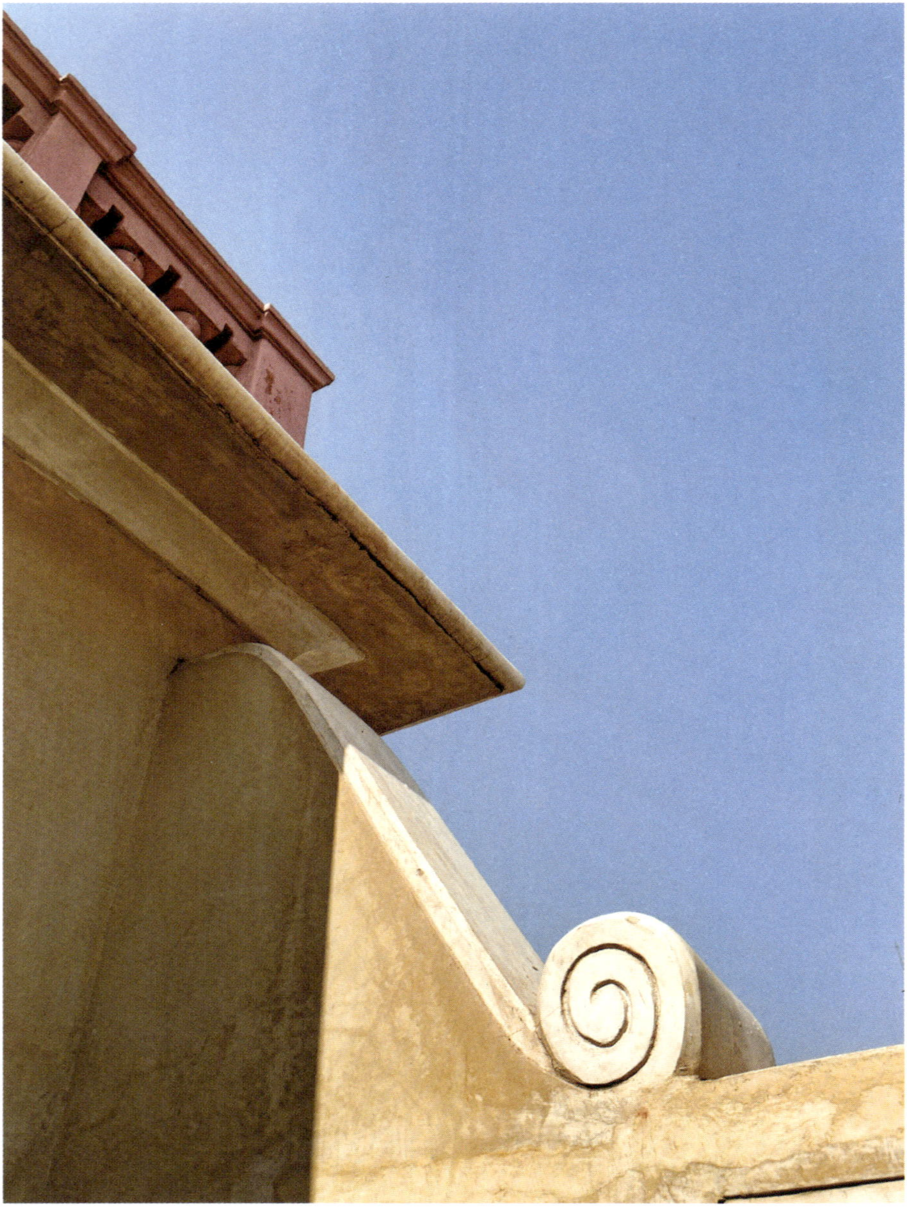

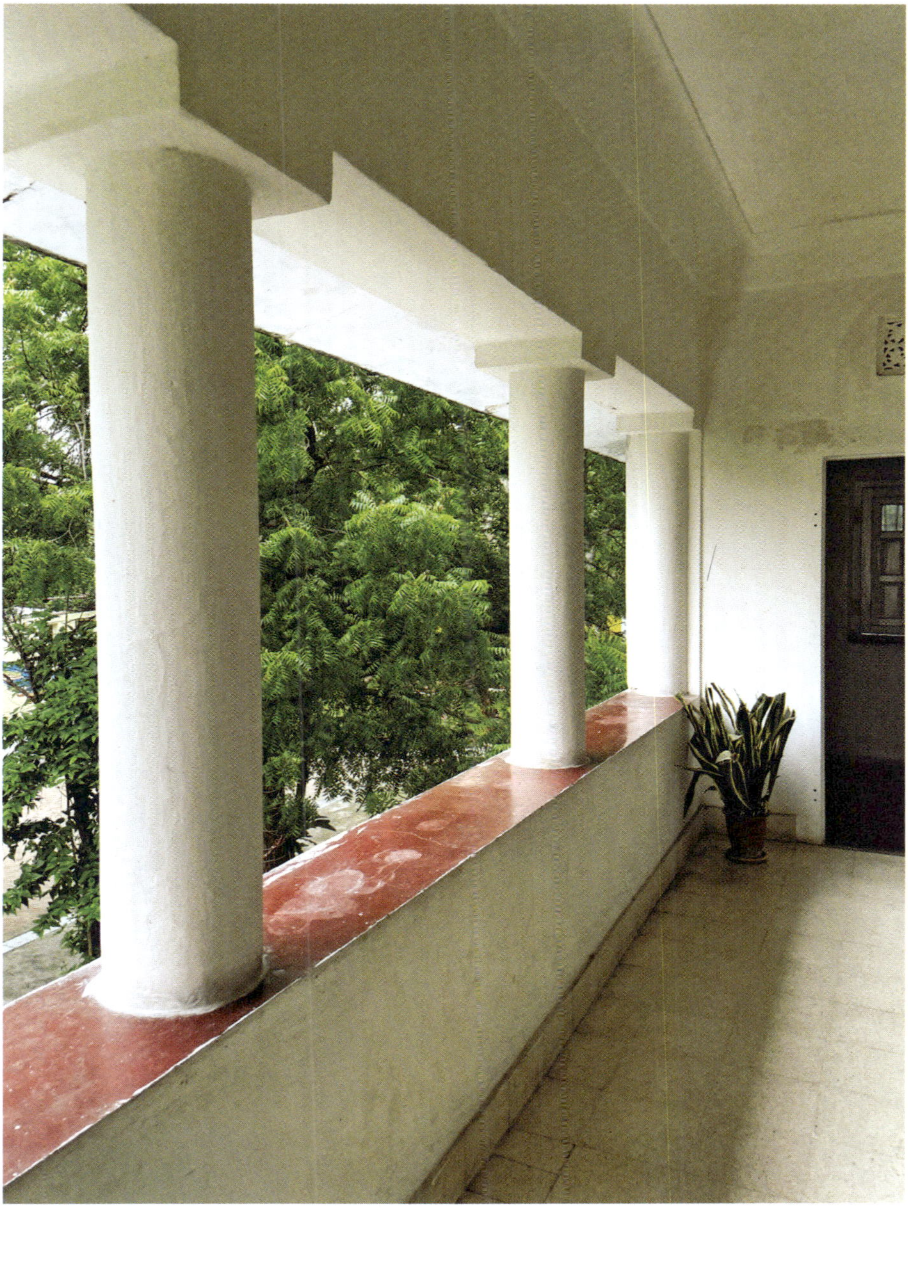

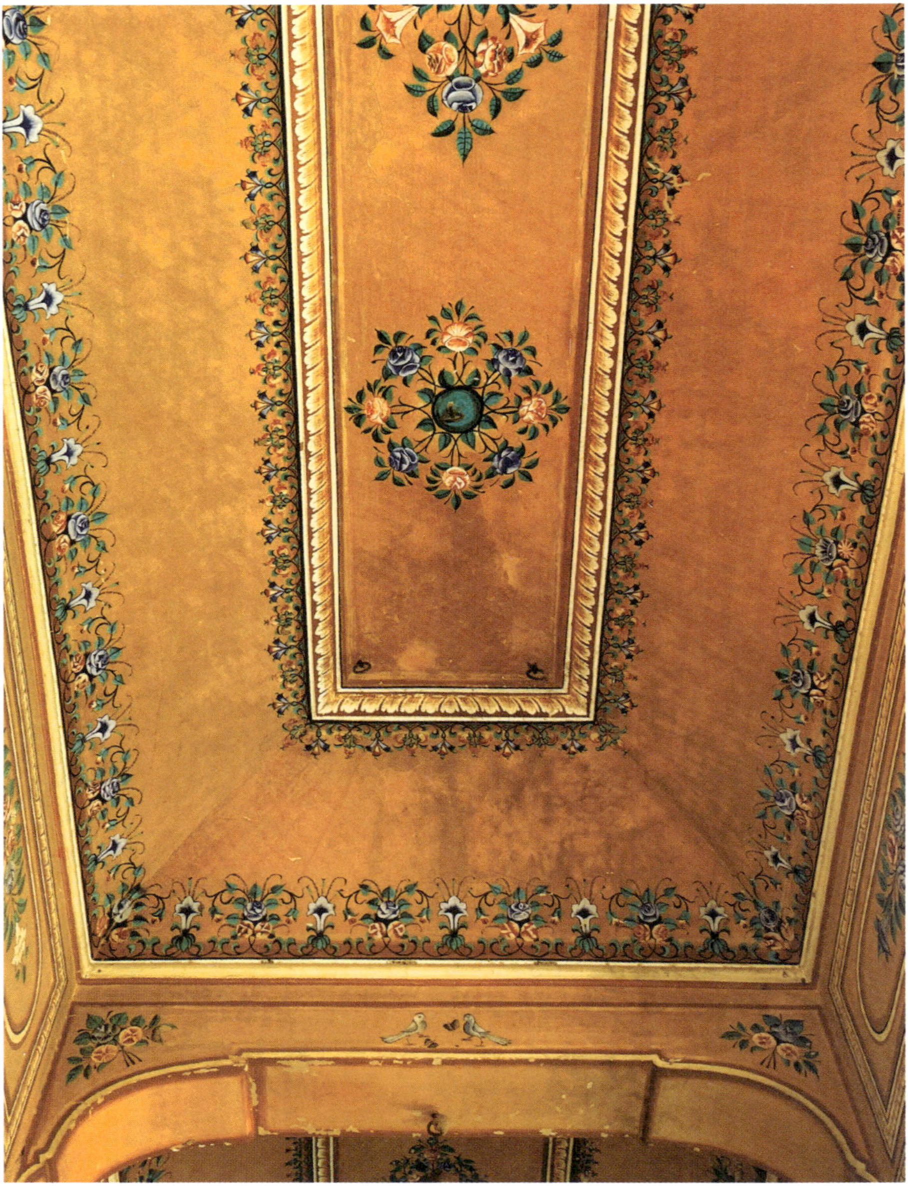

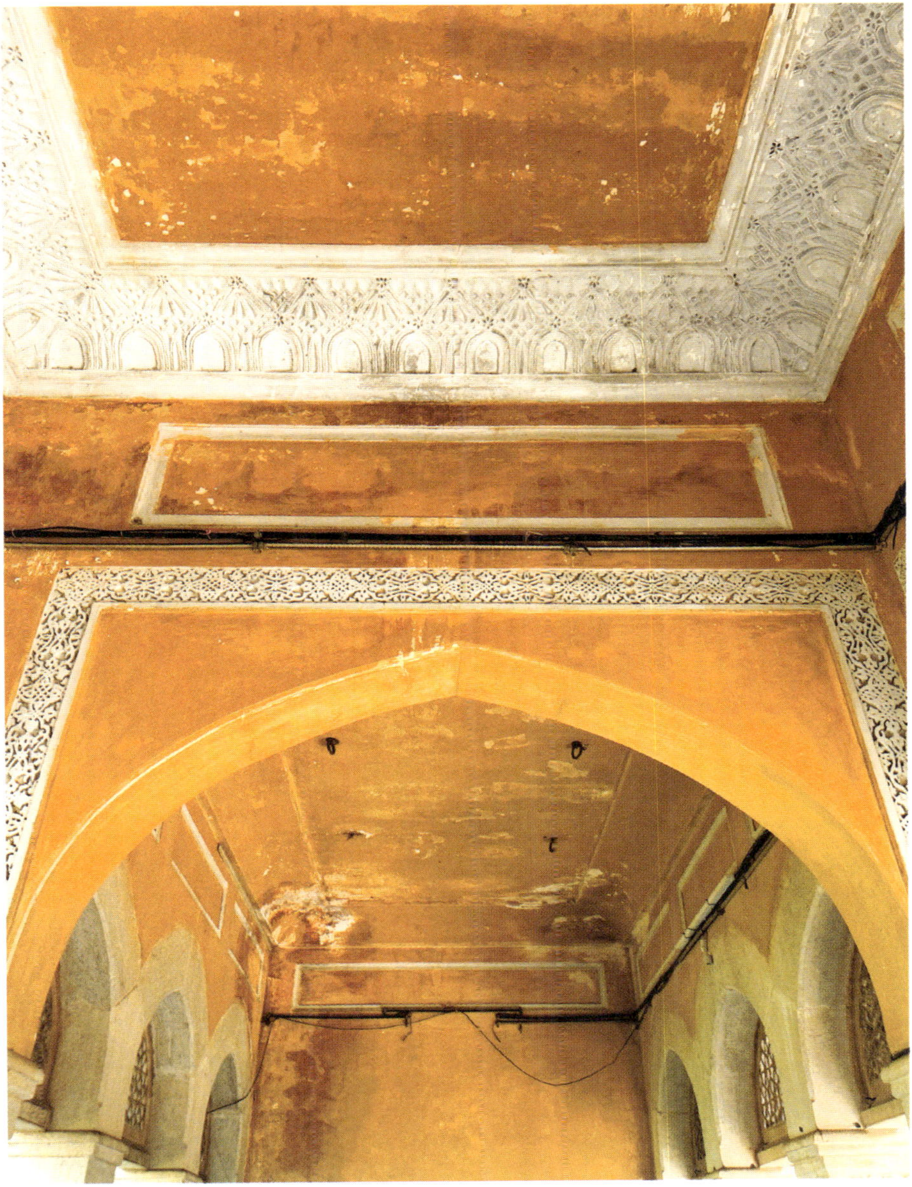

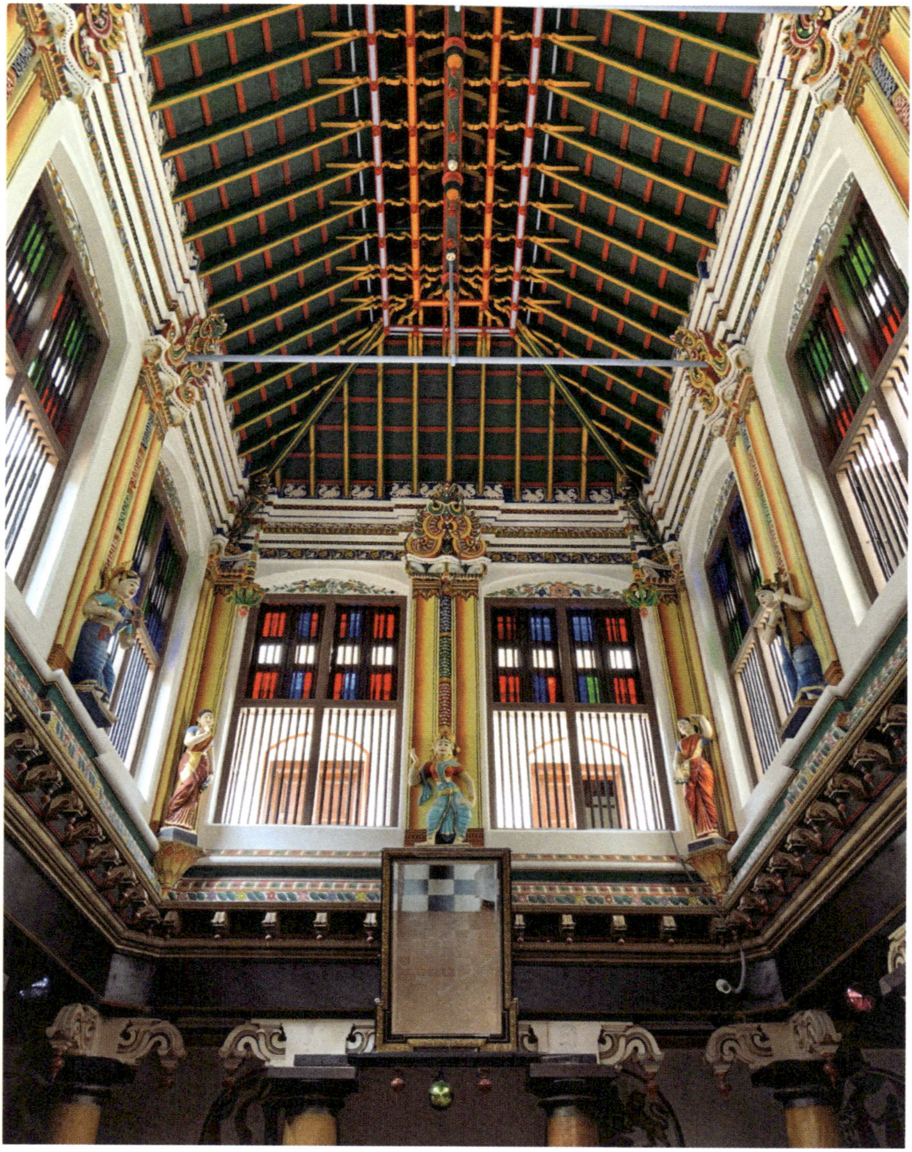

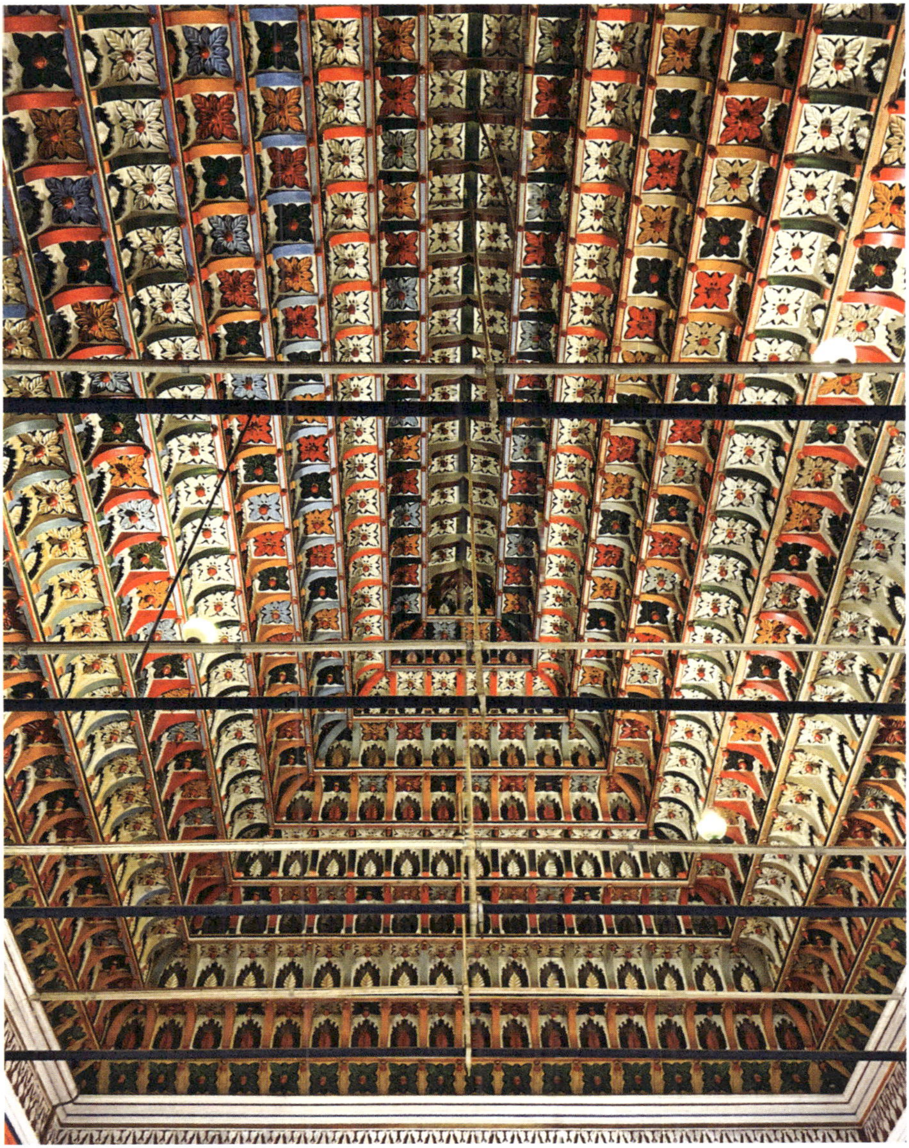

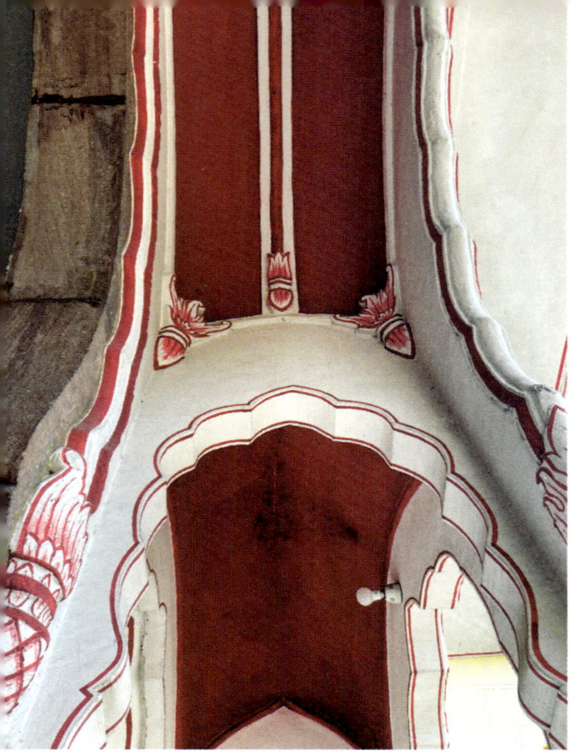
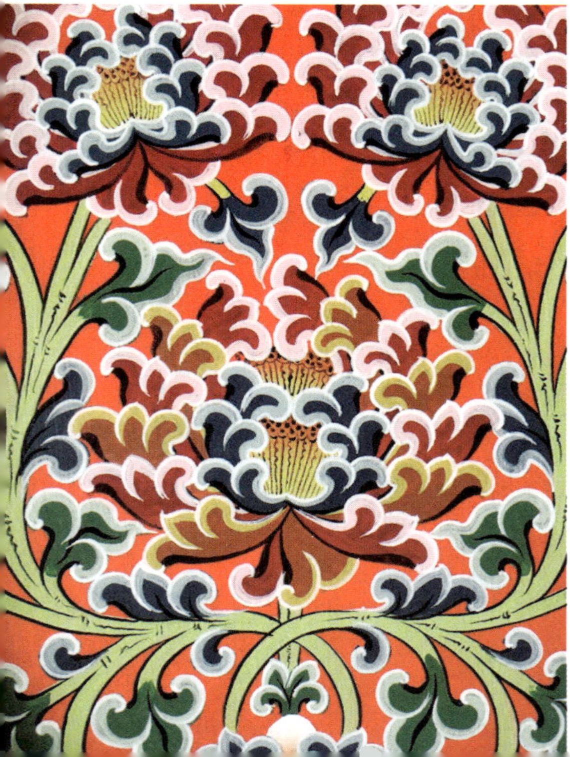

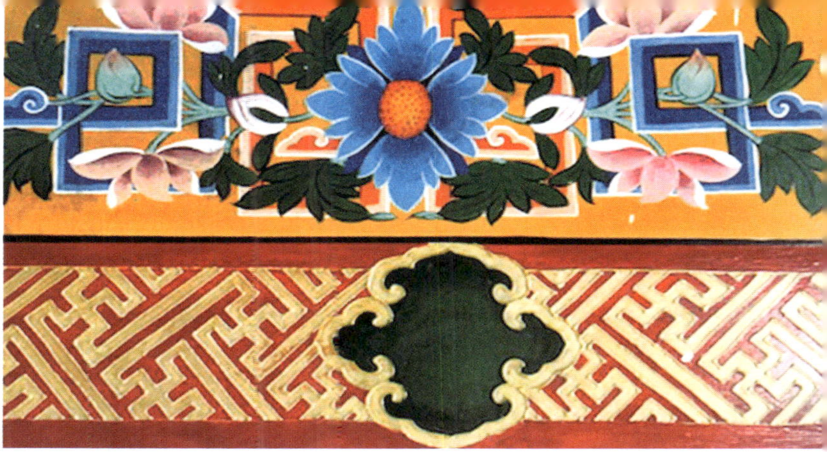

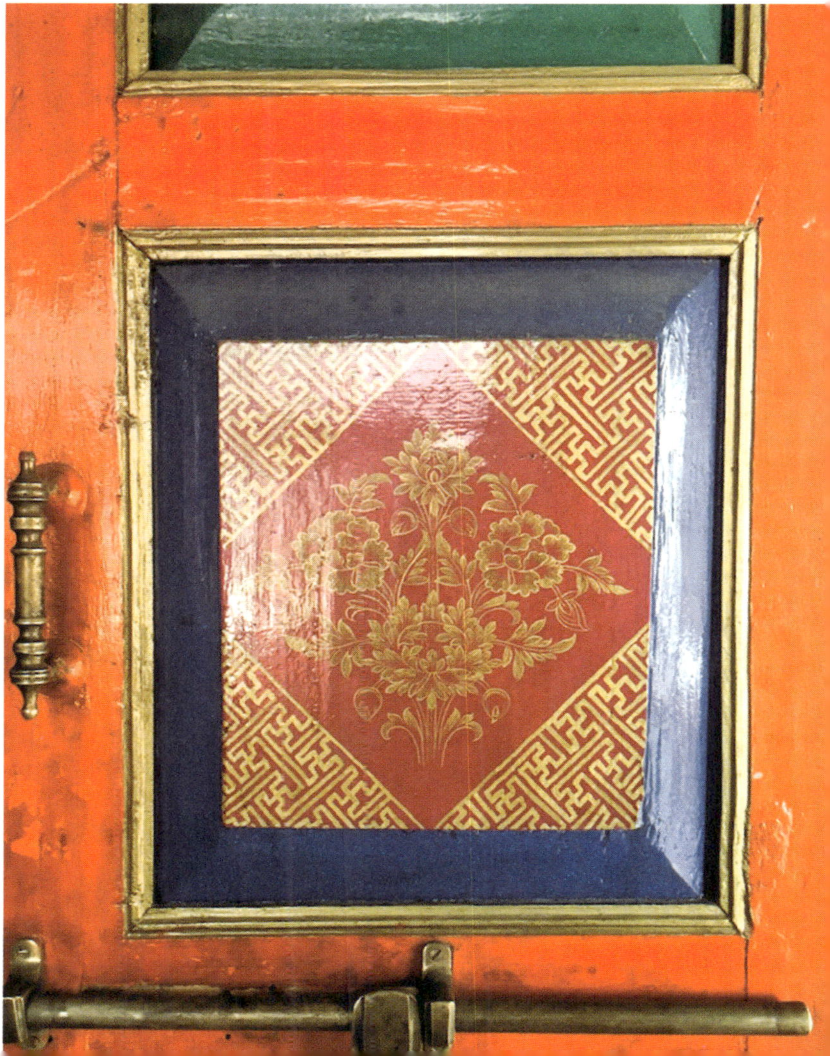

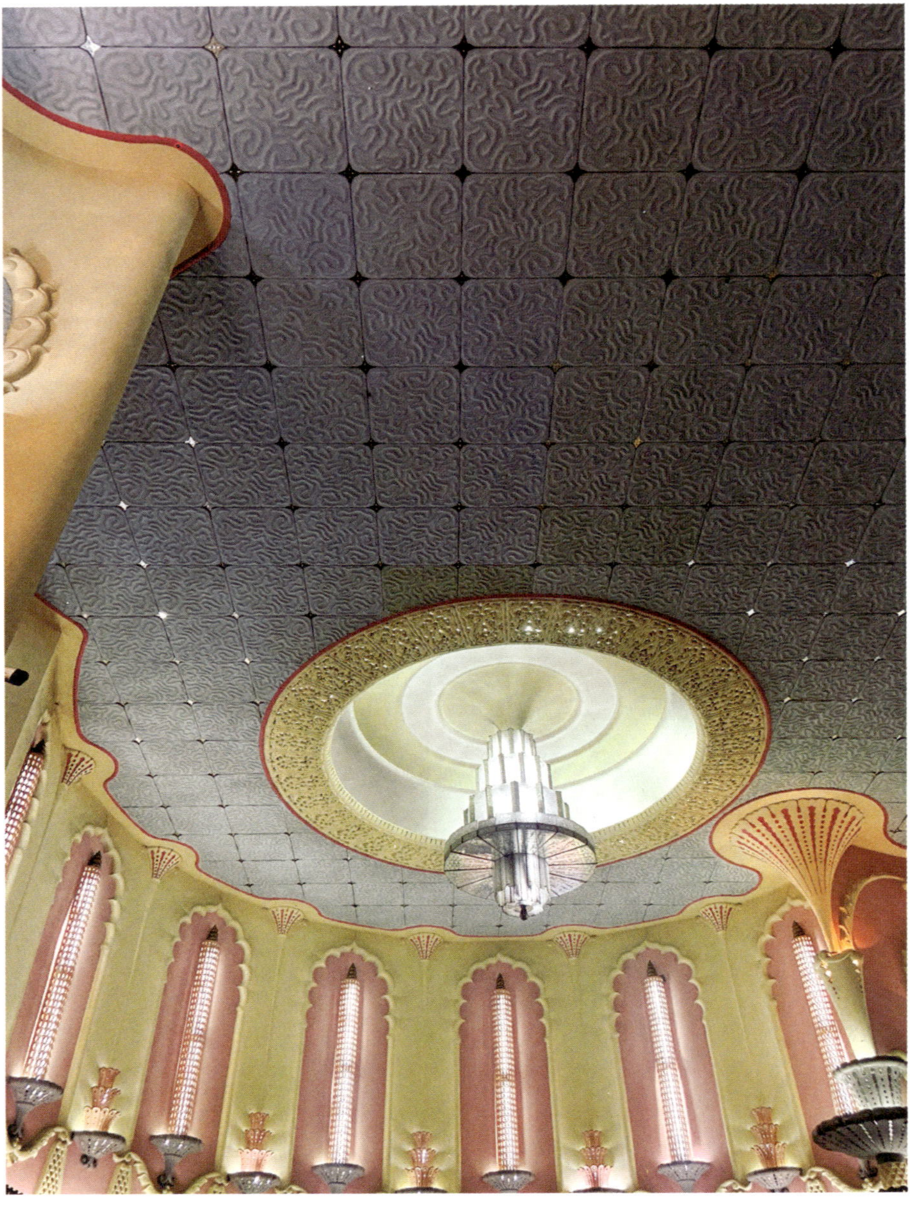

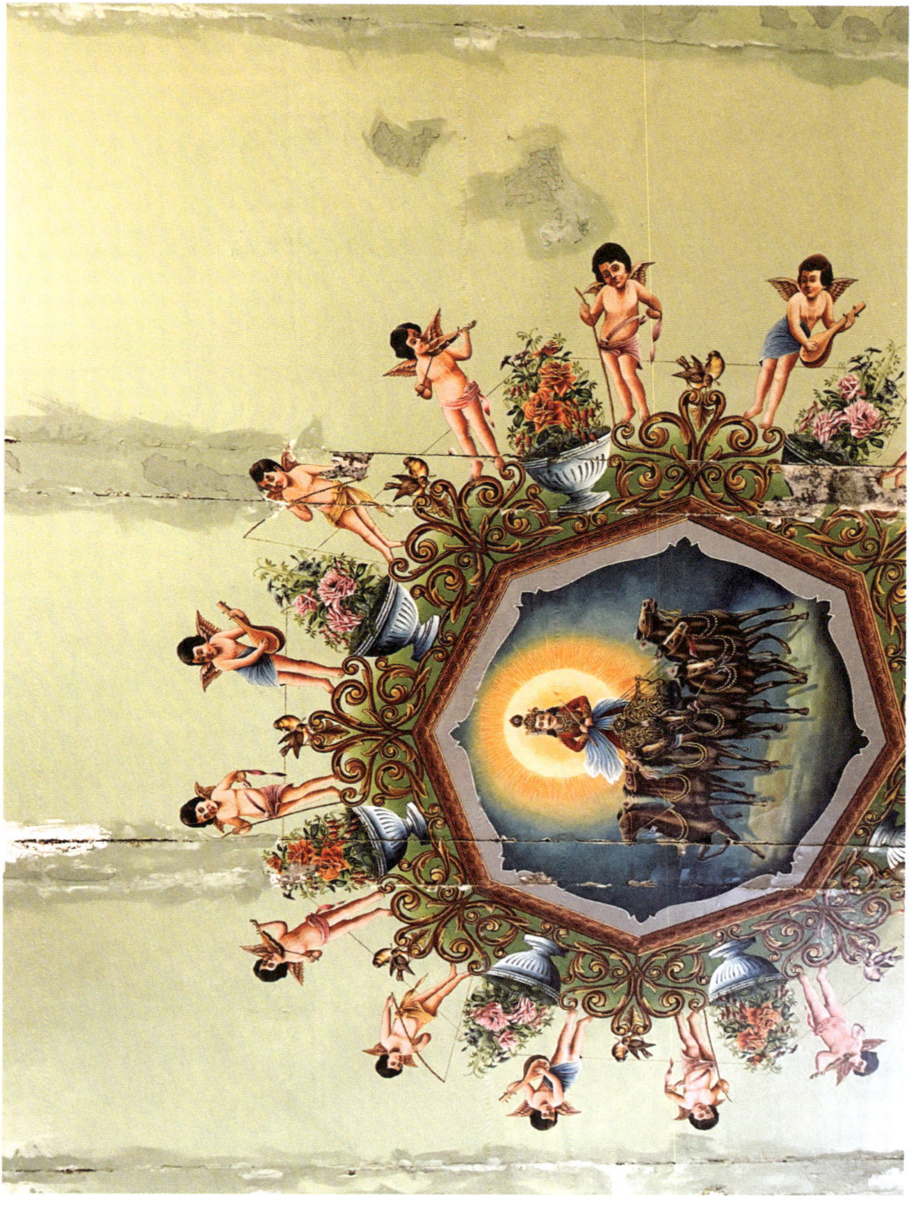

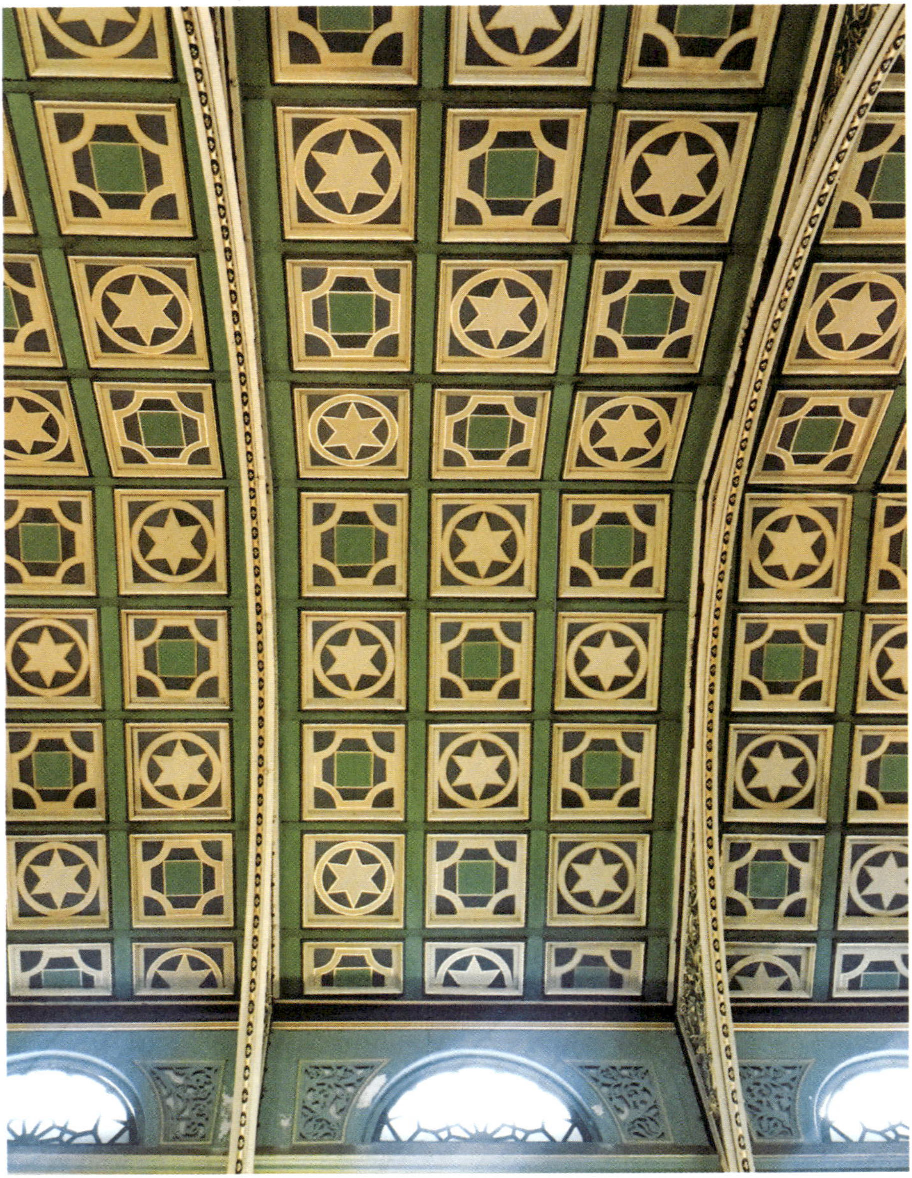

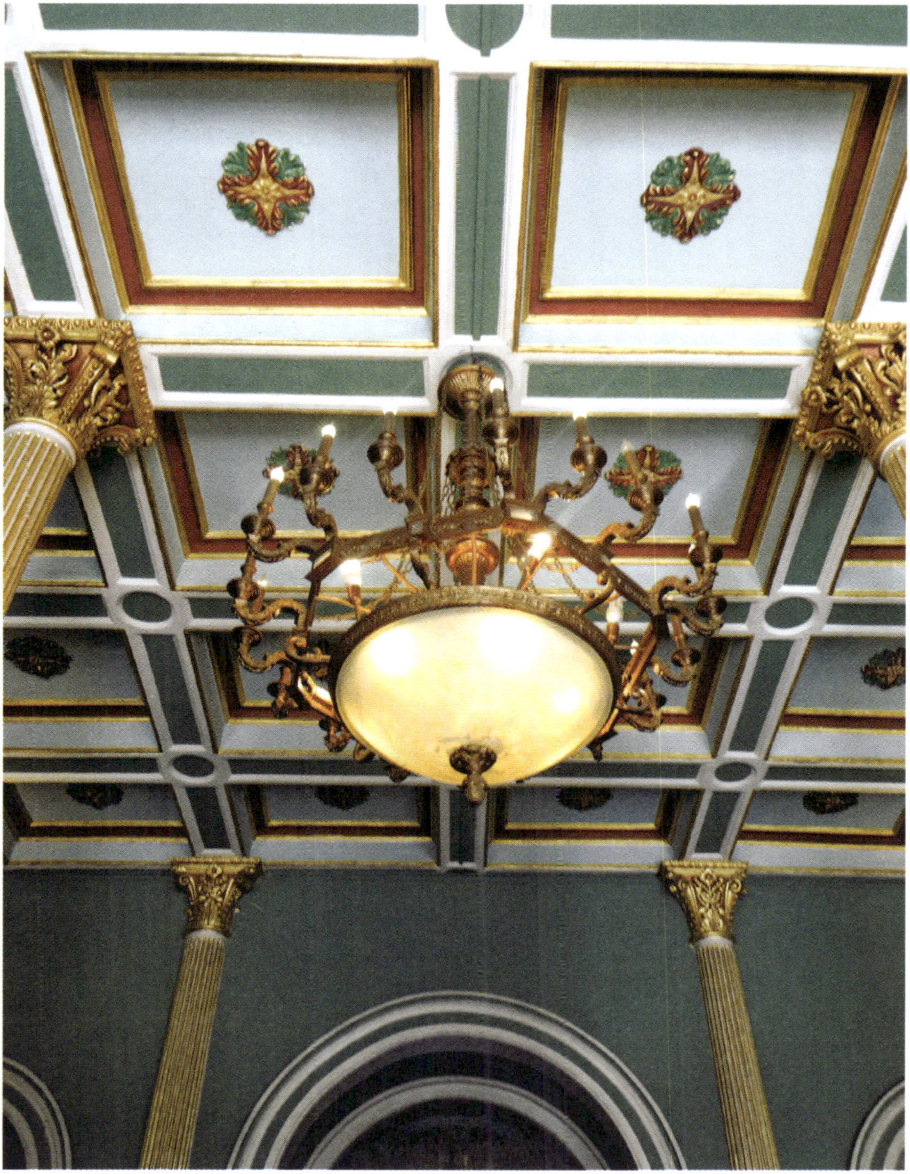

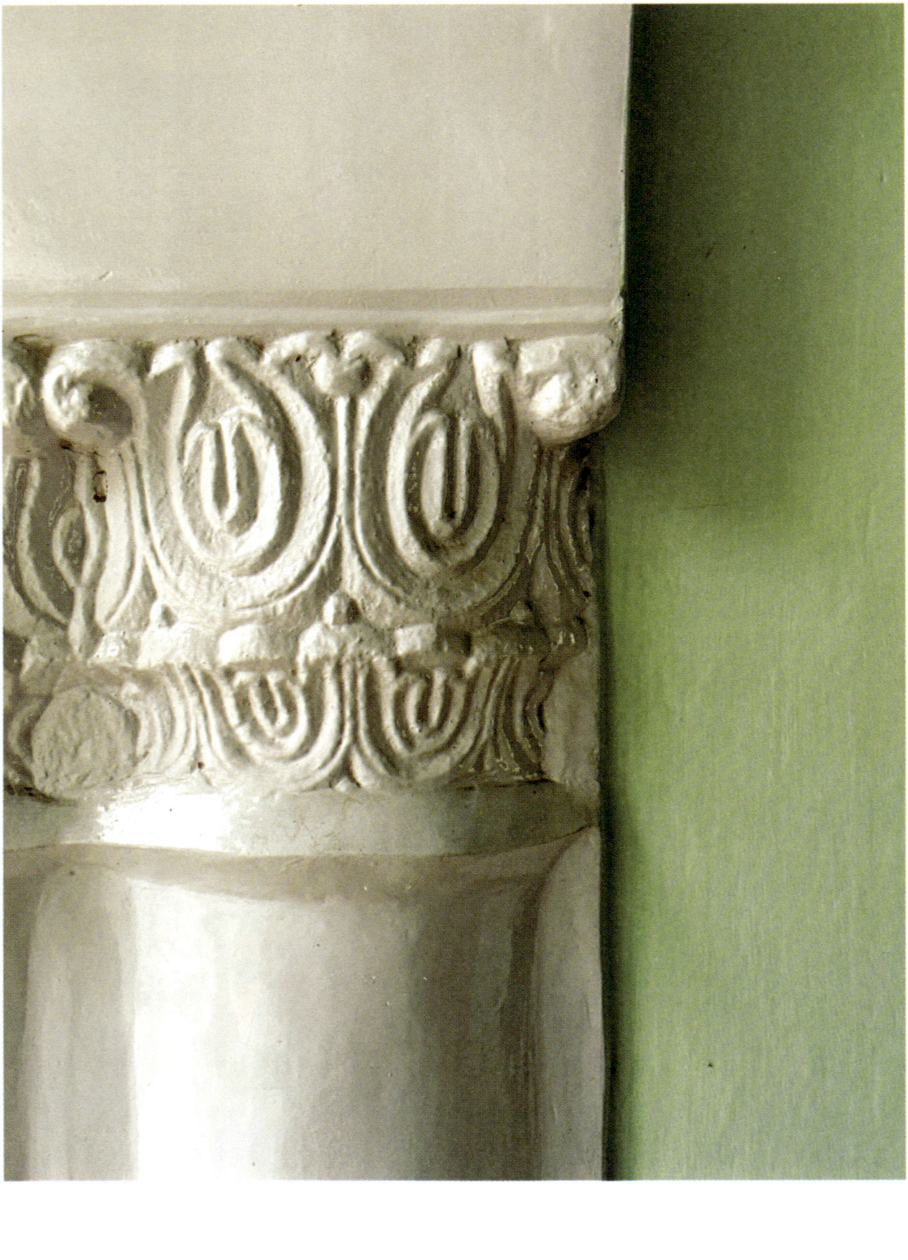

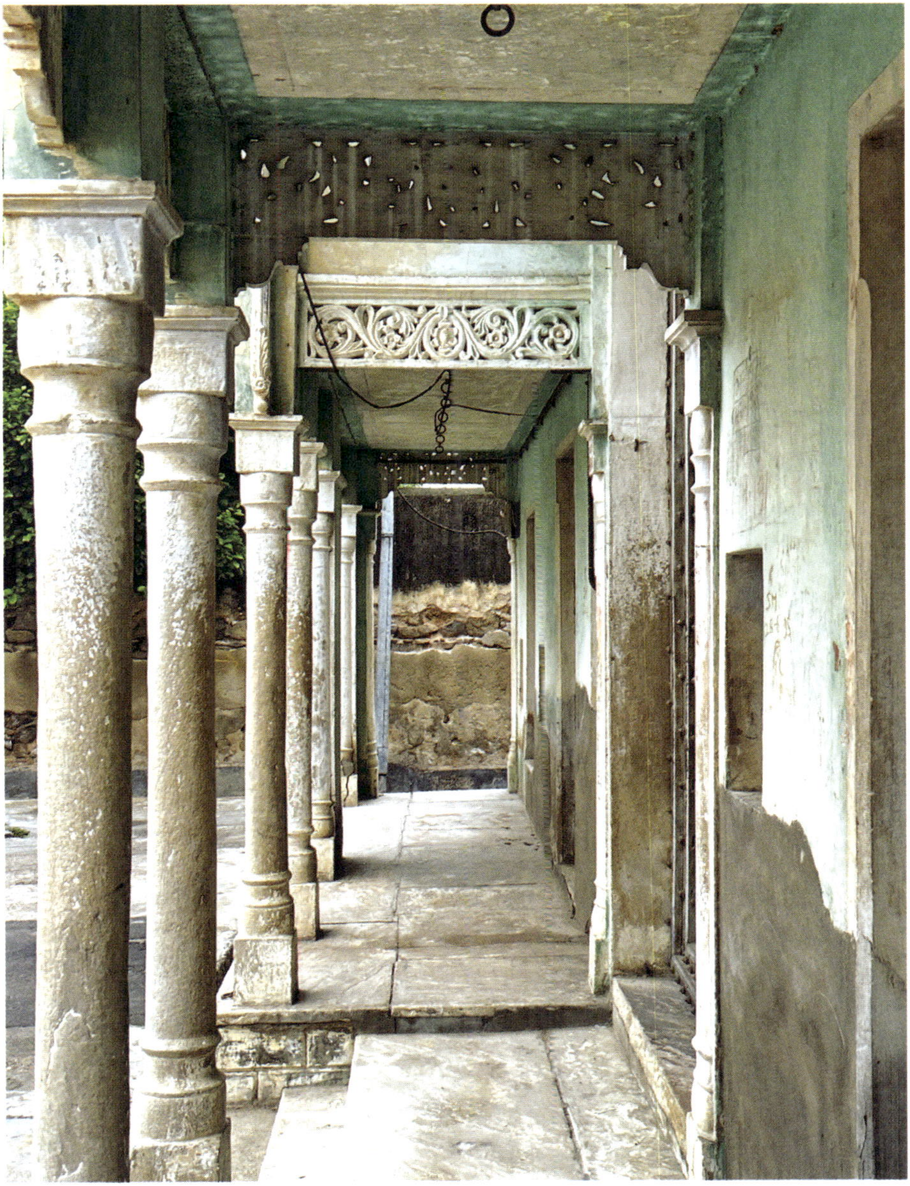

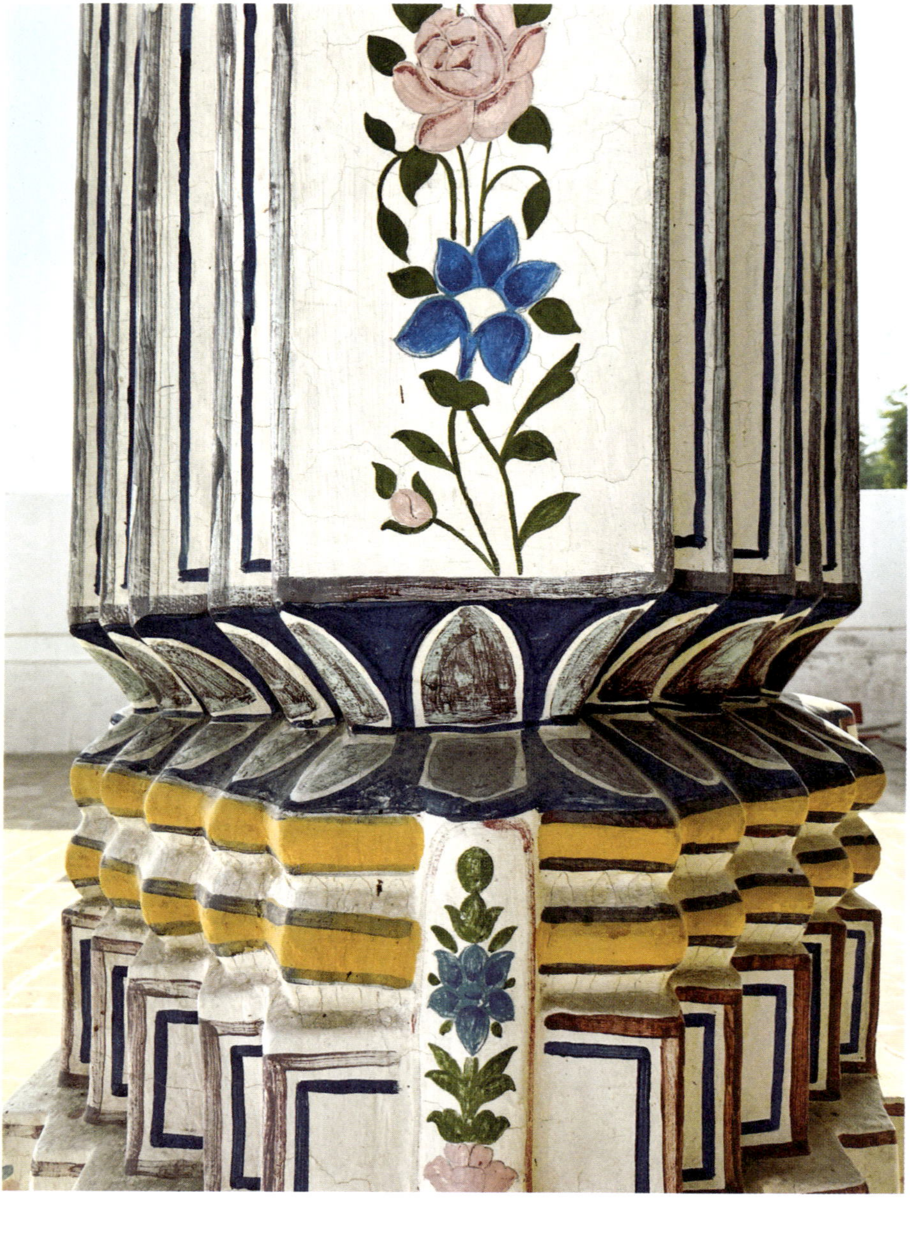

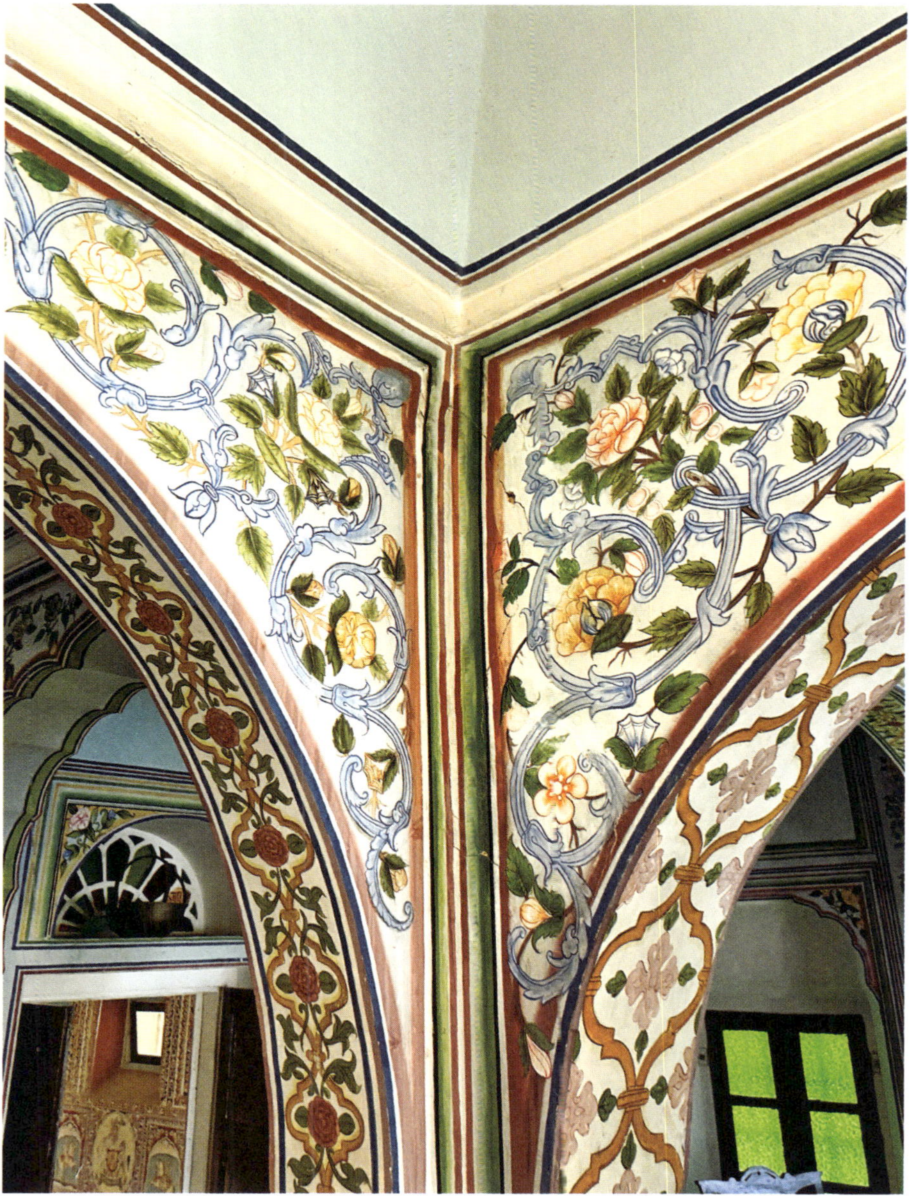

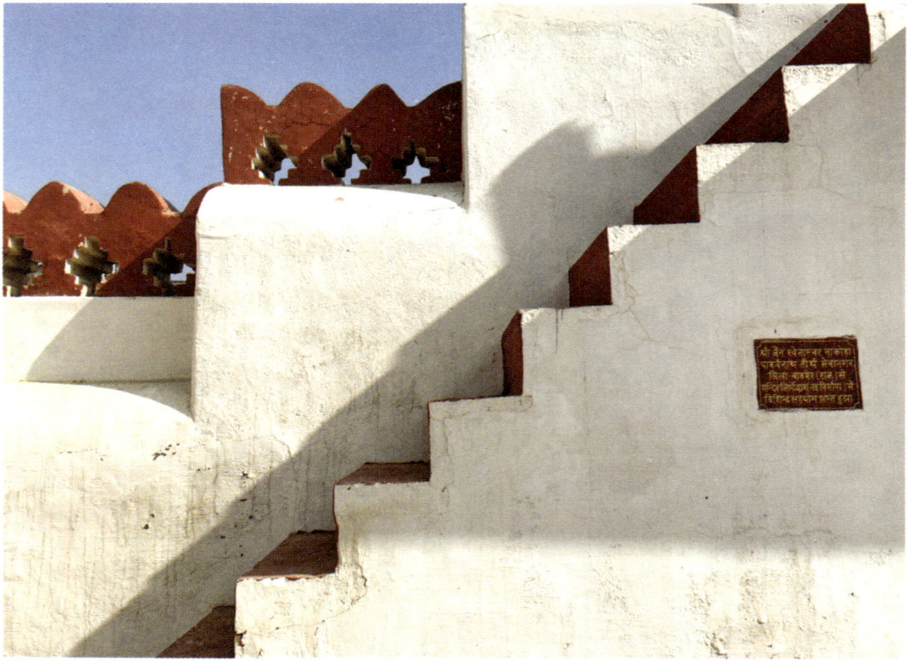

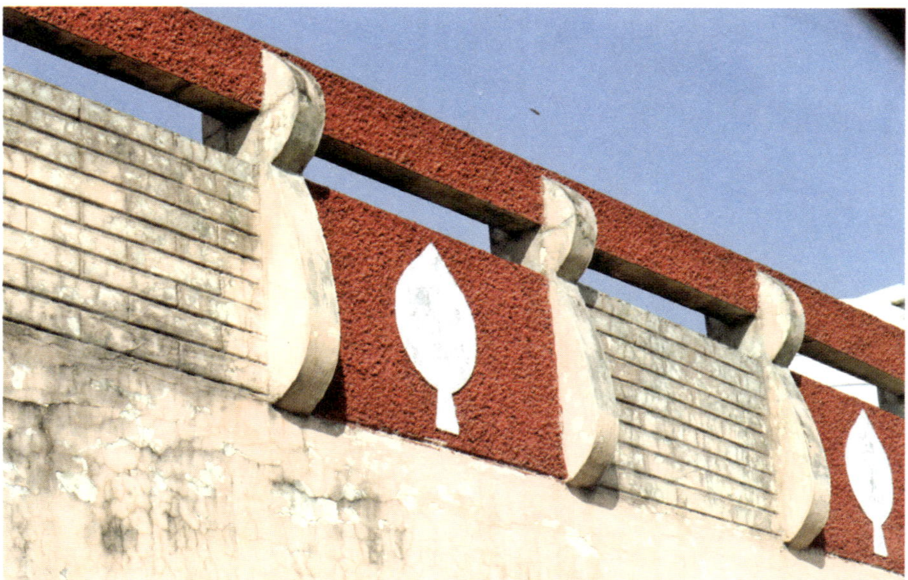

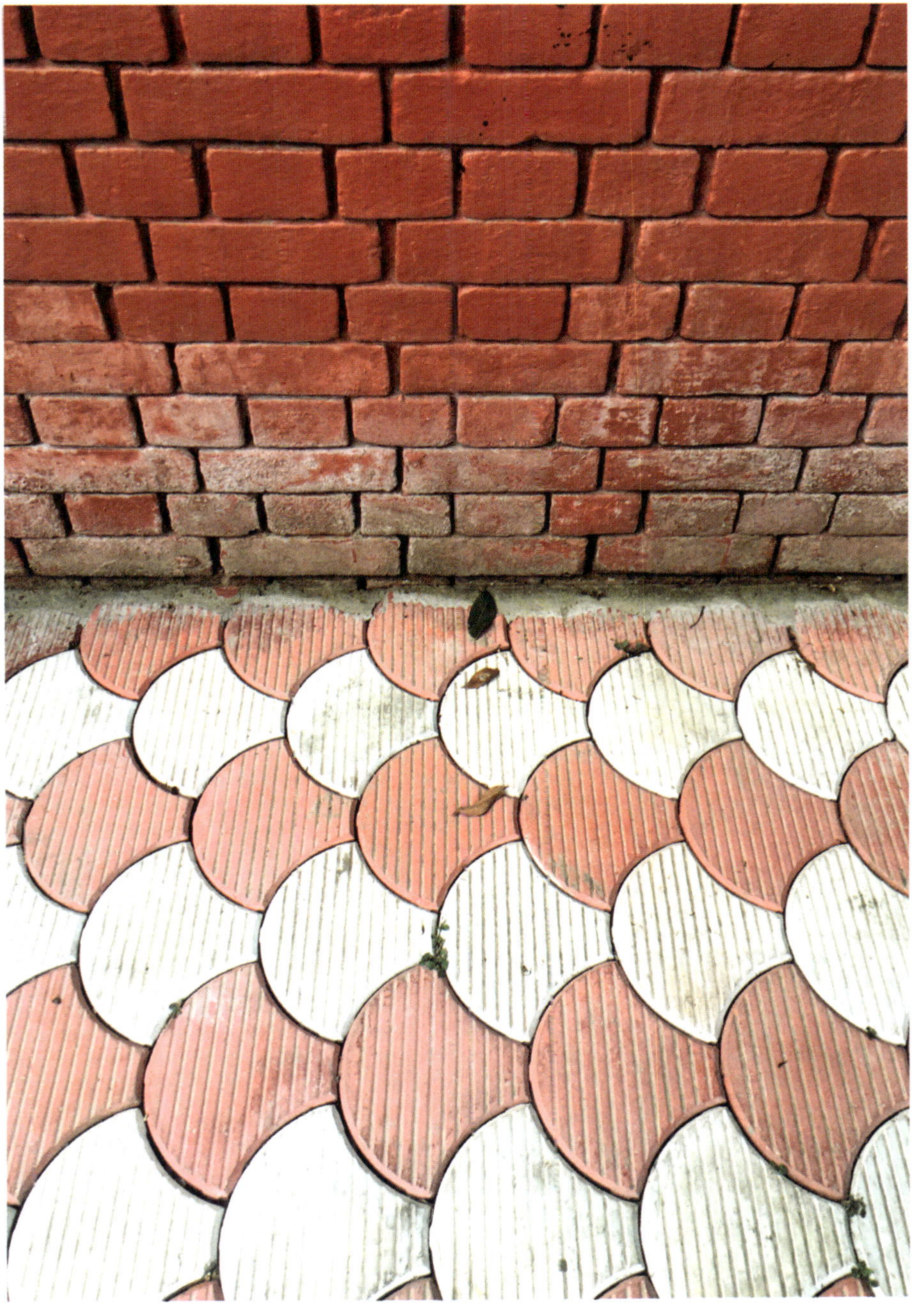

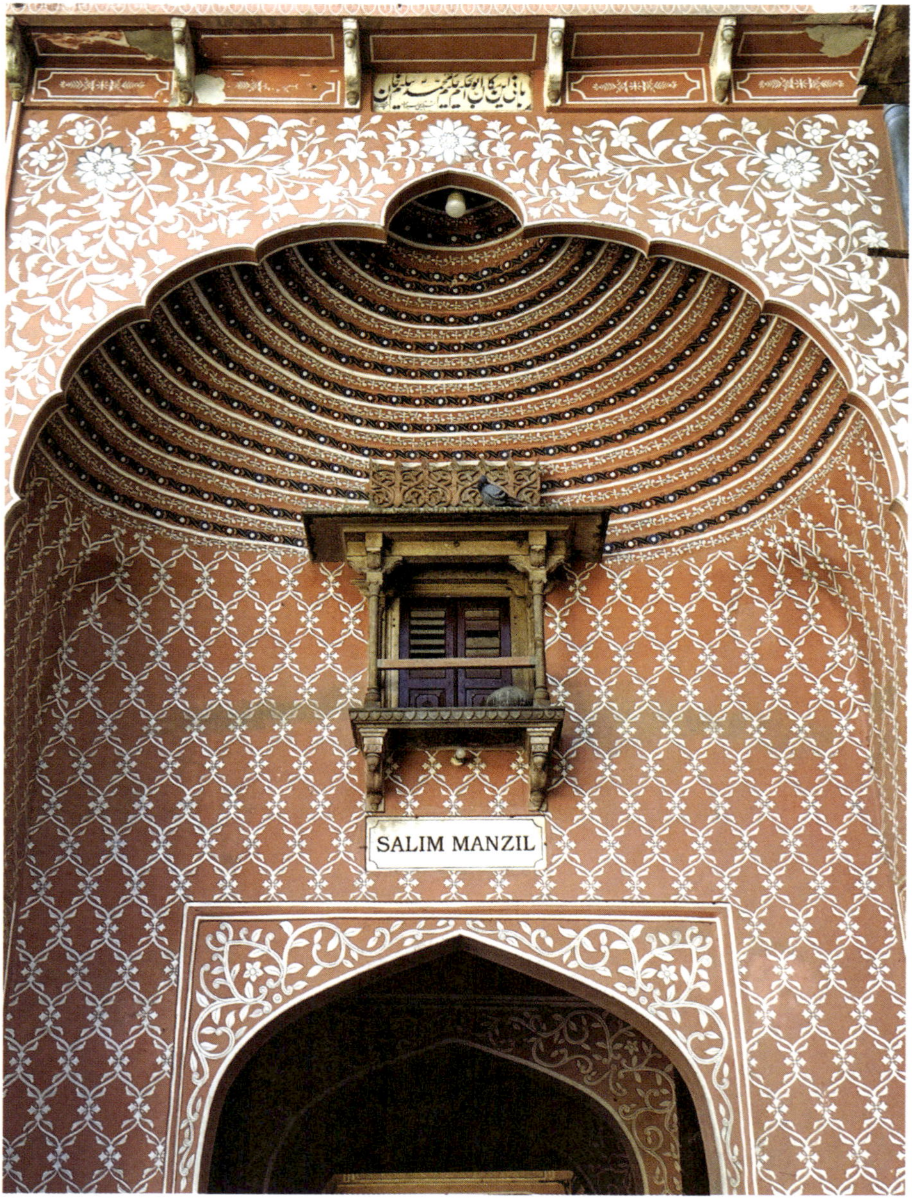
SALIM MANZIL

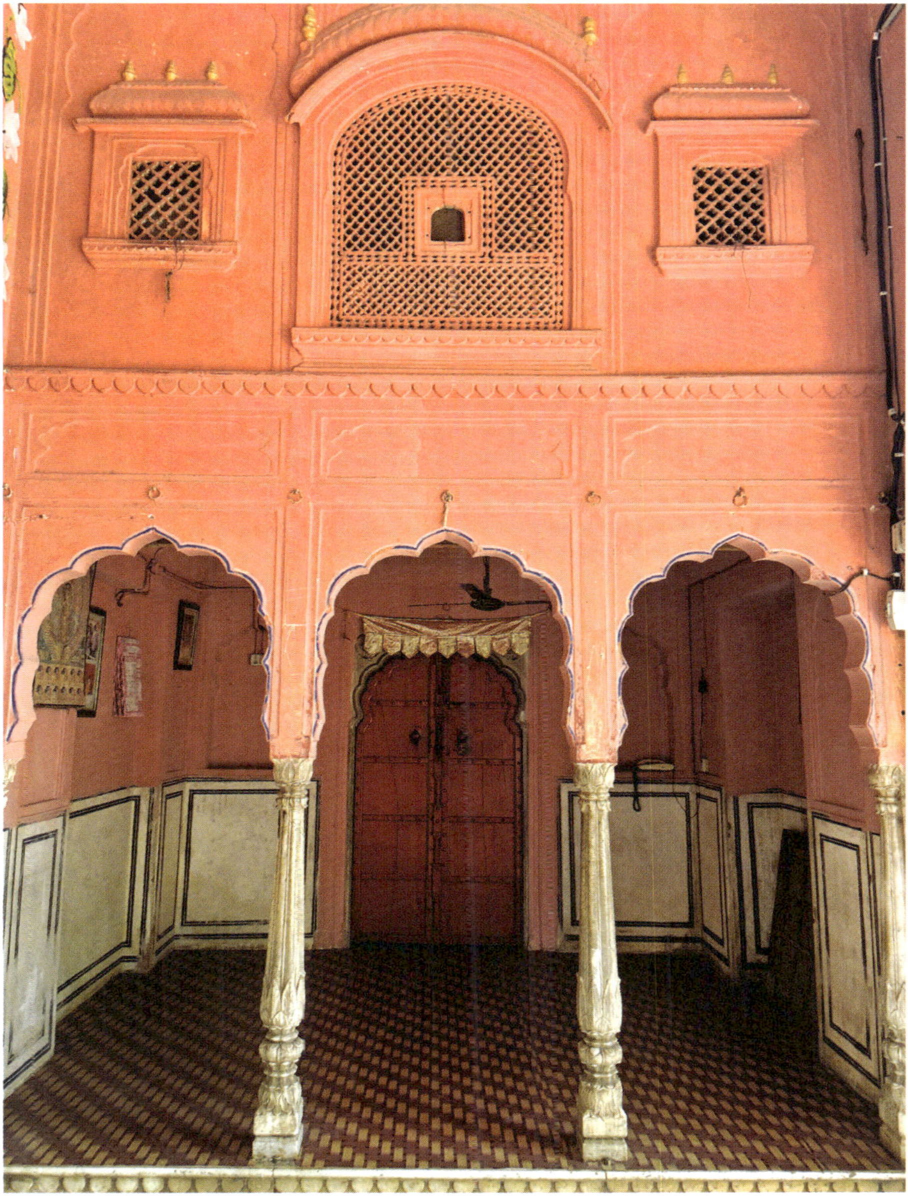

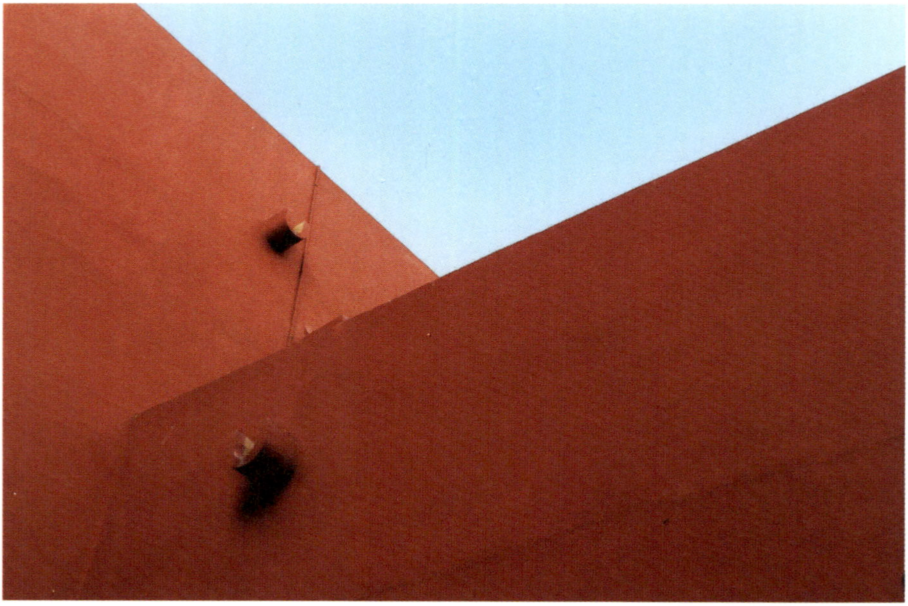

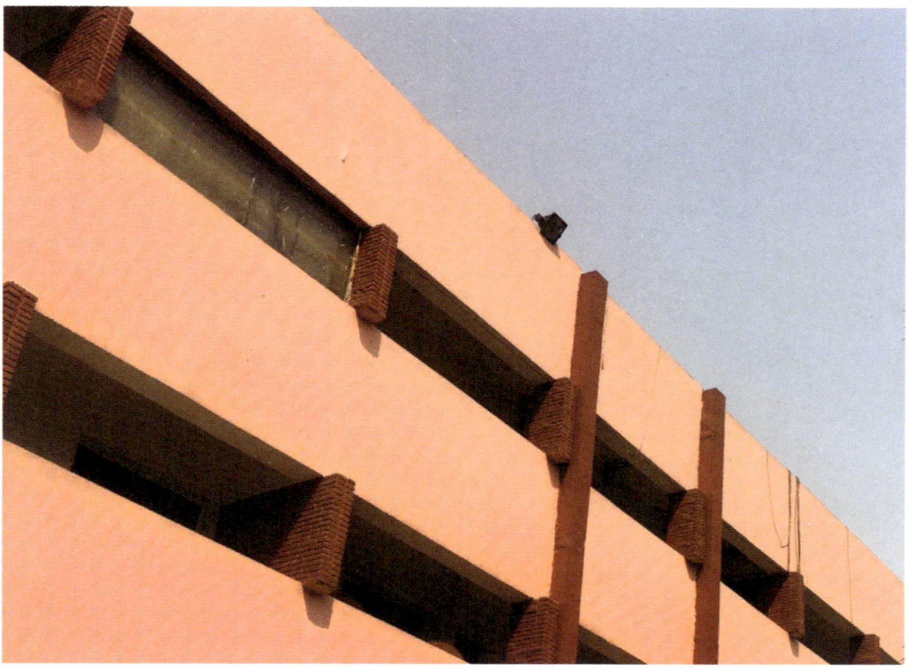

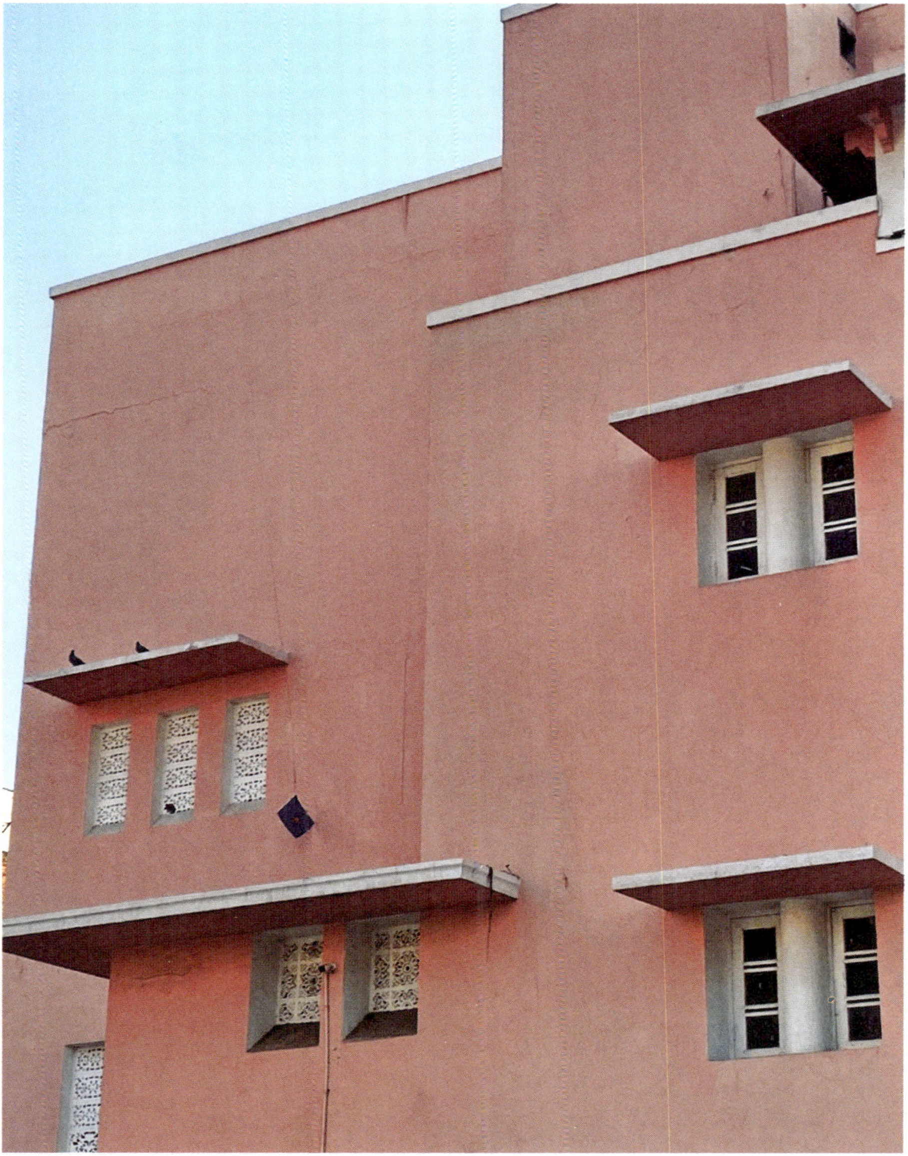

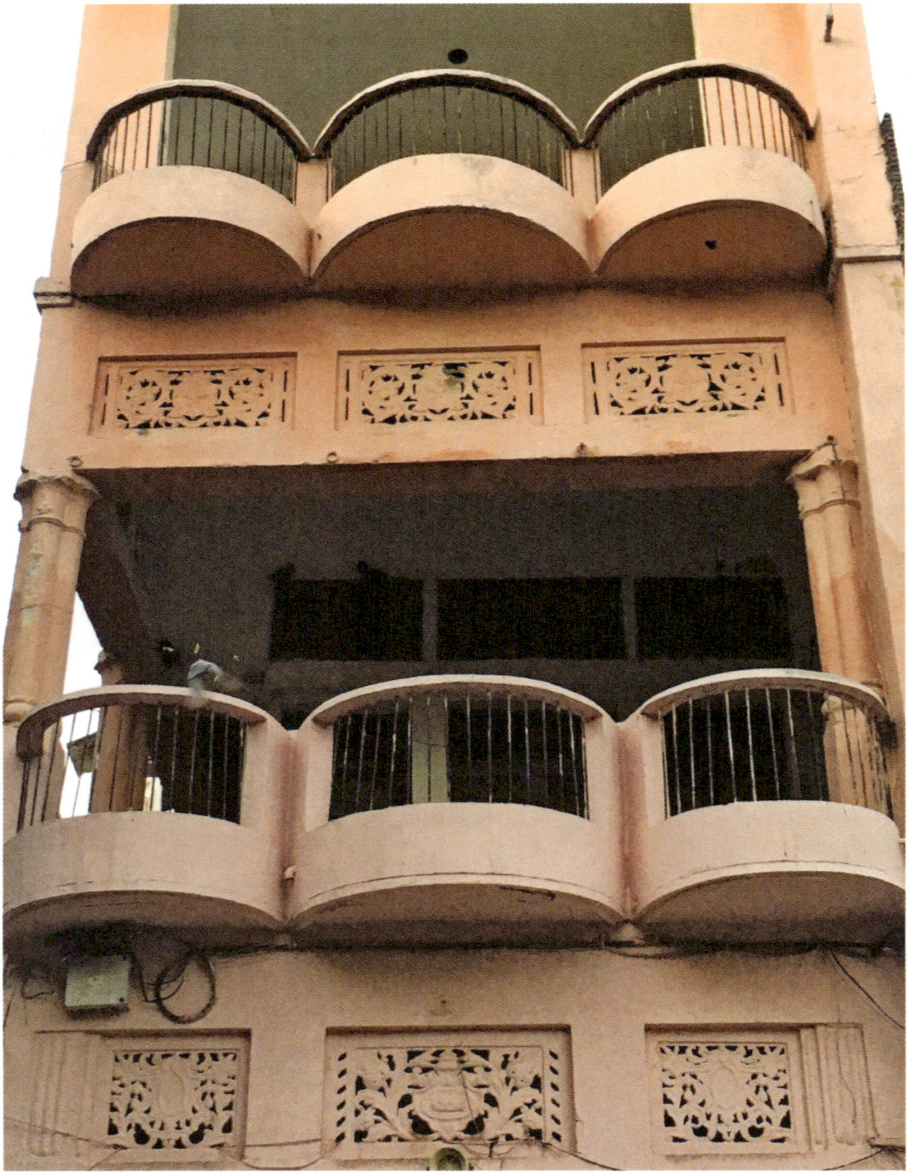

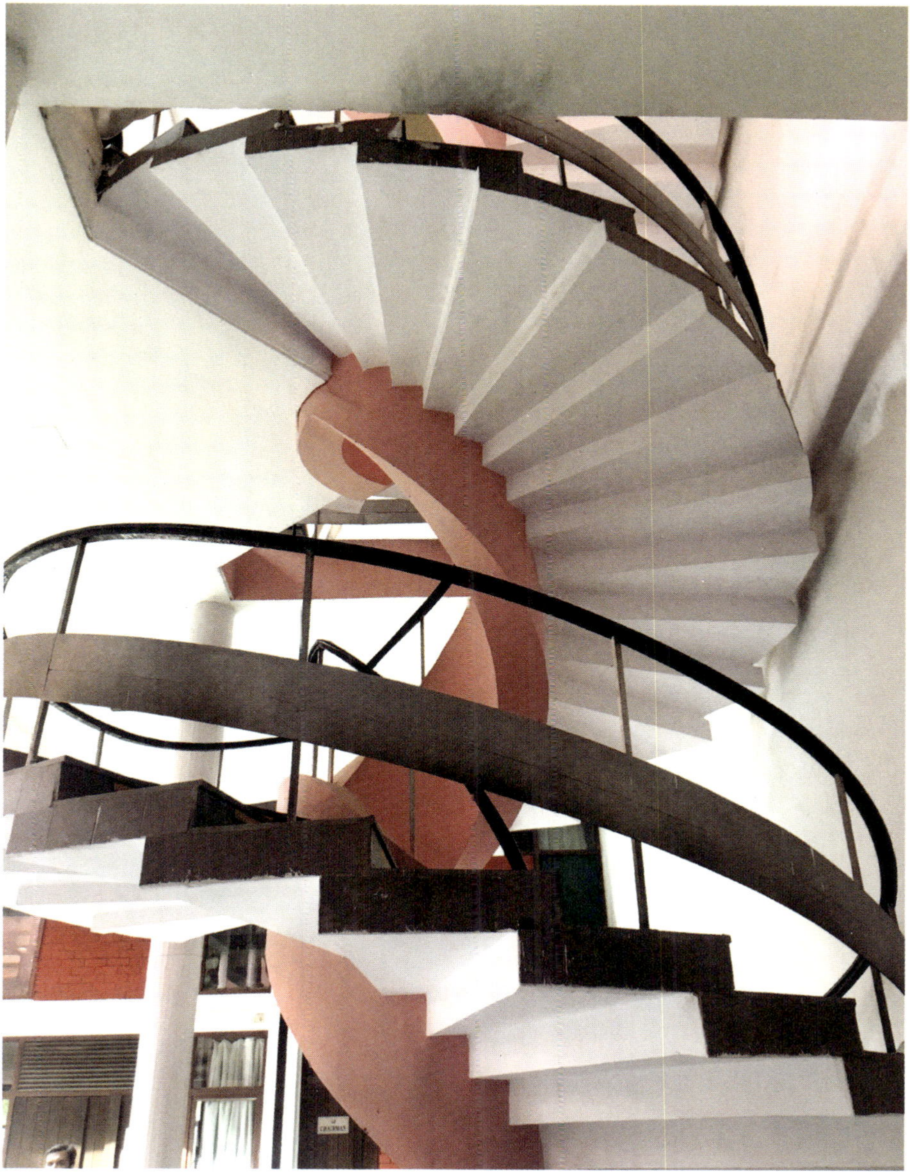

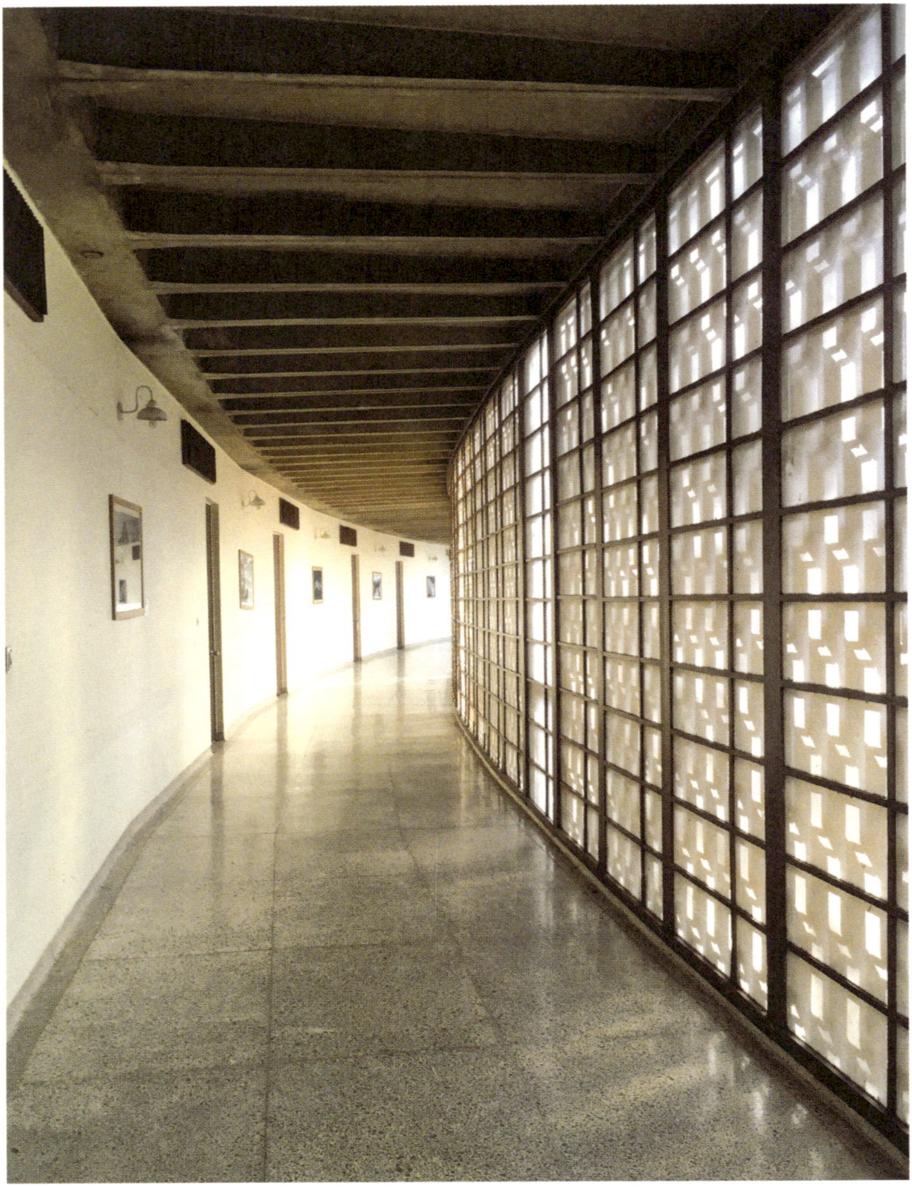

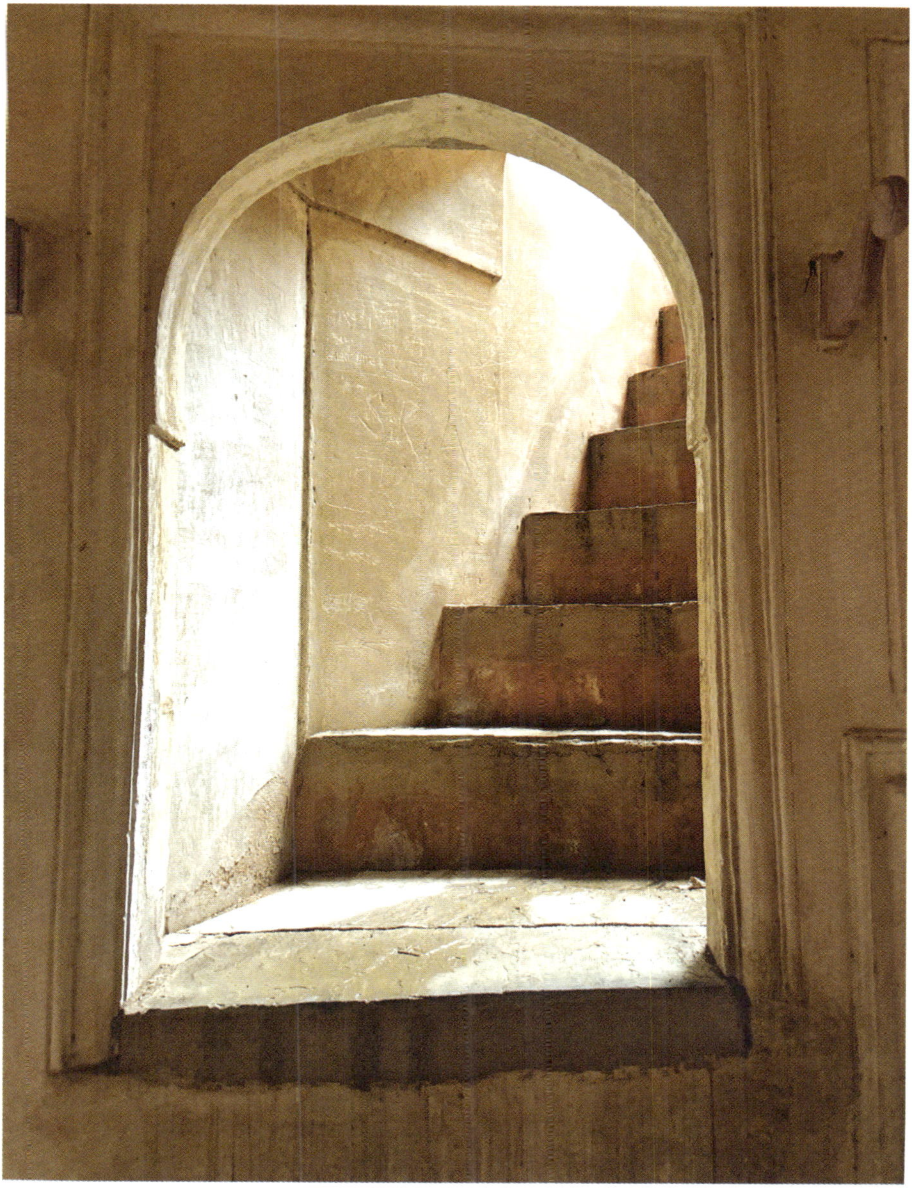

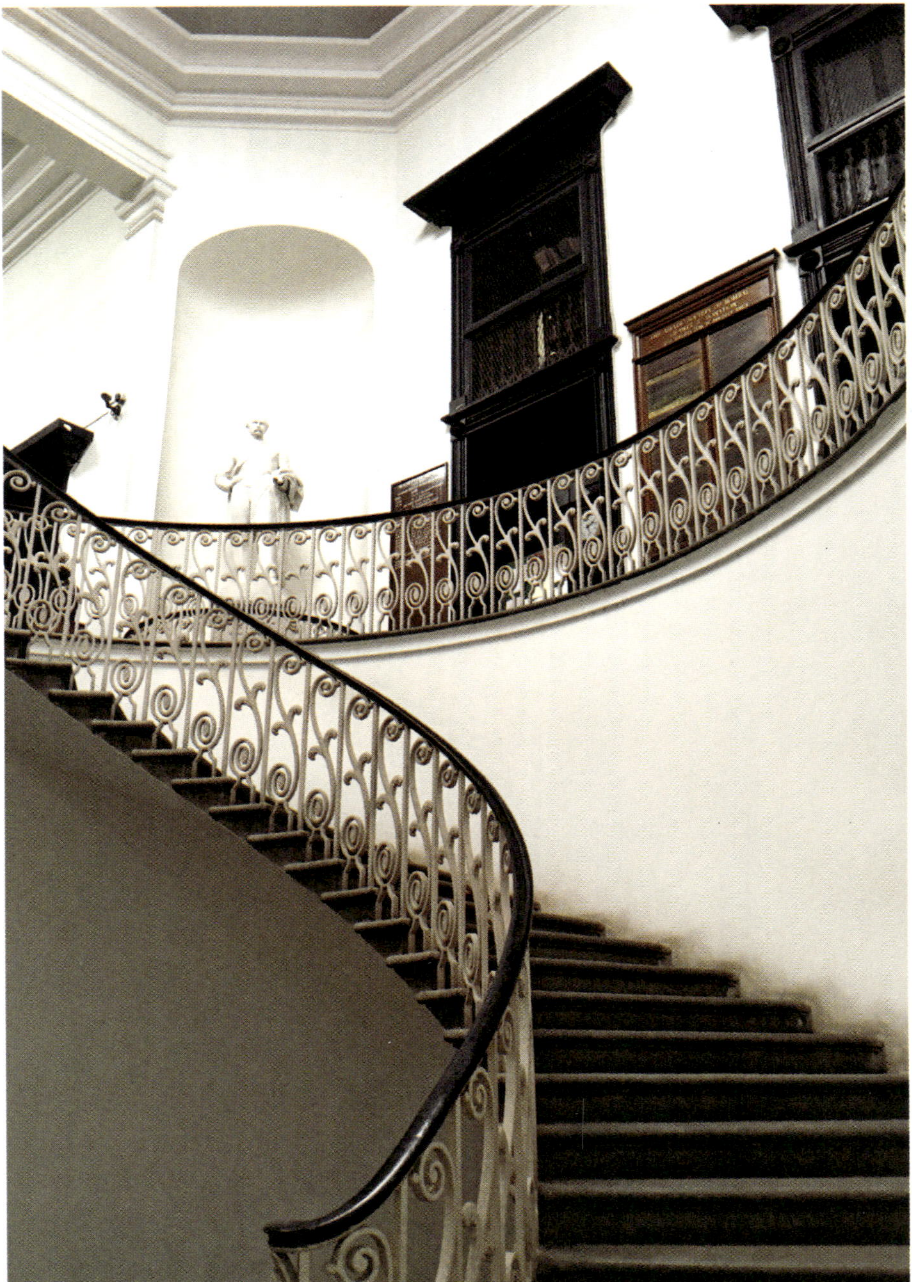

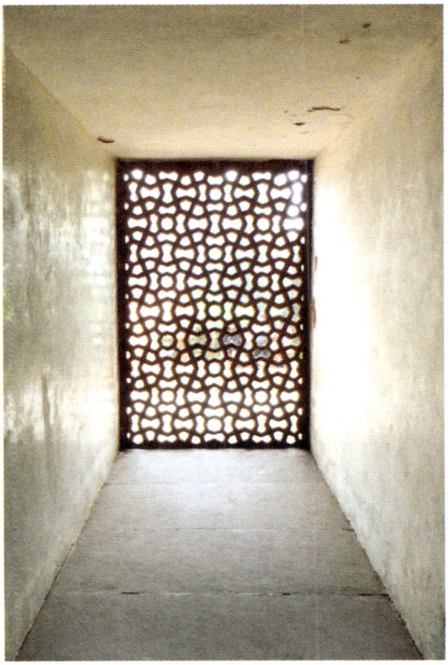

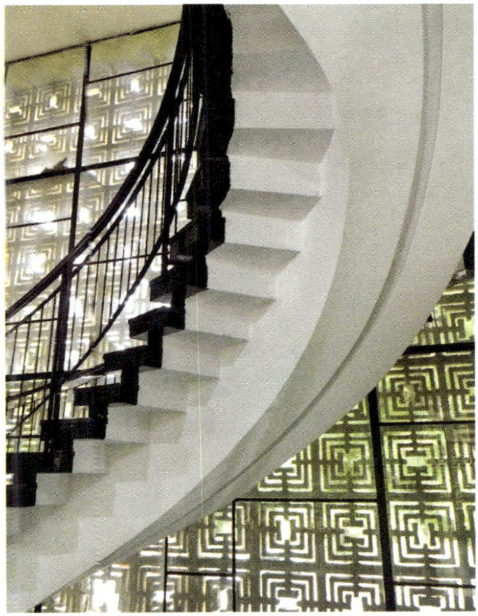

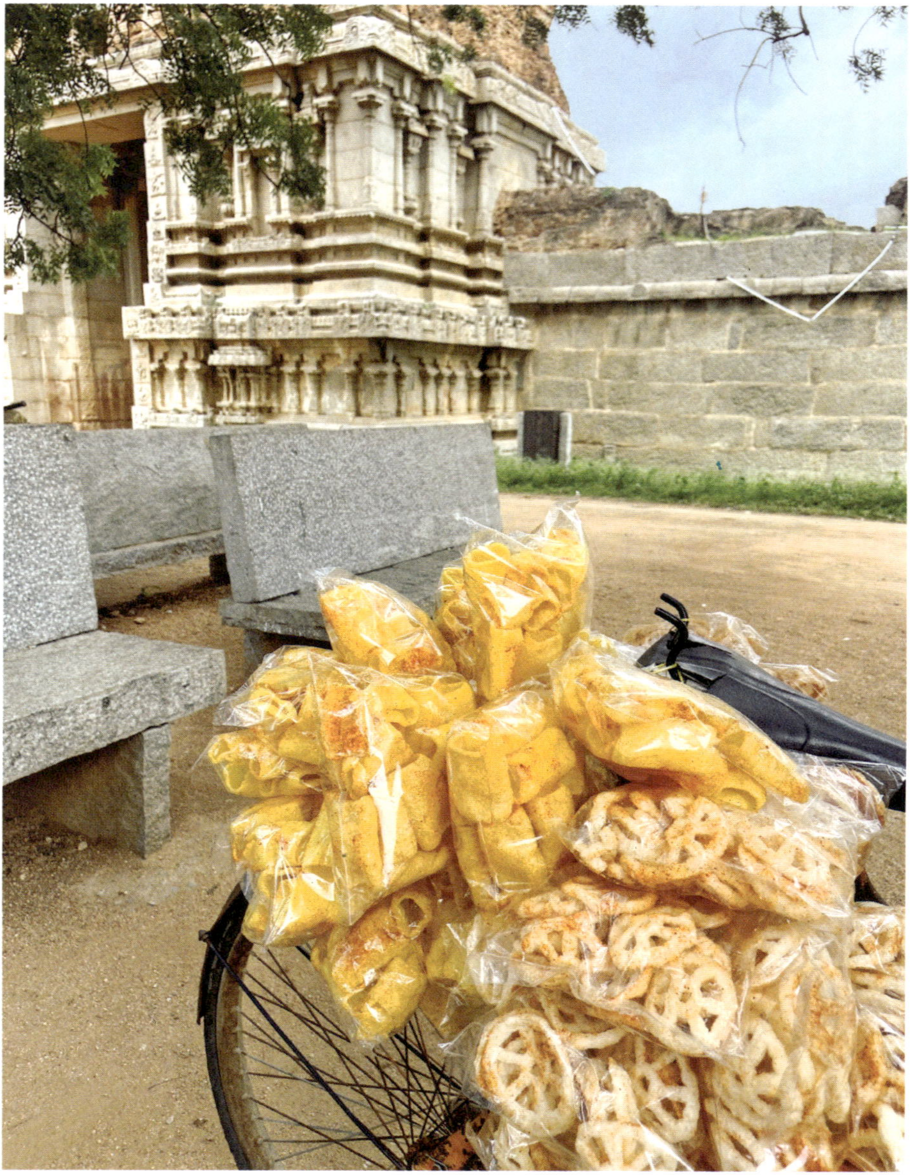

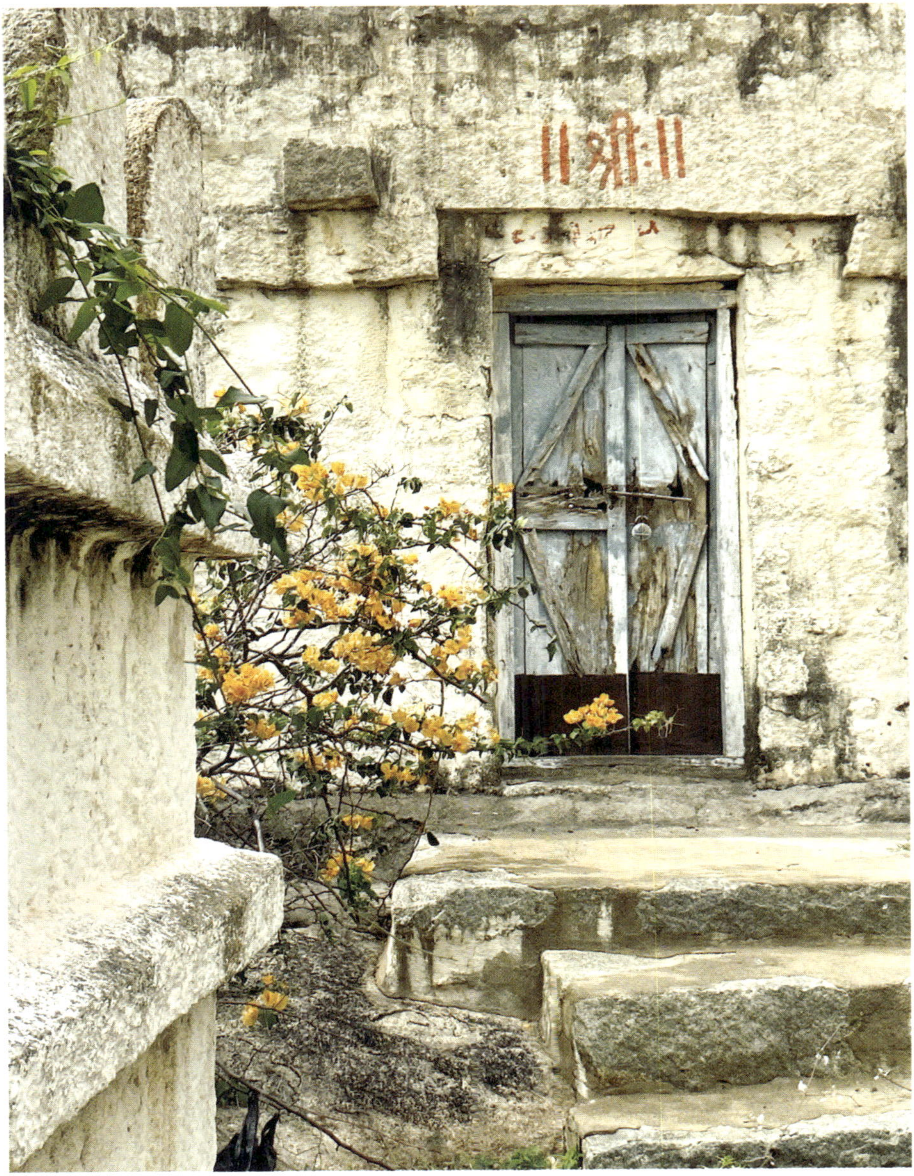
॥ श्री ॥

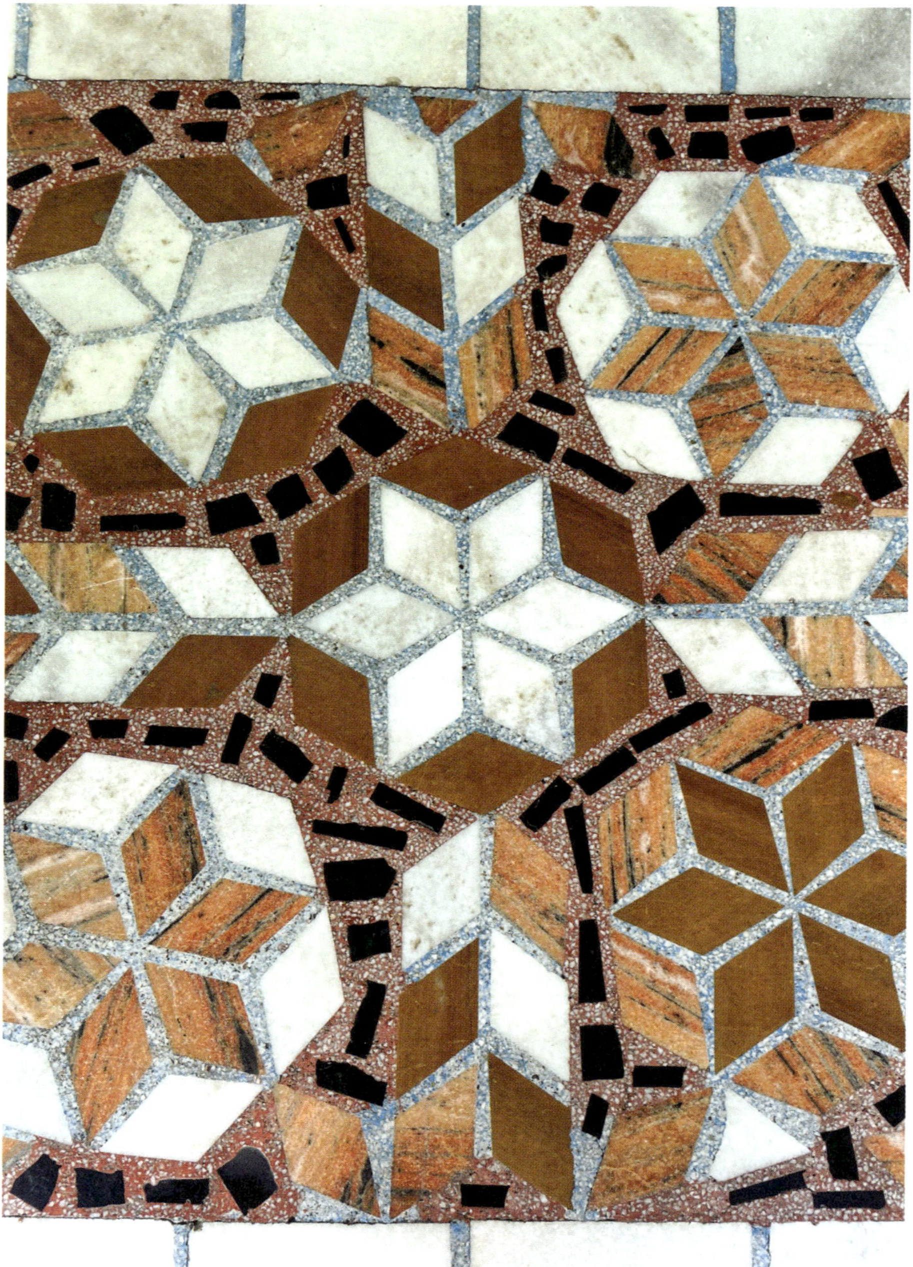

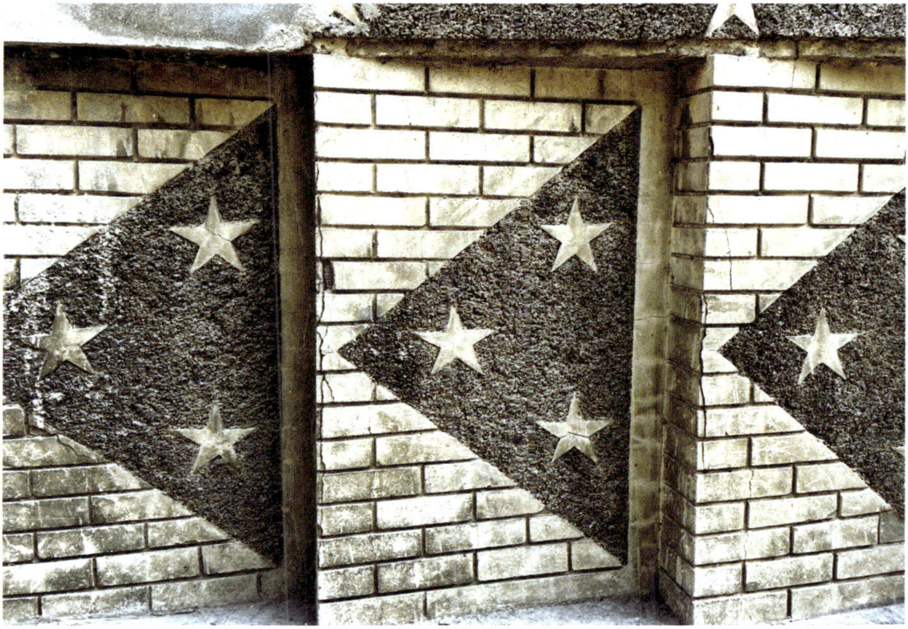

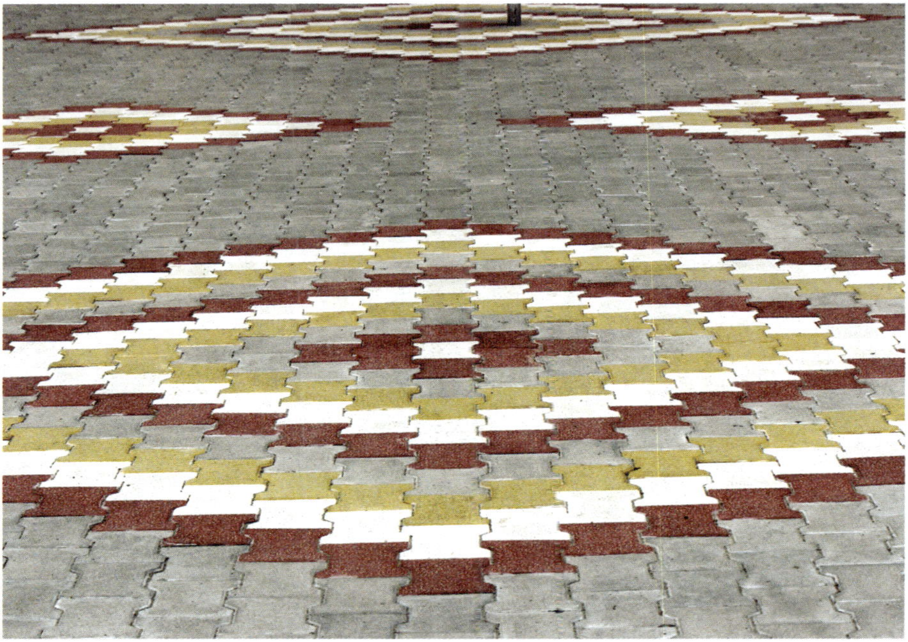

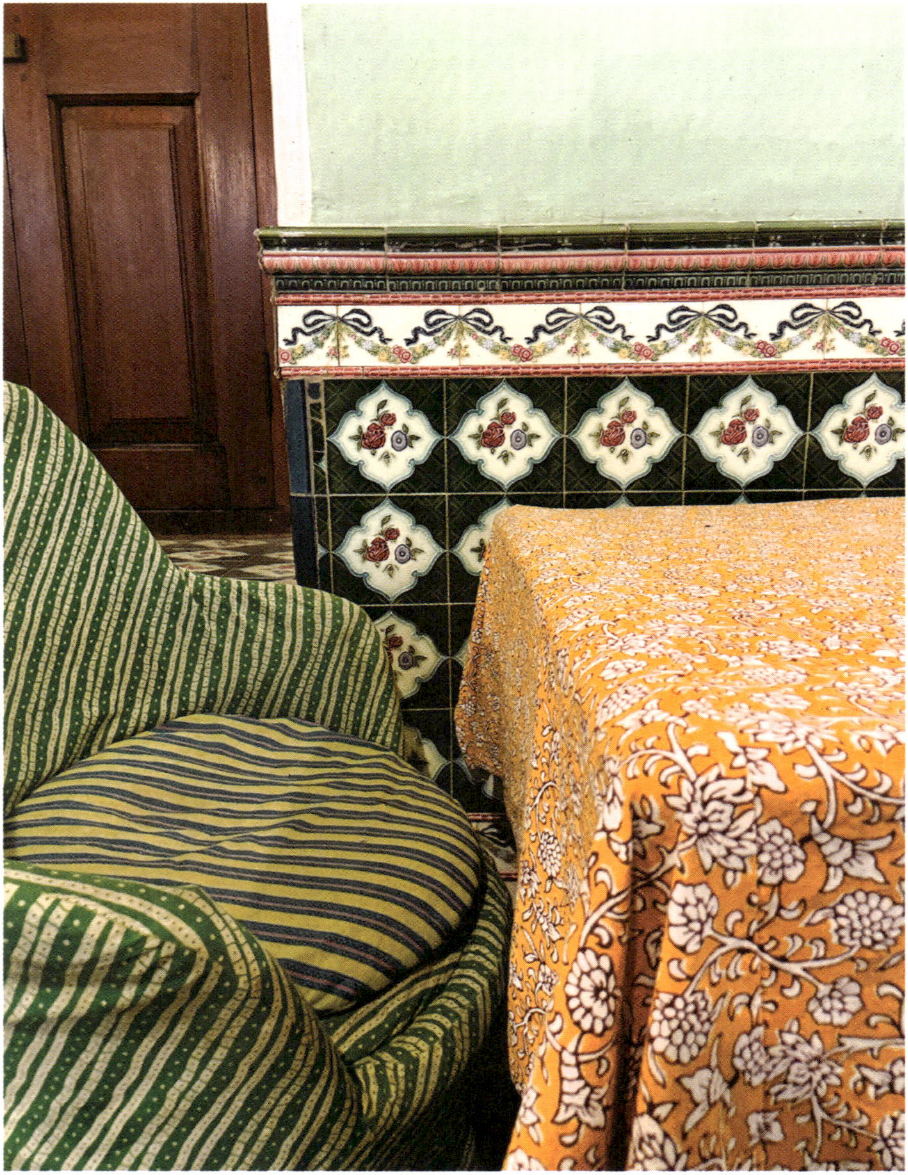

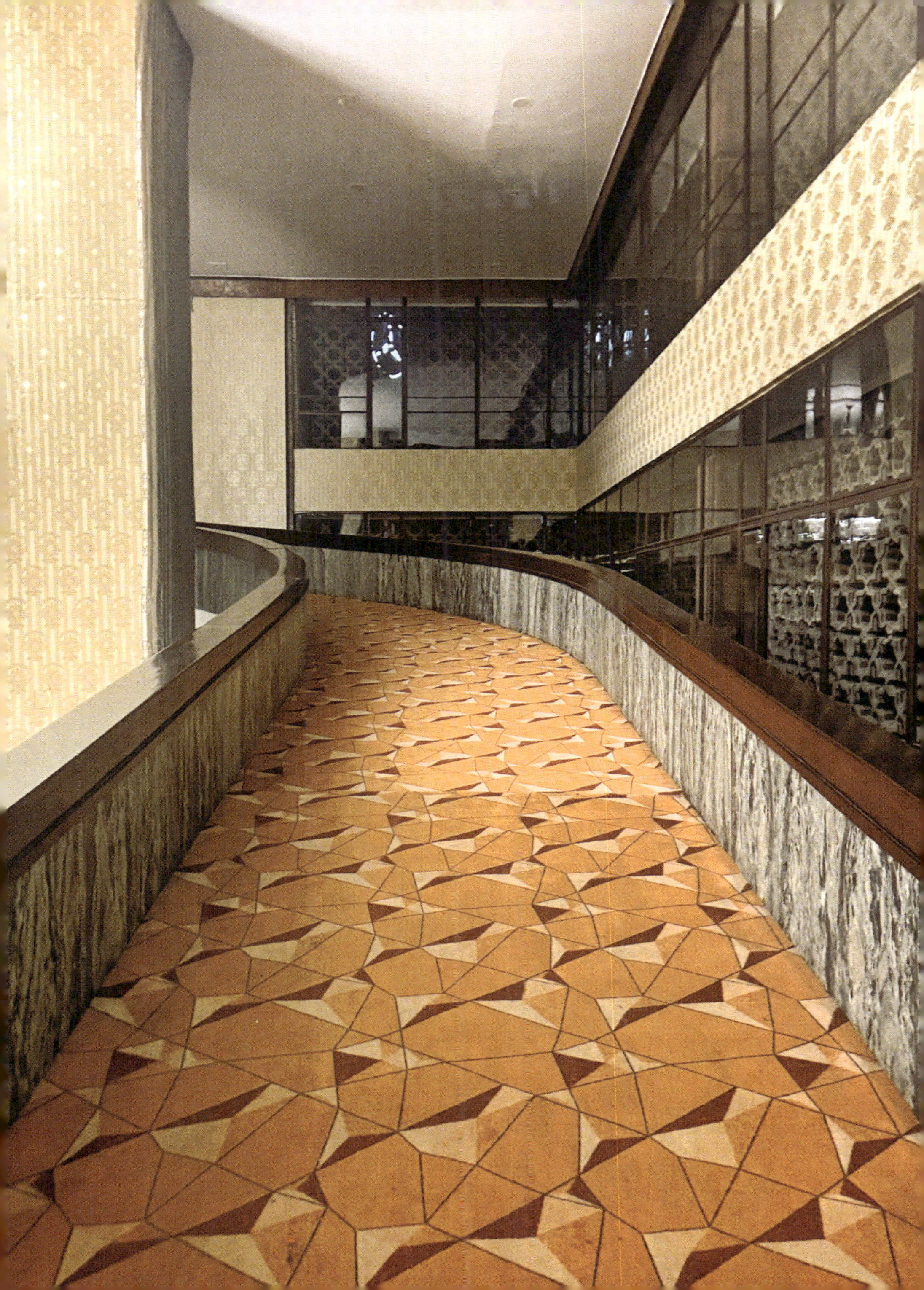

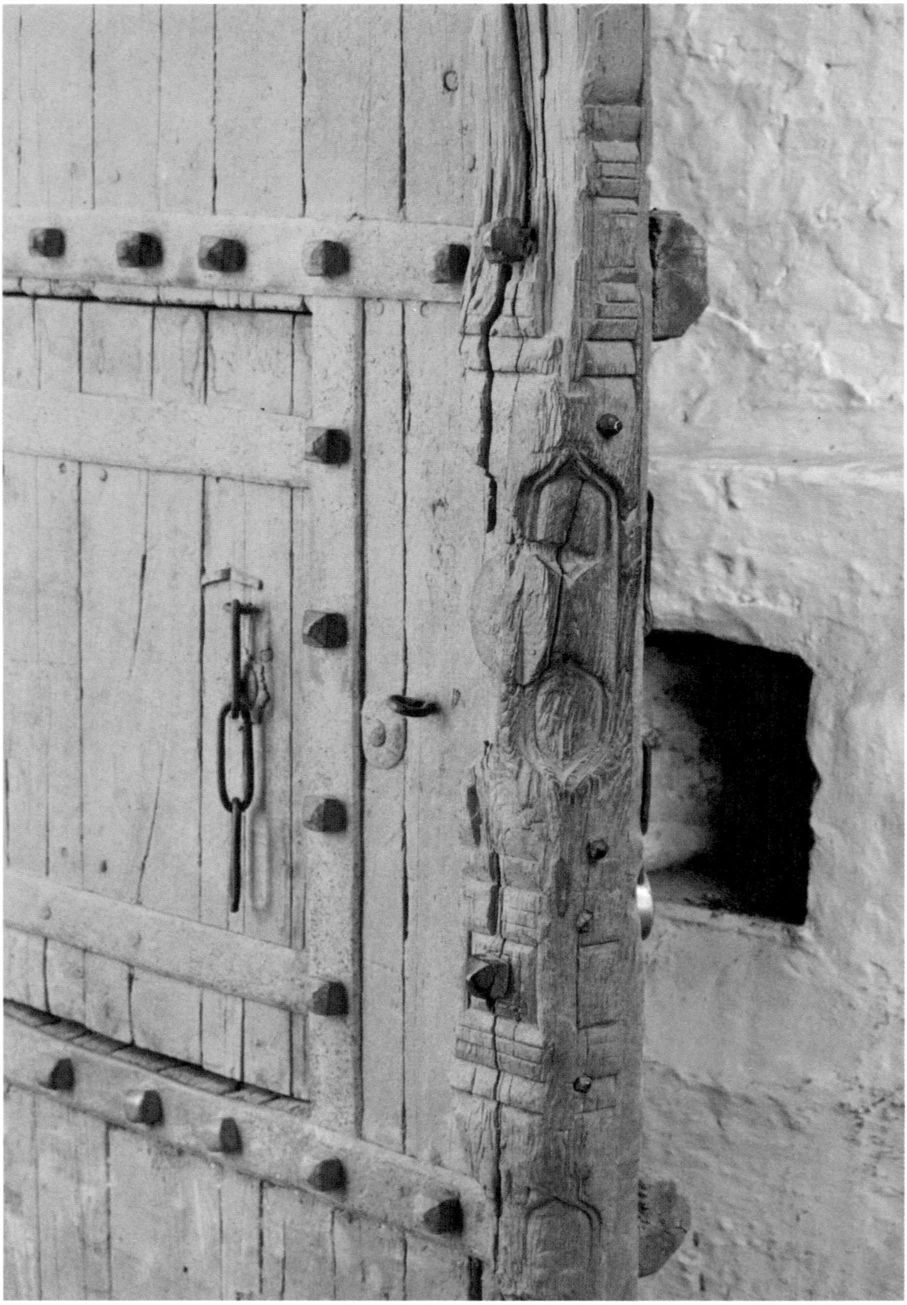

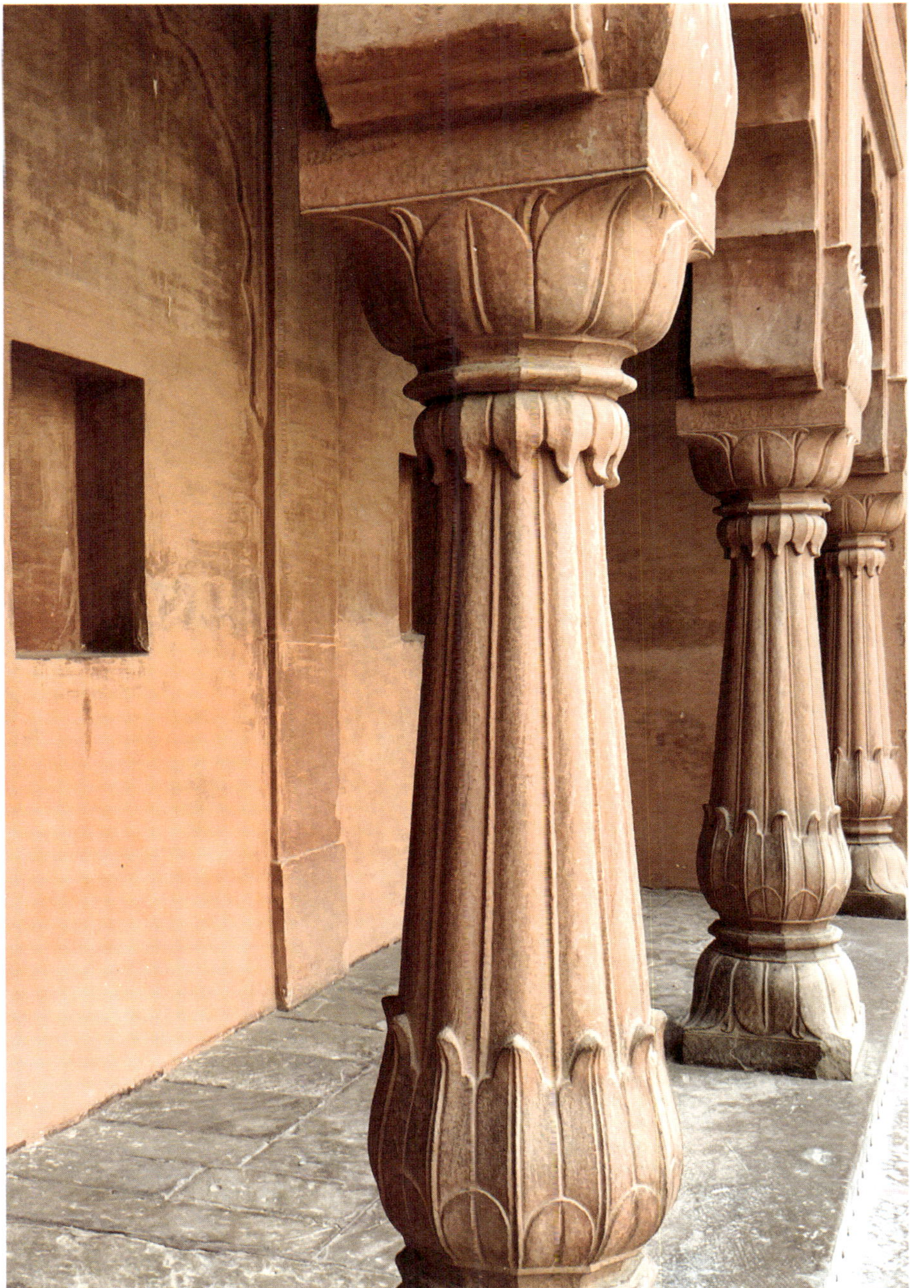

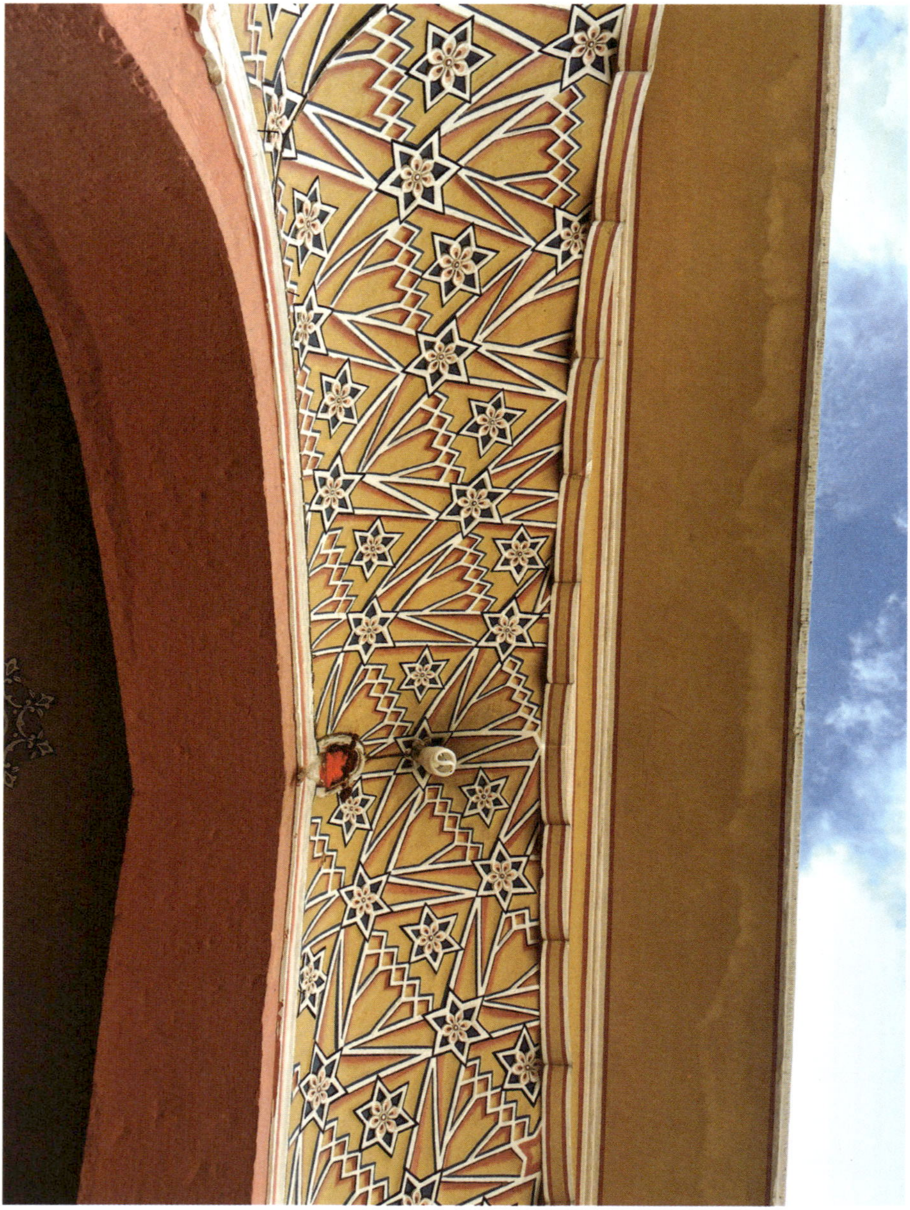

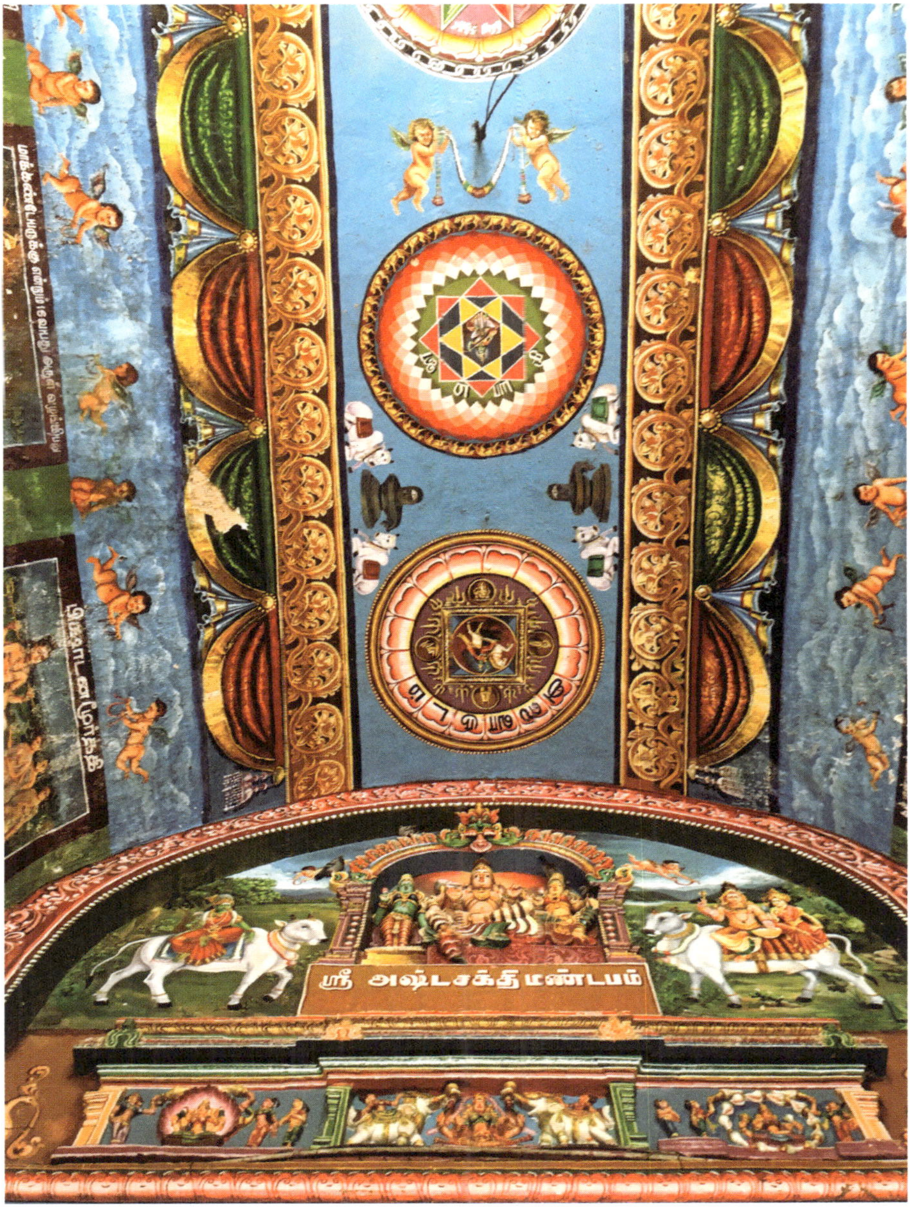
ஸ்ரீ அஷ்டசக்தி மண்டபம்

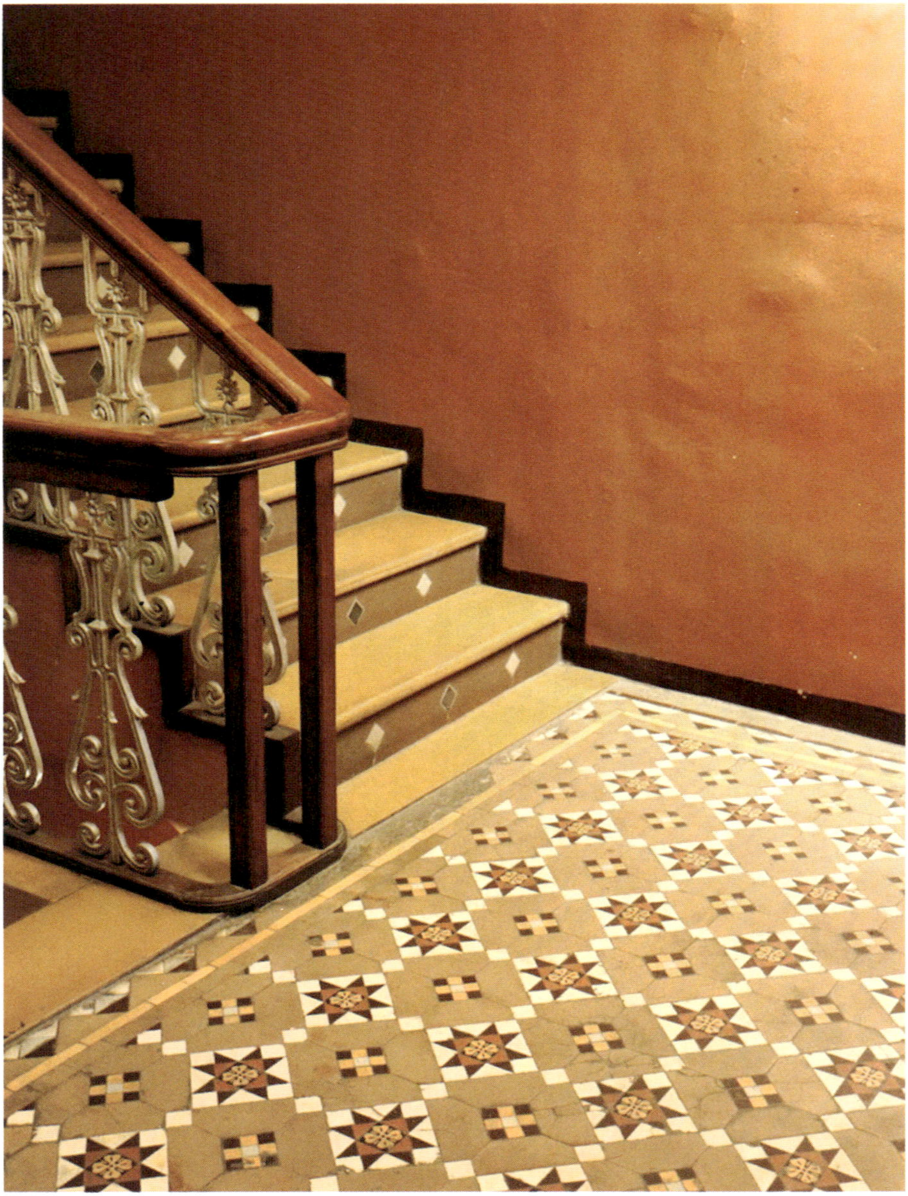

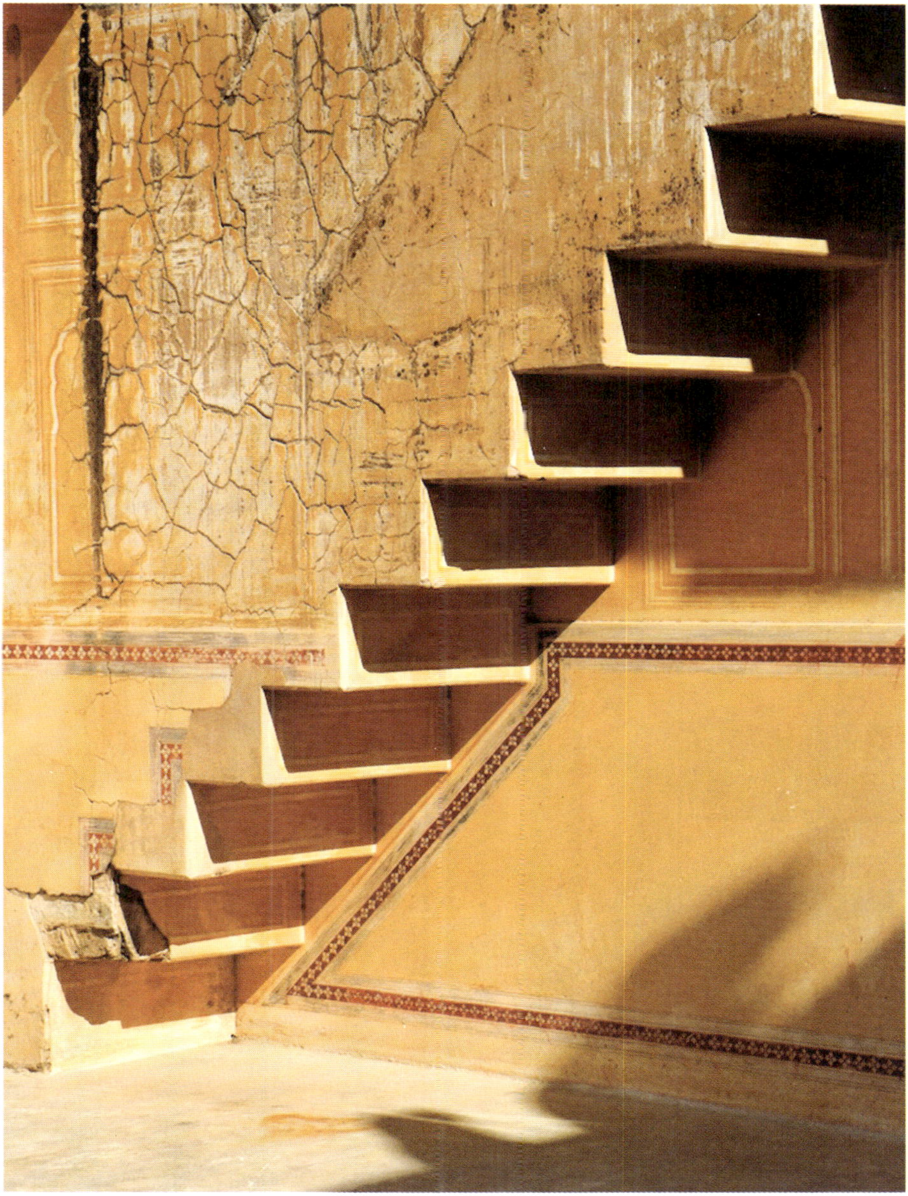

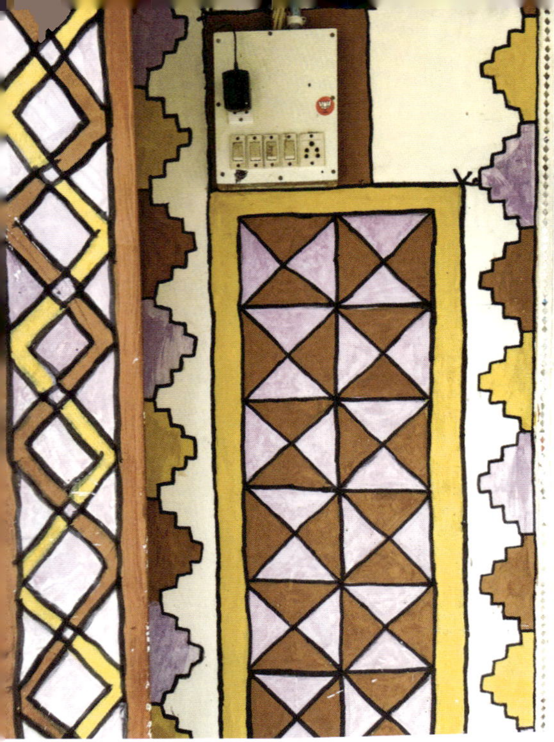
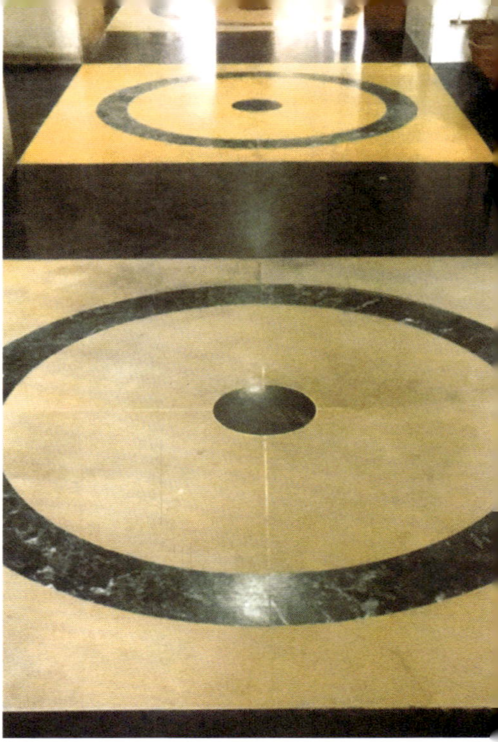
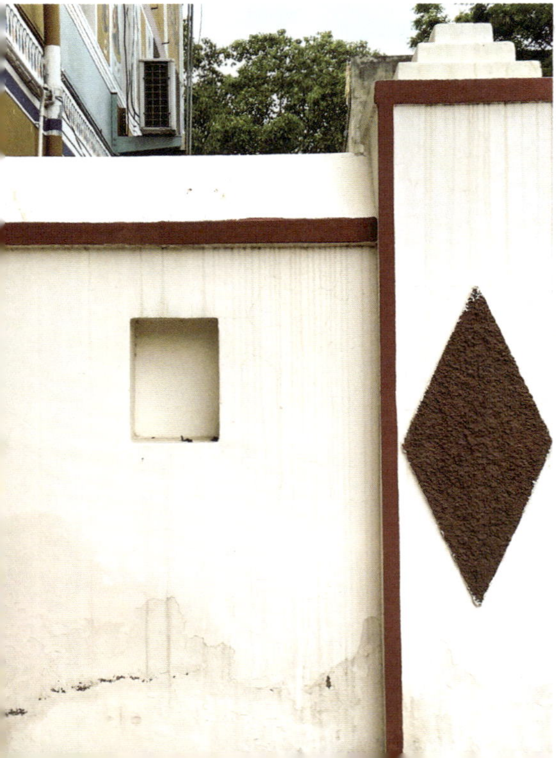
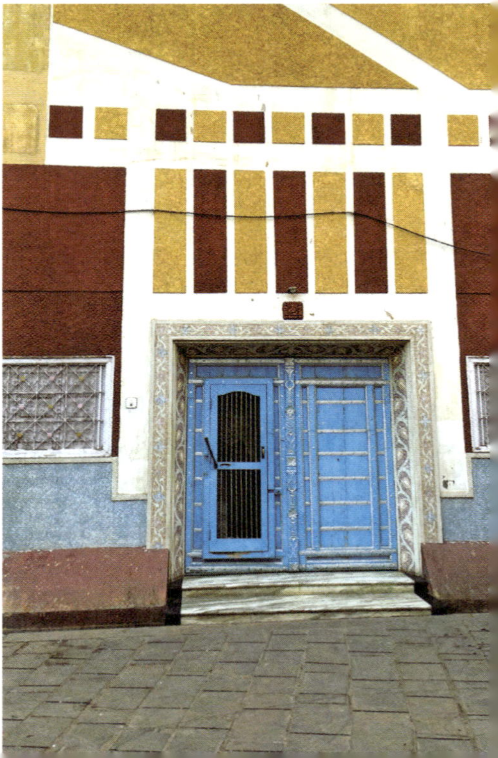

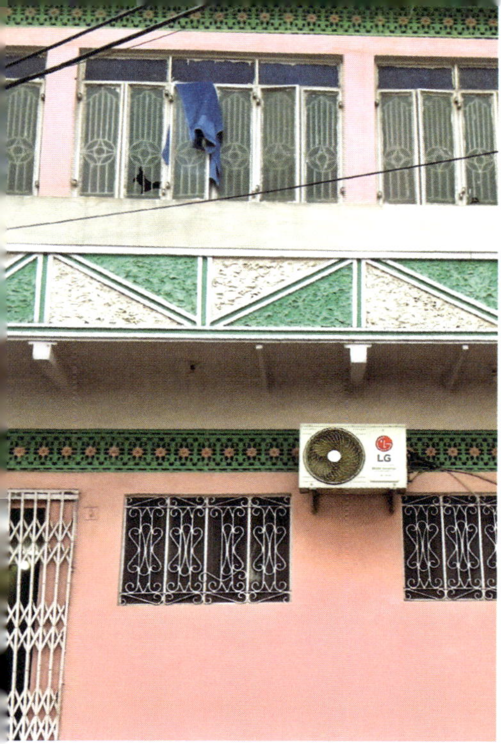
LG
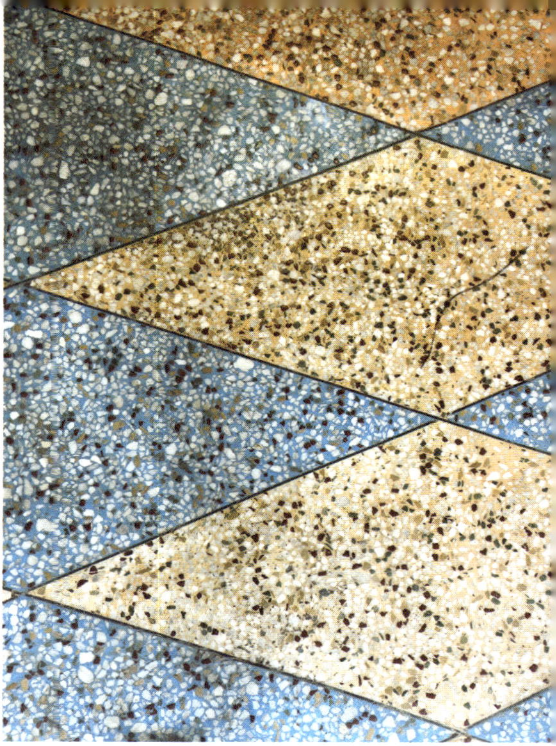
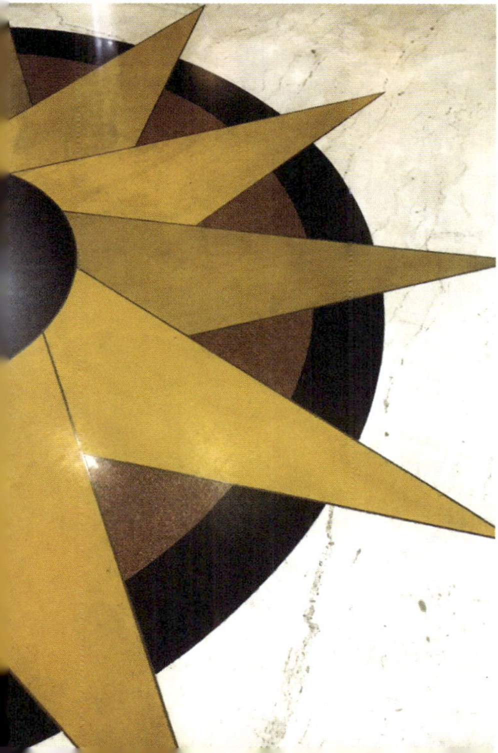
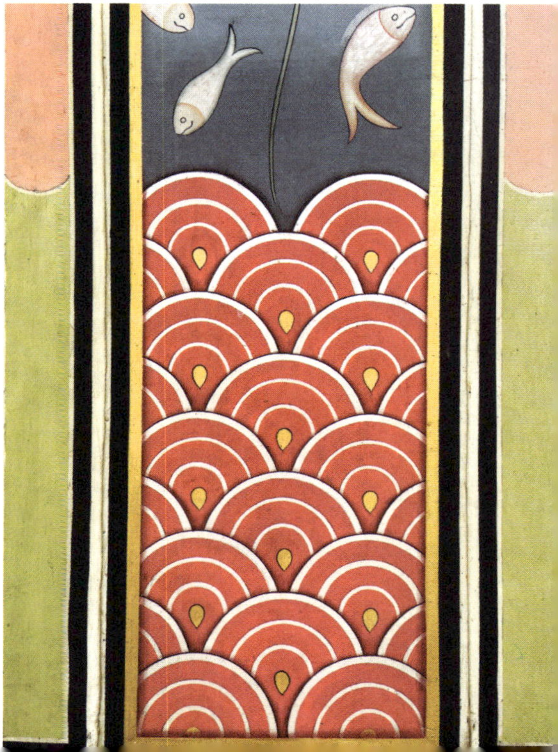

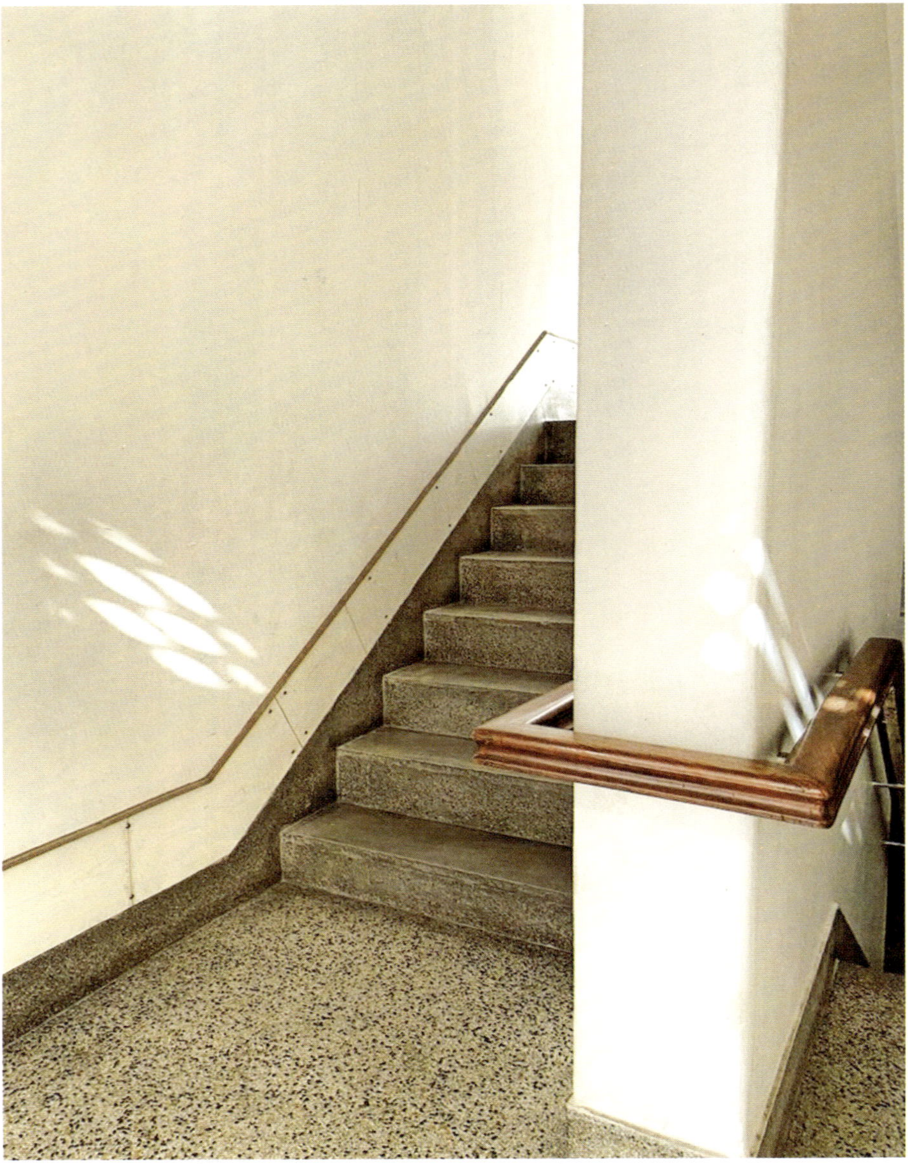

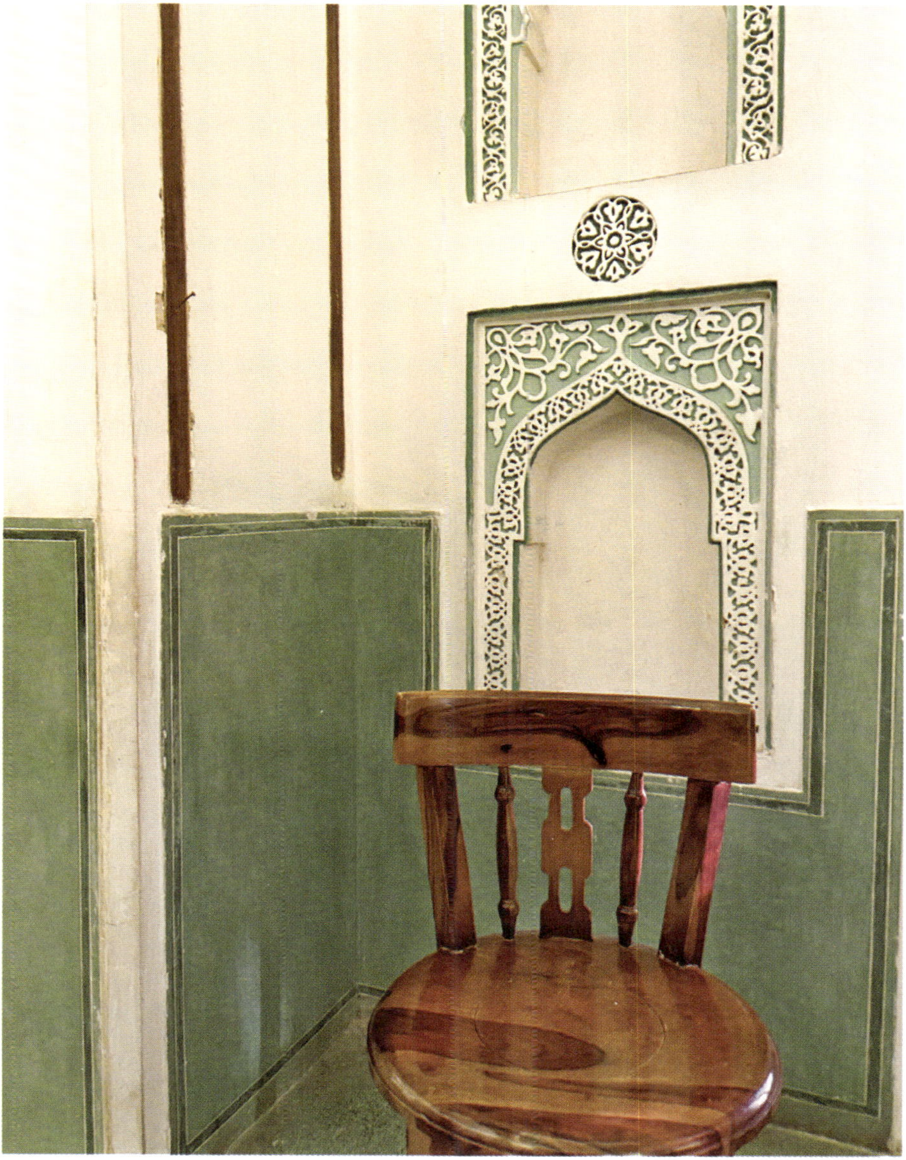

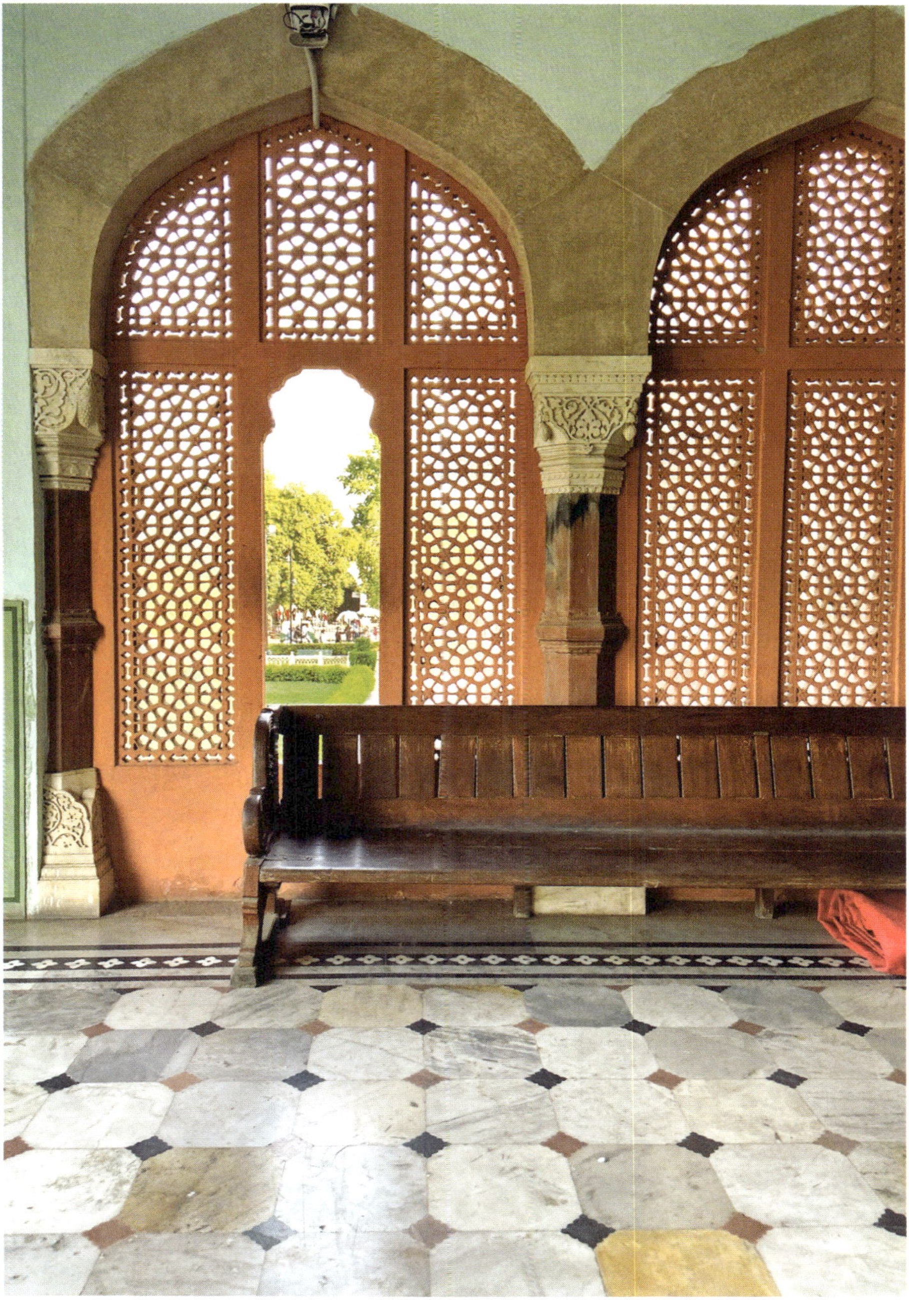

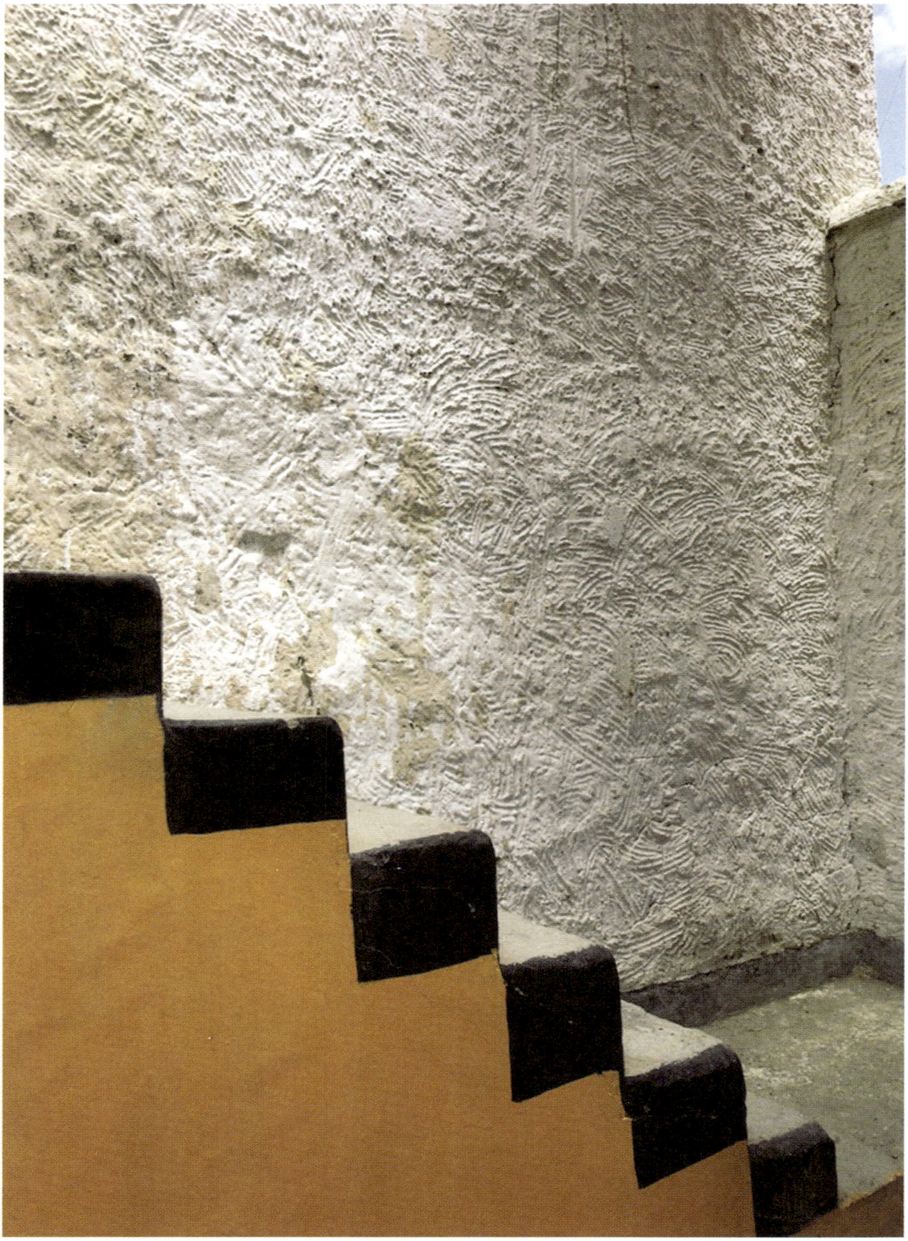

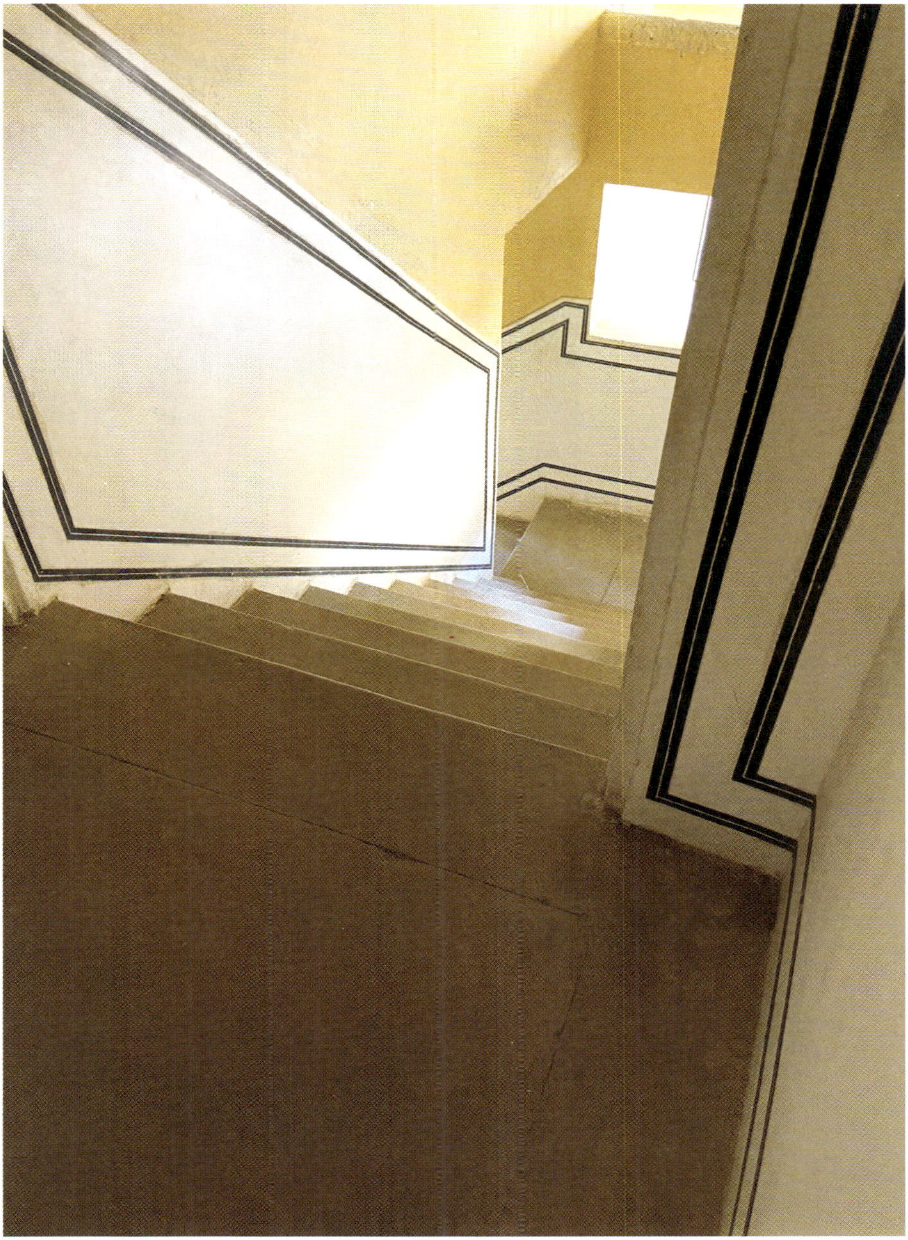

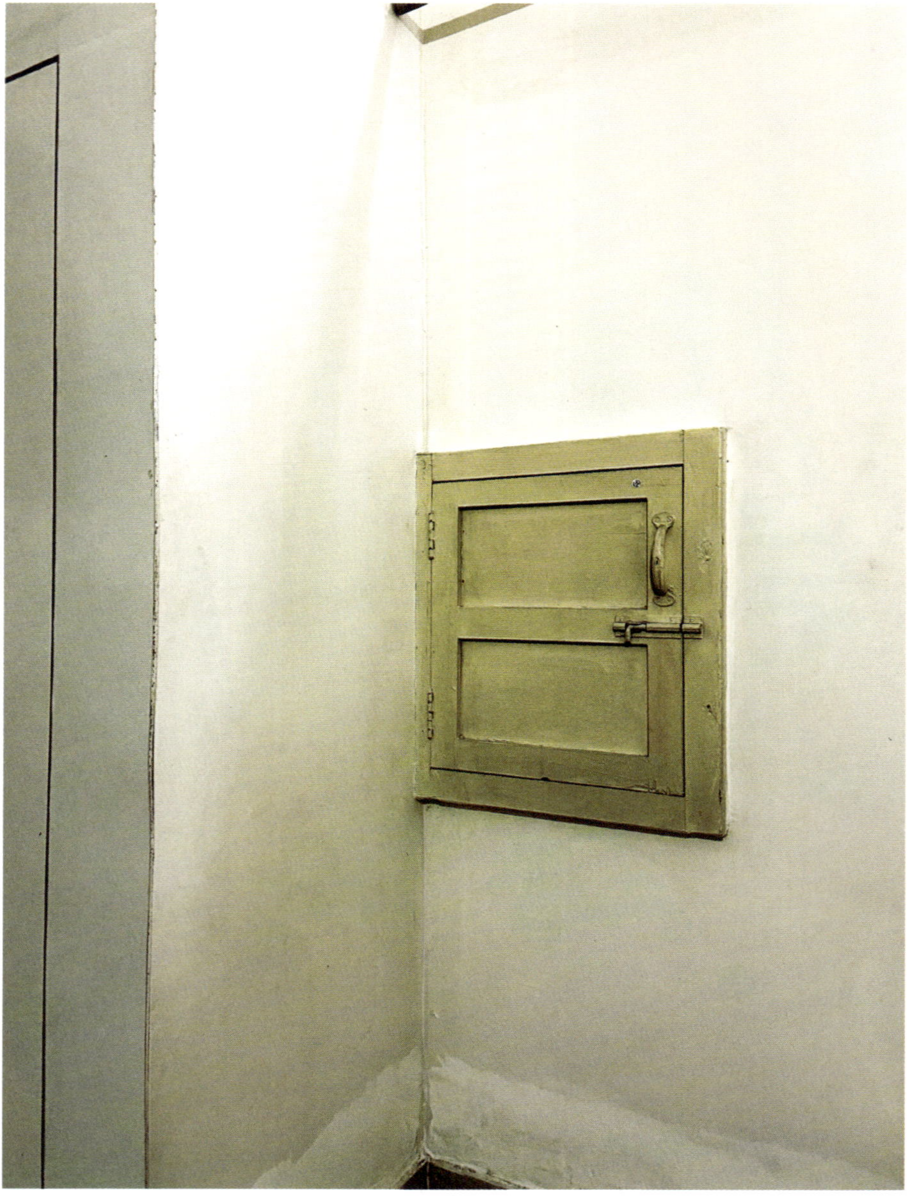

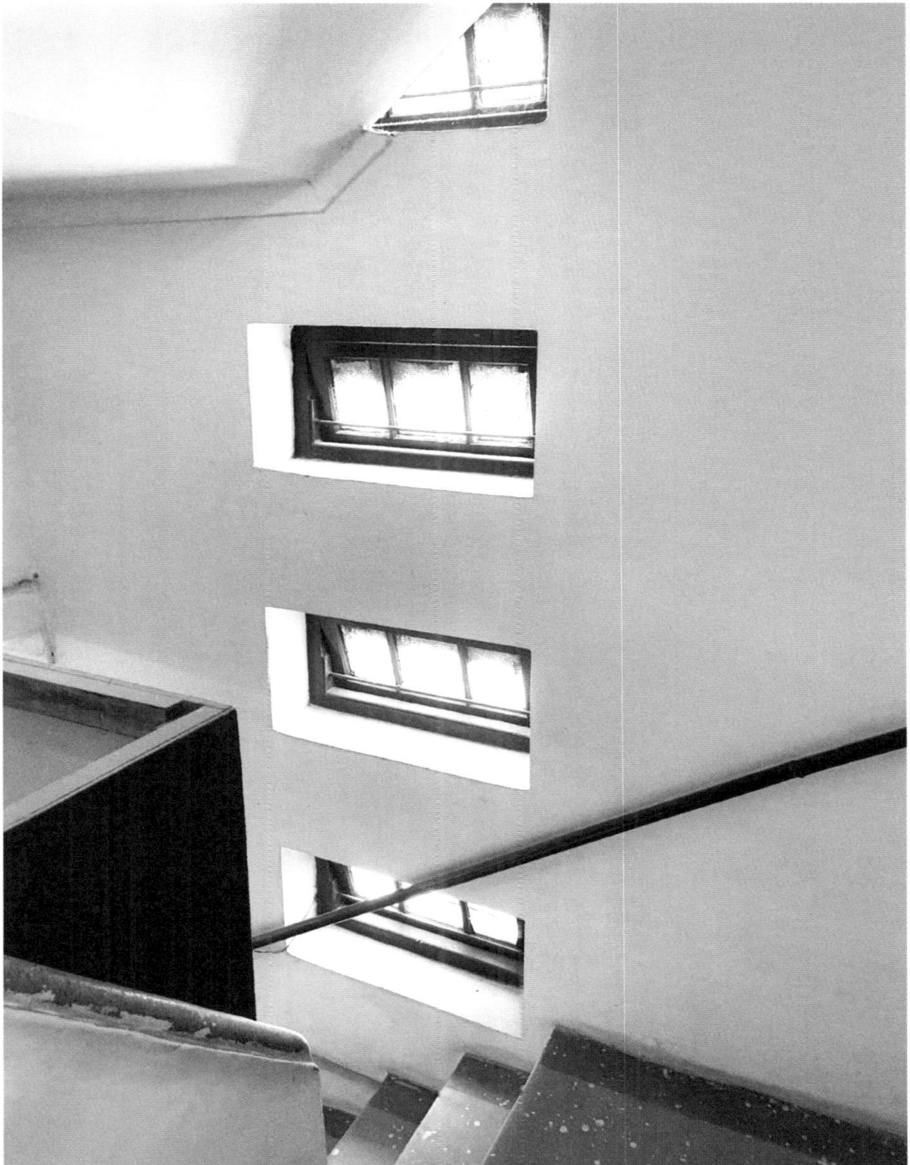

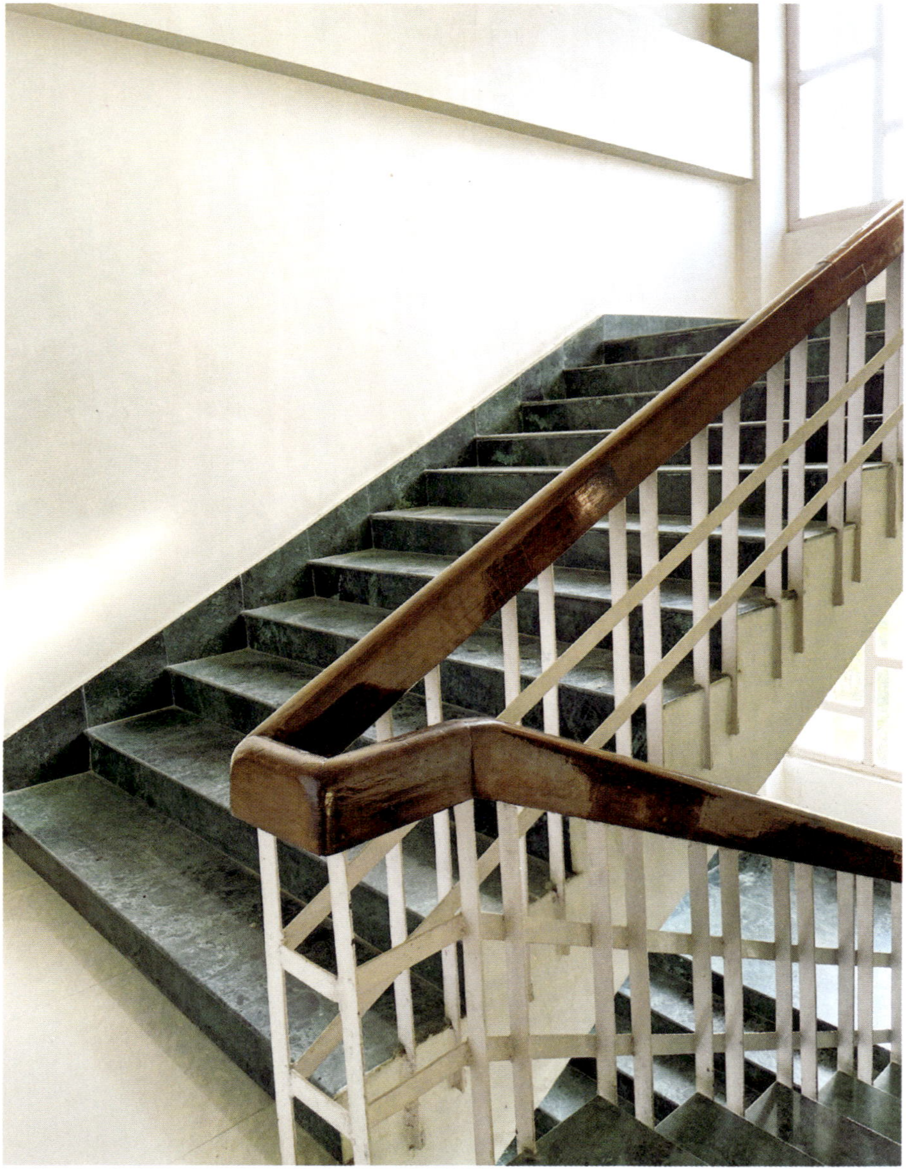

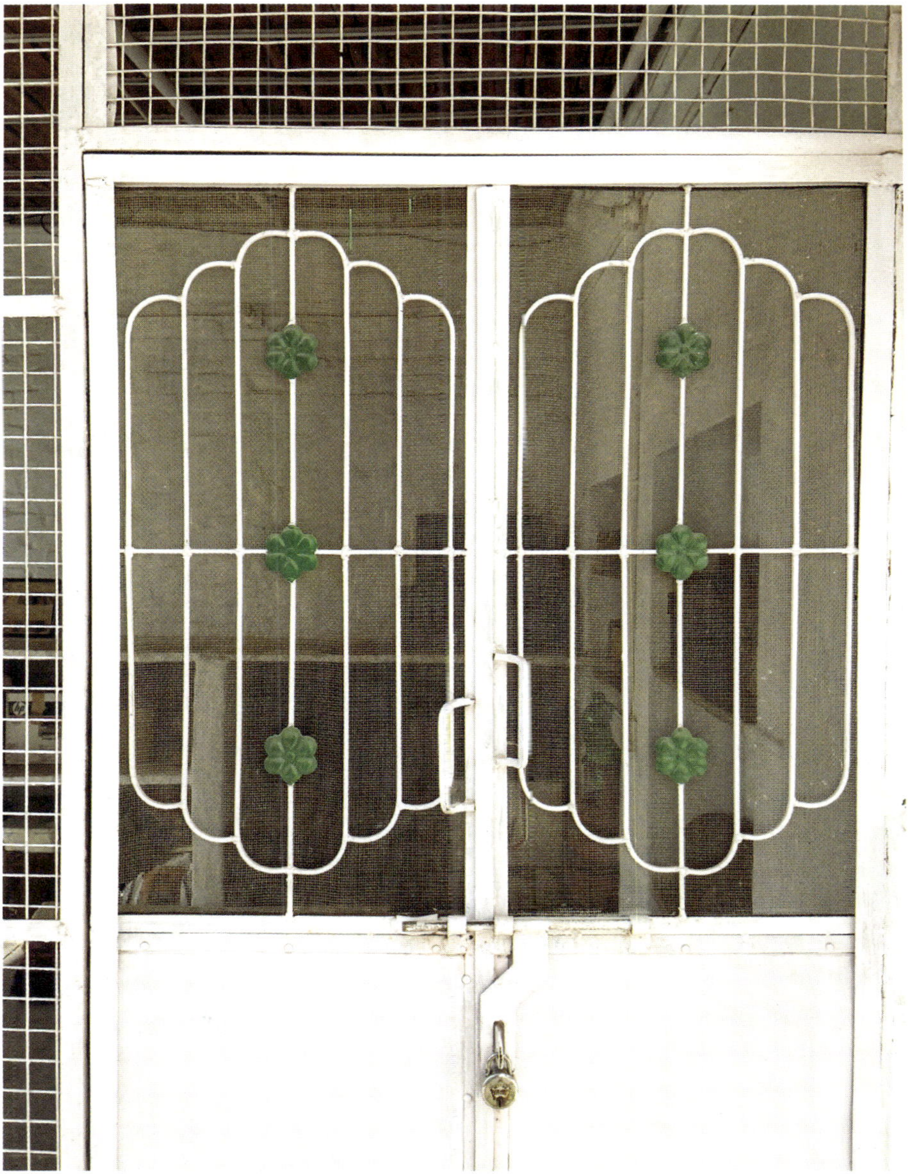

3C1

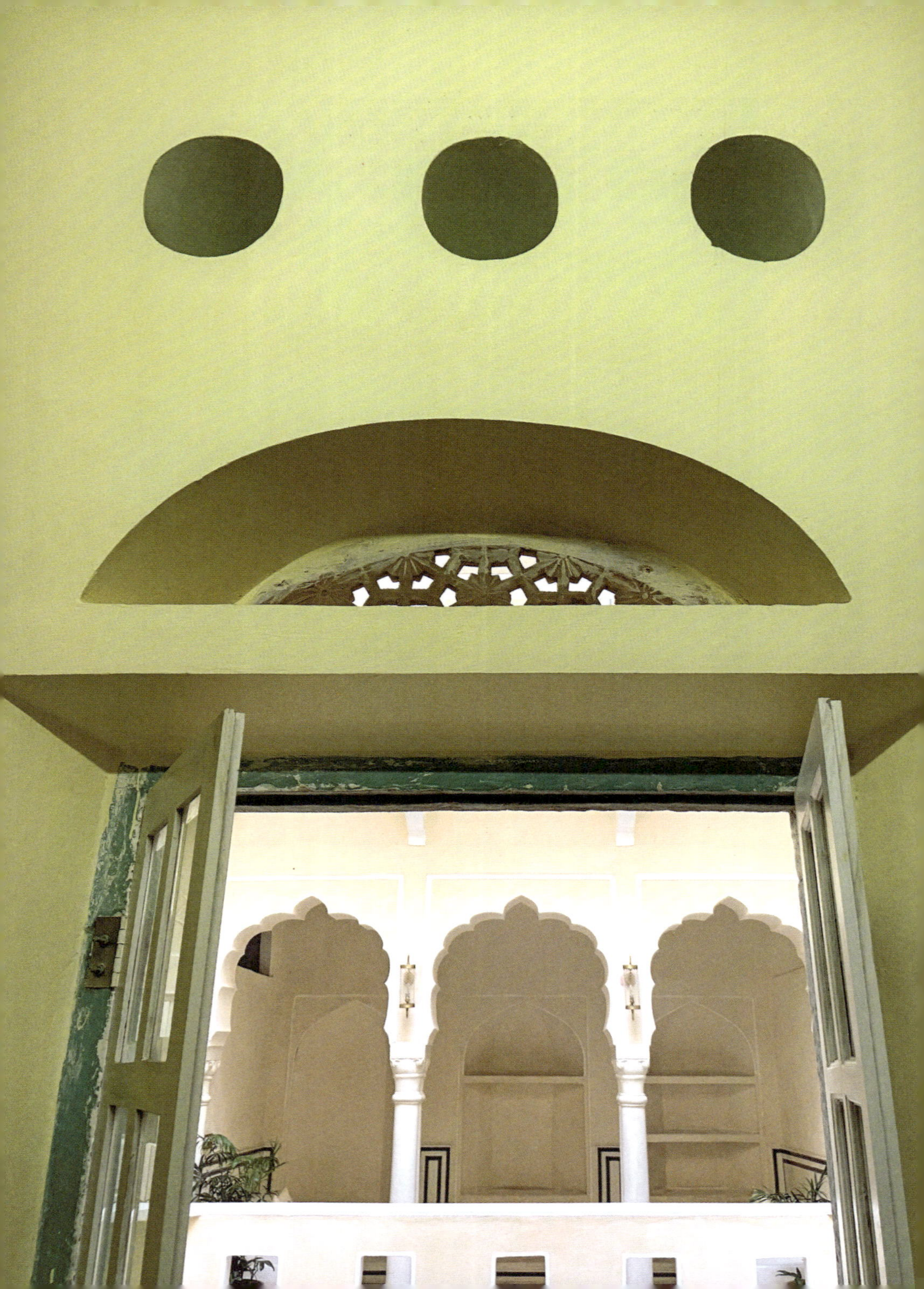

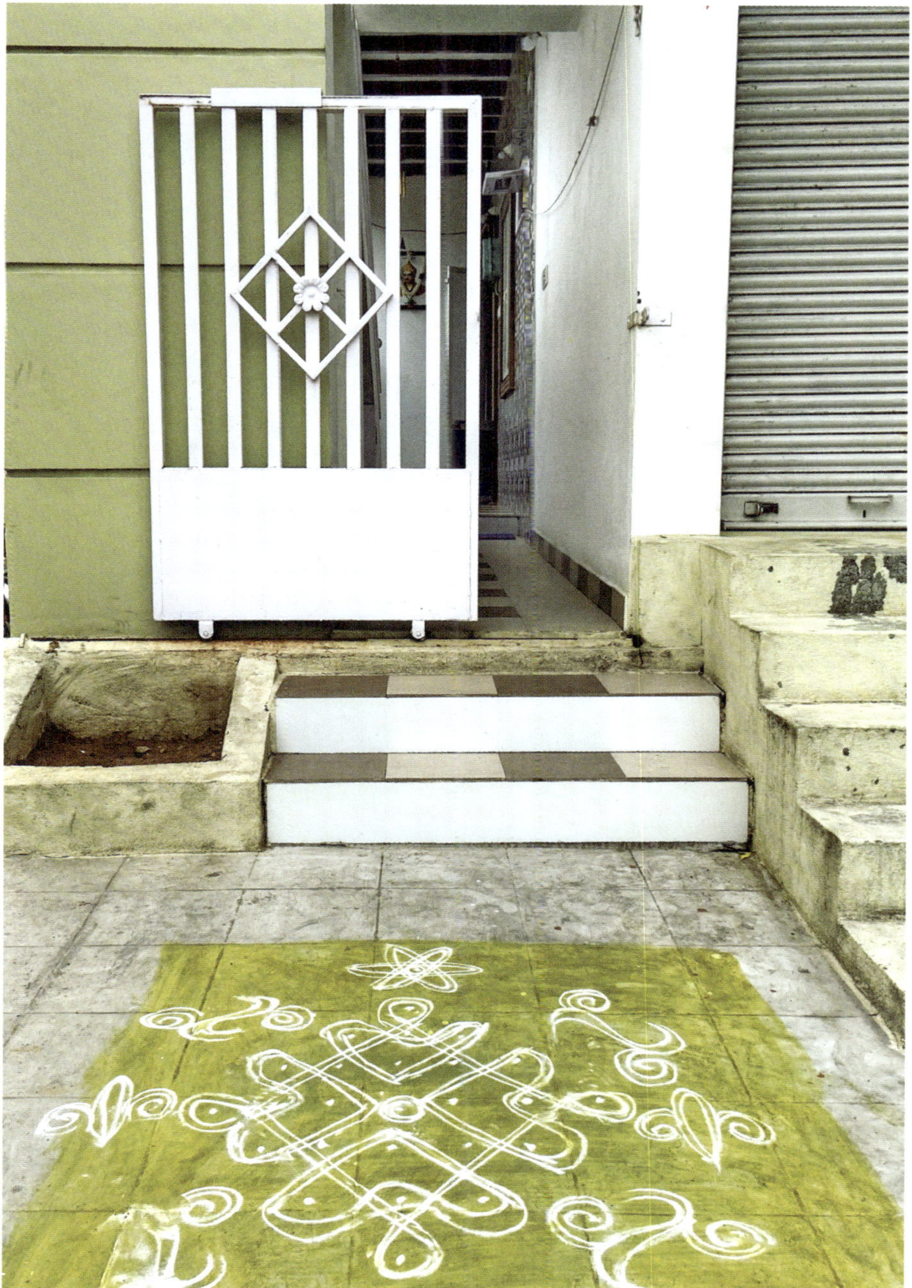

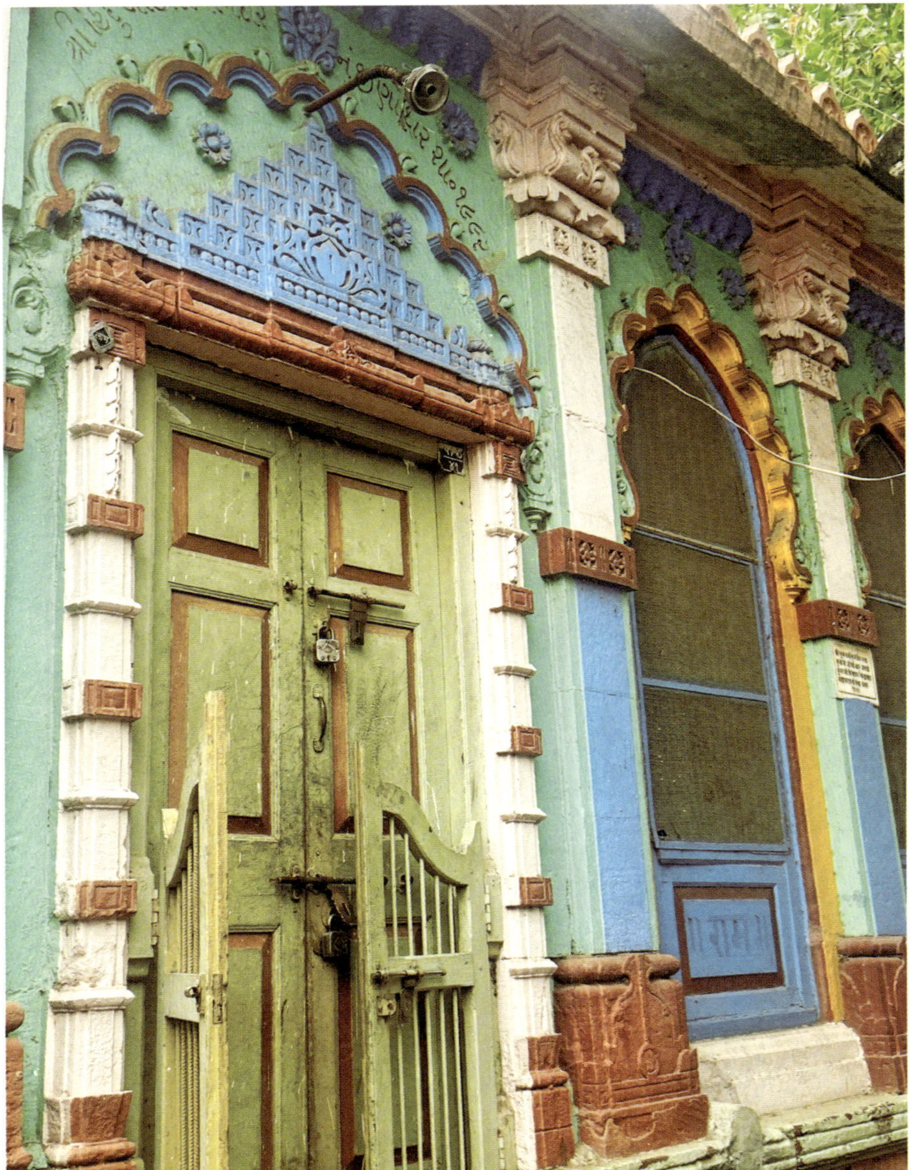

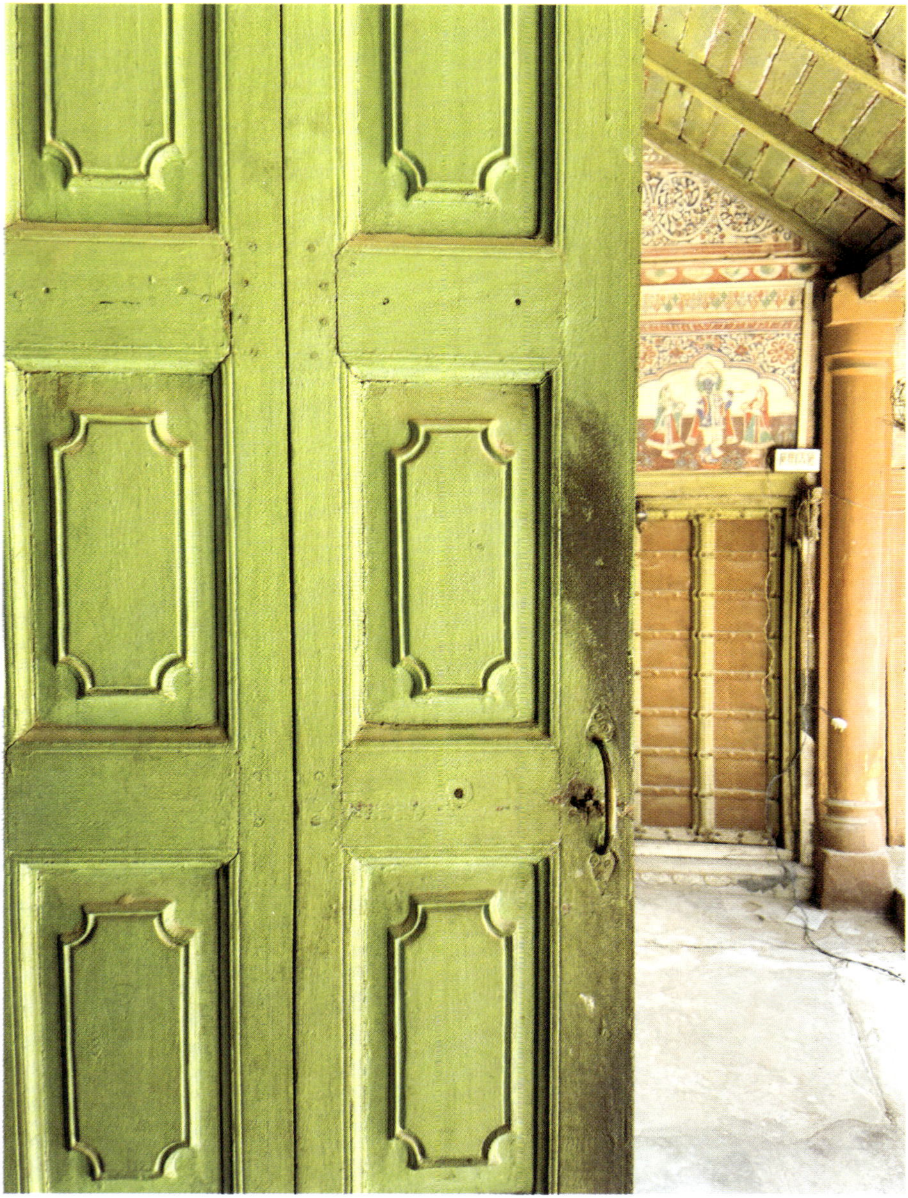

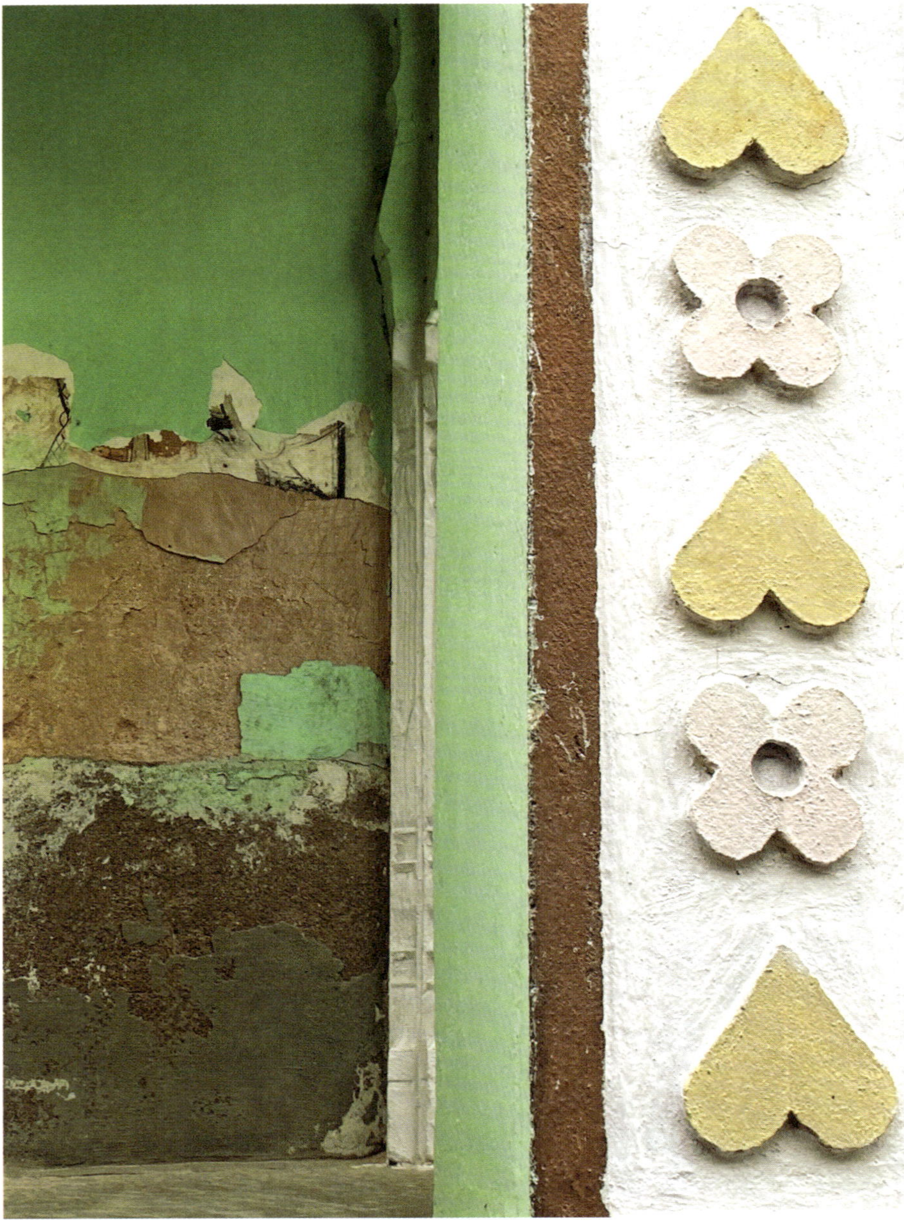

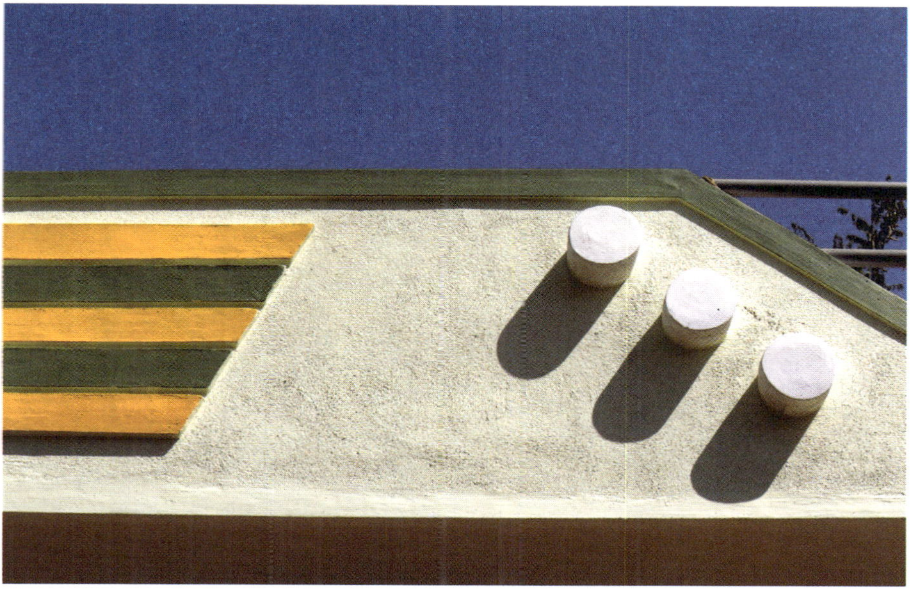

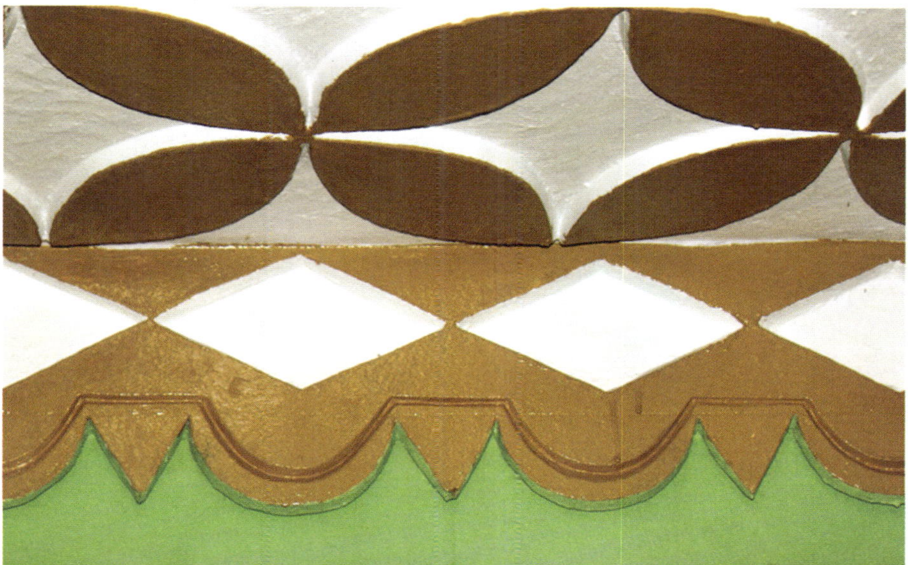

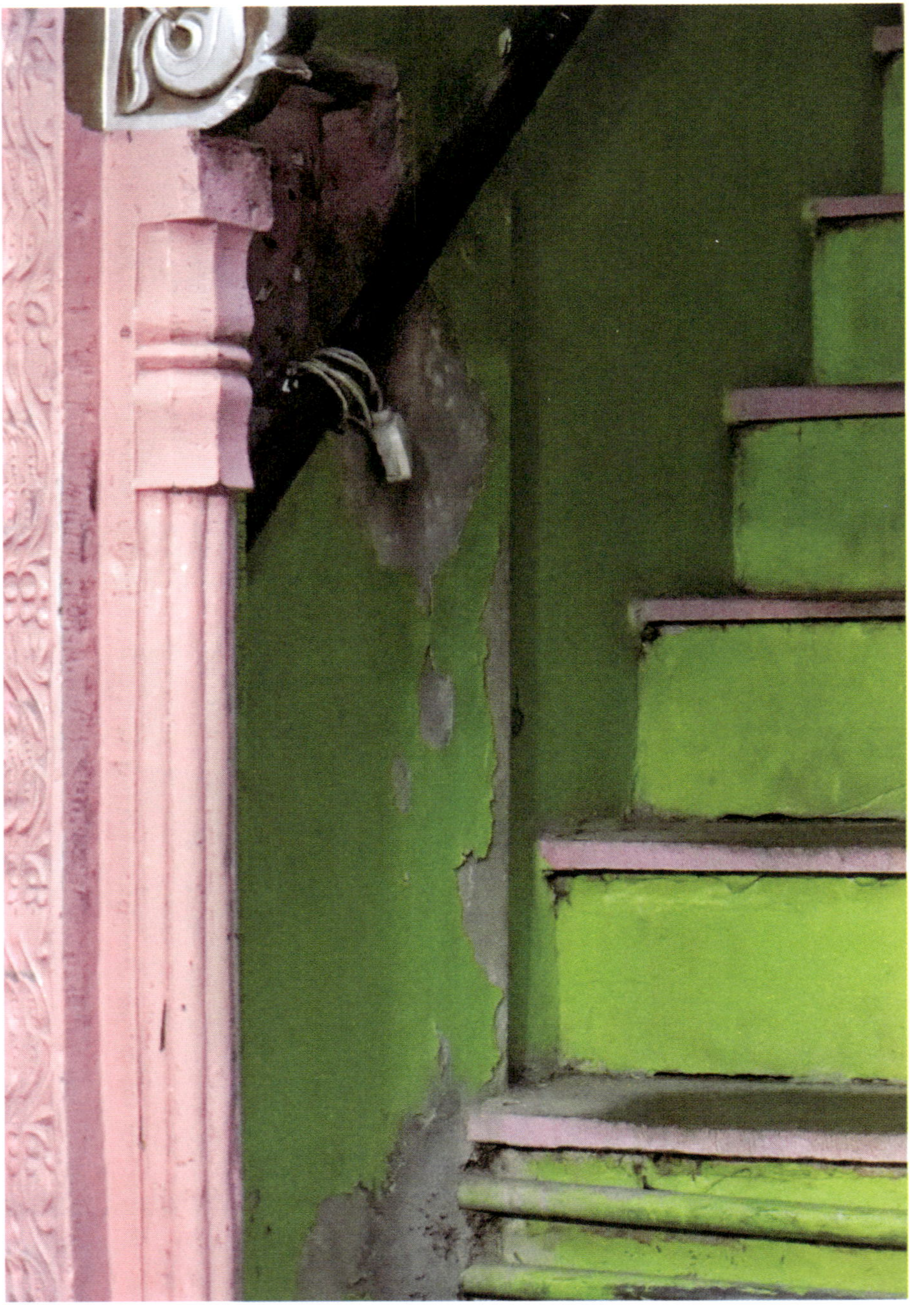

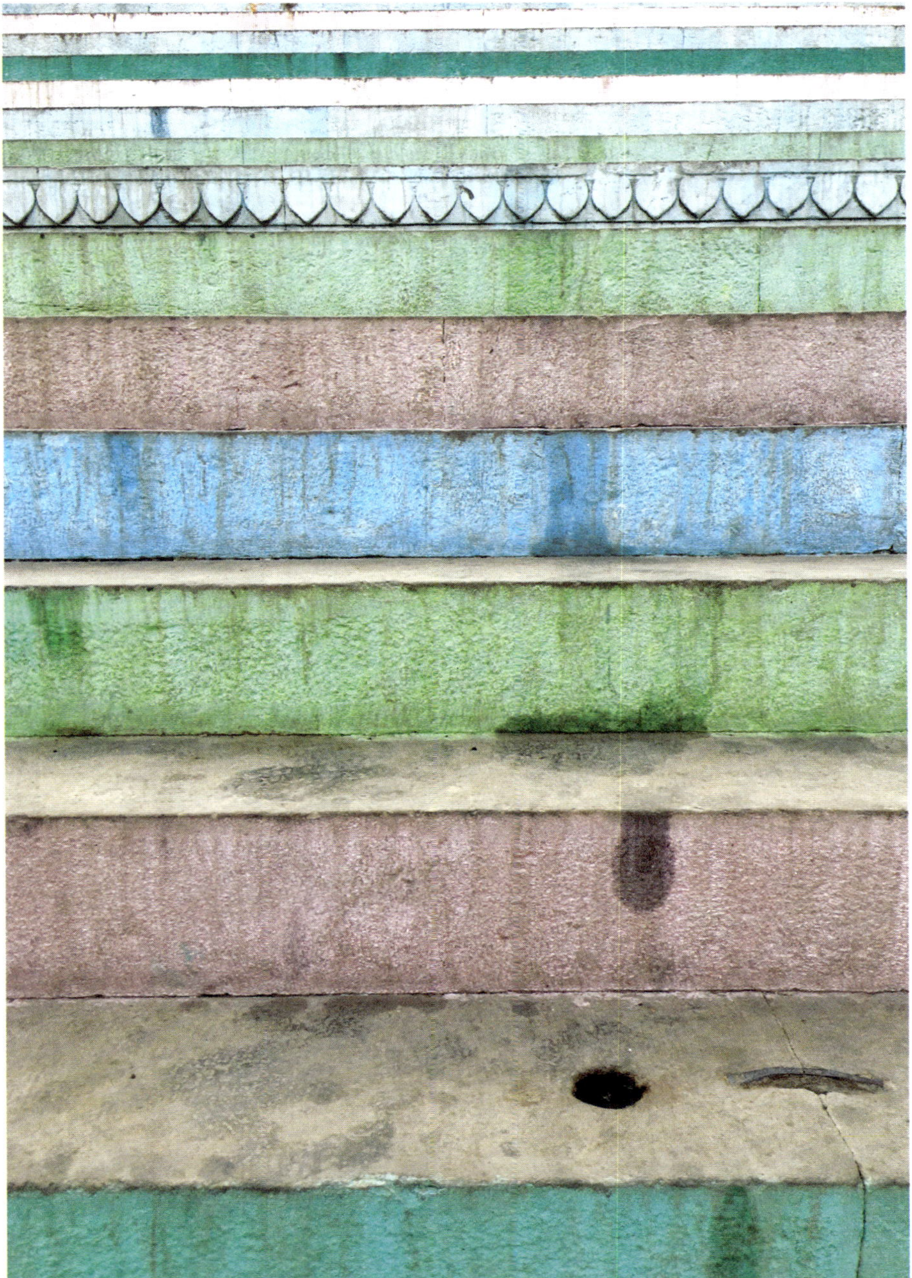

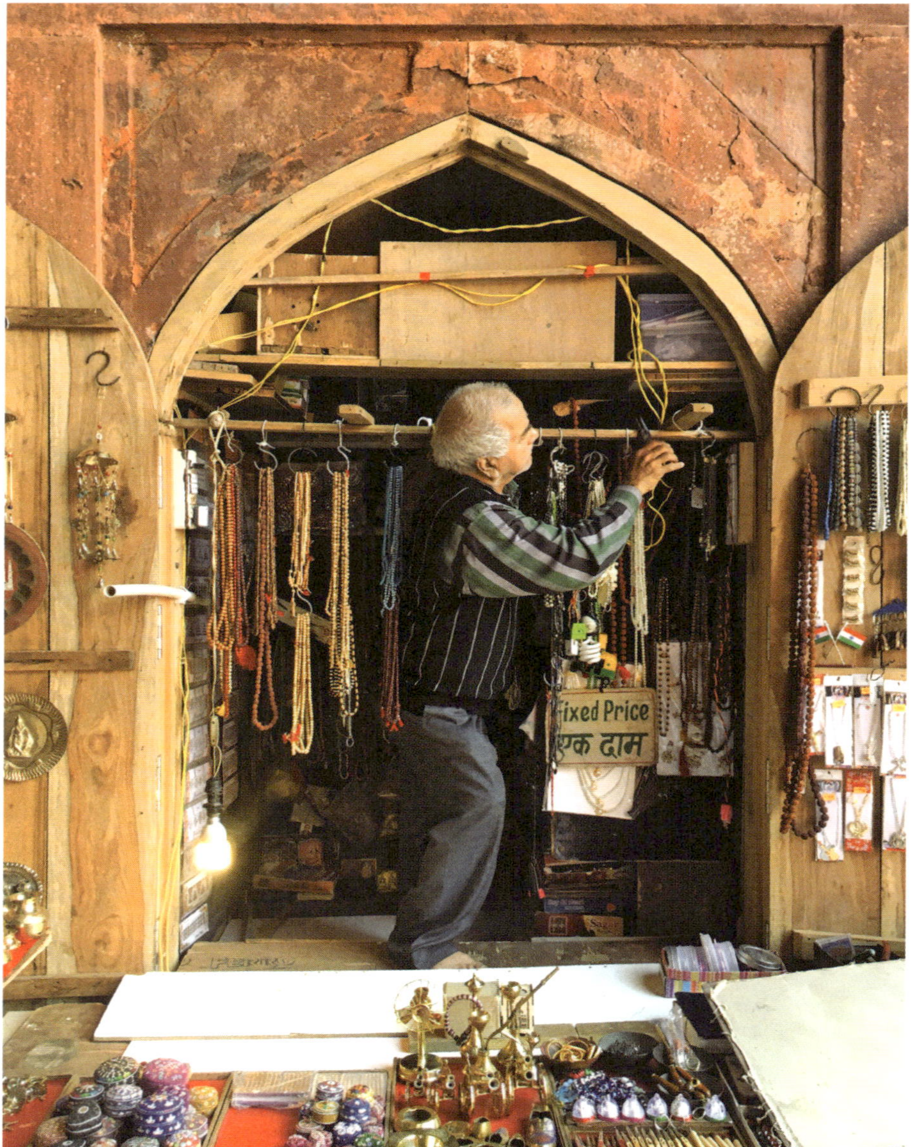
Fixed Price
एक दाम

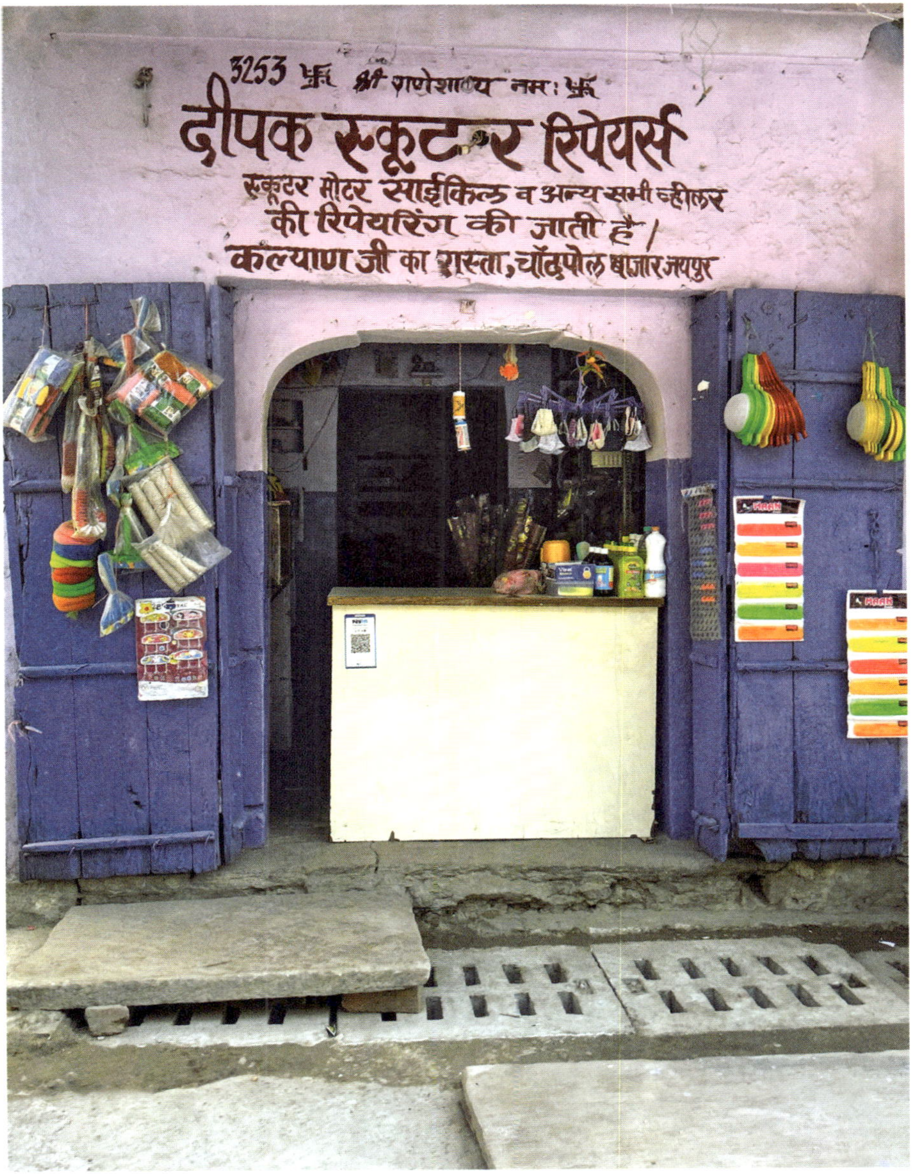
3253 श्री गणेशाय नमः
दीपक स्कूटर रिपेयर्स
स्कूटर मोटर साईकिल व अन्य सभी व्हीलर
की रिपेयरिंग की जाती है।
कल्याण जी का रास्ता, चाँदपोल बाजार जयपुर

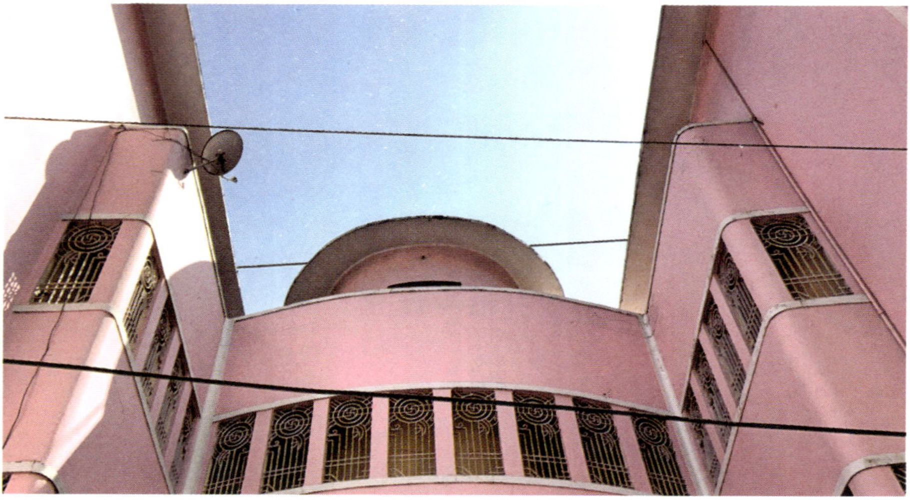

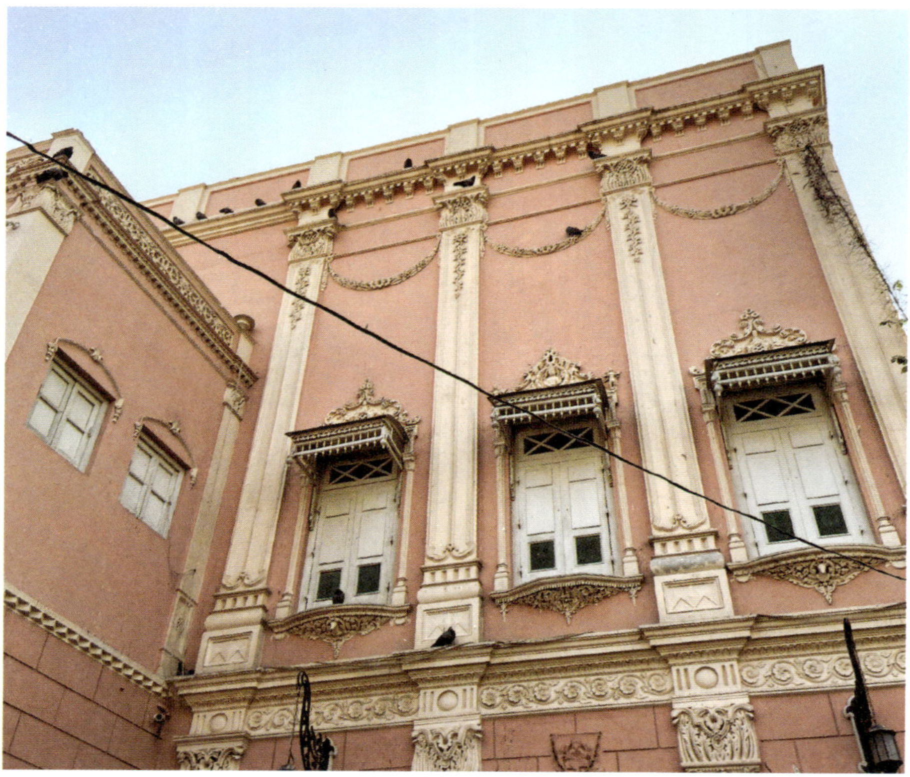

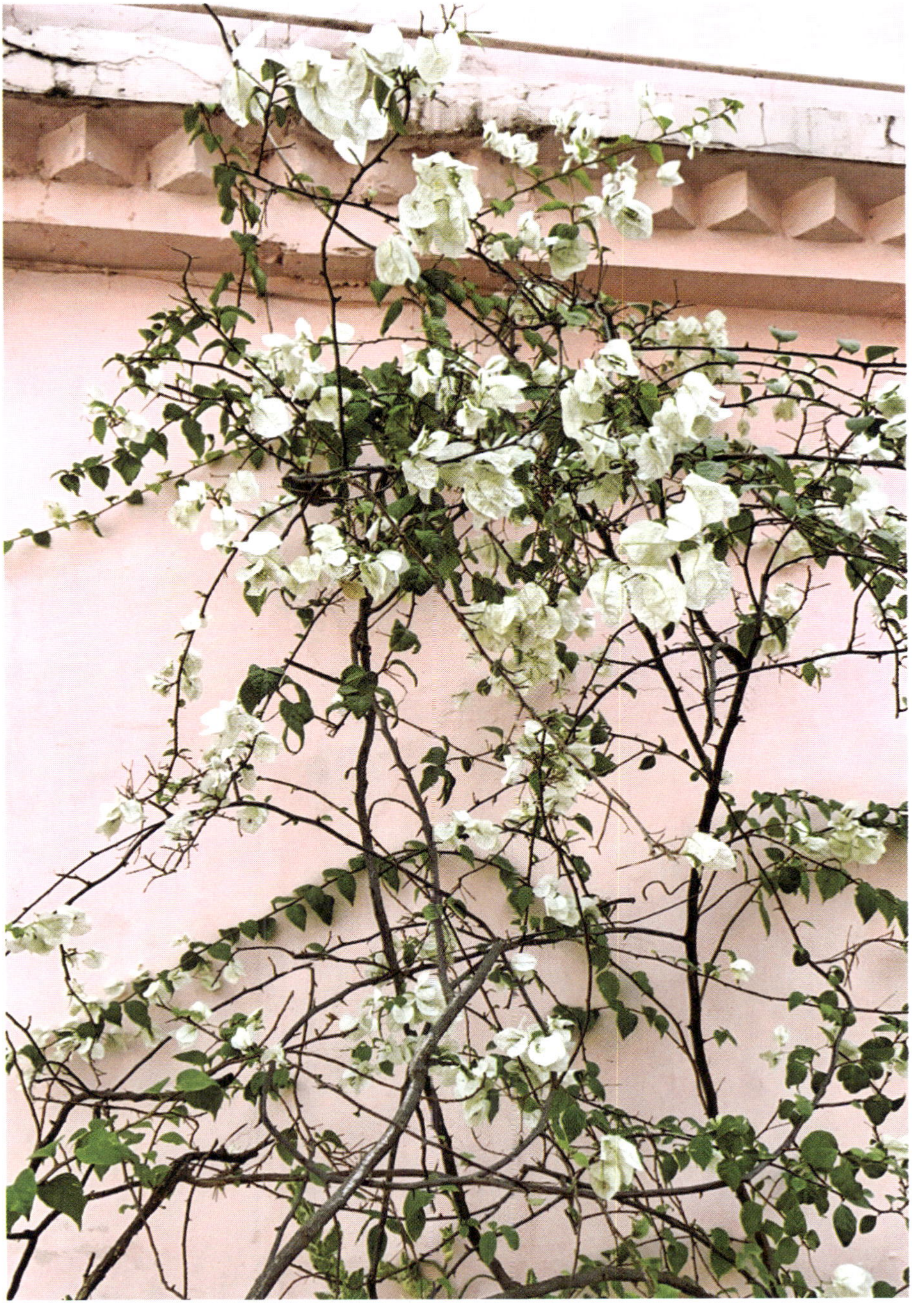

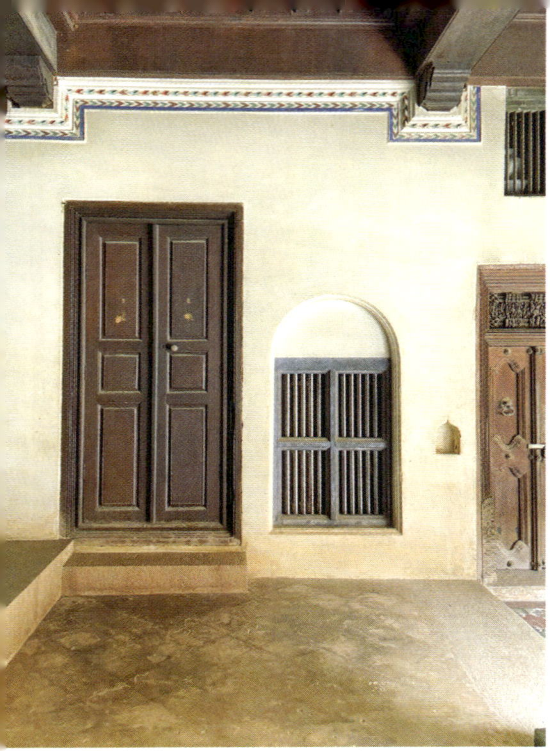
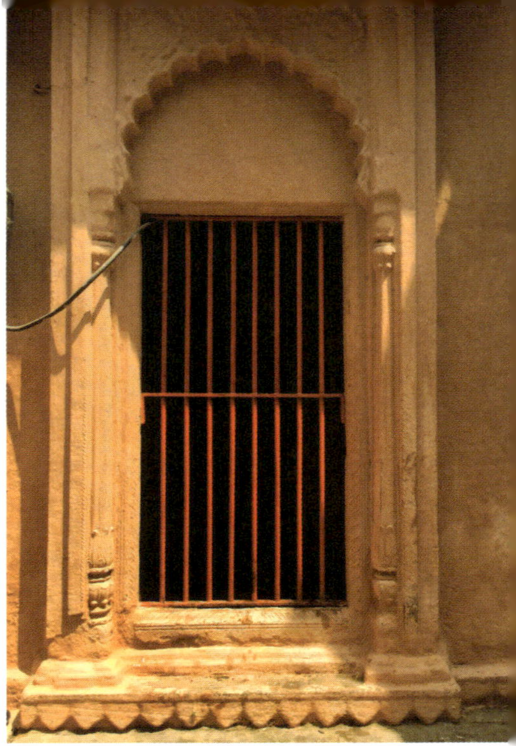
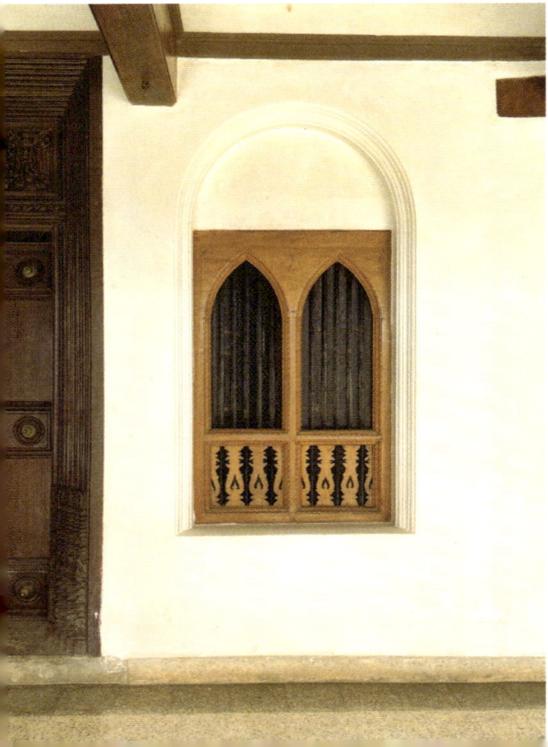
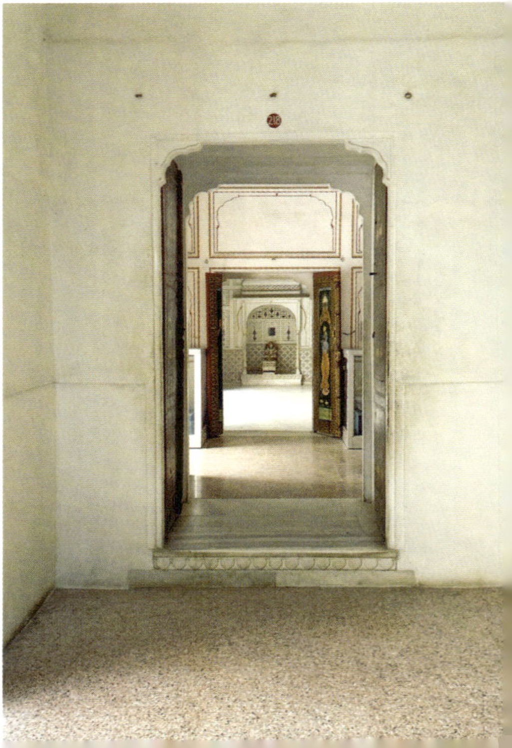

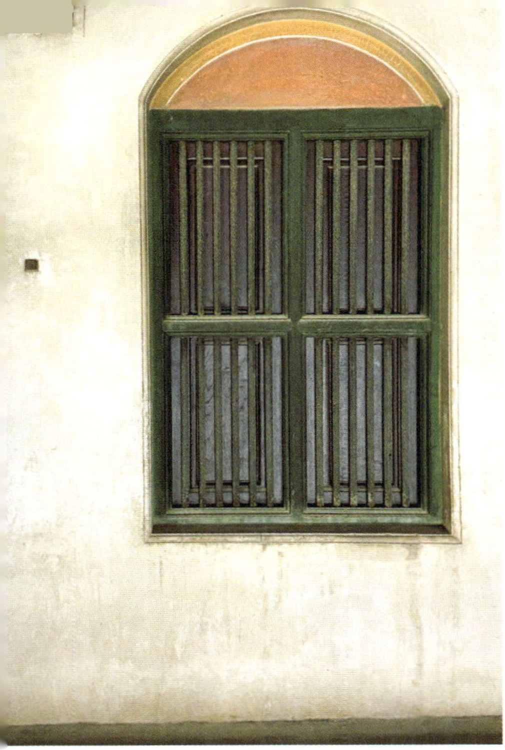
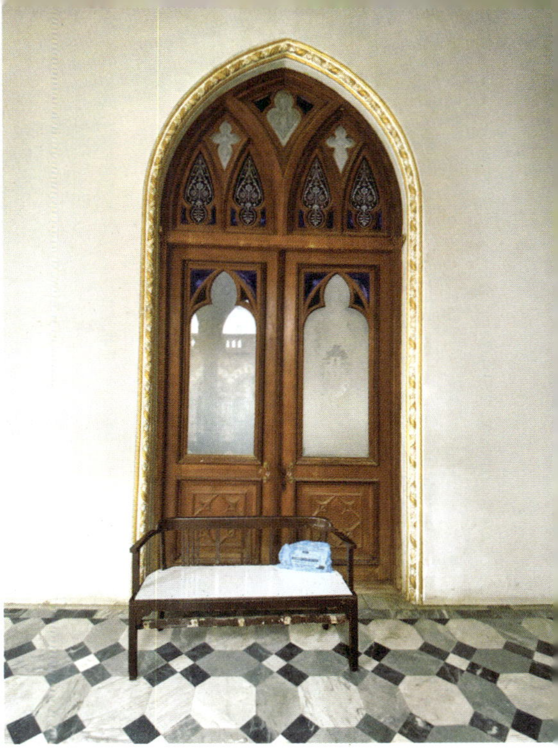
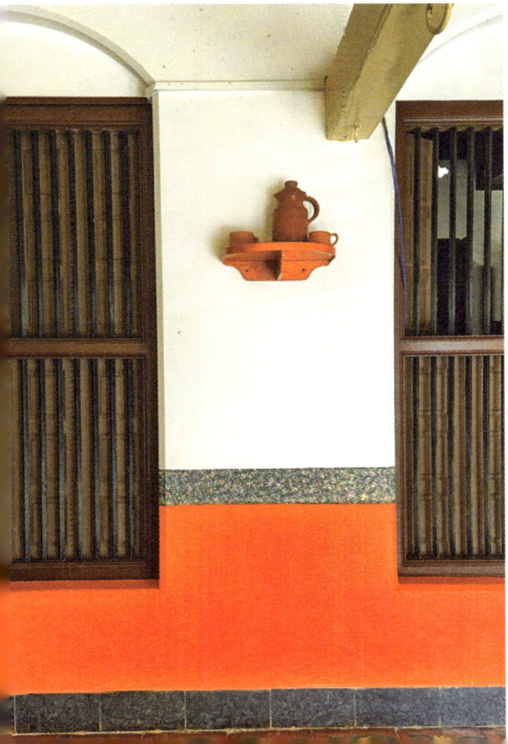
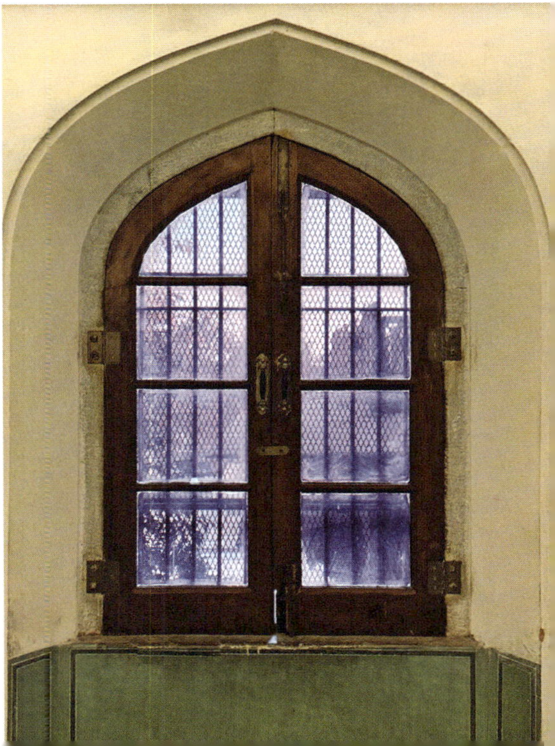

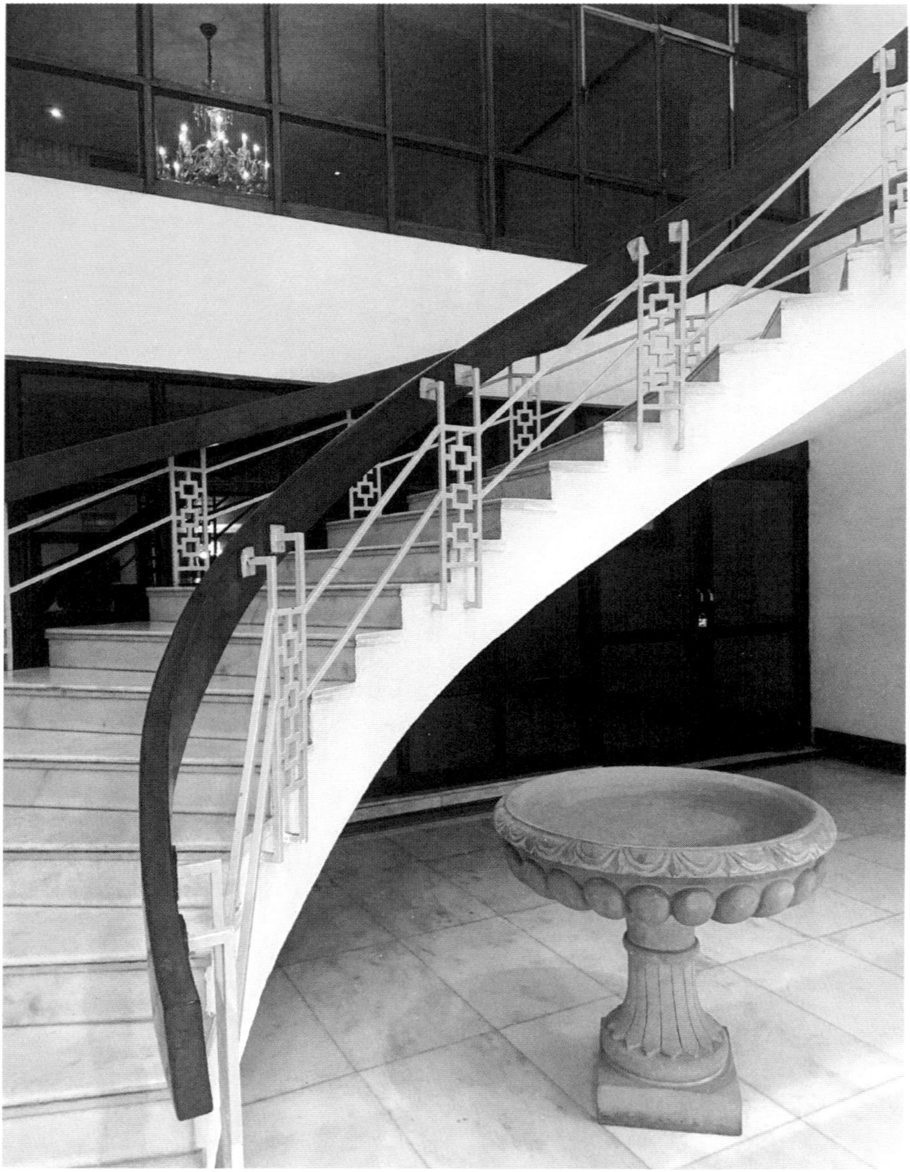

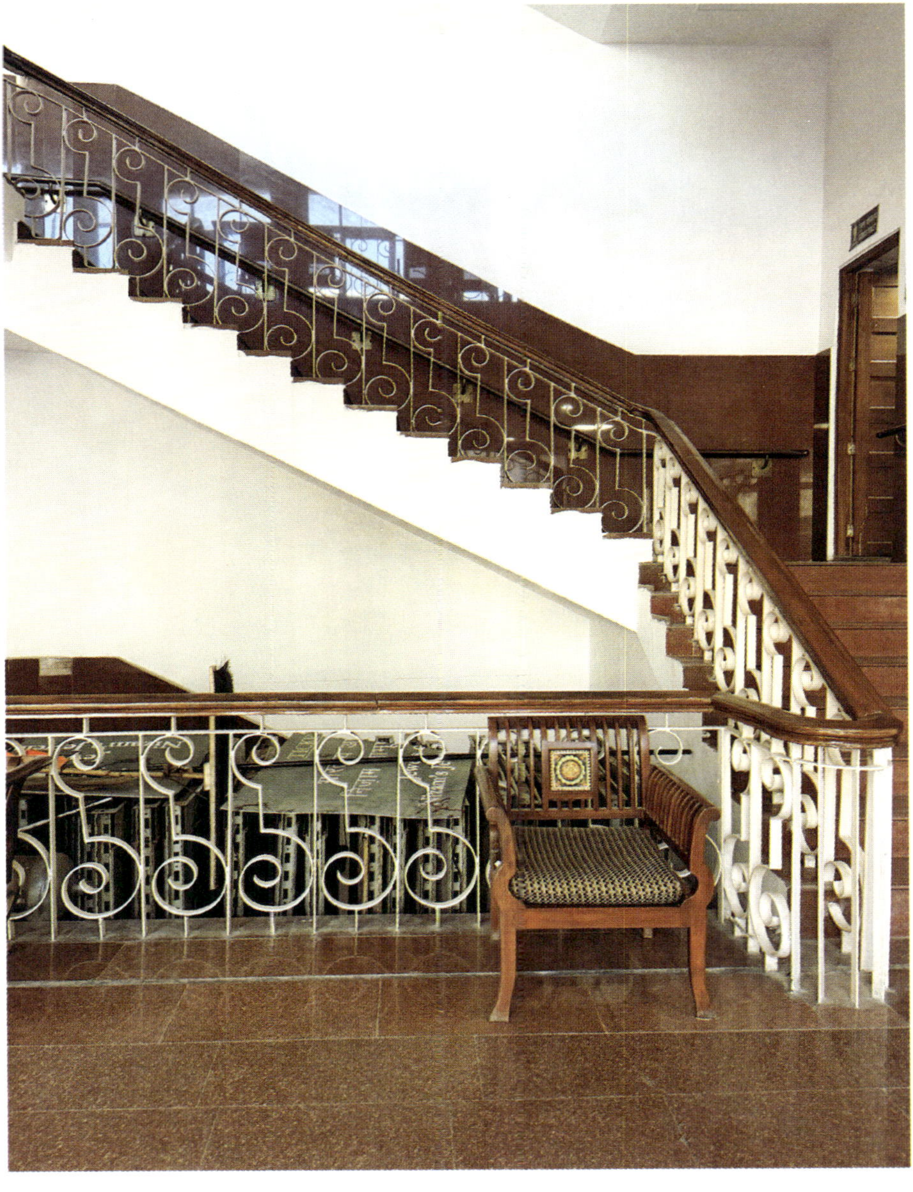

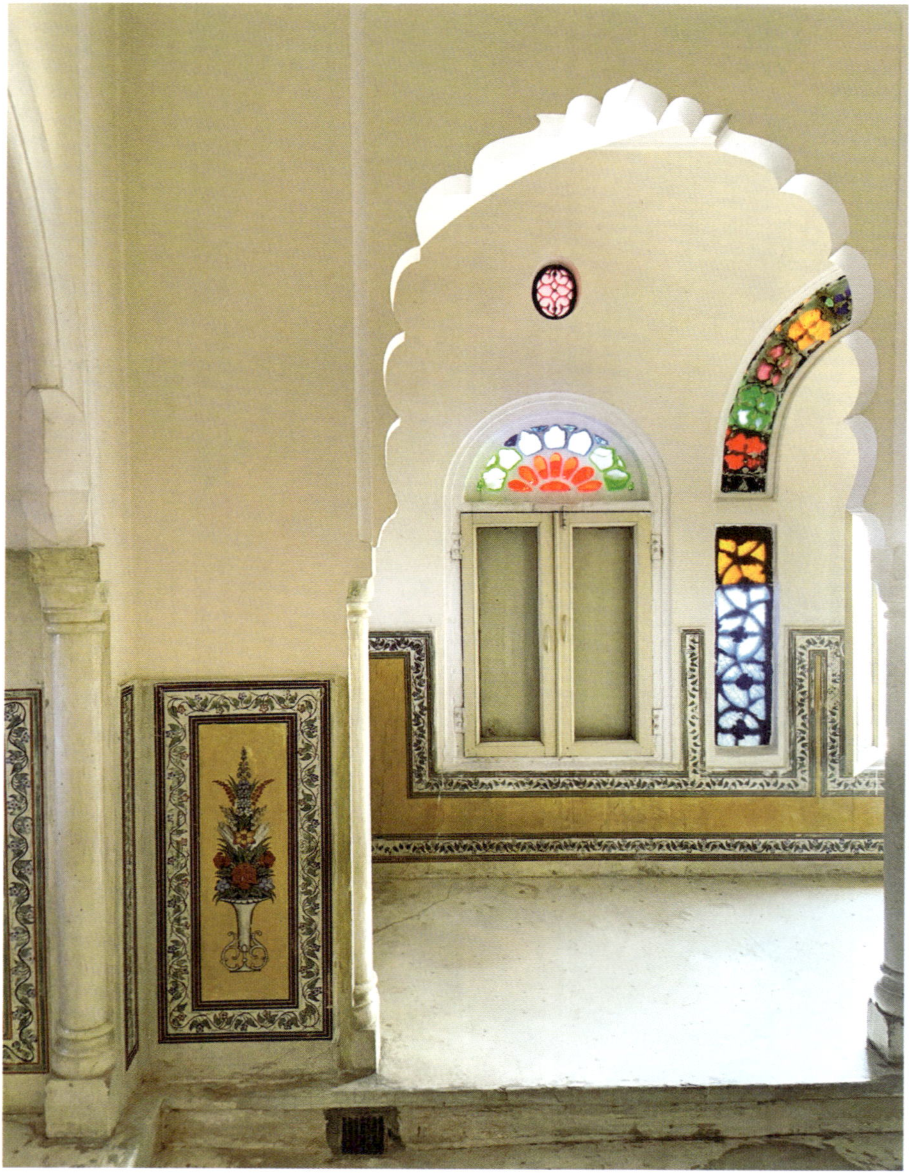

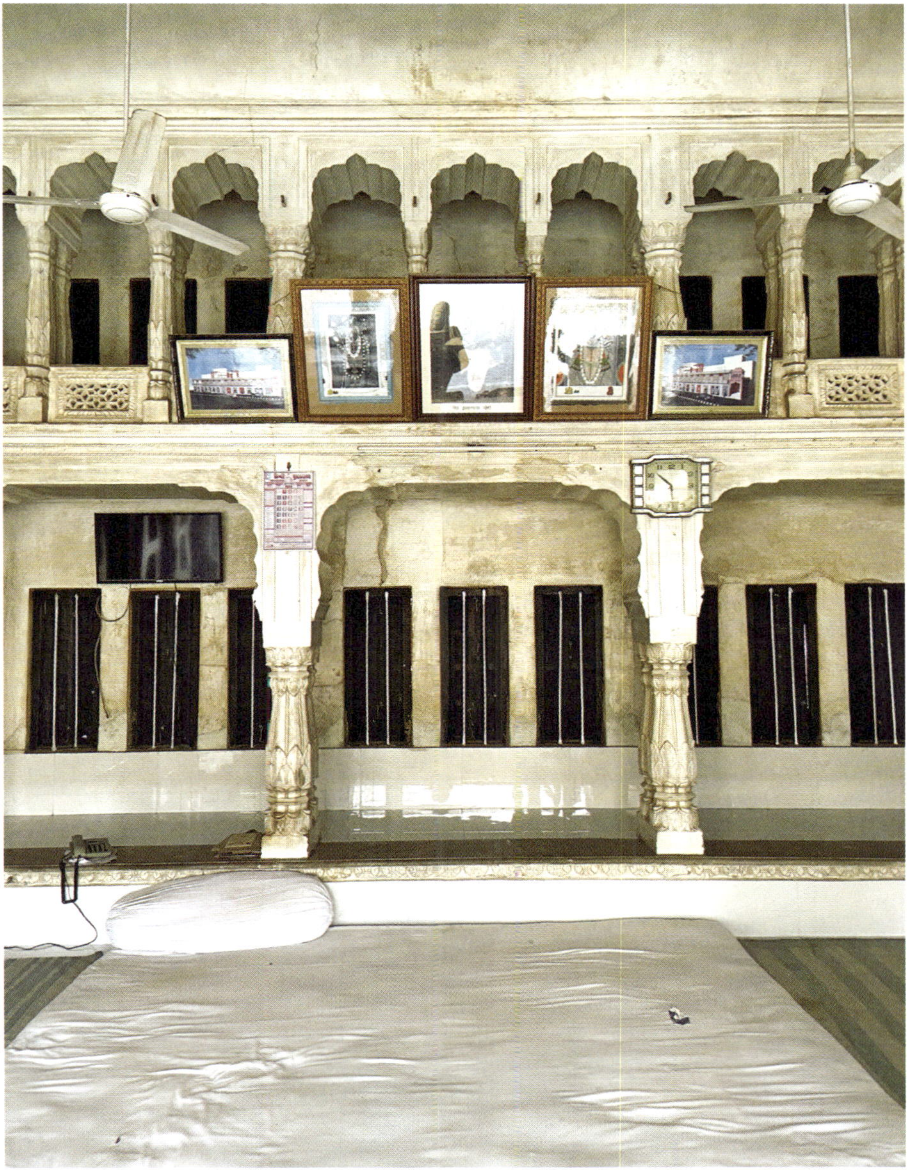

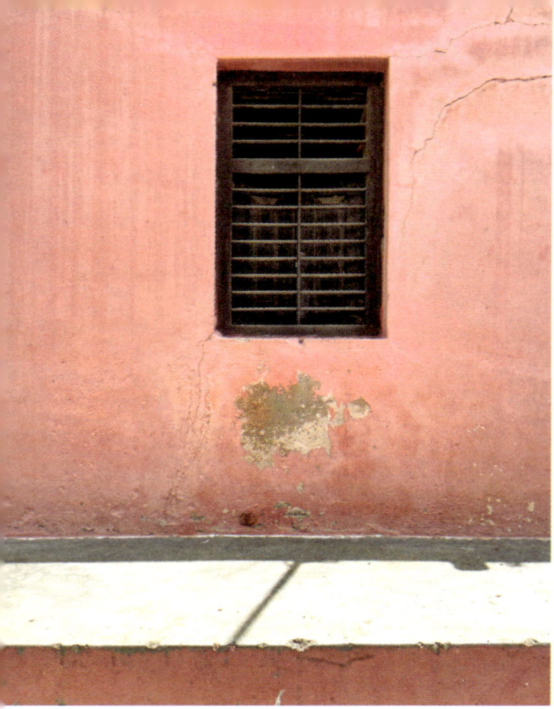
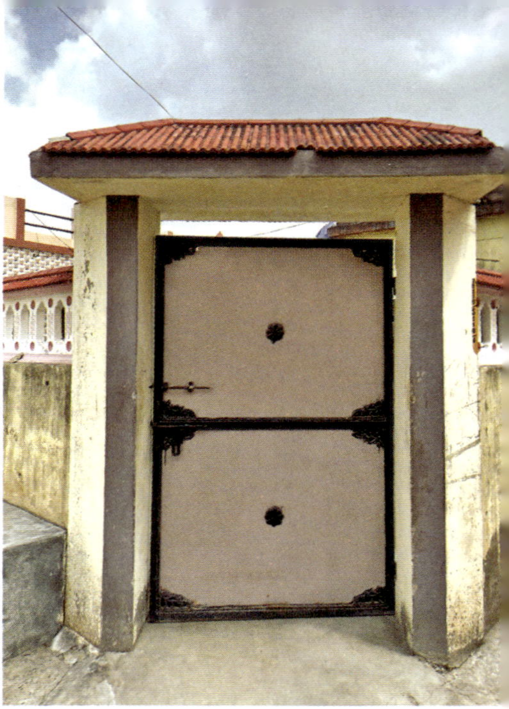
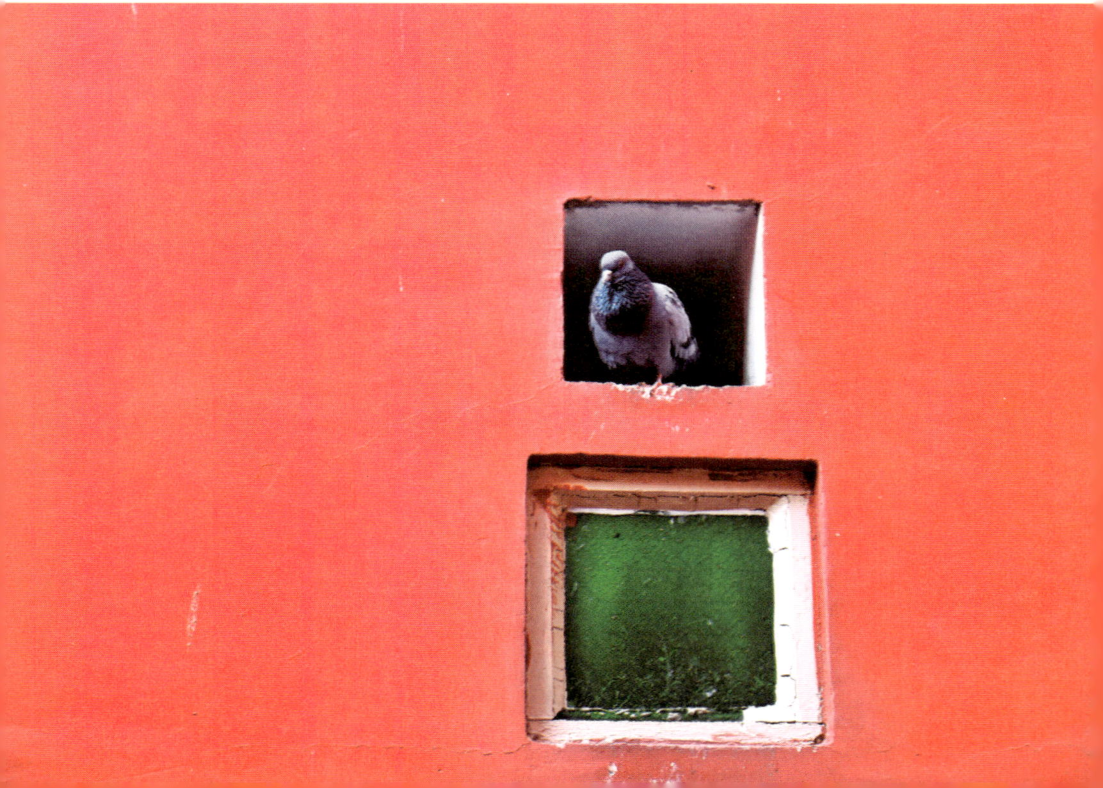

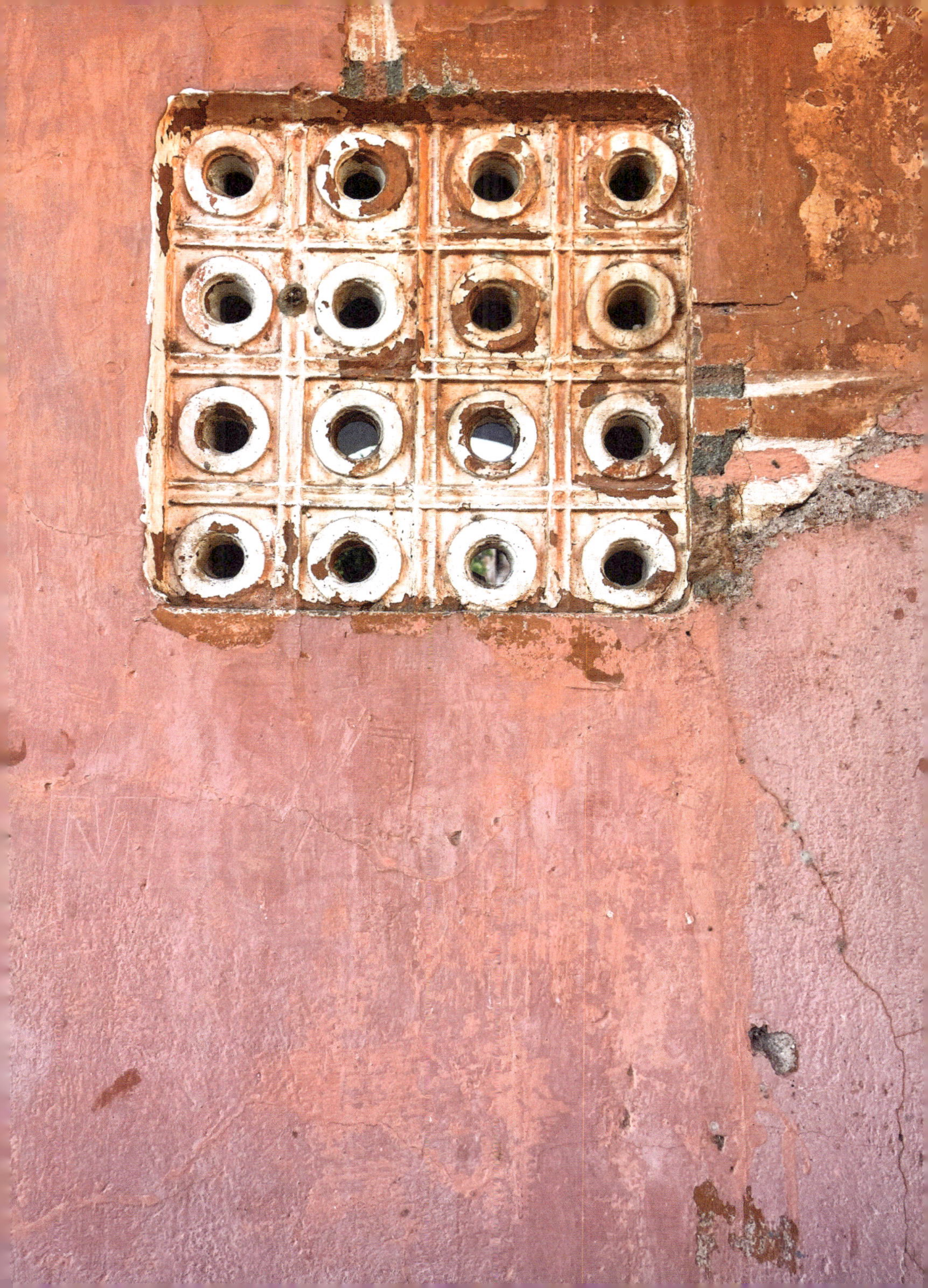

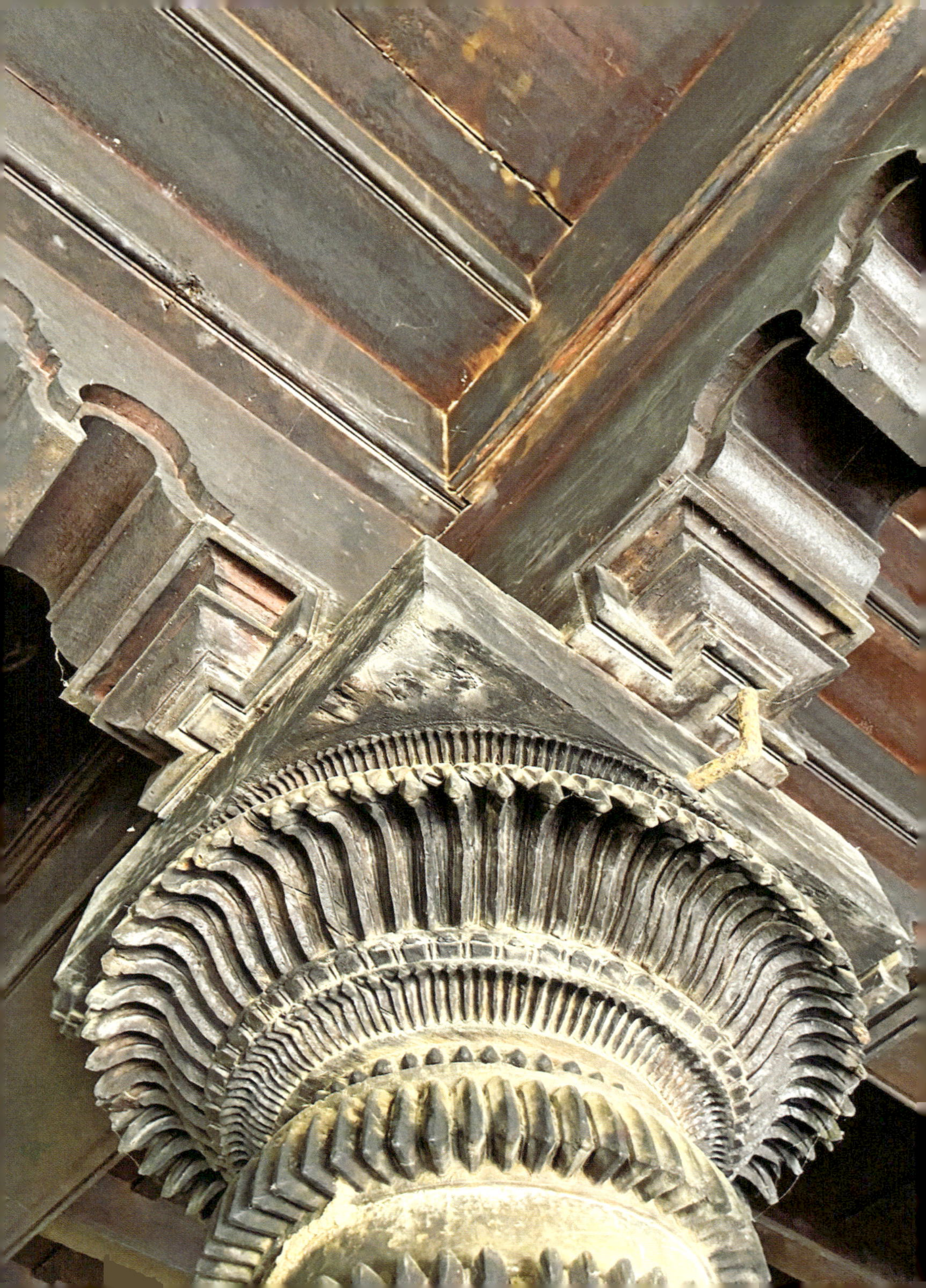

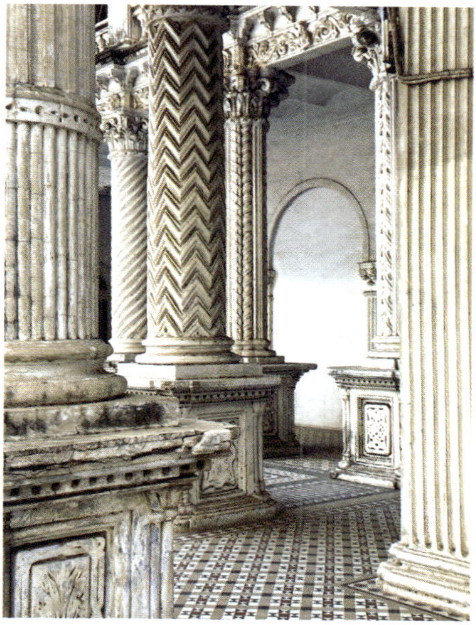

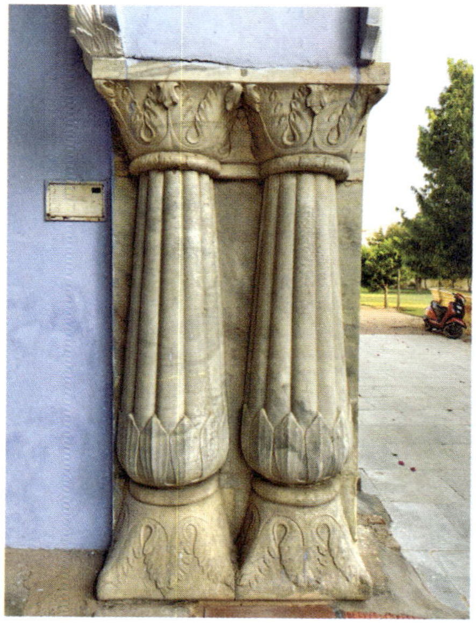

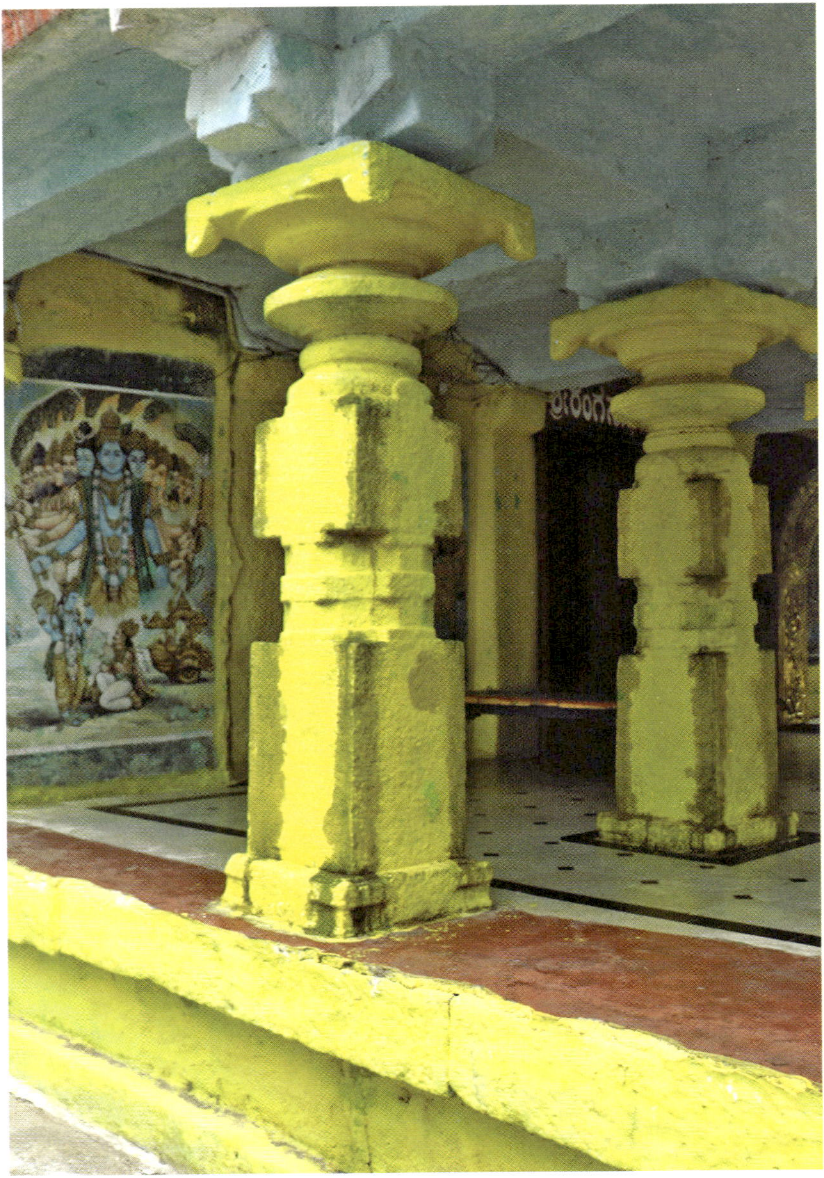

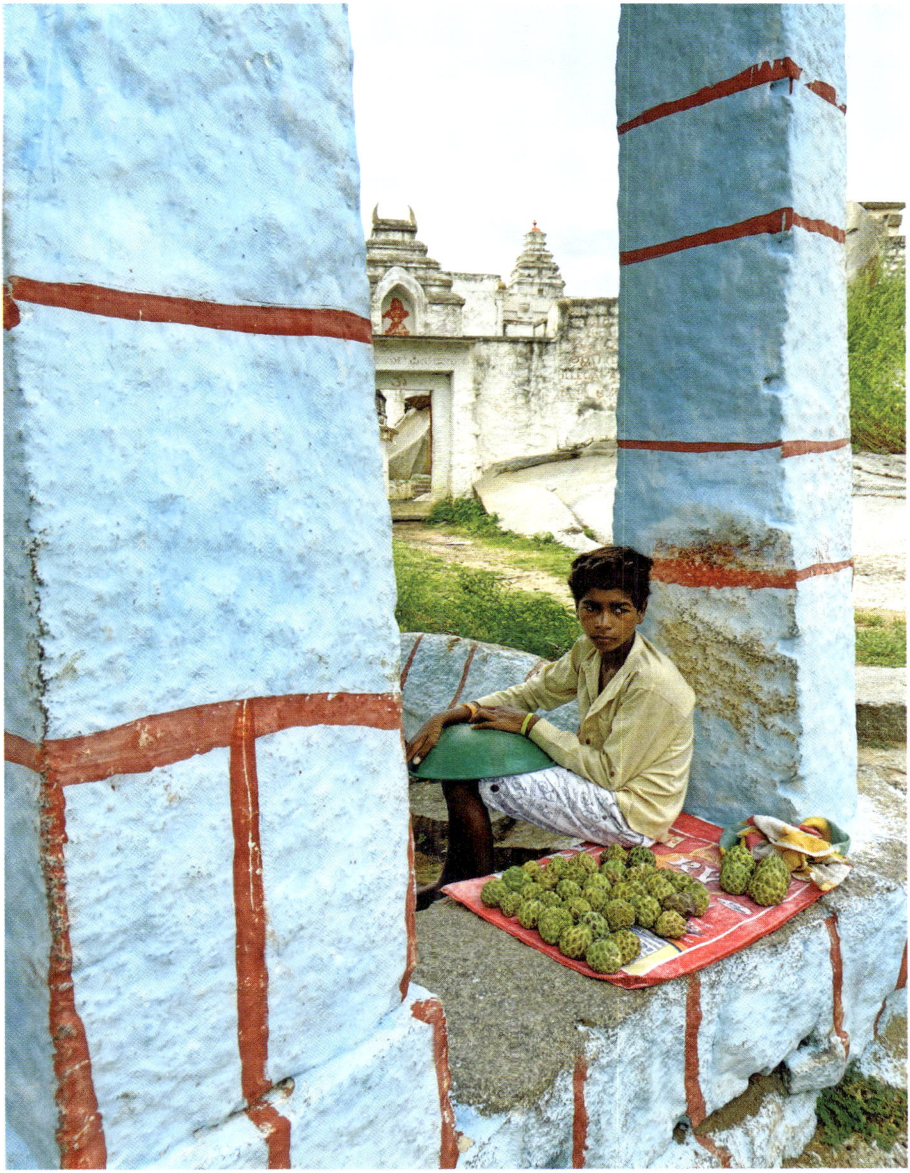

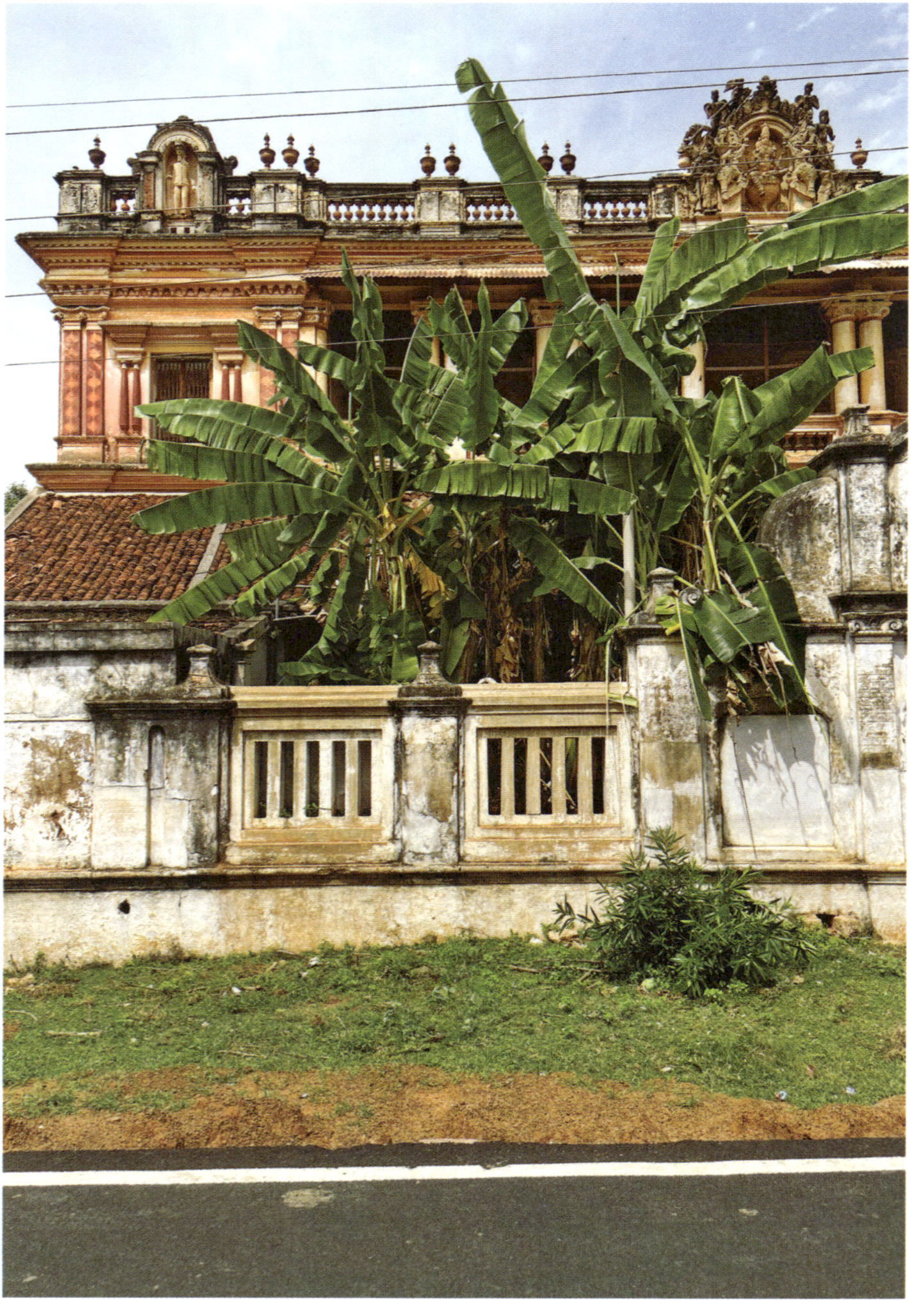

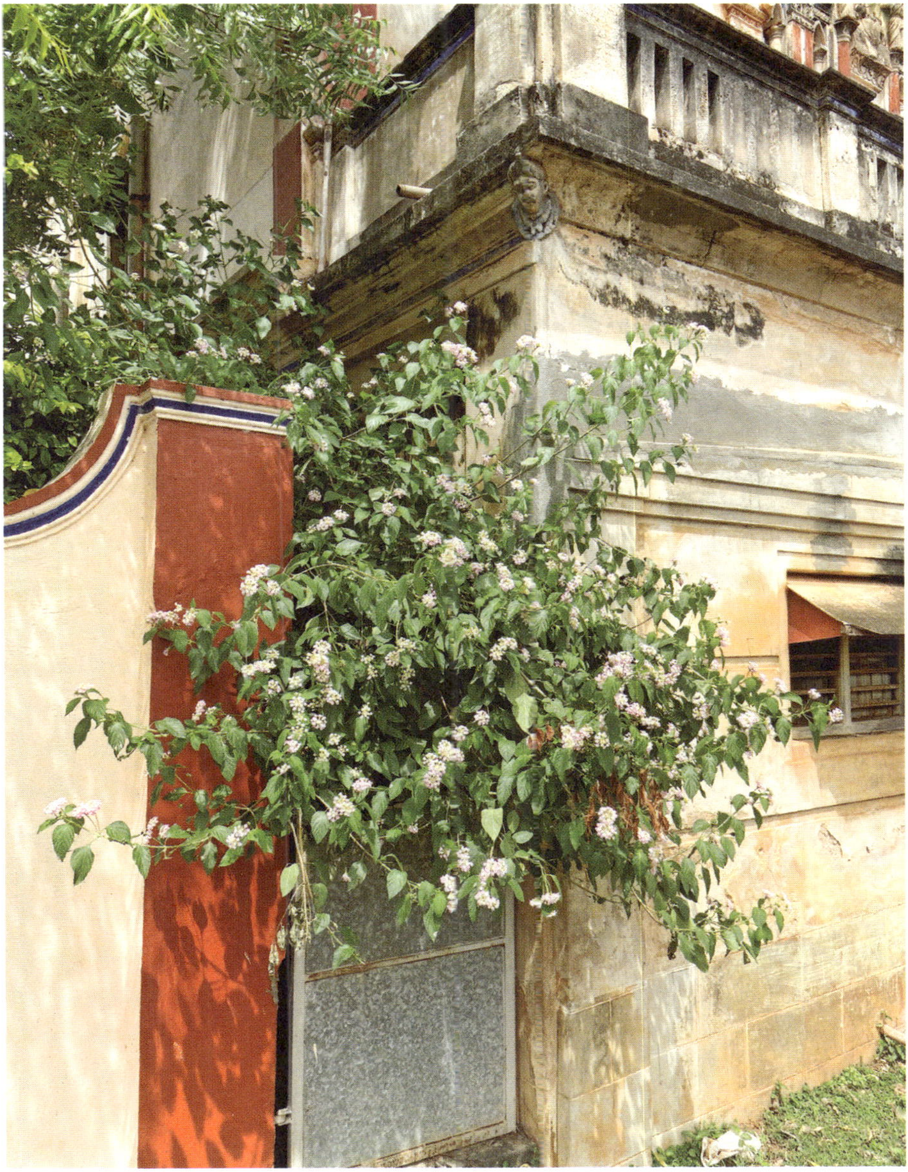

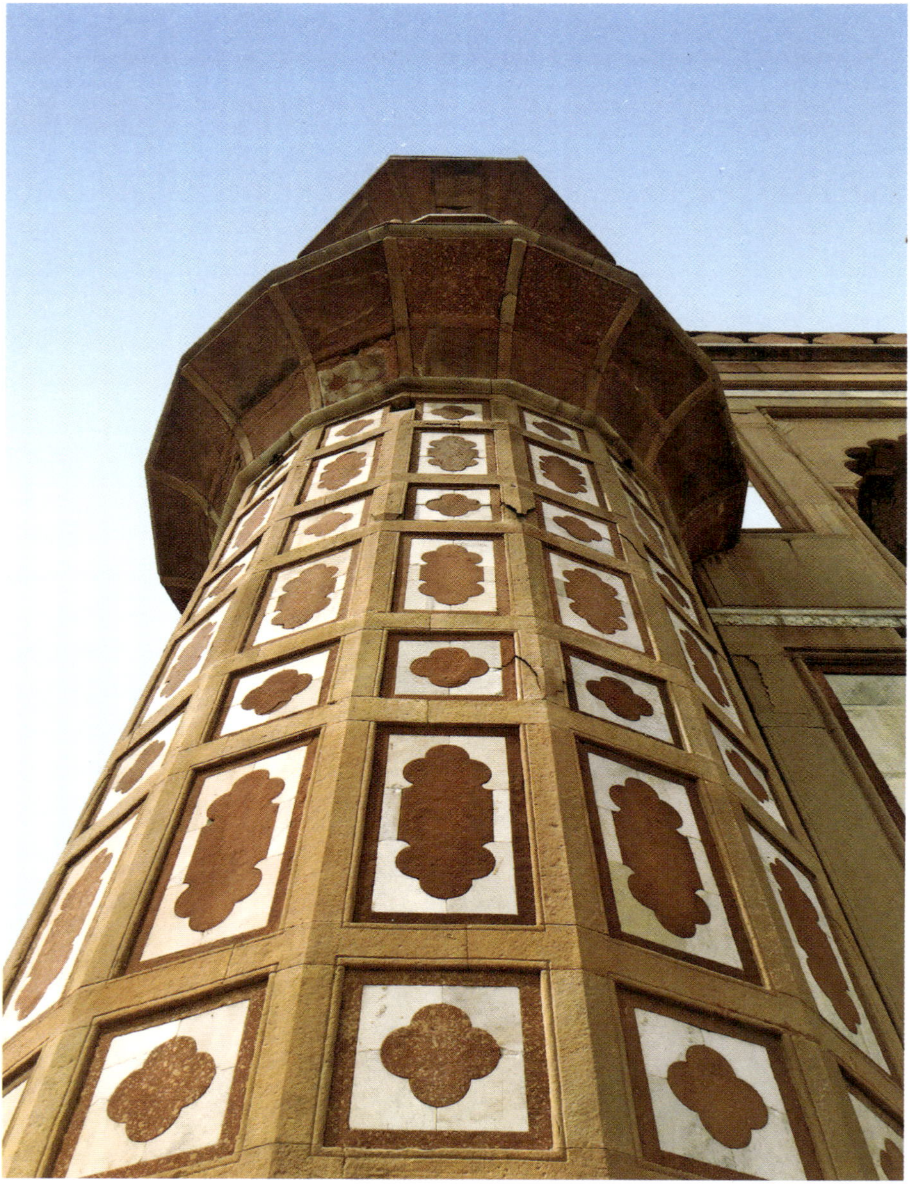

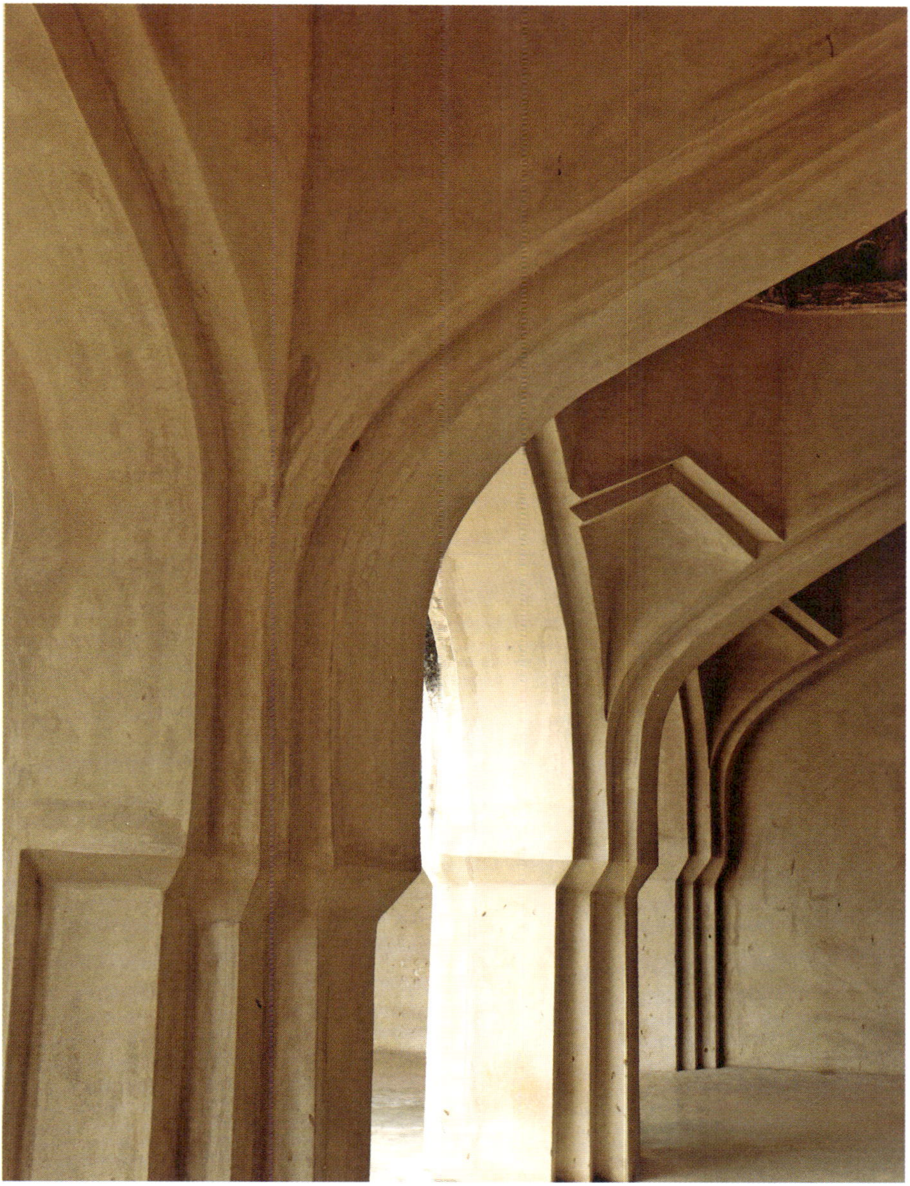

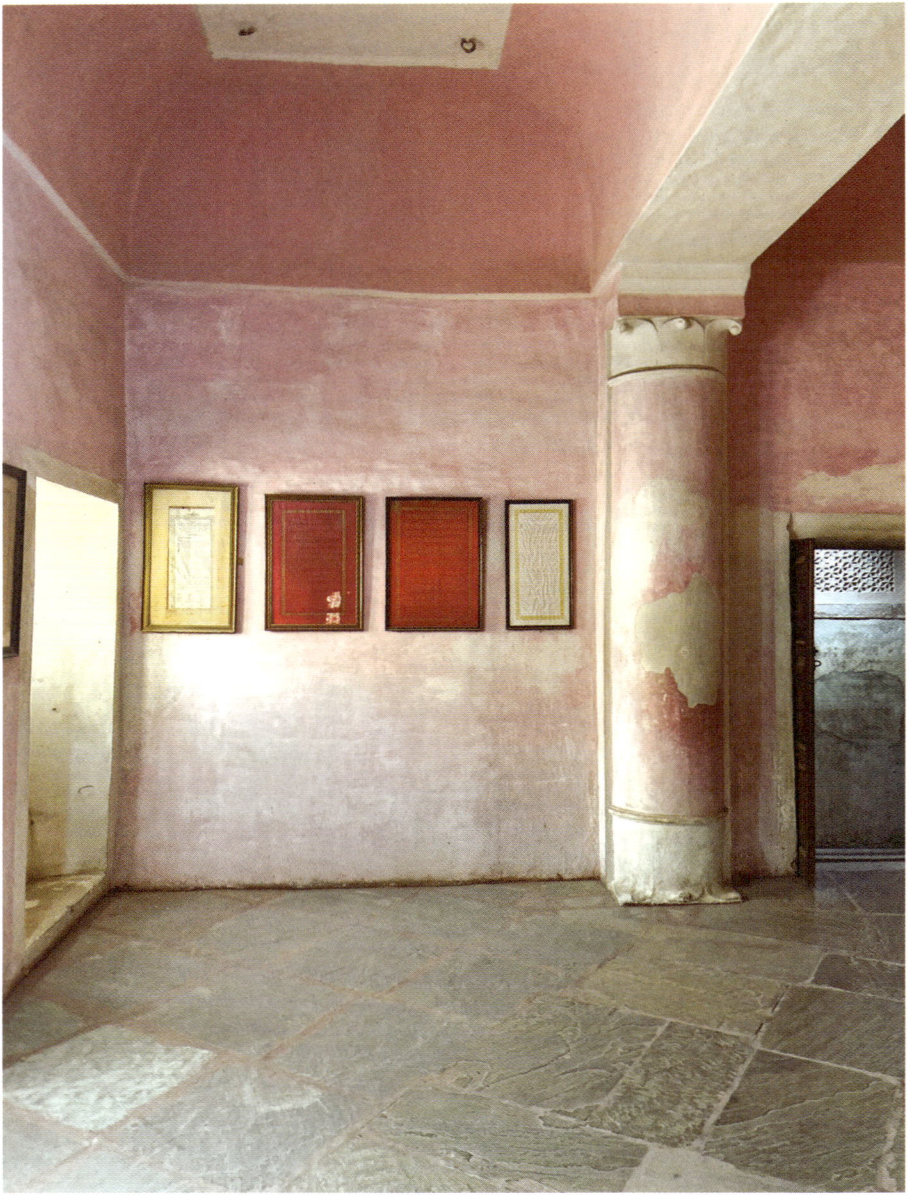

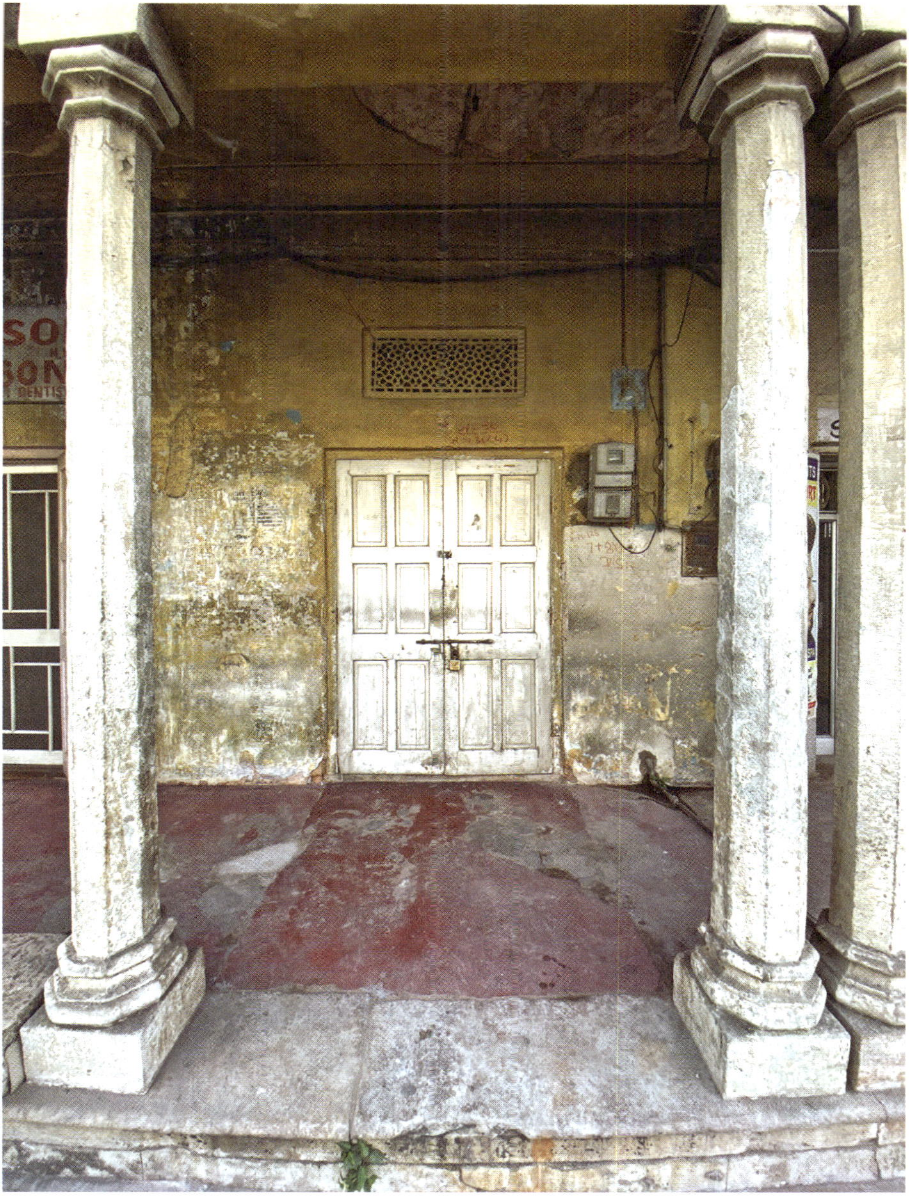

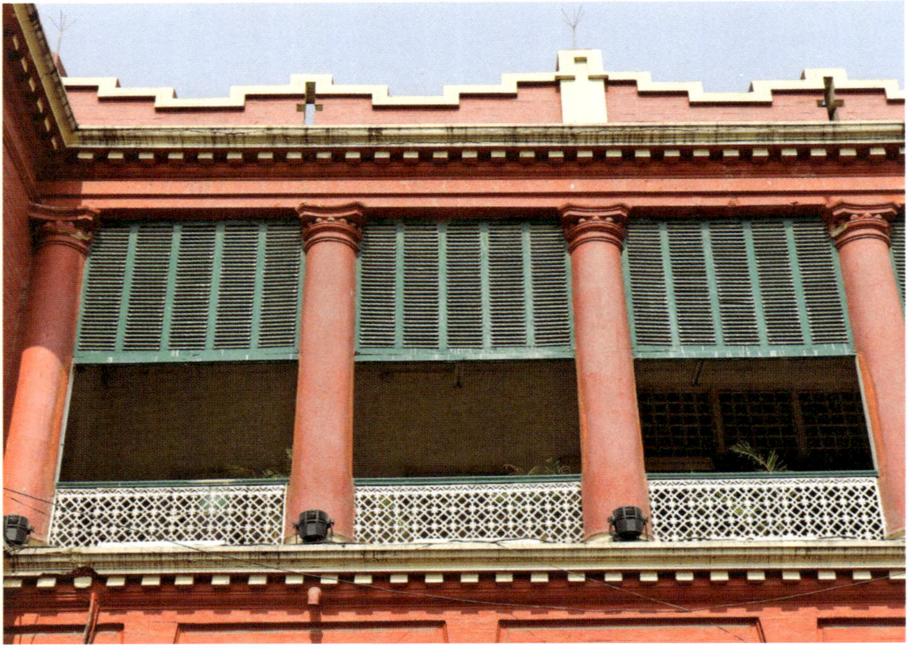

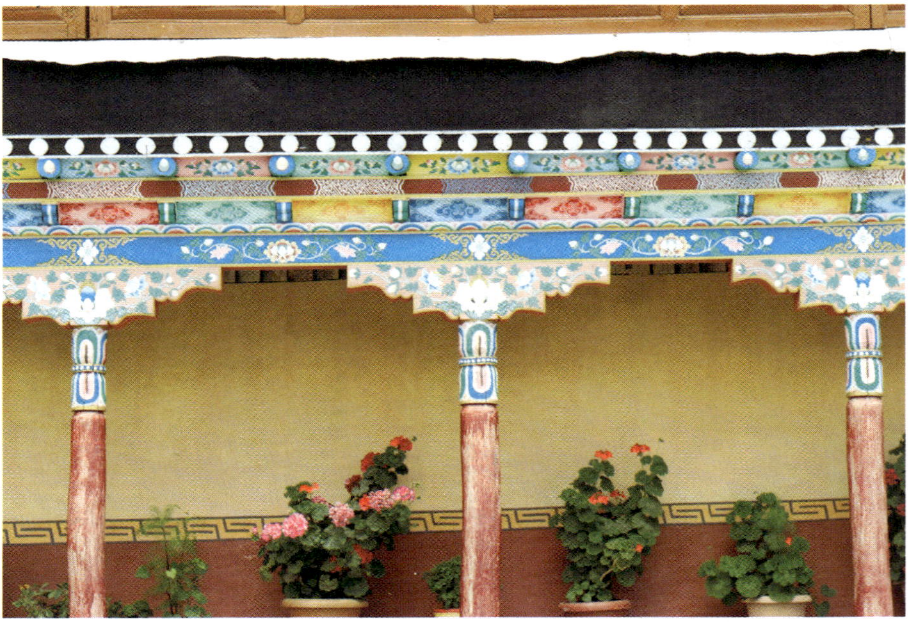

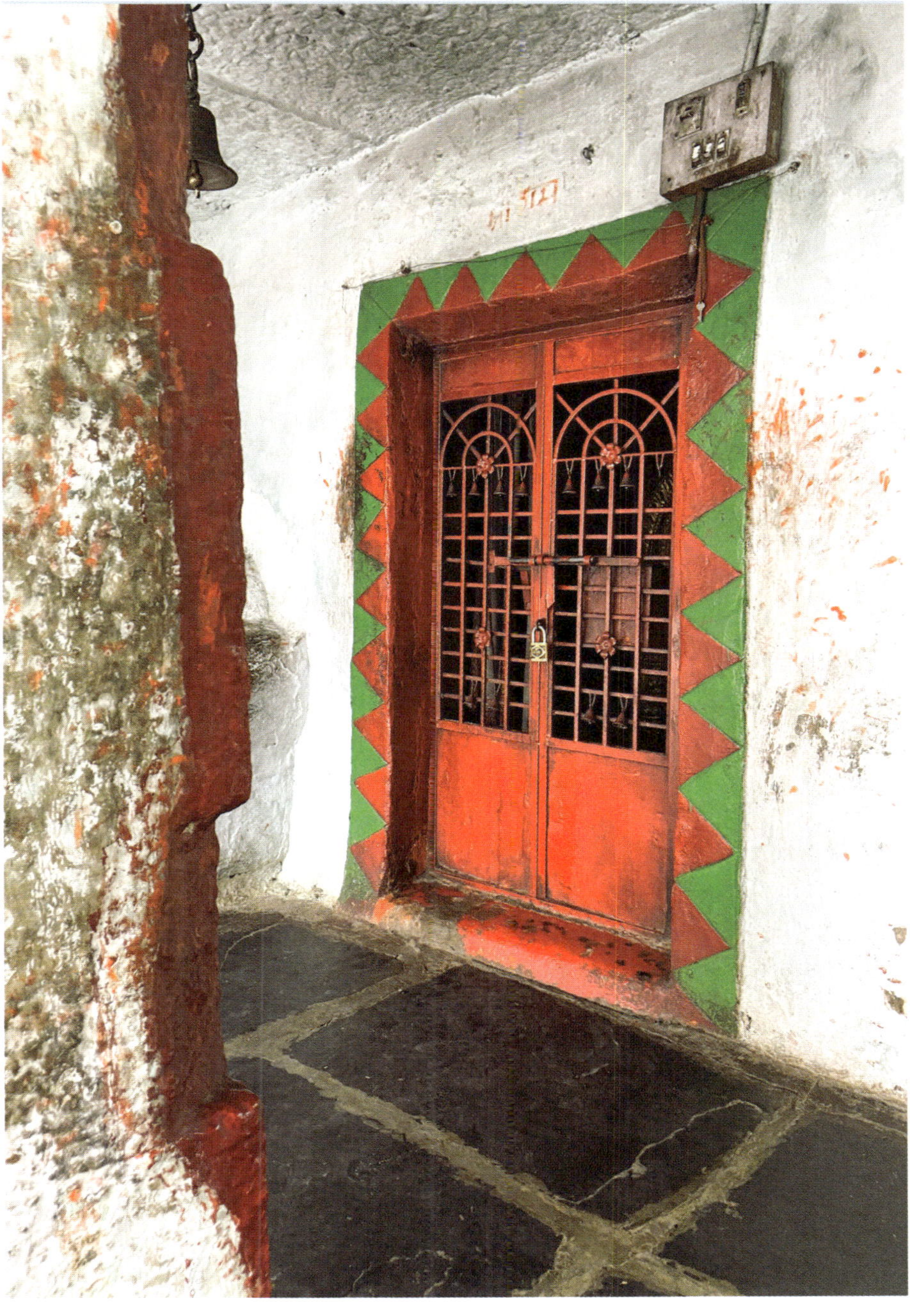

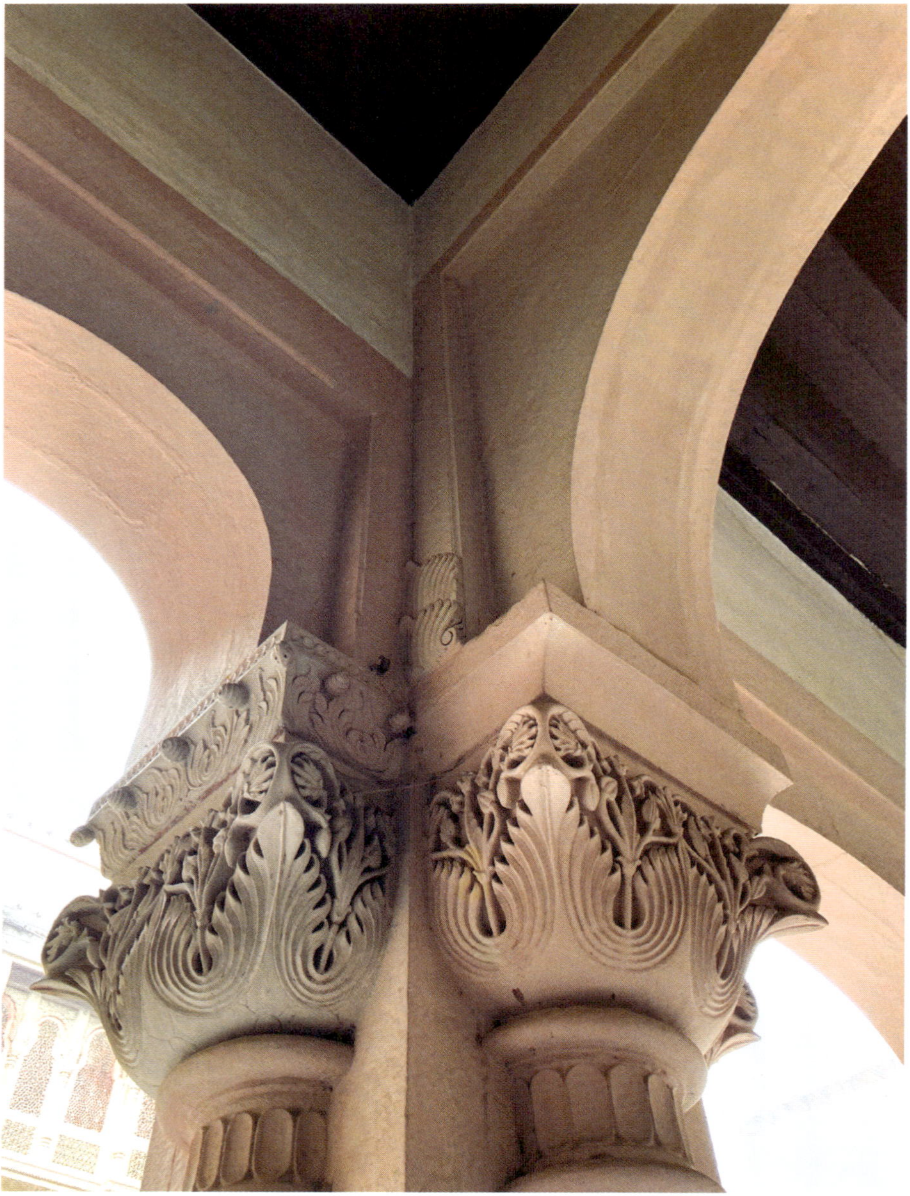

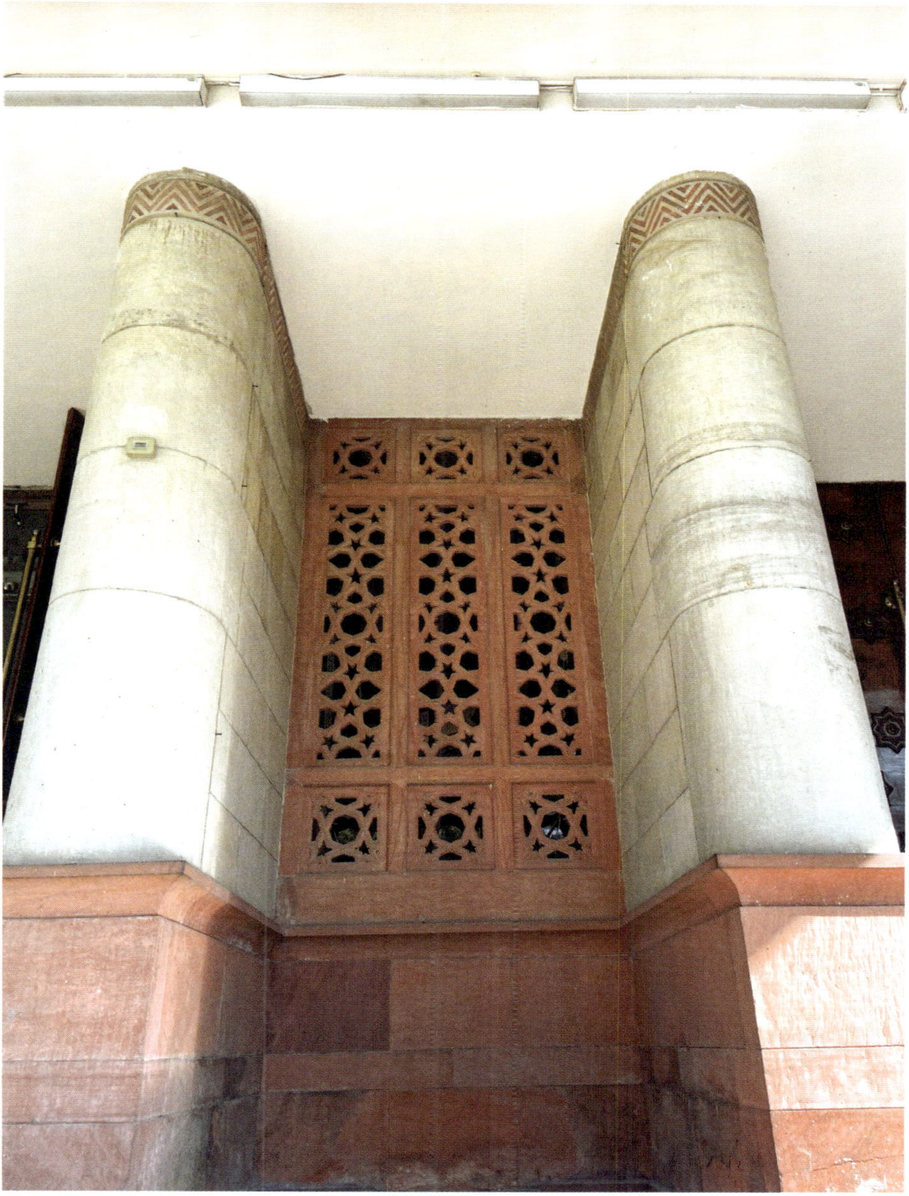

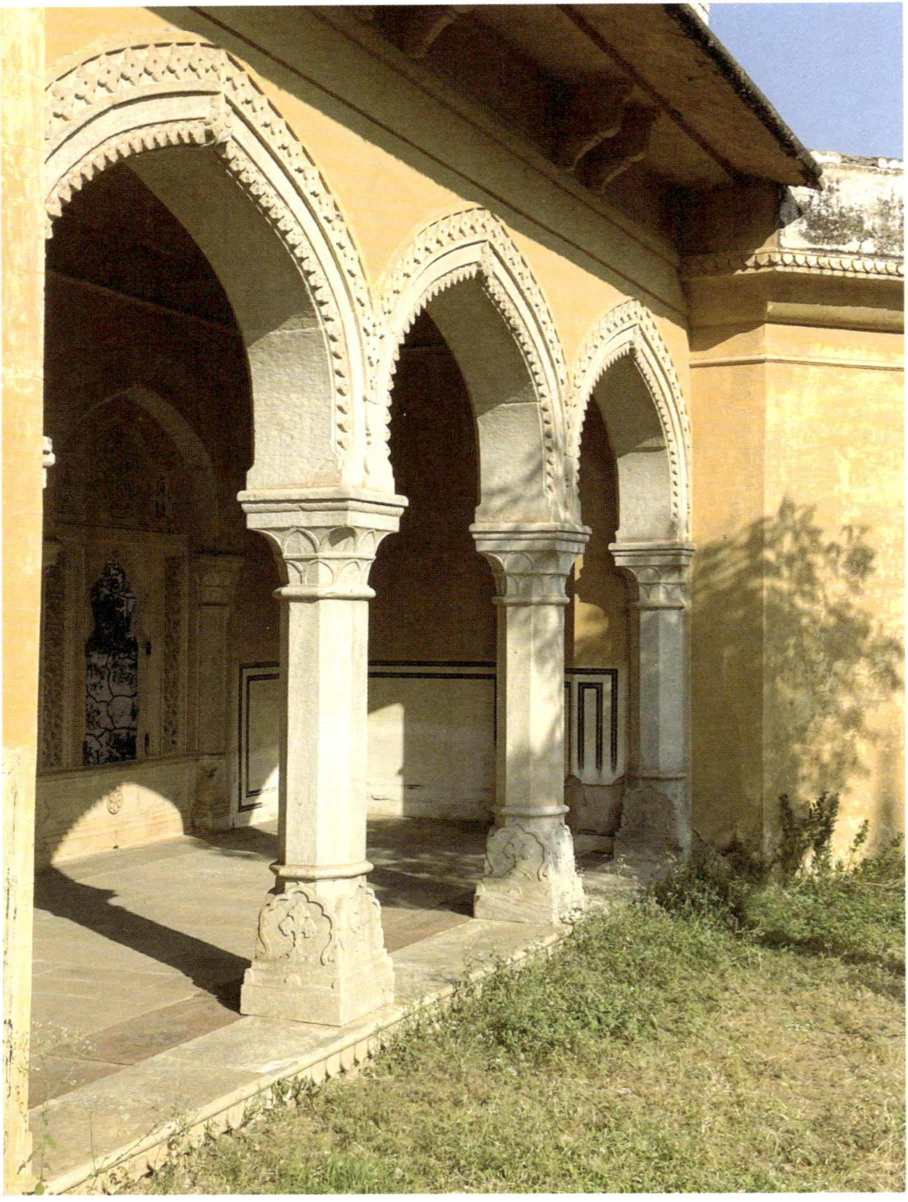

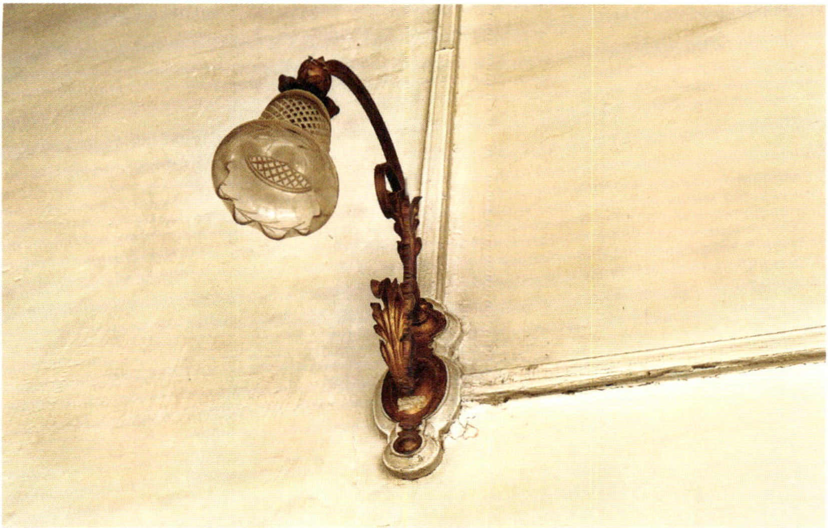

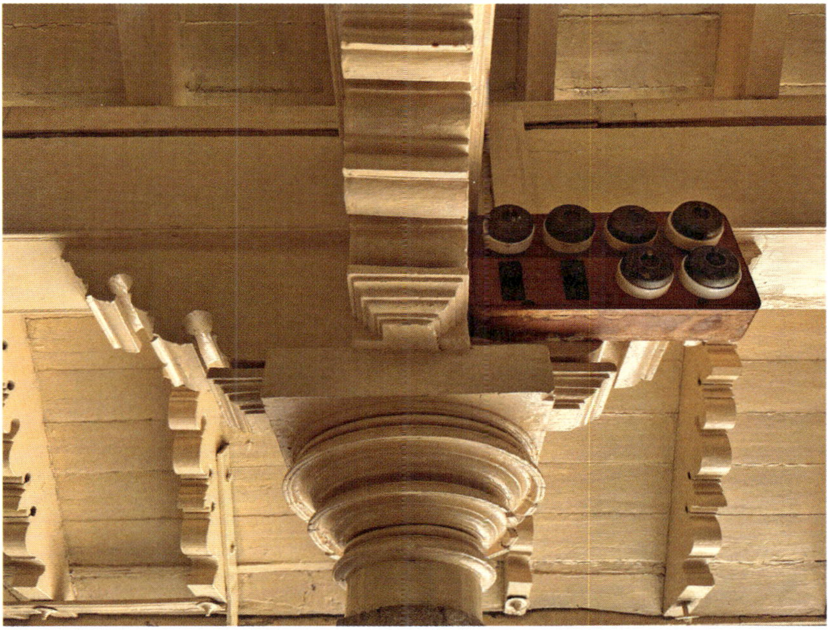

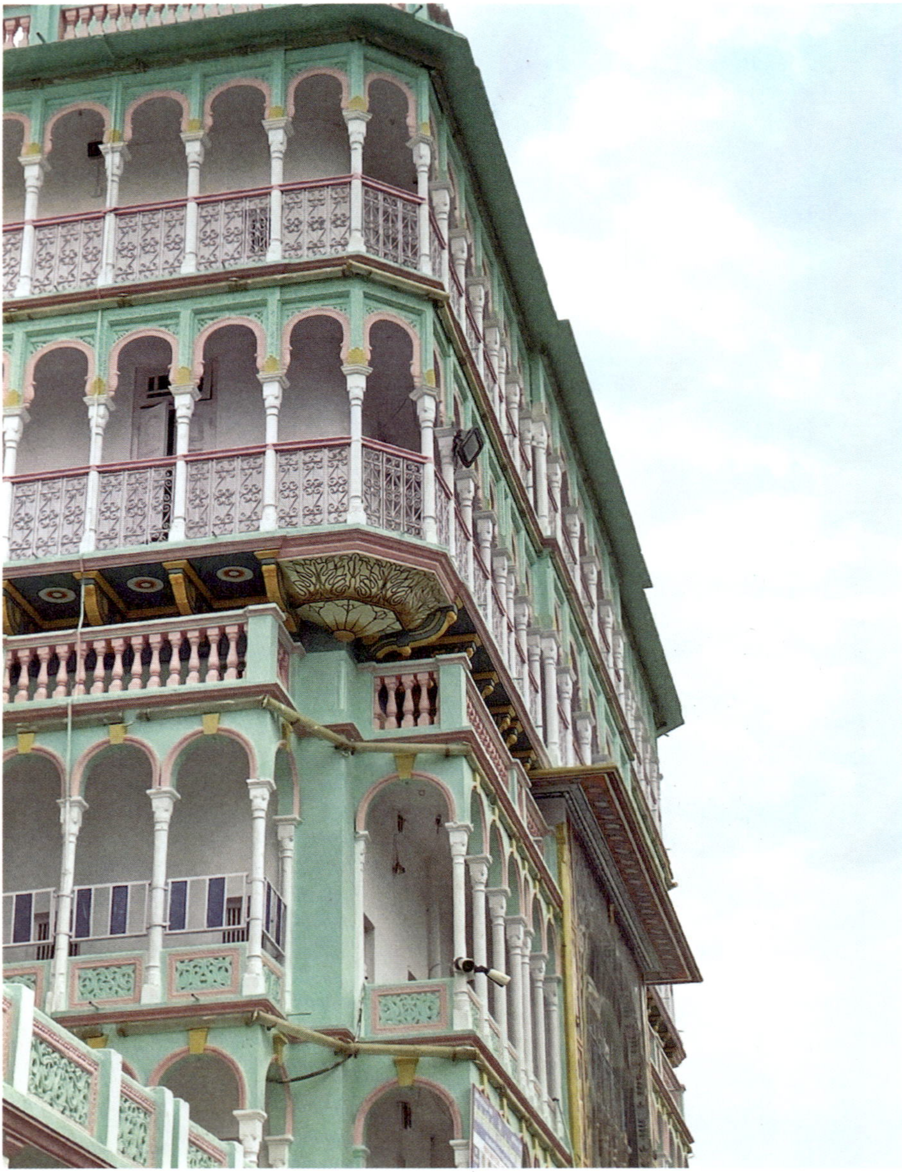

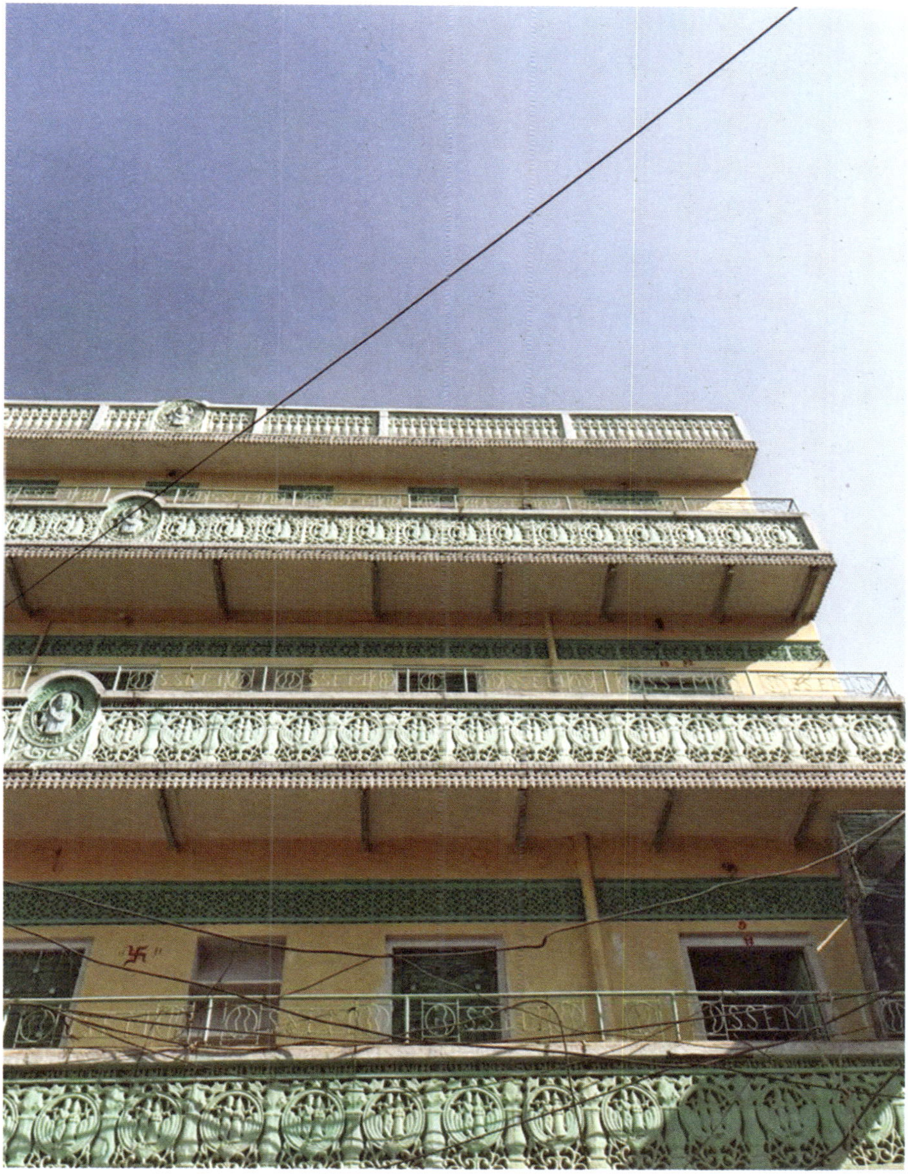
SSEM

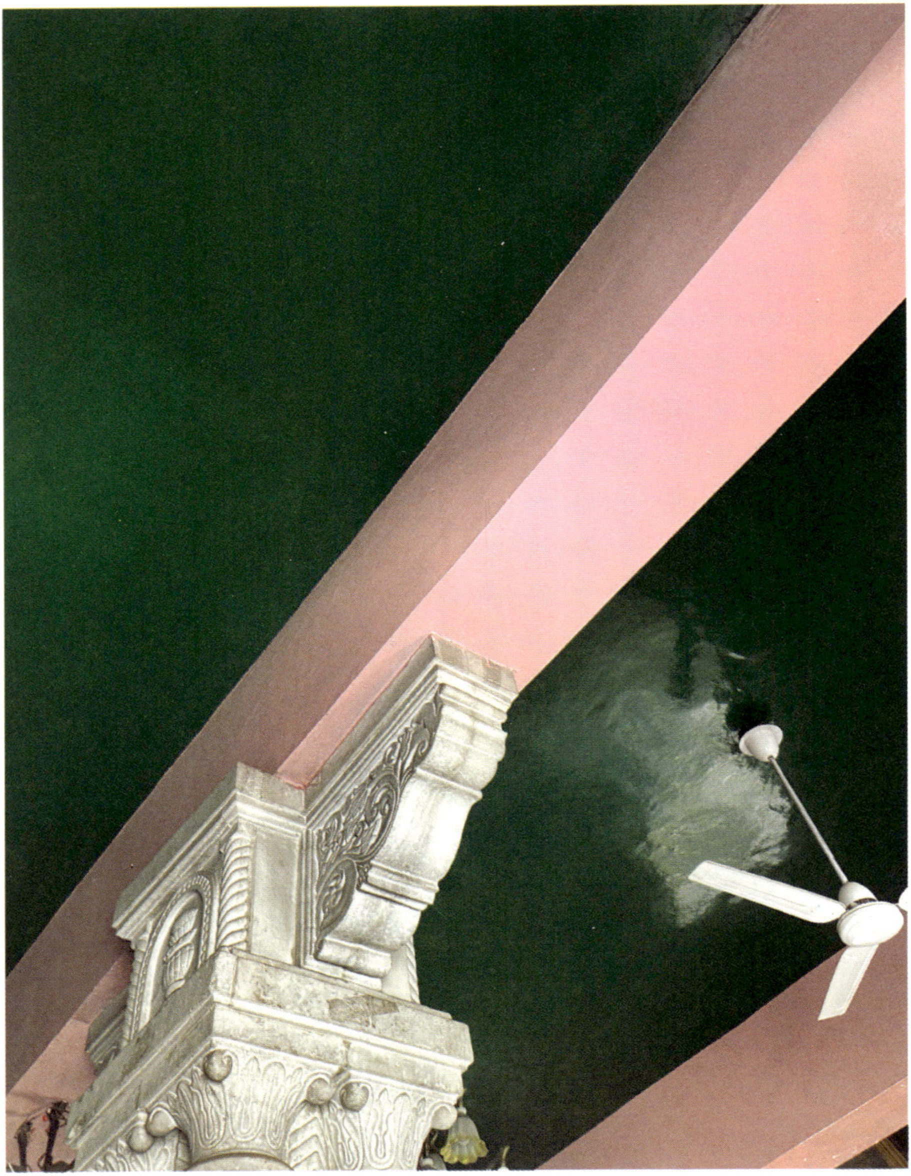

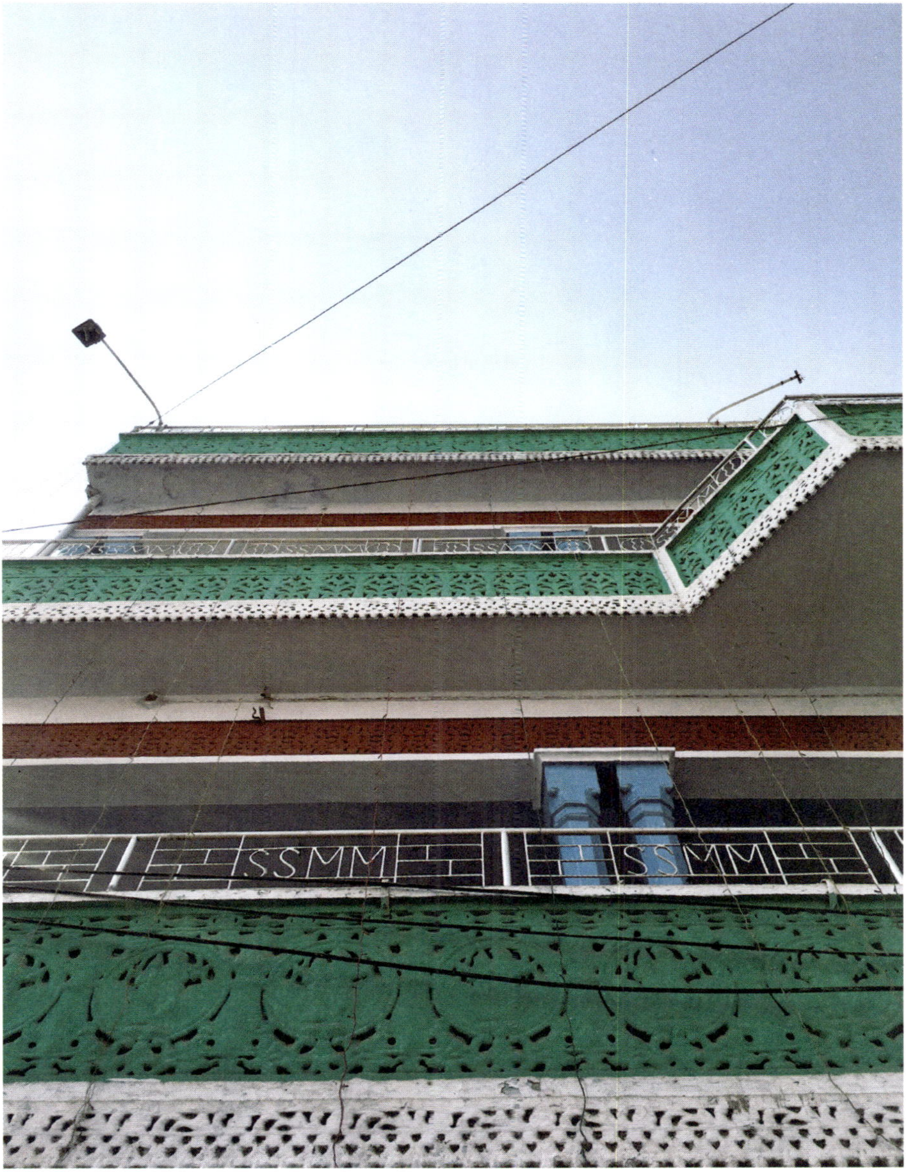
SSMM
SSMM

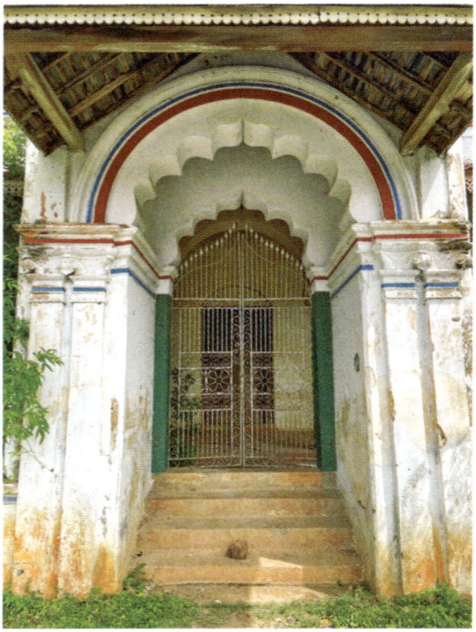
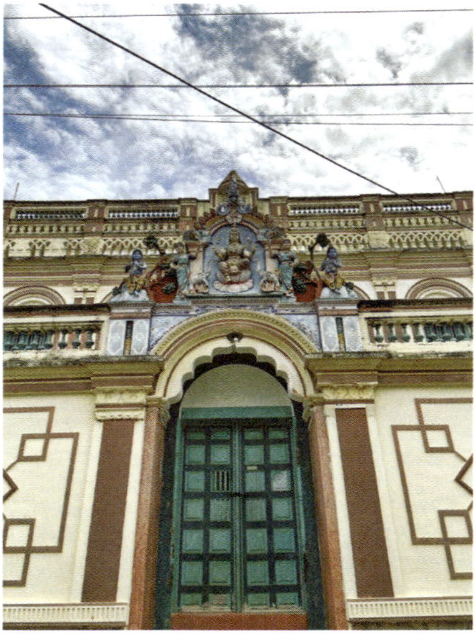
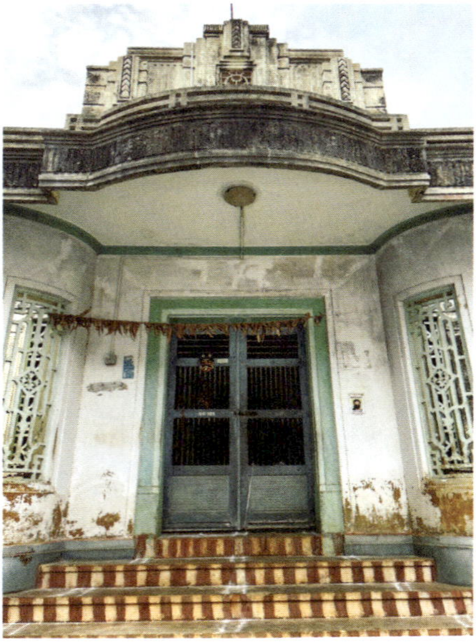
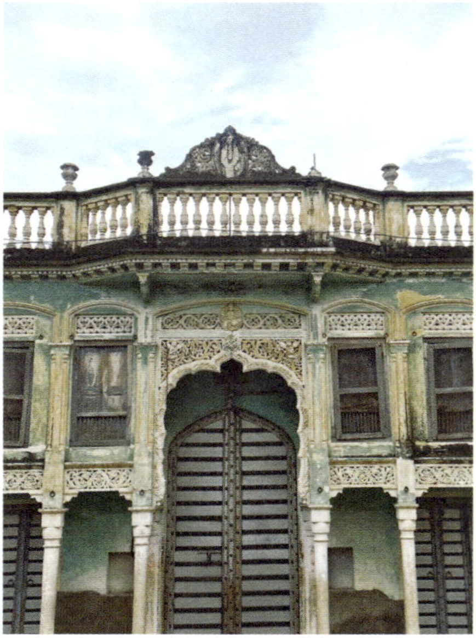

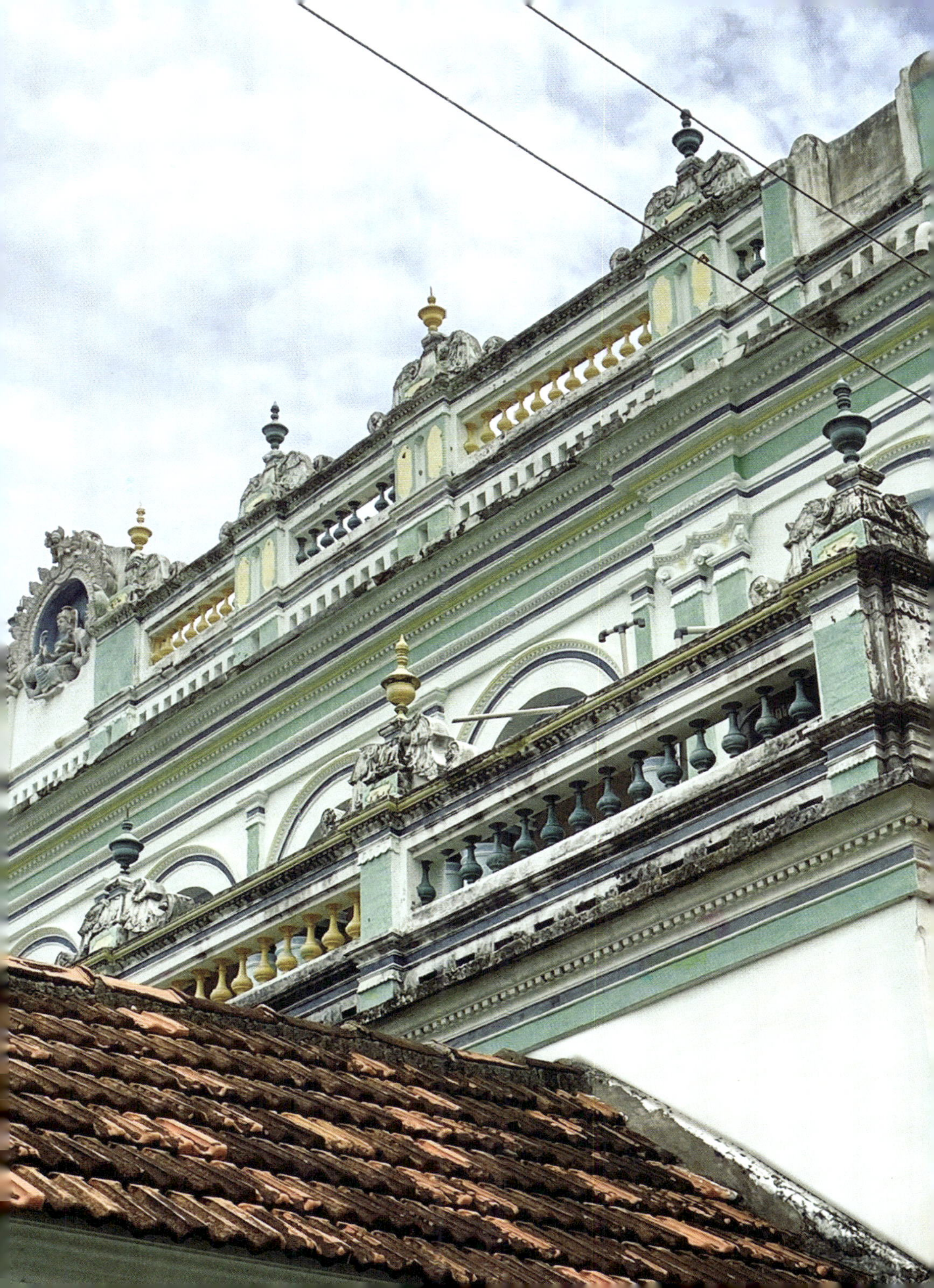

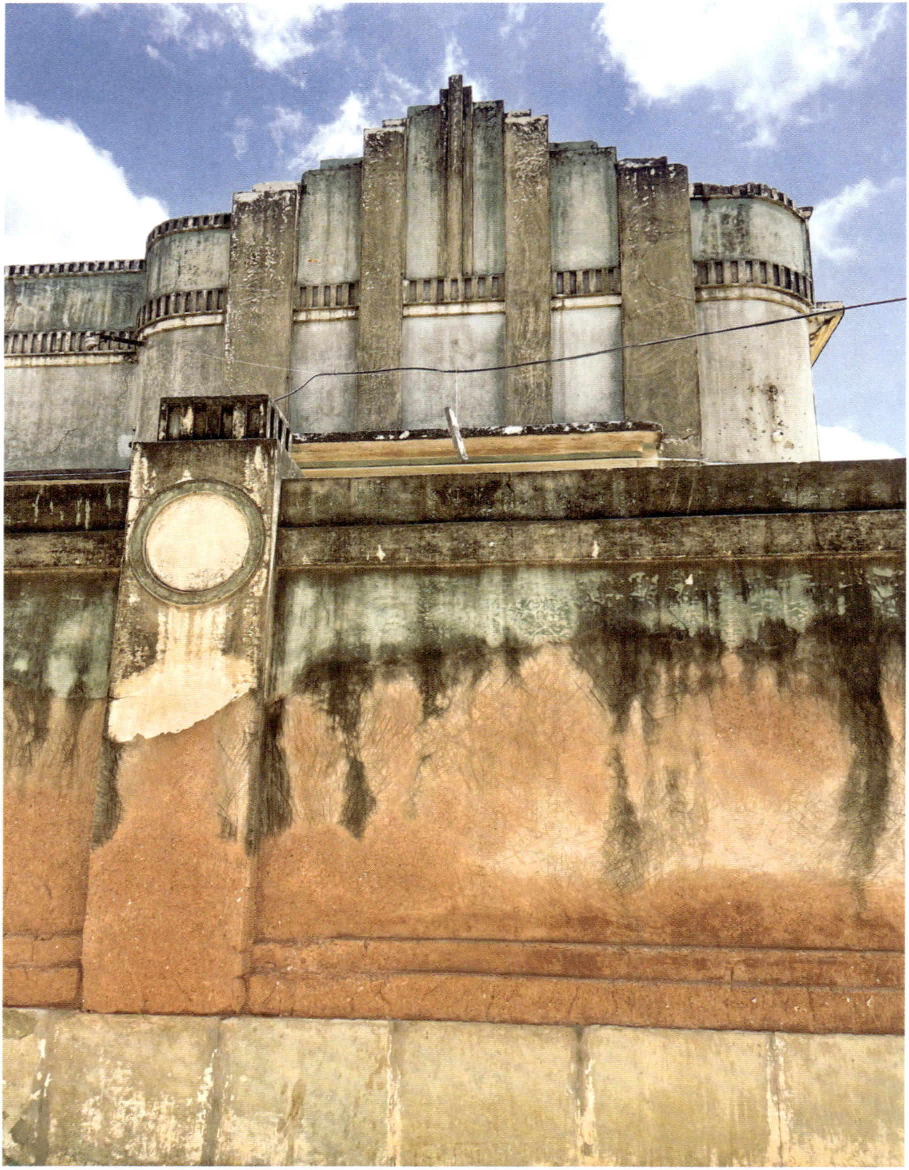

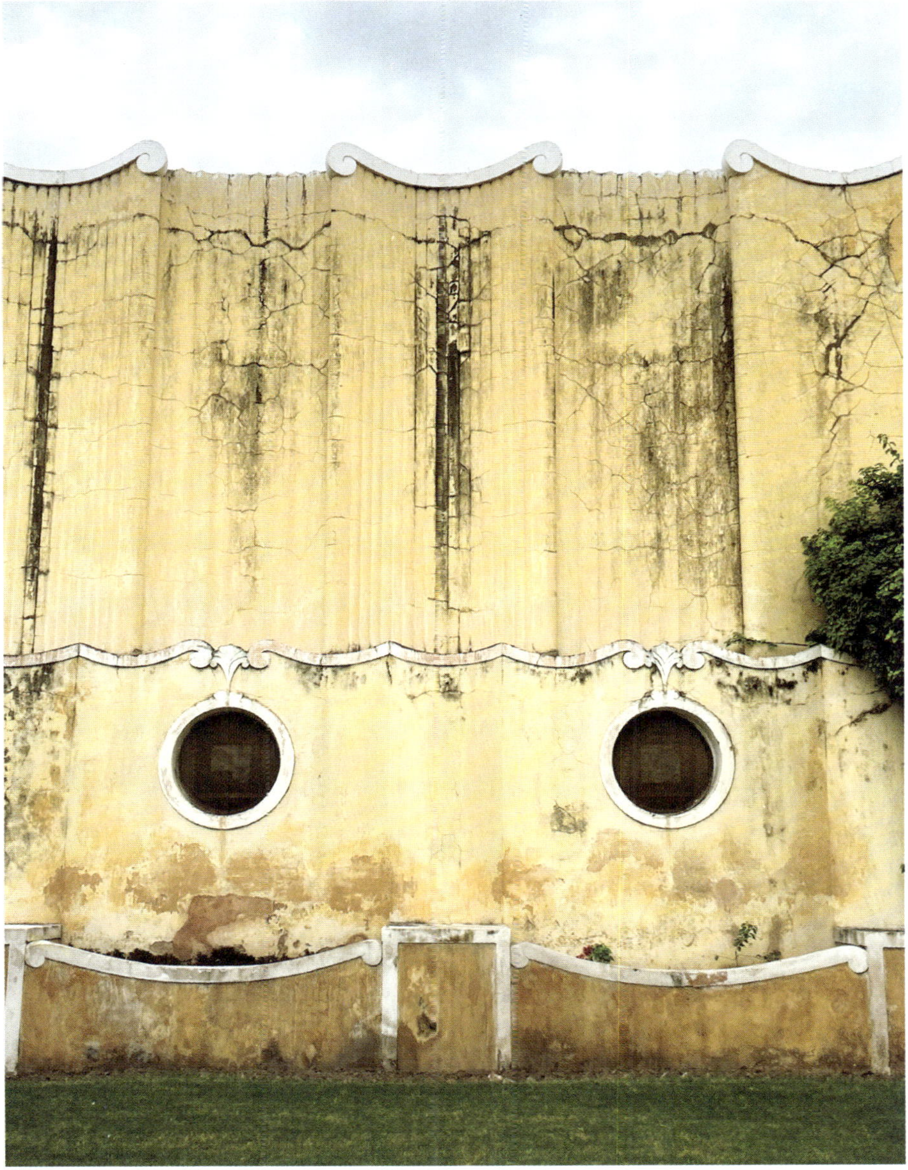

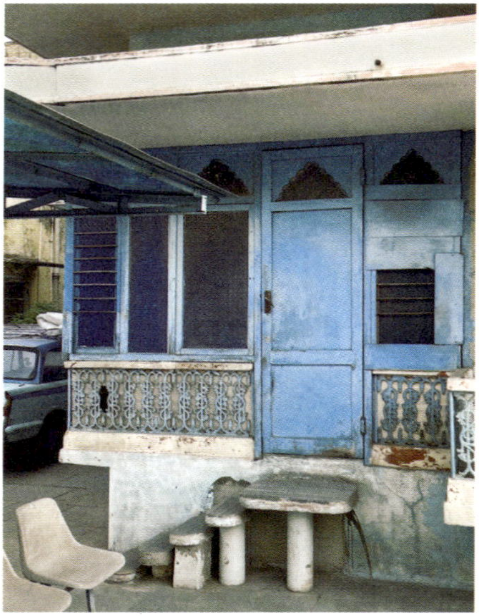
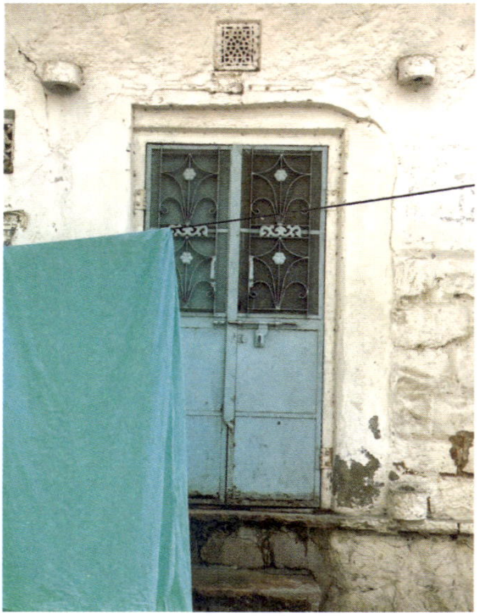
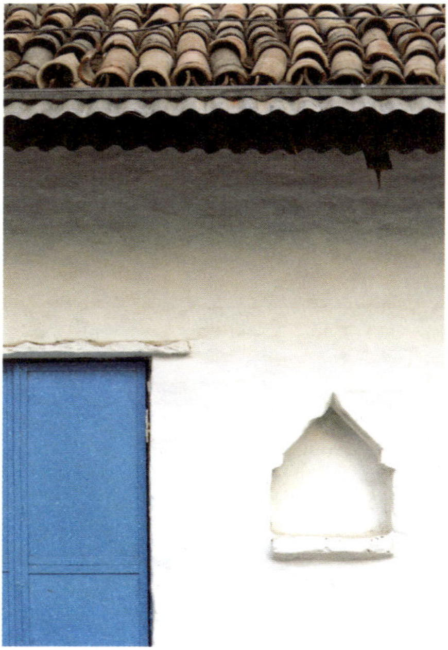
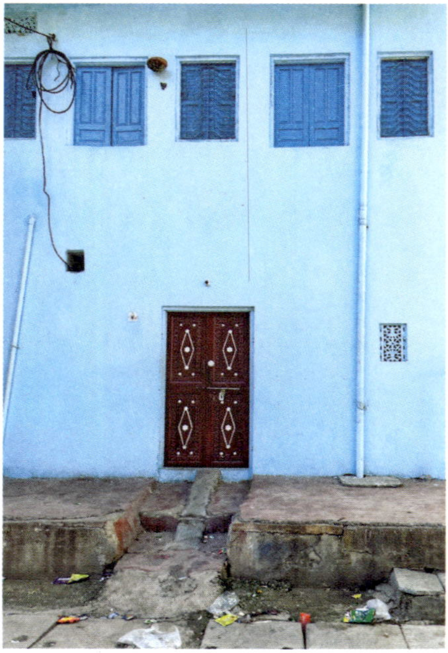

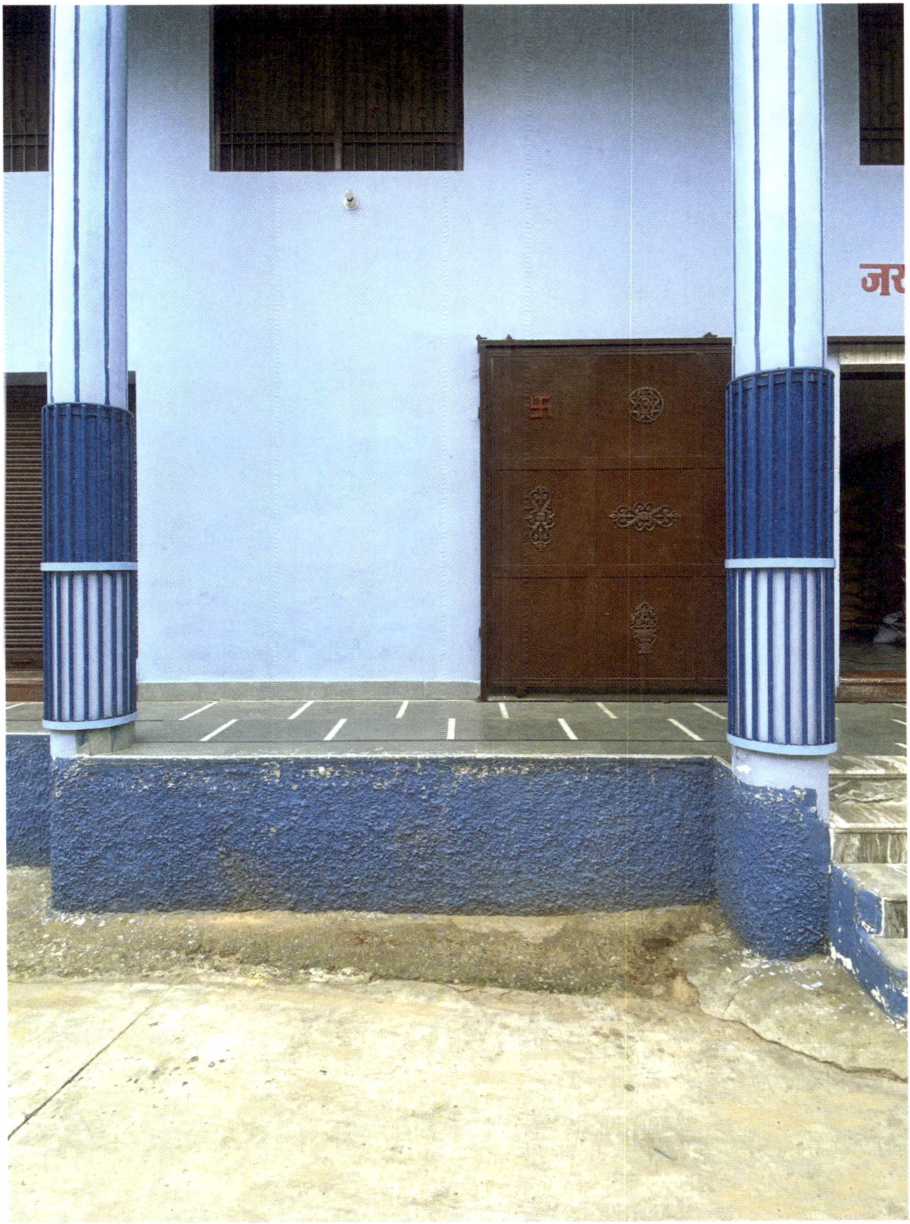

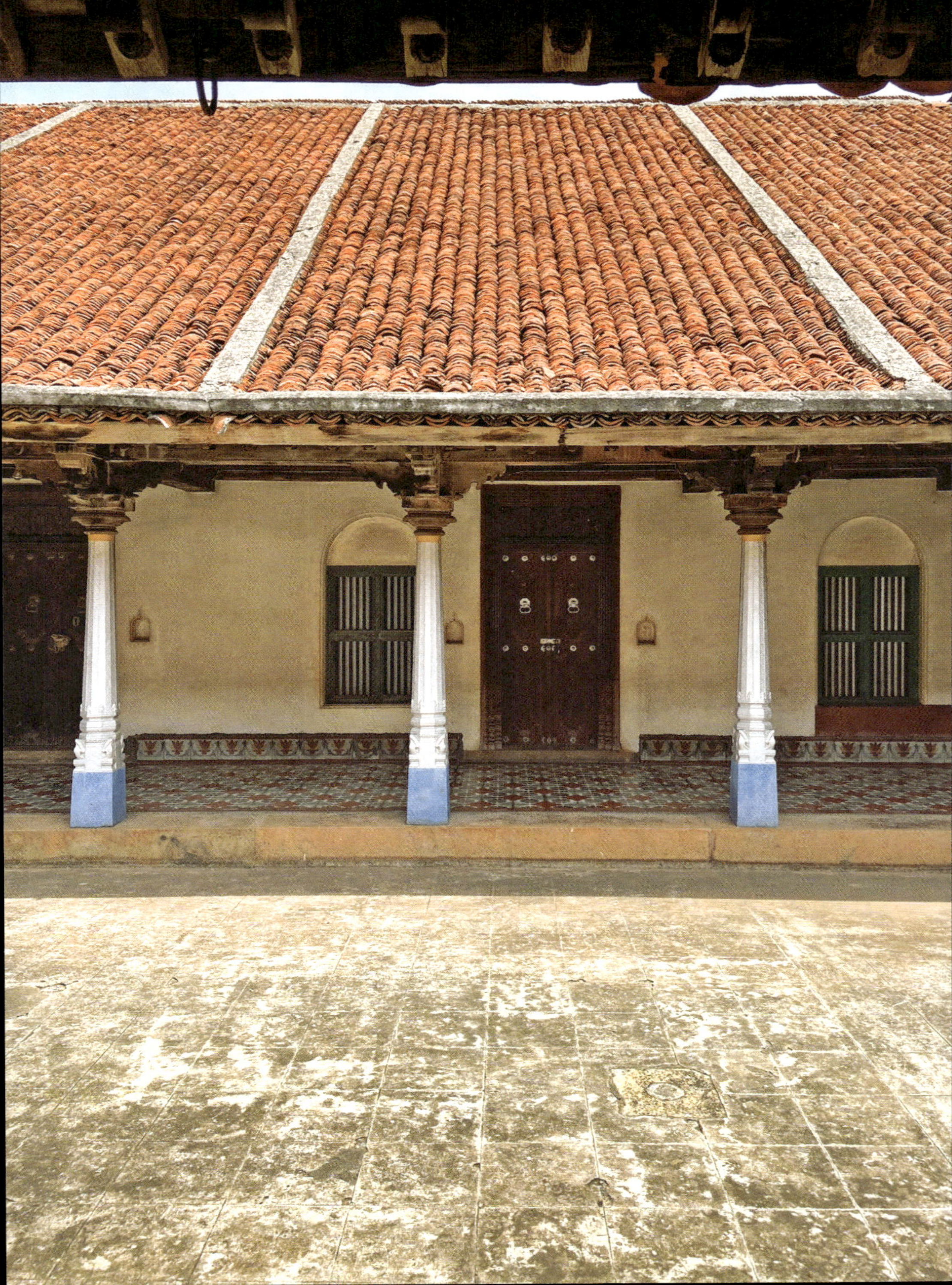

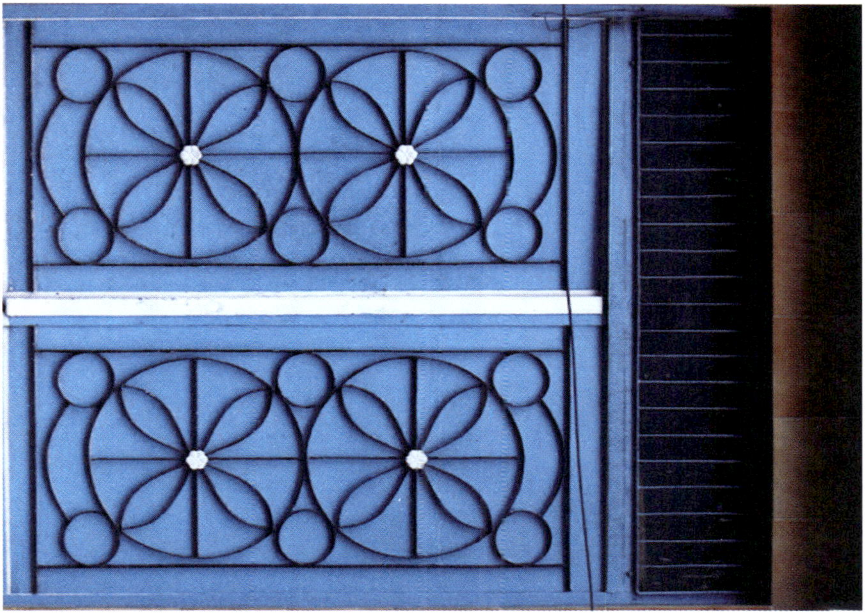

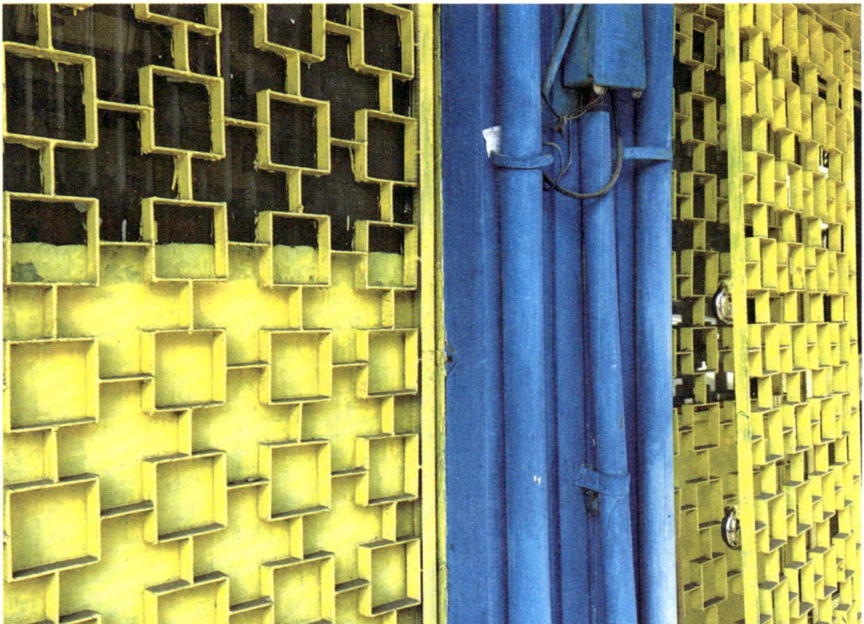

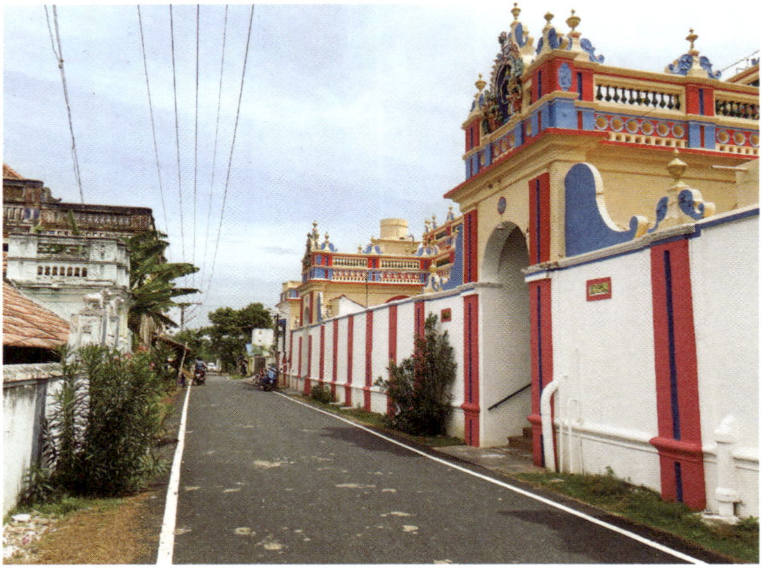

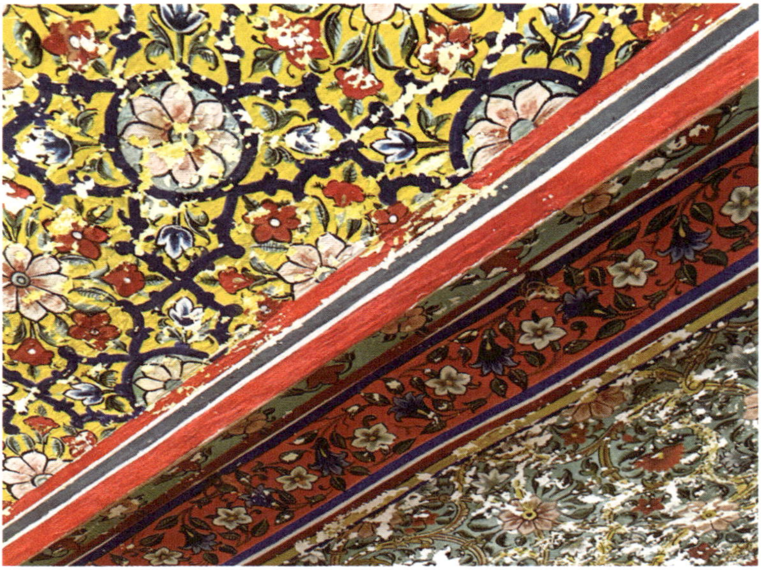

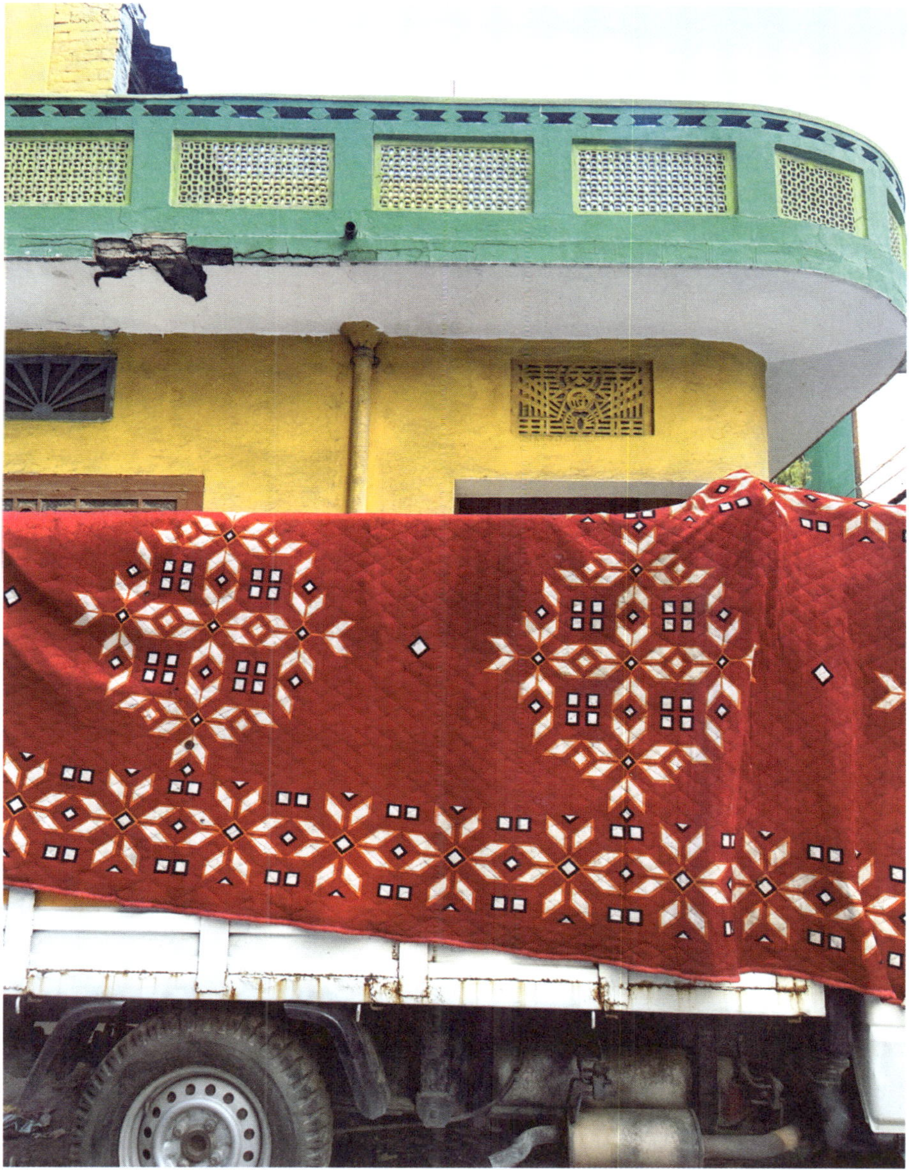

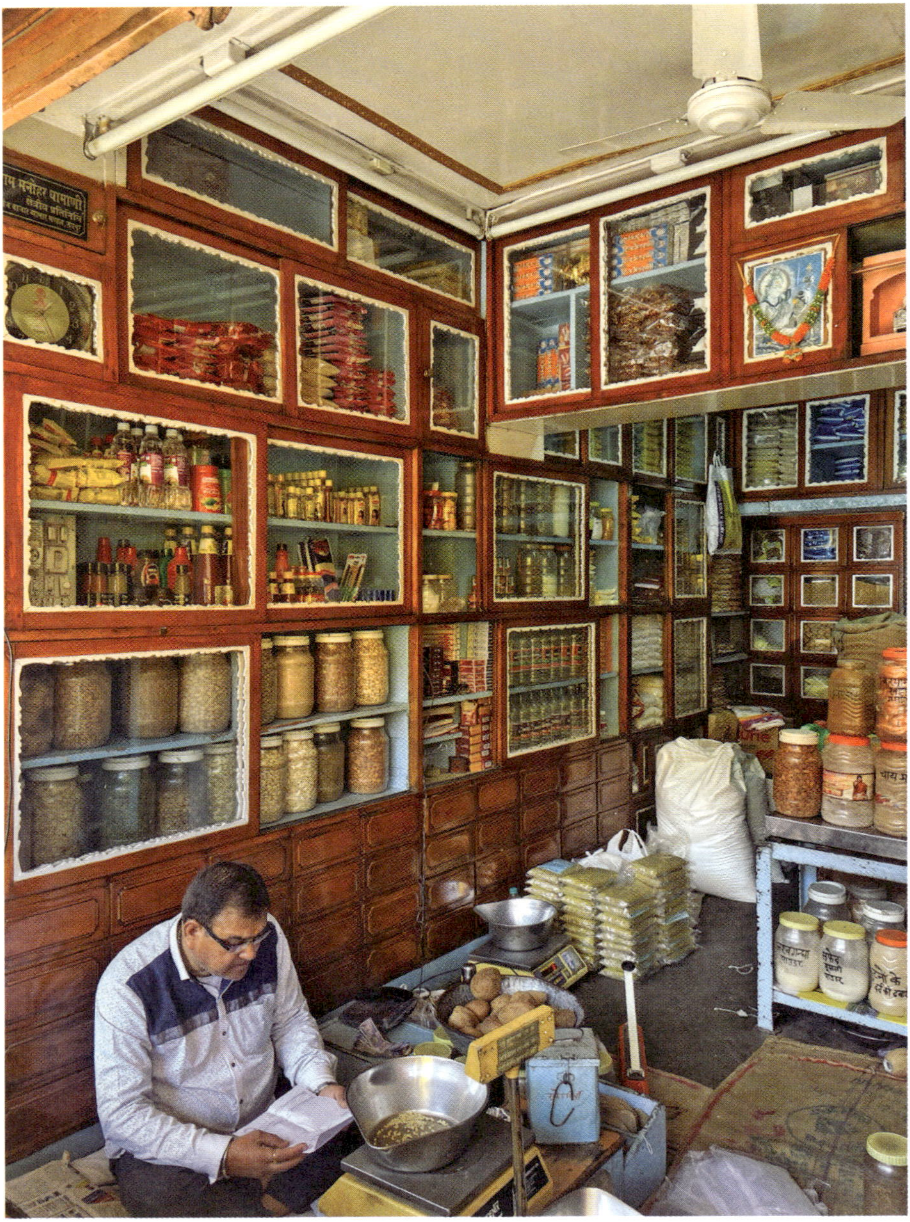

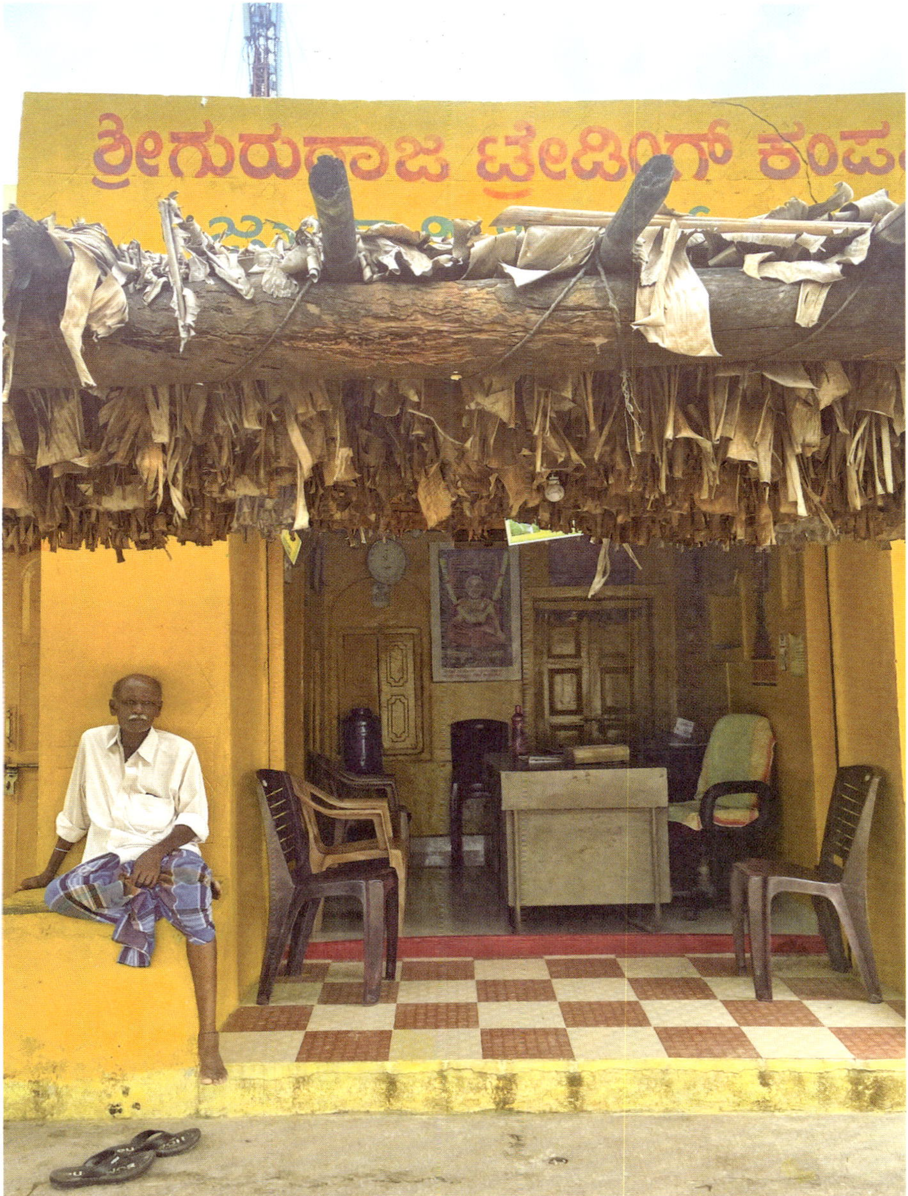
ಶ್ರೀಗುರುರಾಜ ಟ್ರೇಡಿಂಗ್ ಕಂಪ

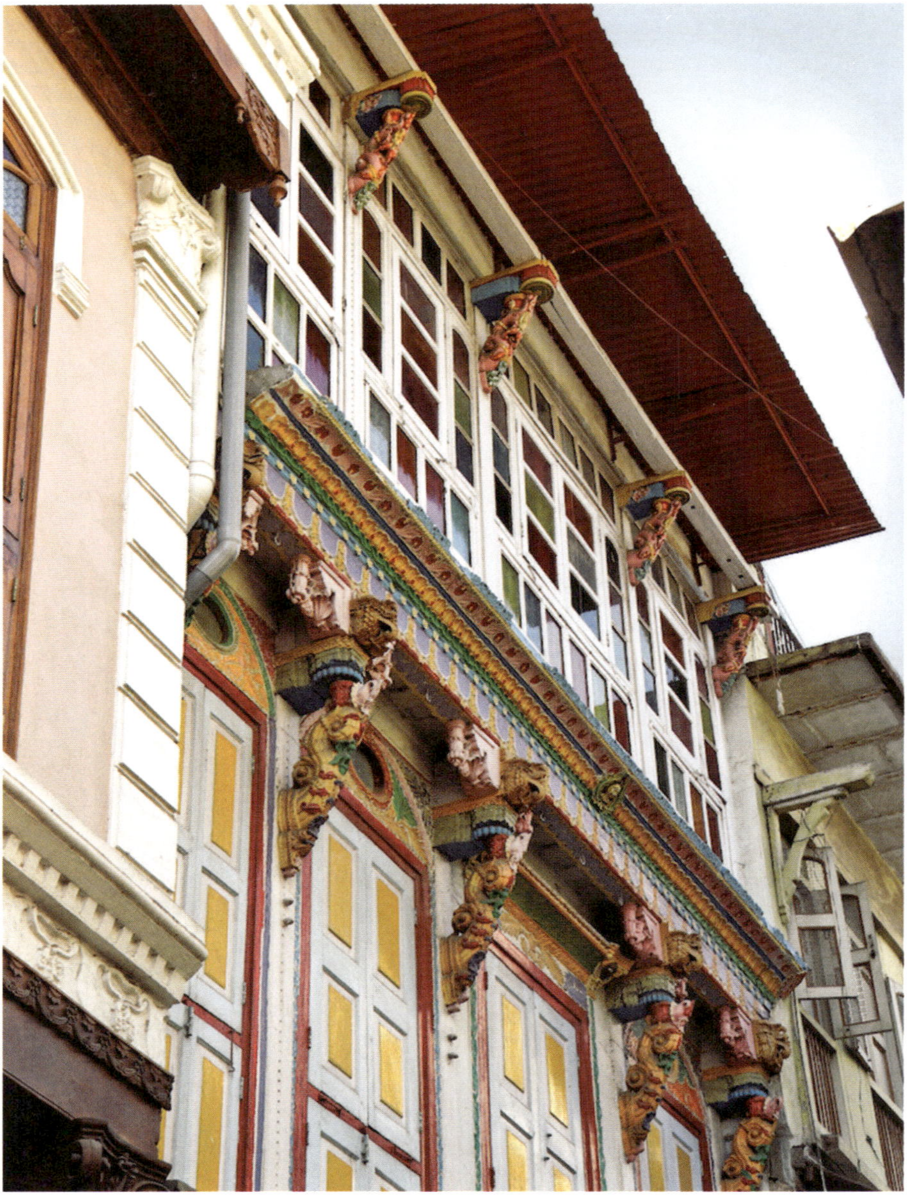

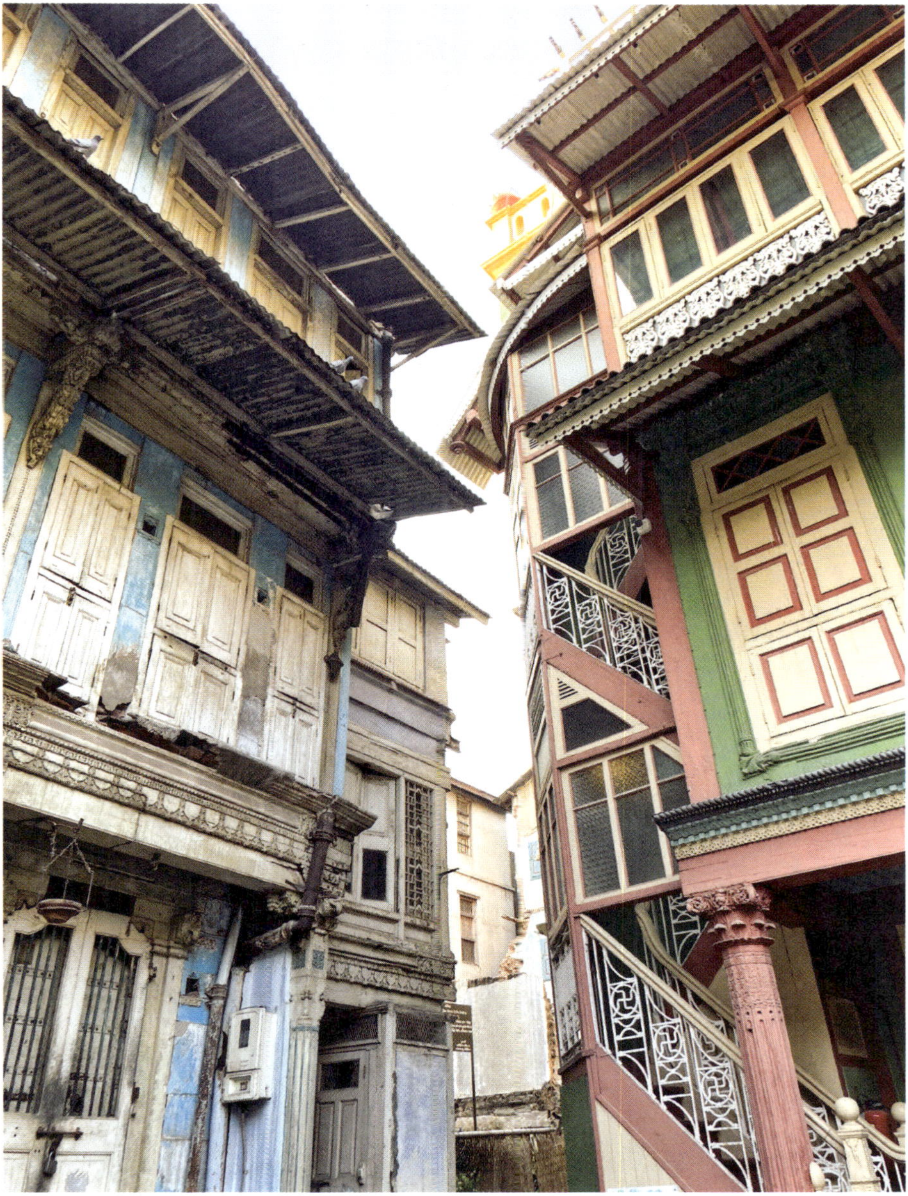

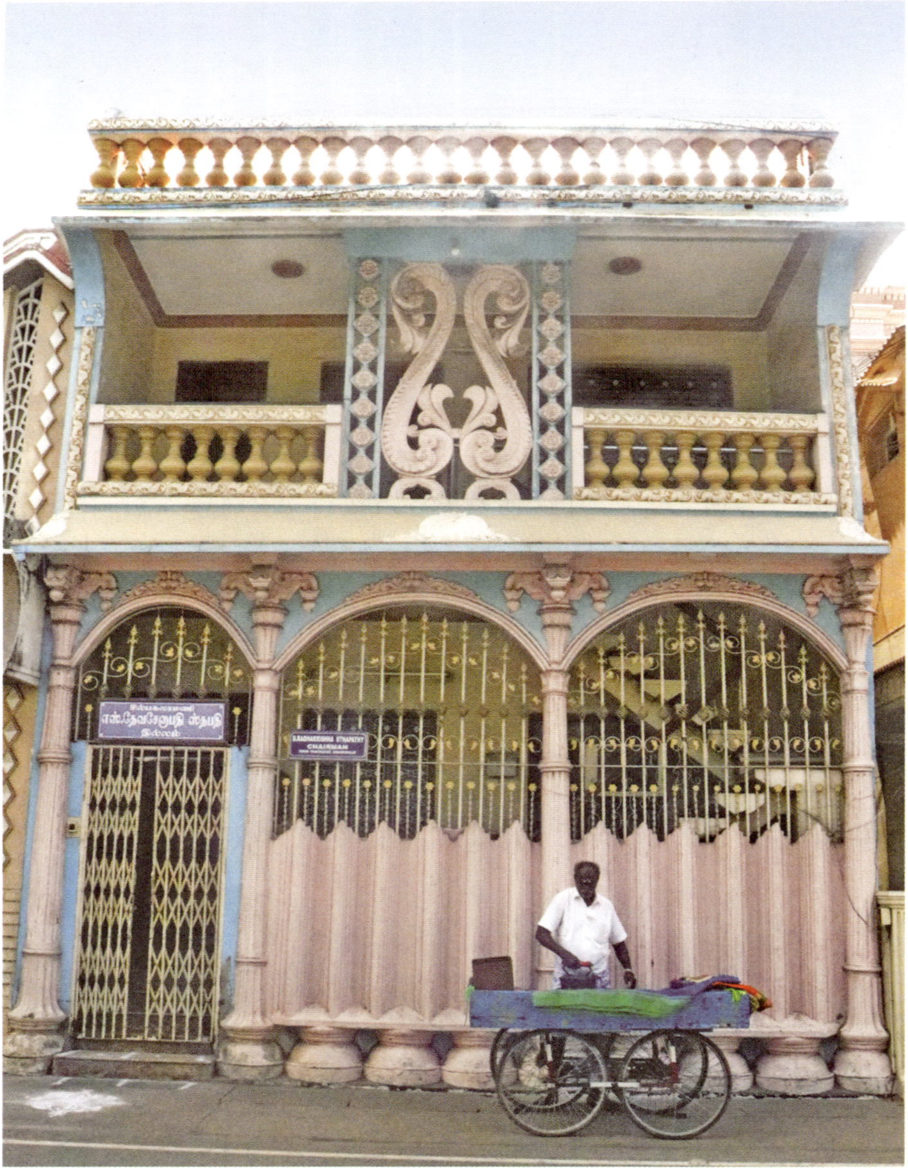
எஸ்.தேவசேனாபதி ஸ்தபதி
இல்லம்
S.RADHAKRISHNA STHAPATHY
CHAIRMAN

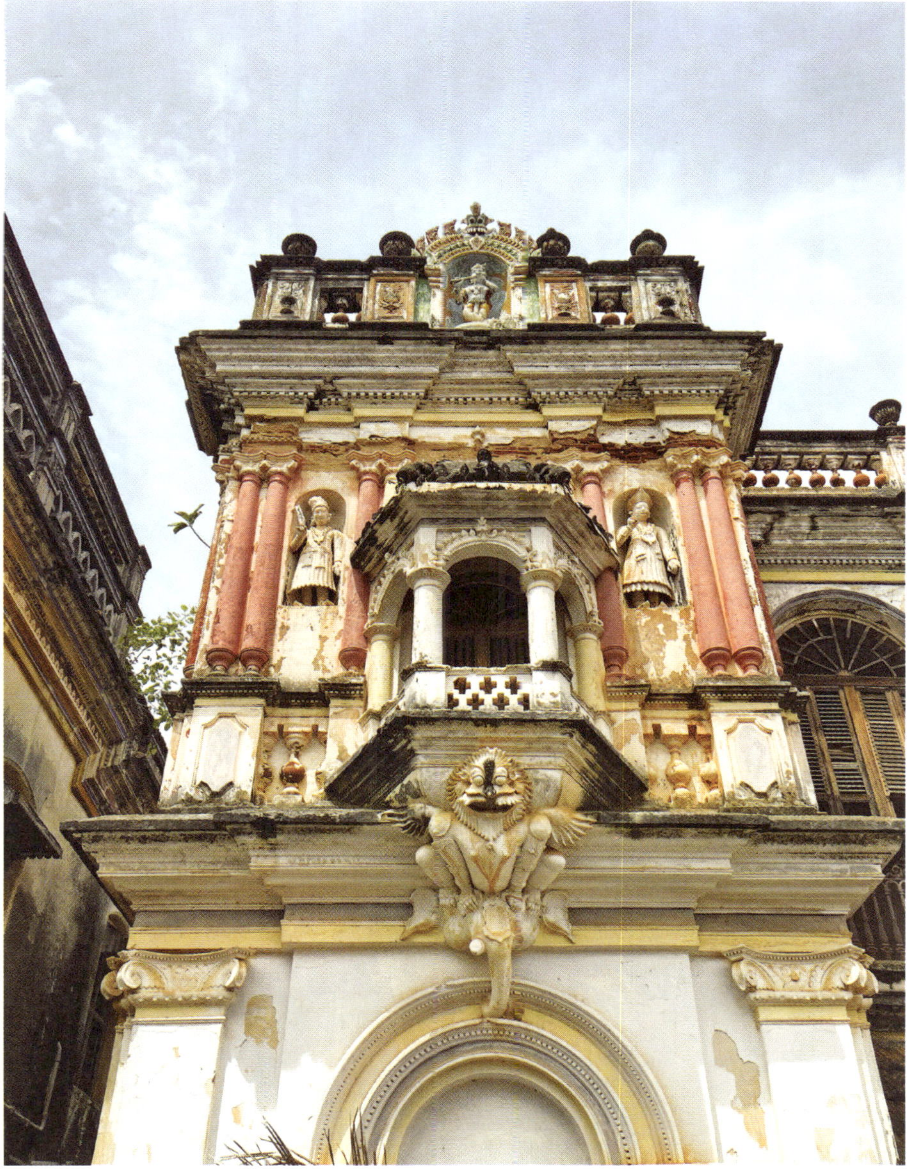

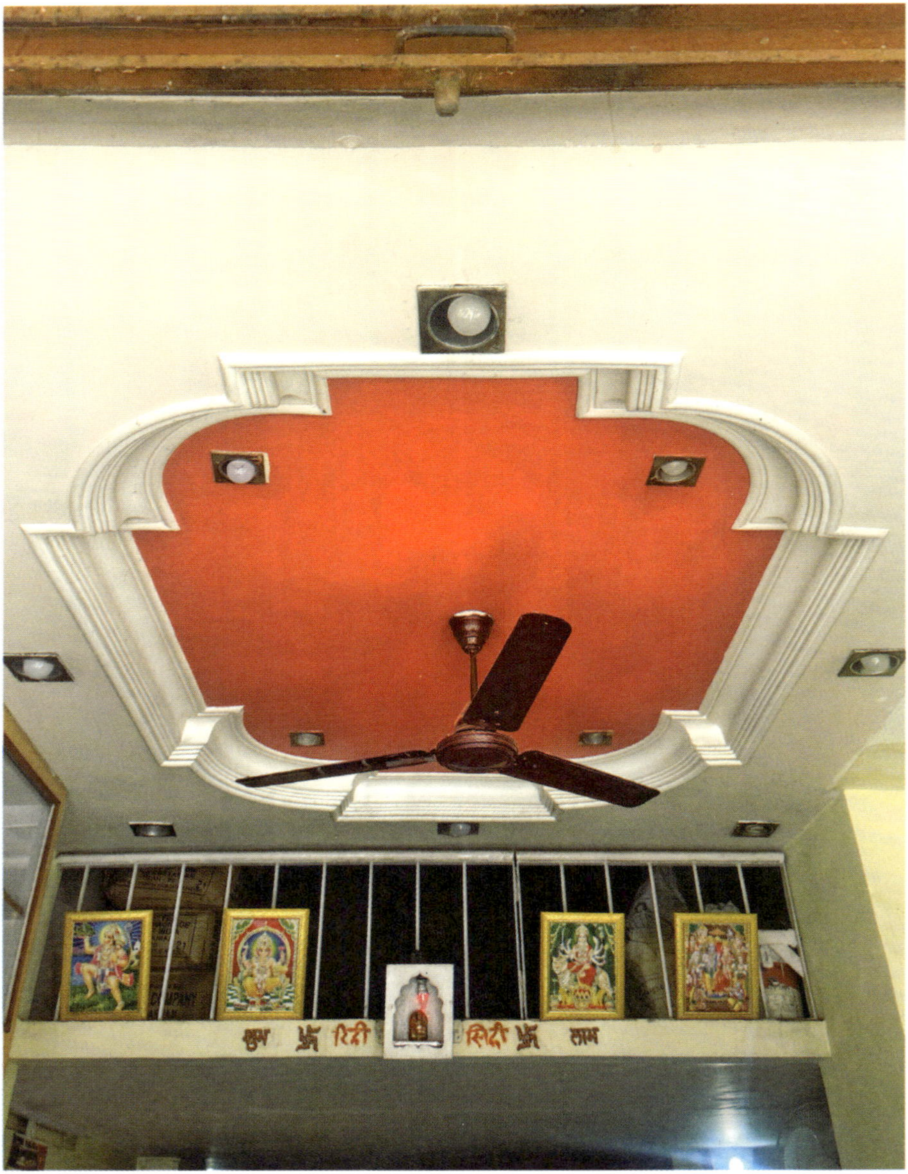
शुभ
रिद्धी
सिद्धी
लाभ

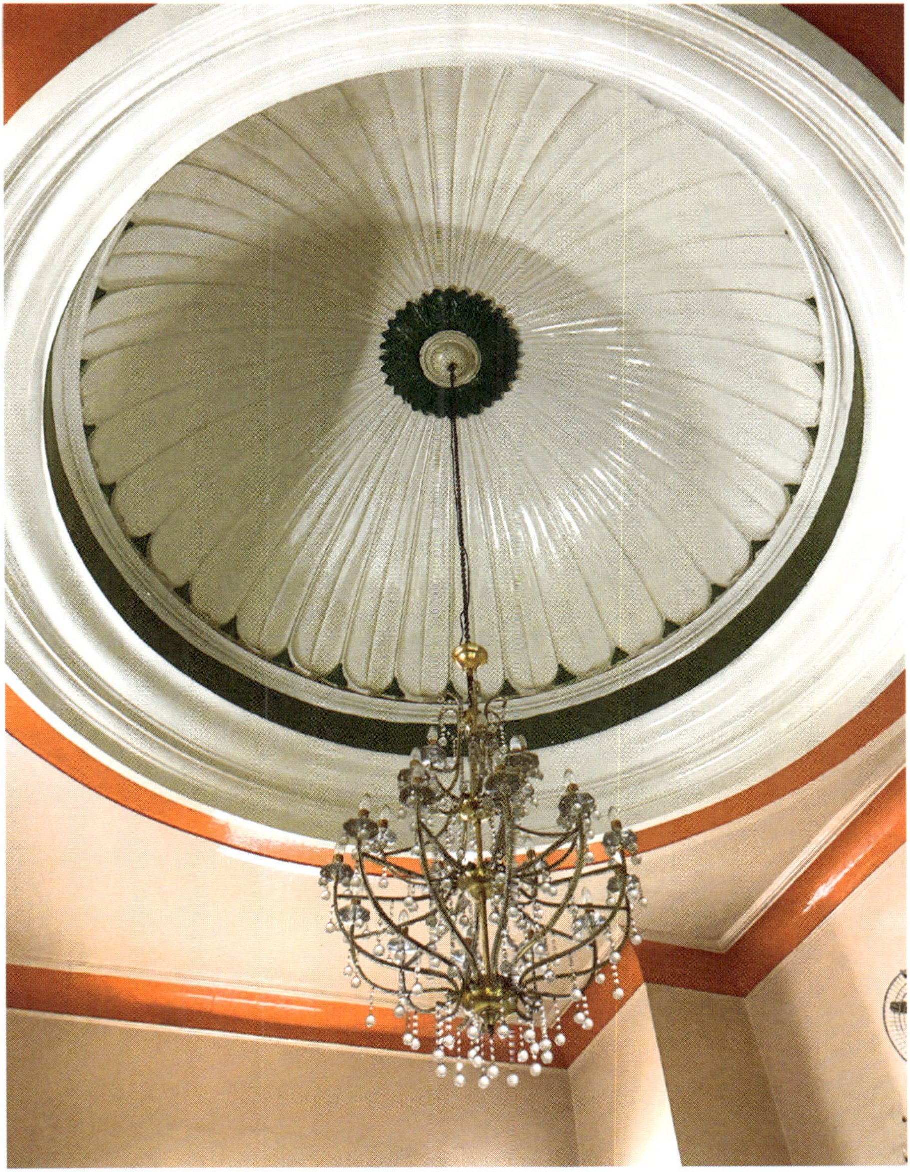

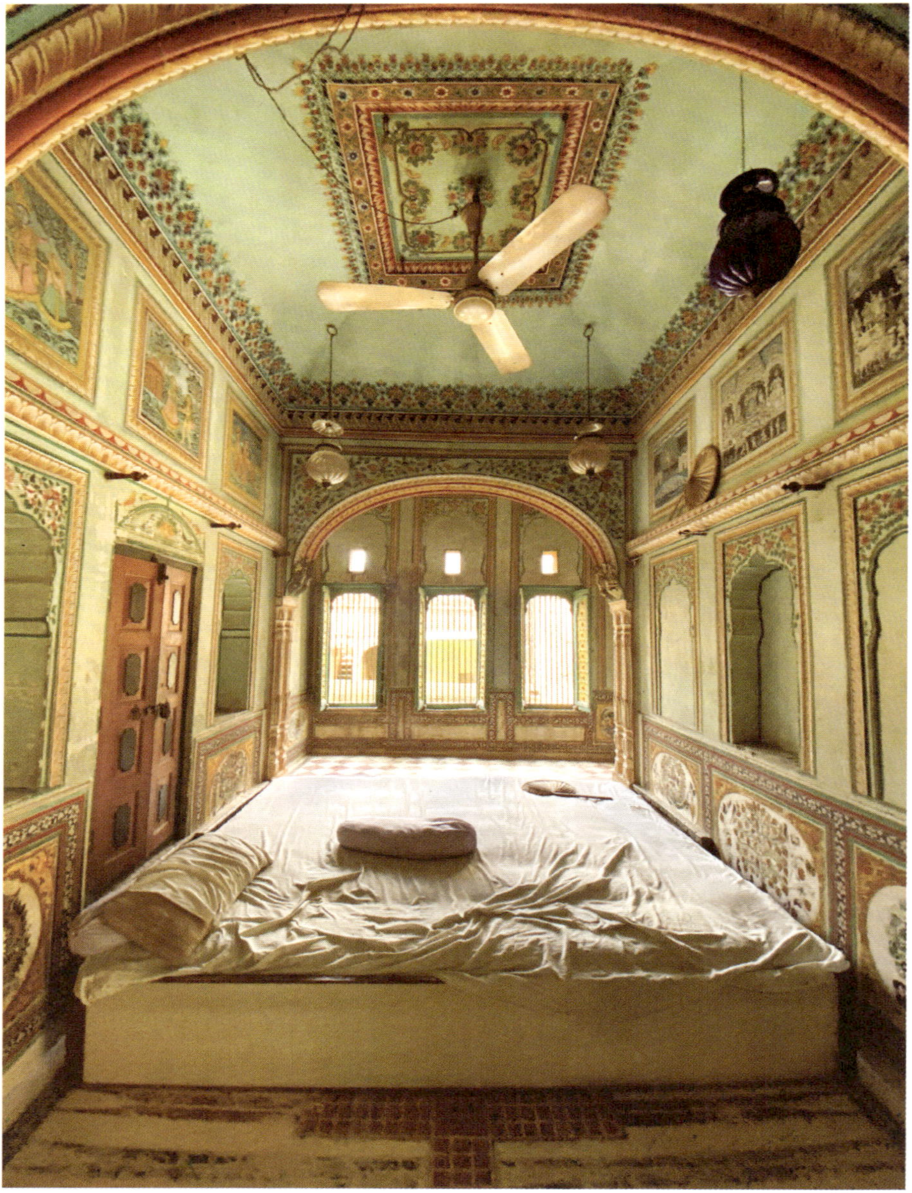

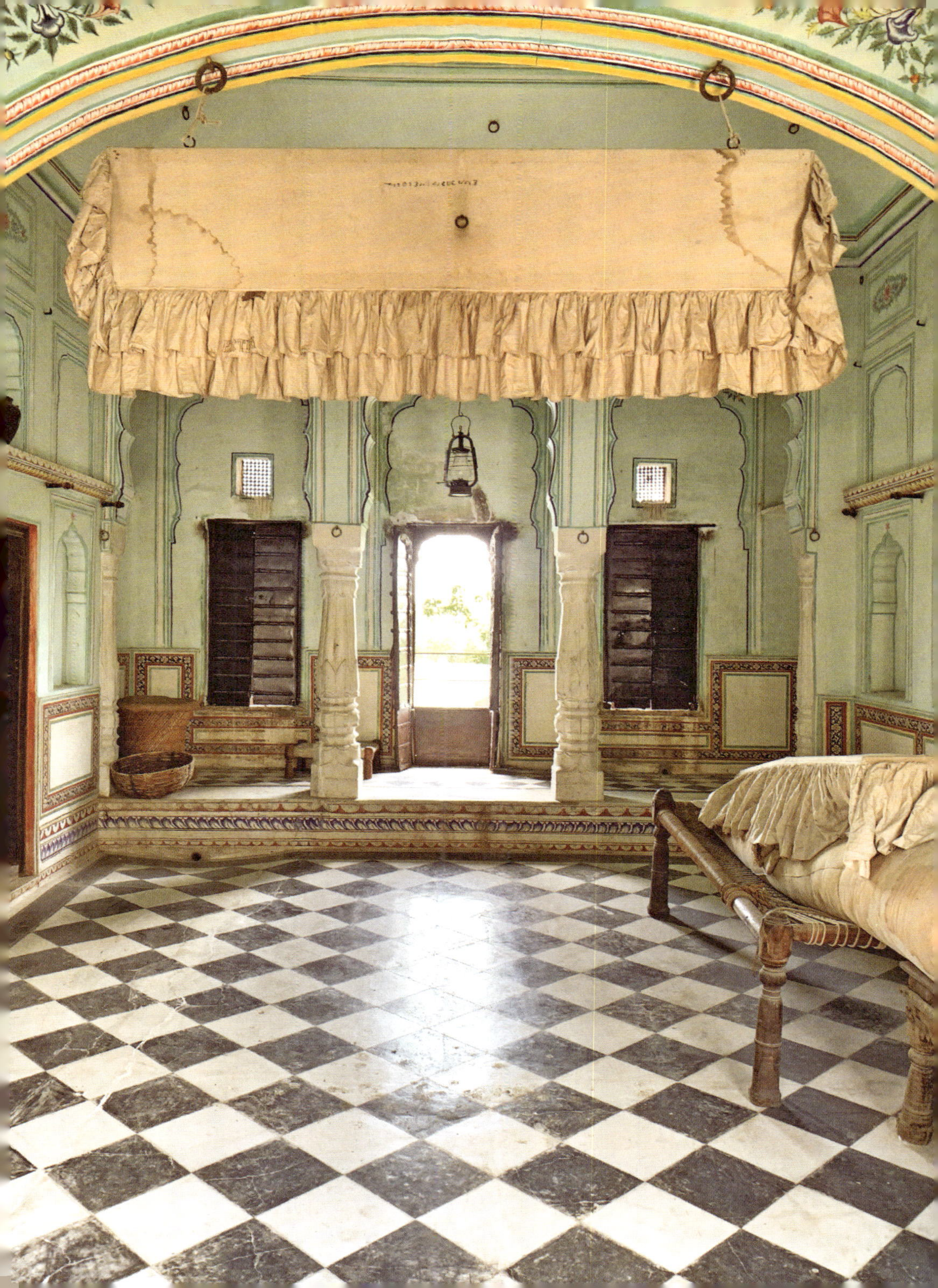

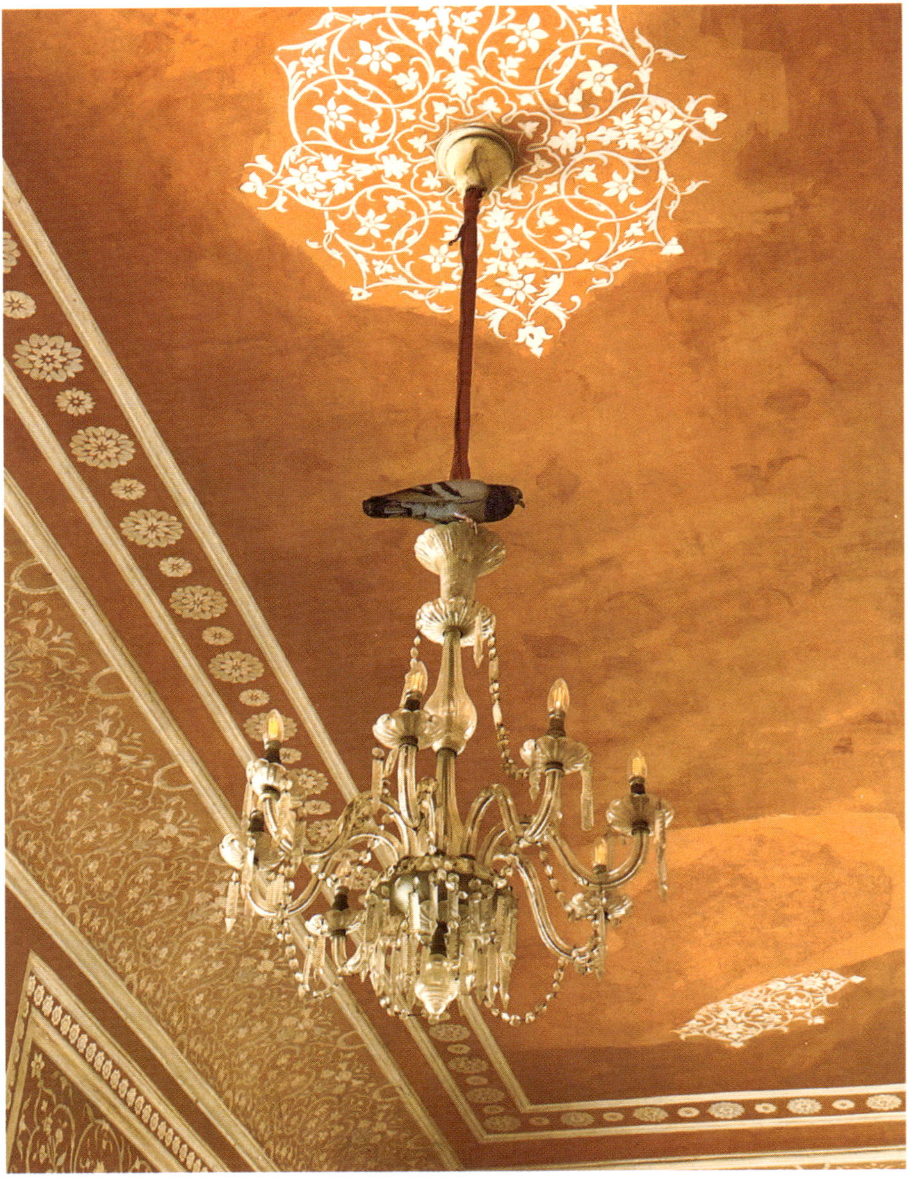

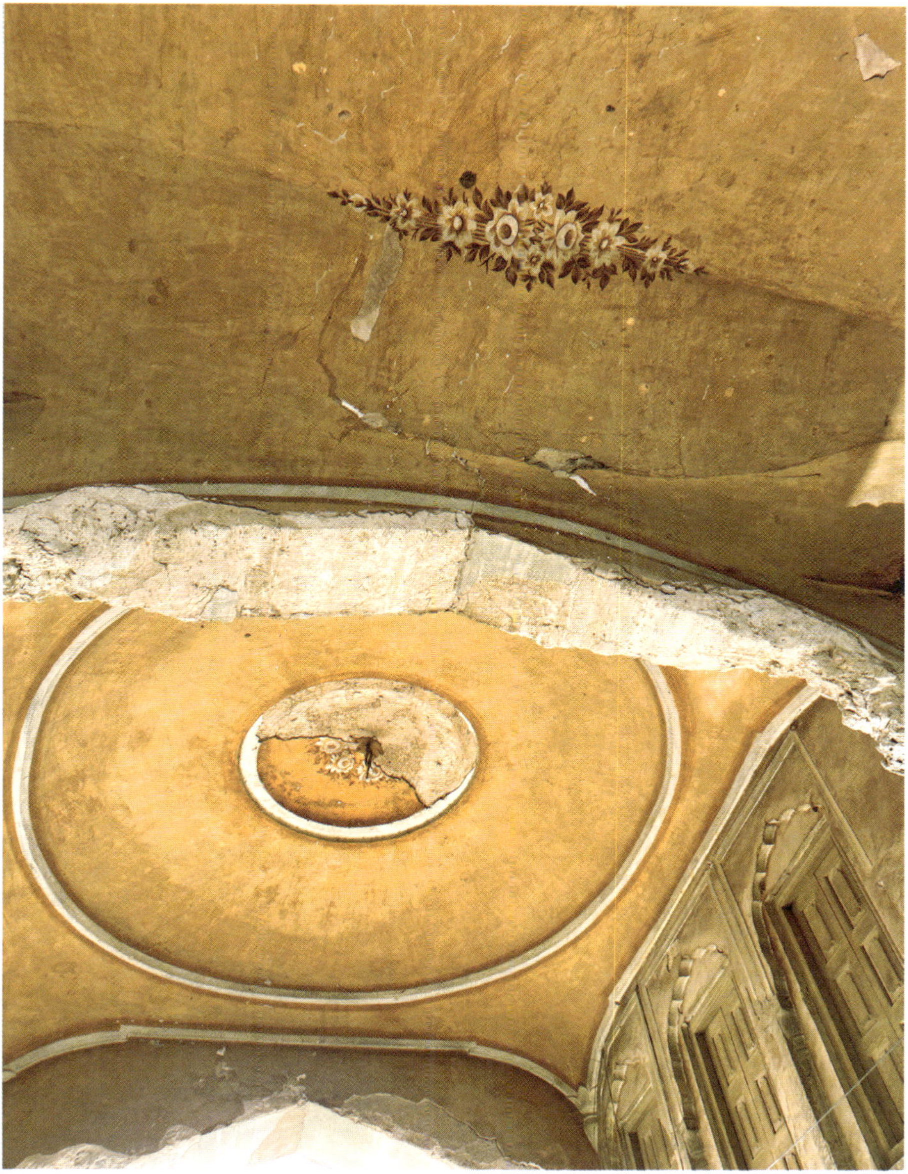

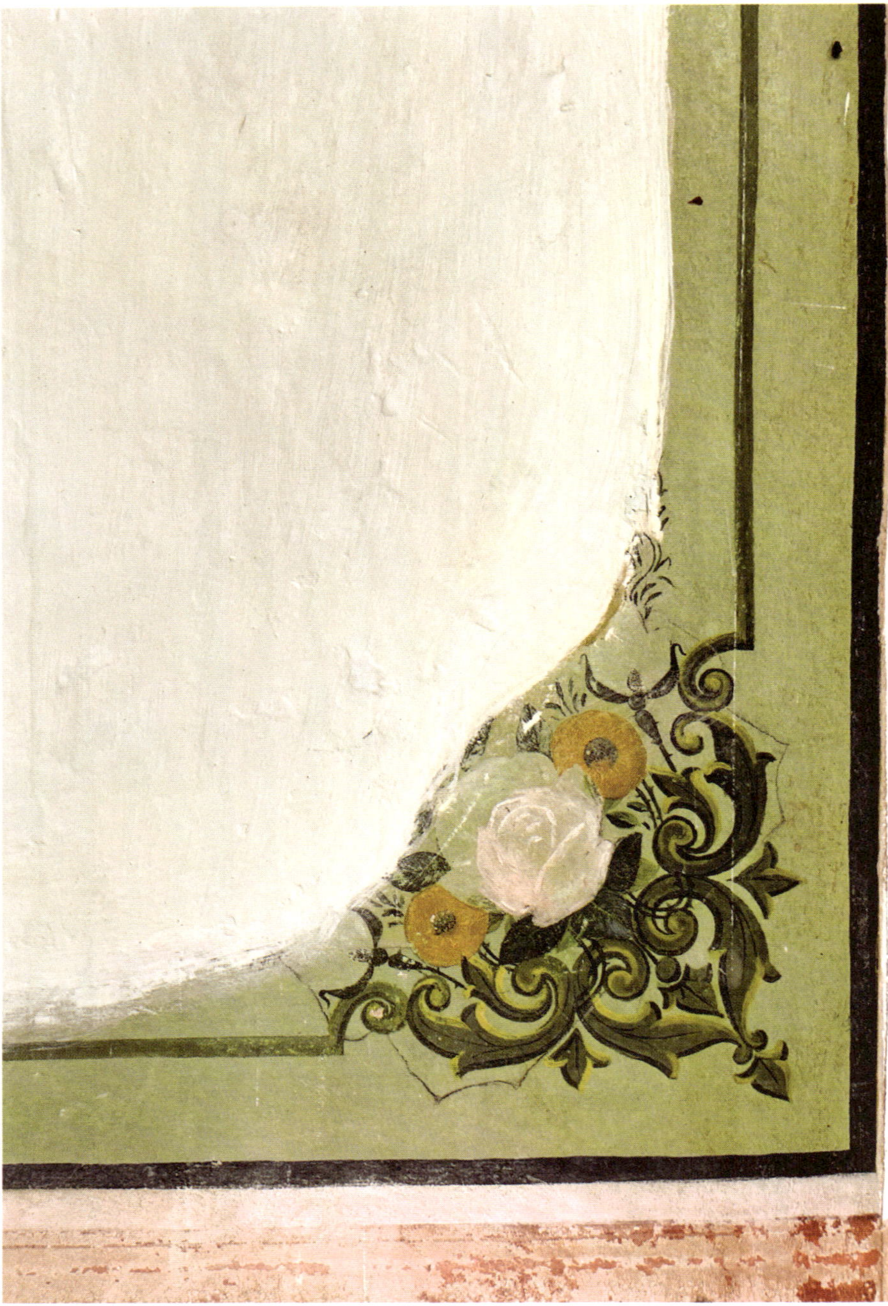

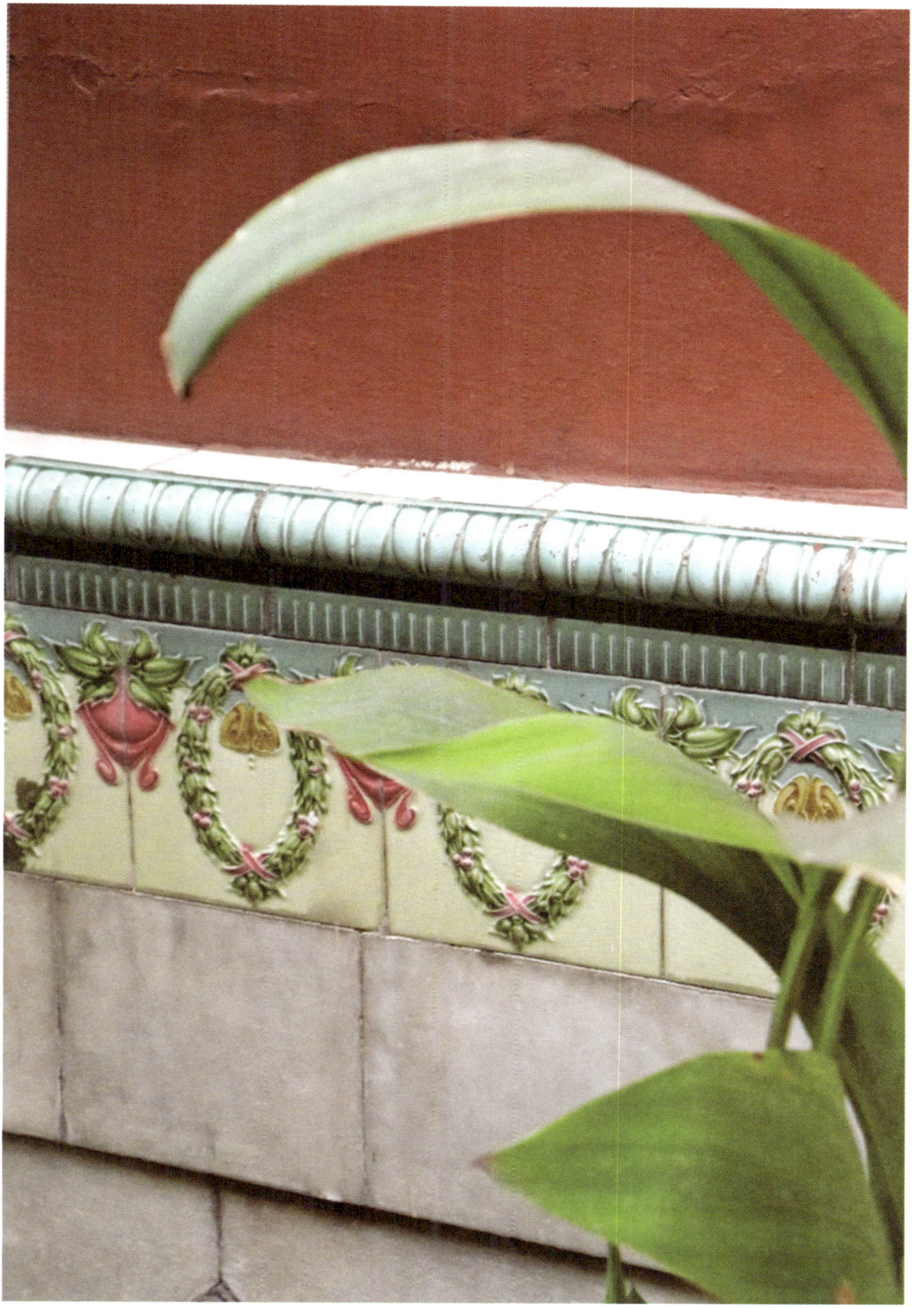

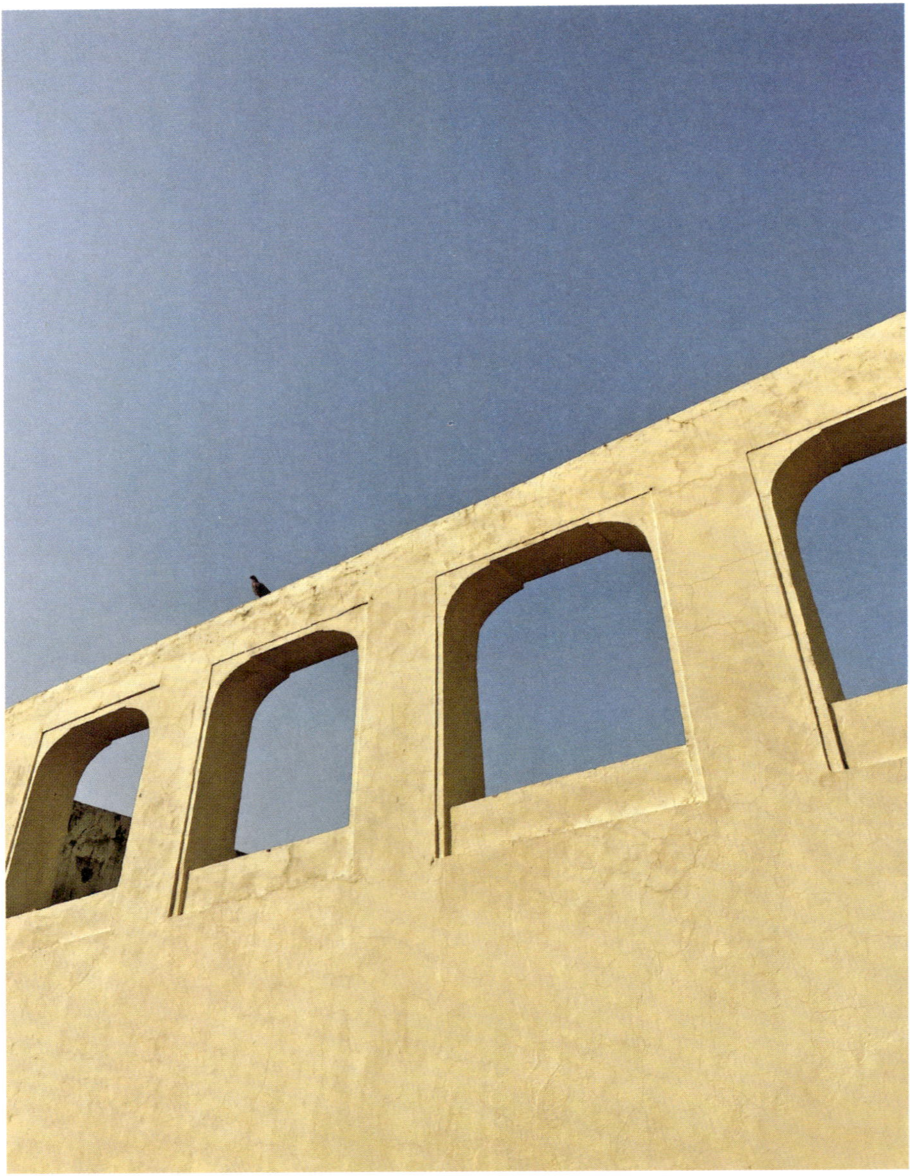

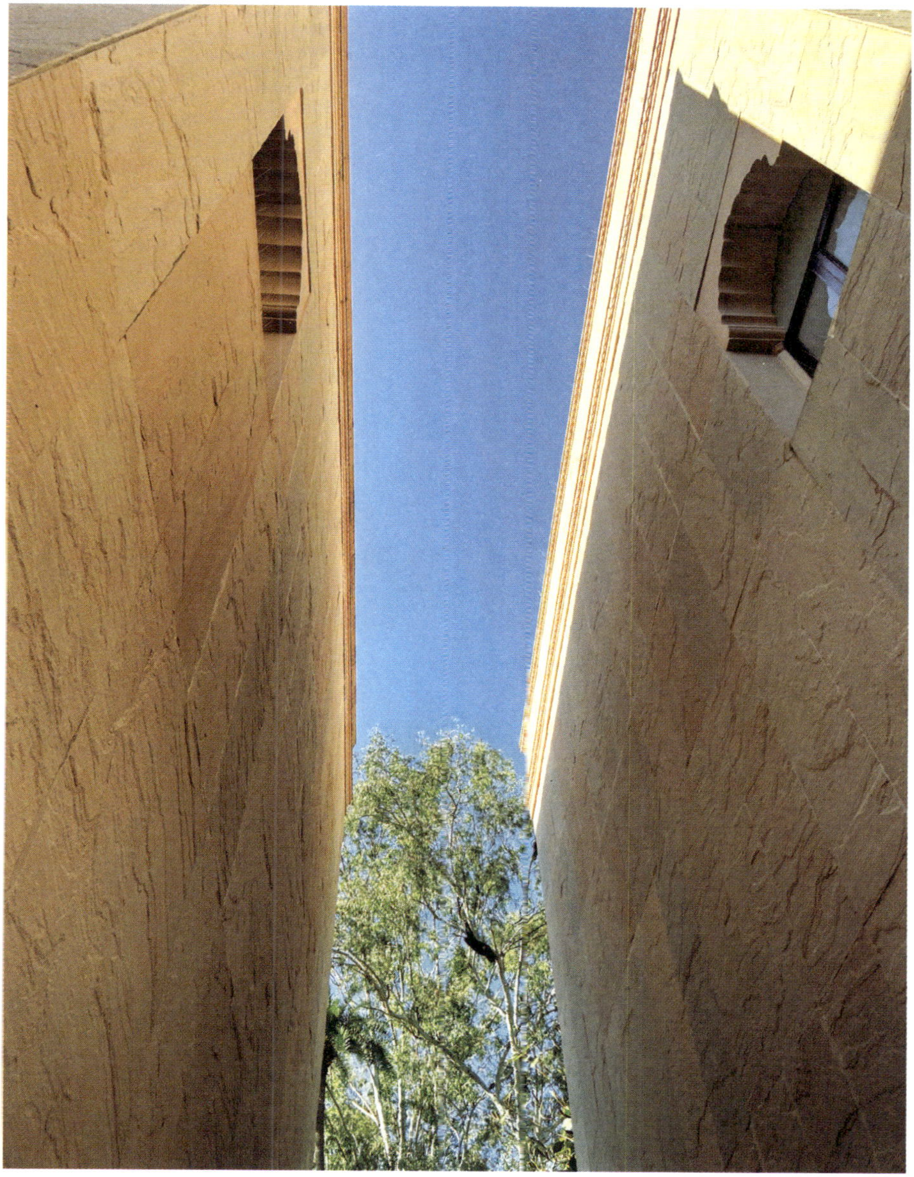

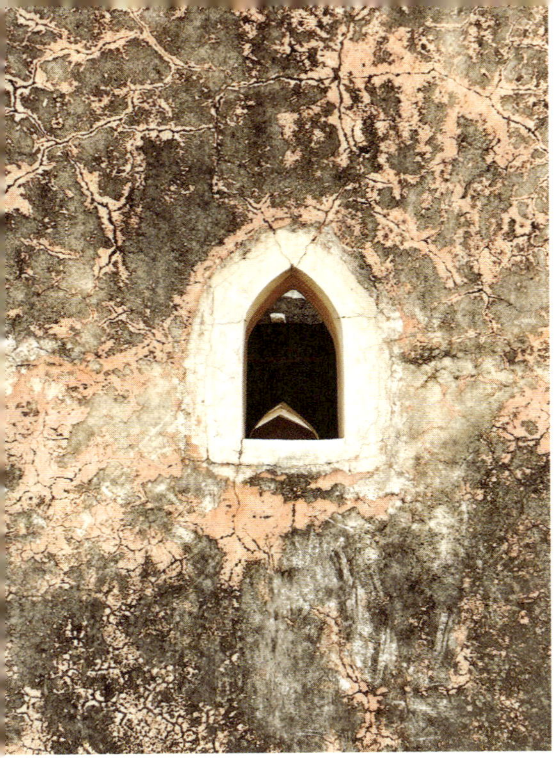
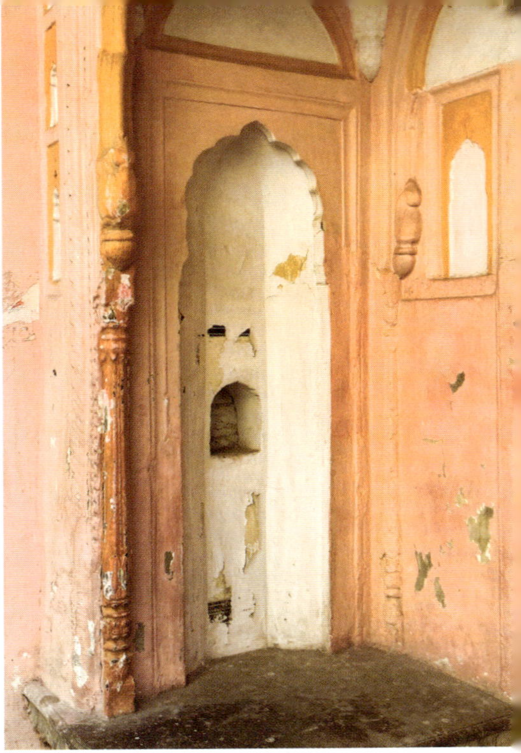
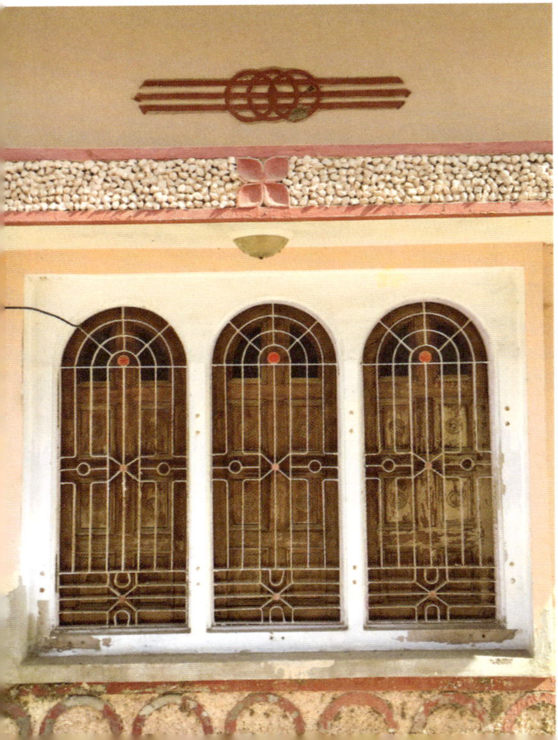
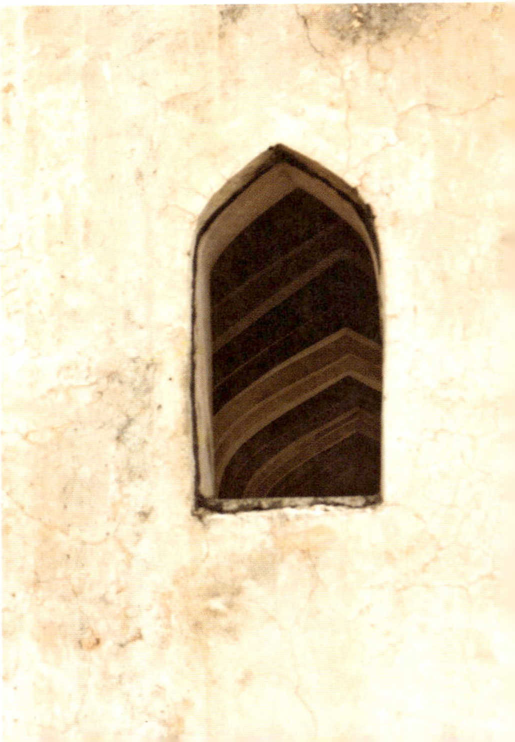

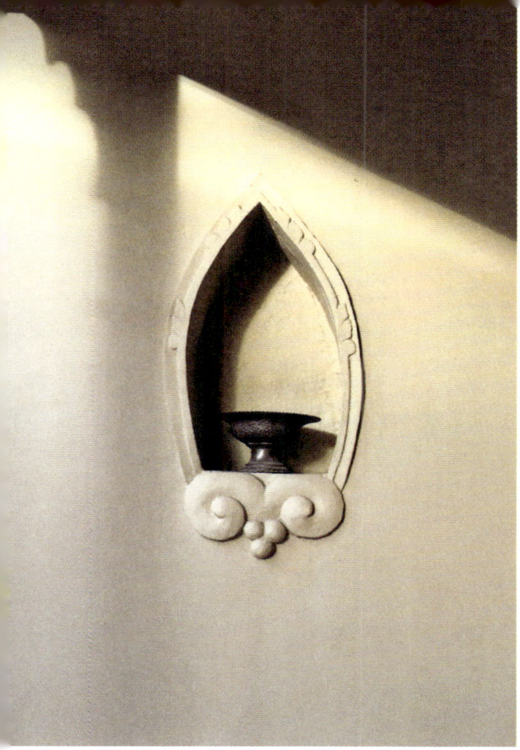
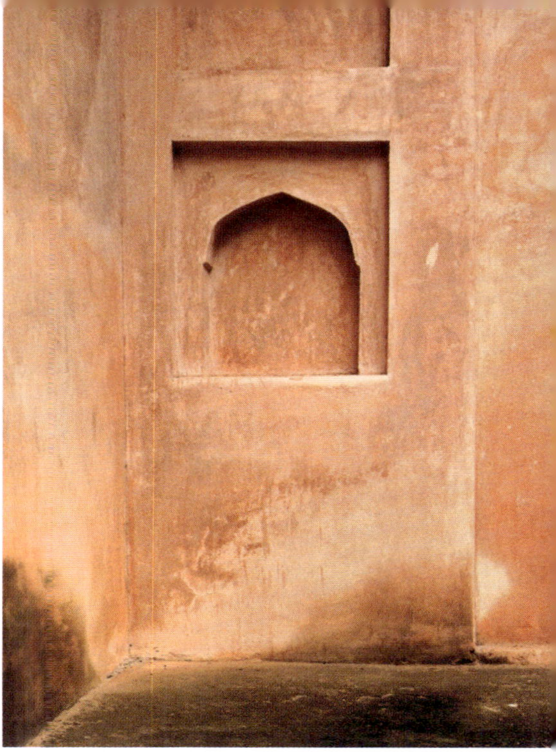
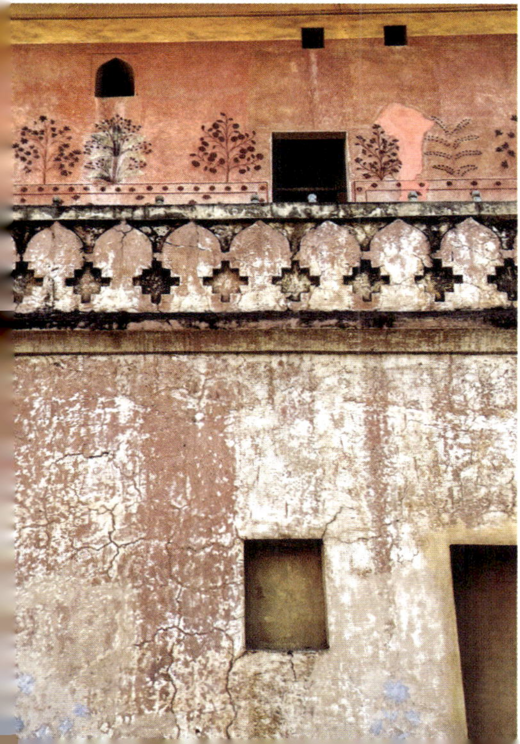
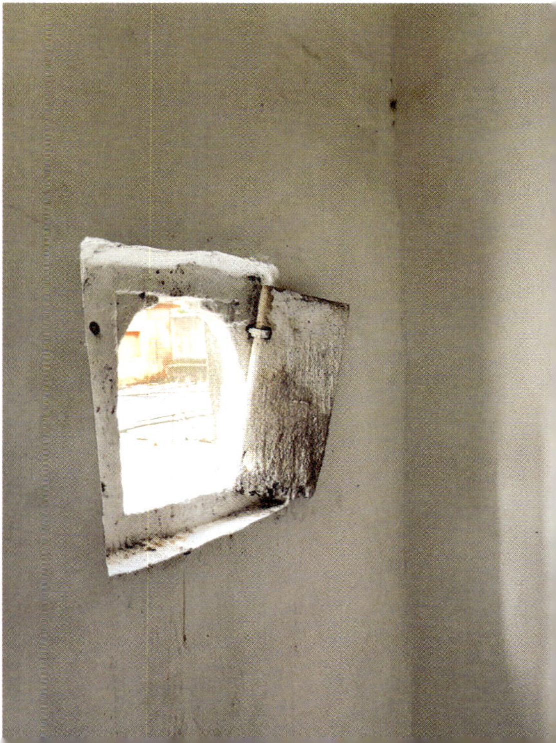

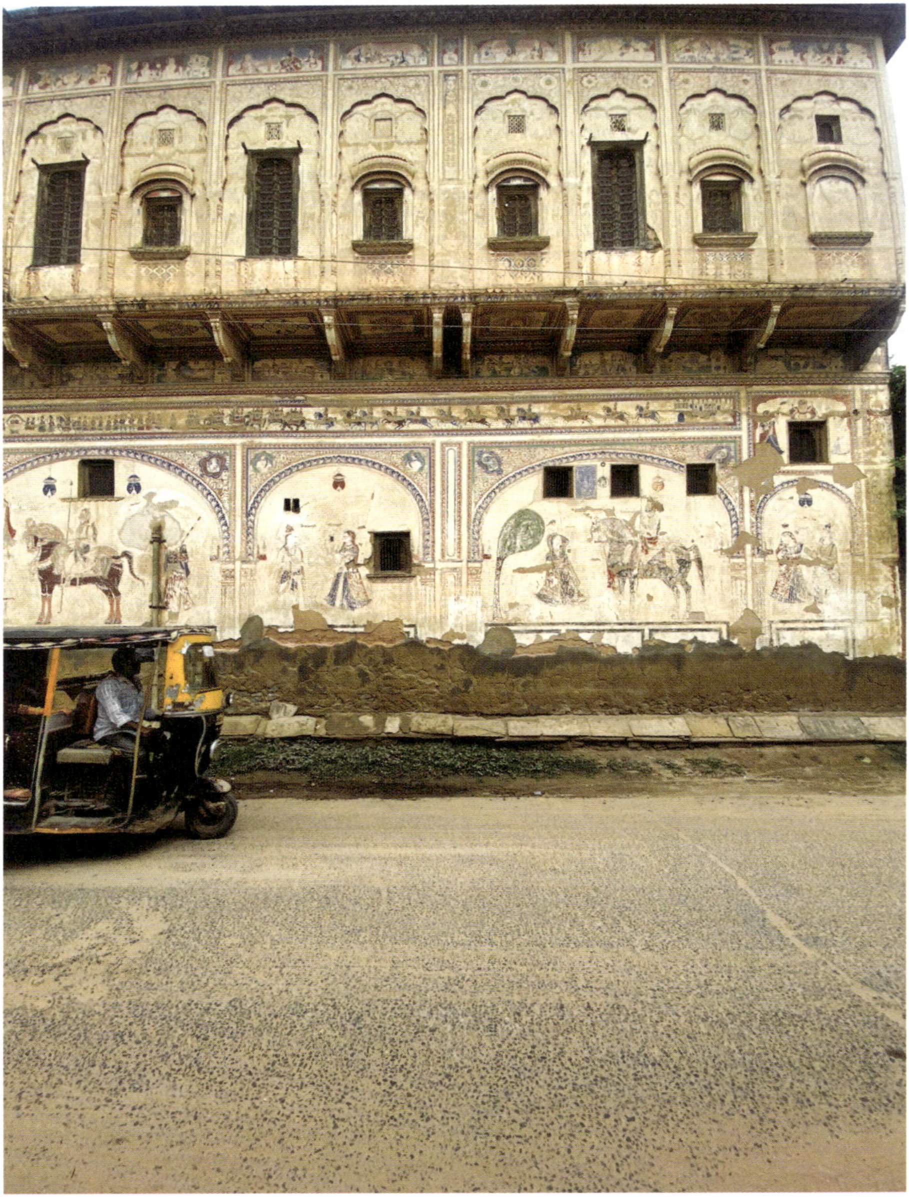

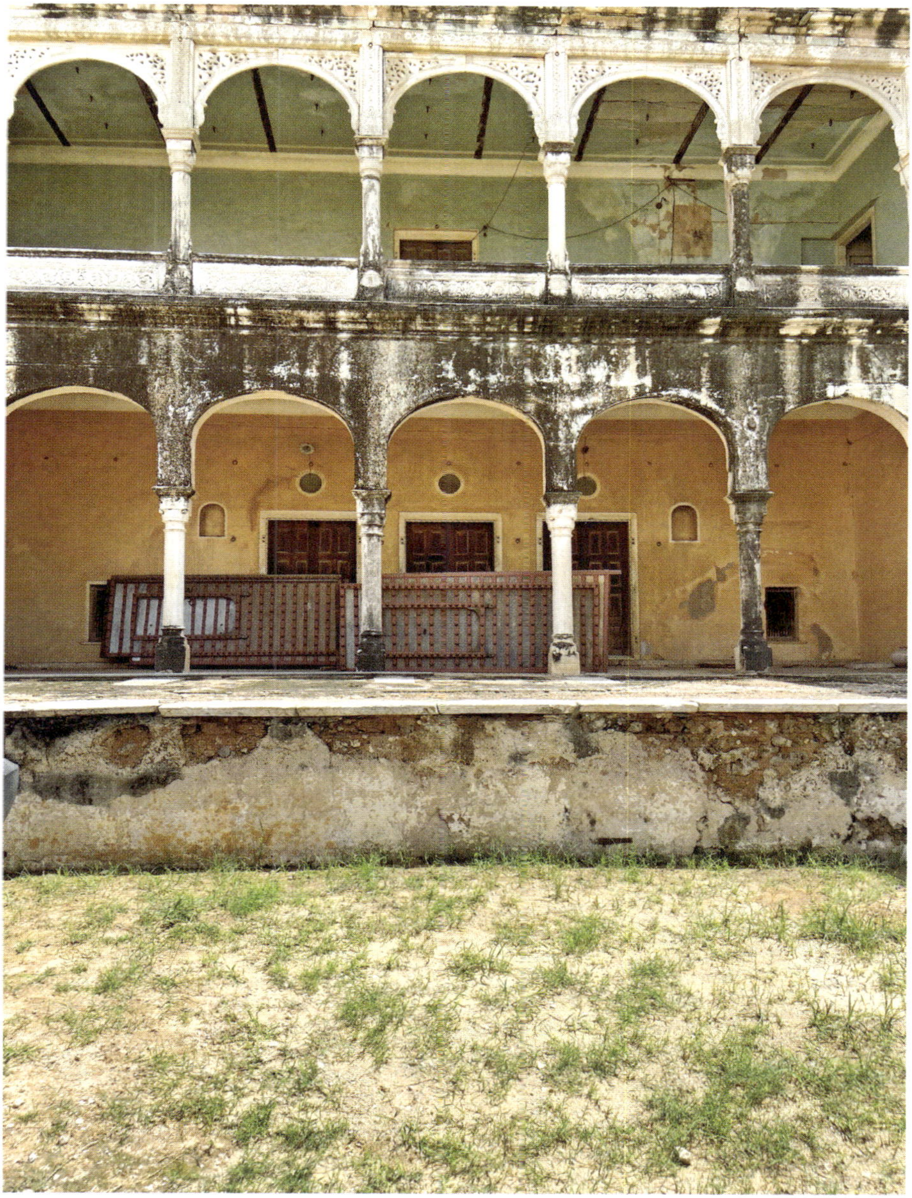

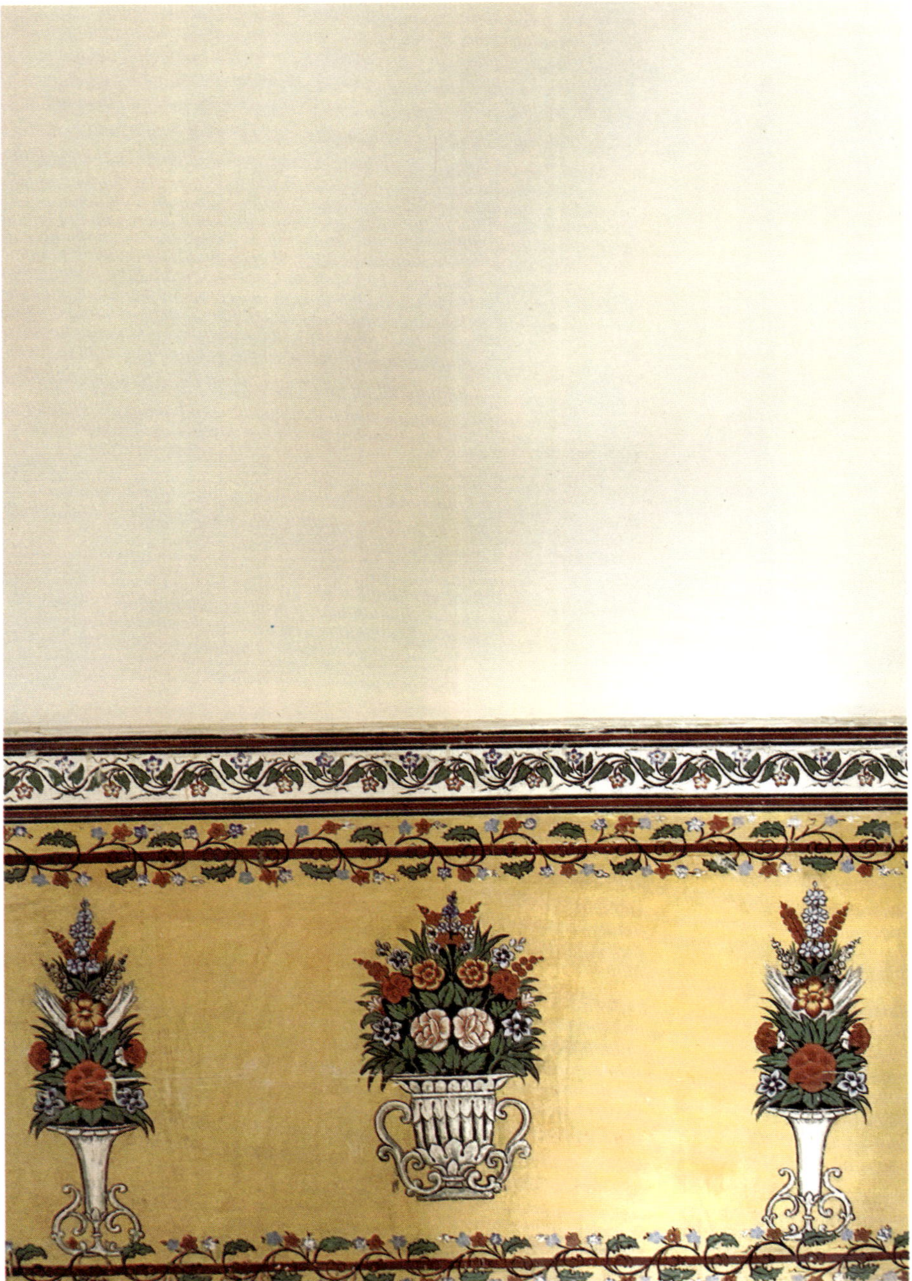

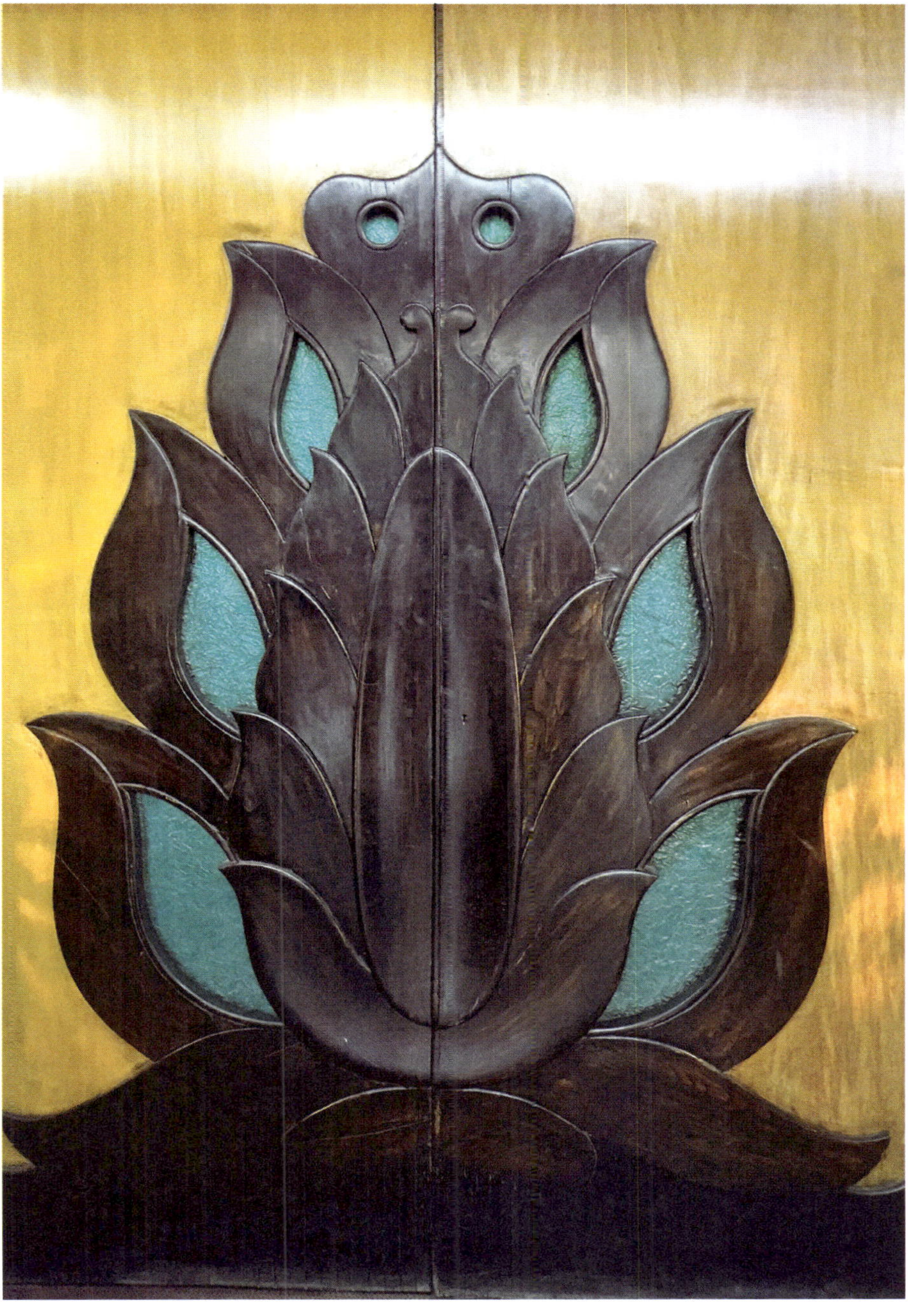

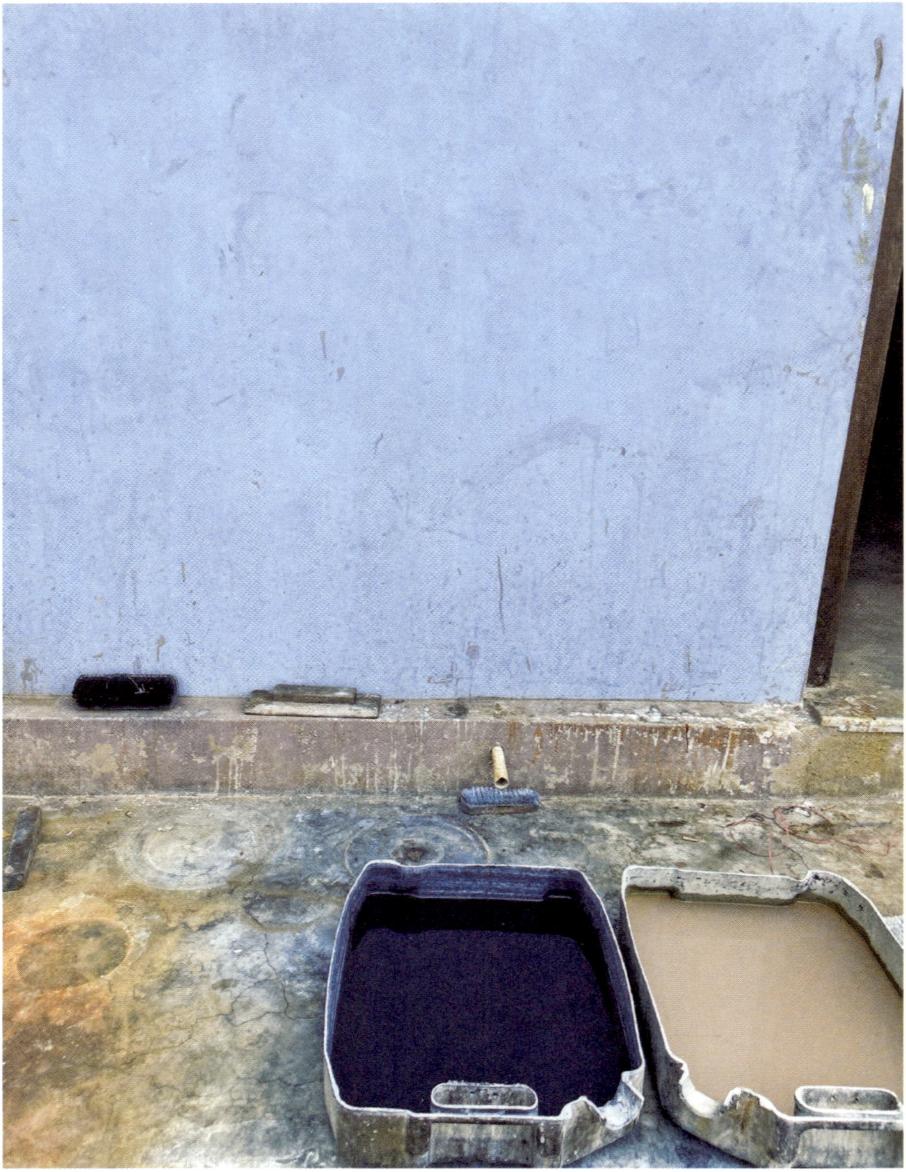

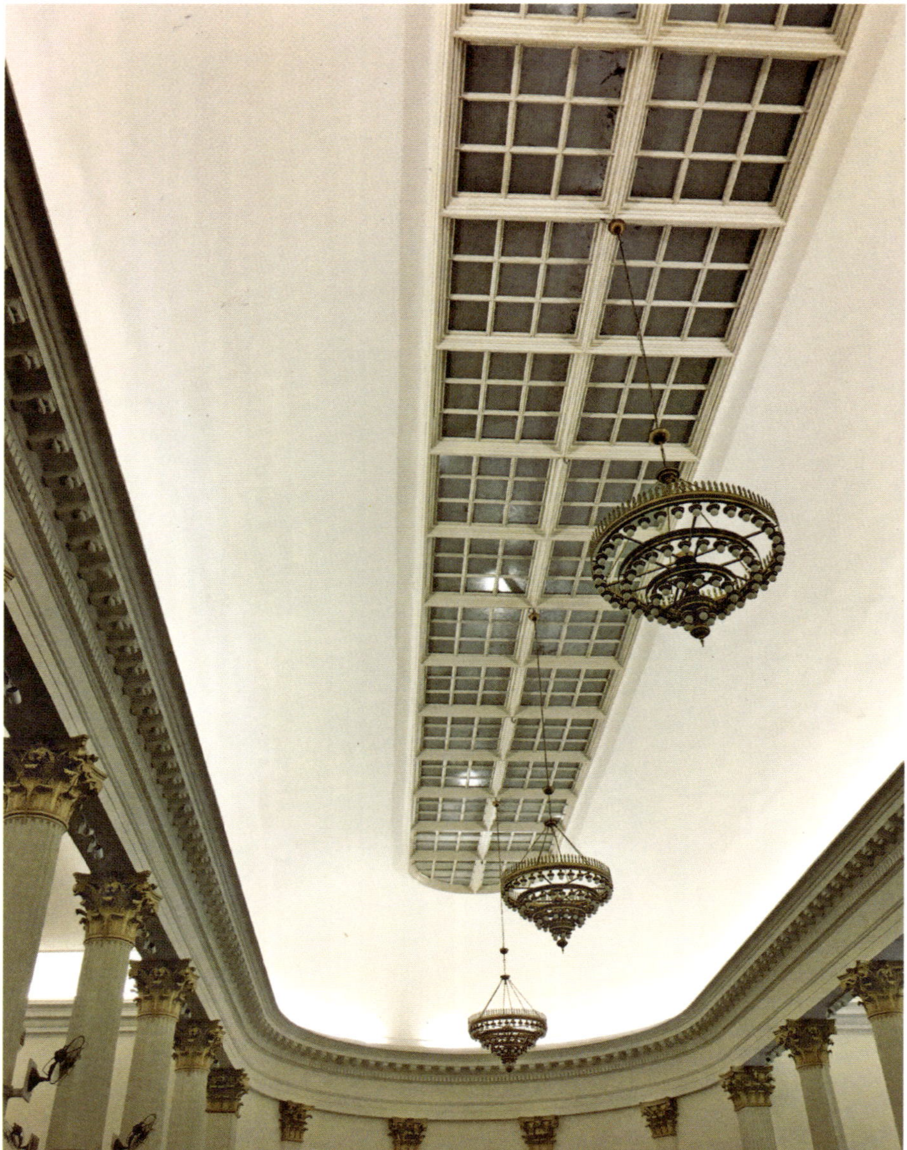

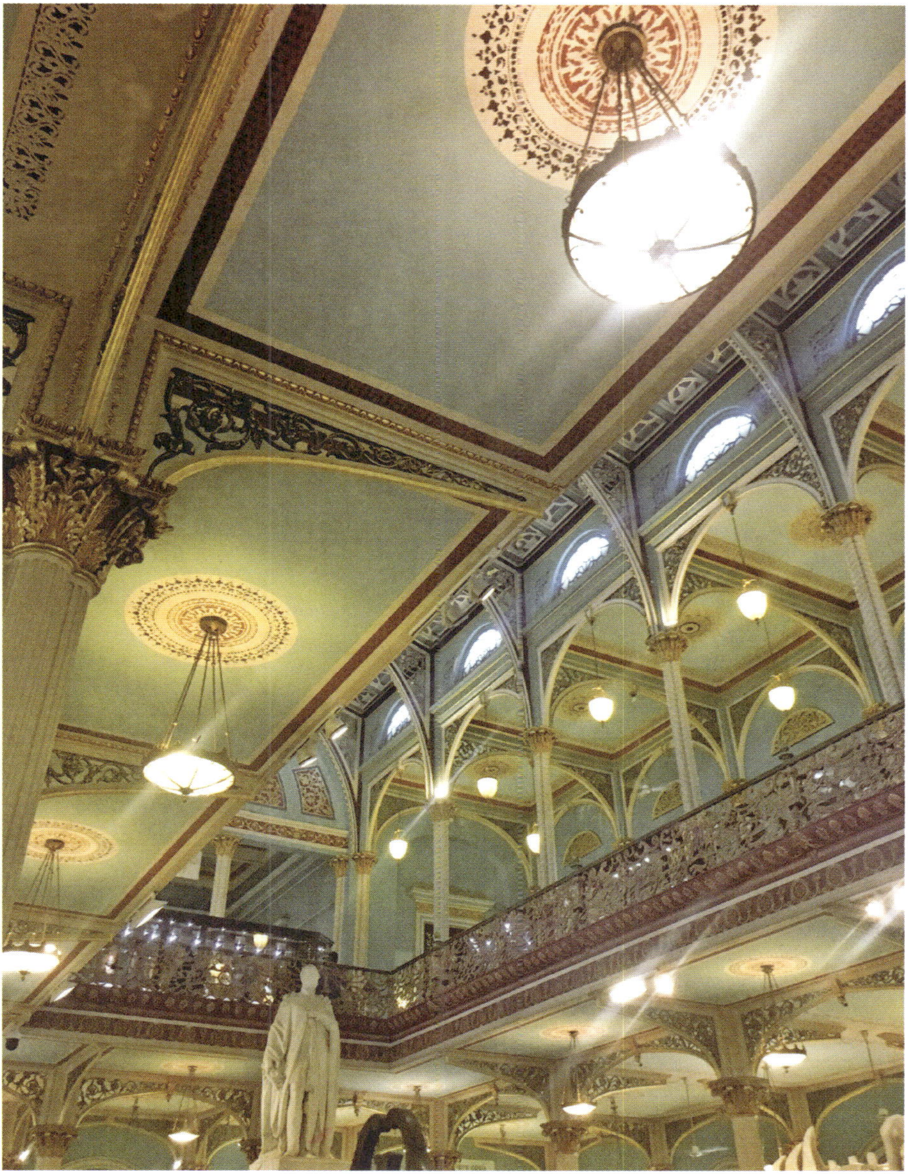

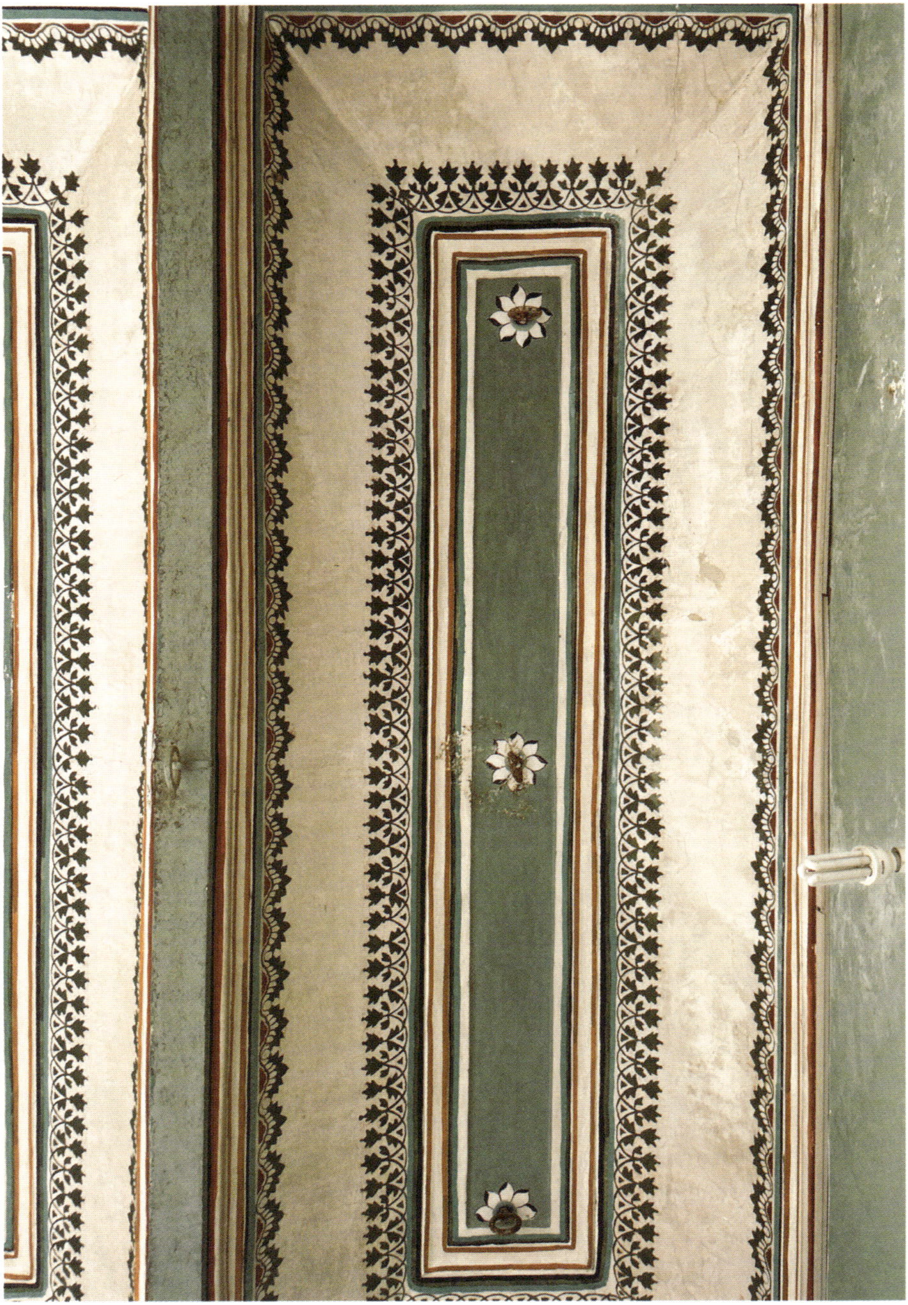

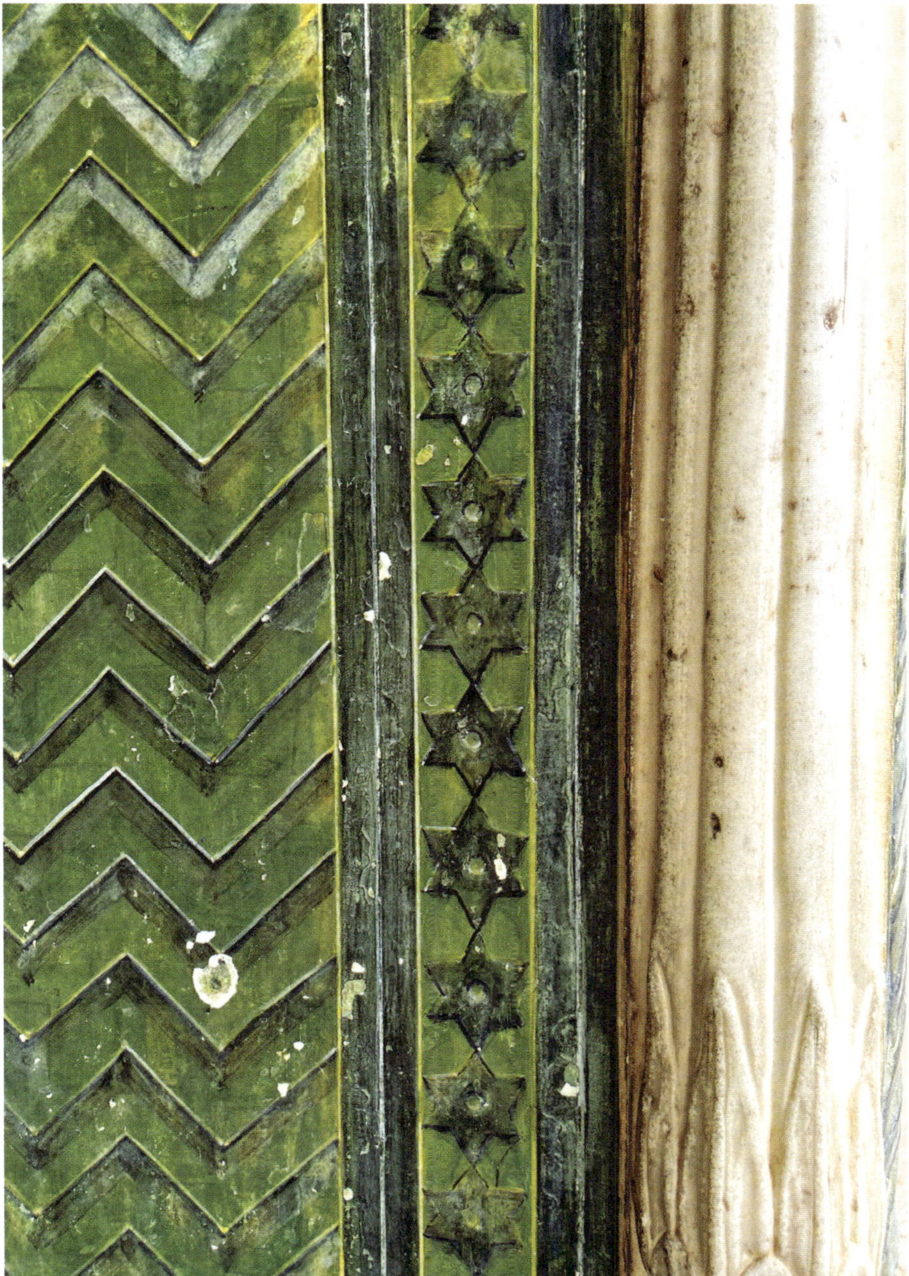

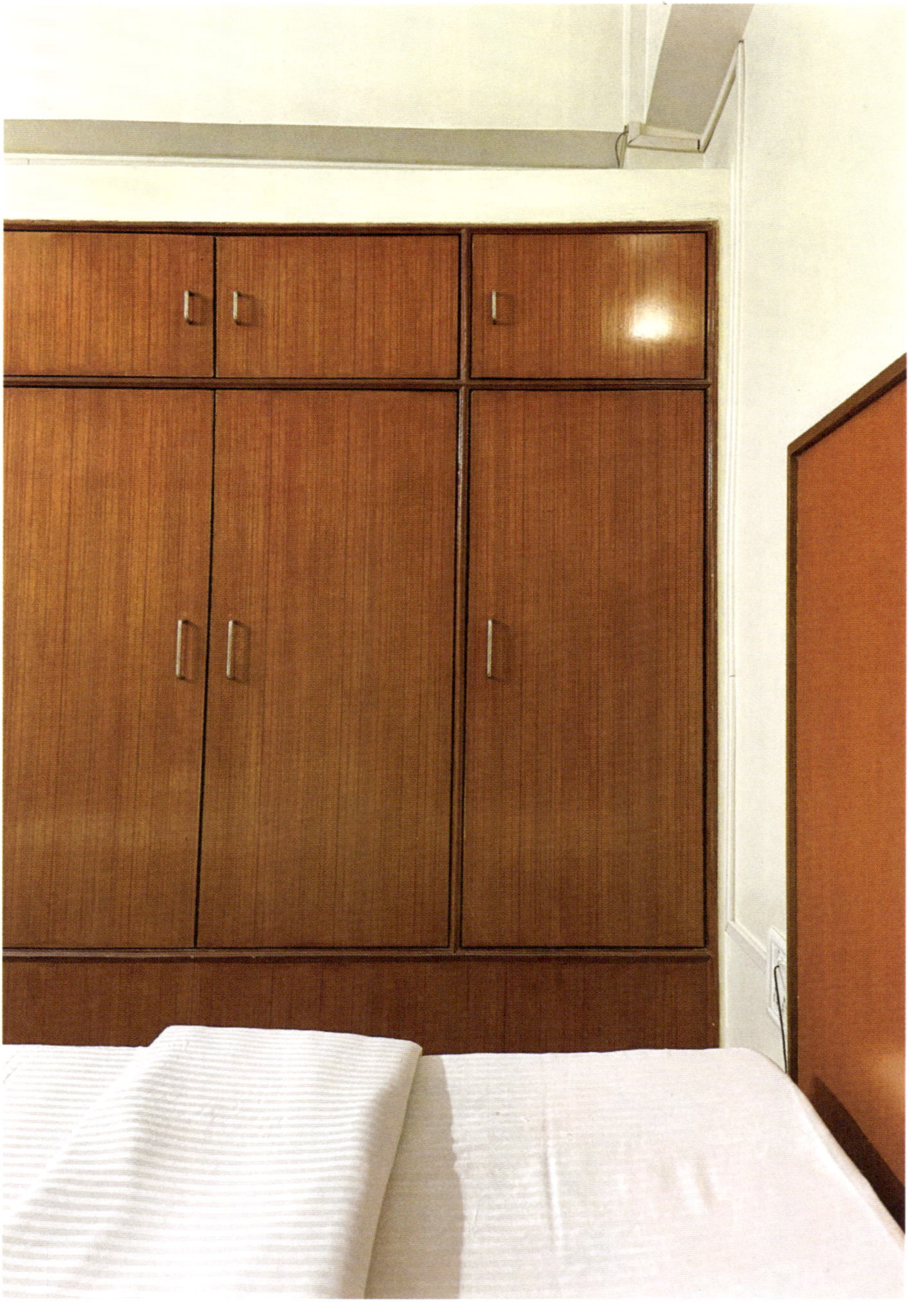

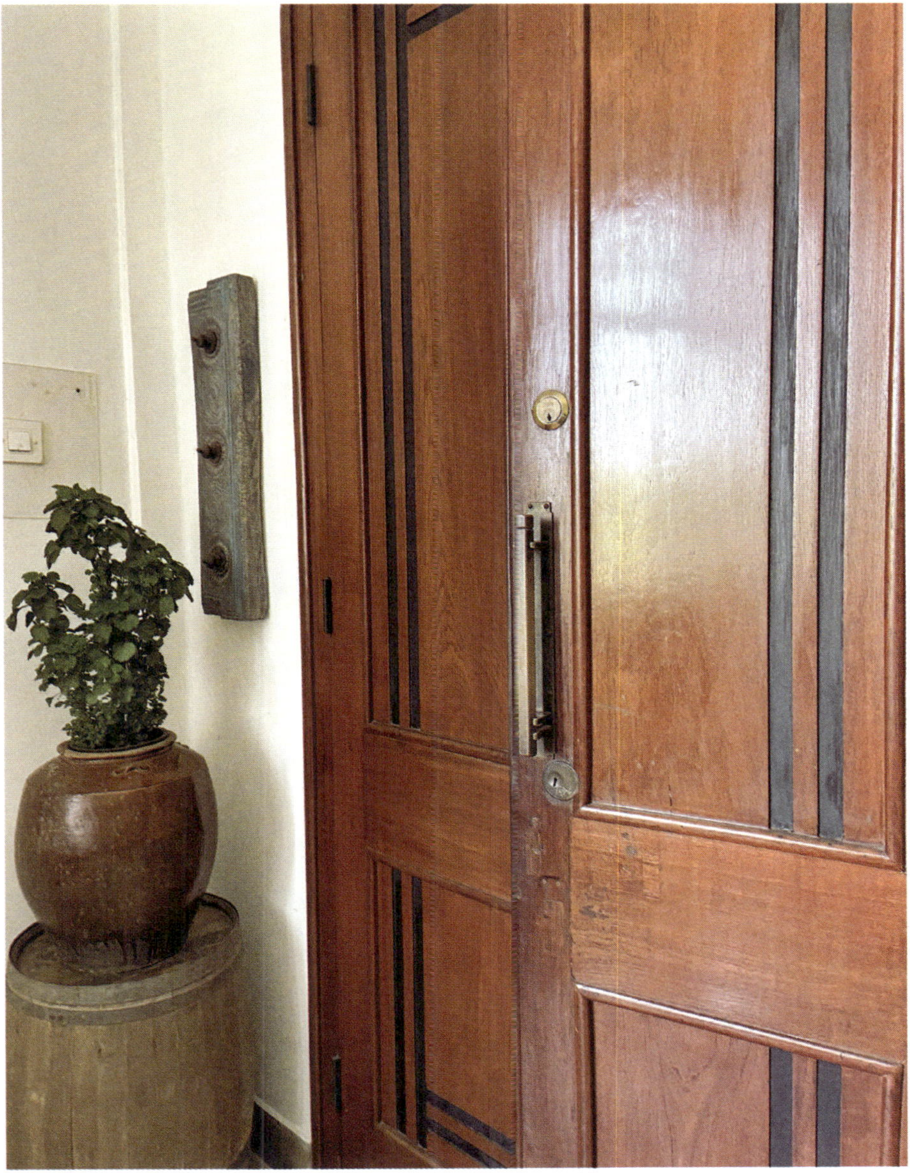

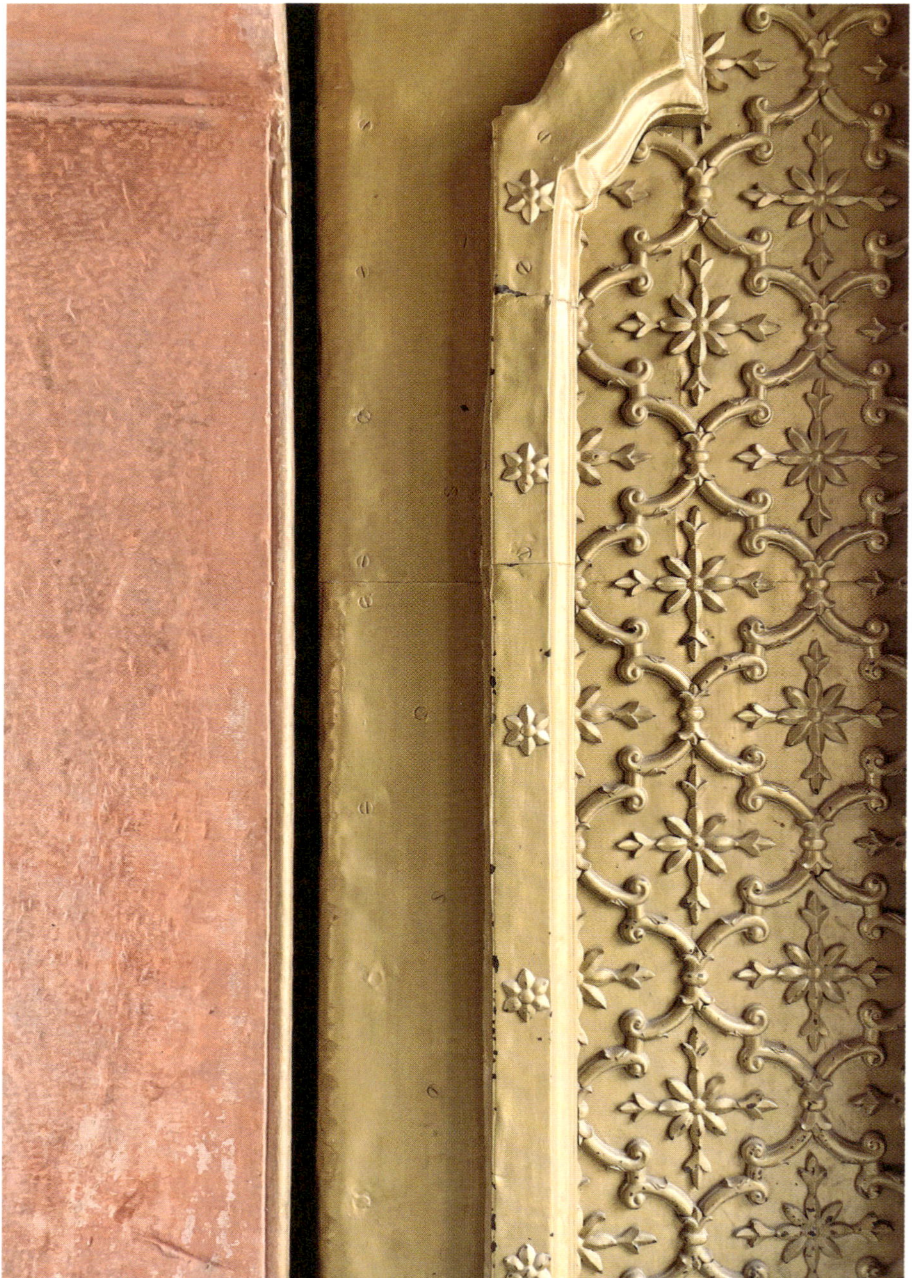

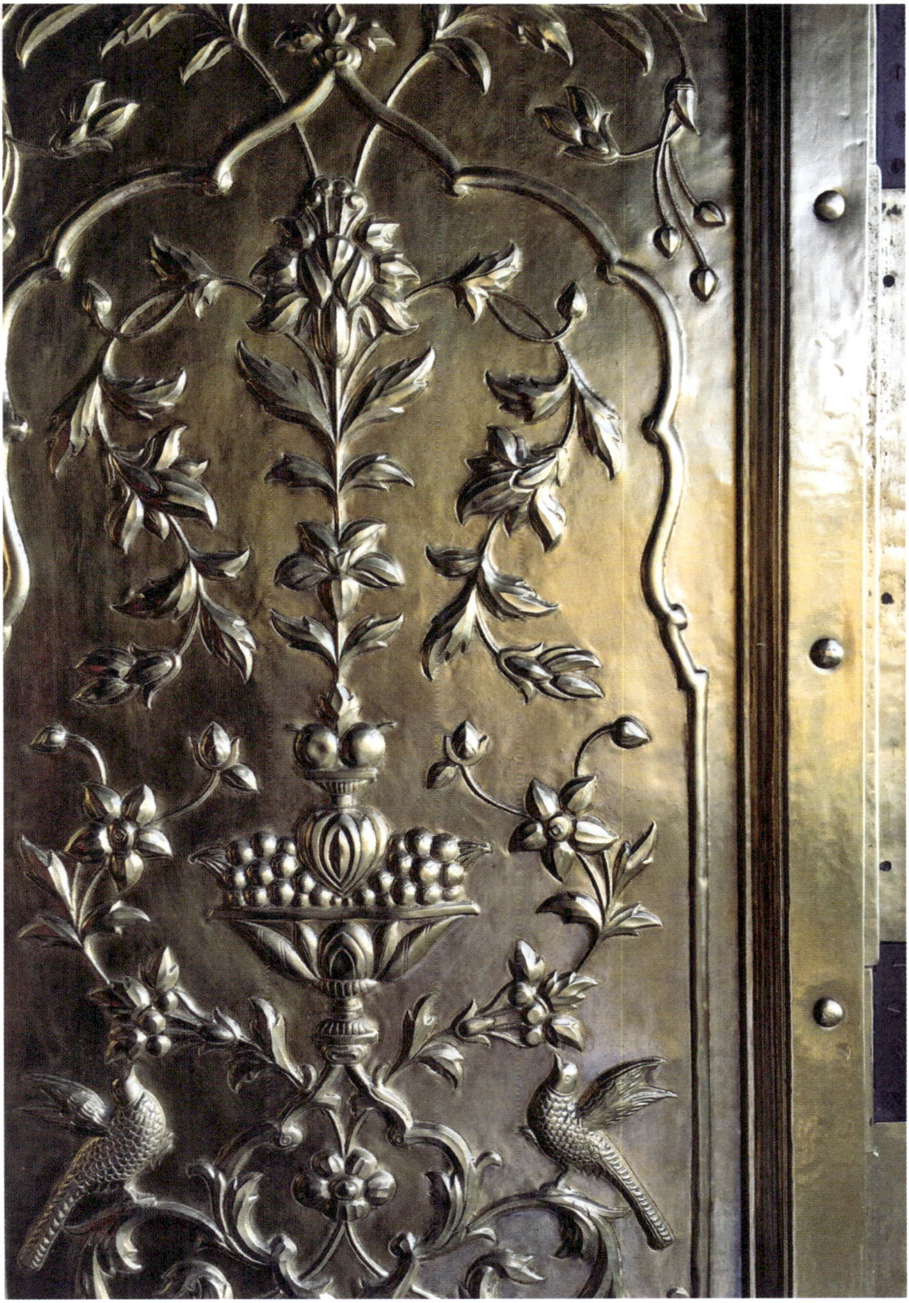

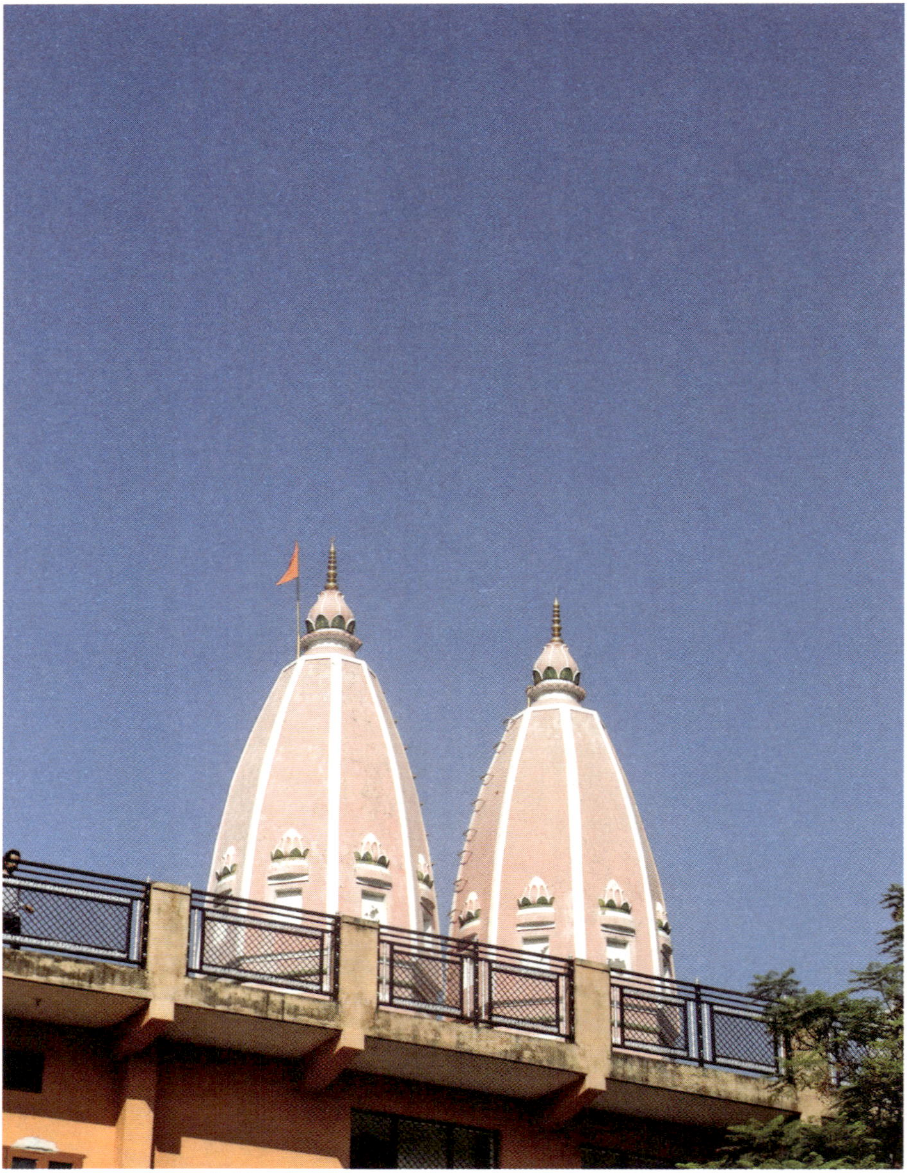

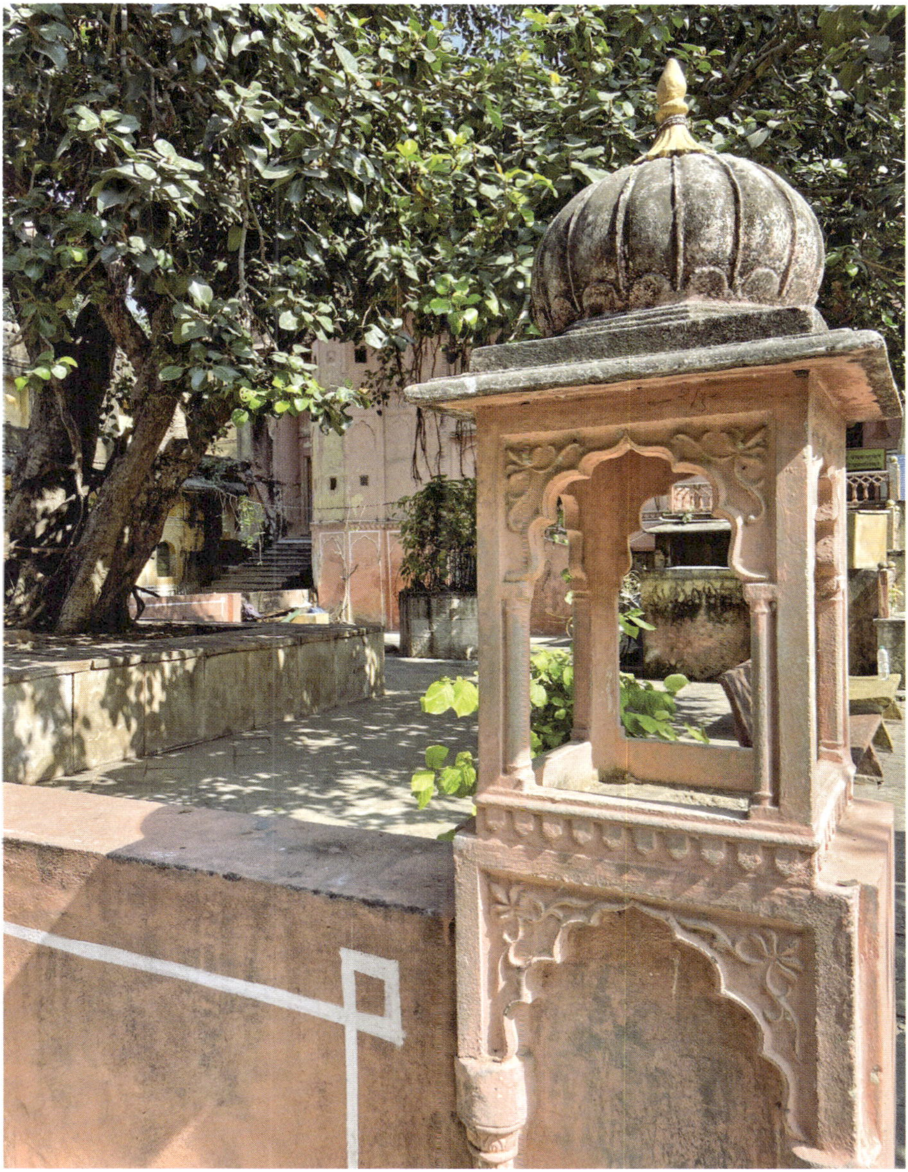

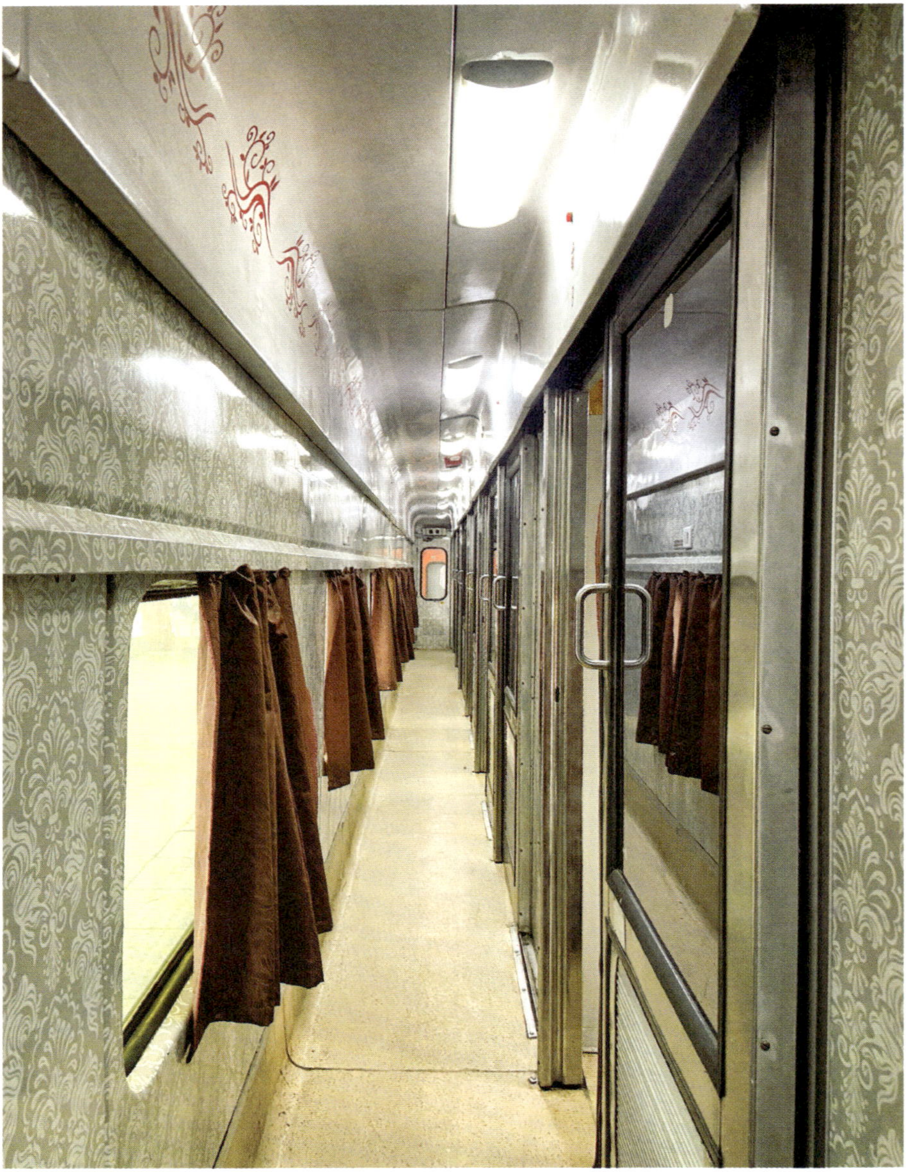

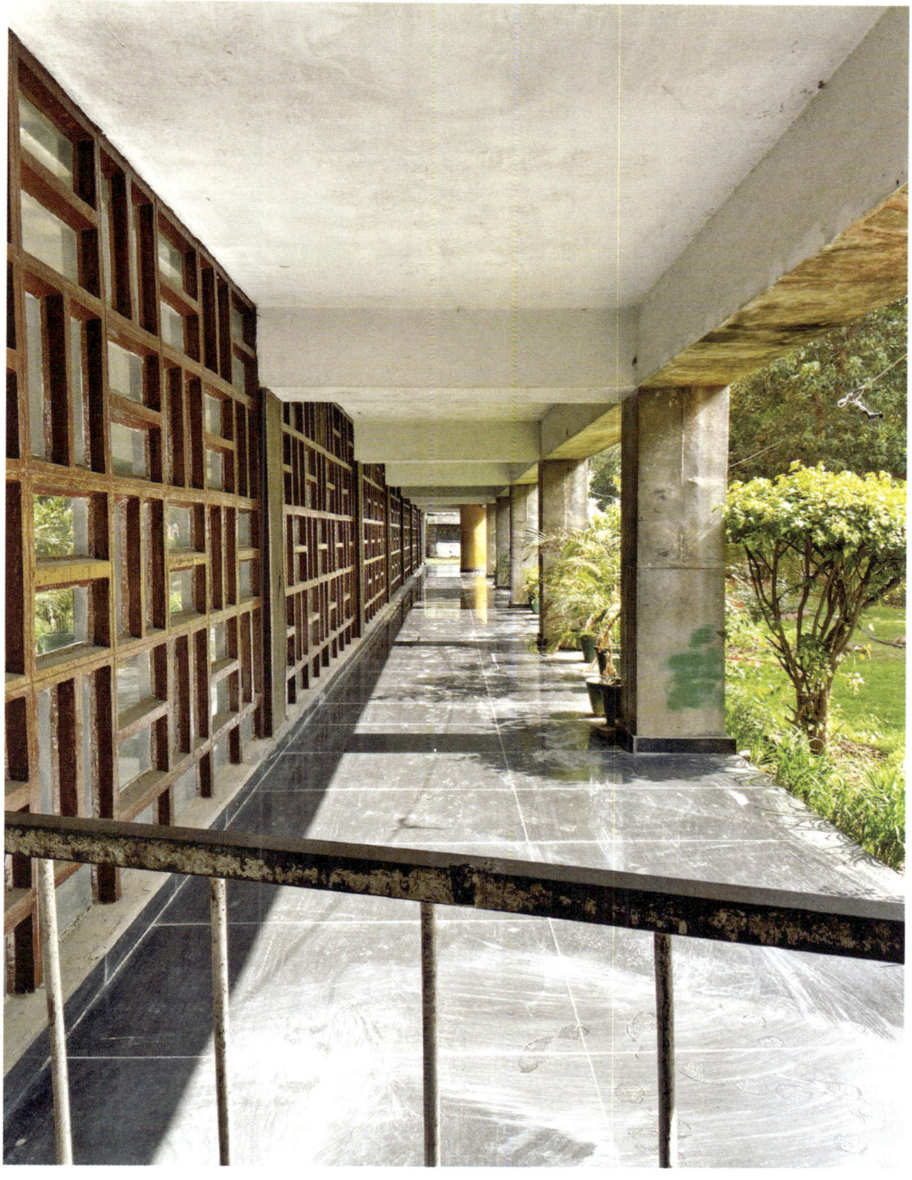

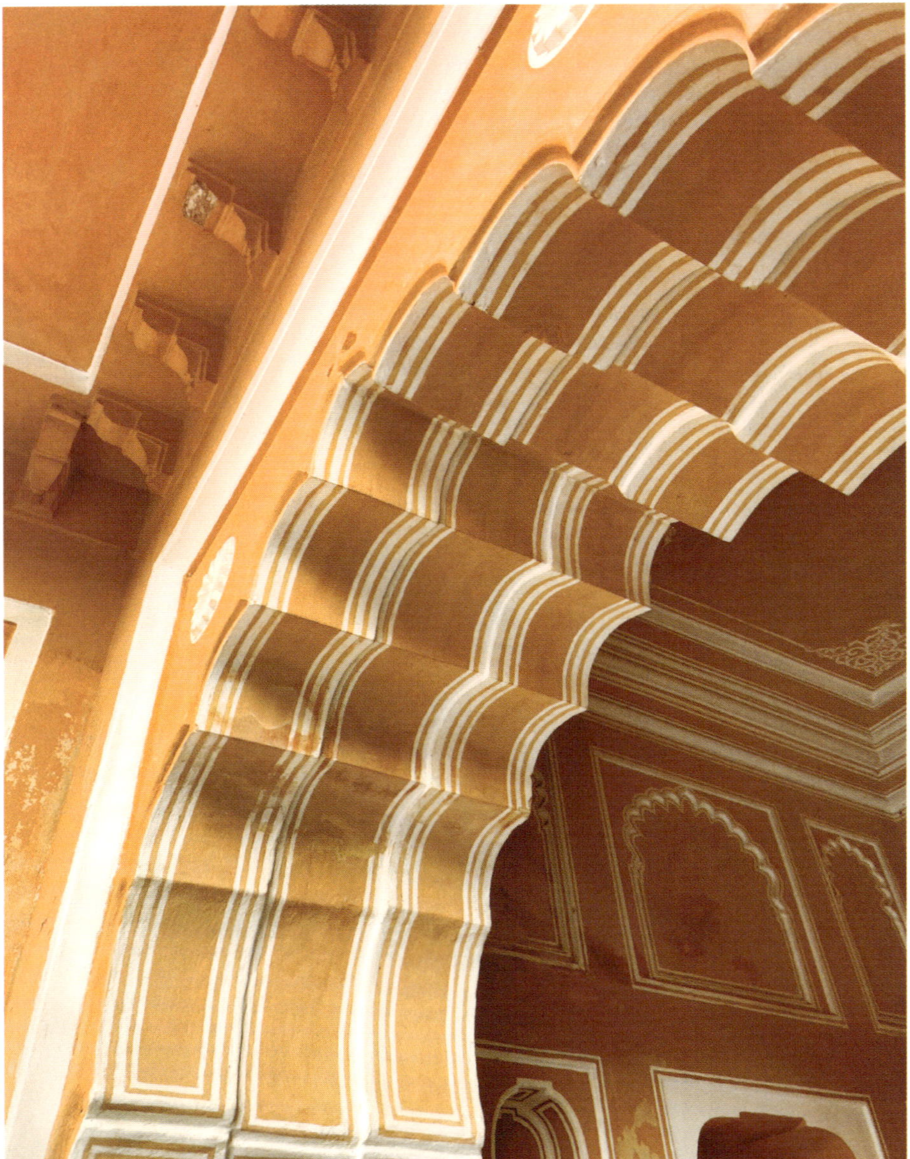

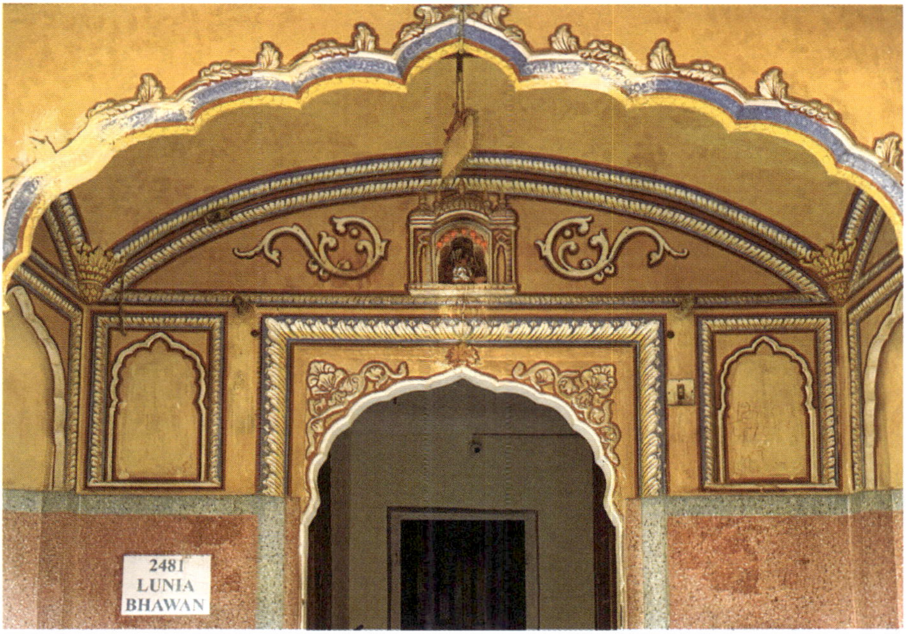
2481
LUNIA
BHAWAN

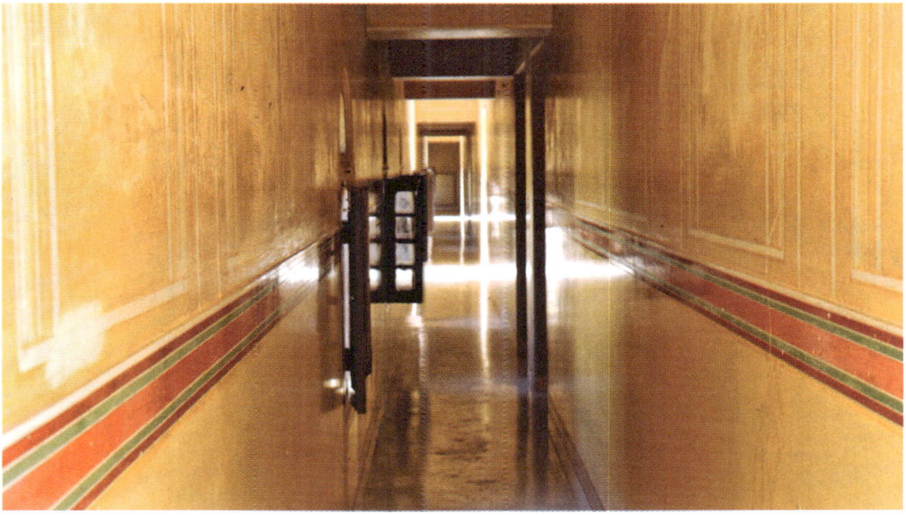

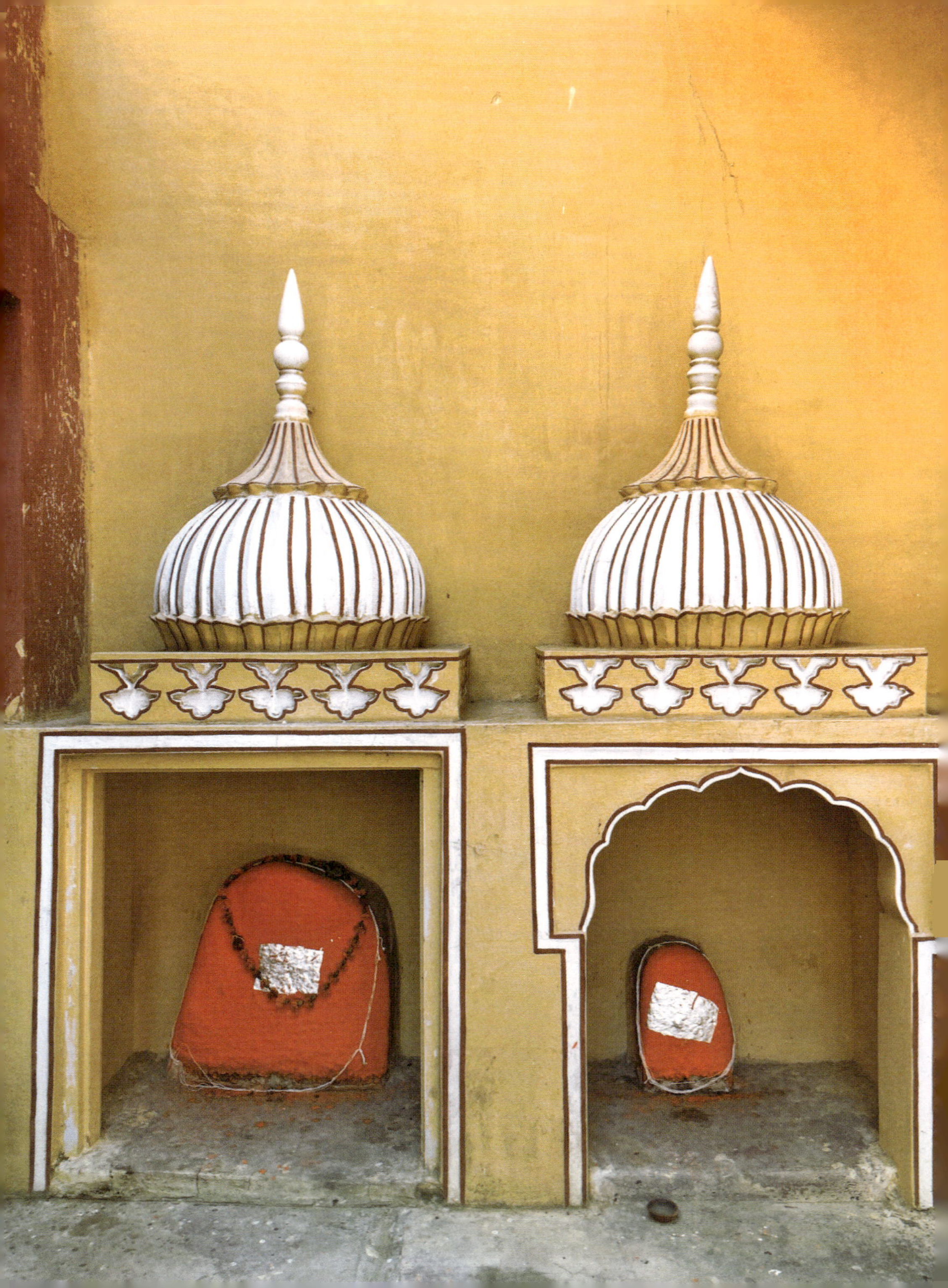

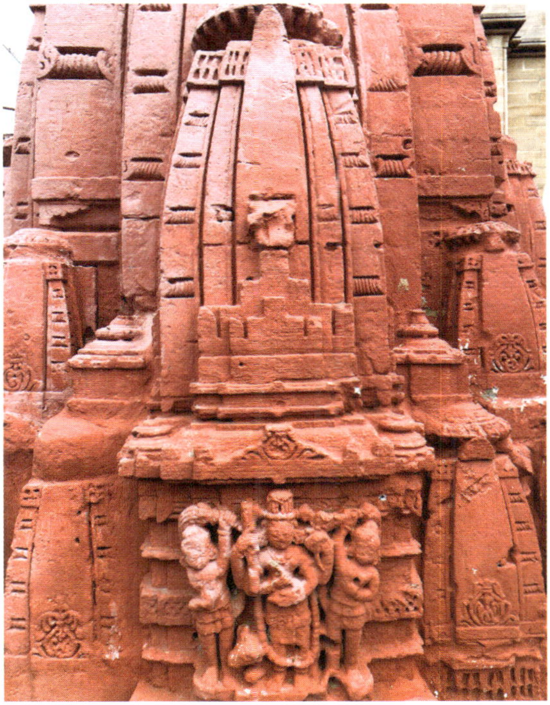

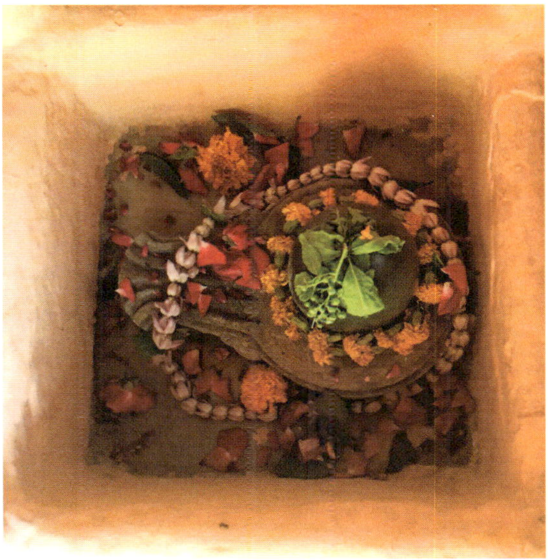

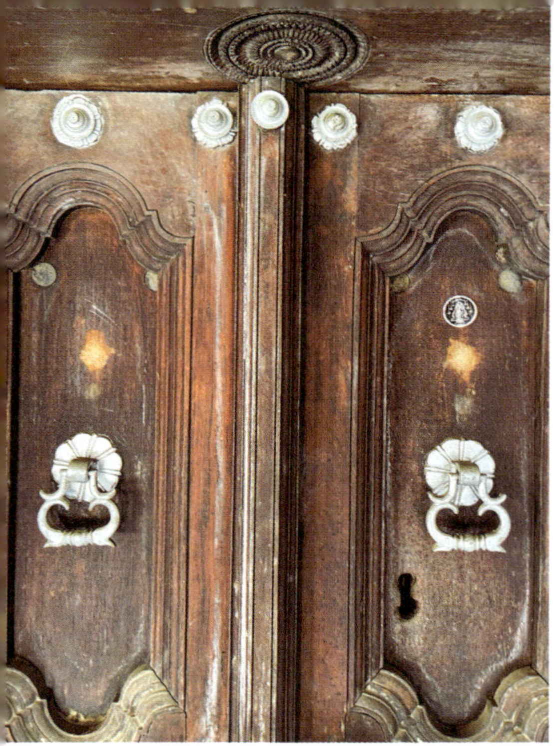
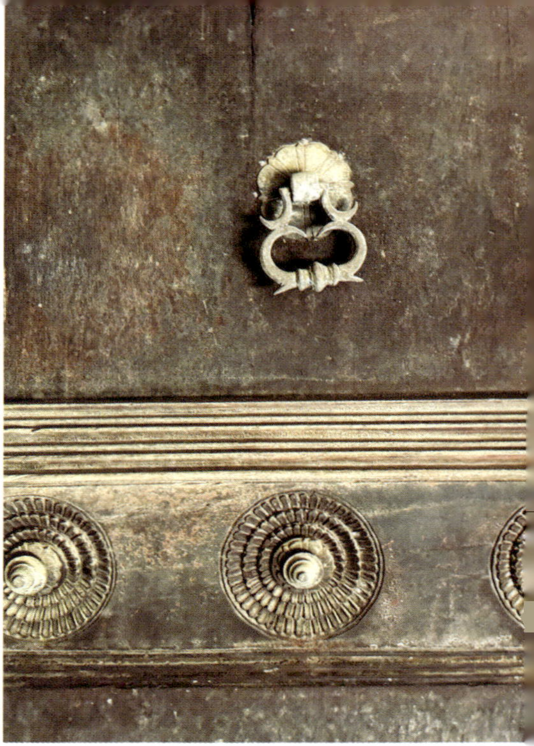
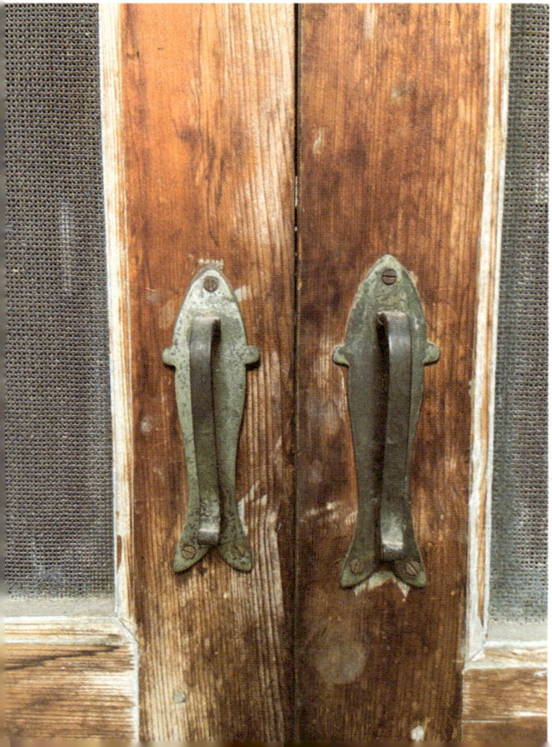
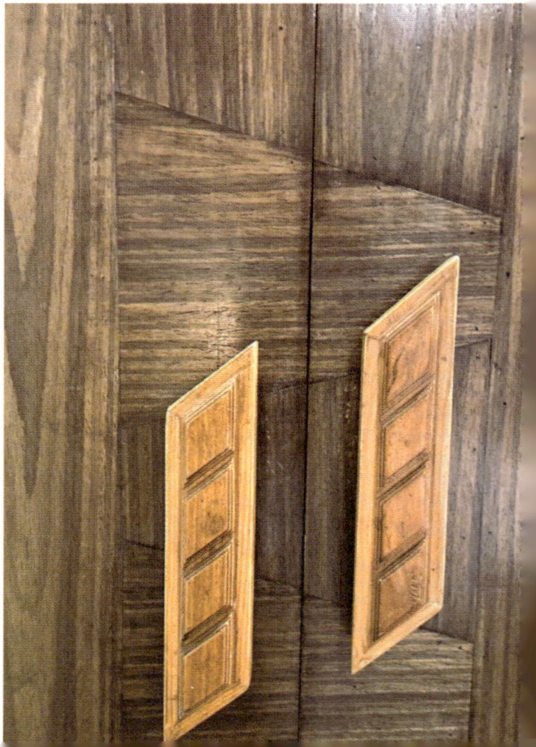

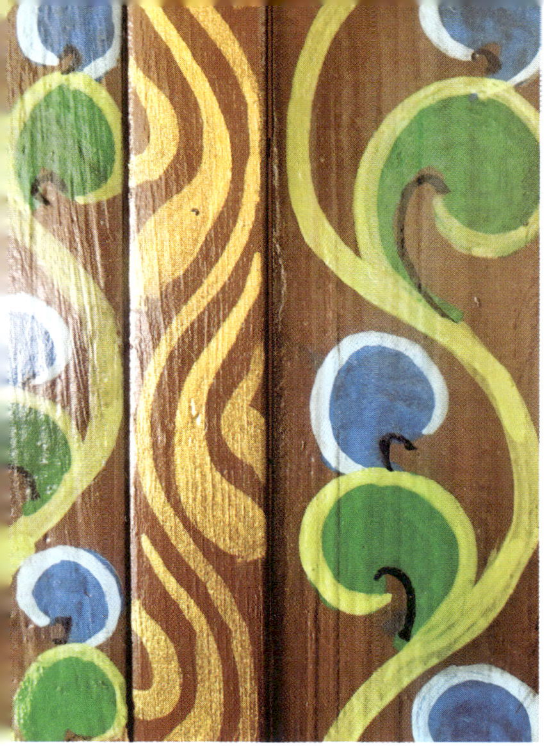
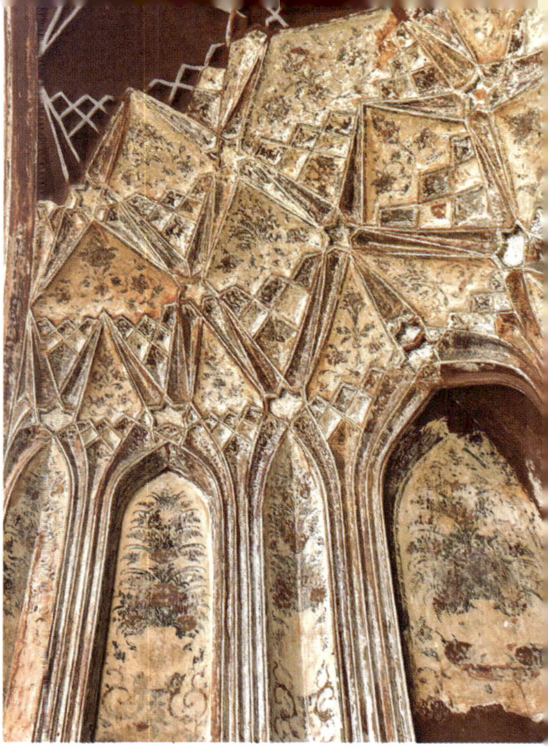
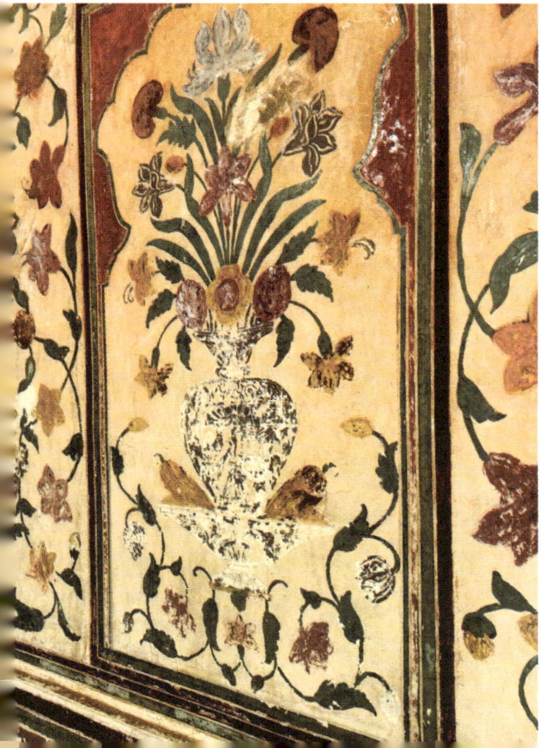
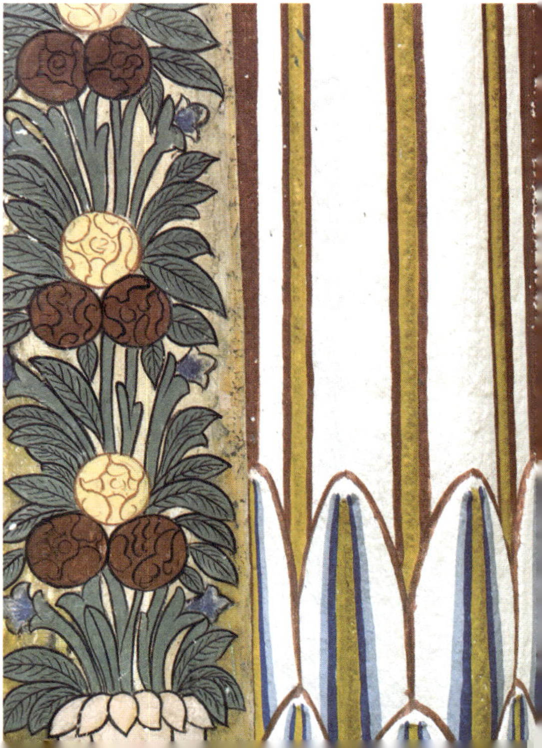

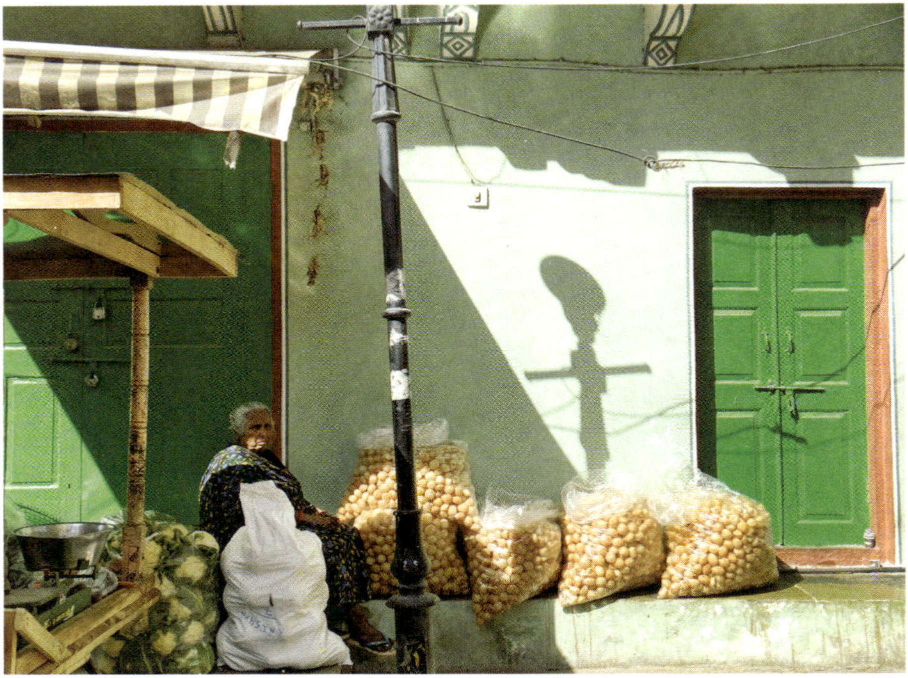

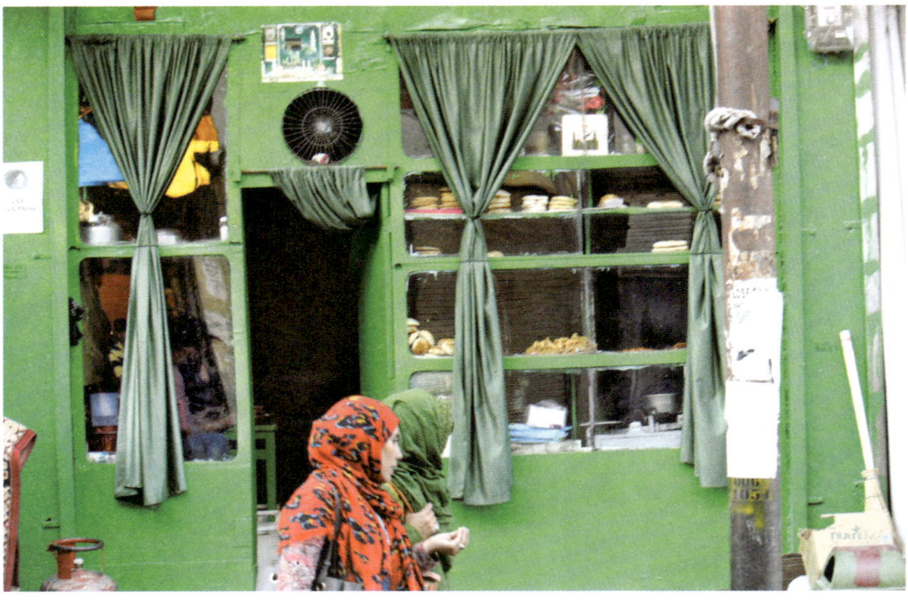

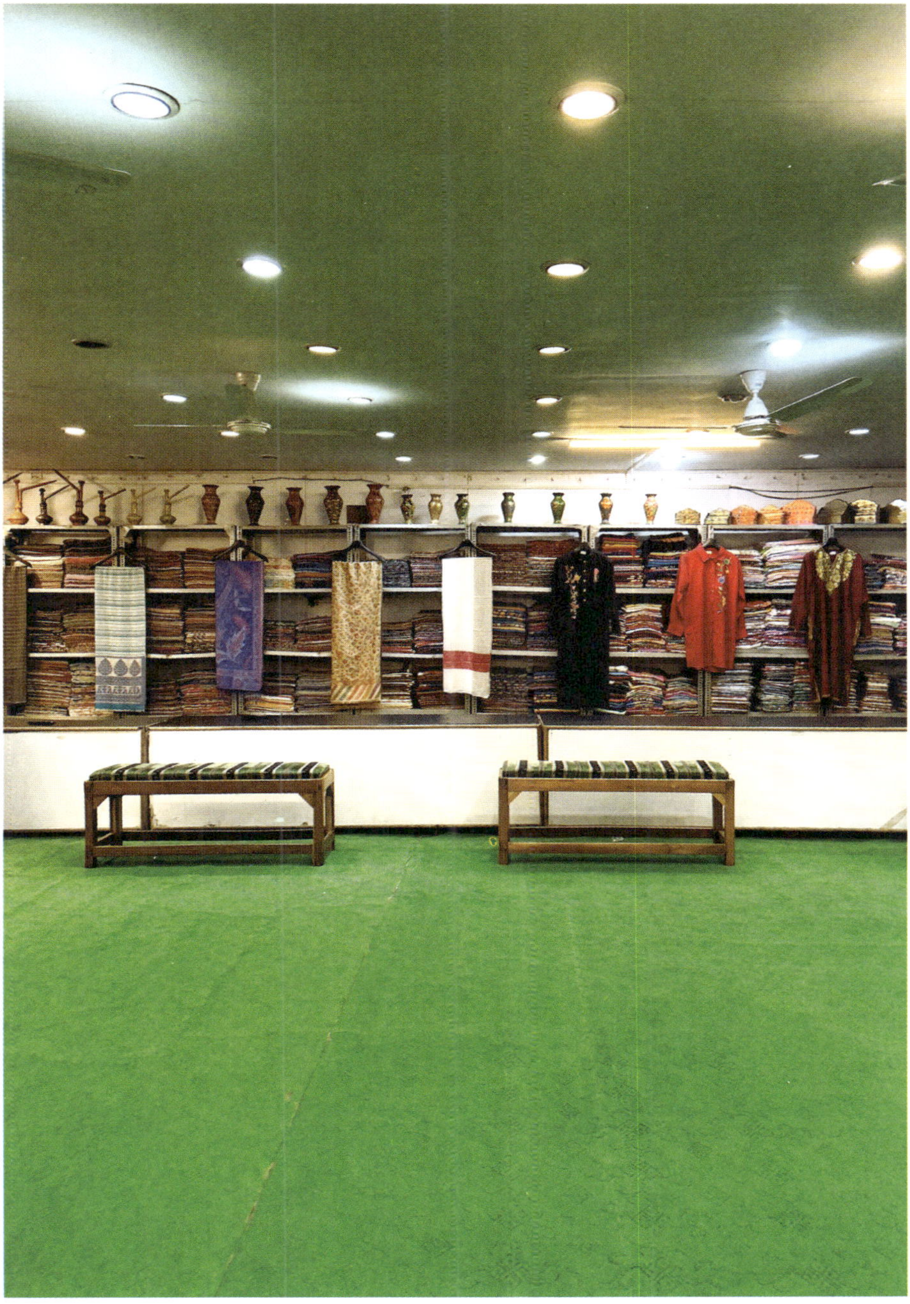

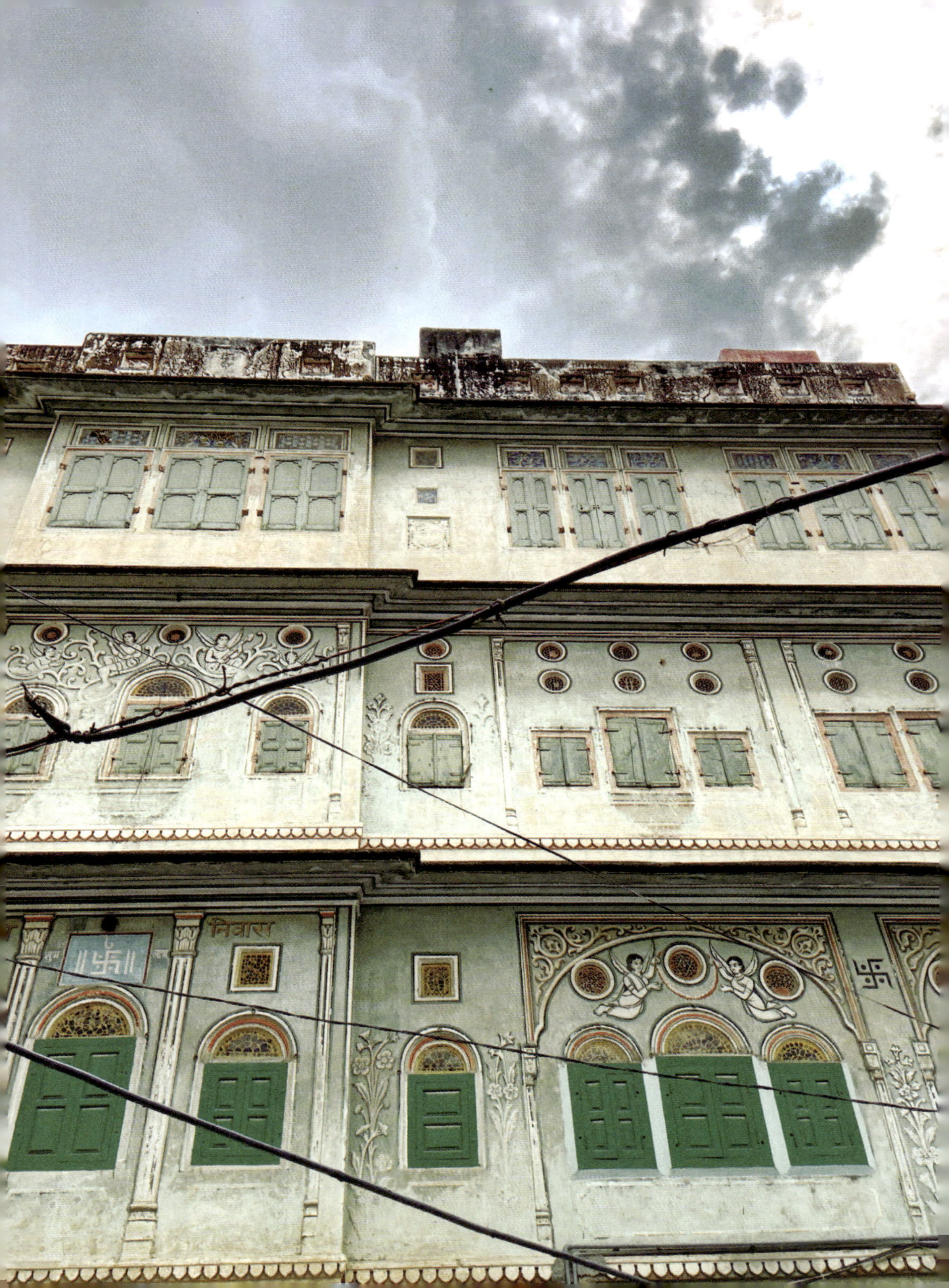
निवास

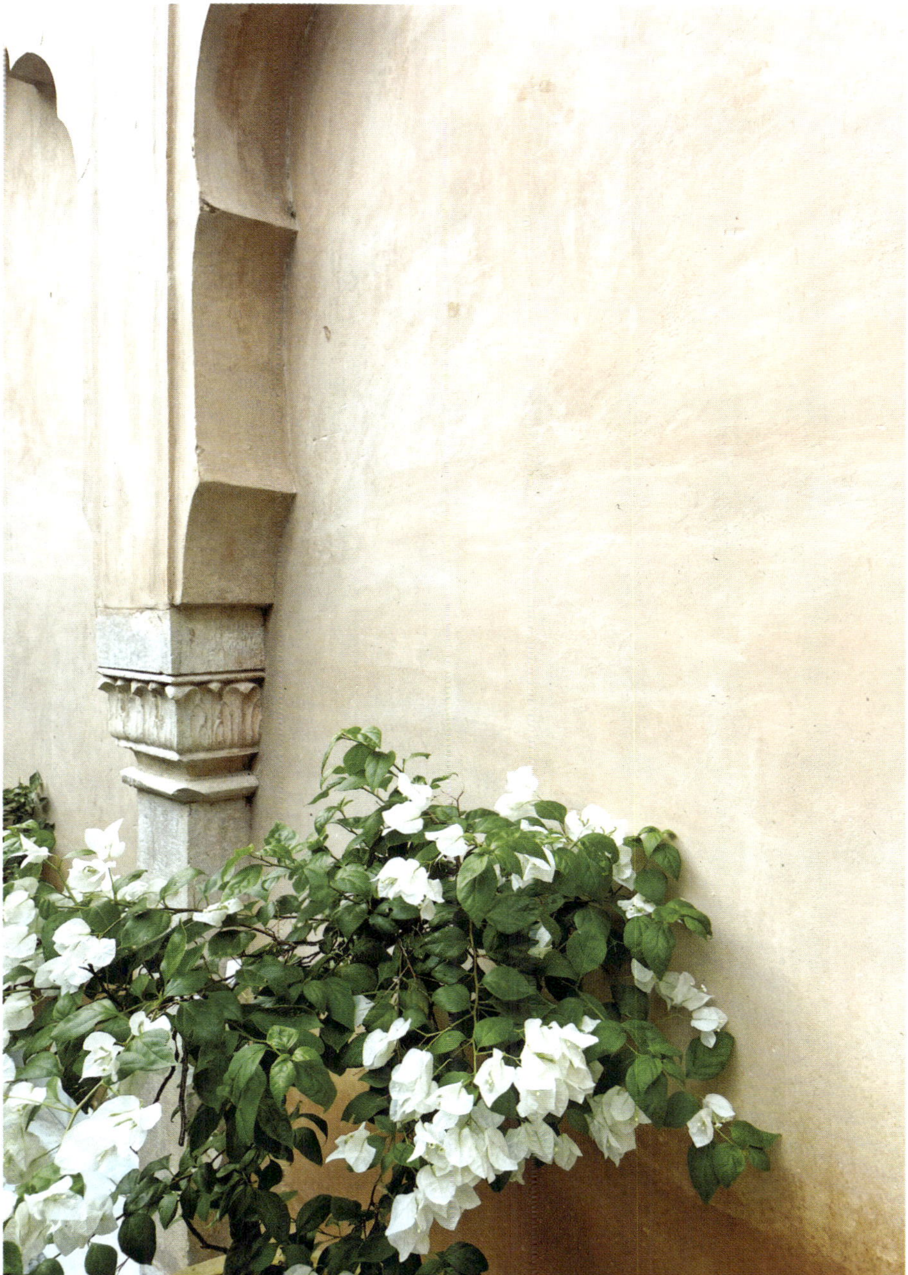

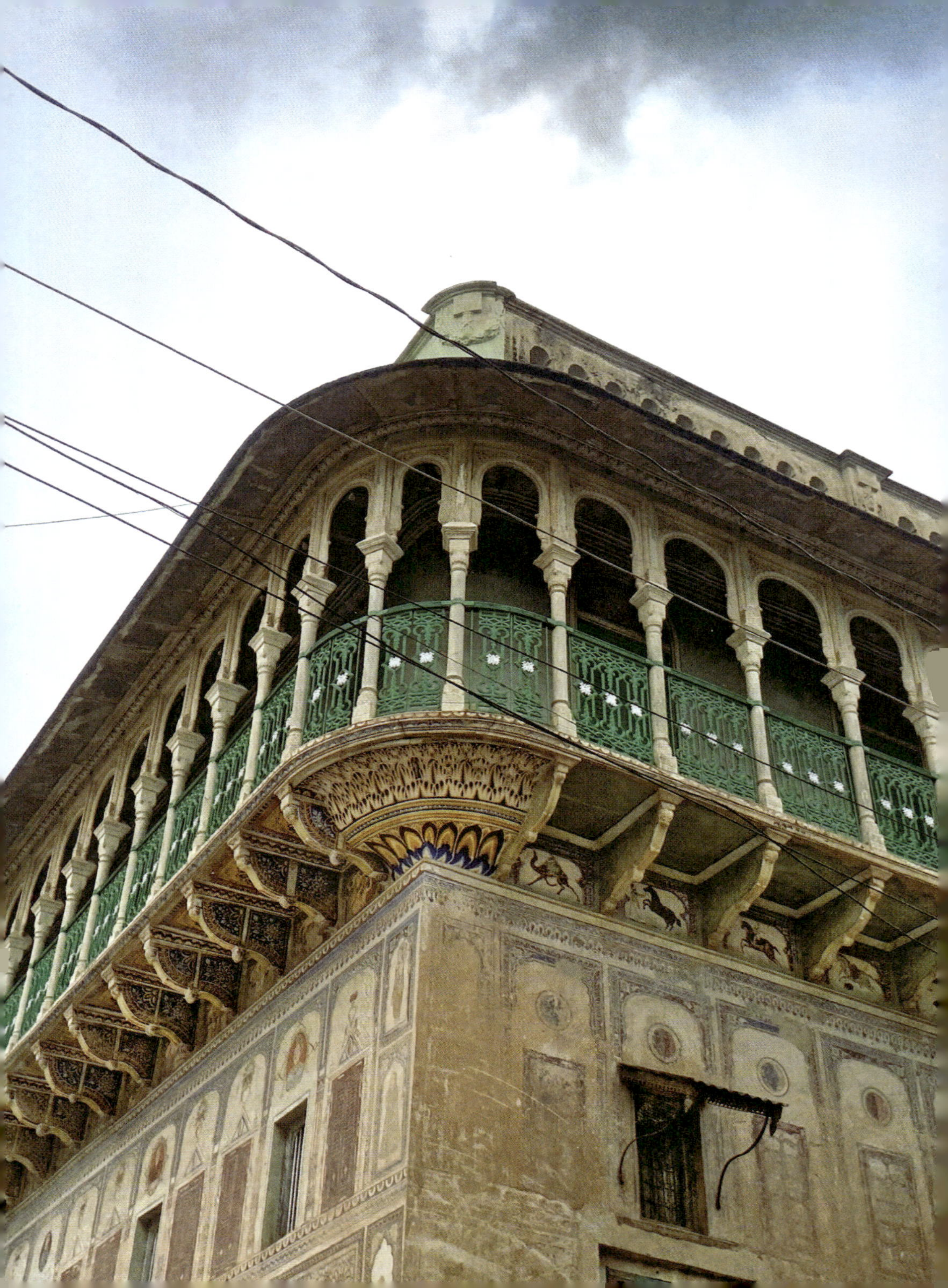

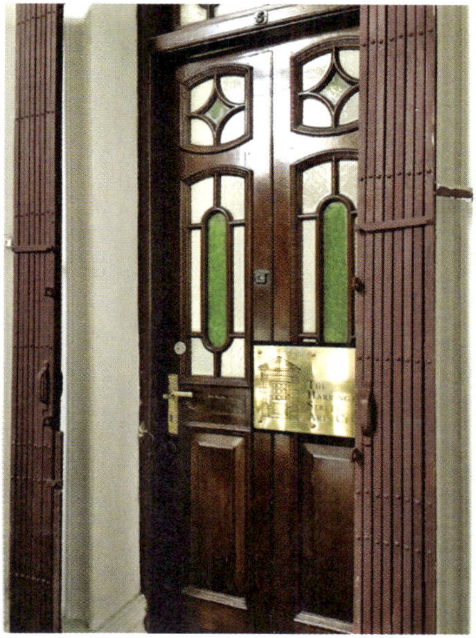

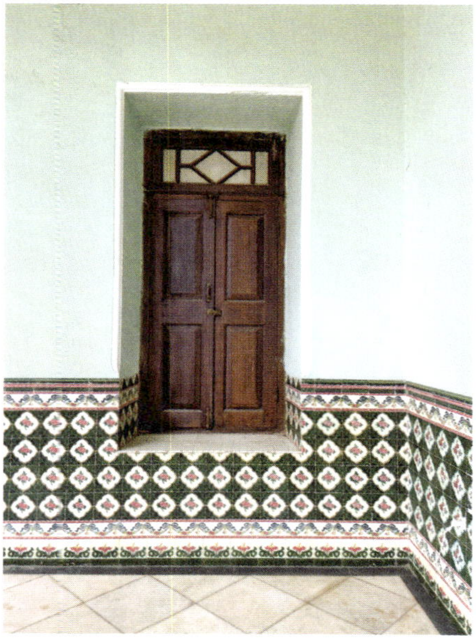

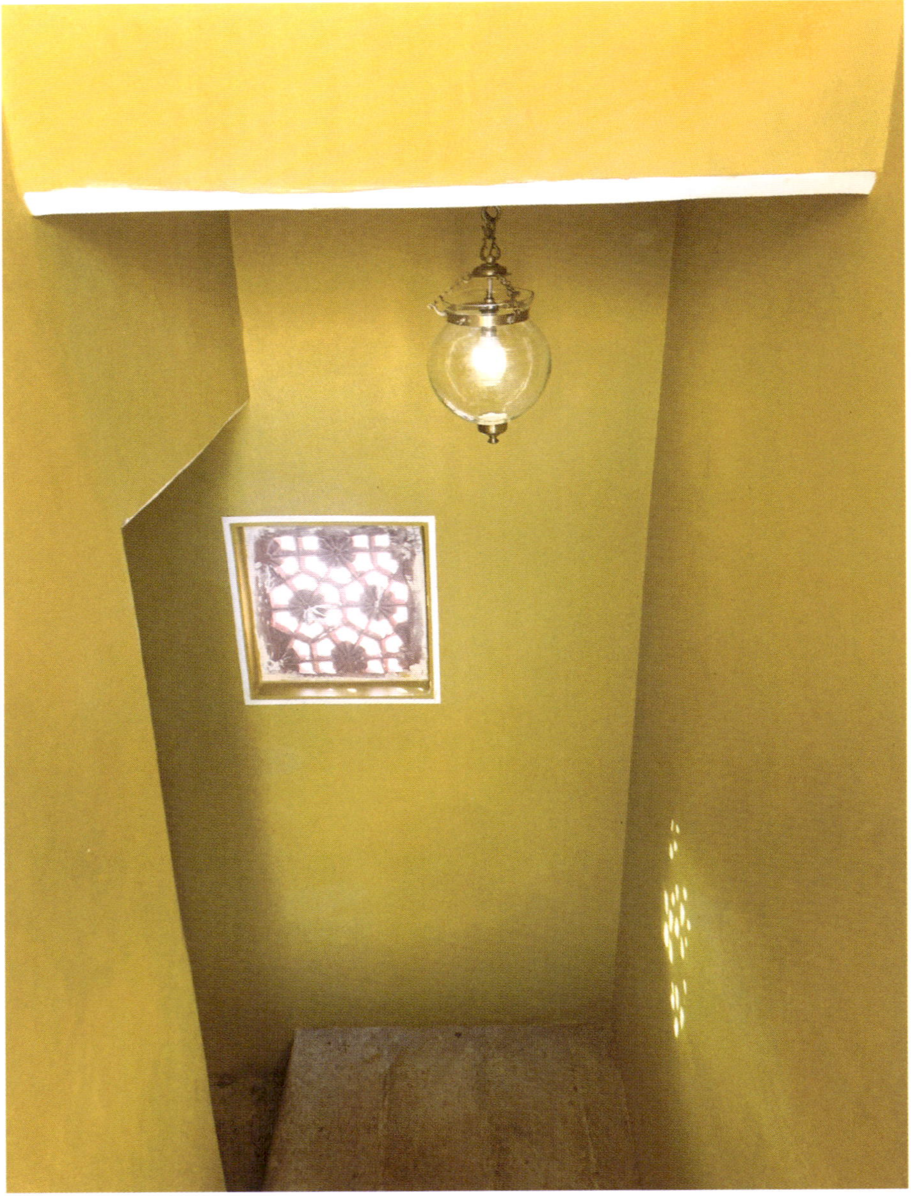

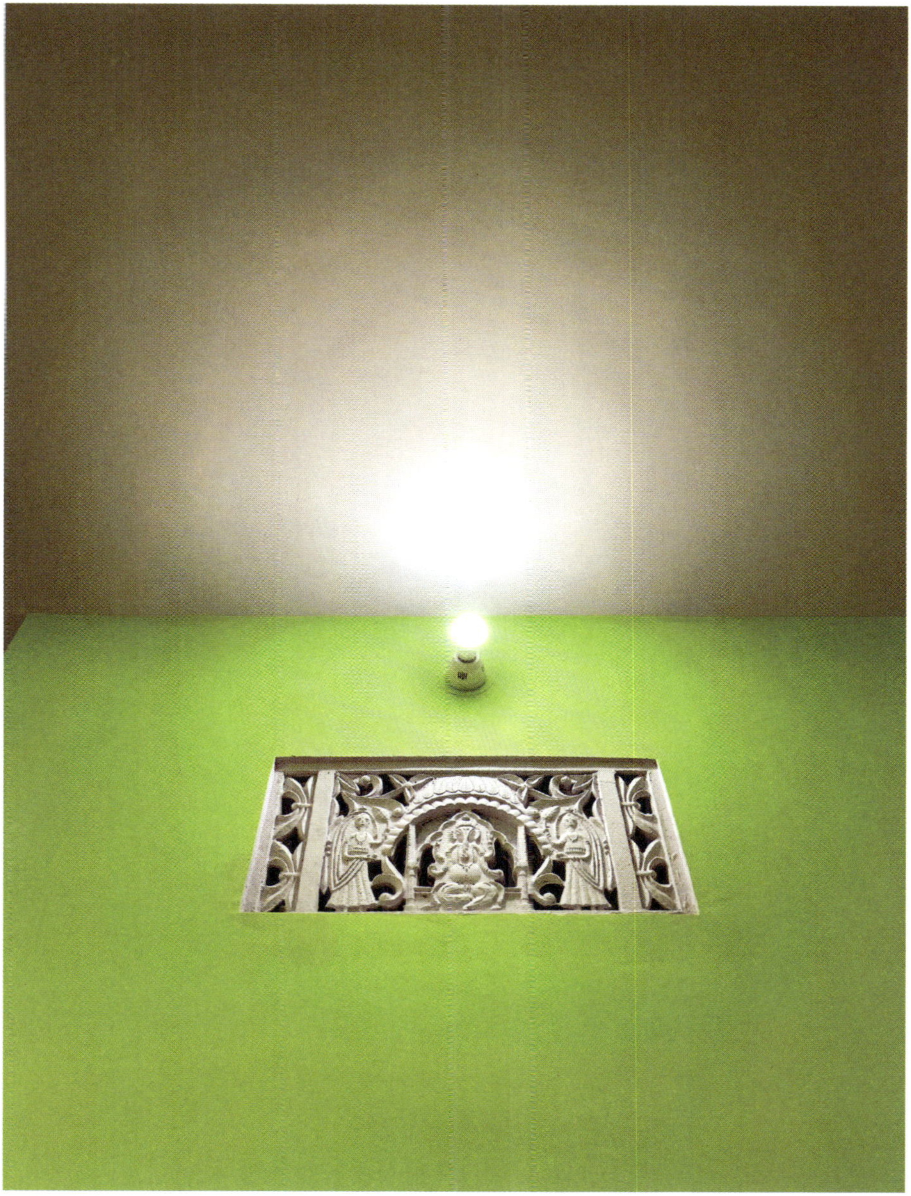

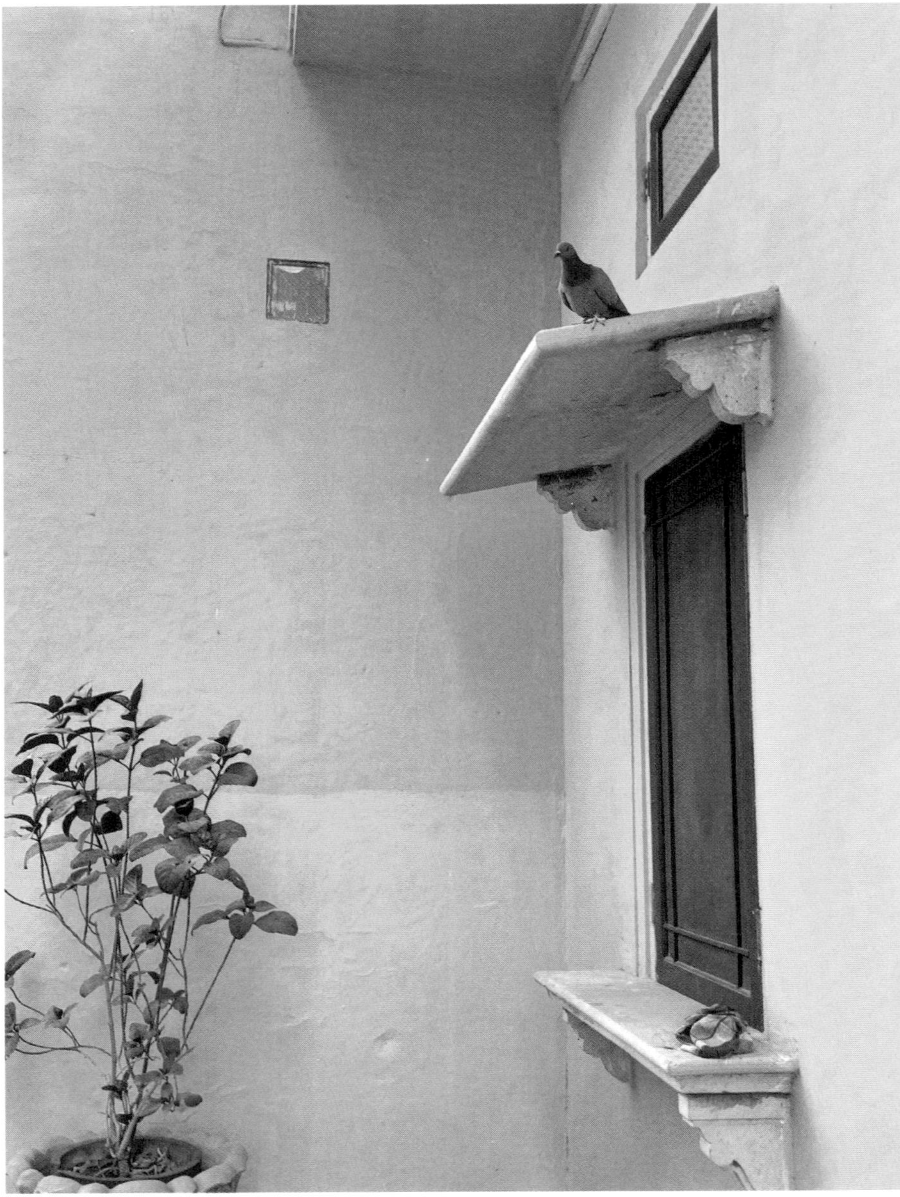

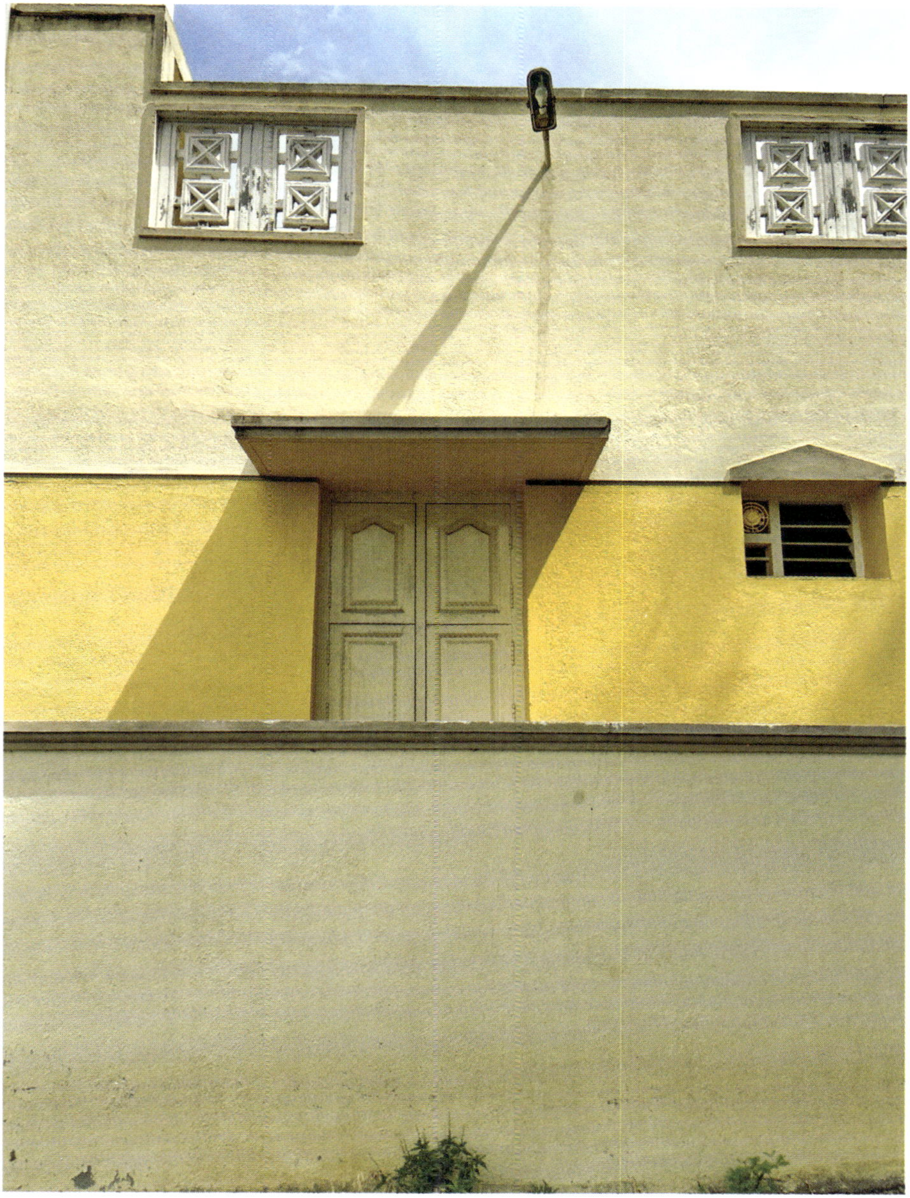

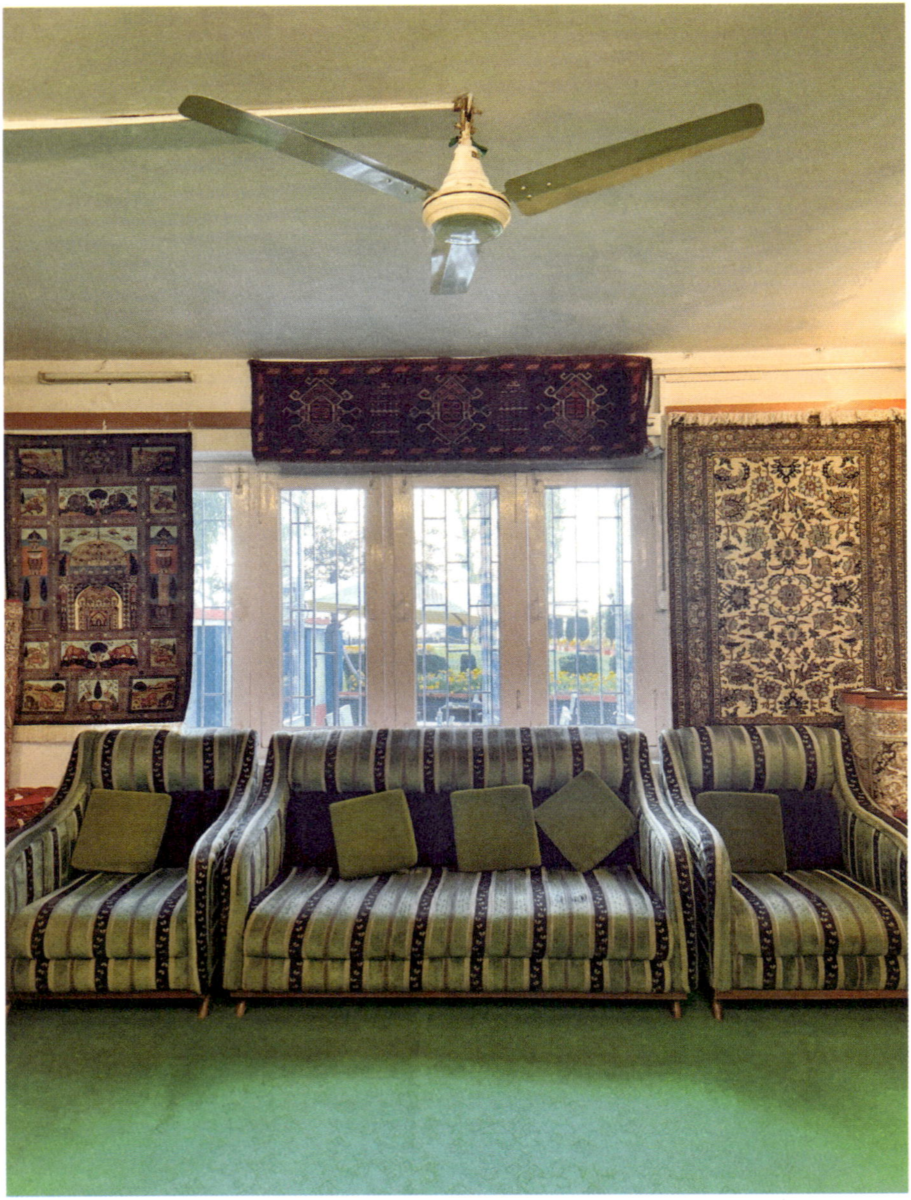

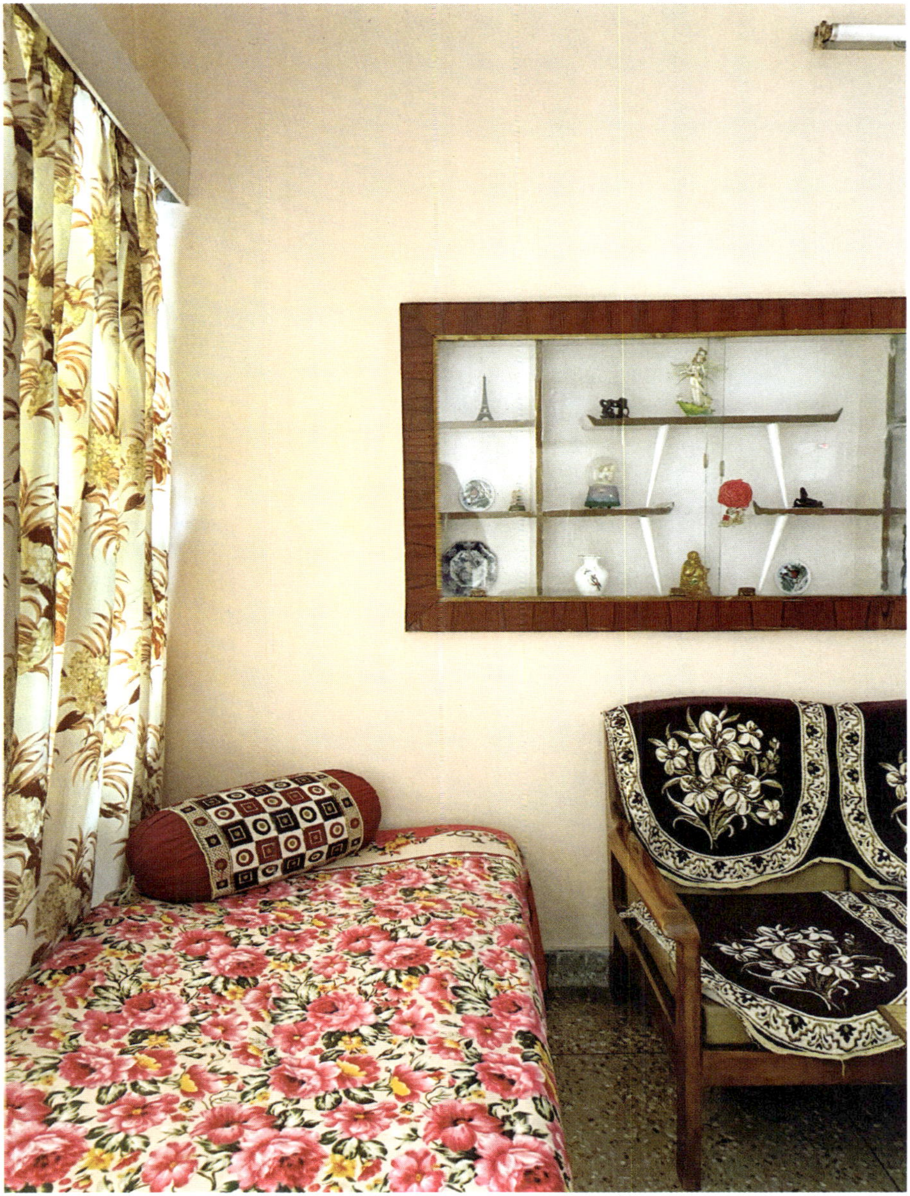

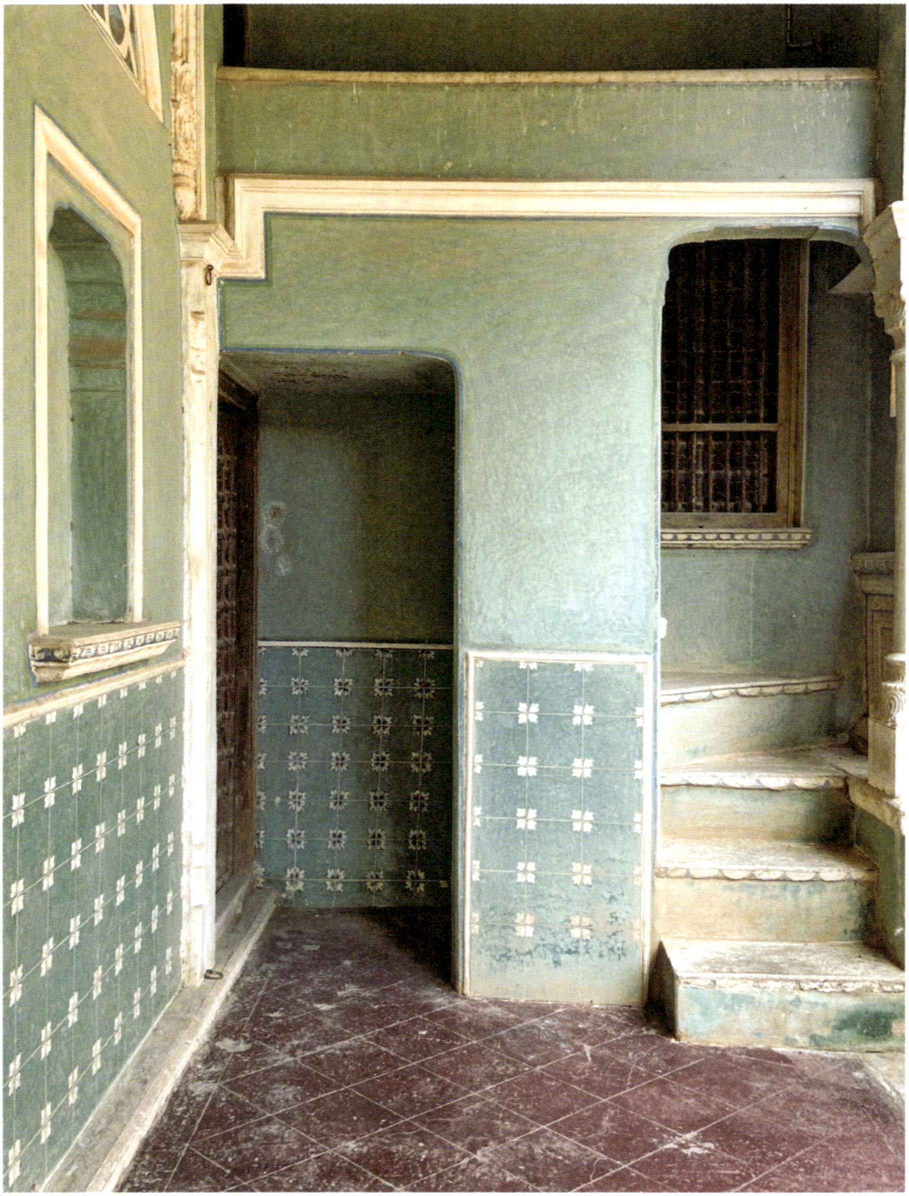

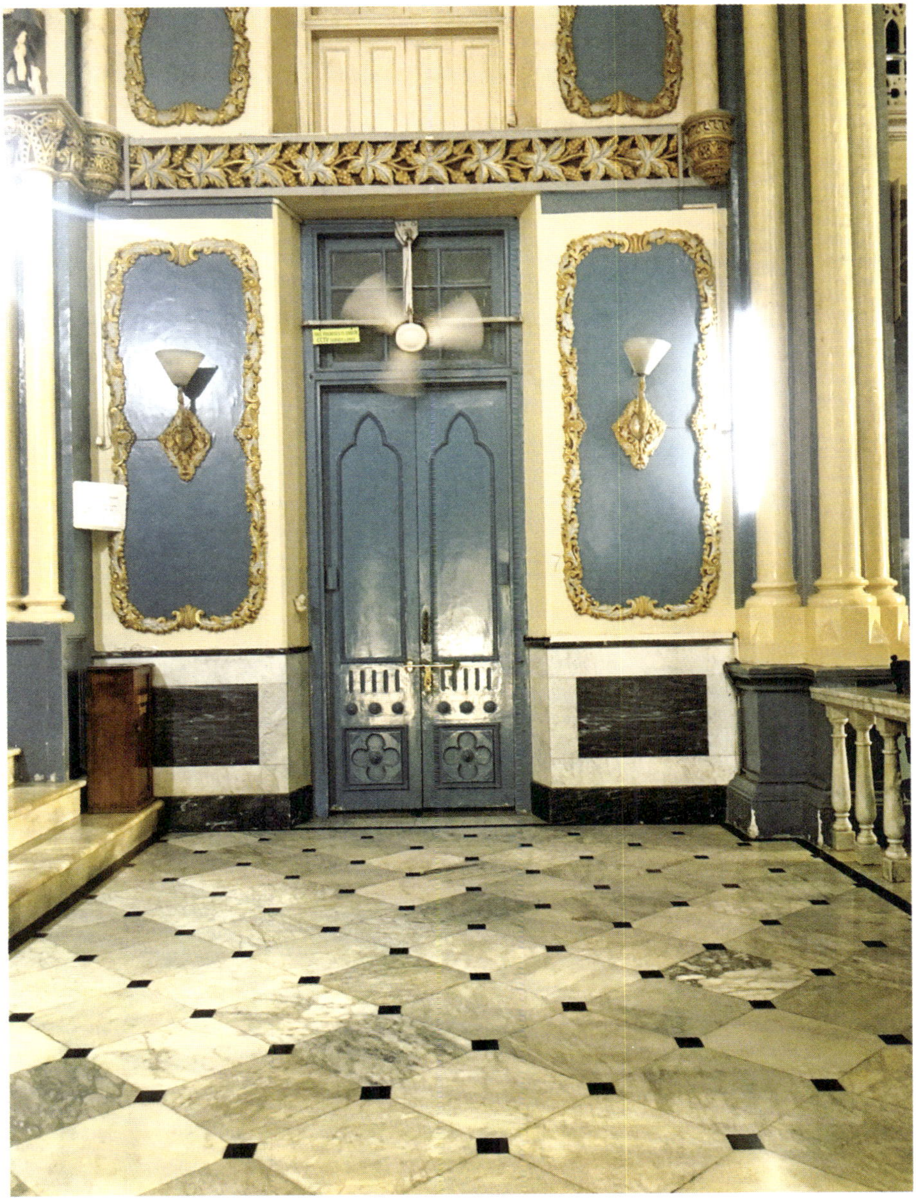

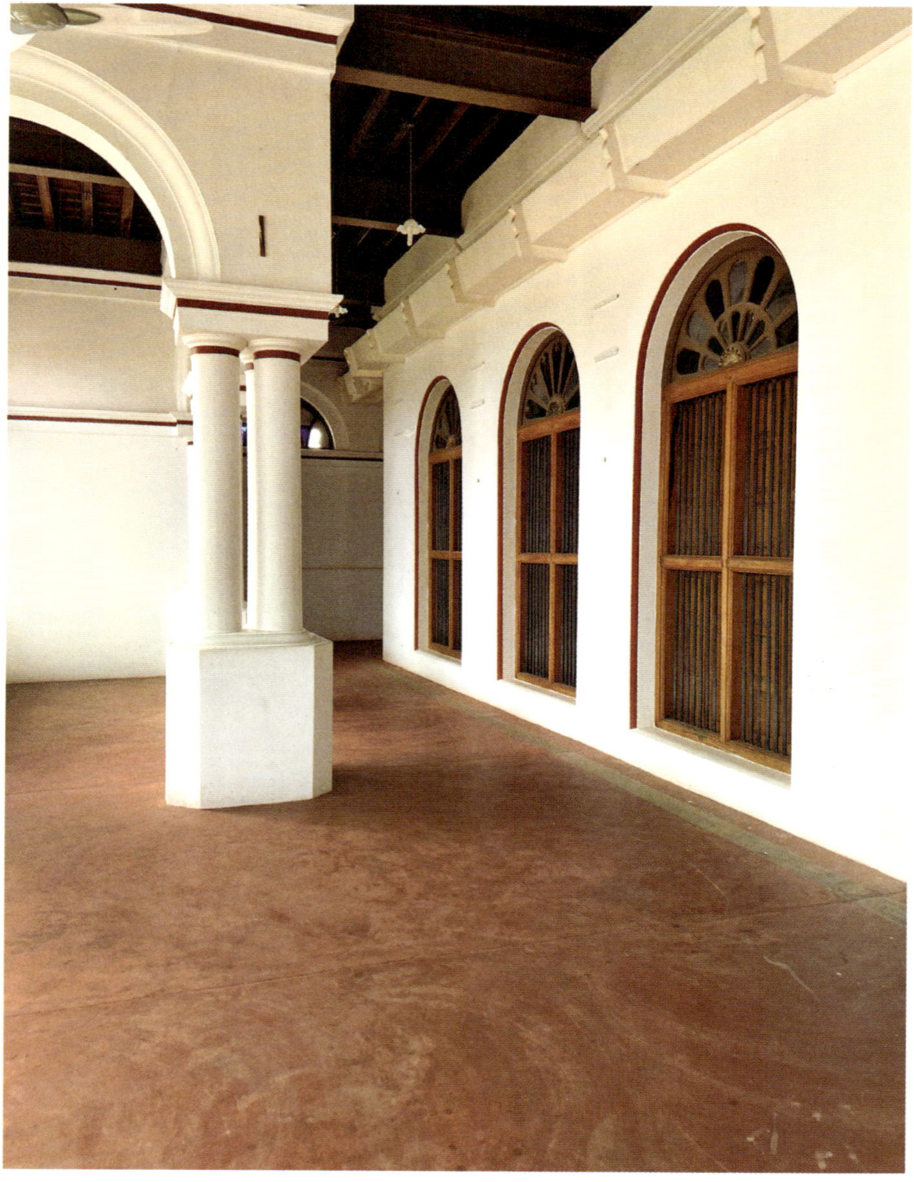

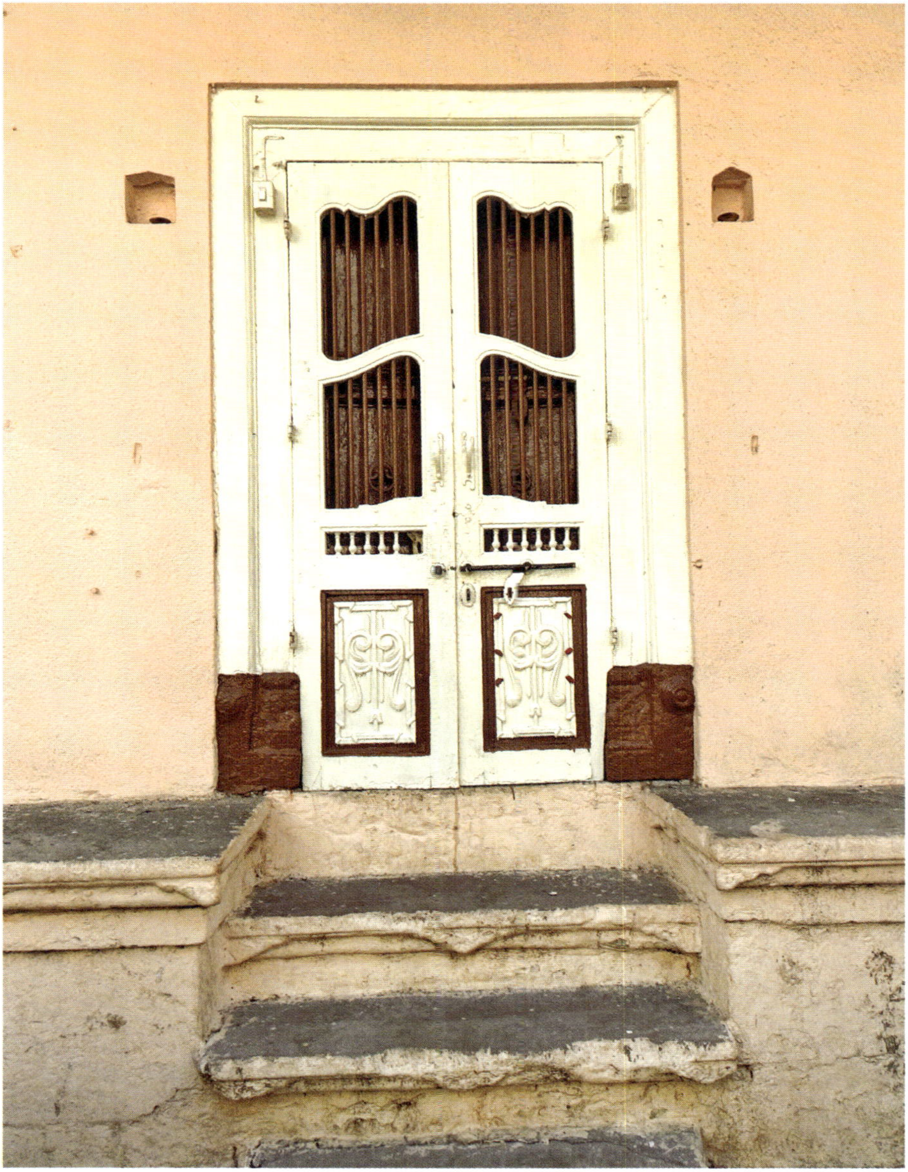

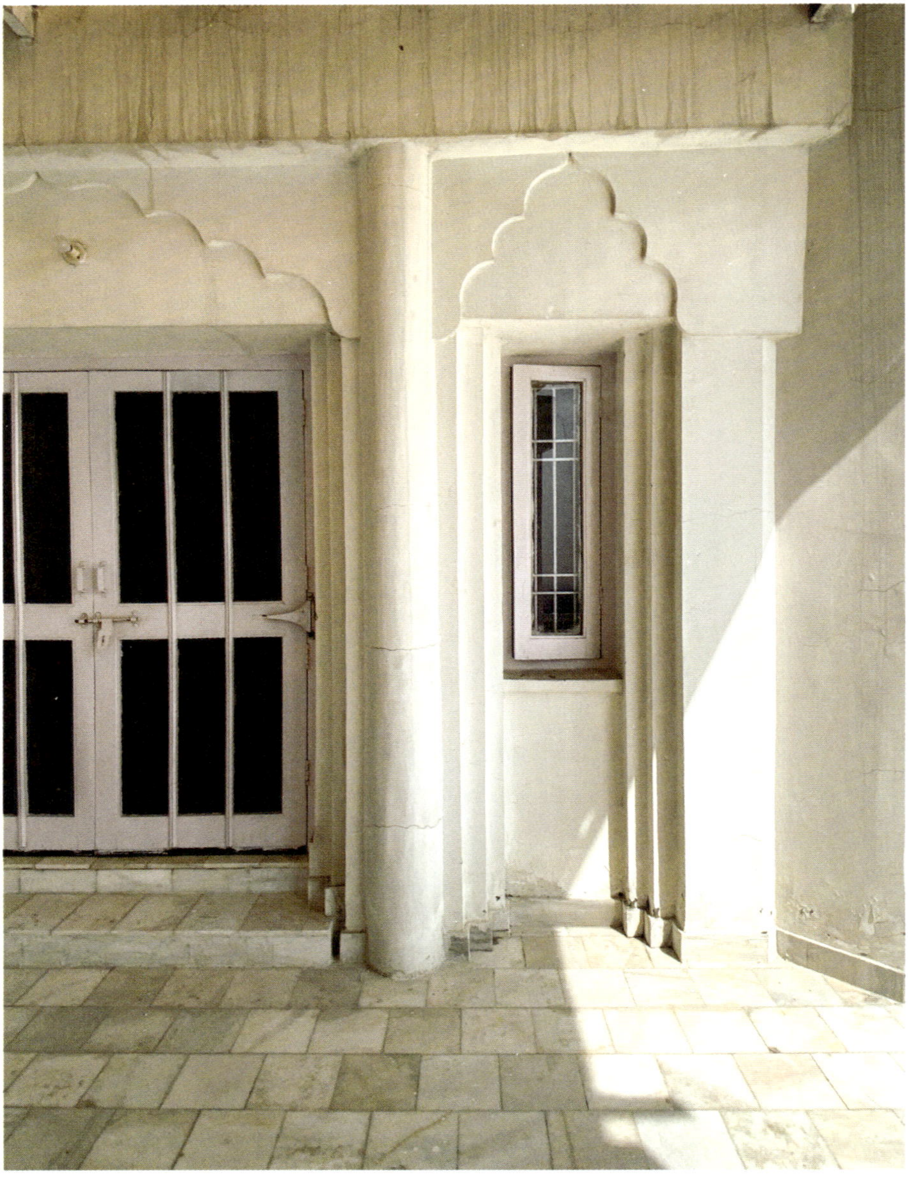

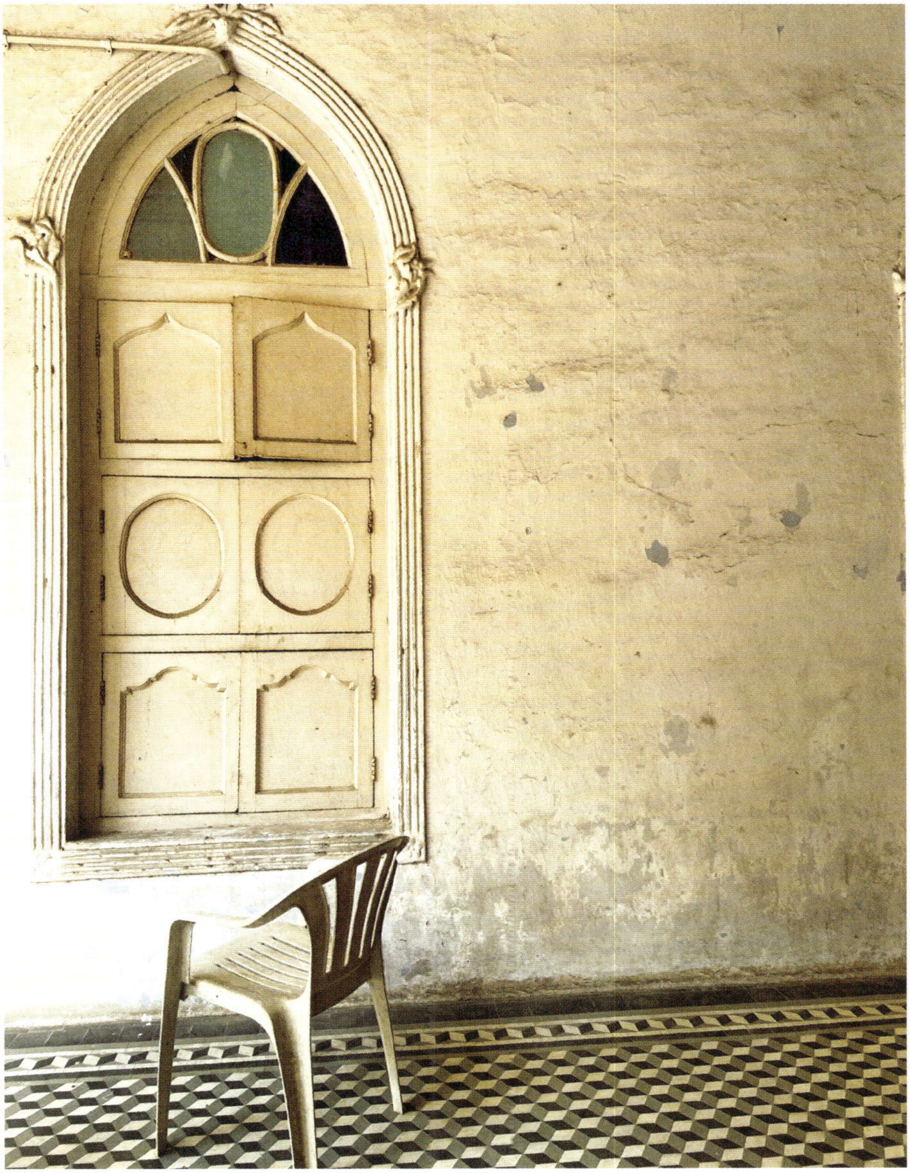

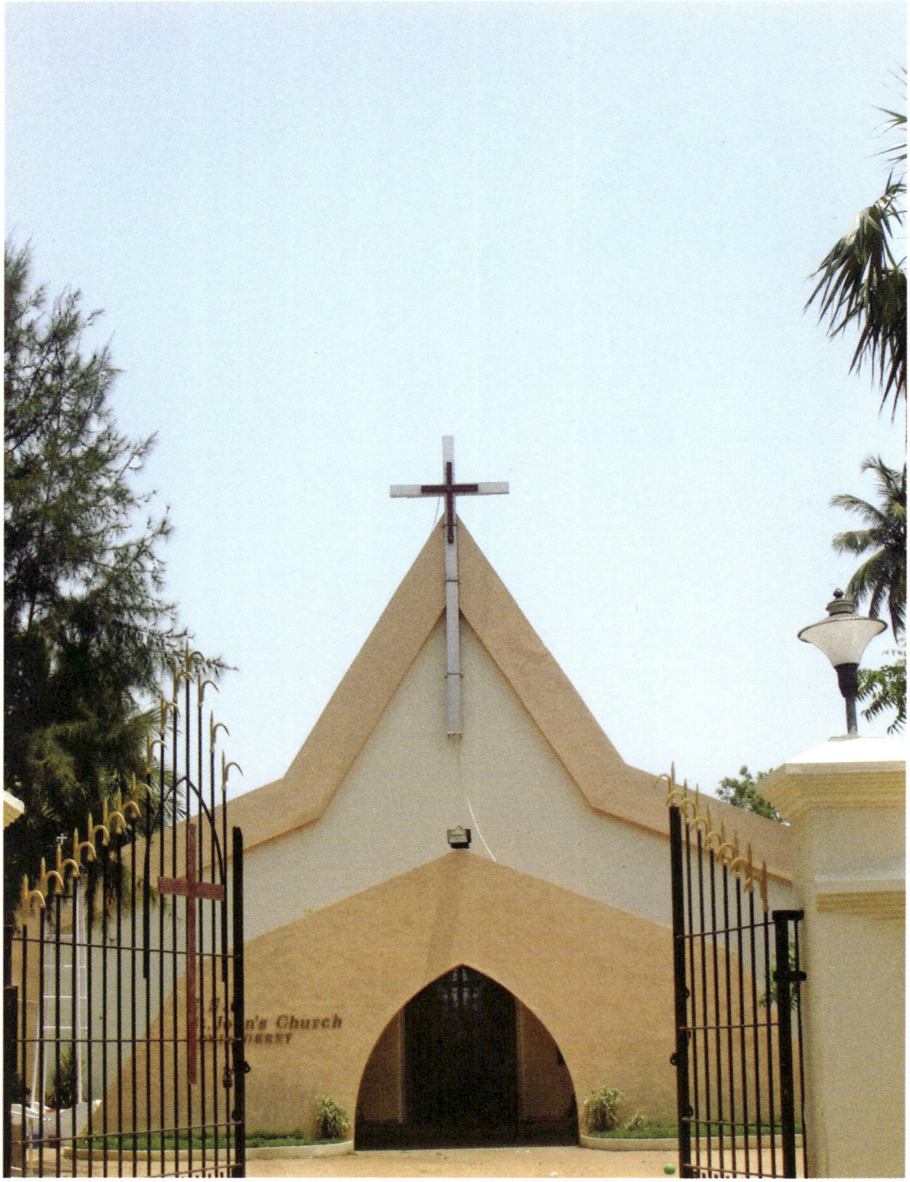
Church

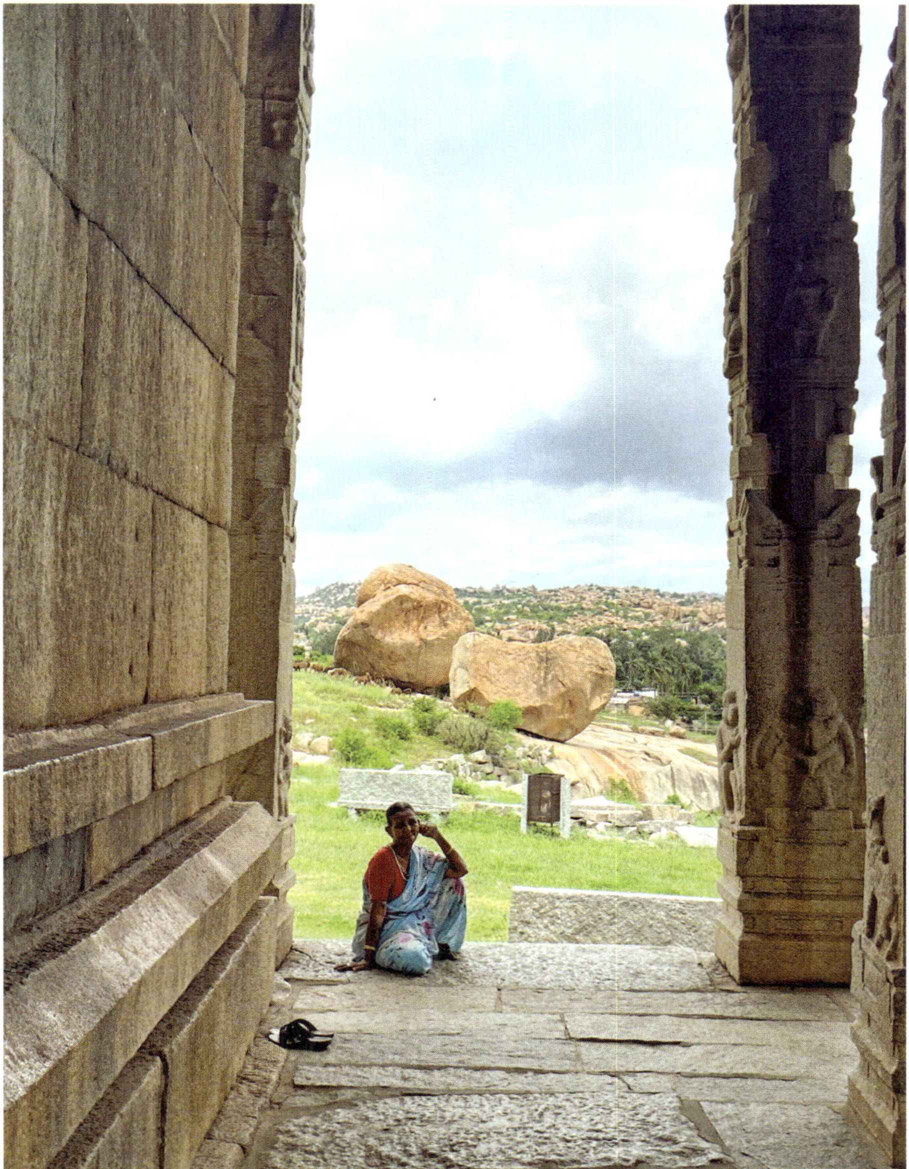

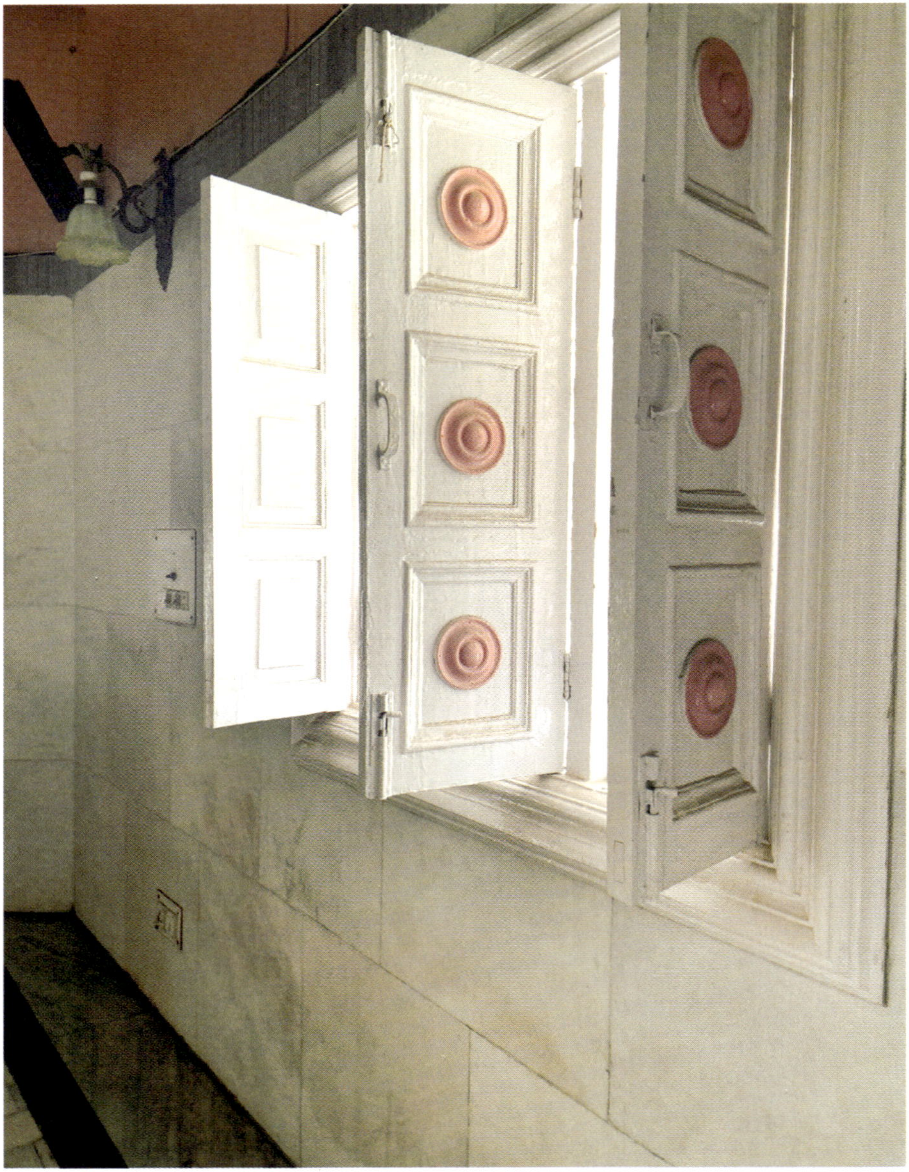

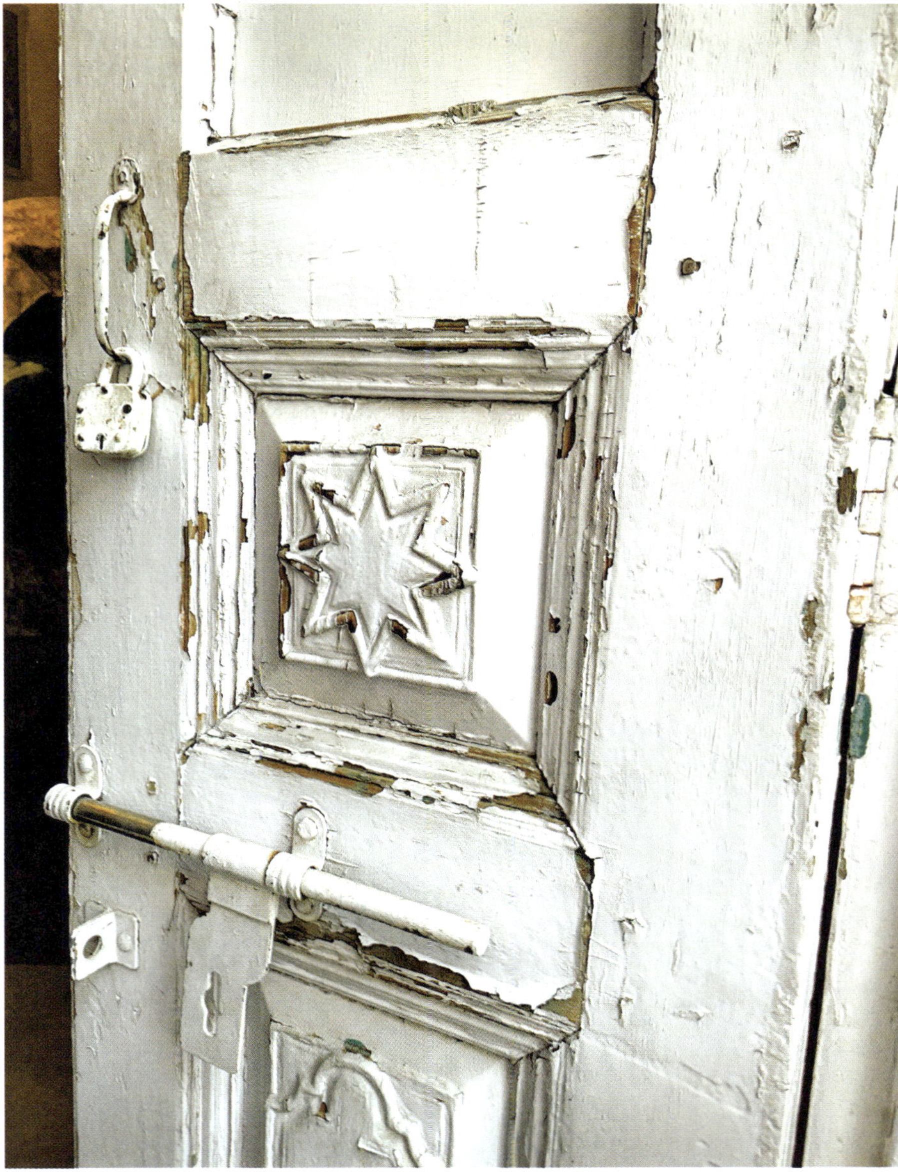

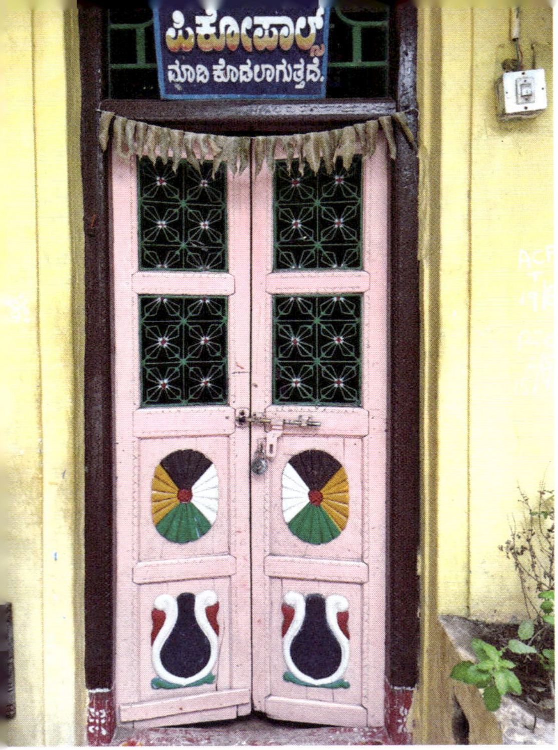
ಪಿಕೋಪಾಲ್ಸ್
ಮಾಡಿ ಕೊಡಲಾಗುತ್ತದೆ.

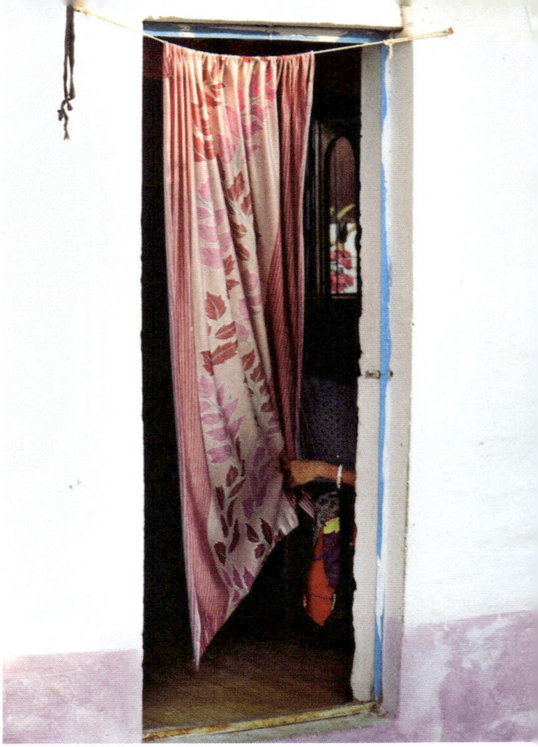

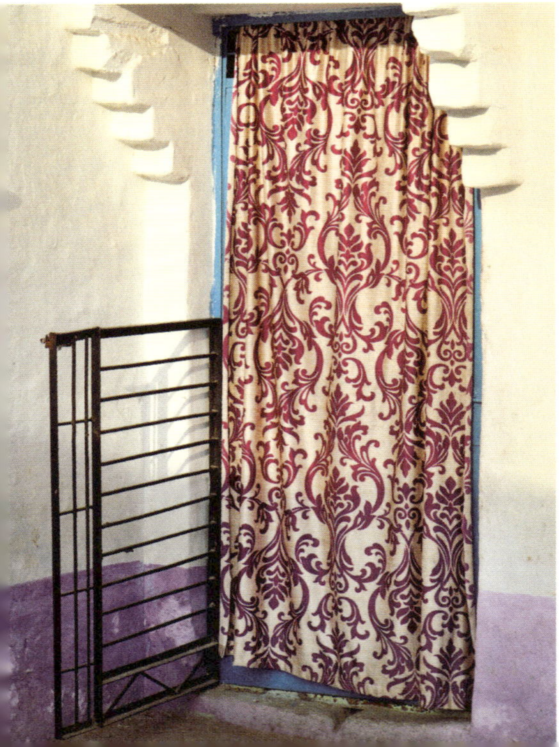

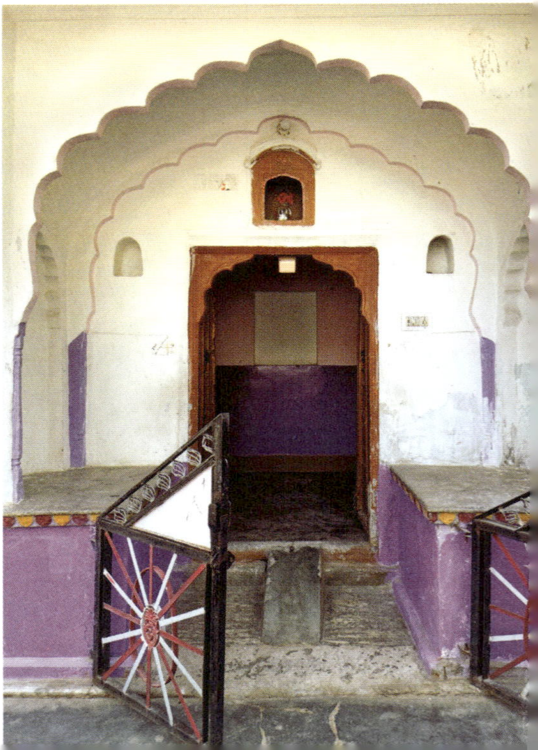

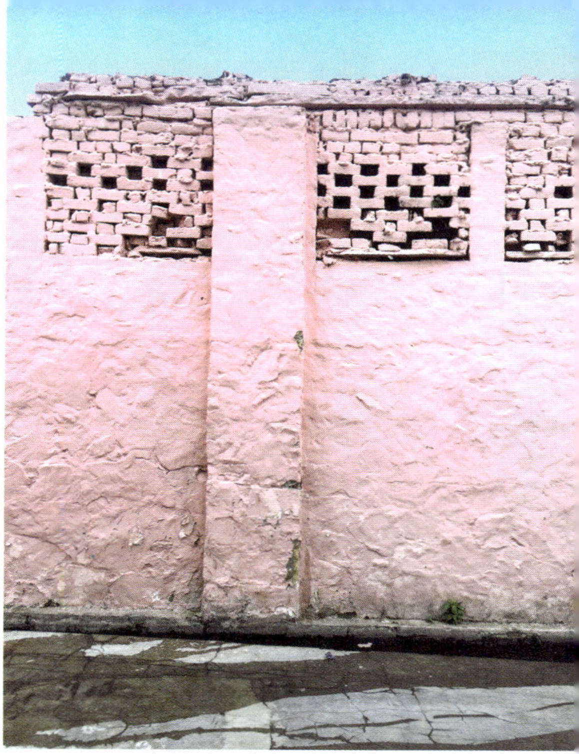

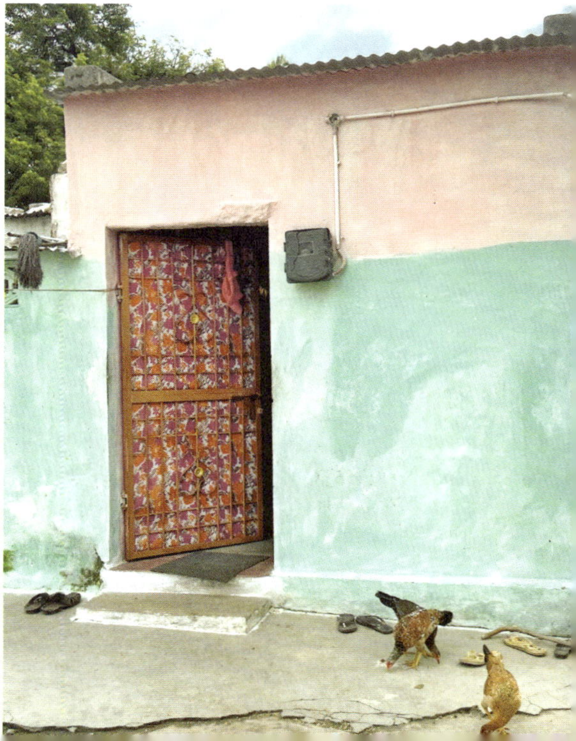

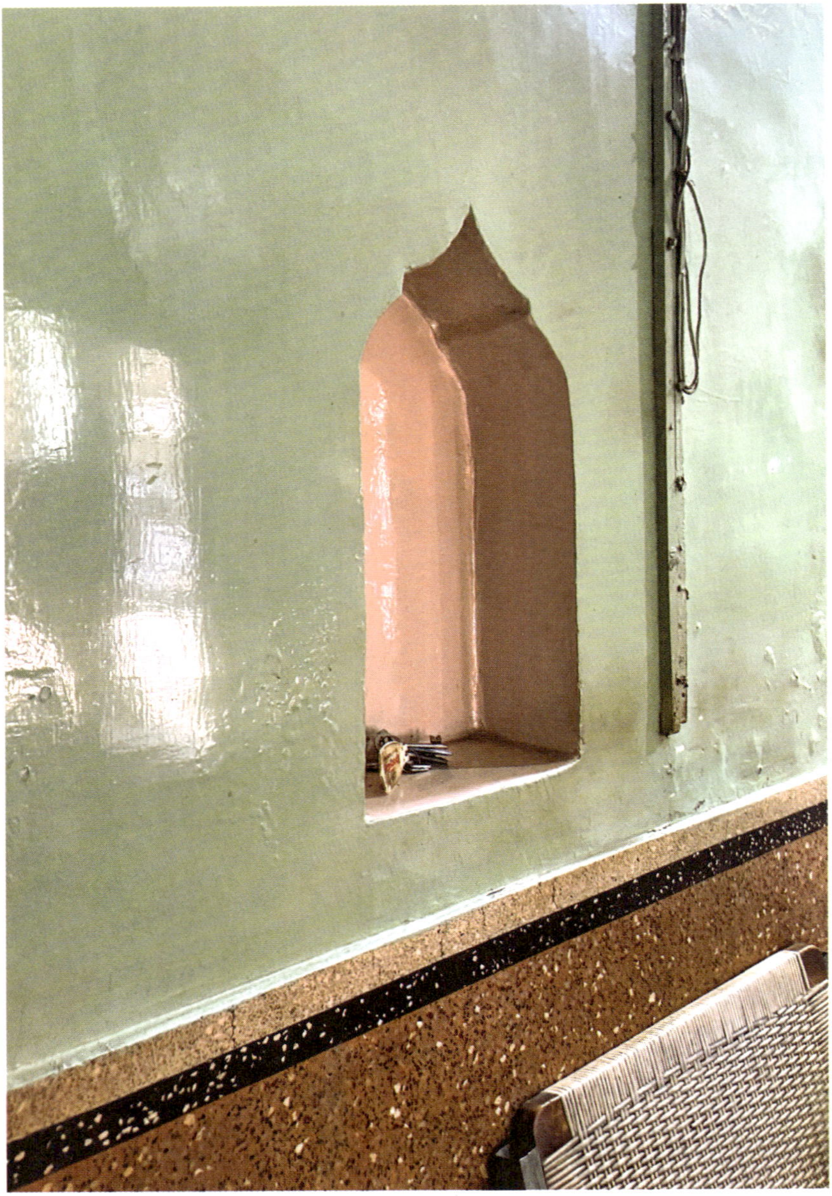

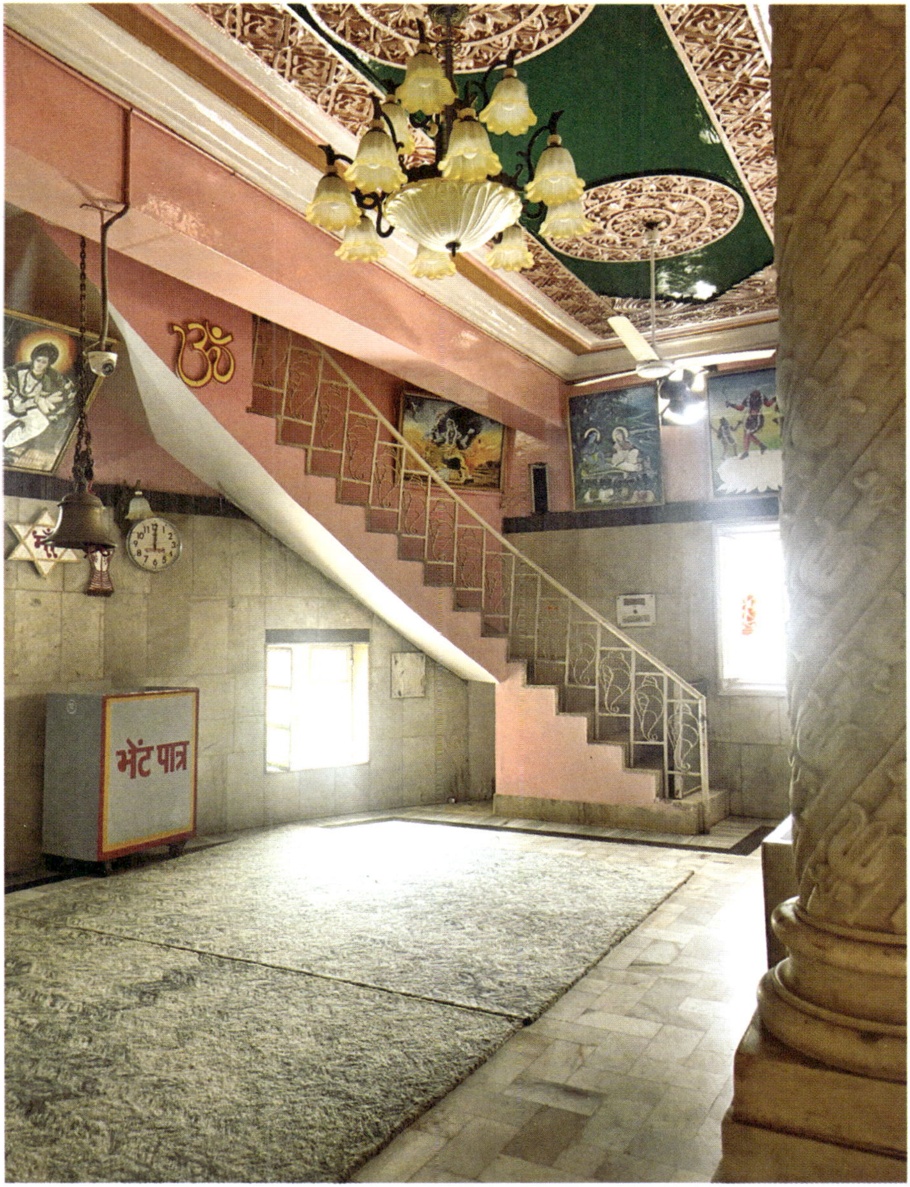
भेंट पात्र

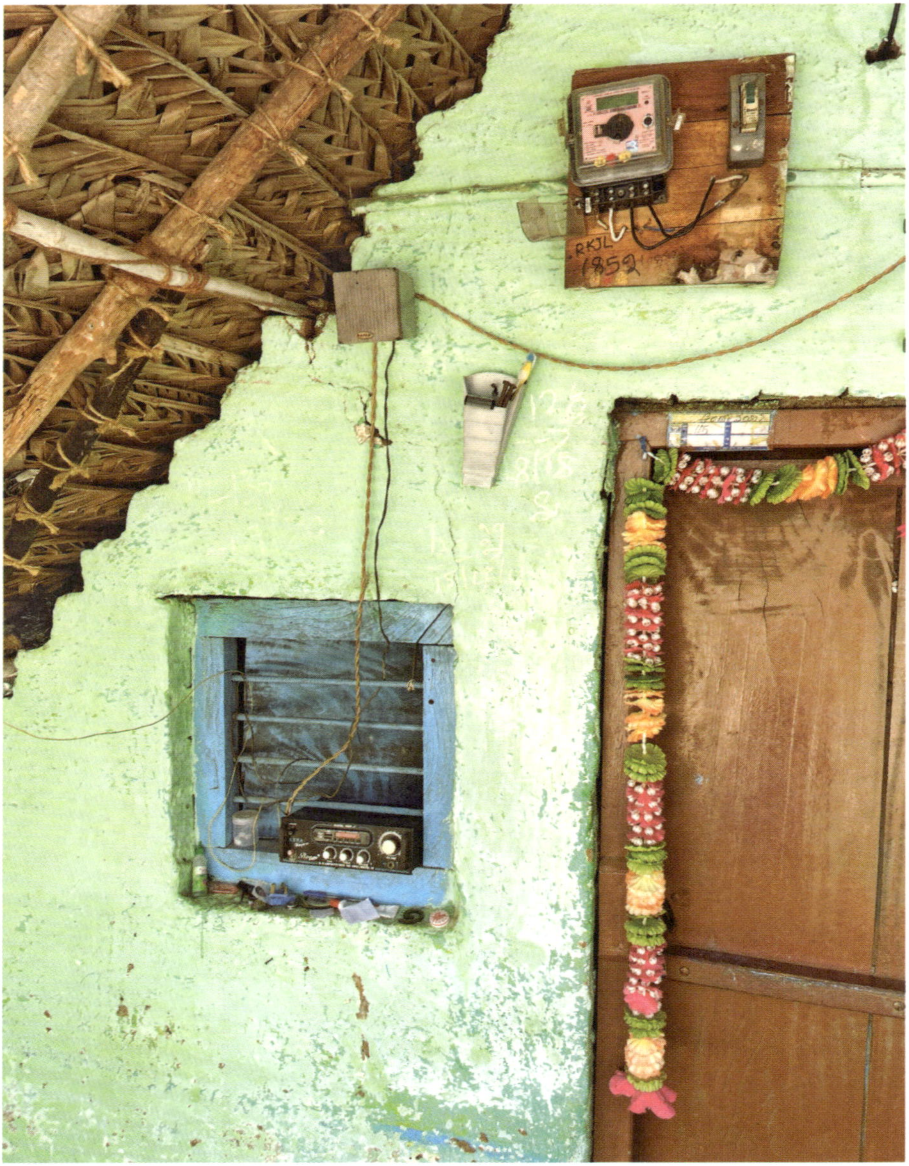
RKJL
1852

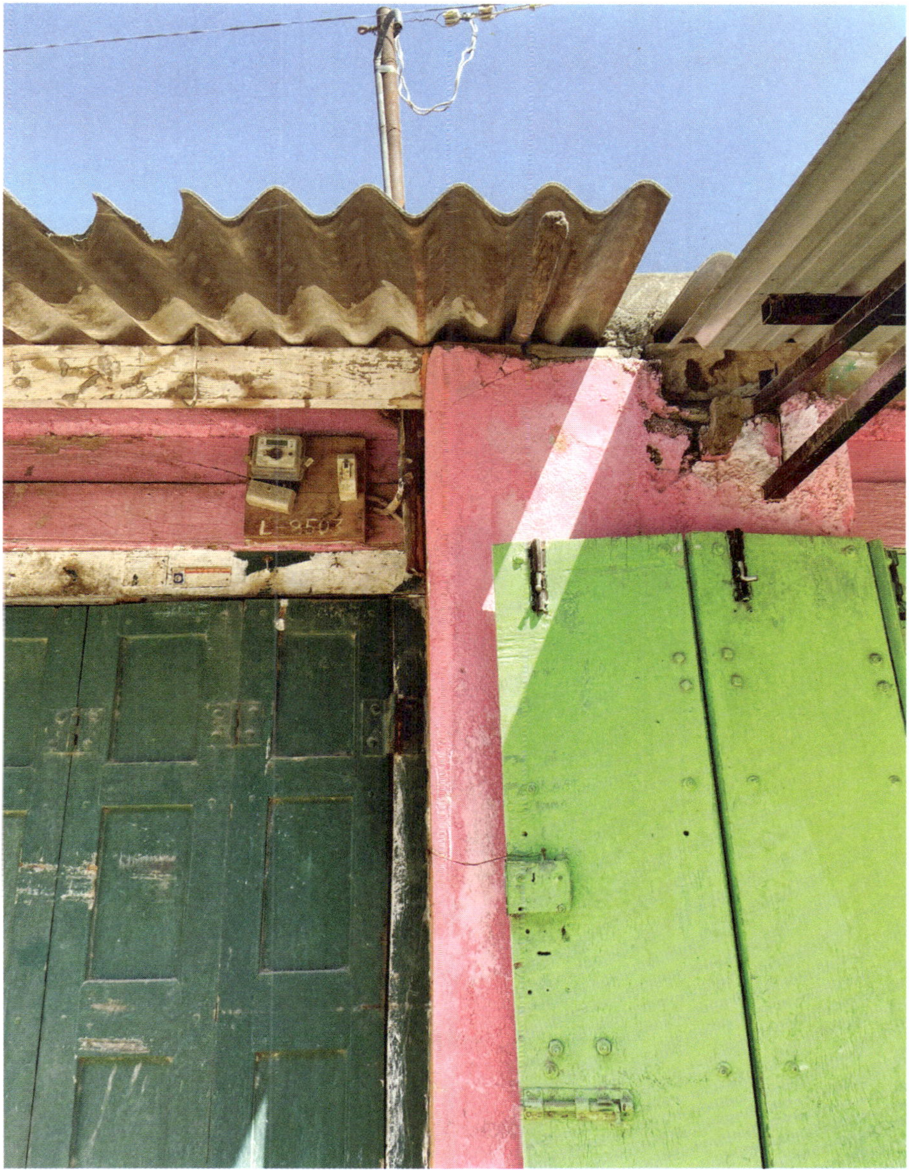
L-9507

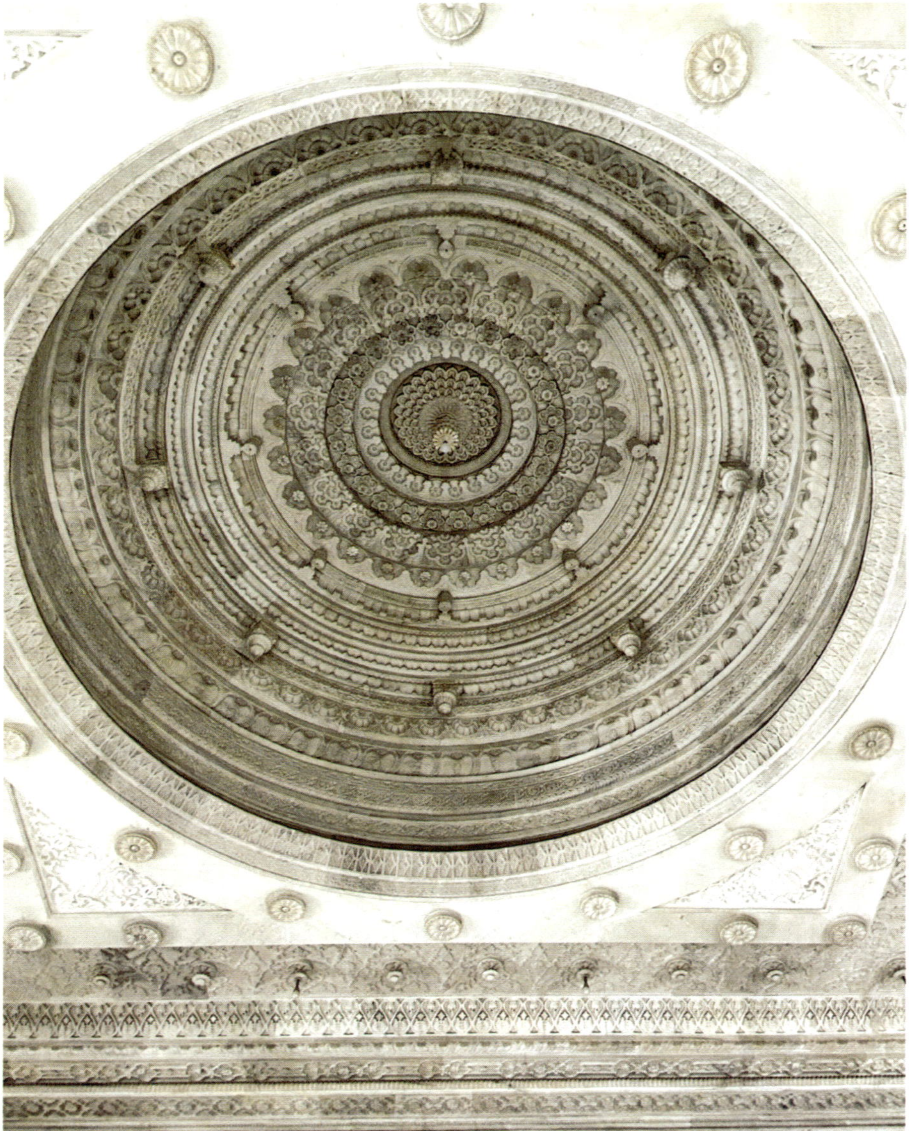

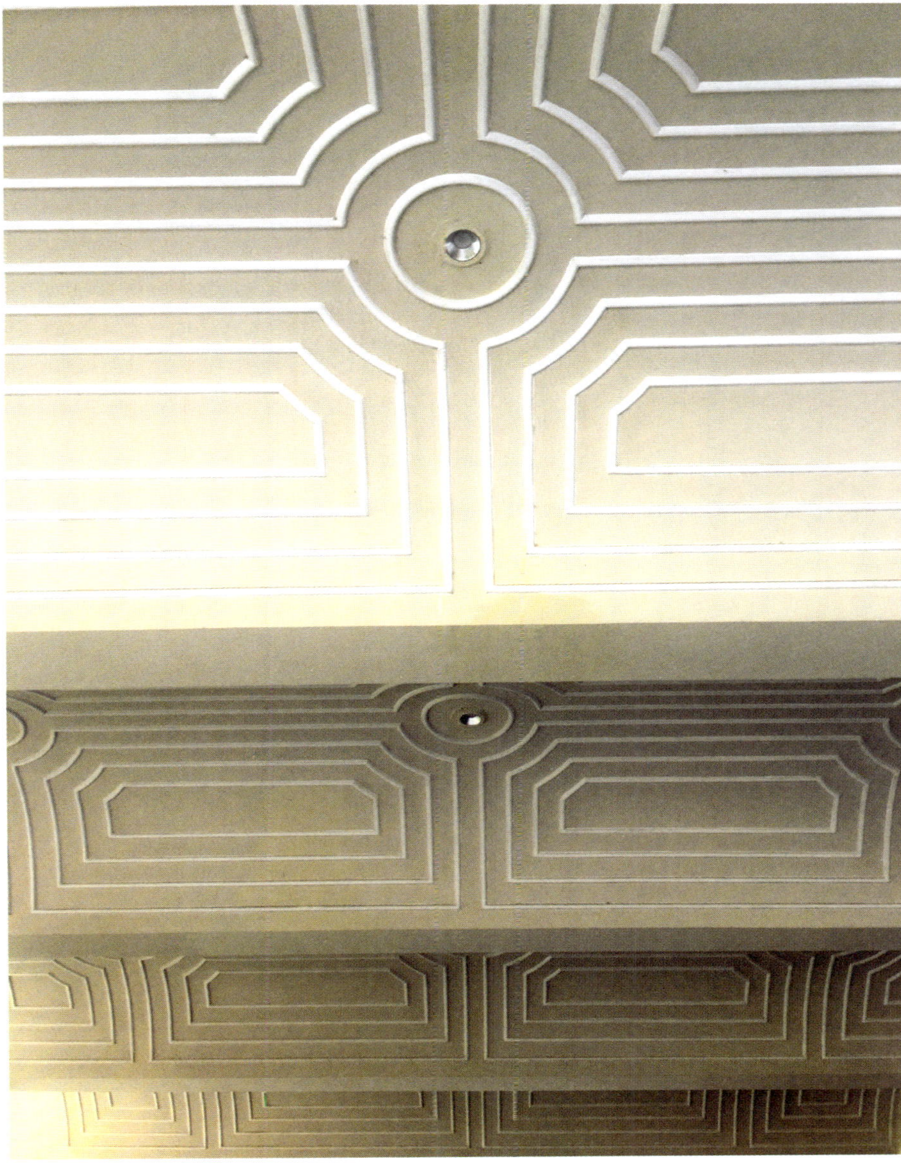

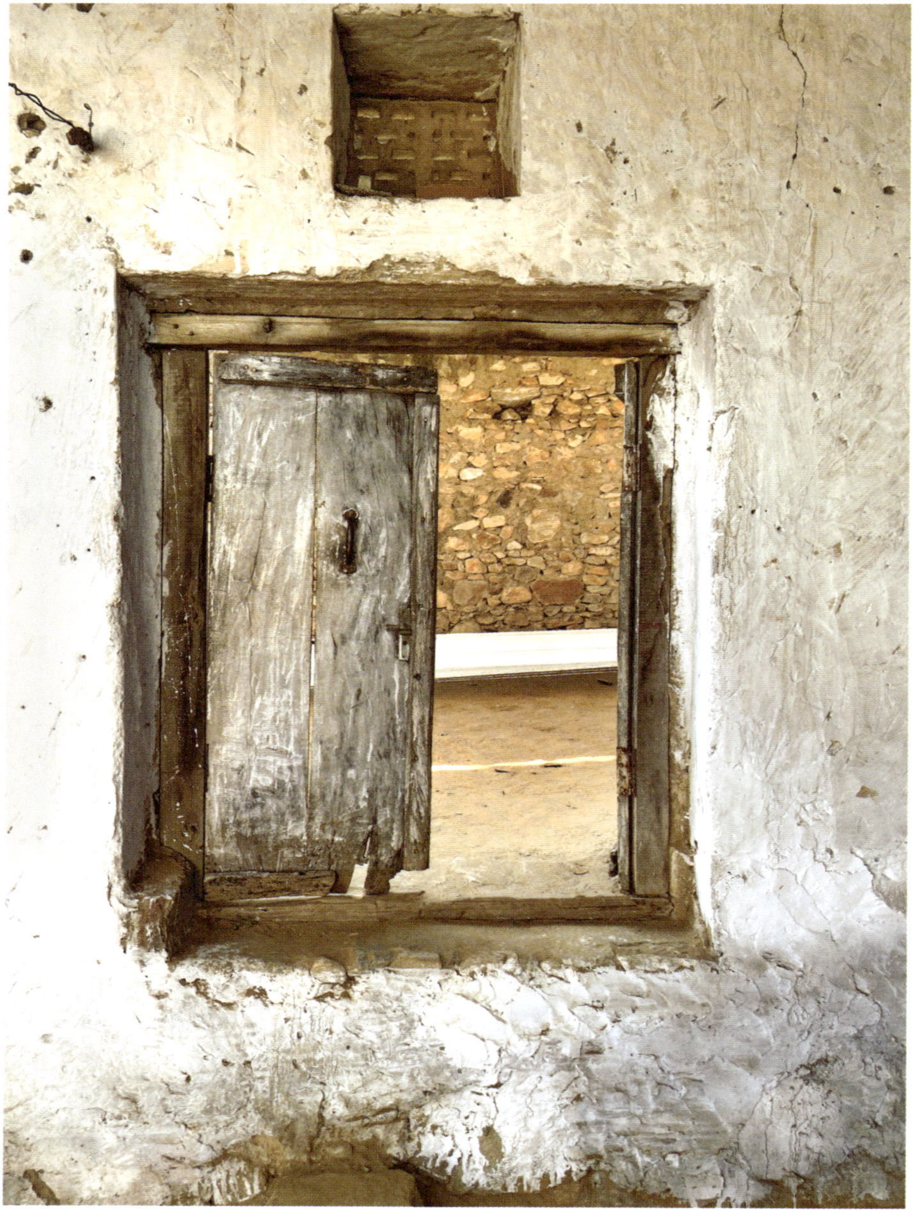

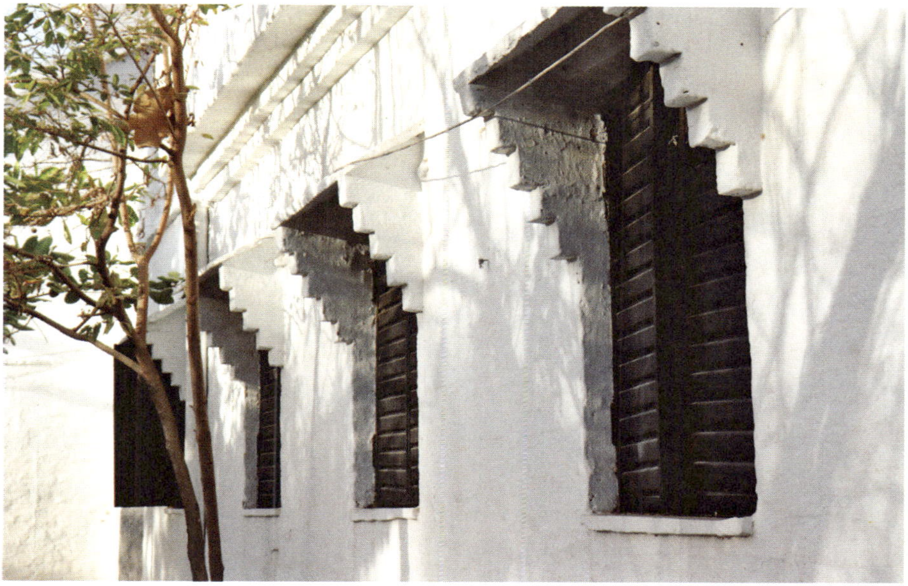

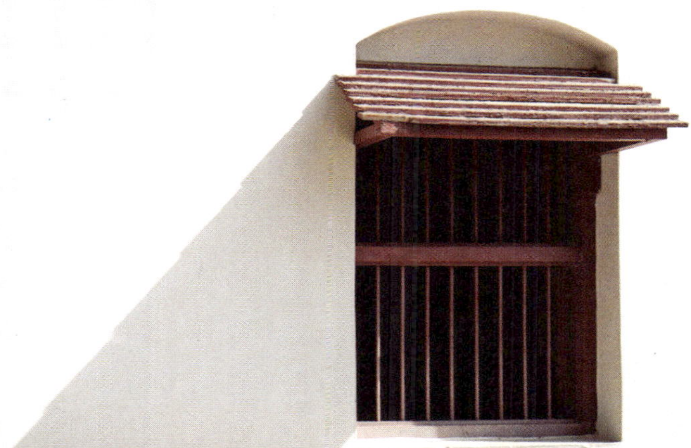

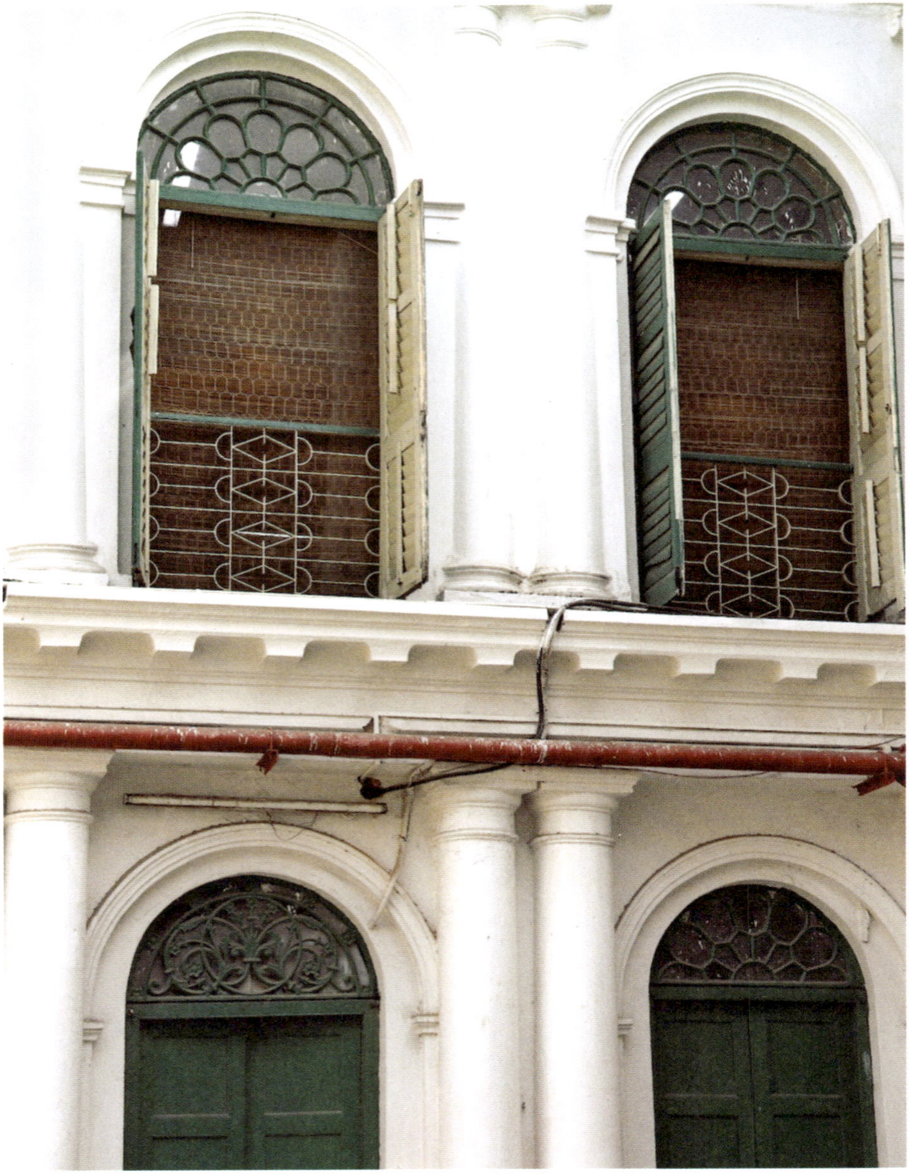

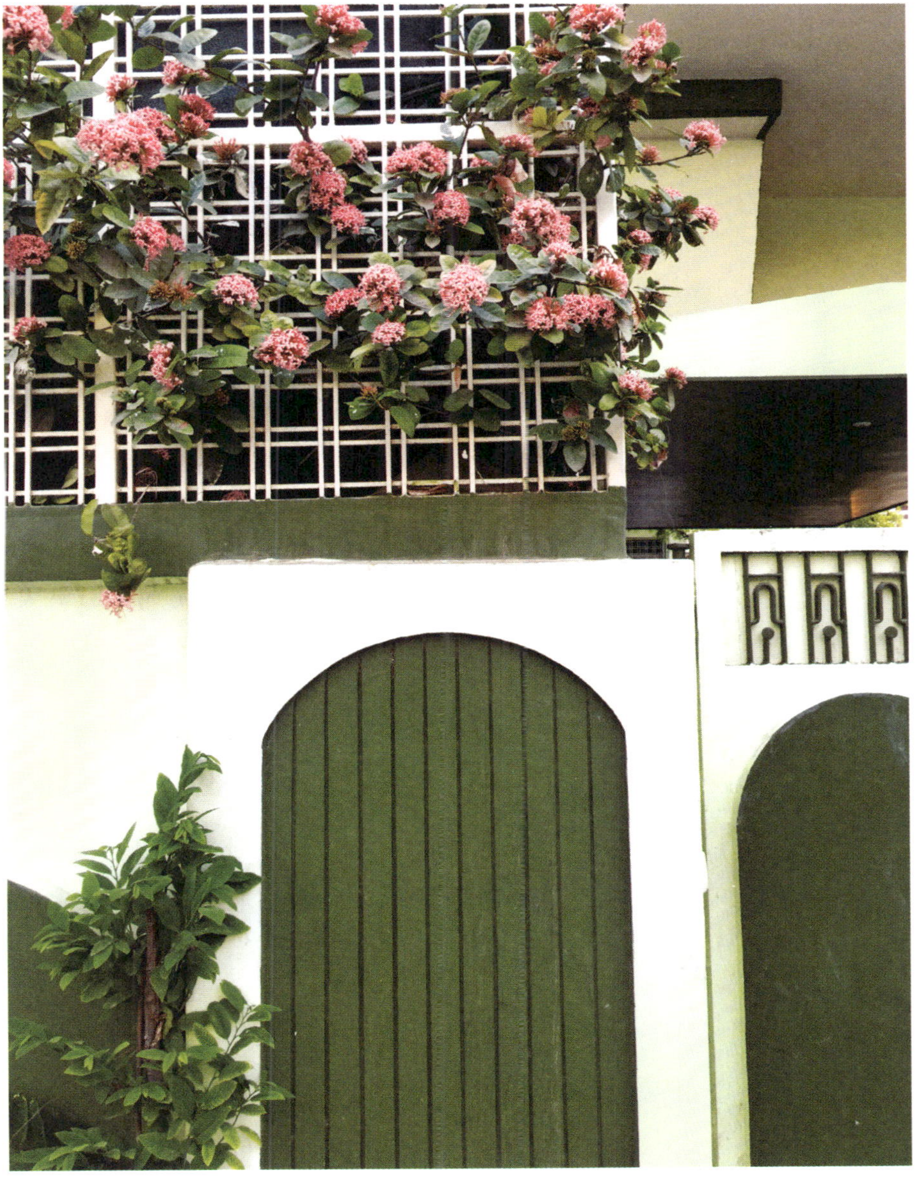

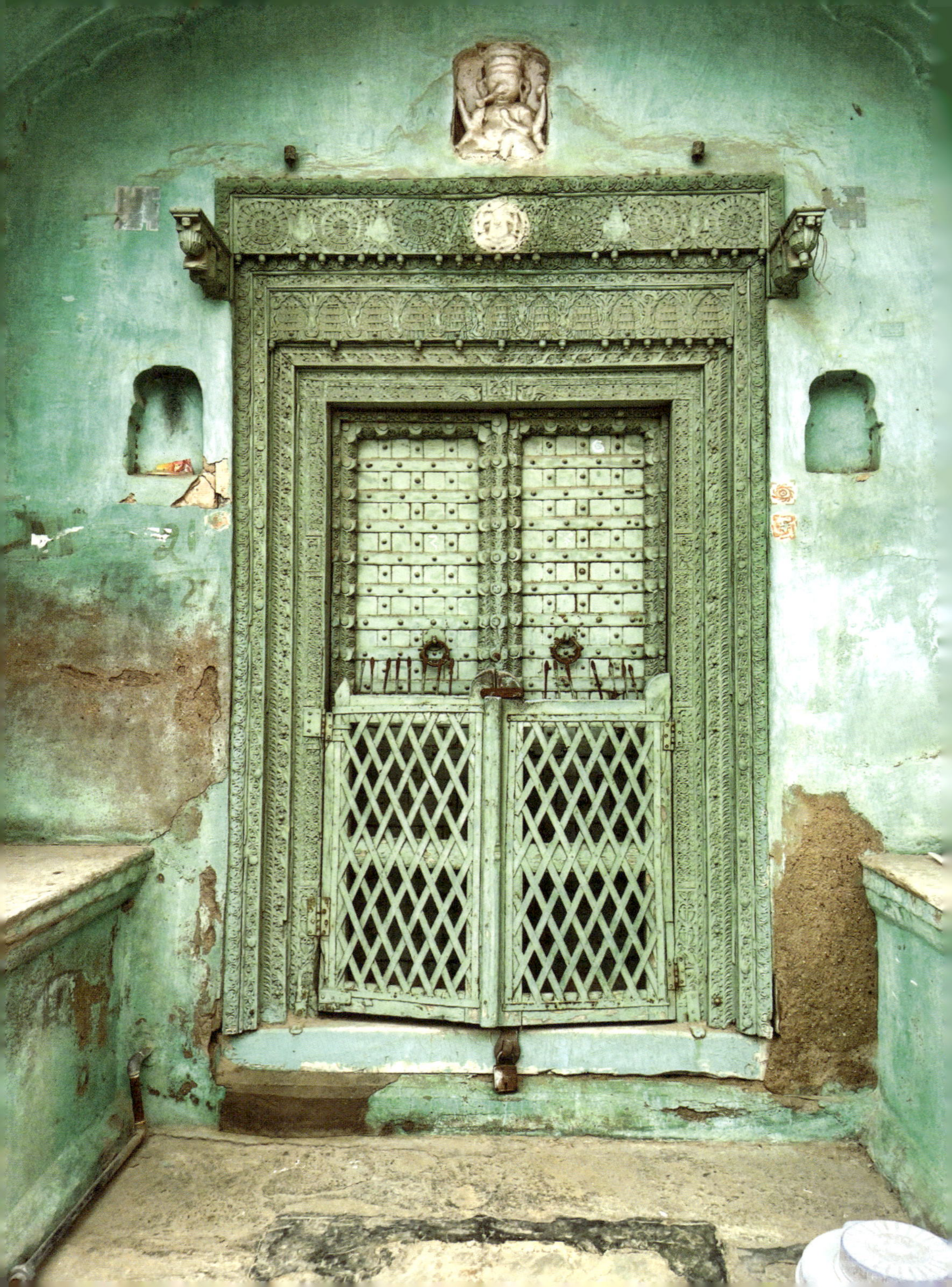

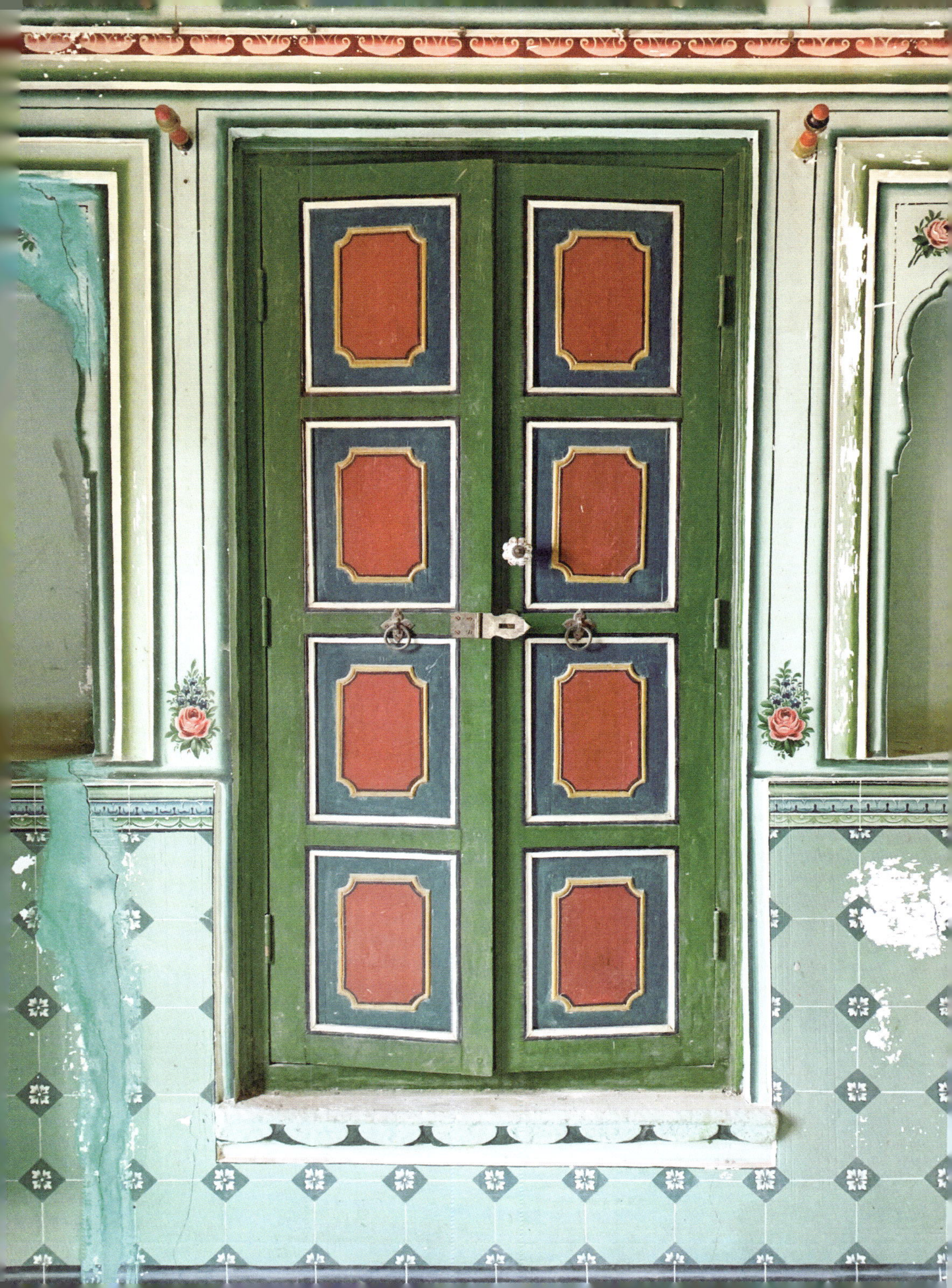

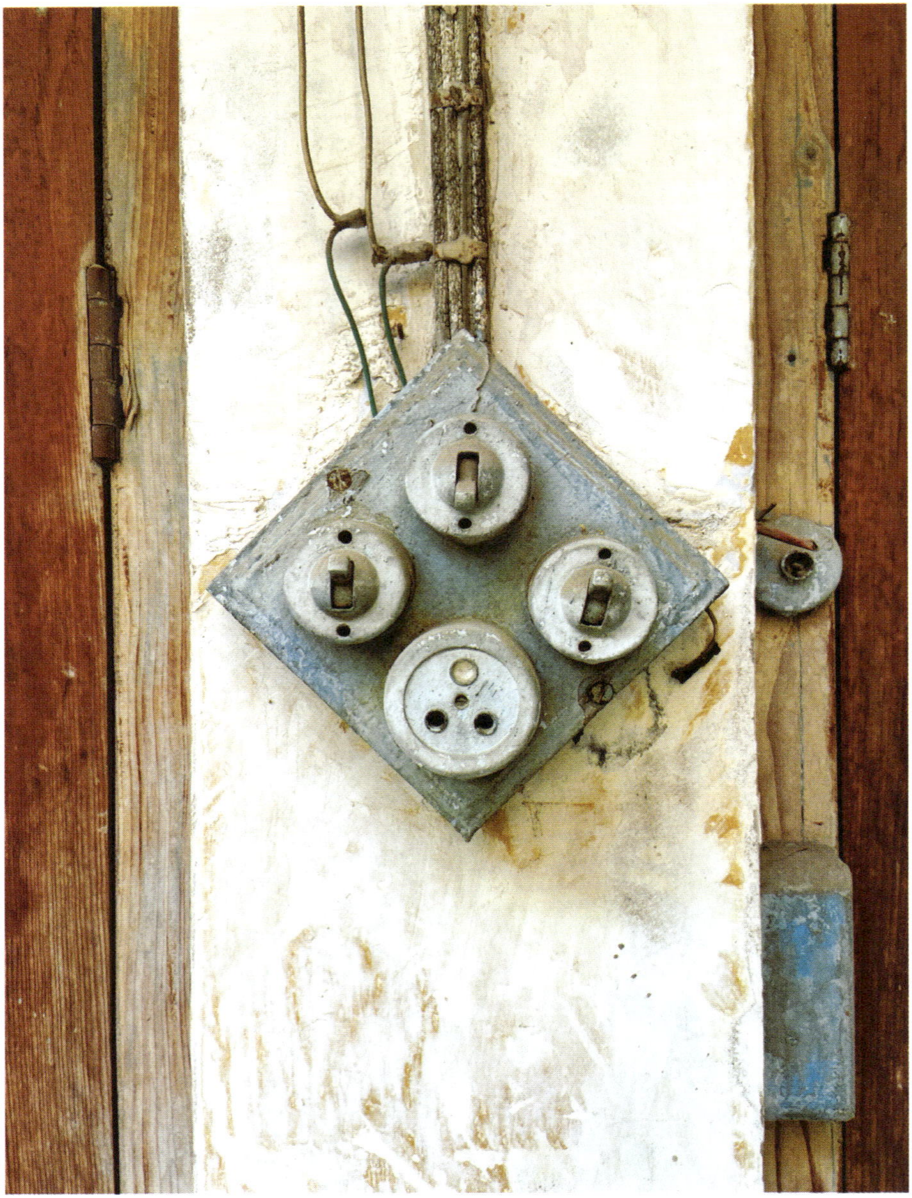

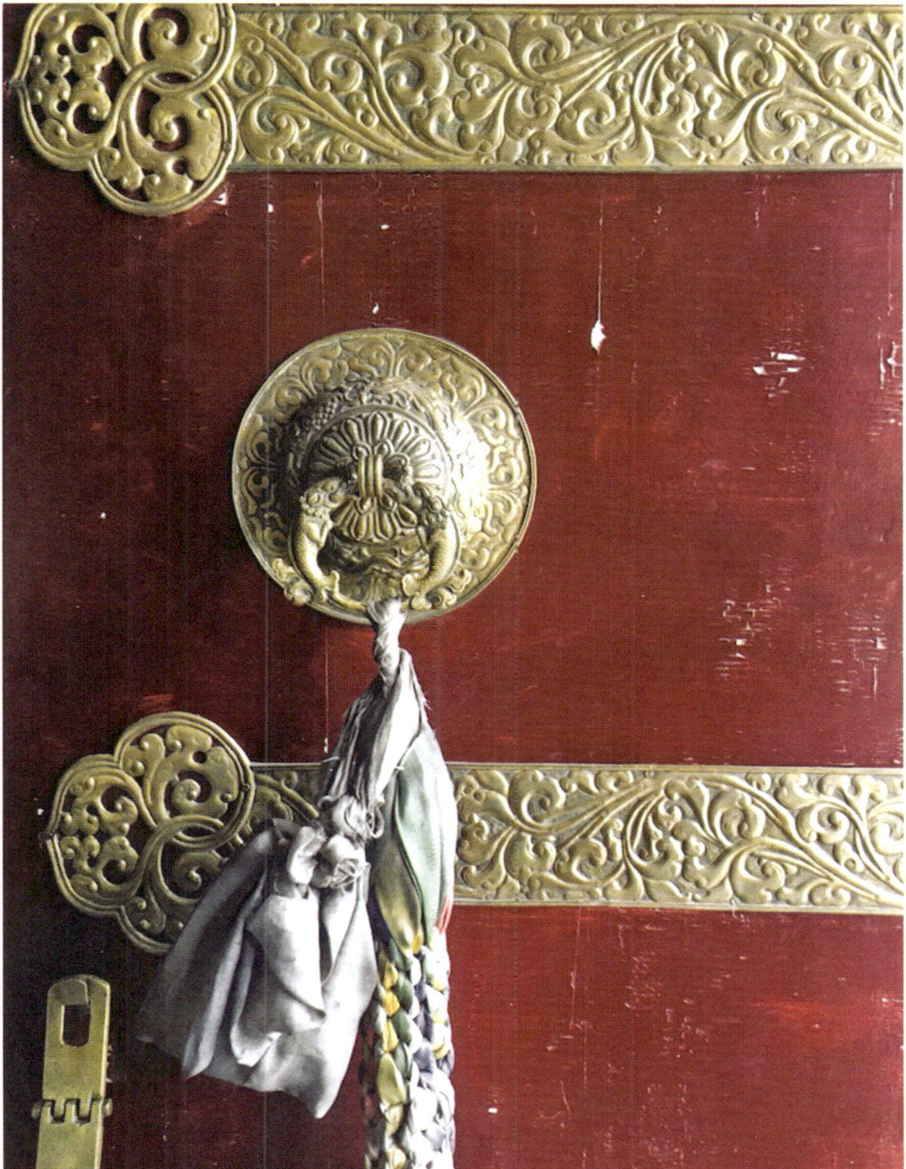

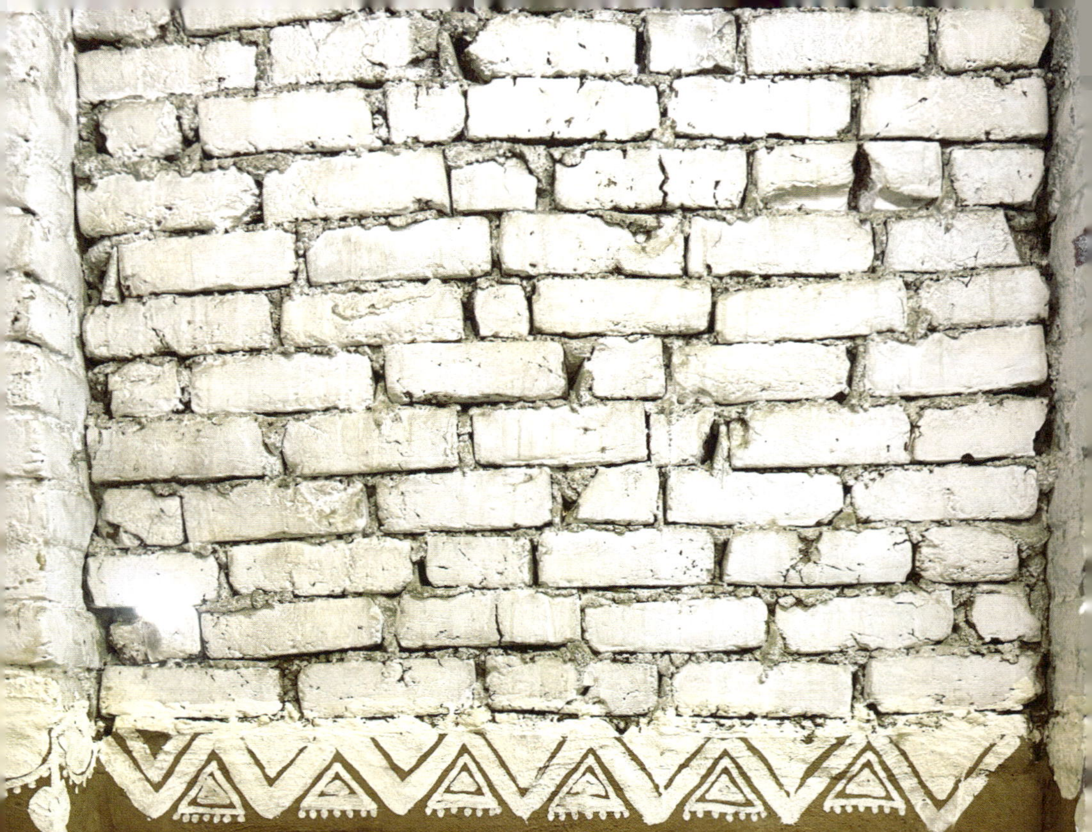

Published in India by Roli Books in 2024
M-75, Greater Kailash II Market, New Delhi-110 048
Ph: +91-11-40682000
info@rolibooks.com www.rolibooks.com

ISBN: 9788196643546

DESIGN & CURATION: SNEHA PAMNEJA
PRE-PRESS: JOYTI DEY
PRODUCTION: LAVINIA RAO

Printed and bound at Naveen Printers, New Delhi